THE RETREAT FROM BURMA
1941-42

OFFICIAL HISTORY OF THE INDIAN ARMED FORCES
IN THE SECOND WORLD WAR
1939-45

Campaigns in the Eastern Theatre

THE RETREAT FROM BURMA
1941-42

The Naval & Military Press Ltd

COMBINED INTER-SERVICES HISTORICAL SECTION
(INDIA & PAKISTAN)

Published by

The Naval & Military Press Ltd
Unit 5 Riverside, Brambleside
Bellbrook Industrial Estate
Uckfield, East Sussex
TN22 1QQ England

Tel: +44 (0)1825 749494

www.naval-military-press.com
www.nmarchive.com

In reprinting in facsimile from the original, any imperfections are inevitably reproduced and the quality may fall short of modern type and cartographic standards.

TO ALL WHO SERVED

ADVISORY COMMITTEE

Chairman

SECRETARY, MINISTRY OF DEFENCE, INDIA

Members

DR TARA CHAND
MR K. ZACHARIAH
DR S. N. SEN
PROF K. A. NILAKANTA SASTRI
PROF MOHAMMAD HABIB
DR R. C. MAJUMDAR
LIEUT-GENERAL D. RUSSELL
LIEUT-GENERAL K. S. THIMMAYYA
MAJ-GENERAL S. P. THORAT
MILITARY ADVISER TO THE HIGH COMMISSIONER
    FOR PAKISTAN IN INDIA

Secretary

DR BISHESHWAR PRASAD

CAMPAIGNS IN THE EASTERN THEATRE

    Campaigns in South-East Asia 1941-42:
        (Hong Kong, Malaya, Borneo)
    The Retreat from Burma 1941-42
    Arakan Operations 1942-45
    Reconquest of Burma 1942-45
    Post-War Occupation Forces:
        (Japan and South-East Asia)

PREFACE

Each major war in the past has engaged the attention of historians who have brought under review the trend of operations and examined the forces and influences which prompted large masses of humanity to diverge from their normal pursuits of peaceful avocations. This tendency is a necessary corollary to the importance attached to political history, for have not wars in the past affected the whole course of political, economic and social life of humanity at large ? An important object of military history, however, is to examine the developments in the science of strategy and tactics and trace their influence on the defence organisation of states. In the present century, two global wars following each other within the span of two generations, and working tremendous changes in the life patterns of the world, have been the subject of study from various angles ; some of these sponsored by governments ; and this has resulted in the preparation and production of numerous accounts depicting prominently the part played by participant nations.

Much before the conclusion of the Second World War, the Government of India had decided to set up an organisation attached to the Chief of the General Staff for collecting and collating records with a view to writing the history of the operations in which Indian forces had participated. The beginning was made with one officer, but by the time the war had come to a close, the cell had expanded into the War Department Historical Section. Subsequent to the partition of India, it was agreed upon by the Dominions of India and Pakistan that the project of recording the glorious achievements of the Indian Armed Froces in the Second World War should continue as a joint venture of the two states ; that this combined organisation should function under a civilian historian and that it should be named the Combined Inter-Services Historical Section, India and Pakistan. This joint body was chartered to produce the official history of the part played by the pre-partition India and its armed forces in the World War of 1939-1945. The narratives were to deal with military operations and organisational activities, and were to provide a truthful, analysed record of the operations carried out by our armed forces, so as to be an authoritative reference work for the future leaders, a field of study and guidance for the military student, and a written monument to the achievements of the forces who served.

Keeping in view these fundamental purposes, a history in about twenty volumes was planned ; it has been divided into three series, *viz.* the campaigns in the western theatre ; the campaigns in the eastern theatre ; and the activities pertaining to organisation and administration. The campaign volumes narrate the part played by the Indian armed forces in Africa, Italy, the Middle East, Burma and South-east Asia, but while doing so, the achievements of the forces of the Allied nations fighting alongside have also been sufficiently highlighted, for the operations have been studied as a whole in their geographical setting. The volumes relating to the campaigns in the western theatre cover the theatres of war in North Africa and Western Desert, East Africa, the Middle East comprising Iraq, Syria and Iran, and Sicily, Italy and Greece. The other series gives the story of the war in the east beginning with the conquest of Hong Kong, Malaya, Borneo and Burma by the Japanese to the recovery of these countries by the Allied nations. Two volumes have been assigned to the reverses while three volumes cover the story of the reconquest of Arakan and Central Burma. The activities of the Occupation Forces in Japan and South-east Asia also find a place in this series. In addition to the narratives of campaigns, volumes in the third series discuss the policy and planning of the defence of India, expansion of India's armed forces and the general headquarters, the development of technical services and supply organisation, and the war economy, including industrial production and finance. All operations have been studied from the inter-service aspect, but the history of the two infant services, the Royal Indian Air Force and the Royal Indian Navy has been traced separately also.

India's role in the war was one of subordinate co-operation, for she was not the architect of policy either in determining the influences which heralded the war or in steering its course. Her line of action was laid down by His Majesty's Government in the United Kingdom, and, later, with the integration of Allied command, higher strategy was planned by the Combined Chiefs of Staffs who disposed the available supplies and war equipment among the various theatres of war. In these narratives, therefore, 'higher direction' or 'Grand Strategy' finds no place as this was the concern of Washington or London. The Government of India, under the direction of Whitehall, was however responsible for devising measures for its territorial defence, and such plans as were then formulated have been discussed in one volume. Yet, the narratives of campaigns have necessarily to be prefaced by an analysis of the general strategic plan as also the strategic appreciations and plans of the local authorities who regulated the course of the campaigns. But the treatment of strategic problems has seldom exceeded the level of the theatre or army commander, and it is from his point of view generally that this history has been written. For the spheres beyond, the reader will have inevitably to depend on the volumes on 'Grand Strategy' planned by the United Kingdom Cabinet Historical Section or those in Washington.

We have been allowed full access to the official records of the Government of India, and the Historical Section has almost a complete set of War Diaries and despatches and reports of the commanders in the field. But, unfortunately, a large mass of high level records was destroyed at the time of transfer of power to the two Dominions, which has handicapped us in finding many important documents relating to policy and decisions. We were unable to make good this deficiency by drawing upon the resources of Whitehall, as the agreement with the War Office precluded reference to any papers beyond the army level. Within these limitations, however, we were able to derive considerable information from the War Office, the Admiralty and the Air Ministry, where our Liaison Officers worked for some years, as well as from the Cabinet Historical Section. Their co-operation, on a reciprocal basis, has been of considerable benefit in enriching our sources of knowledge. We have also received documents from the archives of Canada, Australia and New

Zealand under arrangements for mutual information on subjects of common interest. The exchange of drafts of narratives between the Commonwealth countries has been of great advantage in reducing points of controversy and eliminating wide divergences as to fact. Yet, on the whole, this history is based on the records in our possession of which free and full use has been made.

History, at best, is a narrative ; to present an accurate narrative of events has been our endeavour. Yet, it is not a mere chronicle of events, for we have analysed the factors and influences which have produced them and thereby interpreted facts in their correct perspective. Our viewpoint has been one of objectivity, but in the sifting of material subjectivity cannot altogether be eliminated ; in relating the exploits of our own troops we may have been at times led to emphasise their glorious achievements. Yet a panegyric is not our object and we have not hesitated to record reverses or recount inconvenient situations in which the troops were placed. However, as a civilian organisation, we have refrained from speculating on what a commander in a particular position should have done or passing judgement on his appreciation of the situation. We have marshalled facts to reconstruct the situations as we view them, and lessons as emerging from them have been deduced.

The present volume is one of the series of Campaigns in the Eastern Theatre, and narrates the circumstances in which Burma was lost to the Japanese in 1942, so soon after the start of their putsch in South-east Asia. Yet, it is not merely a story of continuous reverses but of successful retreat as well. The mettle of an army, the morale of its troops and the character of its commanders are best revealed in retreat, when the first concern is to extricate the force to enable it to fight later in better circumstances. That the army in Burma managed to save itself from the Japanese pincers and succeeded in getting behind the hills screening Assam from the land of pagodas was no mean achievement ; it offsets the initial inability to stop the Japanese from over-running the Valley of the Irrawaddy. Why did the disaster come? The answer to this question is to be found in the lack of effective military preparations, inadequacy of the apprehension of danger and the faulty conceptions of defence. These have been analysed in the earlier chapters, while in subsequent pages the details of operations have been given in the background of strategical and tactical plans.

In this campaign the Indian, British, Burmese and Chinese units fought side by side or in different but contiguous sectors. Hence it has been necessary to plan the story as a whole, for the strategical picture would not be made clear without bringing into full review the fighting in the different zones. The operations of the Burcorps and the Chinese Armies, therefore, find due mention in this volume. So also has an assessment been made of the work of the Royal Air Force which was somewhat conspicuous in the early stages. In the main, however, it is an account of the fighting of the Indian divisions who struggled to stem the tide of Japanese advance and who, against all odds, saved themselves from the prospect of extermination which faced them. In our analysis of the ugly situations and estimate of the facts responsible for them, some commanders may not appear in the best of lights, but it is far from our intention to deprecate their zealous endeavours to stop the Japanese on the borders of Burma. Their failure is no reflection on their generalship, but was, no doubt, the result of lamentable deficiency of military resources in the east, both in men and equipment. The first reverses, however, paved the way for later preparations to fight the Axis Powers successfully.

This narrative is based largely on the War Diaries, reports and despatches of the commanders and the records of the Government of India which have been, where necessary, mentioned in the footnotes. The nature of basic material has been indicated in the bibliographical note at the end. Some of the important documents have also been given in the appendices, where also will be found location statements of the forces and the orders of battle on several dates. Maps and sketches have been interspersed in the text to illustrate the strategy of the campaign, or the tactics in a particular engagement. The spelling of place-names conforms generally to the system approved at the informal conference of British and American experts in October 1947, a report of which was communicated to us. In the maps conventional symbols have been used to represent the Allied and Axis troops, though coloured maps have been kept to a minimum as a measure of economy. In the text, the Japanese units have been mentioned in italics to distinguish them from the Indian, British or Chinese forces. We have also eschewed the use of the word 'enemy' to indicate the Japanese. Military abbreviations have, as far as practicable, been avoided. Nonetheless, some of these have been used and a glossary has been included.

Initially, the material for this narrative of the first campaign in Burma was collated by Colonel E.C.V. Foucar, M.C., who was placed on special duty to collect the documentary material and seek information from the various military officers pertaining to this campaign. His draft was revised and enlarged by Dr. K. Gopalachari, M.A., PH.D. who served as Narrator in the Historical Section in 1948-49, before the final editing when additional material was incorporated. To these officers I must express my indebtedness. I am also thankful to Lieut.-Colonel N. N. Madan and Lieut.-Colonel P. C. Bharucha of the Historical Section for their assistance in editing and for the valuable suggestions for the improvement of the narrative. I am grateful to Mr. P. N. Khera, Narrator, for revising the proofs and Mr. T. D. Sharma, the Cartographer, for preparing the maps. Mention may be made of the assistance rendered by other members of the staff of the Historical Section, particularly by Mr. K. N. Pradhan who made a search in the records to ensure the maximum accuracy of facts and figures.

The narrative has been shown to the commanding officers who were responsible for the campaign in Burma, as a whole or in part, for their opinion. I am particularly grateful to Major-General W.D.A. Lentaigne, CB, CBE, DSO, Major-General R. G. Ekin, CIE, Major-General J. Bruce Scott, CB, DSO, MC, and Brigadier R. T. Cameron, DSO, for their comments which have been extremely helpful in clearing many obscure points and resolving doubts. I must express my gratitude to Brigadier H. B. Latham of the Cabinet Historical Section, London, for reading the script and making suggestions for its improvement. The typescript was also seen by Lieut.-General Sir Dudley Russell, KBE, CB, DSO, MC, Chief Adviser, Army Headquarters, India, to whom I am obliged for his valuable suggestions for its improvement.

The Government of India has set up an Advisory Committee consisting of some leading historians and senior Service officers, under the chairmanship of the Defence Secretary, for professional guidance and to scrutinise the narratives and authorise their publication. There is a representative of the Pakistan Government on it, which Government has also appointed a committee of its own to examine the narratives before they are authorised for publication. The members of the Advisory Committee have given me the benefit of their experience and judgement in planning the history and reading the draft of the volume. To them I am indebted for their advice which has greatly compensated for the handicaps of a civilian editor responsible for the production of military history. But, for statement of facts and expression of views, I accept full responsibility.

In conclusion, I must acknowledge the encouragement and support which I have received from the Ministries of Defence of India and Pakistan, without whose constant guidance and co-operation this project would not have been possible. I am specially grateful to Mr. H. M. Patel, Secretary, and Mr. B. B. Ghosh, Joint Secretary, Ministry of Defence, India, for their interest in the work and constant support which they have given to the Historical Section.

December, 1952.   BISHESHWAR PRASAD

CONTENTS

		Page
INTRODUCTION		xxiii

Chapter

I.	BURMA—THE LAND AND ITS PEOPLE	1
II.	BURMA—HISTORY AND POLITICS	12
III.	JAPANESE AGGRESSION IN THE FAR EAST	21
IV.	DANGER OF THE INVASION OF BURMA	31
V.	ARMED FORCES IN BURMA	42
VI.	FIRST ATTACK	61
VII.	LOSS OF MERGUI AND TAVOY	80
VIII.	ACTION IN KAWKAREIK SECTOR	92
IX.	DEFENCE OF MOULMEIN	106
X.	SALWEEN LINE—MARTABAN AND PA-AN	118
XI.	BILIN LINE	139
XII.	BATTLE OF THE SITTANG RIVER	157
XIII.	OPERATIONS IN THE PEGU AREA	184
XIV.	FALL OF RANGOON	202
XV.	OPERATIONS IN THE SHAN AND KARENNI STATE	223
XVI.	REGROUPING OF FORCE AFTER THE FALL OF RANGOON	233
XVII.	ENTRY OF THE CHINESE EXPEDITIONARY FORCE	252
XVIII.	WITHDRAWAL FROM PROME	260
XIX.	RACE FOR THE OILFIELDS—MINHLA-TAUNGDWINGYI LINE	272
XX.	RACE FOR THE OILFIELDS	287
XXI.	THE BEGINNING OF THE END—RETREAT NORTH OF MANDALAY	303
XXII.	PURSUIT—ACTION AT MONYWA	323
XXIII.	END—RACE FOR KALEWA	336
XXIV.	THE CHINESE FRONT—2ND PHASE	348
XXV.	CAPTURE OF AKYAB	358
XXVI.	CAMPAIGN IN THE AIR	365
XXVII.	CIVIL AND MILITARY ADMINISTRATION	381

APPENDICES

Group I	396
Group II	417
Group III	469
Group IV	482
BIBLIOGRAPHY	490
INDEX	495

LIST OF APPENDICES

GROUP I
                                                                                             Page

- A. Location Statement, Army in Burma as on 1 December, 1941 . . 396
- B. Burma—Order of Battle at Commencement of Hostilities. December, 1941 404
- C. State of Infantry 17th Division on the evening of 24 February, 1942 406
- D. Chinese Expeditionary Force in Burma, Order of Battle. 31 March, 1942 407
- E. Order of Battle, Army in Burma. 1 April 1942 410

GROUP II

- A. Extracts from the Covering Memorandum to Far East Appreciation by the Chiefs of Staff Committee, August, 1941 417
- B. Singapore Defence Conference, 1940. (Review of Defence Requirements of India and Burma in the light of possible Japanese threat from Thailand) 418
- C. Singapore Defence Conference, 1940. (Note on India's position in regard to the Japanese threat in general and against Burma in particular) 425
- D. Telegram from G.O.C., Burma to G.H.Q., Far East. 25 February, 1941 427
- E. Telegram from G.O.C., Burma to G.H.Q., Far East 429
- F. F.E.C.B's. appreciation on Joint Planning. 17 April, 1941 . . . 430
- G. Discussion of joint Sino-British action to be taken in the event of war between the British Empire and Japan. July-August, 1941 433
- H. Telegram from Governor of Burma to Viceroy. (Appreciation from G.O.C., Burma). 12 December, 1941 437
- I. Appreciation of the situation in Burma by General Staff, India. 15 December, 1941 438
- J. Appreciation by General Hutton, G.O.C., Burma Army, made at Rangoon on 10 January, 1942 444
- K. Telegram from Rangoon, Burma to Secretary of State, Burma. 22 December, 1941 454
- L. Cable from War Office to C-in-C., India. 26 December, 1941 . 455
- M. Extract from Cable from War Office to G.H.Q., Far East. 8 January, 1942 456
- N. Telegram from Burmarmy to ABDACOM. 18 February, 1942 457
- O. Telegram from Burmarmy to ABDACOM, and India. 20 January, 1942 457
- P. Telegram from Burmarmy to ABDACOM Batavia. 20 January, 1942 458
- Q. Telegram from General Wavell in Batavia to C.O.S. and to Washington for Combined C.O.S.. 26 January. 1942 460
- R. Telegram from ABDACOM to Burmarmy (Personal for Hutton from Wavell). 21 February, 1942 461
- S. Telegram from War Office to ABDACOM. 21 February, 1942 . 461
- T. Telegram from Wavell to War Office, G.H.Q., India and Burma. 22 February, 1942 462
- U. Telegram from ABDACOM Batavia to Armindia (For Hartley from Wavell). 23 February, 1942 462
- V. Telegram from General Wavell to C.O.S. 7 March, 1942 . . . 463

		Page
W.	Telegram from War Office to G.H.Q., India. 13 March, 1942	464
X₁.	Telegram from ARMINDIA to Chiefs of Staff. 15 March, 1942	464
X₂.	Telegram from General Wavell to C.O.S. 25 March, 1942	466
X₃.	Telegram from General Wavell to C.O.S.	467
Y.	Telegram from General Wavell to General Alexander. 14 April, 1942	467
Z.	Letter from Gen. Sir H. R. L. G. Alexander to Gen. Sir P. A. Wavell, C-in-C, India. 29 April, 1942	467

GROUP III

A.	17 Div Operation Instruction No. 5. 1 February, 1942	469
B.	Divisional Commander's Instruction H.Q. 17 Ind Div. 6 February, 1942	471
C.	17 Div Operation Instruction No. 12. 14 February, 1942	472
D.	17 Div Operation Order No. 3. 10 March, 1942	473
E.	17 Div Operation Instruction No. 19. 14 March, 1942	476
F.	Directive based on Burma Army Appreciation. 26 March, 1942	477
G.	1 Burcorps Directive No. 2. 27 April, 1942	479

GROUP IV

A.	A brief account of the Defence of Martaban and subsequent withdrawal	482
B.	Some notes on the withdrawal from Prome. April, 1942	487

LIST OF MAPS

		Page
1.	Rainfall in Burma. Mid-May to mid-October	5
2.	Dispositions of troops for defence of Central Burma and Tenasserim area December, 1941	38
3.	Action at Tavoy. 13-19 January, 1942	87
4.	Brigade area of responsibility 1 February, 1942	119
5.	Dispositions of forces. 5-9 February, 1942	123
6.	Dispositions of forces defending Bilin river line. 15-16 February, 1942	141
7.	Retreat from Rangoon 7-10 March, 1942	219
8.	Operations in the Shan States and withdrawal of 1 Burma Division. 23 February—24 March, 1942	230
9.	1 Burcorps defence zone. 10-14 March, 1942	235
10.	Dispositions 1 Burcorps. 28 March, 1942	239
11.	1 Burcorps counter offensive plan (Phase 1). 29 March, 1942	244
12.	Minhla-Taungdwingyi area. Dispositions of 1 Burcorps. 9 April, 1942	273
13.	Japanese thrust to the oilfields 8-10 April, 1942	275
14.	Yin Chaung dispositions. 14-16 April, 1942	284
15.	Situation on 26 April, 1942 following Japanese break-through in Shan States	312
16.	Battle of Monywa. 30 April—2 May, 1942	330
17.	Kalemyo, Kalewa & Tamu area. Route of withdrawal of Allied Forces. 5-11 May, 1942	340
18.	Action at Shwegyin. 9-11 May, 1942	344
19.	The Japanese Advance from Mawchi to Myitkyina. April—May, 1942	352
20.	Dispositions on Chinese Front. 5 April. 1942	356
21.	Japanese advance and withdrawal of Indian forces from Akyab. 1-4 May, 1942	362
22.	Sketch of Martaban	483

Facing page

23.	South-west Pacific & South-east Asia. Showing extent of Japanese occupation	31
24.	Tenasserim-Siam Area. Showing routes of Japanese attack. 27 November to 28 December, 1941	67
25.	Map of Mayawadi-Kawkareik area. Operations of 16 Ind Inf Bde. 20-25 January, 1942	97
26.	Defence of Moulmein. 26-29 January, 1942	111
27.	Moulmein Town and Environs. Operations of 2 Burma Brigade. 30-31 January, 1942	113
28.	Operations Kuzeik-Duyinzeik-Thaton. 11-13 February, 1942	135

Facing page

29.	Withdrawal from Duyinzeik-Thaton. 14-15 February, 1942	137
30.	Operations in Danyingon. 16-17 February, 1942	139
31.	Withdrawal from Bilin line. 20 February, 1942	155
32.	Pegu dispositions on 5 March, 1942. Operations by 17 Div & 7 Armoured Bde in Waw area	191
33.	Defence of Pegu by 48 Ind Inf Bde. 5 March, 1942	193
34.	Action at Shwedaung. 29-30 March, 1942	249
35.	Prome dispositions. 29 March—2 April, 1942	263
36.	Kokkogwa-Thadodan. Operations of 48 Bde and 7 Armoured Bde. 11-14 April, 1942	281
37.	Action by 1 Burma Div 9-13 April, 1942	283
38.	Operations in the Yenangyaung area. 16-17 April, 1942	289
39.	Yenangyaung and Environs. Operations of 1 Burma Div., 7 Armoured Bde and Chinese 38 Div. 18-19 April, 1942	295
40.	Battle of Kyaukse	321
41.	Burma. Showing geographical details of mountains. rivers, communications, ports, airfields, mines and oil wells etc.	502

Abbreviations

A.A.	Anti-Air-craft
ABDA	American British Dutch Australian
ABDACOM	American British Dutch Australian Command
AFV	Armoured Fighting Vehicle
AIB	Army in Burma
ARP	Air Raid Precautions
ATIS	Allied Translator Interpreter Section
A/Tk	Anti-tank
A.V.G.	American Volunteer Group
B.A.F.	Burma Auxiliary Force
B.A.S.C.	Burma Army Service Corps
Bde	Brigade
B.F.F.	Burma Frontier Force
B.M.P.	Burma Military Police
B.O.	British Officer
B.R.N.V.R.	Burma Royal Naval Volunteer Reserve
B.T.F.	Burma Territorial Force
Bty	Battery
BURIF or Burif	Burma Rifles
C.C.S.	Casualty Clearing Station
C.G.S.	Chief of General Staff
C.M.P.	Corps of Military Police
C.O.S.	Chief of Staff
C.R.E.	Commander Royal Engineers
C.S.O.	Chief Signals Officer
D.W.R.	Duke of Wellington's Regiment
'E' Signal	Evacuation Signal
Fd Bty	Field Battery
Fd Coy	Field Company
FEC	Far East Command
F.F.	Frontier Force
F.F.R.	Frontier Force Rifles
G.O.	Gurkha Officer
G.O.C.	General Officer Commanding
G.R.	Gurkha Rifles
H.Q., ALF	Headquarters Allied Land Forces
H.M.G.	His Majesty's Government
I.A.	Indian Artillery
I.A.F.	Indian Air Force
I.A.O.C.	Indian Army Ordnance Corps
I.E.	Indian Engineers
Ind	Indian
Inf	Infantry
I.O.Rs	Indian Other Ranks
KOYLI or Koyli	King's Own Yorkshire Light Infantry
L.M.G.	Light Machine Gun
L.N.D.	Light Naval Defence
L/Nk.	Lance Naik
Lt. A. A. Regt.	Light Anti-Aircraft Regiment

M.G.	Machine Gun
M.I.	Military Intelligence
M.Ls.	Motor Launches
M.M.G.	Medium Machine Gun
M.O.	Military Operation or Medical Officer
M.T. Coys	Mechanical Transport Companies
Mtn Bty	Mountain Battery
N.C.O.	Non-commissioned Officer
O.C.	Officer Commanding
P.O.L.	Petrol Oil & Lubricants
P.W.O.	Prince of Wales' Own
Q.A.O.	Queen Alexandra's Own
Q.O.H.	Queen's Own Hussars
R.A.	Royal Artillery
R.A.F.	Royal Air Force
R.A.P.	Regimental Aid Post
R.A.S.C.	Royal Army Service Corps
R.D.F.	Radio Direction Finding
R.E.	Royal Engineers
R.G.R.	Royal Gurkha Rifles
R.H.A.	Royal Horse Artillery
R.I.A.S.C.	Royal Indian Army Service Corps
R.I.N.	Royal Indian Navy
S & M.	Sappers & Miners
S.E.A.	South East Asia
S.E.A.T.I.C.	South East Asia Translation and Interrogation Centre
S.I.S.	Security Intelligence Section
S.S.S. or sss.	Southern Shan States
Tps	Troops
USAAC	United States Anti-aircraft Command
V.C.O.	Viceroy's Commissioned Officer
W/T	Wireless Telegraphy
W/T Set	Wireless Transmitting Set

Introduction

The Second World War had not long entered its third year before the eastern lands became a theatre of war, and India had the prospect of danger so close to her borders in the east. Japan had kept out of the war in its early stages though from early 1941 Germany had been prompting her to fight against England by striking against Singapore, ostensibly for the purpose of gaining Japanese collaboration in the invasion of Russia as much as to use Japanese intervention in the long-term war against the British Empire. But Japan feared American participation and did not desire to attack Singapore unless Germany had already invaded England. It is however clear that in Hitler's Grand Strategy there was provision for Japanese paramountcy in South-East Asia; and during the pendency of the war with Russia Hitler's Government had constantly desired Japanese belligerency against the Union of Soviet Socialist Republics. It is also known that Japan had been kept fully informed of Hitler's plans for a three-pronged attack on the Middle East. Germany had, meanwhile, overrun Western Europe and had directed her blows against the Balkans; she was led to declare war on Russia, and was involved in a grim struggle with the British forces in Northern Africa, where the battle swayed from the borders of Egypt to Libya. In Asia itself Syria, Iraq and Iran were threatened with Axis influence and only if Russian resistance had not prevented the flanking of the Caucasus, or Turkey had yielded the right of way, the German forces would have entrenched themselves on the Persian Gulf or advanced eastwards to batter on the western frontiers of India. However, a stroke of strategic imagination and timely intervention in Iraq and Iran by India had forestalled Axis approach and strongly blocked any possible movement eastward. Meanwhile, the unyielding resistance of Russia was straining the German resources to the utmost, and this prevented the Nazis from launching on any bolder adventures in Asia. In Africa itself the year 1941 had witnessed the collapse of the Italian empire in the east under the blows of the Indian Army, and by December, Rommel's offensive had been repulsed leaving Cyrenaica temporarily to General Auchinleck. The Axis fortunes, though not exactly at low ebb, were not meeting with spectacular successes and a stalemate, perhaps involving prolonged war, was in sight. It was in this hour that Japan beat the war drums in the east and inflicted a cruel blow on the British prospects of victory.

Japan had been engaged in war with China since 1937 but had failed to achieve her object of establishing "The Great East Asia Co-Prosperity Sphere", which in the words of Fuller would "make her the sun of an economic planetary system extending from Manchuria to Australia and from the Fiji Islands to the Bay of Bengal." She had failed to break the Chinese will to fight, and in 1941 the problem before her was to beat a hasty retreat or strangle China by cutting her supply lines. The latter course demanded a bold military adventure involving the closing of the ports of Indo-China, the blocking of the Burma Road and thereby preventing the United States from rendering effective assistance to China. The weakness of France afforded an opportunity for Japanese occupation of Indo-China in July 1941. This resulted in economic reprisals by the United States, England, India and the Netherlands, which was in essence "a declaration of economic war". Pearl Harbour soon followed and the unofficial participation of the United States in the war was overnight converted into open, active and determined hostility to the Axis, for eliminating Japan from rivalry in the Pacific and ousting Germany as a competitor for world supremacy. For Japan it would have been no easy decision as Russia had not yet withdrawn her eastern armies and Germany had not yet triumphed in Europe, while the combined war potential of the Anglo-American powers was not inconsiderable. But for Japan the choice was between economic ruin and resort to the sword for safe existence. If she had to fight the time was then when by diverting the Allied forces and supplies from the west, there might be an off-chance of crippling Russia, defeating British resistance in Africa, and enabling Germany to execute the big pincer from west and east against India, whose manpower and economic resources were then being utilised to sustain the war in the Middle East, where Germany's strategy to defeat Britain was then in operation.

Japan's immediate objects were to isolate China and to develop such a defence in depth as would preclude for many years the entry of England or America in east Asia, which would enable her to exploit to the full the natural resources of the countries within the Co-Prosperity Sphere. This necessitated rapid capture of Singapore and mastery over the Bay of Bengal and the occupation of Burma, Malaya and the Netherlands East Indies along with the myriad of islands stretching between India and Australia. She timed her advance well for at the moment the United States Navy was stunned and England was wholly unprepared for war in the east owing to the prior and heavy commitments in the Middle East. All equipment was earmarked for campaigns in that theatre and Indian forces were being trained for desert warfare. In the absence of effective American intervention for some time and the weakness of British navy, air force or army to stop her triumphal march westwards, it was easy for Japan to over-run Indo-China, Thailand, Malaya, Borneo, Java and Sumatra one by one, in quick succession, before directing her victorious army against Burma, the last of her victims in the western perimeter.

What was Japan's aim in conquering Burma? Whether it was merely a necessary consequence of the China War, for the purpose of closing the Burma Road and enveloping the Chinese forces from behind, or it had the object of invading India also, it is difficult to assert dogmatically. That Japan stopped short of the Indian frontiers and even when Indian military weakness was apparent and the eastern frontiers were almost undefended, Japanese forces did not advance further and their navy did not stage a landing on the long Indian coastline, give the impression that India was not at the moment included in the programme of her conquests. This makes Japanese offensive a limited one and motivated by the considerations of Pacific defence. But it may be surmised what her action would have been in case Germany was successful in the Middle East and Russia would not have staged the drive back of the Axis forces in the winter of

1941-42, thus enabling Germany to approach the western frontiers of India. Hitler had informed the Japanese Ambassador in Berlin on 14 December 1941 about his plan to attack South Russia in the spring of 1942 and, after seizing the Baku oilfields, to move eastward against India, and he was sanguine about his victory over Russia. In the event of the success of that strategy, it is probable that Japan would also have moved further westwards and India would have been enmeshed within the big pincer. But in the situation as it developed, the Japanese forces, owing to various factors, did not encroach on the soil of India. Burma alone remained the main objective and towards that Japan, as soon as she was free from Malayan preoccupation, directed her available strength.

Burma's defences were wholly inadequate to meet the new onslaught. Since its separation from India in 1937, the responsibility for Burma's security had devolved entirely on His Majesty's Government in the United Kingdom and the subordinate Defence Department in Rangoon. India had neither a share in this defence nor a say in it. Only when the clouds of war were looming in the eastern horizon and Japanese intentions were believed to be aggressive, that India was burdened with the liability of sending a force of two infantry brigades to Burma to reinforce its meagre army of Frontier Force, Auxiliary Force and Military Police personnel. But even after the declaration of war in Europe, and later when Japan had occupied Indo-China, no substantial endeavour was made to strengthen the garrison in Burma. It was not merely the lack of means which was responsible for this sad inadequacy, for if the threat to Burma had been clearly realised the resources might have been available. The strategic appreciation, which was most zealously adhered to by the British Government, was that Burma would at the worst be the victim of air raids and that her land frontiers were unlikely to be assailed. The Allied Conference in Singapore fortified this assurance, and even when the General Staff in India clamoured for effective aid for Burma in the interest of India's own security, it was a cry in the wilderness. Burma's importance was deemed to be only as a line of communication either in the chain of aerodromes between India and Singapore or in the protection of the Burma Road. With these notions of strategy it is not surprising that even when the Japanese forces were thundering at her gates, not much was done to substantially increase the armed strength of the country in time for effective defence. Reinforcements came, and these were not negligible, but they came rather late and failed to avert early disasters.

The plans for defence were governed by an erroneous and uninformed view of Axis strategy and resources. In all appreciations of 1940, the utmost extent of danger for Burma was computed as air threat though not on a heavy scale, but land attack was generally left out of count. However, in 1941, limited land action also figured in the military appreciations. At the end of October 1941, the Commander-in-Chief in India and the General Officer Commanding the Burma Army had concurred in the view that Japan could assemble up to eight divisions in Thailand, but the actual scale of attack against Burma from that direction was, owing to the maintenance difficulties, not estimated at higher than two divisions and twelve squadrons of aircraft. It was their appreciation that the main threat would develop against the Shan States from the direction of Chiangrai and Chiangmai and would be aimed against the road Thazi-Kengtung and Thazi-Mongpan, in north-eastern Burma. The comparative goodness of roads in that region of Thailand had been the basis of such appreciation. At the same time, it was assumed that only minor threats might be directed against Moulmein, Tavoy, Mergui and Victoria Point in Tenasserim, with a force of a brigade or two. The threat to Burma Road was also discounted. On this basis stock was taken of the forces available as also of the most suitable disposition of troops. At the time there were available two brigades, and two more were expected to arrive soon as reinforcements from India. General plan of defence was to stage delaying action if pitted against a superior force and finally to hold the line of river Salween at all costs. Defence was to be based on demolitions which were to be prepared. In the calculations for defence at that stage, of course, the prospect of receiving 3000 Chinese troops was taken into account, but a large force, it was held, could not be maintained in Burma. But their definite deployment was not then determined upon and it is probable that Burmese prejudice against Chinese forces may have influenced the plan to defend Burma single-handed.

Even after Japan's entry into the war full extent of the gravity of the situation was not appreciated. Lack of air support had been realised as also the fact that Bangkok had become a base for the landing of Japanese land forces, which would increase the scale of hostile attack. Burma Army appreciation on 12 December estimated that one or two divisions might be directed on the southern Shan States and one division on Tenasserim, and that air attacks would be serious. It was also assumed that owing to the lack of bombers, British offensive potential was considerably reduced. Hence a demand was made for two additional brigades, one for each area. The General Staff in India also in their detailed appreciation of the situation on 15 December 1941, failed to forecast the direction of attack. In their calculations though Tenasserim figured more prominently, attack on which was believed to be auxiliary to the war in Malaya and had a subsidiary purpose, the main operation was envisaged as advance by land against Kengtung and Taunggyi from north Thailand, combined with an advance on Moulmein from Rahaeng. This appreciation assessed the importance of Rangoon, but still considered the Burma Road as the objective of Japanese operations for eliminating China from the war, which pointed to the northern sector as being the chief objective of invasion.

The plan of defence had, therefore, a dual aspect, the preparation of "defence on the frontier at all places where useful routes lead from Thailand into Burma", and carrying out offensive operations into Thailand by air and on land. Static prepared defences on the main routes, particularly on the northern frontier, which might be used as pivots of manoeuvre for mobile guerilla columns were to be the defensive element. But the main effort was to be directed towards offensive operations by heavy bombing attacks against Japanese aerodromes and troop concentrations in northern Thailand, and advance into the region. It was to be effected by pushing forward into northern Thailand to draw the maximum hostile force there, and then to stage the main advance by the route Moulmein-Rahaeng-Sawarngalok, to cut the railway line and isolate the

Japanese forces in northern Thailand before liquidating them. It was as things should be. But the General Staff were not oblivious of the impracticability of this step owing to the paucity of troops and aircraft in Burma; hence for the moment they emphasised defensive preparations "designed to hold the main approaches into Burma", with a view to building up later the offensive potential of two divisions to be used in conjunction with the Chinese troops for defeating Japanese aggression in Thailand.

Gradually, however, the seriousness of the situation was dawning. On 22 December, General Wavell deplored the lack of air force on whose strength the defensive plan had been largely based and emphasised the importance of the defence of Rangoon against attack by air, sea or land. Henceforth also began the wail for more reinforcements which, as it was, had been considerably delayed. In January 1942, the apparition of the looming invasion began to haunt the Burma Army, though the complacence of the higher commands had not yet been completely shaken; and when Japanese infiltration had started in Tenasserim, the Burma Command realised that Malayan commitment and paucity of communications would not prevent the Japanese from employing large forces against Burma. Old estimates of the scale of attack therefore were invalidated and realities began to be faced. But even late in January, they had failed to comprehend fully the Japanese object of war in Burma or the basic elements of Axis strategy. That would account for their inability to appreciate that Rangoon would be the main objective of Japanese attack and that South Burma was primarily threatened. ABDACOM was more grievously ignorant of the real issues.[1] Only the General Staff in India, without having direct responsibility for Burma, had a clear view of the situation. Their reading on 21 January was that Japan would readily recognise danger to her communications from Burma, and would therefore be keen to stop the flow of supplies to China as well as the reinforcements from India of the garrison of Burma and air defence of Rangoon. Hence she "will lose no time in anticipating us and exploiting our resources". The General Staff, therefore, believed that with ample land forces in Thailand for further operations, Japan would initiate attack against the southern front, and after capturing Moulmein would infiltrate towards Rangoon, and that any major attack in the northern front was unlikely. This warning was late but it is problematical if it was immediately heeded.

From the above analysis of some of the early appreciations it will be evident that, up to the zero hour, the defenders of Burma had no clear comprehension of the war picture. Firstly, the danger was minimised and adequate preparations were not made. Secondly, the direction of attack could not be forecast for many British commanders were unable to rise above the notion that an attack would follow mainly well built lines of communication. They had been unable to realise the potentiality

---

[1] Wavell's statement on 21 January, based, in his own words, on "an error of judgment", was that "large scale effort against Burma seems improbable" and further his reprimand to Hutton "Am not quite clear why you regard situation as suddenly so serious" and "you should surely be able to hold Moulmein against considerable scale of attack".

of the Japanese soldier to march light and his tactics of infiltration and envelopment for which the difficult terrain of the southern front was most suitable. Hence, the plan of defence which was not fully developed showed every symptom of weakness and failed to afford protection.

A well recognised principle of defensive strategy is so to organise the defences as to admit of their easy conversion into bases of offensive operation. This involves the limiting of the axis of defence and organising it in depth, for every extension would lead to weakness. This principle appears to have been generally overlooked in planning for defence in Burma. Owing to the earlier appreciations defining the focus of attack to lie in the northern sector, a large force was concentrated in the Thazi-Kengtung region. Similarly, when danger was believed to grow against Tenasserim, two brigades were stationed in the southern area. This caused a dispersion of the limited force. Further, river Salween in its long course was considered to be an effective line of defence, and had to be consequently watched in its entire length. But the earlier dispositions had neglected the essential principle of linear defence resulting in failure to maintain the continuity of line. A large gap intervened between the northern and southern defences. Moreover, all defences had not been prepared or the routes leading into Burma blocked. There were few entrenchments or fortresses or even prepared static defences which as pivots of manoeuvre were capable of being used in holding the hostile force to enable the mobile formations to defeat the attacking columns. This drawback further accentuated the weakness of the small force in Burma. But the most glaring mistake was to ignore the capacity of the Japanese to stage a surprise, an essential element of offensive action. The northern sector, by virtue of its communications, would naturally indicate to the defence the direction of attack and thus lead to its preparedness. Whereas the southern sector, owing to its difficult terrain and pregnability of forward protective screen, would afford successful chances of infiltration and enveloping the weak defence before it could fully mobilise. The Japanese were adepts in these tactics and had been reported to be independent of the beaten roads in their movement in Malaya. It was dangerous to discount the resourcefulness of the Japanese.

An analysis of the operations also reveals departure from the principles of defensive warfare. Initially there was dispersal of the meagre forces between Moulmein, Tavoy and Mergui, each separated from the other by long distances and without any adequate means of communication. Emphasis on the defence of these widely separated towns so close to the Thailand frontier and exposed to attack from sea, air or land, without the possibility of their rapid reinforcement, may be justified by the opportunist principle of defending the aerodromes there to maintain the line of air communication with Malaya intact, but was not wholly justified from the point of view of the defence of Burma. The inevitable happened, the small garrisons in Mergui and Tavoy were cut off, and the fighting value of these useful troops was completely lost.

Next, when the main threat developed in the Moulmein-Kawkareik area, the gateway to Rangoon and south Burma, the organisation of defence exhibited weakness. There were two brigades in that region and reinforcements were not far. The region was screened by a high mountain range covered with dense jungle, and in the area behind it there were three main rivers which offered no easy obstacles. General Hutton wished to fight "as far forward as possible between the enemy and Rangoon so as to have room in which to deploy the expected reinforcements". With that object his first line of resistance was fixed at the Dawna Range, and the Salween was to be the next obstacle. This was expected to leave the area in the rear for the expected reinforcements which might have provided defence in depth. But before the new forces could arrive and the defenders had the assistance of armoured force, the Japanese had struck and pierced the mountain passes. The forward defences were thrown back on the Salween. But here, in spite of the initial emphasis on holding the Salween line, little use was made of that natural obstacle, and the seriousness of Japanese threat was not fully appreciated. Opinions may also vary regarding the wisdom of dispersing a small force in holding the passes in a country which provided chinks for infiltration almost anywhere without sufficient depth in the rear which alone would have prevented envelopment. The absence of armoured force made the task doubly difficult, and in the circumstances as they developed, the Salween became a trap instead of being a deep ditch protecting the entrenched positions behind it.

The withdrawal from the mountain barrier together with the loss suffered at Kyondo, owing to the river being in the rear, exposed the whole region up to the Salween to the Japanese. Subsequent phases of the campaign occurred in the Salween-Sittang-Pegu area where also no effective preparations for defence had been made beforehand. It was then clear that the main Japanese thrust was directed against South Burma with Rangoon as their objective, and that the attack in this sector would be their principal effort. It was also evident that with the available forces every line of approach could not be manned in strength, and that every delay in retiring behind a natural screen and containing the hostile thrust would endanger the security not only of the weak forces but also of the main centre of civil and military activity. Yet, despite the obvious weakness of defending Moulmein, the decision was made to hold it "at any rate", and not conform to the suggestion of the Divisional Commander to move the 17th Division "right back to the area Bilin-Kyaikto-River Sittang." The stand at Moulmein could have two objects, firstly that of preventing easy crossing of the Salween at a point which commanded the main communications to Rangoon, and secondly that of gaining time to prepare defences in the rear and enable the armoured force, which was then arriving into Burma, to take up its positions. But full use was not made of the Moulmein stand, though it enabled the force after reinforcement to deploy in the Salween-Bilin area, which then became the main area of resistance. This step would have been a sound strategic decision if there were a large force to man the long Salween line, watching the ferries, and to prepare hedgehog defences in depth from where mobile armoured columns could radiate along lateral communications to contain the infiltrating Japanese troops and liquidating them in their progress towards Rangoon.

The Divisional Commander had not been quite happy with the new situation and desired withdrawal to the Sittang. But he was over-ruled and General Hutton stuck to the line of the river Salween where no ground was to be given. Martaban was to be held securely and the entire disposition of troops was directed against landings from the Gulf of Martaban. The 17th Indian Division was to hold Martaban, Thaton, Paan, Bilin, Kyaikto and Papun, and the main road and railway from Martaban to Sittang Bridge were to be patrolled. The area was much too extensive for a small force without armoured support. At best it could afford merely a thin cover which would leave the individual units disconnected, and, in a country of no lateral communications, exposed to hostile envelopment and liquidation one by one. Moreover, their disposition was directed against sea-landing, for more troops were concentrated on the rail-road line from Martaban to Kyaikto with smaller forces in the triangle Bilin-Papun-Paan where terrain facilitated infiltration. By this means the line had been extended. The Divisional Commander requested permission to shorten his line, on the dictum that extension limits the depth, and desired to withdraw on the Bilin line. But it was decided to hold Martaban and there was justification for it, too, if the Salween line was to be the main line of resistance. However, Martaban did not hold out; Paan on the eastern bank of the Salween was surrounded; the Martaban-Thaton road was cut; and the Japanese forces crossed the Salween by ferries between Paan and Papun. The next halt was made on the Bilin river, but exhausted troops could not long endure on that line which had not been previously prepared and which provided room for infiltration, and were compelled to retreat in disaster beyond the Sittang river, behind which the Pegu force had been prepared and the 7th Armoured Brigade was in position.

It has been necessary to go into some detail to show the strategy adopted in the first stage of the campaign, which may be termed the stage of resistance. This stage has lent itself to the comment that it was divorced from the object of war. If Rangoon was the vital point of defence which had to be retained as long as possible to enable reinforcements to arrive, it would have been more reasonable to organise defences towards that end. Once the Sittang-Bilin position was pierced, Japanese advance towards Rangoon could not be easily checked. The policy of fighting so far away from Rangoon would be feasible, if a large force was available for deployment in depth which would be able, at every stage of infiltration of the hostile columns, to contain them and liquidate them. Linear defence on the ultimate frontier without adequate reserves, and not based on prepared entrenched positions and having the main obstacles behind it, afforded weak protection and led to disaster, for by the time the defence force could retreat to the line of resistance nearer the centre of defence, the troops were exhausted, demoralised and unable to protect the main object. And when Pegu force was by-passed and Japanese troops had pierced through this gap between the 17th Indian Division and the 1st Burma Division positions, the fate of Rangoon and that of Burma was sealed. There was no alternative left to the evacuation of Rangoon and withdrawal northwards.

The resistance had been made feeble not only by the lack of effective reinforcements and support of armoured and air force, but also by the opportunist strategy which dispersed meagre strength. Building up of a force on a strategically sound and strongly defensive line of resistance might have staved off the danger, and by delaying Japanese advance would have afforded the chance for reinforcements to arrive. But that was not done, and instead of waiting for the attack to develop in the area most suitable for defence, close to its base and feasible for armoured forces, behind a natural obstacle with outposts fanning out for observation and delaying action, the defence had to meet the Japanese, forward on an extended line without any depth behind, and lost the game. A prepared defence in the Sittang-Bilin area, with the supporting reserves in Pegu, might have been a better plan, as it might afford contact with the force in the northern sector. But weakness in numbers, absence of armoured support and lack of information about the Japanese, together with the non-availability of adequate Chinese support at the moment, weakened the defence and made long resistance impossible in an area which had not been already prepared for defence.

After Pegu the evacuation of Rangoon and retreat northwards became inevitable leaving South Burma to the Japanese. The loss of Rangoon made it difficult to receive reinforcements and supplies from India or elsewhere, for the land link with India had not yet developed and airlift was not adequate. The only choice before the Burma Army was to withdraw to Upper Burma on the way to India; but until the road from Assam to Burma was constructed and supplies could flow in, its "retention was dependent on the amount of force which the Japanese decided to employ in that theatre". And all that could be done by the Allies was to delay Japanese advance and compel them "to expend resources which he might have employed elsewhere." The retention of Upper Burma therefore became an important object of strategy, for which a regrouping of forces was essential. The retreat was to be no rout and, as long as practicable, every endeavour was to be made to counter-attack the hostile advance, make a stand in strategically defensive areas and to save as much force as possible to fight again from India. Clausewitz has defined the characteristics of proper retreat and has compared it to the retreat of a wounded lion. According to him "the retreat is continued up to that point where the equilibrium of forces is restored, either by reinforcements, or by the protection of strong fortresses, or by great defensive positions afforded by the country, or by a separation of the enemy's forces". He commends "a slow retreat, offering incessant resistance, and bold courageous counter-strokes, whenever the enemy seeks to gain any excessive advantage". The retreat from Burma as directed by General Alexander may be judged by this dictum.

The retreat was effected in three stages depending on the areas where counter-attack was to be delivered. The first stand was planned in the area around Prome in the Irrawaddy valley where all Indo-British forces were to be concentrated, leaving the protection of the north-eastern sector to the Chinese Armies. But the defeat at Toungoo and the inability of the Chinese to hold the Japanese forces beyond, in time, compelled a further retreat. The second region was the dry zone south of Taungdwingyi where the terrain was more suitable for armoured warfare. This could also screen off the oilfields. The third stage was the Mandalay-Meiktila area where resistance was to be offered preliminary to the withdrawal to India behind the defensive wall of the Chindwin and difficult mountain screen. But in none of these zones was there available any strong fortress protection or great natural defence. Reinforcements were also not expected there. Hence the only object was that of slow retreat, strengthening the morale of the forces and arranging organised withdrawal to India. The defence of Upper Burma as a base for future operations was doomed to failure owing to the weakness and exhaustion of the Indo-British forces and the inability of the Chinese Armies to stop the Japanese from reaching Lashio and Bhamo in their rear. The situation in the Shan States and the inevitability of Japanese infiltration north of the Irrawaddy, as well as their encircling movements towards the Chindwin, all demanded hasty withdrawal from Mandalay. At that stage the main object was to provide for the defence of India, but momentarily maintenance of touch with the Chinese and getting across a maximum force to India for reorganisation, were also no minor objects. The plan of operations provided for the detachment of two brigades astride the Chindwin to delay Japanese advance, as far south as possible, for the defence of India.

An analysis of the events connected with the retreat and the plans and operation orders reveals its success and orderly character. At every stage till the evacuation of Mandalay, counter-offensive dictated the trend of operations. Defensive harbours in strategic areas were prepared where the forces were concentrated to delay hostile progress, inflict maximum injury on the Japanese and prevent them from blocking further retreat. From stage to stage the retreating divisions were instructed to occupy defensive positions from which strong mobile and armoured columns were to be detached to engage the Japanese forces in the area. The defensive positions were themselves based on a series of brigade areas in which battalions and companies were sited for all round defence. These harbours were formed on the model of a fortified position with trenches and tactical wire entanglements. Concealment and ambushing were the main methods of dealing with hostile troops. Deep patrolling by armoured forces and mounted infantry was the keynote of such defence. For this purpose the retreating force was grouped occasionally between Striking Force and Defensive Force, and coulmns were formed for particular tasks to keep the retiring zone clear of the adversary. Contact was also maintained with the Chinese Armies and every care was taken to prevent the flanks being exposed. When it became clear that counter-attack would not avail and continuous retreat was essential, bridgeheads and layback positions were always planned and executed which enabled the army to get back up to the Chindwin without being completely enveloped and destroyed. It must be admitted that the strategy of retreat was well planned and successfully executed so that a large portion of the army, even at the expense of its equipment, withdrew to India, a feat which was highly creditable for the commander and his force.

The woeful retreat from Burma brings prominently into view the importance of early preparations, sound training and concentration of force. It also reveals the dangers of under-estimating the adversary and over-optimism. The defence of Burma had long been neglected and though reinforcements were rushed, equipment was promised and communications were developed, all came so late as to be unable to affect the ultimate fate. Preparations made early and reinforcements sent in time might have made considerable difference and afforded prospects of a prolonged resistance. Then also there was lack of training for the task involved in the terrain of Burma. There was no training in jungle warfare and very often the most serious handicap was the lack of air protection and the absence or weakness of armoured element. In the first stage of resistance armoured force was not available, and when it arrived, it could not move beyond the rear-most area and was thus incapable of modifying the trend of battle. In retreat it played a considerable part and very often saved the army from being easily overrun. But owing to the tactics of road-block continuously employed by the Japanese, its effectiveness was greatly limited. Lack of air umbrella also lowered morale and made the Indian infantry easy victims of Japanese air action. Yet, perhaps the greatest factor in the defeat of the Allies was the complete apathy or even hostility of the local population, which was believed to be assisting the Japanese. Whatever may have been the cause of this attitude, it cannot be denied that the Indo-British forces, in the event, were compelled to fight a defensive battle, not in their territory but almost in a hostile land. It involved fighting on a double front which is always productive of disaster.

On the contrary, the Japanese had made long preparations and effective training for the task of conquering Burma. Their forces had become expert in jungle fighting and adopted with great dexterity the tactics of infiltration, envelopment and rapid light marches through little known tracks. Their improvisations were also a surprise to their foes, and in Burma they got wide support of the population of which they made fullest use. They were adepts in the art of concealment which afforded great advantage in village fighting and avoiding the Allied tanks. But the most characteristic feature of their warfare was the frequent employment of road-blocks both for protecting their own flanks and cutting off the Allied forward troops and transport. The road-blocks themselves were never substantial, being made of broken vehicles or felled trees, etc. but they were always strongly held and were effective against a mechanised force. Japanese strategy was direct and had the object of dividing the opposing forces and encircling them by turn to neutralise their fighting power. Terrain and local knowledge helped them in their movements which allowed them ample use of the element of surprise. Utilisation of local resources and assistance of the Burmese population, which was hostile to British domination, proved of immense value to them and enabled them to develop easily and successfully their tactics of infiltration and envelopment. Their first objective was Rangoon and they concentrated on it. When that had been achieved their object was to destroy the Allied force in Burma, and for that they raced towards the bridgeheads to India and China. But the resistance was stout and their forces failed to be in time to anticipate and cut off the Allied forces. However, they were able to inflict a severe blow to the Allies whose force reached India with considerable loss and in great disorganisation. The Japanese advance was three-pronged, subsequent to the capture of Rangoon, one, towards the Chindwin by the west coast of the Irrawaddy, second, up the Shan States towards Lashio, Bhamo and Shwebo, and the third, up the Irrawaddy chasing the Indo-British force. That was well calculated to encircle the hostile force and had gained immense success.

A word may also be added about administration. Owing to its position and as the centre of communication system, Rangoon was the main base of supplies. But this concentration led to serious problems in later stages. However, when war was in sight an alternative base was also constructed in the north, and in Prome, Toungoo or Mandalay, large stores had been collected. This involved constant back-loading of supplies which caused considerable strain on the transport, and very often induced the Japanese force to find easy targets. Retreat was handicapped by this obstruction. Yet it will have to be admitted that the retreating force had no dearth of supplies except in certain engagements where lack of communication or close hostile pressure might have prevented the supply organisation from functioning. After the evacuation of Rangoon, when contact with India was not possible by land or sea, air transport was utilised to convey essential supplies. Food was available otherwise in the country. Nevertheless, transport was not adequate for the needs of the army, and railway and water transport had ceased to function effectively. This revealed the drawback of not militarising the essential transport services in the defence zone.

The retreat from Burma was an essential consequence of faulty appreciation, inadequate preparation and defective strategy. Political factors aggravated the situation further and the result was that Burma, the eastern bastion of India, was rapidly overrun by the Japanese and thus the Indian frontier was exposed to aggression. The trend of defence in Burma was not calculated to ensure the security of India, for that had not been realised as the object till practically the fall of Mandalay. Neither was Upper Burma provided with strong defences nor was Arakan guarded, and these afforded chinks for entry into India. It was fortunate that India did not have to meet Japanese onthrust immediately, otherwise the loss of Burma would have been dangerous to the security of her own eastern provinces. The defeat of the Indo-British forces in Burma and their retreat, on the one hand, highlighted the intimate relationship of India's security with the protection of Burma and, on the other, exposed the weakness of basing defence on an unwilling and politically dominated population. The Japanese had to halt on the Chindwin and, though immediate threat to India was recognised, the onset of monsoon, long lines of communication in the rear, the need for reorganising forces for a major venture and opposition of the main political organisation in India to any external aggression, prevented the Japanese from extending their conquests beyond Burma. The loss of Burma, however, brought India face to face with grave danger on her eastern frontier which had never before been adequately defended. The India Command had not only to organise defence there but also to plan for the reconquest of Burma to drive back the Japanese army from the periphery of India's security. The Retreat from Burma thus became a strategic withdrawal to the line where reinforcements might be available and from which the invader could be hit back.

BISHESHWAR PRASAD

CHAPTER I

Burma—The Land and its People

Lying between China and India, yet separated from both by high mountains, Burma forms an important part of the Indo-Chinese peninsula. At the outbreak of the Second World War, the country had an area of 261,610 square miles, and was bounded on the north by Tibet, on the east by China, French Indo-China and Thailand, on the south and west by the Indian ocean and on the north-west by the State of Manipur and the Indian provinces of Assam and Bengal.

Topographically, the elevated part of Burma, which divides itself into ranges stretching southward, is an extension of the mountain mass of Central Asia. The country is encircled on three sides by mountains. It is marked off in the north-west by the Chin Hills and in the north by the Naga Hills and the Kumon Range. The Kachin, Shan and Karen Hills cover the eastern area. A land of great length and modest width, Burma has been described as the head of an elephant with Tenasserim and Malay Peninsula as its long trunk.

Politically, British Burma was till 1937 a part of India and continued to be almost so militarily till the end of the Second World War. Strategically it is not a mere corridor but a vast road-block thrust between China and India. It is a barrier of mountains, monsoon and malaria, and of rivers and jungles. Some tracks led from Burma to India; but there was at the start of the war not a single road worth the name. With the opening of the Burma Road and the air-line running from Calcutta through Myitkyina to Chungking, Burma eventually became the back-door of China when the latter's treaty ports were closed one by one by Japan.

Culturally, Burma has been the bridge between the ancient civilizations of India and China. While Annam to the east has been greatly influenced by China, in Burma the predominant role has been played by India. Religious and commercial contacts across the Bay of Bengal are very old. Burmese Buddhism derives directly from the parent centres in India. Its texts are written in Pali, and the script of Burmese has been borrowed from South India. The religious architecture of Burma is essentially Indian, especially in Pagan, the centre of the oldest and in many respects the greatest of Burmese ruling dynasties; and the heroes of literary legend, and folk-tale alike, are often reflections from Indian epics and myths.

---

[1] The best contour maps of Burma are those prepared by the Survey of India, Calcutta. E. A. Spearman's *British Burma Gazetteer* (Rangoon 1880) deals with the physical geography of Lower Burma. Though somewhat obsolete in nomenclature, the treatment is authoritative.

GEOGRAPHICAL DIVISIONS

Though a geographical unity Burma has within itself much diversity. Some would divide it into two distinct regions—Lower and Upper Burma. The former corresponds roughly to those parts of Burma which were brought under British control by the Anglo-Burmese Wars of 1824 and 1852 and include the great plains and deltas of the Irrawaddy, and the plains of the Sittang and the lower Salween rivers in addition to Arakan. Here is centred the agricultural wealth of Burma, its world-famed rice fields. It includes also the Tenasserim peninsula. Upper Burma, quite a different country, consists in the main, of the upper Irrawaddy valley and the hill tracts which surround it. Apart from what was yielded by the oilfields of the central zone, northern Burma produced most of the mineral wealth of the country.

Others would divide Burma into three belts:—
- (i) the western hills,
- (ii) the central belt or Burma proper, and
- (iii) the Shan Plateau in the east with a southward continuation in Tenasserim.[2]

The Western Hills

The western hills stem from the vast mountain knot in the Tibeto-Chinese border-lands and swing southwards in a great arc to the sea; they consist of numerous north-to-south ridges whose extreme parallelism is very striking from the air. The Naga and Chin hills constitute the centre of the arc and the Arakan Yoma (Yoma mountain) falls to the south. Lying as they do athwart the rain bearing monsoon winds, the hills throughout get a heavy rainfall. In the tropics this leads to dense jungle and often extremely malarious conditions. The hills are, therefore, sparsely peopled by the tribes such as the Chins and the Nagas, whose primitive agriculture on small burnt-out clearings, abandoned once every three or four years, destroys forest cover and leads to the growth of scrub and bamboo jungle, a great obstacle to communications. In the coastal strip of Arakan, some of the bigger streams have built up small lowlands, which are densely populated. The coastline is creek-and-island-fringed and life is amphibious.

The Central Belt—Rivers and Plains

The central belt or Burma proper consists of the valleys of the Irrawaddy, the Chindwin, the Sittang and the Delta. They have a general north-to-south direction with the important exception of the great east and west bend of the Irrawaddy from Mandalay to the Chindwin confluence. South of Mandalay, the Sittang carries on the line of the upper Irrawaddy. These are the most actively eroding and depositing streams in the world.

Irrawaddy. The Irrawaddy is the life-giving stream of Burma. It traverses the centre of the country practically throughout its entire length of 1,300 miles. At its widest point it is three miles broad and it divides

---

[2] Alleyne Ireland divides Burma into four distinct areas: littoral, deltaic, central and sub-montane. *The Province of Burma.*
See also *British Burma* by Forbes, Vol. I, p. 3.

and subdivides itself, converting the lower portion of its valley into a net-work of inter-communicating tidal creeks, and reaches the sea by eight principal mouths. The area of its catchment basin is 15,800 square miles.

The river is navigable for 800 miles up to Bhamo by large steamers all the year round. Before the war, the Irrawaddy Flotilla Company steamers sailed up and down the stream twice a week. From Bhamo to Myitkyina country-boats can sail, but above Myitkyina navigation is difficult. As a natural source of irrigation its value is enormous but no artificial system of irrigation was built out of it.

Sittang. The Sittang river which drains the valley to the east of the Pegu range is greatly inferior to the Irrawaddy both in the length of its course and in its width. But it possesses similar characteristics. Its chief peculiarity is the great tidal wave or bore which renders navigation in the lower part very dangerous.

Chindwin. The largest tributary of the Irrawaddy is the Chindwin whose entire course lies in Burma. Rising in the far north of Burma on the borders of Assam, it flows south-west on the eastern side of the Naga and Chin hills. Turning south-east it joins the Irrawaddy just above Pakokku, south of Mandalay. Through the greater part of its length until reaching Monywa its course is through rugged and dense jungle country very sparsely populated. Much of its valley is malarial, and in 1941 had no road connection with the rest of Burma, and the river was the only link.

Delta. The delta region has a rainfall of 80 to 130 inches a year. It covers an area of 10,000 square miles including the lower portion of the Sittang which, however, has not formed a delta. Of the eight main distributaries of the Irrawaddy, the most important is the westernmost on which stands the port of Bassein. Most of the delta is one flat level plain seriously exposed to the risk of floods. Here and there are uplands of older alluvium such as the Twante Upland and the long ridge at the end of which stands Rangoon. But even these are rarely higher than 40 to 70 feet above the sea-level. Near the coast which is covered by forest, the villages tend to align themselves on long low ridges or along the sides of the creeks. For the rest, the delta is a sea of paddy, of wide spaces, and magnificent skyscapes.

The Shan Plateau and Tenasserim

East of Burma proper lies the tableland of massive limestone and crystalline rocks, most of which was occupied by 34 Shan and 3 Karenni States. Its average elevation is over 3,000 feet. The tableland is intersected by deep gorges of the Salween and its tributaries. This river, longer than the Irrawaddy and wild in its course, offers a very formidable natural obstacle. It does not admit of navigation and not being spanned by any bridge is crossed by ferries at a number of points.[3]

The general grain of the country is north and south. In its western part there are many wide flat bottom straths, silted floors of old lakes and fantastically craggy hills. The rainfall of 60 to 100 inches is enough to support a fairly dense jungle of bamboo brakes. The thickly wooded

---

[3] *Haward Journal of Asiatic Studies* III, 1938, pp. 31-36.

ranges of Tenasserim, a southward continuation of the Shan Plateau, consist mainly of granite bosses and limestone crags running in a north-to-south direction. Like Arakan, Tenasserim is a narrow coastal strip lying between the Salween and the Bay of Bengal in the west and the hills forming the Thai frontier in the east. Like the Arakan coast its coastline is studded with numerous islands. The Dawna Range, a long narrow range with peaks exceeding 6,000 feet in elevation, separates Tenasserim from Thailand and forms the watershed of the Salween. The low lying lands are mainly under rice cultivation. But the rest of the country is one vast area of dense jungle.

RAINFALL

Burma is a typical monsoon country with alternate wet and dry seasons. The entire rainfall is concentrated in five months from mid-May to mid-October and, except in the central zone which is dry, is plentiful in all parts. In Arakan, Tenasserim and in the mountain ranges along the upper reaches of the Irrawaddy as also the hills which form the Chinese frontier, it exceeds 200 inches a year; the delta has an average of 110 inches. But in the dry zone the rainfall does not exceed 30 inches. A point of interest to the military authorities may be that owing to the north-south grain of the country, monsoon clouds from the south-west are deflected by the hills to a northernly course. When they arrive at a cul de sac in the hills at the head of a valley, there is heavy precipitation, chiefly on the southern and western slopes. As a result, rainfall figures vary very considerably between places, only a few miles apart, and with this variation there is a corresponding difference in the vegetation. During the dry season there is little rain and the heat is the greatest from March to May and that too in the centre of the country. Rangoon rarely, if ever, reaches 100°F in April (the hottest month) while in Mandalay, in the tropics, a temperature of 105°F and over is fairly common.

POPULATION

The population of Burma according to the census of 1941 was a little less than 17 millions.[4] But the density (165 per square mile) is less than that of India (295 per square mile) or China. The Burmese who mostly occupied the plains constituted nearly 10 millions, the Karens about 4 millions, the Shans mainly in the eastern plateau about 2 millions and the rest 1 million. The hills were occupied by the Kachins in the north, the Nagas and the Chins in the west and the Karens (a different group from that of the plains who are largely Christians) in the east.[5] Of the non-indigenous population the most important were the Indians and the

---

[4] The 1941 decennial census was taken on 5 March 1941 for the first time under the direction of a Burman. *The Ethnological Survey of Burma* (1917) is brief and incomplete. *The Census of Burma* Part I, App. C. & D.

[5] For the Chins see the volume by B. S. Carey and H. N. Tuck, *The Chin Hills: A History of the People*. Also O'Connor: *The Silken East*. For Kachins see "*A Burmese Arcady*" by C. M. Enriquez. For Karens see "*The Karen People of Burma—study in the Anthropology and Ethnology*" by H. I. Marshall, and "*Burma and the Karens*" by San C. Po.

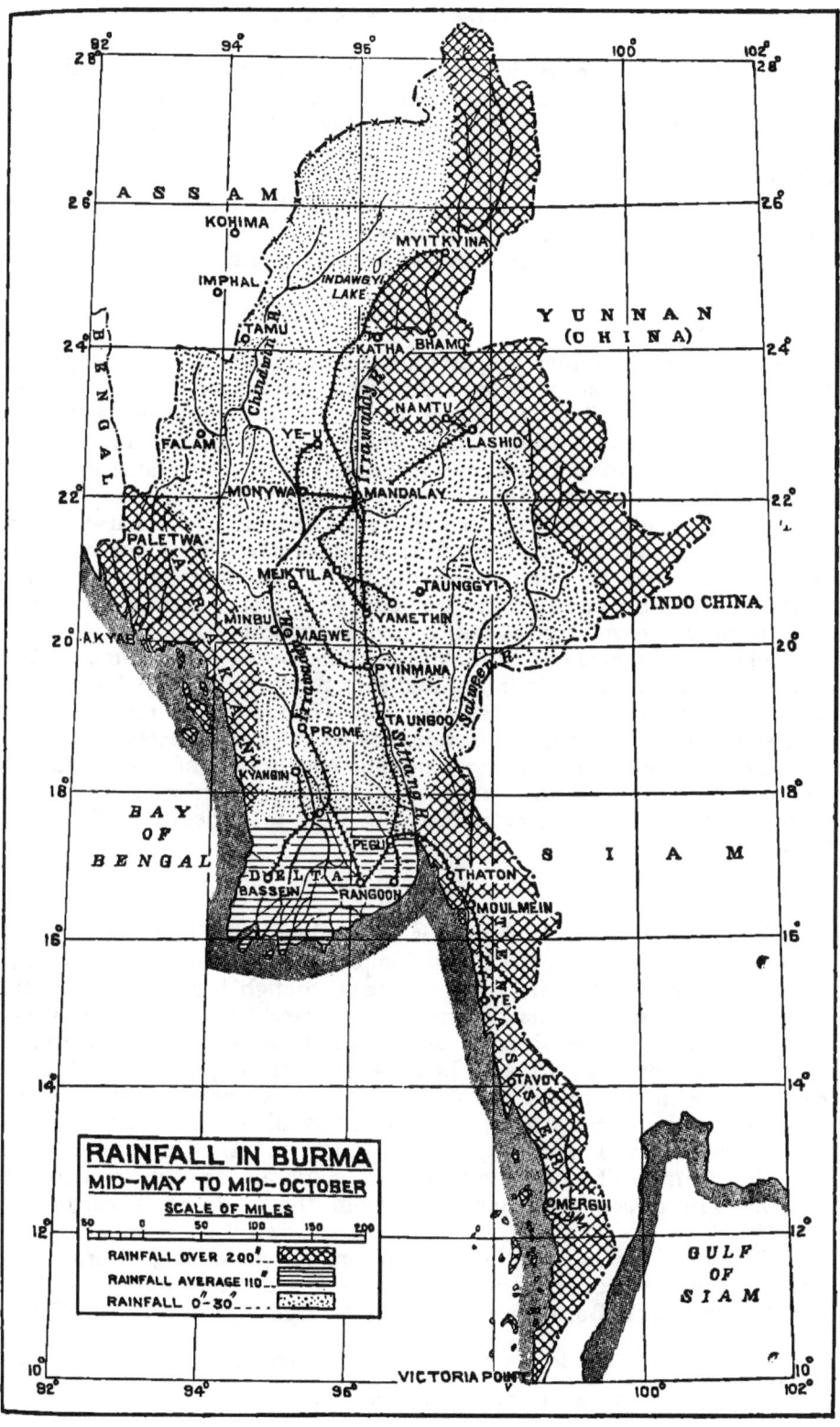

Chinese. In 1941 the Indians numbered about a million consisting largely of traders, professional men, public servants and industrial workers with a strong tendency to urban concentration. The Chinese element of over 300,000 (in 1931) rose steadily after the opening of the Burma Road and fell into three categories:—

(*i*) Cantonese and Fukienese as traders in Rangoon and (*ii*) as tin miners in Tenasserim and (*iii*) Yunnanese in the north. Inter-marriages between the Chinese and the Burmese were frequent.

AGRICULTURE

Agriculture is the most important industry of Burma and the greater part of the population is engaged directly or indirectly in it or in connected occupations. The staple crop is rice. A characteristic feature of Burma is its extensive paddy lands, which cover the delta and a great part of Lower Burma; almost every available piece of suitable flat land throughout the country is under rice cultivation. In the rainy season these lands are under water. In the dry weather after the harvest they are sun-baked and dusty. Each field is surrounded by a low bund of earth which serves to retain water during the planting and cultivating periods. The other crops grown, particularly in Upper Burma, are sugarcane, tobacco, cotton, ground-nut, maize and wheat.

Following the example of Malaya and the Dutch East Indies, rubber cultivation was successfully introduced into Burma. By 1941 large areas in Tenasserim and around Rangoon and Toungoo were under rubber plantation and the rubber production was by no means inconsiderable.

The forests of Burma are large and fine but they are of uneven quality and not very valuable and extensive. They produce the world's main supply of teak. The timber industry is, next to agriculture, the most important.

MINERALS

The mineral wealth of Burma is fairly abundant. She was the only important source of oil in the British Empire and her output of petroleum formed an important item in her economy, though her oil output from 5,000 wells was only a small fraction of the world total. The principal oil-bearing areas were situated along the Irrawaddy at Thayetmyo, Minbu, Yenangyaung, Chauk, Lanywa and Yenangyat. Several large companies were interested in oil production. There were some small refineries on the oilfields but the important refining plants were situated at Syriam, Thilawa and Sikgyi near Rangoon. The largest of these was the Burma Oil Company's plant at Syriam. To this refinery oil was brought direct by a pipe line from the fields at Yenangyaung and Chauk.

The other minerals are tin and wolfram, tungsten, lead, silver, copper and limestone. The production of wolfram was developed greatly during World War I and Burma soon became its largest producer.[*] In Tenas-

---

[*] The Mawchi Mines, in the Karenni States of Bawlake, were the world's most important single source of wolfram. They produced 35 per cent of the world's pre-war needs and about 85 per cent of the British Empire's needs.

serim numerous tin mines and dredging areas were being worked in 1941. Burma also produced about 4,000 tons of tin annually and was the eighth largest producer in the world.

At Namtu in the northern Shan States was situated the silver-lead mine of Burma Corporation. There lead was produced on a very large scale and Namtu was connected by the private railway of the Burma Corporation with the northern Shan States branch of the Burma Railways at Nam-Yao, twenty-five miles distant from Namtu.

TOWNS, VILLAGES AND PORTS

Burma is essentially a land of villages. Rangoon and Mandalay apart there are no big towns, and of these Rangoon is the only modern city. The capital and main port of Burma, Rangoon is not situated on the Irrawaddy, as is often supposed, but stands twenty miles off the sea on the Hlaing river rising in the Pegu Yoma. It is connected by tidal creeks with the delta and some Irrawaddy water finds its way out by this stream. The Hlaing's opposite number on the eastern side of the Pegu Yoma is the Pegu river. Their confluence gives Rangoon its superb water nodality. The town may well be termed as the gateway of Burma since from it radiate all the lines of communication through the country. In 1941 it had a population of about half a million, of which the largest part was Indian. It was the commercial and industrial centre and through its port passed by far the greater part of the country's imports and exports. In it or in its environs were housed large rice and timber mills and a great part of such minor industrial activities as had been established in Burma. The building of the Burma Road had further enhanced Rangoon's vital importance.[7]

Moulmein, Bassein and Akyab, the only other seaports of any size, were, on the eve of the war, badly served by land communications and were of very minor importance. From them was exported rice; Moulmein in addition exported timber and some of the rubber and mineral ore of Tenasserim. Kyaukpyu, Sandoway, Tavoy, and Mergui were still smaller ports utilised mainly by country craft and coastal shipping.

COMMUNICATIONS

Railway

The lack of proper development of communications in Burma was a great handicap to the Burma Army during the campaign of 1941-42. Perhaps, this backwardness was due, to some extent, to the over-reliance on the convenience of coast-wise shipping and on the splendid trunk routes afforded by the Irrawaddy and the lower Chindwin.

The Burma Railway, taken over by the Government in 1939, operated

---

[7] The construction of the famous Burma Road, China's lifeline to the south-west, was begun late in 1937. Actually sections of this road had been open for several years. Between December 1937 and May 1938 the Chinese cut the roadbed from Hsiakwan near Tali to the Sino-Burmese town at Wanting. All construction was directed by Chinese engineers and done with hand tools. The length of the road was 750 miles and the time taken for travel was 5 days. The highway was opened officially on 10 January 1939.

on the metre gauge. The main line ran from Rangoon to Mandalay, a distance of three-hundred-and-eighty-six miles. Of this the first hundred-and-seventy-six miles consisted of a double track, the remainder and all branch lines were single track.

From Pegu, forty-seven miles north of Rangoon on the main line, ran two branch lines, one south to Thongwa through a rich paddy growing area and the other east to Martaban on the west bank of the Salween. A ferry connected the line with Moulmein which then ran south to Ye.

From Pyinmana, two-hundred-and-twenty-six miles north of Rangoon, a branch line ran north-west to Taungdwingyi and Kyaukpadaung, the nearest rail points to the oilfields at Yenengyaung and Chauk.

At Thazi junction, three-hundred-and-six miles north of Rangoon, began two branch lines. The southern Shan States branch ran east to Kalaw and terminated at Shwenyaung just west of Taunggyi, the capital of the Shan States. The other branch was a loop line to Meiktila and Myingyan, an important railway centre on the Irrawaddy. It rejoined the main line at Paleik, twelve miles south of Mandalay.

From Rangoon another line ran north-west via Tharrawaddy to Prome, one-hundred-and-sixty-one miles distant, on the Irrawaddy. From this line a branch at Letpadan connected by ferry with Henzada, on the right bank of the Irrawaddy, and from Henzada a branch ran north to Kyangin, whilst another ran south to Bassein to serve the western portion of the Irrawaddy delta.

Mandalay, next to Rangoon, was, in 1941, the most important railway and communication centre in Burma. It had a population of over one hundred thousand and was the second city in size in the country. Its population was predominantly Burmese. From this city ran a railway through the northern Shan States to Lashio. Another short line ran north, seventeen miles, to Madaya. A third line ran to the Irrawaddy, a few miles south of the city opposite Sagaing. Crossing the river by the recently completed road and rail Ava Bridge, it turned north to Shwebo and Myitkyina. From Sagaing a line branched to Monywa and Alon on the Chindwin river, which terminated at Ye-U.

There was under construction a new line which was to link Lashio with a Chinese railway, then being constructed from Kumming to the Burma frontier. This new line, known as the Burma-China Railway, did not form part of the Burma Railway system but was directly controlled by the British Government. A few miles of the permanent way only had been laid at the end of 1941.

There were several important railway bridges. On the main line there were bridges over the Pazundaung creek, just outside Rangoon, and across the Myitnge river, a few miles south of Mandalay. The Ava Bridge over the Irrawaddy has already been mentioned. This bridge had only recently been completed and was approximately thirteen hundred yards in length.

On the Martaban branch was the important bridge across the Sittang river at Mokpalin, and a smaller bridge across the Bilin river at Hninpale.

The Gokteik viaduct in the northern Shan States was a steel trestle structure, which carried the railway across the deep Gokteik gorge, the bottom of the gorge being several hundred feet below the track. The tallest steel pier of the viaduct was three-hundred-and-twenty feet in height.

Roads

The road system in Burma in 1941 was primitive. There was no real overland communication between the Arakan coastal belt and the rest of the country. A single unfrequented track unfit for motor transport from the right bank of the Irrawaddy near Prome ran west across the Arakan Yoma to Taungup, a village on the coast. Otherwise, the only available routes were along the coast or by air from Rangoon.

Elsewhere there were a few main roads with some feeder roads. Of the main roads the most important was the all-weather road from Rangoon to Mandalay. From Pegu onwards this road followed the railway fairly closely. Twenty miles north of Rangoon at Taukkyan this road forked, the fork running north-west to Tharrawaddy, Prome Allanmyo and Taungdwingyi. Beyond Taungdwingyi the road deteriorated. Traversing the oilfields it turned east near Kyaukpadaung and rejoined the main Mandalay road at Meiktila. This road was metalled and bridged only in parts, and many difficult and dangerous chaungs (water courses) were unbridged. One of these was the treacherous sandy Pin Chaung, just north of Yenangyaung.

There was no through road link between Rangoon and Moulmein, and the bridge over the Sittang river was not a road bridge. The road gap extended from Waw, north-east of Pegu, to Kyaikto, sixteen miles beyond the Sittang. From Kyaikto there was a motor road through Thaton to Martaban, the ferry station for Moulmein.

The Tennasserim division was practically roadless. From Moulmein a road ran south to Amherst through Thanbyuzayat from where a short road branched to Pangna. South of that place there was no road to Ye, but beyond the Ye river a road led to Tavoy and Mergui. This was intersected by numerous wide streams, and rivers crossed by primitive ferries. Beyond Mergui, the normal means of communication with Victoria Point was by sea, there being no roads.

In the programme for defence there was contemplated an all-weather road connecting Rangoon with Mergui. Work was begun on it by the Public Works Department in 1941.[8] It involved the completing of gaps in the existing road system and much bridging and resurfacing. But little progress had been made before the Japanese invasion of the country.

There were no road links between Moulmein, Tavoy or Mergui and Thailand, but there were three recognised routes. The easiest approach was from Moulmein by the Gyaing river to Kyondo, and onwards from that point by road to Kawkareik. In 1941, the inferior road between Kawkareik and the frontier village of Myawadi had been improved. At Myawadi the Thaungyin river, a tributary of the Salween, formed the frontier line. Beyond it lay the Thai town of Mesoht where there was a landing ground. A good cart-track connected Mesoht with the important Thai centre of Rahaeng. Another cart-track from Thailand entered

---

[8] "The gaps in the roads to Martaban and to Ye are to be completed, this will take time".
Administrative Arrangements. 601/2/10/H, p. 4.

Burma by the Three Pagodas Pass, south-east of Moulmein. This track continued until it joined the Kawkareik-Kyondo road. The third route was from Tavoy, from which place a road ran east to Myitta, not many miles from the frontier. Beyond Myitta a track led into Thailand.

From the large town of Toungoo on the main Rangoon-Mandalay road there had been constructed a road running east to Mawchi and Kemapyu on the Salween. On the outskirts of Toungoo this road crossed the Sittang and, traversing a high suspension bridge, turned north to Bawlake and Taunggyi.

Meiktila, a town north of Toungoo on the main Mandalay road, was an important road junction. Eastward led the road through the southern Shan States to Taunggyi, Loilem, Keng-Tung and the frontier village of Tachilek, where it joined the Thai road system linking up with Chiengrai. This road crossed the Salween by a difficult ferry at Takaw. It had several feeder roads running north and south. Some of these were connected with the important Mandalay-Lashio-Wanting road through the northern Shan States. This last named road had recently been considerably improved on the stretch between Maymyo and Lashio and had also been extended from Lashio to the Chinese frontier at Wanting, where it linked up with the new Burma Road to Kunming and the Chinese capital at Chungking. It came into prominence only after 1938, as forming the main line of communication between China and the outside world when the Japanese had cut off the Hankow-Canton Railway.

The Shan States were better served with roads than the rest of Burma, and the Mandalay-Lashio-Wanting Road also had several feeder roads running to the north. The most important of these was to Bhamo and thence by a poor track to Myitkyina.

From Mandalay a road led to Sagaing beyond the Irrawaddy, crossing the river by means of the Ava Bridge. It continued north to Shwebo and Kinu, thence west to Ye-U on the Mu river, a tributary of the Irrawaddy. At Ye-U it moved south to Alon and Monywa on the Chindwin river, then ran east to Myinmu on the Irrawaddy. West of Monywa and Ye-U there were no roads. This Sagaing-Shwebo-Monywa road was the most important on the western side of the Irrawaddy which otherwise was almost roadless. There were a few minor roads in the neighbourhood of the towns of Minbu and Pakokku, but in the main communications were maintained by tracks.

From Kalewa, Mawlaik, and Sittaung, on the west bank of the Chindwin, rough tracks led into the Kabaw valley formed by the Yu river, a tributary of the Chindwin. From the Kabaw valley difficult tracks led over the hills to Imphal in Assam. The most important of these tracks ran from Tamu to Imphal, via Lokchao and Palel. This track followed the line of the Indo-Burma telegraph, and was formed for its maintenance. At Imphal terminated a motor road from Dimapur (Manipur Road) on the Bengal and Assam Railway. Another track from Kalemyo keeping west of the Chindwin connected Pakokku on the Irrawaddy.

In the dry weather many of the tracks were motorable, the flat paddy fields affording a tolerably level surface. These tracks carried an appreciable amount of traffic and to some extent remedied the paucity of roads in the country. In the rainy season, however, with the paddy lands under water, wheeled traffic in Burma was confined to the all-weather roads where too it was not often uninterrupted. Unbridged chaungs were frequently impassable and wash-outs were no uncommon occurrence.

Water-ways

The Irrawaddy has always been an important line of communication in Burma. From the earliest times its valley has been the most populous area in the country, and before roads were built the river was the only convenient highway. It carried men and merchandise, determined plans of campaigns, and formed the main line of advance or retreat for the armies and down its course from Central Asia came the early invaders of the country. Its delta is intersected by innumerable streams where water transport necessarily remains the only form of conveyance.

The Burmese rely largely on their streams and rivers for communications. Particularly in the season of the monsoon small boats and at all times country craft of every size are to be found on all inland waters. On these, too, ply many river steamers, cargo boats, flats, and launches. In 1941 the Irrawaddy Flotilla Company operated a very large fleet. The Company's vessels maintained regular services on the Irrawaddy and throughout the delta, on the lower reaches of the Salween and its tributaries around Moulmein, and on the Chindwin, which is navigable by very shallow draught steamers for a very considerable part of its length.

Airways

Upon the development of commercial aviation in the period following the first World War, Burma became an important link in the Imperial route from Great Britain to Australia. The airport of Mingaladon near Rangoon was built, and a landing ground at Akyab was constructed. Flying boats used Rangoon and Akyab as ports of call. Indian, Dutch and French commercial aircraft also called at these two places, and in 1941 an air service started operating between Chungking and Rangoon. There was an intermediate stop at Lashio where an airfield had been built. There were emergency landing grounds at Moulmein, Tavoy and Mergui, and in connection with the defence scheme for Burma other airfields and satellite air-strips had either been completed or were being built.

CHAPTER II

Burma—History and Politics

EARLY HISTORY OF BURMA

The Burmese are an Indo-Chinese people with the physical characteristics of the Mongoloid races who originally inhabited the eastern Himalayas and western China. They are supposed to have formed part of a vast migratory swarm that spread outwards to Tibet, Assam, Burma, Malaya and Thailand. In Burma they followed the course of the Irrawaddy to the plains.

Their early history is obscure, but by the eleventh century they were firmly established with a splendid capital at Pagan on the Irrawaddy. The magnificent architecture of this capital city is still discerned in its ruins, which lie some twenty miles north of Chauk on the east bank of the river. The city and the dynasty were destroyed in a Mongol invasion during the reign of Kublai Khan in 1284 A.D. Thereafter, for a long period, the country was divided into petty, warring principalities, until the 16th century when the kingdom of Pegu rose into prominence. Its supremacy was later challenged by a new dynasty in Ava in Upper Burma. Eventually Ava under the leadership of Alaungpaya, a native of the Shwebo district, subdued Pegu, united Burma and embarked on a scheme of conquest. Alaungpaya took Mergui and Tenasserim from Thailand, and then laid siege to its capital Ayuthia. He was wounded and retreated to Burma where he died. In the years that followed his death, his son, Sin-Byu-Shin, also sought to enlarge the kingdom. The war with Thailand was continued and Manipur was also invaded.

BRITISH ASSOCIATIONS

Prior to the time of Alaungpaya, European settlements had commenced in Burma. The Portuguese were the earliest to enter the country and establish themselves at Syriam. They were followed by the Dutch, the French, and the English who set up their trading stations.

The growth of Burmese power in Arakan and expanding British interests in India inevitably led to frontier disputes. The first of these was in 1795 when a large body of Burmese troops entered the district of Chittagong. The matter was, however, amicably settled and for a time peace prevailed. But it could not last long and the increasing border incidents led to a state of hostility between the Burmese King and the East India Company's Government in Calcutta; eventually in 1824, the Company's Government declared war.

ANGLO-BURMESE WARS

An Indo-British force sailed up the Hlaing river, reduced Rangoon speedily and took the Tenasserim provinces of Tavoy and Mergui. Other operations were carried out in Assam and Arakan. The main difficulty facing the Indo-British troops was that of climate, and the ranks of the invading force were considerably thinned by disease.

Late in 1824, the Burmese General, Maha Bandula, assembled a large army and marched on Rangoon. He was defeated and later killed when retreating on Prome. The British soon occupied Prome and remained there for the rainy season of 1825. By the end of the year the Burmese were compelled to sue for peace, but they employed the respite they thus obtained to prepare for a renewal of the war. Consequently, Sir Archibald Campbell, who was in command of the Indo-British forces, advanced up the Irrawaddy. When he was within four days' march of Ava, the capital, the Burmese accepted his peace terms and a treaty was concluded. By this treaty Burmese Government *inter alia*, surrendered to the East India Company the provinces of Arakan, and Ye, Tavoy, and Mergui. It gave up all claims to Assam and its contiguous petty states, and agreed to pay an indemnity and to receive a British resident at the capital. British ships were no longer required to unship their rudders and land their guns when calling at Burmese ports.

This treaty had been made by King Ba-gyi-daw and as long as he reigned it was observed in the main. He was deposed by his brother Tharawadi who made no attempt to conceal his dislike of the treaty and hatred and contempt for the British. His example was followed by the Court, and the British Resident was eventually withdrawn from Burma. Tharawadi's successor, Pagan, maintained the same attitude. Acts of violence were reported in Rangoon against British ships and seamen. The mounting strain led, in 1852, to the Second Burmese War.

From Moulmein, in British Tenasserim, Martaban, on the west bank of the Salween river, was bombarded, attacked and captured. A force also sailed for Rangoon under Gen. H. T. Godwin. The town was taken on 14 March after a sharp fighting round the Shwe Dagon Pagoda. Bassein was later seized, and after some resistance Pegu was taken. The British advanced to Prome and in 1853 King Pagan was informed that thenceforth the province of Pegu would be British territory. There was no treaty.

King Pagan was deposed by his brother Mindon who was prudent enough to realise the power of the British and avoid a fresh conflict. At the same time he bitterly resented the annexation of Pegu and long refused to acknowledge it by a formal treaty. But his relations with the British were not otherwise unfriendly, although they deteriorated in later years. He built himself a new capital at Mandalay where he died in 1878. He was succeeded by one of his younger sons, Thibaw, who began his reign by the arrest and massacre of all possible rivals to the throne. Relations with the British became strained. Once more the Resident was withdrawn. The government of the country fell into disorder which was believed to affect the peace of the British frontier. Some British subjects in Burmese territory were subjected to violence. The British Government resented the embassies sent by Thibaw to France and Italy, as British interests were believed to be threatened by this measure. Matters came to a head when the Burmese Government imposed a fine of £230,000 on the Bombay Burma Trading Corporation which held certain forest concessions in its territory. The Government of India suggested that the matter should be referred to arbitration. Thibaw, urgently in need of money and determined to obtain it, rejected the suggestion. In October 1885 the British Government delivered an ultimatum. Thibaw was obdurate, and war followed.

A British force had been assembled at the frontier station of Thayetmyo on the Irrawaddy. Under the command of Maj.-Gen. H. N. D. Prendergast V.C., it moved up the river by steamers and flats provided by the Irrawaddy Flotilla Company. The Burmese fort at Minhla was carried after a brisk engagement, after which there was little resistance. On 28 November 1885, in less than a fortnight from the declaration of war, Mandalay had fallen and Thibaw was a prisoner. Upper Burma was formally annexed on 1 January 1886.

On the disruption of the organized government, Thibaw's soldiery dispersed. Many took their arms with them and began to prey upon the countryside. The suppression of these bands and the pacification of the country was a far more difficult task than had been the defeat of Thibaw. Reinforcements had to be sent to Burma and for some years the Indo-British forces were engaged in jungle warfare against large bodies of malcontents. "It took an army of 30,000 men five years to suppress the sporadic resistance which broke out all over the country and spread to Lower Burma."[1]

A somewhat similar situation, though on a smaller scale, had also developed after the Second Burmese War. Then it had been the area about Tharrawaddy where order had to be re-established. These two periods of pacification, following on alien domination, clearly illustrate the opposition of the Burmese to foreign rule and their readiness to take advantage of any relaxation of authority in an emergency.

BRITISH RULE

From the time that Arakan and Tenasserim had been annexed after the First Burmese War, British Burma was included in the administrative charge of the Governor-General of India. In 1862 British Burma became a province of India, and was administered, first by a Chief Commissioner, and later, from 1897, by a Lieutenant Governor with a Legislative Council of nine nominated members, of whom five were officials. This form of government continued substantially unchanged until 1923.

Prior to 1897 all legislation was effected by the legislative authority of the Central Government, in which the Burmese people had no hand. After 1897, when the Legislative Council was established in Burma, its members were all nominated "and had little real power, in particular the vital power of finance remained with the Central Government". "In 1909 a non-official but nominated majority was provided, but the powers of the Council remained little more than those of an advisory body of the Lieutenant Governor."[2]

During the period of British rule, economic development of Burma was carried on by the foreign rulers largely in their own interest. Cultivation of rice for export was encouraged, roads and railways were

[1] *Burma Handbook* 1944, p. 101.
[2] *Ibid*, pp. 101-2.

constructed. Exploitation of mineral wealth, particularly of petroleum, progressed. The establishment of a stable foreign government throughout the country attracted British and Indian capital. Rice milling and export, timber industry and oil extraction were developed. Concessions were secured by the British companies for all these developments.

GOVERNMENT OF INDIA ACT OF 1919

The Government of India Act of 1919 introduced a certain measure of responsible government in India. For each of the major provinces, which did not initially include Burma, it provided a Legislative Council consisting of a large majority of elected members. There was also created a Central Legislature with a majority of elected members. The entire field of government was divided by the Act into central and provincial subjects. The latter, again, were sub-divided into 'transferred' and 'reserved' subjects. Reserved subjects were the responsibility of the Governor of a province aided by two official councillors or advisors, whilst transferred subjects were administered by the ministers responsible to the Legislative Council. Broadly speaking, matters relating to the administration of law and order and to finance were not transferred. Of course, the defence of India and matters connected with the armed forces, foreign affairs, and other subjects of intimate interest to India as a whole remained entirely under the Central Government.

In 1923 Burma also became a Governor's province and its constitution was moulded according to the Government of India Act of 1919. A Legislative Council with 103 members, of whom 84 only were elected, was established. Subject to the veto of the Governor, the Council had the final power of legislation in transferred subjects and controlled the Ministers. Thus the representatives of the people elected by a restricted franchise had a partial share in the government of their land. At this time there was a great political awakening, and Burmese young men in particular became active in political matters. Students and priests took prominent part in political demonstrations and gave expression to the anti-British sentiments and the growing nationalism of the people.

SEPARATION FROM INDIA

Burma had been linked to India as a matter of administrative convenience but it could not have any deep roots in her people's imagination. In later years, along with the opposition to British rule, hostility to this connection with India became an important factor of the political life of Burma. There was a feeling in the country that a disproportionate share of Burma's revenues went to India and that little was received in return. Fear of Indian domination and the feeling of intense nationalism fanned the demand for separation from India. The Indian Statutory Commission, popularly known as the Simon Commission, appointed to inquire into the development of representative institutions in British India was satisfied that the claim of Burma for separation from India was justified. This finding was embodied in the Report of the Commission published in 1930. This desire for separation and anti-Indian sentiment were further accentuated by the economic depression of the thirties, when it became difficult for the Burmese agriculturists to eke out a satisfactory living. They were led to ascribe their sufferings to the Indian community which was employed in labour, both agricultural and industrial, or trading and money lending activities. A fair portion of land was also owned by Indians. Combined with these economic grievances were political reasons for the riots which broke out in 1930 and again later in 1938. These were generally directed against Indian settlers. In Tharrawaddy these assumed a serious form when one Saya San proclaimed himself king. These riots were an indication of the political attitude of the Burmese who desired freedom from British rule as well as separation from India.

ACT OF 1935

In 1935 the British Parliament passed the Government of Burma Act, which came into force in April 1937 and effected the separation of Burma from India. Burma became a separate territory under the British Crown, and a new Secretaryship of State for Burma was established in the United Kingdom. The Act enlarged the powers of the Burma Government. All the former central subjects were allocated to it while the control of the legislature and the Ministers was greatly enlarged. But the defence of Burma, the control of the armed forces, external affairs, monetary policy, Christian ecclesiastical affairs and scheduled (frontiers) areas, and some other matters were retained under his direct control by the Governor and were thus withheld from the Ministers and the legislature. In these matters the Governor was to be advised by three Counsellors, one of whom in 1940 was a Burman. Joint consultation between the Ministers and Counsellors was provided for, while a Defence Council consisting of the two elements was formed. The important subjects of law and order and finance were placed in the charge of Ministers who were responsible to the legislature. The legislature was bi-cameral, consisting of the House of Representatives and the Senate. The House of Representatives or Lower House had 132 seats and was composed entirely of members elected for five years. Of the Senate half the members were elected by the House of Representatives whilst the remainder were non-officials nominated by the Governor. The Act provided for a maximum of ten Ministers, and the members of the Ministry were drawn from the majority party or groups in the legislature. Franchise was widened and roughly 20 per cent of the population had votes. The principle of communal representation was maintained, 25 of 132 seats being reserved for the minority communities. This constitution brought Burma generally, in so far as its internal government was concerned, nearly to the level of the Dominions. But the special powers of the Governor and the exclusion of vital subjects like defence and monetary affairs, as well as the restrictions placed on the powers of the legislature, detracted from that status. Moreover, the exclusion of the scheduled areas further limited the scope of self-government. The scheduled areas "were in effect the hills surrounding Burma on the west, north and east. These areas were excluded from responsible government on the ground of their political backwardness. These areas comprised the Federated Shan States, the Shan State of the Chindwin and Myitkyina districts, the Chin Hills district, the Kachin Hill Tracts, the Naga Hills, the Hukawng Valley, the Triangle and the Salween district." "These were to be governed in their traditional manner under the supervision of the Burma Frontier Service, and supreme legislative and executive power in respect of them rested with the Governor."

The first election to the House of Representatives was held in December 1936 prior to the coming of the Act into force. This was the only general election under the Act. The strength of the parties in the new House was as follows:—

United Party (U Ba Pe) 46; Sinyetha (Poor Man's) (Dr. Ba Maw) 16; U Chit Halaing Party 12, Ko-min Ko-Chin (Thakin) 3; Golden Valley Party 2; and Thetpan and Fabian parties 1 each. The balance was made up of non-party members including 17 Burmans, 12 Indians, 9 Karens, 9 Europeans and 2 each of Anglo-Burman and Chinese members.

The party alignment, prior to 1936, had been on the basis of more political reforms and separation from India. The nationalist party known as the General Council of Buddhist Associations (G.C.B.A.) was opposed to separation from India and wished to participate in the Indian Federation, with the right of cessation being recognised.

Separation was, however, demanded by the moderate groups composed of the People's Party under U Ba Pe and the Independent Party led by Sir J. A. Maung Gyi, who participated in working the government under the Act of 1919. With the final settlement of the issue of separation, there was a break-up of the earlier parties, and a number of groups, as mentioned above, emerged in the general election of 1936.

The election marked the virtual disappearance of the Independent Party and evinced the "tendency towards the multi-group system", as in France. The largest group was that of U Ba Pe, but having no clear majority he was unable to form a ministry. Dr. Ba Maw succeeded in getting the support of minority groups and despite his 16 members formed the government and became the first premier. The policy of his Sinyetha Party was to improve the lot of the cultivator. It is reported that he "began to develop distinct Nazi tendencies; he formed a private army known as the *Dahma Tat* and evidently began to envisage himself as the Dictator of Burma". In 1938 U Saw, who had broken away from U Ba Pe, formed the Myochit or Nationalist Party, in opposition to Dr. Ba Maw. He had also his own army, the *Galon Tat*, which gave the impression of developing "the dictator complex". A third party, the Thakin Party, comprised the younger elements largely drawn from the students of the University and had close liaison with the Students Union. The party is said to have been "violently nationalist and revolutionary", inclined towards communism. Its aim was complete independence of Burma.

The year 1938 witnessed widespread unrest and disorder. Labour was restive, students went on strike and anti-Indian riots were frequent in the country. Dr. Ba Maw was unable to restore order, hence he lost the support of the minority groups and his ministry fell. His place was taken up by U Pu who formed another coalition cabinet which comprised, among others, both the Ba Pe and the Myochit parties. In January 1940, U Pu eliminated U Ba Pe from his cabinet, but he was defeated by U Saw in September 1940, who formed his own cabinet. U Saw introduced some important legislation and retained office till January 1942 when on his way back from the United Kingdom, where he had gone to negotiate with the British Government for the grant of Dominion status, he was detained in Uganda on the ground of his contact with the Japanese.

YEARS 1937-41

Thus, between the years 1937 and 1941 the Government was never stable. The Burmese members who held the largest number of seats in the House of Representatives were always divided into small groups. Coalitions of these never held together for long, and there were frequent changes of Government. Personal jealousies were rife with the result that no settled line of policy was pursued. These features were the common effects of partial autonomy where all substantial power was concentrated in the hands of the representative of the British Crown. This led to an intense demand for independence in which the major political parties were united. They were opposed to all measures which even indirectly would have increased Imperial authority. This may account for their opposition to the project of the extension of the Mandalay-Lashio road to the frontier to improve the transport of war material and supplies generally into China when that Republic was attacked by Japan. They resented every increase in defence expenditure, advocated the Burmanisation of the armed forces and opposed all aspects of Imperial defence.

On the outbreak of war with Germany in 1939, the Burmese regarded the conflict as of little concern to themselves. The Burmese press was either indifferent or anti-British in tone, and frequently emphasised the fact of British injustice to Burmese aspirations. The expression of such views was ascribed by the British rulers to Communist, Japanese or other anti-British sources. They failed to recognise the intensity of feeling arising out of political frustration and ignored the writing on the wall.

JAPANESE INFLUENCE

It is not surprising therefore, that Japanese influence secured steady infiltration. Japanese propaganda was at work in the Burmese press. Several leading Burmese politicians were also believed to be in close touch with Japan, even to the extent of receiving funds from the Japanese. This fact, if true, would to some extent account for the general lack of enthusiasm for active co-operation in the British war effort. There were notable exceptions, but the general attitude to war was one of indifference. The British Government was not prepared to concede the demand for independence and ascribed it to Japanese influence. The case of U Saw, the Premier, who in 1936 had visited Tokyo is an apt illustration. When in December 1941 he went to Great Britain and America, to press the Burmese demand for independence, the British Government, on the plea that he had made contact with the Japanese in the course of his travels, refused to allow him to return to Burma and detained him. The suspicion of being in league with the Japanese was levelled against the ex-Premier Dr. Ba Maw, who was reported in 1940 to have been among the political leaders approached by the Japanese Consul. It was alleged that the Japanese had offered to pay him for a lecture tour in Japan. In 1941 he resigned his seat in the House of Representatives and then made a speech advocating no help for Britain in the war, unless independence was promised to Burma. For this he was imprisoned and he was in custody when the Japanese invasion of Burma began. He escaped on 14 April 1942. Later, when the Japanese occupation was complete, he was appointed Chief Administrator of Burma.

The Thakin party was also believed by the British to be closely associated with the Japanese, and its active efforts for the achievement of independence were interpreted as the effects of Japanese fifth column. This party starting in the troublous year of 1930 had soon gathered influence. It was nearer the masses, who took part in labour and agrarian problems, and organised a corps of volunteers. It was joined by a large number of students, who did not abhor violence.

After the outbreak of war in 1939, the Thakin party repeatedly asserted its opposition to British interests and a determination to secure the freedom of Burma by force whilst the British were engaged in fighting elsewhere. For the realisation of this object it was not averse to utilising Japanese support if the latter agreed to help in the fight for independence. These sentiments and the presence of one Thakin leader in Tokyo in 1940, where he was suspected of assisting the Japanese Government in the preparation of Burmese broadcasts of anti-British nature, reinforced the conviction of Thakin association with the Japanese.

Finally, when in 1941 several well known Thakins and a number of young men, totalling some thirty odd in all, disappeared from Burma the conviction grew strong. It is said that they had come under the influence of Colonel Minami who trained these men and was later to lead the Burma Independent Army and had spent some months in Burma where he passed as the secretary of the Japan-Burma Association.

The disaffected and nationalist element which had been always there was greatly swelled by Japanese successes. It had powerful support from persons of influence like U Saw, Dr. Ba Maw, and other political leaders. It had no particular love for Japan, but was ready to accept Japanese aid in the fulfilment of its object of independence from the British yoke.

The following official estimate of the situation clearly brings out the character of Japanese influence on the political leaders and parties of the country:—

"It is doubtful whether any of the political leaders or their followers who toyed with Japanese connections had any disposition to bring their country under Japanese control. They were willing to fish in troubled waters and to obtain arms and money from Japanese sources in the hope that if Britain became involved in real difficulties they could blackmail her into granting complete independence; but with characteristic lack of foresight they failed to perceive that instead of their using the Japanese as an instrument for securing independence the Japanese were using them as an instrument for aggression.

The great mass of population were even less disposed to welcome the enemy. Invasion, when it came, was generally resented, and the number of those, whether prominent politicians or others, who aided the enemy formed the merest fragment of the population; in this respect Burma may compare favourably with most European countries."[3]

The Japanese in Burma were themselves a small but prosperous community. In Rangoon they carried on several large business undertakings, and a considerable trade existed between Burma and Japan. Manufactured goods from that country found a ready market in Burma, whilst rice, cotton, and other products were largely exported in return. In Rangoon, as well as in every town of any importance, were to be found Japanese doctors, dentists, and photographers. These professions provided ideal opportunities for contact not only with the Thakins but with people of all classes, which enabled much vital information to be collected. The Japanese in Burma made full use of their opportunities and everyone of them reported to his Consul what he saw and heard. Undoubtedly road reconnaissances were made, and the traffic along the Burma Road to China was checked. Men who had lived in Burma and knew it well are reported to have returned with the invading army. It is interesting to note, too, that many experienced Police Officers held the view that the Japanese had a far greater share in Burma's internal troubles than was generally known. They were suspected of fomenting the serious strike in the oilfields in which the Thakin element was active.

---

[3] *Burma Handbook* 1944, p. 114.

CHAPTER III

Japanese Aggression in the Far East

The rise of modern Japan and her imperialism constitute an important chapter in the history of the Far East. An island state like Great Britain, she was quickened to modern life by German and American contact and inspiration. Geography gave her more advantages than it did to Britain. Her island home was far away from the reach of all her potential enemies except Russia. The times were equally propitious. China was neither united nor industrialised. Great Britain backed Japan as "a stabilising factor in the Far East". The soil of the Far East, dotted with Western imperialism and half awakened peoples stirring uneasily under it, was quite favourable for "the dwarf posing as the champion of the East against the West". Japan was the only nation in the Far East which was thoroughly industrialised. In her army and navy she had the finest fighting machine. Her traditional step-by-step policy enabled her to steal marches. It was only in 1941-42 that she went in for mass conquests with a speed and thoroughness that left the other nations gaping.

IMPERIALISM

Japan's march towards industrial development was rapid. The industrialisation brought in its wake imperialism. The pressure of population brought in the problem of *lebensraum*. There was the demand not only for markets but also for raw materials. Japan was poor in essential raw materials like iron, oil, petroleum, cotton, copper and basic chemicals. In the days of immigration laws, rising tariff barriers, and import and export quotas, Japan felt herself stifled. Manchuria and China would give her markets as also the commodities which the rest of the world needed. Here lay the germs of imperialism.

ARMED FORCES

Hand in hand with the industrial development went the building up of a modernised army and navy. Conscription was introduced and the state maintained a strict control over military or strategic industries as they constituted the flesh and blood of a modernised army. The complete reorganisation and expansion of the armed forces from 1882 to 1884 and the revision of the conscription law in 1883, were further designed to place the army in readiness for a contingency other than an internal one.

The Imperial Ordinance of 1889 gave the Ministers of War and Navy direct access to the Emperor on military affairs of secrecy and grave importance, thus by-passing the Prime Minister. Another Ordinance (1898) limited the appointment of Ministers of War and Navy respectively to Generals or Lieutenant-Generals and to Admirals or Vice-Admirals in active service. The army and navy could, as such, prevent the formation of a Cabinet if they so desired. The power of the armed services was reinforced by the rising tide of nationalism which looked upon the army and the navy as the chief bulwark of the nation, and by patriotic societies. State Shintoism, the cult of the Imperial ancestors and of the nation's heroes, and the exaltation of the Emperor and the race, reinforced this patriotism.

JAPAN'S AGGRESSION

Korea 1895

Economic pressure, military strength and national pride drove Japan along the path of aggression. From 1894, her internal problems did not demand the entire attention of the government. But even before this year Japan had obtained Kurile, Bonui and Kyuku Islands and the Volcano Group. Korea was the next victim. China regarded it as her tributary. Japan regarded it as an outlet for her growing population; in the hands of Russia it would bring an aggressive power at the very doors of Japan. No wonder then that Japan went to war with China over Korea in 1894. By the treaty of 1895, defeated China recognised the independence of Korea and gave Japan Formosa and Pescadores. The 'dwarf' had worsted the 'giant' and demonstrated that he was a factor to be reckoned with in the Far East.[1]

Russo-Japanese War 1904-05

In 1904 Japan went to war with Russia. The latter had refused to withdraw her troops from Manchuria and recognise Korea as the sphere of Japanese influence. Helped by his army and navy, by the London bankers and by the Anglo-Japanese Alliance of 1902 which ensured Britain's neutrality as also virtually that of France and Germany, the 'dwarf' defeated Russia, rolled back her armies, destroyed her fleet and compelled her to sign a favourable treaty. Japan's prestige had now greatly increased in the West. The Anglo-Japanese Alliance was renewed in 1905 and again in 1911. The success in this war also confirmed in Japan's mind the conviction that a great power could be defeated. She was not slow to learn the lessons of military science derived from this war.

Consolidation

After 1905 Japan set herself to the task of consolidating her territorial acquisitions. In Formosa new industries were introduced, old arts were improved, railways were built and administrative efficiency increased. In Korea she maintained a dual government till 1910, when she annexed it reviving the old name of Chosen. Here too she reduced robbery, promoted road and railway construction, multiplied agricultural research stations, encouraged industry and undertook the much needed forestry programmes.

---

[1] This Sino-Japanese war initiated the long string of Japanese acquisitions in China.

Japan's gains in World War I

The Great War was Japan's greater opportunity. She entered it on the side of the Allies, helped England to clear the Asiatic waters of German cruisers and raiders and captured some of the German Pacific islands, which later proved of great strategic importance. That Japan was not slow to profit by the preoccupation of the Allies in Europe was also shown by the Twenty-One Demands she made on China which, if they had been accepted, would have placed the Republic completely under the power of Japan.[1] The Chinese Government staved off the evil day by accepting the less important ones. Early in 1917, Japan obtained from England and France secret assurances to the effect that they would support, at the Peace Conference, her claims to the German islands north of the equator. The military collapse of Russia in 1917, as a result of the Russian Revolution, removed, for the time, one of the main checks upon the aggressive designs of Japan in Manchuria. At the Paris Peace Conference (1919) she obtained the Mariana, Caroline and Marshall Group of islands, and one of the five permanent seats on the Council of the League of Nations.

Washington Agreement

The next three years saw friction between Japan and the United States growing. It was all due to a clash of rival policies in the Far East. Japan was opposed to the open door policy in China and the United States was opposed to Japanese naval expansion. The Washington Conference sought to remove the friction. One treaty limited naval armaments of the Great Powers, and forbade the construction of additional fortifications in the Pacific islands. The ratio for capital ships was fixed at 5:5:3 for the United States, United Kingdom and Japan. They also agreed not to construct new bases or build new fortifications in certain of their Pacific possessions. The Nine-Power Treaty of February 1922 involved Japan in a pledge to respect China's sovereignty and integrity and the preservation of the Open Door. Japan appeared to have not only renounced what she had been struggling to achieve for the past twenty years but even to have bound herself to renounce it for all time.

Manchuria

But in 1931 the old aggressive impulses broke out again into furious energy when the intensification of Chinese nationalism and its resultant anti-Japanese activities manifested themselves in Manchuria. The Chinese looked upon Manchuria as a tributary state. To Japan, it was valuable as a buffer between herself and Russia, a valuable market for exports, a vast field for immigration and an unfailing source of supply of raw materials. In Manchuria the Chinese had been for some time building a transportation system which would make them independent of the Japanese South Manchuria Railroad. In the summer of 1931 clashes occurred in Manchuria between the Chinese and Koreans (Japanese subjects).[2] In September, Japan struck. Within four months her forces

---

[1] The United States and Great Britain protested strongly against this attempt to end the Open Door Policy in China.
[2] The Mukden Incident:—a bomb is said to have wrecked a portion of the Japanese controlled South Manchurian Railway.

[3] The Mukden Incident:—a bomb is said to have wrecked a portion of the Japanese controlled South Manchurian Railway.

succeeded in getting control of southern Manchuria; by the end of 1931 she overcame organised resistance in the north and north-east also. In the entire territory 'an independent' regime was set up under the name of Manchukuo. In 1934 the new state assumed the title of an Empire.[4] A close alliance was formed with Japan and Japanese advisers were prominent in the administration.

At the outbreak of hostilities in September 1931, China had appealed to the League of Nations which, after unsuccessfully attempting first the cessation of hostilities and then the evacuation of Manchuria, appointed a Commission (the Lytton Commission) to inquire into the question on the spot. The Commission reported against Japan. The League also condemned her aggression, and its members and the United States refused to give official recognition to Manchukuo. But no sanctions were applied; for the only power which could have carried out the sanctions in the Far East was Britain and she was not prepared to provoke Japanese hostility. The new state was recognised by Salvador in 1934, by Italy in 1937, Germany and Poland in 1938 and by the U.S.S.R. in April 1941. Soon after the conquest, Japan set about developing the country but the cost of policing it more than offset her economic gains.

The founding of Manchukuo had far-reaching results. Unable to bear the rebuff at the hands of the League and the big powers, Japan notified her desire to leave the League (1933). In December 1934, the Japanese Government notified the United States Government of their desire to terminate the Washington Naval Treaty. All the great powers soon began increasing their navies. This race was still further intensified in 1938 by the United States adopting an enlarged programme of shipbuilding and by the refusal of Japan to deny that she was designing capital ships of an immense size.

China

The formation of Manchukuo was but the forerunner of further expansion on the mainland. In 1933 Manchuria was rounded off by the annexation of Jehol by force of arms. In 1934 the Japanese Foreign Minister announced that Japan "serving as the only corner-stone for the peace of East Asia, bears the entire burden of responsibility". A Japanese naval writer, writing in 1935, said that war between England and Japan was inevitable unless either Japan stopped the policy of expansion that she had been driven to adopt under the most severe pressure, or unless England, with her excessive number of colonies, abandoned her policy of the preservation of the status quo.[5] In 1937 however, Japan used her elbows not in British possessions in the Far East but in China.

In May 1933, China was forced to create a demilitarized zone along the eastern portion of the Great Wall. Here Chinese troops were replaced by the Chinese police force. Late in 1935, an area in the eastern part of Hopei which embraced Tientsein and Peking was separated from Nationalist China by the formation of the east Hopei Autonomous

[4] Pu-Yi, former boy emperor of China, was installed as the nominal head of the puppet Empire of Manchukuo.
[5] Lt. Com. Tota Ishimaru, *Japan must fight Britain*, IX.

Council composed of Chinese under the thinly veiled domination of Japanese military authorities.⁶ In her fear of Russia and communism Japan entered into an Anti-Comintern Pact with Germany (1936) and Italy (1937). She also continued to press Nationalist China to join her in economic co-operation and in stamping out communism from China. Japan was emphatic that she had special rights in China and that she would not brook the efforts of any nation to strengthen the latter. She desired to draw all Inner Mongolia and north-eastern China within her control and there to set up local governments which she could dominate. From the military point of view the purpose was to seek safeguards against an attack from Russia and against Russian overland aid to China. From the economic stand point, the purpose was to get the rich natural resources of the area in order to relieve some of the economic pressure. The Chinese saw through all this and deemed war inevitable.⁷

An excuse was soon found. On the night of 7 July 1937, a local skirmish occurred in the outskirts of Peking between the Japanese and Chinese forces. Thus began an undeclared war between Japan and China which later merged in the World War. In this war the advantages seemed to be with the Japanese. They had full command of the sea and a well-trained, well-equipped and well-officered army, backed by the best industrial structure.⁸ In the beginning Japan wanted to tear off only northern China and not get involved in a long war with the Republic. But in the following months she realized that a local settlement was no longer possible and that the Chinese Govenment and army should be dealt a decisive blow which would destroy their will to fight. War moved with rapidity and the Chinese retired westward. By 1940 Japan had gained the capital of China, most of its seaboard and the most thickly populated and highly industrialized parts of the country. By 1939 Japan had closed all the treaty ports of China. She then attempted a slow strangulation of China by blockading her coast. To close the only two routes of supply left, she next moved into Indo-China, and compelled the British Government to close the Burma-China Road, though only for three months (August-October 1940).⁹ In August 1940 she proclaimed a Chinese National Government for the conquered areas.

Doctrine of Co-Prosperity in East Asia

It was during this war that Japan had enunciated the doctrine of Co-Prosperity in East Asia. As early as November 1938, Prince Konoye

⁶ Maj.-Gen. Kinji Doihara of the Japanese Army and the 'Lawrence of Manchuria' played a leading role in these activities between 1933 and 1936.
⁷ In 1936 Chinese resistance to Japanese demands stiffened and Generalissimo Chiang-Kai-Shek refused to grant additional concessions and insisted that Japan must cease violating China's sovereignty.
⁸ Japan had in 1937 a standing army of 300,000 carefully picked and thoroughly trained troops. A reserve of over 2,000,000 had been built up under a system of compulsory military training. There was in addition the Manchukuo Army of 150,000 Chinese nationals officered by the Japanese. The equipment of this large military machine had been thoroughly modernized. Particular emphasis was placed on mechanised warfare. The Air Force had 2,000 first line planes and an adequate supply of well trained pilots. Japan had above all the third largest navy in the world comprising some 200 warships many of them modernized. *The war with Japan Part I, Department of Military Art and Engineering. United States Military Academy, p. 3.*
⁹ This step shut off every channel of supply to China except the long caravan route to Siberia.

said, "There must be brought about a new peace system, based on realities covering trade, immigration, resources, culture and other fields.... Japan wishes to undertake the construction of new life among the people." On 22 December he went further: "Japan, China, and Manchukuo will be united by the common aims of establishing a new order in East Asia.... Japan demands only minimum guarantees for the execution of her function as a participant in the establishing of a new order."[10] In 1940 she gave a sugar coating to this demand and called it Co-Prosperity Sphere. In September 1940, she signed the Three-Power Pact with Germany and Italy by which the latter countries recognised the leadership of Japan in Eastern Asia. The three powers agreed to assist one another politically, economically and militarily, if one of them should be attacked by a Power not involved in either the European War or the Sino-Japanese conflict.

Aggression on Indo-China

It is necessary to describe Japanese aggressions in Indo-China and Thailand at length as it was there that Japan acquired strong advanced bases for her rapid move southwards.[11]

Indo-China, the chief bastion of France in the Far East, was the pivot upon which Japanese southward drive turned. The country has an area of 729,000 square miles and unlike Thailand is covered with good roads. From this base, with command of the South-Western Pacific, Japan could move west and north-west against Thailand and Burma, south against Malaya and Singapore, or south-east against Borneo and Celebes; and she could also move by short stepping stones, against the rest of the Netherlands East Indies, New Guinea, the islands of the Bismarck Archipelago and the Solomon islands, to within easy bombing distance of Australia.

Northern Indo-China

With the fall of France in the spring of 1940, Indo-China fell a helpless victim to Japan which brought the latter to the gates of Thailand and within quick striking distance of Burma and Malaya. As early as 1939 Japan had seized the Chinese island of Hainan which commanded the northern Indo-China coast. In June 1940, it was reported that the Japanese Government had informed the German and Italian Governments that Japan was concerned both militarily and economically in Indo-China and expected them to refrain from making any alteration in the status of the colony which would prejudice Japanese interests. In the same month she forced on Vichy France an agreement to prohibit the transit of a wide range of goods via Hanoi-Kunming railway; and Japanese inspectors were appointed to supervise the execution of the agreement. The thin end of the wedge was quickly followed in

---

[10] Strategicus, *War Moves East*, p. 99.

[11] It would however seem that the plan for the conquest of South-East Asia was not finally approved until November 1941. The decision to occupy aerodromes in French Indo-China was due to:—
    (i) the desire to safeguard Japan's armies in China by maintaining communications between southern China and northern French Indo-China.
    (ii) the desire to prevent Germany from obtaining the rubber and rice of French Indo-China, an economic move which was inevitable after the fall of France. Advance Headquarters SEATIC—Interrogation of Rear Admiral Chudo. Interrogation reports of Japanese officers (601/7651/H).

July 1940, by a positive demand for the right to establish military, naval and air bases in north Indo-China, as well as facilities for the transport of troops on the Kunming-Hanoi railway. By the agreement signed in September, Japan secured the right to establish three air bases in Tonking at the northern end of Indo-China and 6,000 troops for their supervision; she could also station a certain number of troops at Haiphong and further move troops into south China through a delimited route. To many, these arrangements seemed to be aimed not at Burma and Malaya, but at the Chinese section of the China-Burma Road and southern China.

Southern Indo-China

The turn of south Indo-China came in July 1941 when another agreement was concluded between Japan and the Vichy French authorities. By this the latter agreed to the temporary occupation by the Japanese forces of strategic points in Indo-China in order to defend the country against the De Gaullists, Chinese and British "whose troop concentrations in Malaya, Burma and Yunnan had led France and Japan to fear an Anglo-Chinese attempt to occupy Indo-China". Towards the end of the month it was reported that Japanese warships and troop transports had arrived at Camranh Bay, the French Far Eastern naval base, 720 miles from Singapore, and that Japanese transports and bombers were arriving at Saigon. Soon a Japanese military mission also arrived. Messages from Saigon also stated that a considerable body of Japanese troops would be stationed at Phnompenh, capital of Cambodia, adjacent to the Thai frontier, and that Saigon itself would be used as an air base. Moreover, the Japanese quickly started constructing and improving aerodromes to the south and west of Saigon.

The British Government reacted to the new danger by declaring that they regarded "these developments as a potential threat to their own territories and interests in the Far East". On 25 July, both the United States and Britain, by simultaneous action, froze Japanese assets in Britain and the United States. Corresponding action was taken by Canada, South Africa, India and Malaya. Britain also denounced the Anglo-Japanese Treaty of Commerce and Navigation of 1911 and the Japanese trade agreements with India (1934) and Burma. The Japanese-American Trade Treaty had been denounced earlier. This economic stranglehold, instead of checking Japanese aggression, revitalised it, as Japan was forced to secure other sources for her much needed raw materials.

In August 1941, more troops arrived in south Indo-China and occupied strategic points and aerodromes. Japanese naval personnel took over command of the Camranh Bay naval base. The area was closed and a ban was imposed on newspaper reports concerning the arrival in the colony of Japanese troops and their movements. Two squadrons of long range zero fighters also arrived in south Indo-China. Japanese cruisers and destroyers operated in the South China Sea. There were large-scale movements of motor landing craft from China. In November 1941, Mr. Yoshizawa, accredited with the title of Japanese ambassador to Indo-China, arrived at Haiphong to "reinforce the political and economic ties between Japan and Indo-China". The climax was reached when on 8 December a military alliance was signed between Japan and Vichy

France "for adjusting the measures for the defence of Indo-China to the new situation".

Almost up to the moment of the Japanese attack, the full importance of Japan's strategic position in Indo-China was nowhere appreciated. The Far Eastern Command, which was not totally in the dark about developments in Indo-China, found it difficult "to judge whether this movement signified definite plans for an offensive against us in the near future or it was merely the acquisition of a strategic asset to be used in negotiation, or whether it was the first step towards the occupation of Siam (Thailand). This applied even to the construction of aerodromes of which we were kept fairly well informed." The gradual concentration of Japanese forces in Indo-China vaguely brought home the danger, but Britain was powerless to effect a counter-concentration to meet the threat. British resources in material and proper conditions of convoy had been already strained to the utmost. The little that Britain could send was sent to Libya where a new front had been opened.

Netherlands East Indies

Since the Netherlands East Indies was as much important to the Japanese economically as Indo-China was strategically, it was only natural that Japan should avail herself of the fall of Holland to forge her stranglehold on Insulinde.[12] In September 1940, a Japanese economic mission arrived in the Netherlands East Indies to negotiate for the purchase of large quantities of lower grade oil as well as octane aviation spirit, supplies of which to Japan were interfered with by the United States' embargo on exports otherwise than to the Western Hemisphere. At a conference which took place at Batavia there was great wrangling. The Japanese demands included increase of Japanese migration, mining and prospecting rights, increased import quotas, regular air transport, and additional supplies of oil, rubber and tin. In May 1941, the Japanese Government made formal representations to the Netherlands Government to break the deadlock in the negotiations. In June, Matsuoka (Foreign Minister) declared that the Netherlands East Indies and Indo-China, if only for geographical reasons, should be in intimate and inseparable friendship with Japan. When the Netherlands Government protested against the statement Japan replied that she "did not contemplate any military or political hegemony but only economic co-operation". As Japan's requests to the British and American ambassadors to induce the Dutch to enter into an agreement were not heeded and as the Dutch reply was unsatisfactory, the negotiations were broken off in June 1941. This failure left only one course for Japan in her Naushiraron or "march south"—the military course.

Thailand

The Japanese aggression in Indo-China was but a prelude to the entry into Siam (renamed in 1942 as Thailand). The wonder is it came so late. In the context of Japanese plans for the domination of South Asia, the country assumed much greater strategic importance than even Indo-China, as the road to Burma and the back-door to Malaya. The possession

---

[12] Japan was faced with the possible loss of oil supplies from the United States.

of this country would give Japan not only twenty-two air fields within easy striking distance of targets in Burma, but also Thai roads and railway communications leading into Tenasserim and the Shan States. Railway communications, though not very good, could also be developed rapidly.

Thailand's position was a difficult one, of delicate balancing between two great Powers, Great Britain and Japan. As a small nation, eager to preserve its age-long and incredible independence, her only course was neutrality. But three factors made such a position impossible. After her entry into Indo-China, Japan was well poised for a lightning entry into Thailand. For lack of military resources the British were unable to help the Thais effectively to counter Japanese designs; and Thai irredentist feeling, fanned by its military Government and the Japanese, made her covet, not only those parts of Burma where the Thai group lived, but also Tenasserim over which Thai kings had ruled for a time. The appetite for territory was whetted by her acquisitions in Indo-China.

The importance of Thailand for both the British and the Japanese was realised as early as June 1939 in the Anglo-French Singapore Conference. The neutrality of Thailand was recognised as "a vital factor in the security of Indo-China, Malaya and Burma".[13] It was, however, realised that her strategic situation would eventuate Japanese aggression, a fact which could not be ignored. The Conference recommended, therefore, that by diplomatic action backed by increased land, naval and air forces in the Far East, Thailand should be made to declare her unwillingness for an alliance with Japan. "From a military point of view," it went on, "the ideal would be if we could obtain free passage through the Siamese territory for the troops of both Allied nations and for their supplies and also that the Siamese Government should bind itself to resist any attempt at Japanese landing."[14] But British occupation of Thailand was ruled out by the weakness of the former's forces in the Far East and by a desire not to provoke Japan into a war—a blissful policy of not following either of the two courses—to invade Thailand or help Thailand to resist the Japanese.

But Thailand was fast moving into the Axis camp. On 12 June 1940, she signed a treaty of friendship with Japan. On 8 September, the Thai Government officially proclaimed the country's neutrality in war and the British Government assured the Thai Government that so long as Thai neutrality was respected by other powers, it would, of course, be completely respected by His Majesty's Government.

The fall of France created an unprecedented situation. The weakness of Indo-China tempted Thailand to lay claim to territories annexed by France at the beginning of the century. In December 1940, hostilities broke out on a large scale between Thailand and Indo-China. In the first week of January 1941 fighting extended along the entire length of the frontier. An attempt by the Commander-in-Chief, China Station, and Commander-in-Chief, Far East, to mediate failed; Japan scored a diplomatic victory, when both sides accepted her offer of mediation. In the peace conference at Tokyo, Japan forced her plan on Indo-China. Under the terms of the treaty signed on 11 March, Vichy France ceded to

[13] *Report of the Anglo-French Conference, Singapore, June 1939*, Part I, p. 8, F, 481.
[14] Ibid.

Thailand about 70,000 square miles of territory. Japan had acted the honest broker and in return for her guarantee of the terms of the settlement, the Japanese Foreign Minister demanded and obtained assurance that Indo-China and Thailand would not conclude any agreement with a third power for political, military or economic co-operation against Japan. The Prime Minister of Thailand was reported to have said that his country would for ever remember the friendly efforts of the Japanese. The Thai fish was well within way of being caught on the Japanese hook. When the British Government reiterated in March 1941 that "avoidance of war with Japan is the basis of Far Eastern policy and provocation must be avoided", they seemed to bless the growing Japanese influence in Thailand.

In May 1941, the British Minister at Bangkok reported that the Japanese were said to be considering the idea of a *coup d'etat* in Thailand for placing a more pro-Japanese Government in power; he also advised the Ministry of Economic Warfare to counter this move by giving Thailand oil and credit. In July, the Japanese radio launched a campaign against Thailand alleging British troop concentrations on the Thai frontier and invited Thailand to emulate the example of Indo-China. Next month Bangkok radio declared that it would resist aggression even with poison gas, if needed. The stage was thus well set for a Japanese drive into Thailand but the drive did not materialise till the day after the attack on Pearl Harbour.

In her plan for her southward drive Japan ensured her rear by signing, in April 1941, a Neutrality Pact with Russia, valid for five years during which the parties engaged to "observe neutrality throughout the whole duration of a conflict which should result from either of them becoming the object of military action by one or more states".

CHAPTER IV

Danger of the Invasion of Burma

APPRECIATIONS AND PLANS OF DEFENCE

PRE-1939 APPRECIATION

The danger of a land attack on Burma by an external enemy was long regarded as remote. In an appreciation prepared in 1927 for meeting Chinese aggression in Burma from the province of Yunnan, it was emphasised that such a danger would be preceded by sufficient indications. The General Staff, India, went a step further and considered that no such danger would materialise for a considerable time.[1] Until 1939 the Committee of Imperial Defence took the view that a land attack in force on Burma was only a distant possibility. In that year, however, the practicability of Japanese action in Thailand was visualised and the altered situation considered. The danger of air attack was, however, the main concern of the army in Burma. Maj. Gen. D. K. McLeod, then General Officer Commanding, Burma Army, in a letter to the Deputy Chief of the General Staff, India, in 1939, wrote, "On the Siamese (Thai) border there is not much scope for a larger force (than raiding parties) to attack Burma by land via Myawaddy. This is the only practicable route for a force of any size—say a Brigade. The objective would be Moulmein. But I do not regard the land threat very seriously—air attack by Japan from Siamese aerodromes is the big danger."

FAR EAST CONFERENCES

Anglo-French Conference

In June 1939, an Anglo-French Naval, Military and Air Force Conference met in Singapore, in order to co-ordinate plans for meeting the Japanese aggression in the Far East.[2] The basis of these was a defensive policy of holding on to certain positions and intercepting seaborne supplies to Japan. Only the defence of Singapore and reinforcements to Singapore —the key to Anglo-French position in the Far East—were considered at length though it was realised that the geographical position of Thailand made her a vital factor in the security of Indo-China, Malaya and Burma. It was thought that the Japanese forces in Thailand would, while threatening Malaya and Indo-China by land operations, expose only the oil refineries in Burma to air attack. Soon, however, the basic assumption of active French collaboration with the British from Indo-China vanished with the collapse of France.

---

[1] *Appreciation and Plans of operations for the Defence of North-East Frontier of India*, 1927, pp. 7-10, F. 480.
[2] *Report of the Anglo-French Conference Singapore, June, 1939.*

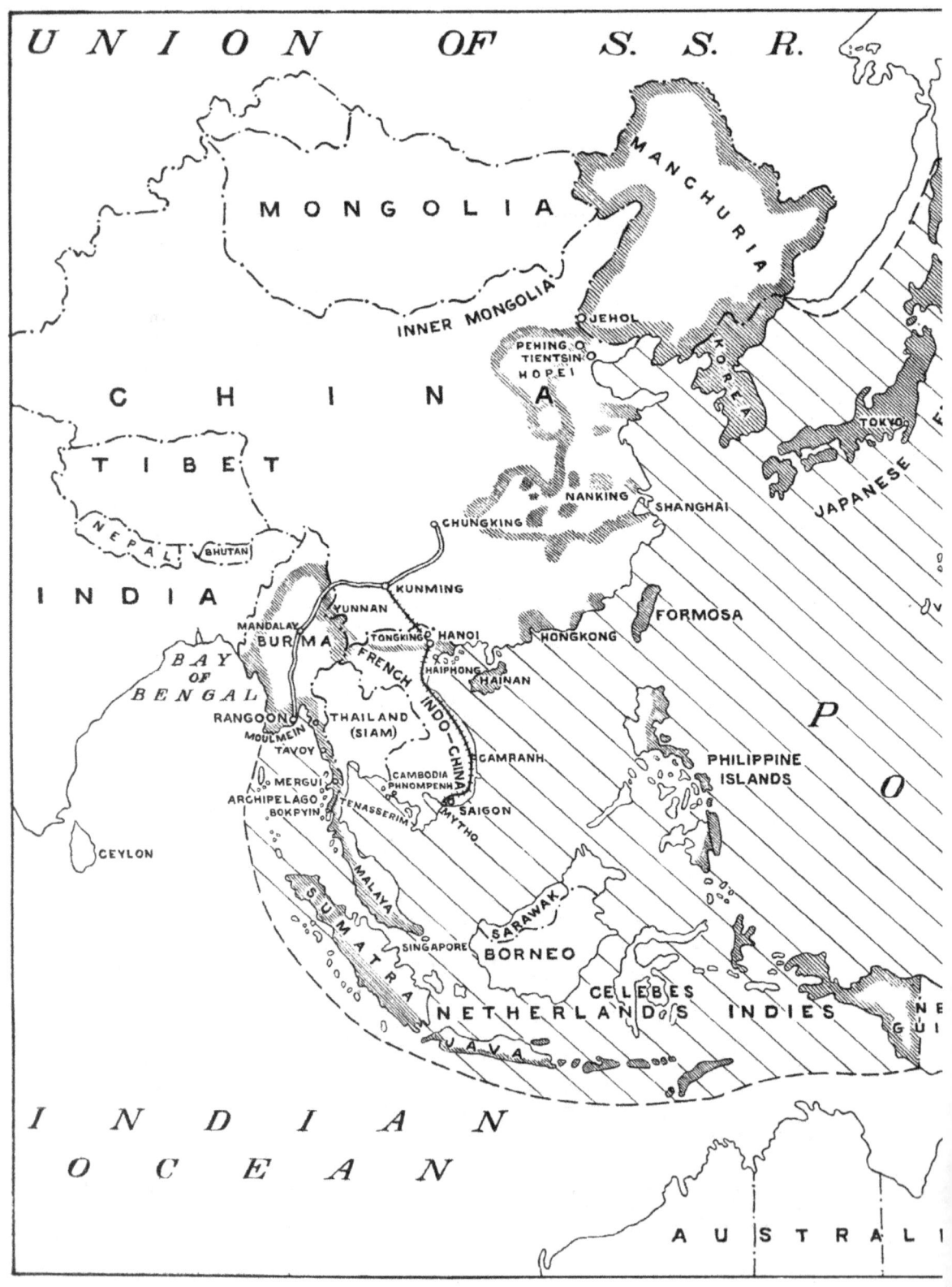

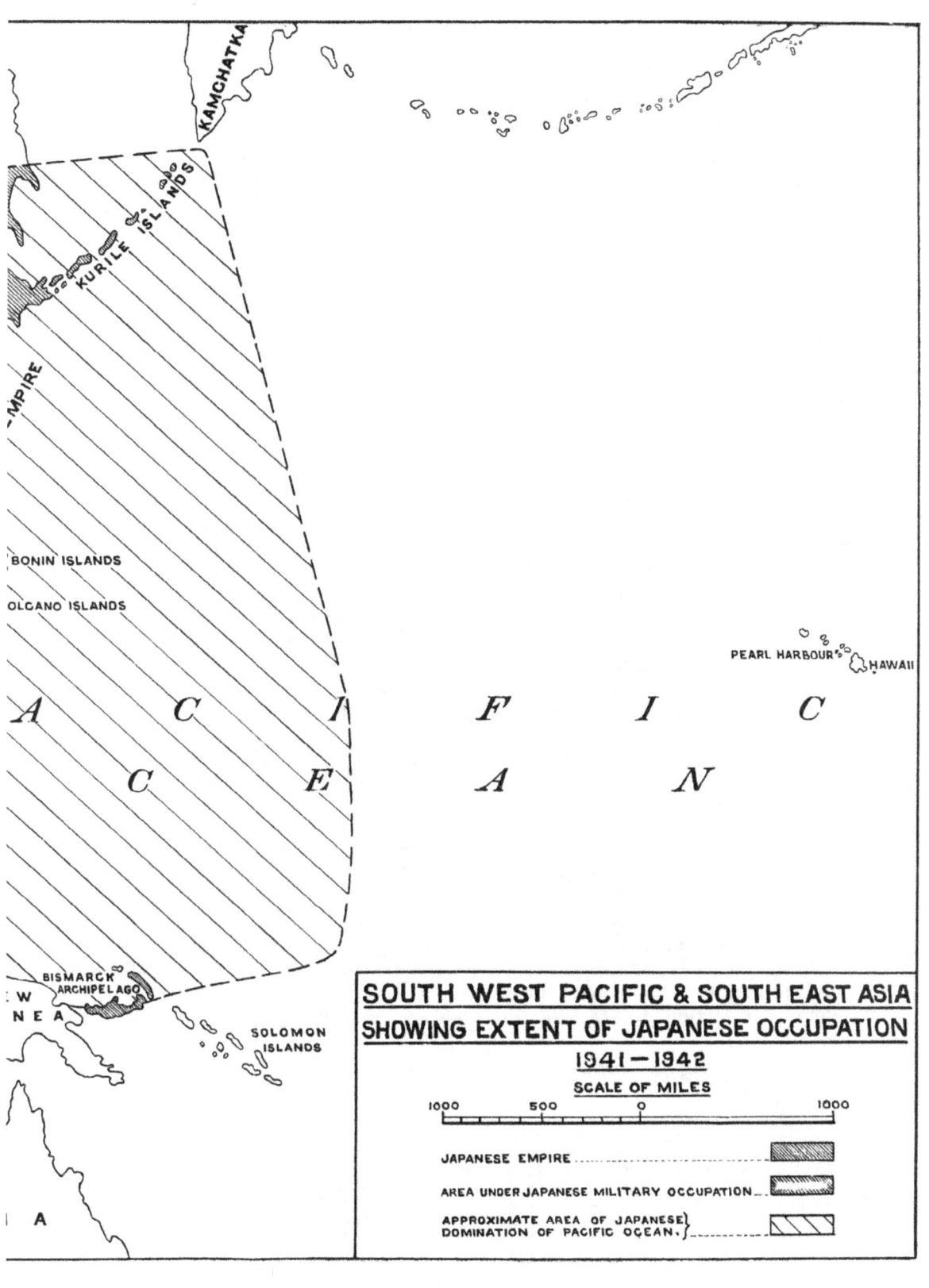

Singapore Defence Conference

In October 1940, the Singapore Defence Conference met to co-ordinate plans for the employment of British, American and Dutch forces in the event of war with Japan.[3] Though it gave greater attention to Burma than the previous Conference, it still harped on the old theory that the foundation of British strategy in the Far East was to base on Singapore a fleet strong enough to provide cover for communications in the Indian Ocean and South-West Pacific and to frustrate large expeditions against Australia and New Zealand and British Far Eastern possessions. The first and the immediate consideration was to ensure the security of Malaya, "a vastly more attractive and important objective"[4] than Burma. Nevertheless, it was recognised that "Burma is of imperial importance because of her oil and mineral resources and because of sea and air communications with Singapore. She is also the channel for supplies to the Chungking Government."[5] It was also admitted that for the purposes of general defence Burma was an outpost of India and that any threat to Burma or the occupation of Burma by the Japanese was a direct menace to Eastern India and the installations of imperial importance situated there.

It was then appreciated that after occupying Thailand, Japan could attack Burma and Eastern India from the east though Malaya should be her primary objective. The immediate threat to Burma and Eastern India was considered to be:

(a) "air attack on the oil refineries and docks at Rangoon and possibly on the vulnerable points in Eastern India, (Digboi, Calcutta and Tatanagar).

(b) land, seaborne and air attacks including air-borne troops on Tenasserim to capture or destroy aerodromes on the Singapore air route, and

(c) attacks on the remainder of Burma's eastern frontier would probably, in the first place, be limited to raids into Burma territory in which the Japanese might be assisted by the Thais. An attack from Chiengrai into the southern Shan States was a feasible proposition for a large force against which defence measures must be taken."[6]

"As a long term project it was further held that the Japanese could attack Burma from Yunnan by land and air."[7]

The Conference also considered the strength of forces necessary for holding and delaying any land attack on Burma until reinforcements arrived and for keeping open the air route to Singapore. Neither Victoria Point nor Mergui, it was thought, could be defended. The defence of

---

[3] *Report of Singapore Defence Conference*, F. 515.
[4] *Ibid*, p. 7.
[5] *Ibid*, p. 4.
[6] *Ibid*, p. 1.
[7] In Dec. 1940, the C.G.S. India wrote to the Headquarters Far Eastern Command that Japan's major objectives were to liquidate the war in China, improve her strategic and economic position in the Far East without becoming involved in war with Great Britain or America. He added, should Japan decide to attack British or Allied possessions in the Far East her main effort would probably be directed to the capture of Singapore and the oil supplies and bases in the Netherlands East Indies. (601/44/H.)

the rest of Tenasserim required four Battalions, a Field Battery, a Mountain Battery, and a Field Company. The defence of the Shan States would require two Brigades with two Field Batteries, a Mountain Battery, an Anti-Tank Battery, a Light Anti-Aircraft Battery, a Light Tank Company and two Field Companies. The defence of aerodromes would require garrisons found by the Burma Frontier Force. The defence of Rangoon area required a Brigade supported by a Field Battery and a Field Company. The report concluded, "with the forces at present available the most that can be done is to hold the northern part of Tenasserim and Rangoon. The vital installations in the Rangoon area, the oil-fields, ... are entirely unprotected from air attack."

The forces immediately required for the defence of Burma were estimated as follows:

Five Infantry Brigades and two additional Battalions. One Field Regiment and one Battery, two Mountain Batteries, one Anti-Tank Battery, one Heavy Anti-Aircraft Regiment of 24 guns, one Light Anti-Aircraft Battery (non-mobile), one Light Anti-Aircraft Battery (mobile), and one Company of Light Tanks.

This was exclusive of the Burma Frontier Force and the Territorial and Auxiliary Forces allotted for internal security duties. It was also stated that an additional requirement for the long term problem was one Division, less certain units, which made the fighting portion of this Division as follows:

Two Infantry Brigades, each of three Battalions, one Reconnaissance Unit; one Field Regiment (24 guns), one Medium Regiment (16 guns), one Light Anti-Aircraft Regiment (48 guns), one Anti-Tank Battery and one Machine-gun Battalion.[8]

The Chiefs of Staff did not agree to this view, and in their note of January 1941 on the Conference proposals they stated that in their view both the threat of attack and the demand for land forces had been overstated.

OTHER APPRECIATIONS

The Conference was not unique in such an appreciation. As late as February 1941, the Governor of Burma was assured by the War Office that it would be a waste of effort to send more troops to Burma as it was so highly improbable that Burma as a safe country would ever become involved in war. In October 1941, Mr. Duff Cooper told the Bush Warfare School at Maymyo that he sympathized with them for being in Burma as they would "never see any war".[9] Even after the war broke out with Japan, both the War Office and the Far East Command informed General Sir A. Wavell that an attack in force against Burma was unlikely until the Japanese had

---

[8] Sir Robert Brooke Popham's *Despatch* on Operations in the Far East, from Oct. 17, 1940 to Dec. 27, 1941. (*The London Gazette Supplement* No. 38183 dated 20-1-48).

[9] Correspondence between Lt.-Col. C. Foucar and the Secretary, Government of Burma (601/1/22/H), p. 2.

completed their campaigns in Malaya and the Philippines.[10] It was often represented that Burma's natural defences and the lack of communications across her frontiers would make a land invasion an extremely difficult and even a hazardous operation.[11] In the Anglo-Dutch Conversations at Singapore in April 1941, it was emphasized that the main effort should be to defend naval and air bases. In his Order of the Day on December 8, 1941, the Commander-in-Chief, Far East, said that the main war against Japan would be an economic one.

DIRECTION OF A LARGE-SCALE ATTACK ON BURMA

The possibility of a big Japanese advance through Thailand could not, however, be completely ruled out. It was necessary, therefore, for the Burma Command to consider the probable weight and direction of such an attack.

Communications between Burma and Thailand were very poor.[12] Only one motor road existed. Much of the frontier country was mountainous and densely covered with jungle, and an invader would also be faced with the formidable natural obstacle of the Salween river. Few tracks crossed the frontier and it was thought that in most places the forests traversed by these would compel an invader to confine himself strictly to the tracks.

The one existing motor road was that from Thazi through Keng Tung and Tachilek to Chiengrai. One of its southern feeder roads from a point about sixty miles east of Taunggyi ran south-east to Mongpan, a town forty miles from the frontier. Tracks linking Mongpan with the road system centred on the Thai towns of Chiengmai and Mehongsohn. Between Chiengmai and Chiengrai and the Burma frontier, the Thais were improving their communications which were comparatively good. This area, therefore, appeared to offer the best line of advance to an invader. Against this were the facts that such an advance would not immediately threaten any vital point in Burma, and would give the defence ample ground for manoeuvre and the fighting of delaying actions. The road passed through a country extremely suited for such warfare. Such an advance, too, would necessitate the maintenance by the invader of very long lines of communication. Thazi, where presumably the main road and railway would be cut, was considerably more than two-hundred-and-fifty miles west of Tachilek on the frontier. Finally, the securing of Thazi by the Japanese would still leave the defenders of Burma covering their main base of Rangoon and with extensive communications behind them.

[10] General Sir A. Wavell's *Despatch*, p. 4.
Lt.-Gen. T. J. Hutton also says that the Commander-in-Chief at Singapore never warned Burma to prepare for a full scale invasion. Nor did H.M.G. issue to the Burma Command any directive setting out what preparations should be made in Burma. The Commander-in-Chief, Far East, only tried to persuade Burma to increase her police force. His defence is: "Admittedly we were working on probabilities and not certainties. But in view of the weakness of our Air Forces, it was essential to concentrate the maximum effort and not try to be equally strong (weak) in both places". *Op. Cit.* p. 540.
[11] *American-Dutch-British Conversations, Singapore—April 1941*, (601/457/H), p. 10. Also *Anglo-Dutch-Australian Conversations, February 1941*, (601/523/H), p. 2.
[12] *Topographical Report*—Routes across Burma Siam Frontier; 601/7267/H.

From Mehongsohn on the Me Pai river, a tributary of the Salween, there existed two possible lines of approach. One was down the Me Pai river itself, the other by tracks across the Salween which joined the Toungoo-Bawlake-Taunggyi road running through the Karenni States. The country there was most difficult.

As against this, further south were the Tenasserim routes, the easiest being that through the frontier village of Myawadi. The Dawna Hills although precipitous and densely covered with forest were of no great depth, and less than twenty miles to the west of Myawadi an invader could emerge into level and comparatively easy country. A successful advance there must constitute an immediate threat to Rangoon, and the immobilisation or fall of that city would strangle the whole defence of Burma. In addition, the moral effect of a blow at the heart of Burma would be far greater than an attack through the distant Shan State of Keng Tung.

Road and rail communications in Thailand indicated Chiengrai and Chiengmai in the north and Rahaeng in the west of Thailand as likely concentration areas and advance bases for an attack. This confirmed the two danger points as the Thazi—Keng-Tung—Tachilek road and the Myawadi route.

INDO-BURMA CONFERENCE, 1941

In October 1941, there was a conference between the Commander-in-Chief, India and the General Officer Commanding, Army in Burma.[13] It was then appreciated that though the Japanese might get up to eight divisions into Thailand it was unlikely, owing to maintenance difficulties, that the scale of attack on Burma would be greater than two divisions, four Bomber squadrons and four Fighter squadrons as escorts for Bombers. The main land threat, it was thought, would be directed against the Shan States from the direction of Chiengrai-Chiengmai towards the roads Tachilek—Thazi—Keng-Tung and Thazi-Mongpan; for in this area the communications in Thailand towards the Burma frontier were comparatively good and were being developed. Recent experience in Europe and Africa had shown the dependence of modern armies on motor transport. Hence combined sea, land and air threats were expected against Moulmein, Tavoy, Mergui and Victoria Point. Towards each of these places there were roads with gaps traversed by jungle tracks to the frontier from Thailand. It was further thought unlikely that the northern Shan States could be directly threatened unless the Japanese captured Yunnan.

FAR EAST COMMAND'S INSTRUCTIONS TO BURMA ON THE EVE OF JAPANESE ATTACK

When war with Japan became imminent, the General Officer Commanding, Burma Army, was instructed by the Commander-in-Chief, Far East, that his first duty was to maintain the Imperial air route to Singa-

---

[13] *Administrative Arrangements, Burma* (601/2/10/H), Appendix 'A'.

pore by providing local protection for the various landing grounds in the south of Burma.¹⁴ His next duty was the safeguarding of the Burma Road and communications with China. At that time it could not be anticipated that Singapore would fall to the Japanese or that the command of the seas in the Far East would be lost. The Japanese, although active in French Indo-China, had made no move against Thailand. The Burma Road, it was feared, would be cut by means of an attack on the northern Shan States through Indo-China.

BURMA COMMAND APPRECIATION OF 12 DECEMBER

As soon as Malaya was attacked, there was a slightly different appreciation by the Burma Army Command (12 December).¹⁵ While sticking to the old view that the terrain limited the land forces that could enter Burma, the General Officer Commanding, Burma Army, estimated that the scale of attack would be greater than previously expected. The defence plan, however, was, as before, largely based on the hope that the air force would make Japanese approach difficult or impossible by bombing. This was contrary to all experience of World War II; and anyway, there were no bombers in Burma.¹⁶ The Far Eastern Command and the War Office also stuck so far to their old opinion that as long as the Japanese were committed in Malaya and the Philippines, they could not stage a major operation in Burma. Even though an attack in strength on Tenasserim was then expected by the Burma Army Command, it was not easy to repair the old error. The main strength of the small forces available had to be shifted hundreds of miles to Tenasserim in the south, and communications and supplies built up to meet the altered plan. It also became necessary to visualize an early situation when Rangoon, the door to Burma, might be closed by hostile action.

APPRECIATION BY GENERAL STAFF, INDIA, 15 DECEMBER

On 15 December, the General Staff, India, made an appreciation for limited offensives into Thailand.¹⁷ It was stated then that the troops in Burma, apart from those engaged in internal security duties, would, with their existing scale of transport and armament, particularly their paucity of artillery, be unable to undertake successfully any offensive operations into Thailand. The Japanese strength in Thailand was estimated at four divisions, two of which were operating in Malaya, and 200 aircraft to be increased by atleast a further 100. In addition, it was necessary to reckon the Thai force which would necessarily be brought into action in case of operations against Thailand. This force amounted to 45 infantry battalions, 15 artillery regiments, 5 cavalry regiments, 2 tank regiments and 1 Anti-aircraft Group besides 214 aircraft.¹⁸ There were two courses open to the Japanese : one was to concentrate on Malaya and sever connections

---

[14] Chinese Armies, Brig. J. C. Martin's *Personal Narrative* p. 1. (601/3/8/H).
[15] *Appreciations and Plans*, (601/2/3/H), pp. 1 and 2.
[16] General Sir A. Wavell's *Despatch*, p. 11.
[17] *Appreciations and Plans*, p. 15 ff.
[18] This was correct.

between Burma and Malaya by cutting the air route down the west coast by capturing Tavoy, Mergui and Victoria Point. The remaining forces in Thailand might be moved northwards to develop and establish aerodromes from which Burma and the Burma Road could be attacked by air. This would have the effect of diverting the Indian reinforcements to Malaya. A second course would be to use the two divisions in Thailand for capturing Tavoy, Mergui and Victoria Point as also for an advance by land on Keng-Tung and Taunggyi at an early date.[19] An advance on Moulmein via Rahaeng could also be combined with it.

PLANS FOR DEFENCE

The plan set out was that of preparing fixed defences on the frontier at all points where usable routes led from Thailand into Burma, for being used as pivots of manoeuvre from which small mobile guerilla columns could operate into Thailand, particularly against aerodromes and railway communications south of Bangkok. As large an air force as could be made available was to be located in Burma at an early date so as to increase her offensive potential. It was emphasised that communications limited land operations from Burma into Thailand to a maximum of two divisions. One division was to be moved into northern Thailand from Keng-Tung via Chiengrai route; two brigades were to be moved from Moulmein via Rahaeng and Sawarngalok to cut off all Japanese forces in the Chiengmai area. The best course was to draw the maximum Japanese forces into northern Thailand by giving the impression of a large-scale attack in that area and then carry out the main advance by the route Moulmein-Rahaeng-Sawarngalok, improving the road as the advance progressed to a standard sufficient to maintain at least one division. This offensive could be best supported by the Chinese forces in Yunnan moving south into northern Thailand. A limited defensive-offensive plan was then in fashion and would have been an effective means of warding off the invader, if only adequate forces were available to implement it. But the forces available in Burma were unequal to this task.

The appreciations were based on an inadequate estimate of the Japanese strength and erred on the side of optimism. The five cardinal mistakes were :—

(1) That the traditional step-by-step policy of Japan would preclude her attacking many countries at the same time.
(2) That the excellent communications in the Shan States pointed to an invasion through the southern Shan States.
(3) "That the natural difficulties of the country on the frontier, the few and indifferent tracks, the hills and thick jungle would restrict the numbers the Japanese could employ and dictate the direction in which they could use them. Actually we found ourselves up against a new feature in warfare, an enemy fully armed, disciplined, and trained on the continental model, using the mobility, independence of communications and the

---

[19] It is noteworthy that even here, a drive on Rangoon from Moulmein is not envisaged.

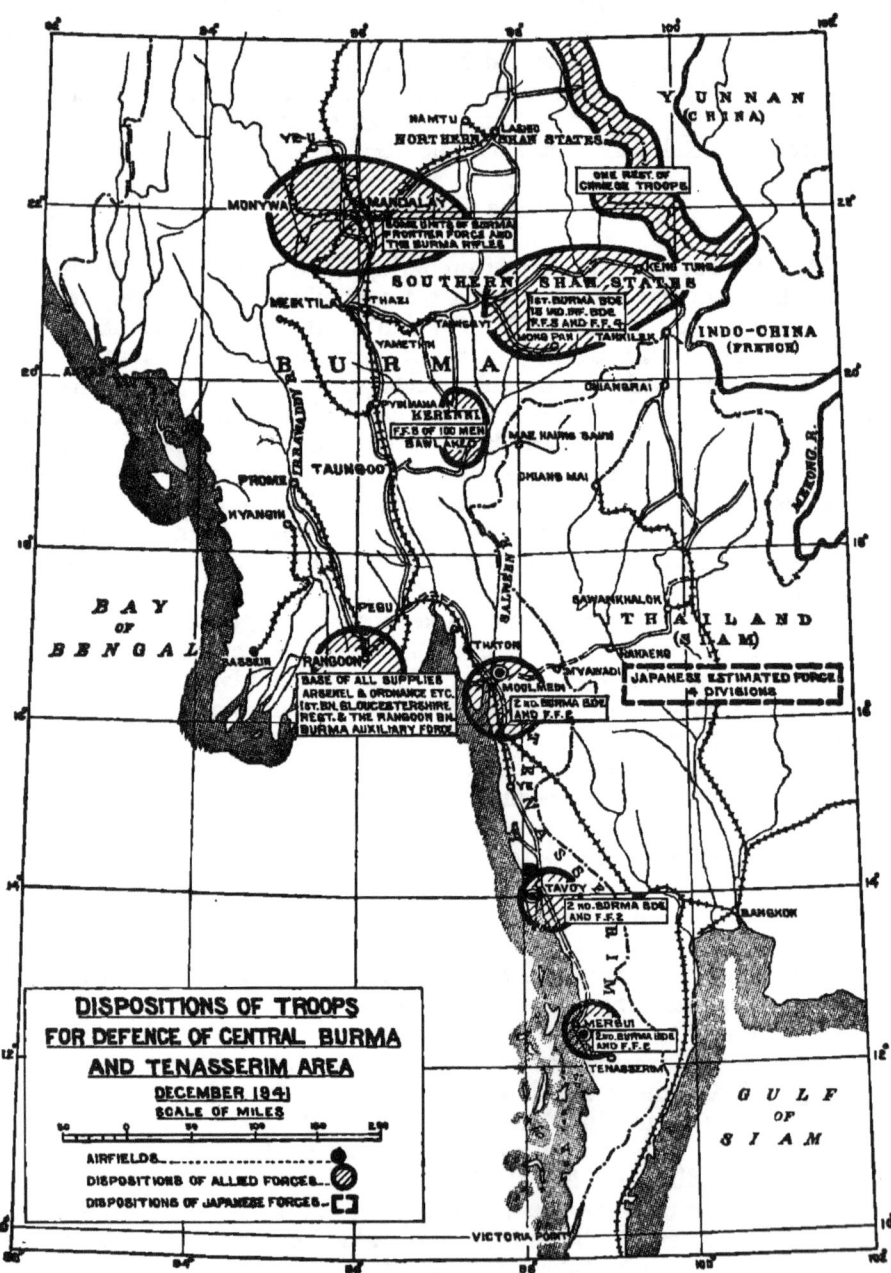

unorthodox tactics of the savage in thick jungle."[20] Indo-Burma troops were consequently out-manoeuvred and became bewildered.

(4) It was fondly believed that the air forces would be able to prevent the Japanese from using even the limited approaches to the frontier. Above all the grand Japanese strategy of closing either end of the Burma Road in Burma (Rangoon and Lashio) was missed.

(5) The unsound premise that Singapore would not fall and that the Allies would retain command of the Bay of Bengal and the Indian Ocean.

TROOP DISPOSITIONS

Upon the Burma Command's appreciation of the situation two Brigade Groups (1st Burma Brigade and 13th Indian Infantry Brigade) had been moved into the southern Shan States. F.F. 3 and F.F. 4 were also in this area. F.F. 5 of approximately one hundred men covered Karenni. The 2nd Burma Brigade with F.F. 2 was given the task of covering the Tenasserim frontier. Both Tavoy and Mergui as well as the Moulmein area with the important landing grounds at these places were to be strongly held.

Internal security was considered to be a real problem. In the event of a heavy Japanese threat, the loyalty of the local population was in doubt. It was necessary therefore to maintain a substantial force to deal with such a situation. Approximately one brigade including the 1st Battalion Gloucestershire Regiment and the Rangoon Battalion, Burma Auxiliary Force, was to be retained in Rangoon; in Central Burma there were available some units of the Burma Frontier Force and the Burma Rifles.

GENERAL PLAN OF DEFENCE

The general plan of defence against a superior invading force was that of delaying action and finally the holding at all costs of the line of the Salween.

Liaison had been established with the Chinese and arrangements were made for one regiment of Chinese troops to be moved close to the Burma frontier early in December 1941. This force would then be available for the defence of the southern Shan States in the event of operations there.

In accordance with this plan, lines of communication to the frontier were organised, the main base being Rangoon where all supplies entered the country. All units were originally supplied with Ordnance equipment from the small arsenal at Rangoon, but on the approach of war administrative plans for the location of Supply Depots, Ordnance and other services were made on the assumption that the main thrust would come through the Shan States. The Tenasserim front was regarded as subsidiary.

[20] Gen. Sir A. Wavell's *Despatch*, p. 11.

DIFFICULTIES PRESENTED BY THE EXTREME SOUTH

Tavoy and Mergui presented difficult problems. As long as Malaya was held, the airfields at these places required protection. They were not only essential to the air reinforcement of Malaya, but also afforded most valuable bases from which attacks could be carried out on the lines of communication of Japanese forces operating in Malaya. The distance from Rangoon to Singapore was too great for modern bombers, even without a bombload, to attempt safely without refuelling. At that time no Flying Fortress aircraft were available. Yet, the isolated position of these airfields, their proximity to the frontier, and the lack of communications between them complicated the task. The total naval forces available were limited to a few motor launches of the Burma Royal Naval Volunteer Reserve (B.R.N.V.R.), and country craft manned by Burmese crews who would be unreliable in the face of Japanese attacks. The single road linking Mergui, Tavoy and Ye and running close to the frontier could very easily be cut by an invading force. Eventually it was decided that in the case of a serious threat, the Mergui garrison would be evacuated to Tavoy which could then be held. Ultimately Tavoy Force, if necessary, could withdraw on Moulmein to stop the one track leading in from Thailand.

It is surmised that if Japan had been in a position to launch an immediate major attack on Burma in December 1941, her success would have been speedy and the fall of Rangoon must have rapidly ensued.[21] But there was to be no immediate serious attack and the respite that was gained gave time for a certain amount of regrouping of forces, the entry into Burma of Chinese troops, and the landing of reinforcements. The delay in the Japanese invasion until the break up of the monsoon also gave India time to organise her defences. But all this made little difference to the final outcome of the campaign in Burma itself, though it did have a definite bearing on the general conduct of the war in the Far East.

COMMAND

A major defect in all the plans was introduced by the frequent changes of Command, most of them adversely affecting Burma. In November 1940, the Far Eastern Command with headquarters at Singapore was created; Air Chief Marshal Sir Robert Brooke-Popham was made the Commander-in-Chief. He was responsible for operational control and general direction of training and for the co-ordination of plans for the defence of Hong Kong, Malaya and Burma. But the General Officer Commanding, Burma Army, who was previously directly under the War Office came under the new control only for matters of major military policy and strategy. Administrative and financial responsibility and normal day-to-day functions still pertained to him, and for these purposes he remained under the War Office. Moreover, the Commander-in-Chief, Far East, was given control and command over matters which,

---

[21] Japan was handicapped by lack of proper communications between Thailand and Tenasserim. This factor delayed the full scale invasion by a month.

under the Act, belonged to the Governor.[22] He was, therefore, required to resolve conflicts by being in close touch with the latter and by free consultation.

"So much, however, was the security of Burma of concern to those charged with the defence of India that several attempts were made by successive Commanders-in-Chief in India to have this arrangement altered and responsibility for the defence of Burma transferred to India."[23] The recommendation made to this effect by Gen. Sir C. Auchinleck was not accepted. His successor, Gen. Sir A. Wavell, personally pressed this change on the Chiefs of Staff who again refused to alter the existing arrangement on the ground that the question had been fully considered when the Far East Command was created. The Japanese had by then invaded Indo-China and brought danger nearer to Burma; but even this fact could not justify the change. During his visit to Malaya and Burma Gen. Sir A. Wavell discussed the same question with the Commander-in-Chief, Far East, the Governor of Burma, and the General Officer Commanding, Burma Army, and in the end cabled to the Chief of the Imperial General Staff on November 11, again recommending the transfer of Burma to the India Command. His arguments were:—

(a) that the defence of Burma was vital to the defence of India but not to that of Malaya;
(b) Bomber squadrons for the defence of India were best located in Burma;
(c) reinforcements of land forces for Burma must necessarily come from India and
(d) administration of Burma Defence Forces could be more effectively done from India than from Burma or the War Office.

But no reply was received to this telegram.

---

[22] Burma Operational Control (601/2/4/H).
[23] Gen. Sir A. Wavell's *Despatch*, p. 1, para 3.

CHAPTER V

Armed Forces in Burma

Prior to separation in 1937 Burma District formed part of the India Command, which had regarded the eastern and north-eastern frontiers with equanimity. On the east beyond Burma no threat was apprehended and even police outposts were seldom maintained there. So secure did Burma seem that no overland lines of communications were established between that Province and the rest of India. The linking up of the Burma and Assam railway systems as also the construction of a road from India had been discussed from time to time, but there were always other and more pressing projects to be carried out. Trade did not require such a link. The Burma Government feared immigration, and military necessity did not appear to demand it. The question was last considered in 1936 and then dropped on the ground that the time had not arrived for considering it seriously.

Therefore, in accordance with the traditional view very small regular forces were maintained in Burma. The District Headquarters was located in the hill station of Maymyo, the Government summer capital, and it approximated to that of a lower scale division. The country was a military backwater and the command was usually held by a General Officer whose last post it was to be before retirement.

ARMED FORCES BEFORE SEPARATION

In the District which covered Burma and the Andaman Islands were stationed an Indian Mountain Battery, a company of Sappers and Miners, two battalions of British Infantry and three, sometimes four, battalions of the Burma Rifles regularly officered by Indian Army Officers and recruited predominantly from Karen Tribes. The Burma Rifles were of course a part of the Indian Army. There were also a few ancillary and administrative units and certain units of the Auxiliary Force (India) and of the Indian Territorial Force. Units were grouped into areas, the Rangoon Brigade area covering Lower Burma and the Andaman Islands, and the Maymyo Infantry Brigade area comprising Upper Burma. This latter area was directly under the command of District Headquarters and had no separate Brigade staff.

Their duties

The primary duty of these forces was the maintenance of internal security and frontier watch and ward. There were also available for these duties nine battalions of the Burma Military Police, a semi-civil organisation not subject to military control and under the command of the Inspector-General of Police, Burma. They furnished guards, acted as a security reserve and were invaluable in times of rebellion. The Karen minority supplied a quarter of the men and the rest were Indians. As an integral part of India, Burma relied on India for large forces to cope with serious internal troubles like the rebellion of December 1930. In spite of the growing threat of Japanese aggression, the strength of the forces in Burma had remained more or less constant for a long period prior to 1937.

SEPARATION OF BURMA AND THE ARMED FORCES

Principle as regards the Armed Forces

What the threat of external aggression could not achieve the separation of Burma from India did. Both the Government of Burma and the Committee of Imperial Defence insisted that the separation must be complete in military as well as constitutional spheres. The proposal for the defence of Burma by the Army in India in lieu of a fixed contribution was dismissed as it would retard Burmanisation and Burmese politicians would regard it as a perpetuation of Indian domination. Like every other portion of the British Empire, Burma was therefore to be primarily responsible for her internal security. Further, to prevent invasion on a large scale by organised land, sea and air forces she was to be responsible for the organisation of resources of defence in the manner best suited for delaying aggression until assistance could arrive from other parts of the Empire or until pressure exercised elsewhere could relieve the situation. The policy was thus laid down that the Burma Defence Force should be organised for the modest triple purpose of internal security, policing the frontier and meeting the first impact of aggression and delaying it. This policy of creating a second line force only, was decided upon in spite of the recognition of the remote danger of Japanese aggression in view of Japan's commanding position in Thailand.[1]

Defence Committee's Report

A Committee was appointed early in 1931 by the Government of Burma to inquire into the future defence arrangements after separation.[2] It recommended that, as before, the defence of the frontier be entrusted to the Military Police but that there should be an increase in its establishments by six battalions, in addition to a Pioneer Battalion. For internal security it recommended the retention of two battalions of British Infantry, three instead of two battalions of Burma Rifles and three instead of one battalion of Indian Infantry, and one Mountain Battery (Indian). Both frontier battalions and internal security troops were to be formed into a Burma Defence Force under one Command and they were to be interchangeable. The most satisfactory method of getting officers was thought to be by secondment from British and Indian armies. There was to be complete, though slow, Burmanisation of the forces. The India Command objected to these proposals on the ground that by this scheme India was committed to supply, for many years, the majority of the officers and the greater part of the other ranks

---

[1] 1932-1936 Government of India, Defence Department G. S. Branch—*'Question of the Separation of Burma from India'*, (601/2/11/H), p. 51.
[2] *Ibid.* pp. 1 & 2.

personnel, a situation which did not well accord with the principle of complete separation.[2]

Controversy over India's help to Burma

Over the question of Indian battalions there was a protracted controversy. The Government of Burma wanted to have three Indian battalions until the Burma Rifles battalions were found fit in all respects. The Government of India was prepared to lend only one battalion and that too for one year after the return of the Burma Rifles battalion from Taiping, and to leave a company of Sappers and Miners for some time after the separation but with the right of recall in the event of mobilisation or on twelve months' notice. However, two battalions were to be earmarked in India for proceeding to Burma at short notice, if necessary, at the discretion of the Government of India.[4] Ultimately it was agreed that the Government of India should lend one battalion which would remain in Burma until such time as the Government of Burma was satisfied that the newly raised Burma Rifles battalions were fit. One battalion was to be earmarked for service in Burma in case of necessity and the Taiping battalion was to be returned immediately.

Final arrangements

Finally, when the separation was effected, by Sections 4 and 7 of the Government of Burma Act, 1935, control of all the Armed Forces of the Crown in Burma was vested in the Governor. A Defence Department was established for their administration. Thus came into being in April 1937 (when the separation actually took place) a small independent military command, carved out of the much larger Indian organisation. Naturally it was deprived of the many advantages possessed by the Indian Army, but political considerations had necessitated such a course.

The severance from India resulted in the transfer of the Burma Rifles to the Army in Burma. It was intended that the two British battalions should continue to be maintained in the country, mainly for internal security purposes, but that the Indian Army units should be ultimately withdrawn. The two Indian Infantry battalions soon left and to replace them the training battalion of the Burma Rifles was converted into an active battalion. Each battalion thereafter trained its own recruits. The Mountain Battery and the company of Sappers and Miners remained on loan from India, but on the raising of the 1st Field Company Burma Sappers and Miners, the Indian company (13th Field Company of the Q.V.O. Madras Sappers and Miners) was withdrawn early in 1940.[5]

The Auxiliary Force (consisting of Europeans, Anglo-Burmans and Anglo-Indians) and Territorial units (consisting of Burmese mainly) were

---

[2] *Ibid.* p. 4. The various details in the organization of the Burma Defence Force were further examined by small departmental sub-committees. 601/9858/H.

[4] The protracted negotiations can be followed in the Notes on the *"Question of the Separation of Burma"*.

[5] 'H. Q. Army in Burma Progress Reports', Pamphlets Nos. 4, 5 & 6. (601/1/16/H).

embodied in the newly created Burma Auxiliary Force and Burma Territorial Force respectively. These units were:—

> Rangoon Field Brigade R.A. Burma Auxiliary Force. (Armament, one Battery of four 18 pounder guns).
> Tenasserim Battalion, Burma Auxiliary Force. (Headquarters, and two Rifle Companies).
> Rangoon Battalion, Burma Auxiliary Force. (Headquarters, and three Rifle Companies, and an Armoured Car Section).
> Upper Burma Battalion, Burma Auxiliary Force. (Headquarters, and two Rifle Companies).
> Burma Railways Battalion, Burma Auxiliary Force. (Headquarters, and four Rifle Companies composed entirely of railway personnel. The duties of the unit were the maintenance and protection of the railway system).
> The 11th Battalion Burma Rifles, Burma Territorial Force. (The composition of this unit was Burmese and Karen).
> Rangoon University Training Corps, Burma Territorial Force.

Early in 1939, the Governor approved the formation of another Territorial Force battalion, *viz.* 12th Battalion Burma Rifles.[6] This, too, was to be composed of Burmese and Karens. At first, Headquarters and two companies were raised, partly by transfer from the 11th Battalion. The remaining two companies were to be raised in 1940-41.

Signals Unit

About the same time it was decided to raise a Burma Army Signals Unit.[7] This was to be completed by August 1941. Later (between April and September 1940) this unit was much enlarged to provide for the needs of the expanded Field Army. Thus came into being two Brigade Signal Sections equipped with motor cycles, line and visual equipment. A scheme was also submitted for its reorganisation on the lines of a Divisional Signal Unit, which was accomplished in April 1941.[8]

WAR-TIME EXPANSION

Rangoon Field Brigade

In September 1939, the Rangoon Field Brigade had been embodied and with its 18 pounder guns manned the Examination Battery at Dry Tree Point. Later, when the 6″ guns intended for the Battery arrived from England, the 18 pounder guns were withdrawn and were then used to provide the armament of 5 Field Battery R.A., B.A.F., a permanently embodied Battery of the Field Brigade, the establishment of which was enlarged. The Field Brigade personnel continued to man the Examination Battery.[9]

---

[6] *Op. Cit.* Pamphlet 5, p. 4, para 10.
[7] The plans contemplated that the unit would begin to take definite shape in October 1939, and that for a long time it would be in the elementary stages of development. Pamphlet No. 4, p. 2, para 8.
[8] Pamphlet No. 7, p. 2, para 6. Pamphlet No. 8, p. 3, para 15.
[9] Pamphlet No. 5, p. 4.

Burma Military Police

Separation effected an important change in the Burma Military Police. Six of its battalions which were largely Gurkha and Indian in composition, became the Burma Frontier Force.[10] This body was administered by the Defence Department although it was under the command of the General Officer Commanding, Burma Army. It was placed under the Inspector-General of the Burma Frontier Force. The three remaining battalions together with the civil police under an Inspector General of Police were administered by the Home Department under the Home Minister.

Garrison Companies

On the outbreak of war, the Burma Frontier Force immediately took over the defence of the landing grounds on the Singapore air reinforcing route, and a detachment of the Rangoon Battalion, B.A.F., was detailed for guard duties at Rangoon and Syriam. At the same time, the formation of Garrison Companies for carrying out these and other guard duties was taken up. These companies were eventually formed into two administrative Garrison Battalions. Their personnel was obtained from ex-regular soldiers and also from substandard recruits. New companies were also raised by 'milking' the existing companies whilst each company also trained a certain number of recruits to complete its strength.

BURMA ARMY AT THE OUTBREAK OF WAR AND ITS EXPANSION

British Units

The main portion of the fighting troops of the Army in Burma consisted of two British Infantry battalions in the country with the Burma Rifles and the Burma Frontier Force and Military Police. Except in the case of the British units a very considerable expansion took place in 1940 and 1941. The quality of these troops was not without effect on the campaign which opened in December 1941. It is necessary therefore to discuss these units in some detail.[11]

Defence of Rangoon and oilfields

The situation in the Far East and the peril of an outbreak of war in Europe led to a review of the measures for the defence of Burma. Early in 1938 an Inter-Services Conference was held in Rangoon and certain recommendations were made. These were considered by the Committee of Imperial Defence which advised the Secretary of State for Burma on them. As a result, plans were made for anti-aircraft defence of Rangoon, the oilfields areas, the oil refineries at Syriam near Rangoon, and other strategic points.[12] Landing

---

[10] Burma Frontier Force (1939-42), Report by Brig. J. F. Bowerman, and Notes by Lt-Col. H. M. Day and by Maj. D. Mostert. Microfilm Nos. 166/260-66; 166/277-281, and 166/303-310.

[11] The 'Army in Burma Mobilisation Scheme (Provisional)' was drawn up in 1940 and by Dec. 1941 the Army was to a large extent mobilized—*'Army in Burma Mobilization Scheme'* 1940. 601/1/18/H.

[12] 'Army in Burma Progress Reports', Pamphlet 4, pp. 4-5, paras 15, 16 and 17.

grounds were to be protected. Moreover, an Examination Battery of two 6" guns was to be installed at Dry Tree Point near the mouth of the Rangoon river. An establishment of the Rangoon Field Brigade was authorised. The desirability of proceeding with air raid precautions was also generally agreed upon but the protection of the civil population was not considered to be a military responsibility which was confined to the oilfields and oil refineries at Syriam and wireless installations in the Mingaladon area. The danger of aerial attack had always been clearly visualised by the military authorities, but prior to the middle of 1941, no substantial measures for the protection of the general population were taken.[13] Then it was too late.

The two British battalions in Burma were, the 1st Battalion Gloucestershire Regiment and the 2nd Battalion King's Own Yorkshire Light Infantry. Both units had been in Burma for some time and had been largely drawn upon to provide not only the necessary British framework for newly formed units and services in Burma, but also experienced officers and other ranks for service in the United Kingdom and in India. Good men thus lost were not replaced. The result was that both were very weak, and neither could produce more than two full companies on parade.

Burma Rifles

The strength of the Burma Rifles had been doubled. The new Battalions were:—

The 5th Battalion Burma Rifles.
The 6th Battalion Burma Rifles.
    Raised from existing Regular battalions by a process of milking. Each had a Burmese company.
The 7th Battalion Burma Rifles.
    Raised from the civil and Military Police. It had a composition of Gurkhas, Sikhs, Punjabi Mussalmans and Burmese.
The 8th Battalion Burma Rifles.
    Composed of Sikh and Punjabi Mussalman volunteers from the Burma Frontier Force.
The 9th Battalion Burma Rifles.
    A holding unit with an establishment of some two thousand designed for the holding and training of recruits who passed out of the 10th Battalion Burma Rifles.
The 10th Battalion Burma Rifles.
    A training unit located at Maymyo with an establishment of about two thousand and five hundred and raised to replace the training battalion.
The 13th (Shan States Battalion), Burma Rifles.
The 14th (Shan States Battalion), Burma Rifles.
    These two units were Territorial Force battalions raised in the Shan States recruiting Shans. These were raised in order to form the necessary troops for the R.A.F. aerodromes which were being established in Burma. They were officered by Shans, Karens and Burmese. Raising of the former commenced in

---

[13] See chapter VI, 'First Attack'.

December 1939 and soon reached its full establishment of Headquarters and four companies, though the 11th and 12th Battalions Burma Rifles continued to be somewhat below strength.

The standard of their training was analogous to that of the Indian units. Brigade training was carried out to the full extent of funds, equipment and facilities available. Yet it is doubtful if they could integrate to the level of the Indian Army, particularly the newly expanded units.

Their officer position also, particularly British officers, was not encouraging. The majority of these were seconded from the British or Indian armies for a four-year tour of duty with the Burma Rifles. But they could not identify themselves with their men owing to language difficulties, and it was only towards the end of the four years with a battalion that one began to be of any real value as a regimental officer. After 1939, however, the majority of the younger officers bearing Emergency Commissions had been previously employed in civil occupations in Burma. These officers were of exceptionally good quality and many possessed experience of conditions in the jungle and a knowledge of local languages. The few remaining regular officers had a very heavy responsibility to carry when fighting began. On the other hand, Governor's Commissioned Officers (the equivalent of the Viceroy's Commissioned Officers in India) and Non-Commissioned Officers were generally inexperienced, some of the former having had not more than two years' service.

Burma Military Police and Frontier Force

The Burma Military Police and, after separation, also the Burma Frontier Force, had earned a well deserved reputation for the part they played in the settlement of internal disorders and in frontier watch and ward duties. Within the limits of the purposes for which they were raised they were reasonably efficient bodies. But they had never been intended to be used as regular troops, or to fight against a first class army.

The Burma Frontier Force had taken over in 1939 the protective duties on the aerodromes of the Singapore air route. But additional aerodromes and landing grounds were built on the eastern frontier, and R.A.F. dumps came into being. All these required protection. So, too, did the vast quantity of stores that had accumulated at the China base at Lashio. For these purposes were raised thirty-nine additional platoons of the Territorial Battalions of the Burma Rifles, the Burma Frontier Force and armed civil police. In 1940 the Kokine Battalion of the Frontier Force was formed to carry out these special duties.

In the following year it was decided to raise mobile units from within the Frontier Force to carry out specific outpost work. There were at first four such units known as F.F. 1, F.F. 2, F.F. 3 and F.F. 4.[14] Later their number was increased. Their role was that of giving a warning of, and harassing and delaying, hostile advance until regular troops could be brought up. They had some motor transport, and F.F. 2, operating in

---

[14] Short Histories of F.F.2, F.F.3 and F.F.4, Microfilm 166/311-329.

Tenasserim and Mergui Archipelago, was supplied with native craft fitted with motor power. Each F.F. unit generally consisted of Headquarters, two troops of Mounted Infantry, and three infantry columns each about one hundred men. Their fire power was increased by allotting to each column five Thompson sub-machine carbines and one mortar. In addition, each platoon was given a light machine-gun. These new weapons were not available until after the war with Japan had broken out, and the units were required to employ them in action before they had time to learn their use efficiently. F.F. 5 and the mobile units subsequently raised were very hurriedly formed and were incompletely equipped. Officers and men had no opportunity of becoming acquainted with each other before going into action. These factors all affected efficiency.

The formation of these new units, and the drafting of personnel, including officers, to them and to the 7th and 8th Battalions of the Burma Rifles caused a very considerable lowering in the efficiency of the existing battalions. All Regular Assistant Commandants were posted to newly raised units as were the best of the Governor's Commissioned Officers and other ranks.

Burma Auxiliary Force

The recruiting field for the Auxiliary Force was much enlarged by the issue of a Governor's Ordinance[15] making eligible for service all British subjects in Burma. This opened the force to Burmese and other indigenous races as also Indians settled in Burma.

Army in Burma Reserve of Officers

An Army in Burma Reserve of Officers was formed, partly by the transfer to it of officers resident in Burma who were on the Army in India Reserve of Officers list and partly by the acceptance of new entrants. Before the end of 1939 the first of a series of officers' training courses had begun in Maymyo. After September 1940 the normal channel of entry came to be through the Militia and Officer Training Cadet unit. The National Service Act 1940 made it obligatory for the European British subjects of military age to join it.

By the beginning of 1942 the Army in Burma Reserve of Officers had increased to a strength of over nine hundred. In addition, about one hundred and fifty gentlemen had received Emergency Commissions. Of all these the very great majority were European British subjects who had been resident in Burma.

Emergency Commissions

After the entry of Japan into the war the demand for junior Staff Officers, officers for Supply and Transport, and other services and posts increased enormously. Many gentlemen were then commissioned direct from civil life and placed in appointments for which they were suited by training and experience.

Burma Army Service Corps

Originally the Burma Army Service Corps had no mechanised

---

[15] Army in Burma Progress Reports, Pamphlet No. 5, para 9.

transport sections, but eventually provision was made for twenty-nine such sections. Much of the personnel was taken from the Burma Rifles. After Japan had entered the war additional Auxiliary Transport Units were formed by taking over fleets of civilian lorries, notably in Lashio and elsewhere in the Shan States. Numerous miscellaneous Burma Army Service Corps units were also required and accordingly raised.

It was necessary to expand or raise on a considerable scale the Burma Military Engineering Service, the Burma Corps of Clerks, Medical, Ordnance, Provost and other ancillary and administrative units. In 1941 it had become clear that in the event of a campaign in Burma, the Government Posts and Telegraph Department would have to be militarised. This was actually carried out early in 1942.

Observer Corps

The Army controlled Observer Corps was formed to man a series of posts throughout the country to give warning of Japanese air raids. The location of these posts was largely dictated by the existing telephone and telegraph systems to which they were linked. As far as possible the whole eastern frontier was covered. A somewhat similar system of coast-watchers was also organised.

Air Defence

For defence against aerial attack a new Auxiliary Force unit, 1 Heavy Anti-Aircraft Regiment, was raised in 1941. It was armed with 3" and light Bofors anti-aircraft guns. These only arrived after the outbreak of war with Japan. Prior to the formation of this unit an Anti-Aircraft Light Machine-Gun Battery of the Burma Auxiliary Force had been formed. It was disbanded when the Anti-Aircraft Regiment was raised.[16]

1st Burma Brigade Group—Shan States

After the outbreak of war in 1939 the formation known as the Maymyo Infantry Brigade Area was divided, and the Maymyo Infantry Brigade with its own Headquarters was formed. This assumed command of the Regular Infantry battalions in the Old Brigade Area, the remaining units being grouped under a new Upper Burma Area.[17]

When the attitude of Japan became more menacing the Maymyo Infantry Brigade was moved into the southern Shan States for the defence of the eastern frontier. Later, the units were regrouped under the Southern Shan Area and 1 Burma Brigade Group. The latter, commanded by Brig. G. A. L. Farwell, M.C., comprised the 2nd Battalion the King's Own Yorkshire Light Infantry, the 1st Battalion Burma Rifles, and the 5th Battalion Burma Rifles.

2nd Burma Brigade Group—Tenasserim

Further south, in Tenasserim, additional troops were also made available for frontier defence. Some of the newly raised Burma Rifles battalions were employed for this purpose. There was first formed the Tenasserim Brigade Area and then, in addition, 2 Burma Brigade Group,

---

[16] *AIB Progress Reports* No. 8, para 22.
[17] Commenced functioning on Nov. 6, 1939.

which was commanded by Brig. A. J. H. Bourke and included the 2nd, 4th, 6th, and 8th Battalions of the Burma Rifles. Later, in December 1941, two companies of the 3rd Battalion Burma Rifles were moved to Mergui and came under the command of 2 Burma Brigade Group. The Tenasserim Brigade Area was also commanded by Brig. A. J. H. Bourke and, after the formation of 2 Burma Brigade Group, this comprised little more than the Tenasserim Battalion, B. A. F.

Formation of 1st Burma Division

In April 1941, the 13th Indian Infantry Brigade Group (Brig. A. C. Curtis) landed in Burma, the first reinforcements to enter the country. The Infantry units were the 5th Battalion 1st Punjab Regiment, 2nd Battalion 7th Rajput Regiment, and the 1st Battalion 18th Royal Garhwal Rifles. These were stationed in Mandalay and later in the Shan States since it was considered that the main body of any invading force would enter the country by the Chiengrai-Kengtung road.

The three Brigade Groups (1 Burma Brigade, 2 Burma Brigade and 13 Indian Infantry Brigade) intended for the active defence of the frontier were then formed into the 1st Burma Division in July 1941.[18] Divisional Headquarters were at Toungoo, midway between the Tenasserim and Shan States areas and considerably removed from both of them. The Division was commanded by Maj. Gen. J. Bruce Scott.

ARRIVAL OF 16TH INDIAN INFANTRY BRIGADE

Towards the end of November 1941 the first elements of the 16th Indian Infantry Brigade Group arrived[19] and were moved to Mandalay. These were placed under the direct command of the Army Headquarters. Brig. J. K. Jones was in command and its Infantry battalions were the 1st Royal Battalion 9th Jat Regiment, the 4th Battalion 12th Frontier Force Regiment and the 1st Battalion 7th Gurkha Rifles.[20] These were the last troops to enter the country before the Japanese invaded Burma, and it will be noted that the greater part of the available forces were mainly disposed to cover the Shan States. Several formations were still directly controlled by the Army Headquarters. The Location Statement for December 1, 1941 (Appendix 'A') and the skeleton Order of Battle for December 8, 1941 (Appendix 'B') give details of their composition and disposition.

DEFICIENCIES

Lt.-Genl. D. K. McLeod, c.b., d.s.o., who was in command, had been in Burma for some years and in the normal course would have proceeded on leave early in 1942 prior to retirement. He had made great endeavours in spite of a very limited staff and resources to prepare the country for war. But the staff was totally inadequate and a few overworked staff officers were struggling to compete with problems quite beyond their capacity. There was no intelligence organisation worthy of the name.

---

[18] It was itself a miniature United Nations consisting as it did of British, Burmese, Chin, Kachin, Punjabi, Rajput and Garhwal forces.

[19] The 1st Royal Battalion 9th Jat Regiment and the 4th Battalion 12th Frontier Force Rifles.

[20] The last mentioned battalion arrived in Rangoon on January 18 and was diverted to Moulmein the same night.

Owing to the policy adopted by His Majesty's Government no proper arrangements existed for external intelligence and, as a result, there was usually complete ignorance of what was happening in Thailand. The possibility that Burma might be invaded and the necessity of leaving behind a suitable intelligence organisation had not been considered.[21]

Army Headquarters was at the same time a War Office, a Corps Headquarters, and Lines of Communication Headquarters, this last owing to the absence of any lines of communication staff. Army Headquarters, as such, had responsibilities which covered exactly the same field as that covered by General Headquarters in India. It was therefore impossible for the General Officer Commanding, Burma Army, with his vast responsibilities to keep detailed operational control of the forces in the field.

The nucleus of base and administrative or of lines of communication units, as it existed, consisted of locally raised units partially trained and very weak in Governor's Commissioned Officers and Non-Commissioned Officers. There were few trained reserves.

The recruiting reserve was insufficient and casualties could never adequately be replaced. The 'milking' of all regular units had necessarily lowered the general standard of efficiency. The system whereby administrative control of Frontier Force units remained vested in an independent Inspector-General was unsound.

The problem of equipment and that of transport vehicles was also serious. The urgent requirements of the armies in Great Britain and of the active theatres of war naturally had preference, but the result was a shortage in Burma. Ordnance had no real reserve of small arms. Thomson sub-machine carbines, mortar ammunition, grenades, and anti-tank mines were particularly lacking. The total target of twenty-four heavy and sixty-eight light guns for anti-aircraft units was never attained. There was a general shortage of war-equipment, steel helmets and numerous other items. Transport was not up to full scale, and arrangements for supplies were largely carried out by means of requisitioned vehicles.[22]

OTHER ARMED FORCES AVAILABLE

Brief mention must now be made of the other armed forces available in the country.

Supply Base

A small organisation known as the Supply Base (Burma) had been set up by the War Office under the General Officer Commanding, Burma Army, for the conduct of operations in China in the event of war with Japan. It was intended to maintain guerilla companies and also Bomber squadrons of the R.A.F. in China. These were to be supplied by several motor transport companies operating along the Burma Road. A training school and depot for the guerilla companies was established at Maymyo under the name of the Bush Warfare School. Several companies were trained and sent to China.[23]

[21] Gen. Sir A. Wavell's *Despatch*, p. 11, para 29. The lack of 'external' intelligence in peace time was partly responsible for the faulty appreciations.
[22] *Administrative Arrangements, Burma*, 601/2/10/H, Appendix G.
[23] Report on the Administrative Layout of the Army in Burma with particular reference to 'Q' Services and Units. Para 9.

The course of actual operations largely frustrated the objects of the Supply Base and it was closed before the end of December 1941, but the remaining personnel of the Bush Warfare School were converted into Commando units.

Air Force

Air attack being regarded as the main danger to Burma it was intended that a considerable force of aircraft should be maintained in the country. In fact, there were very few. India, almost denuded of modern aircraft, had nothing with which to reinforce Burma.

Early in 1941 one squadron of Blenheim Bombers was stationed at Mingaladon, the airfield on the outskirts of Rangoon, and a small Royal Air Force command was set up. In the course of 1941 the aircraft of the Blenheim squadron were flown to Malaya and were not returned. When war broke out with Japan the only effective R.A.F. unit in the country was No. 67 Squadron with some sixteen Buffalo aircraft. New operational airfields were under construction at Heho and Namsang in the Shan States and at Toungoo. Those in the Tenasserim area were extended, and satellites to the main airfields were built.[24]

Intended for service in China was an air force known as the American Volunteer Group (A.V.G.) with a personnel composed of American subjects. It was formed in Toungoo in 1941 and comprised pilots, ground staff, hospital, and administrative unit. It was equipped with P. 40 (Tomahawk) aircraft. The aerodrome at Magwe had also been placed at its disposal. Members of the A.V.G. were to play an important part in the air defence of Burma.[25]

The Burma Volunteer Air Unit was a training organisation stationed at Mingaladon. Selected volunteers from Burma were trained by two R.A.F. officers attached to the unit as instructors. Two Moth type aircraft were used. On the completion of their course with the unit, members were sent to India for advanced training.

Burma Royal Naval Volunteer Reserve

The Burma Royal Naval Volunteer Reserve had been raised in Burma in 1940. Officers were British and Burmese, and the ratings were almost wholly Burmese. It maintained an Examination service at the mouth of the Rangoon river, carried out minesweeping, and furnished a Mergui Archipelago patrol operating in a few armed launches. It had a personnel of about fifty officers and six hundred ratings.[26] Shortly after the outbreak of war with Japan, Capt. J. I. Hallet, D.S.O., R.N., was appointed Naval Officer in Charge, Rangoon. Later, Commodore C. M. Graham assumed the appointment of Commodore, Burma Coast.

---

[24] *AIB Progress Reports*, No. 8, para 28.
[25] Administrative arrangements—Burma, Report 6, para 8.
[26] *Narrative Account of B.R.N.V.R.*, 601/3/6/H. *AIB Progress Reports*, No. 8, Appendix A. Says Gen. Sir A. Wavell, "There was never any effective naval support during the Burma Campaign; and its absence made the G.O.C. always anxious about a landing near Rangoon. Actually the Japanese made no attempt at seaborne invasion.." *Despatch*, p. 11. Says Lt-Gen. T. J. Hutton "In spite of their inadequate numbers they (the Burma Navy) undoubtedly proved a considerable deterrant to coastal operations of the type employed by the enemy with so much success off the coast of Malaya". *Report*, p. 9, para 35.

INDIA'S CONTRIBUTION

It needs to be mentioned that India had no responsibility for the defence of Burma but, being well aware of the weakness of her forces in numbers, armament and quality, she frequently represented the need for reinforcements and the advantages of giving the Commander-in-Chief, India, the task of placing Burma in a proper state of defence. This had been urged in many telegrams from no less than three successive Commanders-in-Chief, and also personally during a visit to the War Office by the Chief of General Staff, India, (Lt.-Gen. T. J. Hutton), in October 1940 and by Gen. Sir A. Wavell during a similar visit in October 1941. The state of unpreparedness of Burma was also strongly represented by various senior staff officers from India and elsewhere, who visited the United Kingdom in 1940 and 1941. In December 1941, it was further stressed by the General Officer Commanding, Burma Army, (Lt.-Gen. D. K. McLeod) and repeated by Gen. Sir A. Wavell after his visit to Rangoon on December 22 in that year. From the time of his arrival as Governor of Burma in May 1941 Sir Reginald Dorman-Smith had also made frequent representations on the subject.

India was, however, herself engaged in the vast expansion which, begun a year too late, was to bring her forces from some two hundred thousand to nearly two million in just over two years. She was almost as short as Burma of all modern munitions of war and motor transport. She was also under very strong pressure to send the maximum number of troops and administrative services to the Middle East, Malaya, Iraq and Persia where they were most urgently required.[27]

Nevertheless, India initiated action regarding reinforcements for Burma, and the second Infantry Brigade to arrive, if not the first, was despatched entirely on the initiative of General Headquarters, India. Administrative units could only be made available at the expense of the Middle East and elsewhere if so decided by the War Office. Consequently Burma was advised to raise as many of such units as she could from available indigenous material. Considerable help was, however, given in various minor directions by the visiting officers.[28]

THE OVERALL SITUATION OF THE ARMED FORCES IN BURMA

To sum up, the Burma Army had had a very short existence dating as it did only from the separation of Burma from India in April 1937. The rapid expansion from 1938 lowered rather than raised its efficiency. From October 1940 peace time expansion became merged in war time expansion. The Headquarters Staff was totally inadequate. The Army Headquarters combined within itself the functions of a war office, General Headquarters and subordinate Headquarters. This organisation or the lack of it clogged the whole machine. The Burma Rifles, though they were of considerable value for reconnaissance and patrol work in the jungle, were not on the whole fit to stand the test of serious operations against a hostile force like that of the Japanese.

---

[27] Gen. Sir A. Wavell's *Despatch*, p. 6, para 15.
[28] *Troop Reinforcements*, 601/2/7/H, Part I. Lt.-Gen. T. J. Hutton's *Report*, p. 4.

Added to this was the political problem. Eventually a large proportion of the Burmans and some of the Karens deserted and the active battalions had to be reconstituted without them. These desertions were likely to have a bad effect on the young Indian soldier fighting far away from his home. As regards equipment and transport the situation was equally serious and no unit had its full scale and some, such as signal units and Anti-Aircraft Batteries, had practically none. There was complete lack of either mechanical or pack transport till 1941 when M. T. Companies were hurriedly raised, yet vehicles arrived with no spare parts and there was no form of maintenance. Reserves were practically nil. The Burma Frontier Force consisted for the most part of good Indian and Gurkha personnel, but was weak in officers; and neither its origin nor its training really fitted it for operations against a first class Power. The force, such as it was, was quite unprepared for war. None of the units was trained for jungle warfare and was therefore tied to roads and mechanical transport. But much of the blame attaches to the higher command which grossly underrated the strength and efficiency of the Japanese and the scale of attack on Burma. Nor did the reinforcements arrive in time or to the full extent promised. "Shuffle and reshuffle was the order of the day and commanders did not know from day to day of what their commands were composed".[29]

REINFORCEMENTS

The Burma Army was built up on the assumption of meeting the first impact of invasion and holding it up till the arrival of striking forces from elsewhere. The problem of reinforcements was therefore vital particularly in view of the threatening mien of Japan. But Burma did not have priority in the matter of troops or equipment owing to the more pressing needs of other theatres. India was the only reservoir which could replenish the deficiencies of Burma in its own interest. But she had to meet the requirements of Malaya and the Middle East. That made it impracticable for her to strengthen the defences of Burma adequately. Yet reinforcements were sent to Burma, though they could not arrive in time for effective service, and reached Burma only when the hostilities had commenced.

The first reinforcement to arrive was 23 Garrison Company. This went to Akyab in December 1941 for the defence of the airfield and port. Later, in January 1942, it was relieved by the 14th Battalion 7th Rajput Regiment. In Rangoon the first reinforcements to arrive were 8 Indian Heavy Anti-Aircraft Battery (less two sections), and 3 Indian Light Anti-Aircraft Battery. These disembarked on the last day of 1941 and at once took up duties at airfields and other vital points around Rangoon and Moulmein.

In mid-December the 17th Indian Division had been selected for service in Burma. It was commanded by Maj.-Gen. J. G. Smyth, v.c. Eventually two of its Brigade Groups went to Malaya,[30] and only

---

[29] Major-General Bruce Scott's words.
[30] 44 and 45 Brigades.

Divisional Headquarters and the 46th Indian Infantry Brigade Group were sent to Burma.[31]

The 17th Indian Division was made up of young troops and had been orginally destined for Iraq where it was to complete its training. It was not really fit for immediate active service and had no experience in jungle warfare. The Infantry battalions of the 46th Indian Infantry Brigade (Brig. R. G. Ekin) were the 7th Battalion 10th Baluch Regiment, the 3rd Battalion 7th Gurkha Rifles and the 5th Battalion 17th Dogra Regiment.

Towards the end of December, the 48th Indian Infantry Brigade Group of the 19th Indian Division was earmarked for Burma. It was commanded by Brig. N. Hugh-Jones, and its Infantry units were the 1st Battalion 3rd Q.A.O. Gurkha Rifles, the 1st Battalion 4th P.W.O. Gurkha Rifles, and the 2nd Battalion 5th Royal Gurkha Rifles F.F. When it arrived in Rangoon on 31 January it was transferred immediately to the area of the 17th Indian Division.

Three unallotted British battalions were also allocated to Burma. These were the 1st Battalion the West Yorkshire Regiment, the 1st Battalion the Cameronians, and the 2nd Battalion the Duke of Wellington's Regiment. The first named battalion landed in Burma at the end of January; the other two battalions in the course of February. Early in March the 1st Battalion the Royal Inniskilling Fusiliers was flown into Burma to the Magwe airfield. Rangoon had then fallen.

Army Headquarters in Burma had been informed that the 14th Indian Division (less one Brigade Group), the 63rd Indian Infantry Brigade Group, two East African Brigades, not then in India and which had done excellent work in the Italian Campaign, and the 7th Australian Division would be available in due course. One East African Brigade had been promised for January, the other for March. Of all these only the 63rd Indian Infantry Brigade Group arrived. The convoy bringing in these troops reached Rangoon on 3 March and was just in time to participate without its transport in the final stages of the battle for the port. It was commanded by Brig. J. Wickham and was composed of the 1st Battalion 11th Sikh Regiment, the 2nd Battalion 13th Frontier Force Rifles and the 1st Battalion 10th Gurkha Rifles.

The 14th Indian Division had not been due to arrive until April, and the African Brigades were diverted elsewhere. The Australian Division, withdrawn from the Middle East, could have been landed in Rangoon at the end of February. However, the Australian Government considered its return to Australia to be essential and accordingly the proposal to utilise it in Burma was negatived. In addition, the Governor of Burma had been informed that a British Division then on the high seas would be available for employment in Burma. This presumably, was the 18th British Division which landed in Singapore just before the fall of that stronghold.

In addition to the anti-aircraft batteries already mentioned the following artillery reinforcements were landed before the evacuation of Rangoon:—8 Anti-Aircraft Battery, R.A., 2 Indian Anti-Tank Regiment,

---

[31] This Brigade (less 5/17 Dogra Regt.) after disembarking at Rangoon was sent to Martaban as a reserve to cover the withdrawal of 16 Indian Infantry Brigade. After four days it was sent to HNINAPLE area.

1 Indian Field Regiment, Headquarters 28 Mountain Regiment and 15 and 28 Mountain Batteries. There were also sent a few Engineer, Supply and Transport, Medical and other units.

On 6 February, Gen. Sir A. Wavell visited the Salween front. On seeing the country he considered that parts of Lower Burma during the dry weather would provide a good going for tanks, which could operate across the flat, sun-baked paddy lands. He therefore proposed to divert to Rangoon the 7th Armoured Brigade Group then intended for service in Java. The Brigade was equipped with General Stuart tanks, its Regiments being the 7th Queen's Own Hussars and the 2nd Battalion Royal Tank Regiment. In the Group were also 414 Battery R.H.A. and 'A' Battery 95 Anti-Tank Regiment, R.A. Brig. J. H. Anstice was in command. The Brigade landed in Rangoon on 21 February and was destined to render great service.

With the evacuation of Rangoon the entry of reinforcements almost entirely ceased. They could then only be brought in by air, or through the very difficult overland route from Manipur Road in Assam via Imphal and Tamu to Kalewa on the Chindwin river. In fact, no reinforcements entered Burma by this route.

The Indo-British forces in Burma were greatly assisted by the entry of Chinese troops. One Regiment entered Burma in December 1941 and later the Chinese V, VI and LXVI Armies were also brought into the country. These troops eventually undertook the defence of the Shan States, Karenni, and the Sittang valley fronts and played an important part in the campaign.

JAPANESE FORCES IN THE CAMPAIGN

It may be pertinent here to give some idea of the force employed by the Japanese in their invasion of Burma. As against two Indo-Burma divisions (1st Burma Division and 17th Indian Division) and two Chinese Armies each equal to one Indian division, the Japanese employed in the Burma campaign the *Fifteenth Army* which ultimately came to consist of four divisions.[32] This Army was under the Japanese South Region Command. First came *55 Division* less one full Infantry Regiment and various ancillary units.[33] In January 1942 came *33 Division* less *33 Infantry Group* and *213 Infantry Regiment*; the latter less the *2nd Battalion* and the *Mountain Artillery Regiment* came in February. The third group consisting of the *2nd Battalion 213 Infantry Regiment* and

---

[32] For the History of the Japanese *Fifteenth Army* we have the following Japanese documents:
1. History of the Japanese *Fifteenth Army* SEATIC Bulletin No. 245, 601/7785/H.
2. History of the Japanese *Fifteenth Army*, HQ, ALF Siam Weekly Intelligence Summary No. 7, 601/7720/H.
3. Short History of Japanese *14 Tank Regiment* Burma Command Intelligence Summary No. 10, 601/7277/H.
4. History of Japanese *33 Division* HQ, ALF Siam, 601/7725/H.
5. A Short History of *18 Division Twelfth Army* Weekly Intelligence Summary, 601/7256/H.
6. History of *55 Japanese Division* 601/7247/H.
7. History of *56 Japanese Division* 601/7249/H.

[33] See below. Chapter entitled "First Attack".

6 Company of the Mountain Artillery Regiment came in March. The two divisions had a total strength of 40,000.[34]

The fall of Singapore released more forces. The entry of the Chinese Expeditionary Force also necessitated further reinforcements for Burma and the fall of Rangoon facilitated such a move. *56 Division* (less the *3rd Battalion, 146 Infantry Regiment* and a company of *56 Reconnaissance Regiment* which had gone to Java) landed in Rangoon in March. It was rejoined by the rest of the Division in Lashio in April. In the same month landed at Rangoon *18 Division* from Malaya (12,000 strong).[35] Along with it came two Tank Regiments,[36] five Independent Anti-Aircraft Companies, two Heavy Field Artillery Regiments, three Anti-Aircraft Battalions and line of communication units.[37]

A Japanese division was almost double the strength of an Indian division. The former consisted of three infantry regiments if the formation was triangular. But if it was square, it consisted of two brigades, each in its turn consisting of two infantry regiments. Each division had its full complement of Divisional Infantry Group, Mountain Artillery Regiment, Engineer Regiment, Cavalry Regiment, Transport Regiment, Medical Section, Divisional Signals and Reconnaissance Unit. Each regiment consisted of three battalions. The Japanese method of training left nothing to chance. In addition to the training at Seinen Gakko (Young Men's School) they had in peace time a training for two years;[38] in war time it was reduced to a period of three months. Most of the soldiers were of peasant stock and were used to hard work and privation.

Their military training, consisting of arduous route marches, tactical training in adverse weather and open air campaign in a rigorous climate, only increased this hardihood. The social system and "spiritual training" also tended to heighten the martial spirit. In infantryman's training, marching played a very important part. Training on the march included discipline, maintenance of communication with other troops, dispersal against air attacks and singing of military songs. When necessary complete silence was maintained and men were taught to find their directions from the stars. Orders were given by the use of signs. Soldiers were taught to merge with the terrain. This might involve crawling close to the ground for a distance of over half a mile. By the end of three months a distance of 25 to 30 miles march per day was attained. Building of camp sites, field hygiene, construction of defensive positions, digging of trenches, duties in the front line, patrolling and construction of dummy positions were also taught. Weapon training included those in the rifle, L.M.G. hand grenades, and bayonet. An offensive spirit was fostered. The Japanese interrogated at Payagyi said that Japanese troops had not received much training in jungle warfare prior to their entry into Burma.

---

[34] The losses suffered since entry into Burma up to the fall of Rangoon are put down by Japanese sources at 500. See History of Japanese *Fifteenth Army* SEATIC Bulletin No. 245, 601/7785. History of Japanese *Fifteenth Army*, 601/7720/H.

[35] It had won the Order of Merit thrice.

[36] Each Regiment consisting of 36 Tanks and 43 trucks.

[37] History of Japanese *Fifteenth Army* 601/7785/H, p. 2 and 601/7256/H, p. 4. A short History of Japanese *18 Division*.

[38] Japanese Methods (601/1251/H), Payagyi Interrogation Report No. 6.

But this was not a fact. In Japanese Operational Orders even for "withdraw" the word "advance" is used. No wonder the Japanese were very "infantry minded".

Some information is available about the Japanese intelligence organisation. Each Divisional Intelligence Unit comprised three sub-sections. Sub-section one, comprising two officers and two Non-Commissioned Officers, dealt with the information regarding the enemy's strength, his weapons and possible intentions. Information was collected from front line units and native agents but the information given by the latter was as a rule unreliable. Sub-section two, consisting of two officers and two Non-Commissioned Officers, dealt with the line of communications and terrain. Sub-section three, consisting of one officer and one Non-Commissioned Officer, dealt with the recording of various actions in which a division had been engaged. All information was submitted to the Operational Planning Section of the General Staff.[39]

As regards air force which played a less spectacular role than the infantry, the Japanese employed one air division (*5 Air Division*). The Japanese army air force and navy air force, each formed a component part of the local area—army or navy, in each theatre of war and operated under its direction. An air division consisted of about 200 first line aircraft; it was subdivided into brigades which in turn were divided into regiments. A Fighter Regiment equipped with single engined aircraft consisted of three squadrons of 16 aircraft each. There were in all 48 pilots and a maintenance and repair company of 320 officers, Non-Commissioned Officers and men. The three squadrons and their maintenance and repair company were under a Regimental Headquarters consisting of 5 or 6 officers, 45 NCOs and men. Each light bomber regiment was equipped with 27 to 37 light bombers (type 99) which carried a crew of 4 each. Each squadron of 9-12 bombers had an establishment of 150 men. Heavy bomber regiments were equipped with 27-37 heavy bombers (type 99 or type 100) which carried a crew of 7 each. The personnel establishment of a heavy bomber regiment was 600. There were also reconnaissance flying regiments, independent flying squadrons, the latter designed to be able to operate from a forward airfield with an advancing army without having to depend on the ground services which the Air Sector Headquarters would set up subsequently. Direct co-operation flying units were small units engaged in reconnaissance.

The strength of the Japanese air force in Thailand in January 1942 was one fighter regiment of 27 planes at Lampang, one light bomber regiment of 27 planes at Phitsanulok, one heavy bomber regiment of 18 planes at Nakhon Sawan, and one reconnaissance company of 6 planes at Lampang. Later it was strengthened by the arrival of reinforcements from Taiwan. There were then two fighter regiments of 45 planes, two light bomber regiments of 54 planes, two heavy bomber regiments of 36 planes and 1 reconnaissance company of 6 planes. One heavy bomber regiment and one light bomber regiment were stationed in Bangkok. One fighter regiment and one heavy bomber regiment were stationed in

---

[39] Japanese Divisional Intelligence 601/7258/H.

Nakhon Sawan. One light bomber regiment was in Phitsanulok. One fighter regiment and one reconnaissance regiment were stationed in Lampang.[40] Even this modest Japanese airforce was numerically superior to the Allied airforce of R.A.F., I.A.F. and A.V.G. put together.

[40] Japanese operations in S.E.A. 1941-46. Ops of *18th Div.* Hukawang & Mugaung Area. FEC, GHQ, ATIS, 601/10/111/H. Answer to Q. 66. The Japanese estimate their losses in January and February 1942 as 20 to 30.

CHAPTER VI

First Attack

The Japanese invasion of Burma which began on 11 December 1941[1] was part of a remarkable surge of power, after the crippling attack on Pearl Harbour. Thailand and Malaya were invaded on 7-8 December,[2] Hong Kong on 8 December, Philippines on 9 December, Guam on 12 December, and North Borneo on 17 December. Wake Island was taken on 24 December; Sarawak was invaded on 25 December and Celebes on the next day. The turn of the Netherlands East Indies came on the night of 10-11 January 1942. Japan leaped to Rabaul and New Ireland on 23 January, and New Guinea on 25 January. This penetration was later extended south.[3]

Burma also became the target of Japanese offensive activity. Whether it was intended to be a strategic-shield for their conquests in the South-West Pacific, or as jumping ground for the invasion of India, or as a means of sealing off China,[4] or as a field for economic exploitation, it is difficult to say categorically. Marshal Terauchi's Report would give the impression that Burma was the limit of Japan's land conquests, and there may be some substance in it.[5] To the Allies, Burma had the value of being an important land base for offensive operations against Japan.[6]

---

[1] *War Diary 2nd Burma Brigade* gives 12 December as the date. But the Situation Report at 0100 hours on 12 December, which was repeated on 15 December, would make us understand that the Japanese had crossed the border on 11 December. *Situation Reports* I, (601/2/1/H), p. 4.

[2] Keesing's *'Contemporary Archives'*.

[3] This plan of campaign—offensive in almost every direction of the compass—was, to put it mildly, unusual. Sound strategy has always dictated that a nation fighting on several fronts should concentrate for a decision on one, while holding on to the rest. The risk in the Japanese 'centrifugal offensive' was the wide dispersion of forces and defeat in detail. On closer scrutiny however we find the plan to be not the insane attacks of a maniac. She had a central position and so could plan a campaign that promised to give the greatest results in the shortest possible time. Her unorthodox strategy was tailor made to fit the unusual conditions in the Pacific. It would take full advantage of the Allies' weakness not only in their armed strength, but also in their divergent interests. Once her immediate objectives were gained, Japan was assured of the complete domination of the Far Eastern Seas. Their reconquest by the Allies, operating at the end of long and tenuous supply lines and without benefit of advanced bases, would be, at best, prolonged.

[4] The decision to invade Burma was taken in November 1941, by the Imperial General Headquarters, consisting of the Chief of the General Staff, the Chief of the Naval General Staff, the Minister of War and the Foreign Minister. (Commander of 55 Division wrongly attributes it all to the *Hayashi Army Headquarters* in Bangkok).

The original plan was to occupy the key positions in Southern Burma, such as Rangoon and Moulmein and to establish strong airfields in that area. In this way, the British bases at Singapore could be isolated, Allied help to Burma prevented and British attacks by land, sea and from air on Japanese forces in Thailand held off.

It was only later that the Japanese decided to occupy Central and Upper Burma, in order to prevent the British and Chinese from joining forces. Far East Command, GHQ Military Intelligence Section ATIS Interrogation of Shinichi Tanaka, Chief of Staff, answers to questions Nos. 36, 37 and 38.

[5] Operations in Burma, December 1941—May 1942. *Despatch* by Gen. Sir A. Wavell, (601/7319/H), Appendix B.

[6] "The main object (of the IMPHAL Operation) was to establish a holding defence

As early as 30 November 1941, all formations under Burma Command were warned that a Japanese attack on Thailand was imminent. As the occupation of Thailand would bring the invader to the gates of Burma, precautionary defensive measures were at once taken. Full signal security was instituted. Orders were issued for the obstruction of landing grounds. Patrol activities were increased. In Tenasserim preparations were made to carry out a raid on Parachuap Khirikhan in order to cut the Bangkok Malaya railway. On 4 and 5 December road patrols from Mergui and Tavoy were also instituted.

On 7 December, the Governor of Burma issued a proclamation in which he said, "We will fight, till we win. We will fight in our hills, on our plains, in our towns and villages. We will defend our land whatever the cost may be. We in Burma will have to face a testing time. The whole future of Burma is at stake."[7] In an Order of the Day Lieutenant General MacLeod, General Officer Commanding, also declared that 'All races were united for the defence of Burma'. These words contrasted strangely with the very inadequate preparations.

JAPANESE INVASION OF THAILAND

On the night of 7-8 December, the Japanese invaded Thailand by land and sea. Thailand had been thrown into the Japanese net when in October 1941 the British Government had decided that they must concentrate on the defence of Singapore, so vital to their interest in the Far East. They wrote, "it is on success of this defence that ultimate fate of Siam depends and it is essential that this should not be jeopardised by dissipation of forces." The existing strength of the Imperial forces in Malaya did not warrant offer of any direct military aid to Siam, and the British Government were in no mood to do so. But they could not be indifferent to the threat to Siam and had "a natural interest in frustrating it", because it amounted to an "indirect threat to security of our own territories which border upon hers". However, a Japanese incursion into Siam was of interest to the British Government as they could not ignore the "obviously strategic interest in Kra Isthmus".[8] It was, therefore, essential that any British effort in that region to counteract the Japanese menace should not be opposed by the Siamese. The Minister at Bangkok was also instructed to tell the Thai Prime Minister that "present indications do not suggest an immediate attack by Japan". With no assurance of British military help and with the prospect of terri-

---

of Burma", Field Marshal Terauchi's *Report* on Japanese Ops in Burma (601/7716/H), p. 1. "Plan of Operations for 1942 came more or less to *the final stage* and we felt bitterly the necessity of reequipping and of strengthening our line of communication. At the same time we had to study how to meet a British counter-attack and to enforce (reinforce) our defence positions in general". Japanese Account of their Operations in BURMA, (601/8255/H),

The object of the operation in the latter part of 1943 was "to upset the British base around Imphal, to strengthen the defence of Burma and to exercise political control over India". *Ibid.*

Japan looked up to Malaya and the Dutch East Indies for their economic resources. At best she could deny Burma oil and lead to India which was surely in need of them.

[7] Keesing's *Contemporary Archives*—1940-43, p. 4924.

[8] *Political—Japan—Threat to the British Empire* Vol. II, 24.10.41 to 1.12.41, (601/479/H), pp. 9-10.

torial gains which an alliance with Japan held out, it is no wonder that Thailand inclined towards Japan.⁹ In November the formation of a Thai High Command was announced. Several classes of reservists were mobilised and Bangkok radio declared that Thailand might be forced to defend herself and abandon her neutrality in which case she would welcome with satisfaction the aid of other nations. In the light of the British reply and the later attitude of the Thais to Japan, it seems more than probable that this was an invitation to the Japanese.

THE JAPANESE FIFTEENTH ARMY AND 55TH DIVISION

The thrust into Thailand was made mainly by the Japanese *55th Division* belonging to the *Fifteenth Army*, with its Headquarters at Osaka under the command of Lt.-Gen. Ilda Shojiro as Commander-in-Chief. The *55th Division* had been organised in August 1940 with Headquarters at Zentsuji and was mainly formed out of the agricultural elements of Shikoku. It was commanded by Lt.-Gen. Thakauchi Hiroshi. In November 1941, the main part of the Division (about 12,000) comprising *112th Infantry Regiment* (Commander Chara), and *143rd Infantry Regiment* (Commander Uno) had been moved to garrison French Indo-China, where it was kept in readiness to move into Thailand. It landed at Saigon on 27 November 1941 and was joined there by *14th Tank Regiment* and the *Imperial Guards Division* which were placed under command. The rest of the *55th Division* comprising *Division Infantry Group, 114th Infantry Regiment, 3rd Company 55th Cavalry Regiment, 1st Company Engineer Regiment, 1st Company 55th Transport Regiment* and part of *55th Division Medical Section* (total strength about 8,000) had been initially moved to Guam, New Britain and New Guinea from where they were to enter Thailand gradually and concentrate in Bangkok in the latter part of December 1941.

The main body of the *Imperial Guards Division* pushed towards Bangkok by the Saigon-Bangkok road while the *3rd Battalion 4th Regiment, the Imperial Guards Division* left by sea. *143rd Infantry Regiment* also left Bangkok by sea and landed at Chum-Phaun and Parachuap-Khirikhan, a clear threat to the Tenasserim peninsula.¹⁰ The landings on the Thai coast were accomplished with remarkable skill, speed and secrecy. Operations on the China coast and along the many rivers in China had already given some indication of the efficiency the Japanese troops had attained in the use of water communications but it was in Thailand and Malaya that their technique was shown at its best. Special attention was

---

⁹ Throughout 1941 Japan was having negotiations with Thailand for landing troops on the Kra Isthmus, the use of Thai railway and the storing of supplies. Thailand has on this count been charged with double dealing. As a weak state she had no course except that of inclining towards one of the Great Powers to ward off the attacks of the other. She did sincerely try to get British help but failed here. Refugees from Thailand who entered Burma on 11 December stated that the Thais were very friendly to Britain and would have welcomed the Burma Army if it had walked in earlier—*War Diary, 2nd Burma Brigade.*

¹⁰ The date is given as 8 December in a short History of 55th Japanese Division, 601/7247/H, and as 9 December in the *Despatch* by Air Chief Marshal Sir Robert Brooke-Popham, Commander-in-Chief in the Far East, 601/10026/H p. 563. (The *London Gazette Supplement* No. 38183 dated 20.1.48).

paid to combined operations. Specially built landing craft existed to facilitate the rapid disembarkation of troops and A.F.V. and specially designed small craft with motor propulsion were carried by both of these craft and on the decks of transports.

THAI RESISTANCE

The Thai forces put up only a feeble resistance against the main body of the *Imperial Guards Division* for five hours at Battembang on the frontier. This was in contrast to their stout opposition to British troops advancing into southern Thailand from Malaya later on the same day. In the end the Thai Government announced that it had given permission for Japanese forces to pass through Thailand and also said that it had received assurances that Japan would respect 'the integrity and sovereignty of Thailand'. The Japanese alleged that their troops had crossed the Thai frontier only after Allied troops had violated the Thai frontier. On 14 December, Japan and Thailand signed a ten-year treaty of alliance. "Towards the end of the month Thailand announced a policy of fullest co-operation with Japan. Thai troops were soon fighting by the side of the invader. Late in January Thailand made a formal declaration of war on the United States and Britain".[11]

REASONS FOR THE JAPANESE INVASION OF TENASSERIM

Once they were in occupation of Thailand, the Japanese were at the gates of Burma.[12] The first phase of their campaign in Burma consisted of subsidiary land and air attacks in Tenasserim, on Victoria Point, Bokpyin and Tavoy culminating in two crippling raids on Rangoon.

Tenasserim, that long narrow finger that Burma pokes down the Kra Peninsula, presented many an advantage to the invader. As the Burma Command expected an invasion through Chiengmai for the purpose of cutting the Burma Road, an invasion of Tenasserim would lend an element of surprise.[13] Secondly, a wooded and hilly country, it presented ample scope for jungle warfare for which the Japanese had been thoroughly trained.[14] The Tenasserim peninsula also provided the shortest route to Rangoon from Thailand. Moreover, it contained a chain of excellent aerodromes forming vital links in the air reinforcing route to Singapore,[15]

---

[11] *The War with Japan* Part I (December 1941 to August 1942), Department of Military Art and Engineering United States Military Academy, p. 37.

[12] The Thai-Burma frontier is a long one extending from the southern Shan States to Victoria Point. The Japanese could attack Burma by many routes, from Chiengrai, Chiengmai, Rahaeng, through the Three Pagodas Pass or through tracks leading from Thailand to Tavoy. Topographical Reports—Routes across the Burma—Siam frontier, *Burma Command Intelligence Summary No. 2*, (601/7267/H) pp. 1 and 2.

[13] Vide Chapter on Appreciations and Plans.

[14] As early as 1934 the Japanese had established a jungle warfare school in the island of Formosa. Here they tried out their theories on the aborigines of the interior, who were largely exterminated. Even the thickly wooded island of Hainan offered a good training ground (for details see last chapter). We cannot place reliance on the statement in the Payagyi Interrogation Report No. 6, Jap Method (601/7251/H, p. 18) that jungle warfare was not included in the preliminary training but that it was practised extensively by troops when they arrived in Burma.

[15] Moulmein, Tavoy, Mergui, and Victoria Point.

which could afford full aircraft protection to the Japanese land forces in their next move upwards. Invasion of Tenasserim had the added advantage of striking the imagination of the Thais and securing their co-operation by promising the peninsula to them.[16] Above all it helped to implement the original plan of the Japanese to conquer South Burma.

To the defenders it was 'an awkward commitment'. No defence in depth was possible in Tenasserim. As soon as the Japanese troops, however small, entered the country they were astride the Allied communications and could cut the forces south of the axis of advance. The communications were also very poor. The easiest means of communication was by sea. On land, it was by rail from Rangoon to Martaban and by ferry from Martaban to Moulmein ; from Martaban a railroad ran to Ye ; from Ye to Tavoy and Mergui there ran only a road which was crossed by ferries at many places.[17] There were gaps in the road between Moulmein and Ye.[18] The lines of communication were also very long. From Mergui to Tavoy it was 120 miles and from Tavoy to Moulmein 170 miles.

ADVANCE ON VICTORIA POINT—11 DECEMBER

On 11 December, the Japanese aircraft raided Tavoy at 1630 hours.[19] The first raid was by a flight of 9 planes which dropped about 12 bombs. This was followed by 23 aircraft (single-engined monoplanes) which bombed and machine-gunned the aerodrome for half an hour. However, communications were not interrupted and the casualties were only seven.

Meanwhile a detachment of *143rd Infantry Regiment—the Uno Branch Unit*,[20] which had landed at Chum-Phaun, quickly advanced to Taplee and Namchoot on the Thai side of the frontier along the all-weather motor road running westwards to Taplee and from there southwards.[21] On 10 December, information was received by a motor launch patrolling the coast (Mergui to Victoria Point) from refugees from Enong (a small town on the eastern bank of the Pakchan river opposite Victoria Point) that the Japanese were in strength at the former place and that they had every intention of attacking in the near future Victoria Point, the southernmost tip of Burma situated at the mouth of the Pakchan river.[22] The Japanese would seem to have made their way thither from the east coast, down the Pakchan river in shallow draught sampans with outboard motors.

On 11 December, the Japanese crossed the frontier from Taplee and Namchoot and occupied the village of Marang. The police outpost was

---

[16] Tenasserim had been the bone of contention between the Burmese and Thai Kings in the fourteenth century.
[17] *Administrative Arrangements Burma*, (601/2/10/H) p. 4. The road ferries were to be improved.
[18] "The gaps in the roads to Martaban and to Ye are to be completed. This will take time". *Ibid.*
[19] *Situation Report.* Part I, p. 1. Keesing's *Contemporary Archives* 1940-1943, p. 4933.
[20] The Japanese account of their ops. in Burma (Dec. '41 to Aug 45). 601/8255/H, p. 1. Named after the Commander of the Regiment (Uno).
[21] *Topographical Reports*—601/7267/H, p. 1.
[22] BRNVR (6/10/3/6/H) p. 6. *Situation Reports* Part I, p. 6. "Unconfirmed report 2,000 Japanese Renong area; operations up coast may be contemplated".

overrun and the local police was forced to act as guides. The Japanese objective was Victoria Point, which lay 35 miles southwest of Marang. The town had an excellent aerodrome, and to occupy it was to cut the Allied air link to Singapore.[23] On 12 December, Victoria Point registered an air raid, while it was reported that the Japanese had concentrated, at Namchoot, country boats driven by outboard motor and armed with machine-guns. These crafts were easily transportable and some were capable of carrying a considerable load. A double advance on Victoria Point, one across the Pakchan river from Renong and the other down the Pakchan from Marang, was apprehended. It had been earlier realised both at the Singapore Conference (October 1940) and at the Conference between the Commander-in-Chief, India and the General Officer Commanding, Burma Army, (October 1941) that Victoria Point could not be held if "seriously attacked."[24]

On 11 December, the small detachment (a platoon of Kokine Battalion, Burma Frontier Force) at Victoria Point made preparations for the destruction of the aerodrome to the north of the city and for the withdrawal of the garrison by sea.

EVACUATION OF VICTORIA POINT BY ALLIED TROOPS—13 DECEMBER

From Marang the Japanese moved down to Pakchan river in eight motor-boats and entered Maliwun, a village on the motor road 20 miles north of Victoria point. A combined attack was expected at the dawn of 13 December on Victoria Point, on the aerodrome across the river from Renong and on the town by road from Maliwun. A plan was agreed upon between the officers commanding the detachment guarding the aerodrome and the motor launch 1101.[25] It was arranged that the former would set fire to the petrol dump to indicate that the enemy had attacked, and thereafter would retreat fighting a rearguard action up the coast to the rendezvous in Hastings Harbour, north-west of Victoria Point. The refugees and the troops in retreat would then embark in small motor boats and making their way up the coast close inshore would contact the motor launch. The commander of the motor launch had on his part undertaken to lay off the mouth of the Pakchan, guard the aerodrome against a water-borne attack and assist the embarkation of troops into the motor boats lying in the creeks by providing them with covering fire. The time and place of embarkation were to be signalled by lighting fires on the beach.

On the morning of 13 December, Victoria Point and its aerodrome were bombed and machine-gunned heavily. This caused panic and resulted in the desertion of the civil police.[26] Even though no Japanese attack had really materialised the petrol store was set fire to at 1650 hours and shortly afterwards the aerodrome and wireless installations were also

---

[23] On 11 December this aerodrome had been ruined and rendered unsafe for landing All other aerodromes and their satellite runways were also blocked by carts, which however could be quickly withdrawn.

[24] Report Singapore Defence Conference (601/515/H), p. 2. *Administrative Arrangements—Burma.* Appendix A, p. 1.

[25] BRNVR, 601/3/6/H, p. 6.

[26] Not mentioned in *Situation Reports.* They however refer to the demolitions.

on fire. The motor launch took it as a signal of enemy attack and patrolled between the aerodrome and Woody Island close inshore. It met canoes full of frightened people who could give no reliable information as to the state of affairs in the town. No fires were seen on the beach. In fact, the troops fought no rearguard action, but embarked in motor boats without lighting fires and sailed up to Mergui using inland waterways. They reached the destination on 16 December. Thus no rendezvous could be kept.

The motor launch 1101, did not know all this and so frantically searched for the troops. On 14 December, she picked up at Woody Island[27] a few officials who said that the town had been evacuated on 13 December, and shortly afterwards occupied by the Japanese.[28] The motor launch then set course for Mergui in order to land the refugees and take fresh supplies.

The officials who stuck to their posts at Victoria Point were the Sub-Divisional Officer and the police sergeant, mainly because the communication suspending the instructions to government servants which enjoined on them to stick to their posts of duty, did not reach them owing to the demolition of W/T. On the morning of 15 December, an advance guard of the Japanese troops entered the town and threw them into prison, where they were starved to death.

AIR RAID ON MERGUI—13 DECEMBER

On the day on which Victoria Point was evacuated, Mergui was raided thrice, first by 2, then by 6 (at 0630 hours) and finally by 27 aircraft (at 1150 hours).[29] The targets were the aerodrome and the harbour. Practically every building around the aerodrome was hit, the Operations Room burnt, the hospital and barracks damaged, and two petrol dumps containing 150,000 gallons of petrol and oil hit. The R.A.F. telephone exchanges and circuits were left behind as a tangled mass and the telegraph system running north to Rangoon was put out of action for a day. Propaganda leaflets were also dropped.[30] The town was also raided, the target probably being Burma Oil Company Depot. But the casualties were only six and the hostile aircraft made off swiftly enough at the approach of R.A.F. fighters which had been summoned from Rangoon by a wireless message from a motor launch lying outside the harbour.[31]

Though the town had not been touched, about two-thirds of the population deserted to neighbouring islands and villages along the coast. Some government servants, the majority of members of the Civil Defence Services and considerable labour left the town the same night. The next day the District Collector was given powers to impress labour, but there was no labour to be impressed. It is likely that some of them would have soon returned but the news of the capture of Bokpyin led to their flight again. As Mergui town and district were far from being self-sufficient in

---

[27] *Situation Reports* Part I, p. 5.
[28] In fact, the Japanese entered the town only on 15 December.
[29] *The Situation Reports* Part I speak of only two raids. Eighty bombs are said to have been dropped.
[30] *Ibid*, p. 3.
[31] BRNVR (1601/3/6/H), p. 6.

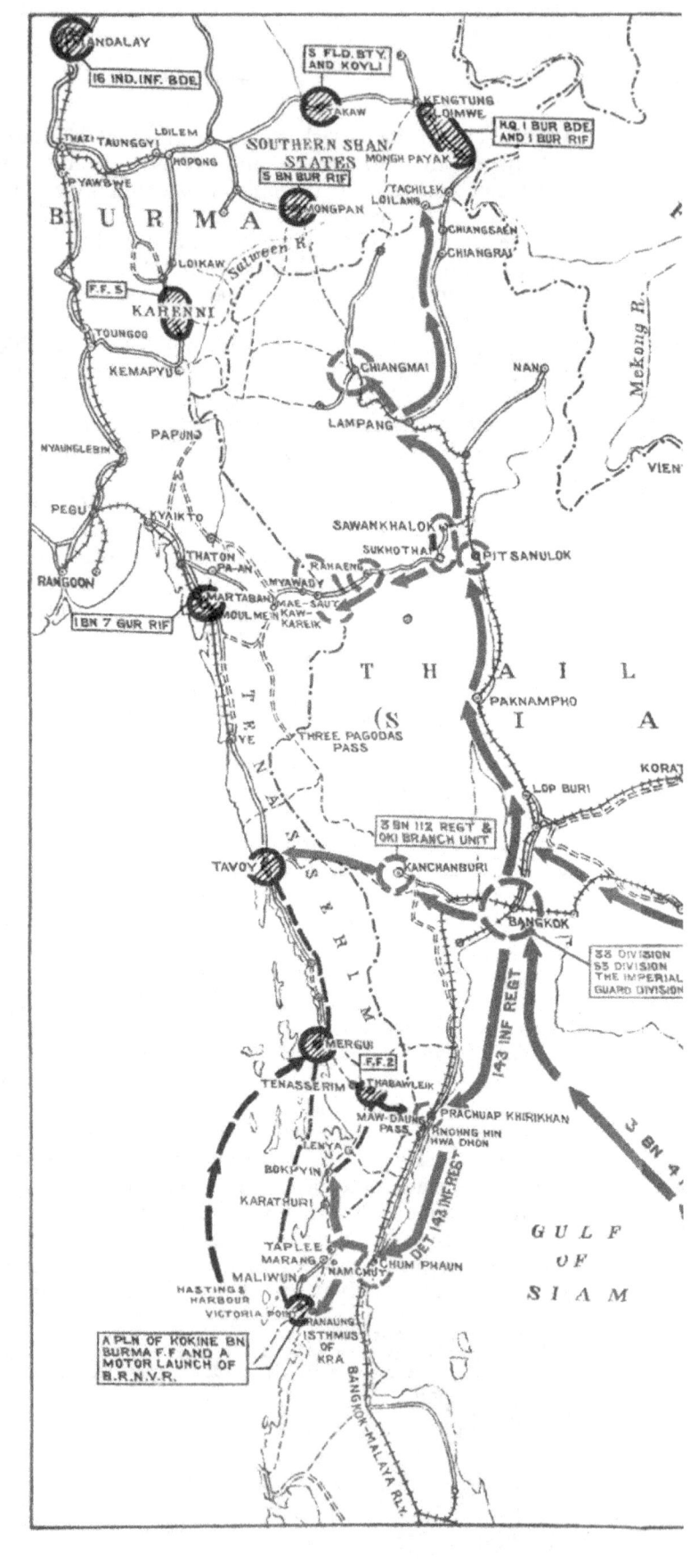

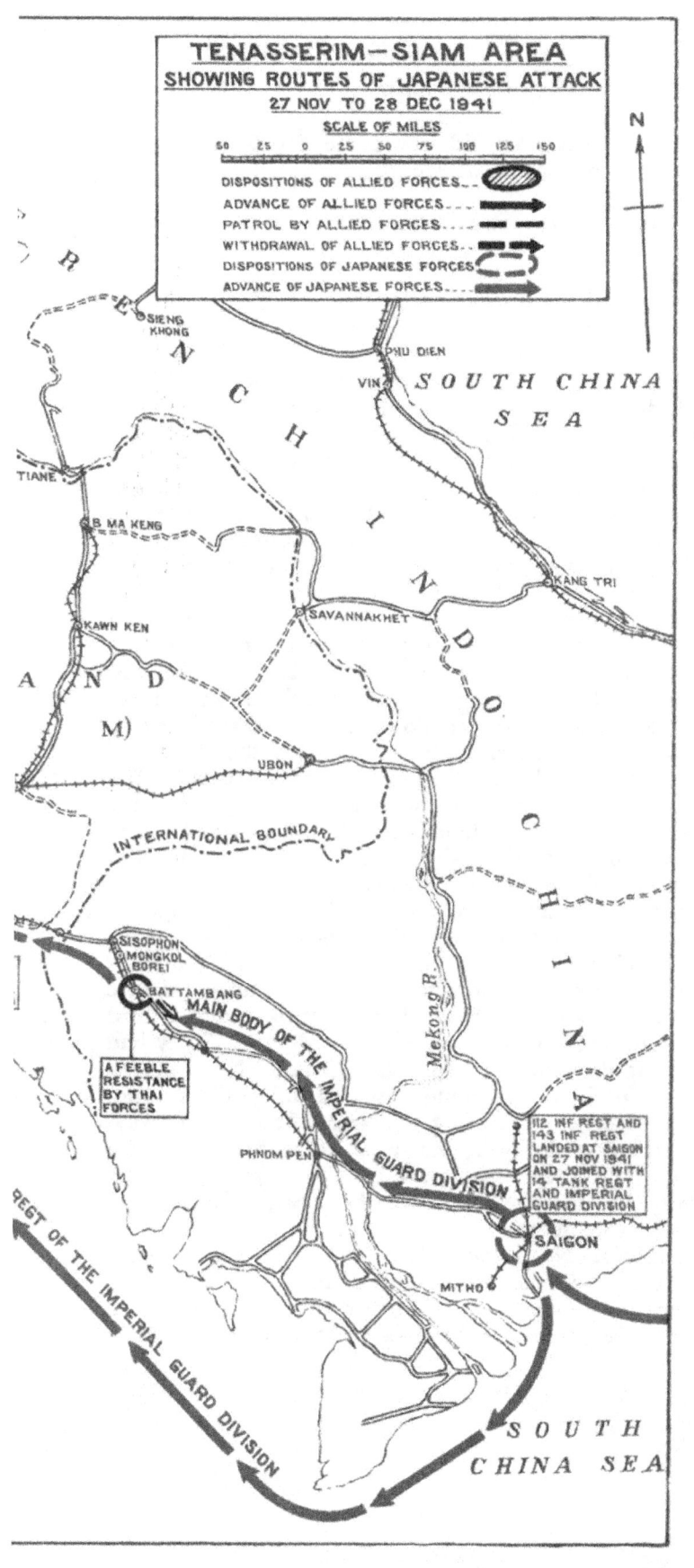

food and as supplies from Rangoon did not come the food position remained critical up to the evacuation of Mergui.

SCHEME 'YACHT'—12-16 DECEMBER

A day after the Japanese had crossed the Thai border into Burma, there was launched by units of the Burma Army the first offensive in the First Burma Campaign. This plan known as scheme 'Yacht' had been prepared as early as October 1940, and was to be carried out before war had actually been declared.[32] The object was to cut off the advance of the Japanese southwards from Bangkok by demolishing two railway bridges on the Bangkok-Malaya Railway, south of Parachuap-Khirikhan near the villages of Hnohng Hin and Hwadon respectively. The task was entrusted to three columns of F.F. 2, each of three platoons and with column Headquarters 120 strong. The fighting men were all Gurkhas though the Headquarters personnel and command were a mixed lot—Sikhs, Madrasi (boatmen), Chinese (muleteers) Karen, Kachin, Chin, Burmese, Welsh, Scottish and English. Just before sunset on 'A' day, column No. 1 and column No. 3 were to proceed over the Maw Daung Pass to the road junction 10 miles away. No. 1 column was then to proceed down the track which led to the village Hnohng Hin and demolish the fifty-yard Box Girder Bridge, 7 miles south of Parachuap-Khirikhan. Column No. 3 was to proceed down the track which led to the village of Hwadon, 7 miles further south, and destroy the sixty-yard Box Girder Bridge, opposite the village. Column No. 2 was to take up a defensive position on the Maw Daung Pass with a view to covering the withdrawal of columns 1 and 3. The whole plan was to be carried out at night. Each column was to do its allotted task and not attempt to offer assistance to the column involved with the enemy.

For a long time the columns were encamped in the village of Thabawleik, about 50 miles south-east of Mergui and near the Thai-Burma border. Later it was decided that one column was to guard the Maw Daung Pass and do reconnaissance of the whole area. Another was to do reconnaissance of the routes from Thailand into Burma and the third was to reconnoitre the seaboard between Bokpyin and Mergui. They had three kinds of transport, mule, elephant and boat. Column No. 3 moved down to a jungle camp near the Maw Daung Pass and did reconnaissance of the area for months together "following up rivers, finding new ways into Siam (Thailand) exploring the hills, but never going forward of the Siamese border", though only a few miles away from the Thai border ran the road and the railway, its objective. In December 1941, column No. 3 was joined by the other two columns.

On 11 December, column No. 1 was ordered to move to the vicinity of Parachuap-Khirikhan to report on the strength of the Japanese there;[33] but it was on no account to become involved with the hostile forces. On 12 December, the other columns received the operational message "carry

---

[32] Capt. E. J. Stephenson, *Personal Narratives of Operations*—Parachuap-Khirikhan (601/3/18/H).

[33] The Japanese had landed here on 8 December. Reports of this landing had been received the next day.

out scheme Yacht". A message was also received that the Japanese had landed at Parachuap-Khirikhan. The two columns then set off over the pass at dusk and at the track junction split as columns 2 and 3. Each column had a W/T through which it communicated with the Force Headquarters in the Pass. But very soon both W/Ts went out of action; the W/T sections were therefore sent back. The columns finding it difficult to make headway in the jungle in the dark, waited till dawn. Soon after dawn they reached the second track junction where they waited for Capt. J. O. V. Edwards, commander of column No. 1, to join them and lead the Hnohng party. Capt. E. J. Stephenson of column No. 3 was to lead the Hwa Dhon party. About 1500 hours the two parties heard the sound of heavy firing four miles away to the north-east. Capt. E. J. Stevenson rightly concluded that Capt. J. O. V. Edwards was in trouble and so decided to move on to his objective with both columns without waiting for Capt J. O. V. Edwards.[34] A little later the party saw men of Capt. J. O. V. Edward's column in flight and at 1700 hours sighted Japanese planes searching the scrub jungle for them. Their discovery was accidental. Major S. W. A. Love at the Force Headquarters had informed Captain Edwards by W/T of Capt. E. J. Stephenson's movements. Just when Capt. J. O. V. Edwards's men were deciphering the message, the set and the message were captured by the Japanese. Though completely outnumbered, Edwards's column fought its way out but after losing 15 of their men killed or captured. The Japanese were now fully aware of Capt. E. J. Stephenson's movements and had sent planes in search of his column.

Every time the planes came, the party had to take cover. With the approach of darkness the planes went away, then, with a compass bearing the column proceeded south-east in search of the river which according to their map (of 1909) ran past the Hwadon. At midnight, instead of the river, they came against a motor road. Capt. E. J. Stephenson decided to cross the road, and move south in an effort to hit the river and then follow its bank to the bridge. Throughout the rest of the night, the party moved on without getting to the river. They were by now hungry and tired. At 0400 hours they struck east in an effort to reach the railway. At dawn they reached a village and later the railway line. "North and south, not a blessed bridge was in sight".[35]

On the third day, the column marched west in a desperate effort to strike the elusive bridge. A party of the Japanese closely pursued them and forced them to take cover for a long period. In the evening the column again marched in search of the bridge. But many had by this time become casualties through fever and weakness. So they decided to return to the camp without their task being completed. After marching for a whole day the column reached the jungle camp on 16 December.

The puzzle about the bridge was cleared up when Capt E. J. Stephenson learnt from an officer having up-to-date maps that the river that originally ran past the Hwadon was tidal, and that for years the land

---

[34] *The Situation Reports* speak wrongly of two columns, one going north and the other south. *Opt. Cit.* p. 2.
[35] *Personal Narratives of Operations*, 601/3/18/H.

had been reclaimed and consequently was overgrown with paddy fields quite close to the bridge. The tragedy of this episode is heightened by the fact that the Burma Army Headquarters' message cancelling 'the Yacht', as the Japanese were already in occupation of Parachuap-Khirikhan, had been received too late—a needless and blundering operation. In the jungle country, night operations presented great obstacles to those who had not been specially trained for them. Moreover, the breakdown of W/T, lack of animal transport and the capture of the message to Capt. J. O. V. Edwards, sealed the fate of the scheme. The Situation Report has the entry that the Frontier Force columns withdrew as "opposition too great and heavy rain".[36]

BURMA REVERTS TO INDIA COMMAND—12-15 DECEMBER

A day after the Japanese had commenced their campaign in Burma there was a wise change in command. On 12 December, a telegram was received by the Far Eastern Command from the Chiefs of Staff that the defence of Burma was to be transferred from the Commander-in-Chief, Far East, to the Commander-in-Chief, India, including air defence and all relations with China.[37] But it was stressed that the constitutional position of the Governor in relation to defence should not be infringed except in so far as operational requirements demanded. Burma actually reverted to India Command on 15 December.[38] The telegram from the Prime Minister to the Commander-in-Chief, India, placing Burma under his command allotted for Burma the 18th British Division, then on passage to the Middle East. India was released from the commitment to send the 17th Indian Division to Iraq. She was also promised a special allotment of anti-tank and anti-aircraft guns and four squadrons of fighter aircraft to be diverted from the Middle East to India. A little later the Chief of the Imperial General Staff promised two African Brigades also. It looked as though very soon ample forces would be available for the defence of Burma.[39]

JAPANESE RAID ON BOKPYIN—19-30 DECEMBER

Next to Victoria Point, the Japanese objective was Bokpyin, a small Burmese village in the Mergui sub-division, 100 miles north of Victoria Point. The Japanese might have intended it either as a feint or as a plan to draw forces south when they planned an attack on Tavoy and Moulmein; or it might have been merely a nuisance raid. On 19 December, a policeman reported that he had seen a party of 50[40] Japanese with one machine-gun on the landing ground near the village. They had moved thither up the coast by sea in a motor boat towing a country boat behind

---

[36] *Situation Reports* Part I, p. 3. *War Diary 2nd Burma Brigade* says that the columns "were unable to cut the railway as it was too heavily guarded."
[37] *Burma Operational Control* (601/2/4/H), pp. 1, 6, 7. C-in-C India was to determine the date on which the transfer was to take place.
[38] *War Diary 2nd Burma Brigade* gives 16 December as date of transfer.
[39] *Operations in Burma,* December 1941—May 1942, *Despatch* by Gen. A. Wavell, (601/7319/H), p. 2.
[40] Later verified as 80.

it. It was later found to be a mixed force of Thais and Japanese fully armed with three machine-guns which they had set up on the jetty. Not unnaturally the people of Bokpyin fled into the jungle. The Japanese took the village and looted it, tortured a villager, and rifled the treasury. The Officer Commanding, Mergui garrison, treated rumours of the occupation of the village with scepticism and even thought that the party might be the 'missing platoon' from Victoria Point.[41] Air reconnaissance had also revealed nothing.[42] But on 22 December he received definite information about the occupation of Bokpyin; and at once ordered a company of F.F. 2 retreating under Maj. S. W. A. Love from the Thai border towards Mergui,[43] to go to the relief of Bokpyin. It moved south in a motor boat but unfortunately failed to contact the craft which had been sent with mortar bombs required for the attack. The craft was sent again from Mergui but arrived too late to be of use to the attacking party.

At dawn on 26 December, Maj. S. W. A. Love began the attack on Bokpyin even though he had no mortar ammunition. The Japanese had ensconced themselves in the strongly built Police Station which was at the western end of a hill 147 feet high; it was therefore difficult to capture the position by direct assault without the use of mortar or artillery. This force attacked the Police Station with hand grenades, and though three of them reached the Police Station they could not force entry owing to heavy counter-fire. At the Court House machine-gun fire held up the attacking platoon.[44] To crown it all the RAF gave no support. The force fell back to the jungle on the outskirts of the village to the southwest in order to re-organise for fresh attacks, but there it found itself under fire from the rear as well as from the village. Major Love was killed by a machine-gun bullet and his second in command was wounded in the shoulder. Shortly afterwards all ammunition becoming exhausted, the company had to withdraw to its left flank through dense jungle after losing four killed and four wounded. They then boarded the motor launch 1100 and sent a signal to Mergui from where a relief force was sent in motor boats. The column had marched through jungle with insufficient food and was in no form to attempt an assault. The desired result could easily have been achieved by denying the Japanese water supply for a day or two.

A company of the 2nd Battalion Burma Rifles was sent from Mergui to attack the Japanese in Bokpyin. As information of the despatch of the relief force reached motor launch 1100 it slipped up the creek to the north of the village on 28 December and effectively shelled the jetty, where the Japanese had posted some machine-guns. The Japanese officer in command of these posts was killed, and after suffering 10 to 12 casualties the Japanese force retired overland across the Thai frontier on the night of 28-29 December through Karathuri, a tin mining centre. Bokpyin was entered by the relief force on 30 December and occupied without

---

[41] *Situation Reports* Part I, p. 8.
[42] The Japanese were good at the art of night movement and camouflage.
[43] This was the force which had, though unsuccessfully, tried to carry out scheme 'Yacht'.
[44] It would have been of immense help if the RAF had bombed the Court House.

opposition. By the first week of January only a small garrison and Military Police were left in Bokpyin, the remainder of the detachment having returned to normal roles. The village was finally evacuated by the Burma force towards the end of January 1942.

PATROL CLASHES ON THE BORDER IN DECEMBER

Apart from the Japanese occupation of Victoria Point and Bokpyin, the month of December witnessed some border patrol clashes. On the evening of 13 December, the patrol near Myawadi encountered a Thai outpost and exchanged shots. Three days later reconnaissance patrol of the 4th Battalion Burma Rifles crossed the Thai border at Tachilek near Meshot and was fired upon by a platoon believed to be of Thai gendarmes. On 28 December, Thai police accompanied by two Japanese officers entered Loilang on the Burma-Thai frontier north-west of Chiengsen; the majority withdrew a few days later.[45]

OPERATIONS IN THE SHAN STATES AND KARENNI, DECEMBER, 1941

December saw only a few minor operations in the southern Shan States and Karenni. The former was guarded by the 1st Burma Brigade. 3rd Frontier Force with the 1st Battalion Burma Rifles, and one section of 2nd Mountain Battery were forward of Loimwe watching the Thai frontier to the south. At Loimwe were Headquarters 1st Burma Brigade and 2nd Mountain Battery (less one section). At Mongpan was stationed the 5th Battalion Burma Rifles. 5th Field Battery and Koyli were at Takaw and the 13th and 14th Shan States Battalions were assigned to line of communication defence. The appreciation at that time was that the main thrust into Burma would be via Chiengrai—Keng-Tung—Takaw. Loilem. There were known to be considerable numbers of Japanese as well as Thai troops in northern Thailand. Above all there were persistent reports indicating an early invasion through the Shan States. The role of the 1st Burma Brigade was largely to delay the Japanese to the utmost along this route mainly by means of demolitions. The mountainous and thickly wooded country through which the road ran, lent itself admirably to the preparations for demolitions. Several small patrol clashes took place between F.F. 3 and Thai or Japanese troops or both. A raid into Thailand up the river Kamapyu yielded useful information. Defensive positions were prepared along the road by the 1st Battalion Burma Rifles in the area between Mongh Payak and Loimwe. The 5th Battalion, Burma Rifles did the same in the Mongping area, and the Koyli on the Salween river at Takaw. The Chinese 93rd Division also undertook some raids across the Mekong river and inflicted considerable casualties on the Japanese. In Karenni the small force F.F. 5 was strengthened by the transfer of the 1st Battalion 18th Royal Garhwal Rifles to that area. The district was most malarial and the troops on patrol and in the outposts suffered severely from fever.

[45] *Situation Reports* Part I, pp. 5 and 38.

FIRST ATTACK

AIR RAIDS ON RANGOON—24 AND 25 DECEMBER

Importance of Rangoon to the Allies

The first phase closed with two devastating air raids on Rangoon—the ultimate objective of the Japanese in their South Burma operations. The focal point of rail, road and water routes, Rangoon was the only effective means of entry into Burma. To close it was to prevent supplies for the Burma Army and block the bottleneck of the Burma Road. The importance of Rangoon was well stressed in an appreciation by the General Staff, India, who considered "its protection of the utmost importance".[46] The War Cabinet had also informed the Commander-in-Chief, India, that "he should proceed immediately with administrative arrangements for the development of Rangoon as a base for a force which might ultimately reach four Divisions and fifteen Squadrons".[47] But Rangoon was not only a tempting but also an easy target. It lay within a comparatively short range of the airfields in Thailand.

The Raids

Though Rangoon had an air raid alarm on 13 December, the actual raids came off on 23 and 25 December. These were preceded by Japanese radio warnings of 'raids to come', which with variations and exaggerations, were extensively quoted amongst the local public and played a large part in creating panic. In the first raid the Japanese used a large force of 54 bombers, operating in formations of 27, escorted by a dozen or so fighters. The captured maps showed that aircraft had come from Saigon via Bangkok.[48] The bombers flew in very tight formations consisting of a line of Vs, each V consisting of 3 or 4 bombers. British and American fighters intercepted the raiders just before the latter reached the city whereupon the raiders broke formation. In the second raid there were 80 bombers and 20 to 40 fighters.[49] The fighters operated above the bombers and independently of them. Though the former succeeded in driving away the RAF fighters and bombing took place almost unmolested it was not actually as accurate as in the first raid.

Japanese objectives and the results of the raids

These raids were directed against the docks, the aerodrome, the Power Station and the congested parts of the city. The primary object of the raids would seem to have been to break the morale of labour by frightening

---

[46] *Appreciation and Plans.* (601/2/3/H), p. 4.
[47] *Ibid,* p. 27.
[48] The Japanese give the number as five bombers and eighteen fighters. They also say that all bombers were shot down over Rangoon. The bombers, they say, were sent out from the airfield in Bangkok and fighters from Nakhon Sawan.
[49] The *Despatch* by A/V/M D. F. Stevenson on Air Operations in Burma, makes out that on both occasions the bombers numbered between 70 to 80 with an escort of 30 fighters. (601/9555A/H), pp. 17-19.
The A. A. Defence was very weak with an initial strength of but one battery of locally raised troops whose equipment arrived towards the close of December. On 23 December, they were in action for the first time.
The Japanese Bombers were Army Type 97 and fighters Navy Type 96. Fighters had belly tanks.
The *Situation Reports* make it that the Japanese bombers during the second raid came in three parties of 18, 30 and 34 with fighter escort estimated at 20 to 40.

it.[50] Material damage would seem to have been only secondary. Actually the docks were undamaged except for one transit shed which was hit and the roof destroyed. No ships were hit. Great damage however was done to the Mingaladon aerodrome against which the greatest weight of attack was directed. The runway was hit in several places, all communications in the landing ground area were destroyed, and the Japanese fighters came low and machine-gunned the buildings and the aircraft on the ground. The Power Station was not hit but several extensive fires were caused in the residential houses in that area. Extensive damage was caused by fires among the wooden houses and huts. Civilian casualties were heavy. In the first raid 1250 were killed on the spot and 600 died in the hospital.[51] In the second raid which was as heavy as the first only 60 were killed and 40 wounded. This very low mortality was due to the fact that by then the town had been largely emptied. The reason for the high rate in the first raid was that the people came into the streets on finding the unlighted and unventilated shelters uncomfortable; and the Japanese used anti-personnel bombs which are devastating against people who stay in the open but practically harmless when they take cover.[52]

The most serious effect of the bombing was however the exodus of 75% of the population. For three days from the evening of 23 December frightened people with minds completely numbed by real and imaginary horrors moved away slowly on foot and in all types of vehicles; the Burmese went to their villages and the Indians walked straight up the main road north 'to walk to India'. However, propaganda helped by fatigue stopped the mass of Indians in or near Prome.

The city was denuded of all servants, menials, subordinate employees and coolies. All essential services, air raid services, municipal services, transport services, Post and Telegraph clerks, the Ordnance and Military Works and Telephone Exchange personnel and above all dock labour, left Rangoon. The dead were left unburied for three days, the railways ceased working in the dock and town areas, delivery of mails ceased, shops, markets and hotels were closed and food supplies broke down. As all dock labour to a man had left, the docks went completely out of action. This was a serious blow as there were many ships loaded with military stores for the Burma Army and Lease and Lend stores for China, awaiting unloading. The very small military force available had too many demands on it. Only sailors of BRNVR unloaded the ships and the available troops were used to clear the town.

The return to town of the population began only on 2 January, and continued to grow greatly in volume during the next three or four days. 50% of the labour came back, but rumours of further raids and of the intention of the military to take over the city led to a second flight of labour. "Taken on the whole, however, the situation was never restored. Military units for essential work became available only on a very limited

---

[50] The Japanese however say that their aim was to destroy the British Air Power over Rangoon—FEC, GHQ, ATIS Interrogation Report, Answer to Question No. 69 by Sato Shoichi, 601/10111/H.
[51] Lt.-Gen. T. J. Hutton's *Report* gives the number as approximately 1,700.
[52] 75% of the bombs dropped were anti-personnel. The rest were high explosive ones.

scale, and the working of all Transportation works, labour, etc. for services was most precarious throughout the period prior to the fall of Rangoon".[53]

If the raids paralysed Rangoon they also gave a nasty jolt to the Japanese. During the first two air raids over Rangoon the RAF and AVG fighters were most successful and accounted for a total of 37 Japanese aircraft besides a considerable number probably destroyed or damaged. A larger number was shot down during the subsequent raids. This heavy loss made the Japanese abandon large day light raids and take to night raids with a small number of bombers.[54]

Civil Defence Organisation

The raids also revealed the defects in the civil defence organisation of Rangoon.[55] The air raid precaution (ARP) of Rangoon had been originally organised by a member of the Burma Civil Service, who had some experience of the previous war. On his arrival the Governor, Sir R. D. Smith, found that the civil defence preparations in Rangoon were crude and inadequate, and outside Rangoon virtually nothing existed. He cabled to the Secretary of State for an officer for this new and highly specialised job to be sent by the quickest means. The new person came on 23 August 1941. There was then no ARP equipment. The personnel enrolled were only names on paper. The fire service was totally inadequate. Only peace time medical resources existed and complete reliance for first aid was placed on the St. John's Ambulance Brigade in Burma—a non-official body. There were neither equipment vehicles nor trained parties to undertake rescue operations. Nor were there shelters as it had been declared impossible to provide any. There were no arrangements for the dissemination of air raid intelligence. The warning system was in its infancy. A scheme for the evacuation of 90,000 non-essential persons had been prepared, but no machinery existed for determining who were essential persons.

The new Civil Defence Commissioner re-organised the ARP arrangements of Rangoon entirely, basing his new organisation on that which had been proved to work well in England. His work was far from being complete when the first air raid occurred. According to some members of the local civil service, had there been six months more to complete the organisation it might have produced better results than it actually did. But the Commissioner's opinion is "that the material was unpromising and disintegrated on the first signs of any attack". There was a great shortage of fire fighting equipment as also trained disciplined personnel and transport.[56] Canteen organisation and transport to feed the services while at work, were equally poor. There were no dispersal camps for

---

[53] Lt.-Gen. T. J. Hutton's *Report*, p. 3.

[54] After the second raid the Japanese directed their attention to the Mingaladon aerodrome. "It is significant to note that on no occasion were the oil installations in the Rangoon area attacked and later we were able to remove with confidence for use elsewhere a portion of the anti-aircraft equipment detailed for the defence of Syriam".

The Japanese maintain that the long pause in aerial operations over Rangoon between 3 January and 24 January was due partly to lack of bombs and fuel and to the concentration of air power over Singapore. ATIS Interrogation Report 601/10111/H, replies to question 72 by Chief of Staff with 5th Air Division by Taka Shita Masahiko.

[55] Civil Defence Administration of Burma (601/3/14/H), Extracts.

[56] *Ibid.*

essential public utility services. Hospital accommodation was still woefully short. Most of the hospitals were not blast and splinter proof. After the first raid the hospital staff (nurses, sweepers and ward-boys) left. The public had no confidence in surface shelters. In short, the preparations were incomplete and the materials undependable.

Refugee camps were too close to the town and refugees received no direction for these camps from either the police or signposts. The ARP plans included a voluntary evacuation scheme, which does not, however, appear to have been fully organised; only advice was given to the population that it would be best if all unnecessary personnel left as soon as possible.

The warning system worked well. Observer Corps Posts were distributed along the eastern frontier of Burma, particularly down the Tenasserim coastal strip. These posts were manned by local inhabitants who passed the warning by pre-arranged codes over the Posts and Telegraphs or railway system, the average time taken for a warning being two minutes. There was a warning of forty minutes for the first and thirty minutes for the second air raid.

JAPANESE PREPARATIONS FOR A FULL SCALE ATTACK ON BURMA

The Japanese, on their side, had made preparations for a full scale attack on South Burma from the middle of December. About that time, the *3rd Battalion 112th Infantry Regiment* and the *Oki Branch Unit* had concentrated at Kanchanaburi and taken Tavoy on 21 December. The main body of the *55th Division* was despatched about the same time by train from Bangkok to Phitsanulok (200 miles further north) and after marching from there by road to Rahaeng-Meshot, it concentrated on the Burmese border near Kawkareik for an attack on Moulmein. Similarly, the *33rd Division* had also arrived at Phitsanulok and concentrated in the neighbourhood of Sakatai and Sawan Kaloke, from where it moved in the direction of Pa-an.[57] Reliable reports stated that before 9 December, heavy guns and tanks were arriving at Lopburi, 100 miles north of Bangkok on the main Bangkok-Chiangmai railway, and that the bridges on this railway up to Phitsanulok were being strengthened.[58] On 12 December, the Japanese were reported at Paknampo on the railway station south of Phitsanulok. It was also reported that the Japanese troops had arrived at Lampang, 60 miles south of the railhead Chiengmai. Some Thais were located near Myawadi. On 19 December, it was reported that the Lampang-Chiengrai road was closed in six places and traffic diverted, presumably for strengthening the bridges. It was also learnt that the Thais living in the Lenya valley, 60 miles south of Mergui, were preparing food supplies in order to assist a Japanese invasion which they expected in the last week of December. On 24 December, 2,000 Japanese were reported at Qayawai, 12 miles from the frontier on the road from Chiengmai to Mongtun. Fighter reconnaissance over Parachuap-Khirikhan had located several torpedo bombers. On 28 December, it was

---

[57] *Japanese Account of their Operations in Burma, December 1941—August 1945* (601/8255/H), p. 17.
[58] *Situation Reports* Part I, p. 3.

reliably reported that Meshai in north-west Thailand was reinforced by 400 troops and many lorries. Thus, the Japanese having already taken Victoria Point and being firmly established at Chum Phaun, Parachuap-Khirikhan, Kanchanaburi, Rahaeng, Meshot, Phitsanulok and Chiengmai, were well poised for an attack on Tenasserim by land, sea and air, from positions directly at right angles to the Burmese main line of communications.

PREPARATIONS ON THE BURMA SIDE

On the Burma side there was very little preparation. To strengthen the forces in Tenasserim the 16th Indian Infantry Brigade, concentrating in Mandalay, was ordered into the area. On 19 December, the 1st Battalion 7th Gurkha Rifles arrived in Martaban. The other two battalions of the Brigade were to move from Mandalay in January 1942. In Karenni the small F.F. 5 force was strengthened by the transfer to the area of the 1st Battalion 18th Royal Garhwal Rifles. In accordance with the arrangements previously made one regiment of the Chinese 93rd Division moved across the frontier to take over the river positions west of the road Kengtung-Mongpayak. The remainder of the Division was at Puerh in China. Also 300 known fifth columnists had been arrested. In his appreciation on 22 December, the following points were made out by Gen. Sir A. Wavell. Owing to the shortage of aircraft and the breakdown of the intelligence system, based on Singapore, information of the Japanese moves and intentions was completely lacking. Little had been done to make defensive works on the main lines of approach. The defensive plans were based largely on the hope that the air force would make Japanese approach difficult or impossible by bombing. This was contrary to all experience of the war but anyway there were no bombers available. From the point of view of defence a great weakness in Burma was the single port of entry which was situated in the most exposed position. The staff was inadequate in number and quality, even though over 20 officers of staff and services had already been sent from India since she had assumed the responsibility for the defence of Burma. If Burma was to be rendered a secure base for future offensive operations the immediate requirements were, two bomber squadrons of Blenheim IV, two modern fighter squadrons for the defence of Rangoon, two brigade groups and a divisional headquarters.

NEW G.O.C.

On 27 December, Lieutenant General Hutton, Chief of the General Staff, India, assumed command of the Burma Army replacing Lt.-Gen. D. K. MacLeod.[59] This change was necessitated by the fact that the extensive reorganisation of the whole military system of Burma required a commander with greater experience of the organisation and administration of troops on a large scale.

[59] *Situation Reports*, Part I, fails to mention this.

BURMA PLACED UNDER ABDA COMMAND

Towards the close of December the South-West Pacific Command (afterwards known as ABDACOM) was constituted and Gen. Sir A. Wavell was appointed Supreme Commander. The first intimation to establish a united command in the South-West Pacific and Gen. Sir A. Wavell's selection to take charge of it was contained in a telegram which he received on 30 December. The official instructions were received five days later. Burma was included in this Command for operational purposes, while continuing to remain administratively under India. It was however realised by the War Office that India was "necessarily closely concerned with defence of Burma as part of defence of India itself and must play a large part in provision and administration of forces in Burma".[60] Conflict of views between the Commander-in-Chief, India, and the Supreme Commander, South-West Pacific Command, was to be referred to His Majesty's Government for decision.

Gen. Sir A. Wavell at once recommended that the defence of Burma should remain the responsibility of the Commander-in-Chief, India. The Governor of Burma also stressed that it would be a grave error to divorce India from any interest in the defence of Burma, especially when the military situation was so unstable; he added, "we must rely on India to continue to supply the necessary means of resistance," and "since India assumed direct responsibility the situation here (Burma) has been positively dynamic."[61] But both were overruled by the Prime Minister and the Chiefs of Staff, "the overriding consideration being that we must give Chiang Kai Shek, the feeling that the new command stretches out his (its) left hand to him. It is of great importance that he should support in every way and the G.O.C. Burma should be placed in direct touch with him."[62] Gen. Sir A. Wavell commented, "I think that this decision was a serious error from the military point of view. From my headquarters in Java, 2,000 miles distant from Rangoon and concerned as I was with an immense area (Burma, Malaya, the Netherlands East Indies and the Philippine Islands), and many international problems, it was impossible for me to give as close attention to the defence of Burma as was desirable; nor had I any reinforcements at my disposal to aid Burma. They must come almost entirely from India. Moreover, administration of the forces in Burma had necessarily to be conducted from India; and it is always wrong to separate operational and administrative responsibility." He added further, "During the five weeks that Burma remained under ABDA Command, I was only able to pay two hurried visits; and owing to faulty signal communications messages and reports from Burma sometimes took several days to reach me in Java. It was during these five weeks that the fate of Burma was decided".[63]

However, Gen. Sir A. Wavell would have protested more strongly had he "thought that there was likely to be an immediate Japanese invasion of Burma in force". He mis-calculated the extent of Japanese

---

[60] *Burma Operational Control*, (601/2/4H), p. 26.
[61] *Ibid*, p. 20.
[62] *Ibid*, p. 21.
[63] Gen. Sir A. Wavell's *Despatch* (601/7319/H), p. 6.

preparations and believed that while engaged in active operations in the Philippines, Malaya and the Netherlands East Indies they would not be able to conduct a serious campaign in Burma.

Gen. Sir A. Wavell took over control of the South-West Pacific Command on 15 January and established ABDACOM headquarters in Java near Bandoeng, a few days later. He then instructed the General Officer Commanding, Burma Army, that the latter's main task was to defend northern and southern Burma against attack by land, pay particular attention to the defence of aerodromes and organise military resources in Burma to a maximum strength of four divisions and fifteen squadrons of RAF so that operations against Thailand could be undertaken.

CHAPTER VII

Loss of Mergui and Tavoy

AIR ATTACKS—1-15 JANUARY

The first fortnight of January 1942 was a period of great activity. It saw a series of air raids on Rangoon, Martaban, Moulmein and Tavoy, surely a softening up process before a large scale invasion of Tenasserim. On 2 January, one Japanese aircraft reconnoitred the Bokpyin area. The next day 9 planes ground-strafed Moulmein, but there was no damage or casualty. An A.V.G. patrol on reconnaissance chased the Japanese to Rahaeng, shot down three and burnt out four on the ground.[1] Information was received from police agents who had been arrested in Thailand and subsequently released, that while in captivity they had overheard some Japanese Officer discussing future plans. These included plans for an attack on Tavoy in three weeks' time. This information proved to be subsequently correct. On 4 January, Rangoon was bombed twice by over 30 planes; and in the dog fight that ensued one Japanese plane and three A.V.Gs were shot down. Mingaladon was bombed on 5, 6 and 7 January. Some buildings and the runway were damaged. But all these were night raids. On 7 January, Martaban, Moulmein, the landing stage at Kyondo on the Haungtharaw river, 30 miles east of Moulmein, were also bombed. At Moulmein the aerodrome and ships were bombed and machine-gunned. At Martaban the station was hit but was not much affected.[2] The object of bombing Kyondo was to make it difficult for the forces at Kawkareik to retreat to Moulmein. On 8 January, local agents reported that the Japanese would attack the Myawadi area in the near future and that this operation would be preceded by a heavy air attack.

But it was not all one-sided. On 8 January, ten Blenheim aircraft attacked Bangkok docks and the commercial area alongside. Two sections of the A.V.G. attached to a small bomber force attacked Japanese aircraft on the Meshot aerodrome and destroyed seven of them. Air reconnaissance over Meshot and Rahaeng was also carried out which showed coolies working on the Rahaeng-Meshot road.[3] On 9 January, Rahaeng was attacked by 6 Buffaloes and 7 Tomahawks of the A.V.G. On the same day local patrols encountered a Japanese force of 50 to 100, on the Burma side of the frontier where Me Pai river cuts the frontier. Reports did not indicate whether the force was Thai or Japanese, but it retired leaving two dead.

On 10 January, attempts were made by the Japanese to bomb the tin

---

[1] *Situation Report*, pp. 32 & 33 (10920-2/1). *War Diary of the 8th Battalion Burma Rifles* says that four of our planes were slightly damaged.
[2] *Situation Report*, p. 39 (10920-2/1). *War Diary of 17th Divisional Signals*. The number of planes was 36 (*War Diary of the 8th Battalion Burma Rifles*).
[3] *Situation Report*, pp. 39 and 40 (10920—2/1). SEATIC Bulletin Noo. 245 *History of the Japanese Fifteenth Army*, p. 1. And *Situation Reports*, Part I, p. 35, 'Small group of workmen on road were ground strafed' by our planes on 2 January.

mines near Myitta on the track from Tavoy to the frontier. The next day, both Moulmein and Tavoy were again bombed. Tavoy was bombed twice, but without damage or casualty. Nor did Moulmein suffer any military damage. On 12 and 13 January, Mingaladon was bombed. On the other hand, the A.V.G. Buffaloes attacked the aerodrome at Parachuap-Khirikhan and shot down a J.U. 87 on reconnaissance on the Tavoy-Mergui road.

On 10 January, Lt.-Gen. T. J. Hutton made the following detailed and almost correct appreciation of the military situation in Burma. It was with a view to stabilising the position against the Japanese attack and to considering steps required to enable an offensive from Burma to be undertaken. The concentration areas and advanced bases in Thailand for an attack on Burma were likely to be Chiengrai and Chiengmai in the northern and Rahaeng in western Thailand. Approaches to Tenasserim from Thailand offered the shortest and most direct approach, with less depth in natural obstacles to a hostile advance. Though Tenasserim is guarded by the Dawna Range, precipitous in places and heavily afforested, the latter has not the depth possessed by the mountains of the southern Shan States. He therefore appreciated that the advance into Tenasserim could be assisted by sea-borne operations on the west coast. But the further the Japanese advanced into Burma the greater would be the difficulty of maintaining communications.[4]

Though the Japanese forces in Thailand were estimated to be three divisions, besides the Thai forces, there was in Lt.-Gen. T. J. Hutton's opinion no reason to suppose that the Japanese could not bring more considerable strength to bear against Burma, as the approaches to it were being rapidly improved.[5] The Japanese could be believed to deploy the greatest possible strength on as wide a front and on as many approaches as possible in order to extend the defence and ensure their penetration. "In attack they are enterprising and prone to take risks and their wide enveloping movements are often carried out without regard to possibility of support in face of determined counter-attack. They move very lightly equipped, require little maintenance, and are prepared to live on the country with little regard to proper maintenance facilities and with no regard to bodily comfort; their tactics to date have been designed to secure aerodrome areas from where they can deploy their air effort to the fullest extent."[6] The need for a rapid decision in Burma before reinforcements arrived and the monsoon set in, might, so Hutton believed, influence Japan to commence operations in Burma alongside those in Malaya. In such a case the offensive was likely to take the form of a land attack against selected objectives by the shortest routes—Rahaeng-Moulmein and Chiengmai-Toungoo—and backed by air support. The probable maximum scale of attack was estimated at one division against Moulmein with subsidiary attacks by the Three Pagodas Pass on Tavoy and Mergui, one division against Keng Tung with Brigade Groups against Toungoo and Mongpan. In the event of the fall of Singapore, the possible scale of attack especially by sea would be heavier. The seizure of Moulmein

---

[4] Appreciation by G.O.C. Burma Army 601/2/5/H, p. 2.
[5] General Hutton's appreciation, p. 2, (10920-2/5). *Ibid*, p. 3.
[6] General Hutton's appreciation, p. 3, (10920-2/5). *Ibid*, p. 8.

would give the Japanese all the Tenasserim aerodromes of Victoria Point, Mergui, Tavoy and Moulmein: and from these places they could bring a practically continuous scale of air attack against Rangoon and render that port unfit for the reception of reinforcements. The seizure of Tavoy would split Allied forces into two, and deny them the only railway and main road between North and South Burma. Heavy Japanese air attack was believed to be mostly directed against Allied communications, the targets being Martaban railhead, the Bilin, Sittang and Pegu bridges, and the railway junctions at Thazi and Rangoon.

As regards the Allied resources, there were for operational roles two divisions, each of two infantry brigades, five battalions of F.F., and about nine infantry battalions for line of communication, internal security duties and protection of aerodromes. The reinforcements which had been promised were four infantry brigades. But these would still leave a big gap to bridge. Lt.-Gen. T. J. Hutton wrote, "We are short of Artillery of all natures, tanks, R.E., M.T., and also infantry for Internal Security and Static roles. So far as Burma is concerned it is unlikely that any additional regular Burma Battalion could be formed owing to the existing paucity of reinforcements and inadequacy of recruitment. The Territorial Force units are of questionable reliability and must be regarded only on the same level as Garrison Companies. There is at present lack of coordination in the Sea, Land and Air Defence of Rangoon and resources available or even foreseeable do not appear to be adequate against anything except a light scale of attack."[7] Militarizing of railways, roads and Posts and Telegraphs was absolutely essential, but was out of the question as it would place a great strain on the military staff and resources. He further wrote, "Even with the foreseeable reinforcements that is up to the period mid-end March our operational resources are so limited as to preclude anything except a defensive attitude possibly combined with very local offensives".[8]

The General Officer Commanding saw early the advantage of the Chinese troops being employed to fill the yawning gaps. Those offered were Vth and VIth Armies. The former was well equipped and considered to be the best fighting formation in the Chinese Army. These troops could be most effectively employed in North Burma either in the Taunggyi-Takaw-Loimwe line of communication; or two regiments could be maintained in the operational area and the remainder kept back as a potential threat to the flank of any hostile advance in the southern Shan States. Lieutenant General Hutton also considered it necessary to prevent Rangoon port from being congested; therefore, Lease and Lend material had to be removed from the dock area to suitable storage accommodation. Further, he desired that shipments should be stopped until existing congestion was cleared and American consent obtained for the use of a part of the material (signal equipment of all natures, explosives, M.T., etc.) for the defence of Burma.

Hutton further wrote, "With our present weakness in troops we must endeavour to concentrate as great a strength as possible at the really vital areas. These would appear to be as follows:—Martaban-Bilin, Ywathit-

[7] *Ibid*, p. 8. General Hutton's appreciation (10920-2/5).
[8] *Ibid*, p. 9.

Bawlake, Mongpan, Takaw".* "All these areas except Moulmein are behind the formidable obstacle of the Salween river and are the main road and track junctions." Hence the main fight was to be in these areas while forward of these there were to be only delaying actions. He wrote, "By denying these four areas we virtually deny every practicable route into Burma from Thailand." The former areas were therefore to be prepared as all round fortress areas stocked and provisioned for protracted resistance, while the forward delaying positions on the main approaches leading to these areas must be occupied. Hutton expressed his fear of the vulnerability of the communications by road and rail between Rangoon and Thazi, and wrote, "the destruction of any one of the main bridges would render movements of reserves very difficult." The plan of concentrating troops for a limited offensive to defeat the Japanese concentration on the Rahaeng route was feasible only if the Chinese Vth and VIth Armies were used on the line Thazi—Keng-Tung. Sooner or later Lt.-Gen. T. J. Hutton hoped to develop an offensive into Thailand based on Moulmein.

But even for this defensive strategy on a restricted scale an additional brigade group, and five un-brigaded infantry battalions with necessary mechanical transport were required, over and above the promised reinforcements. This was for the protection of the line of communication. Military transportation units and labour were also required. All these had to come from India. A separate appreciation was to be prepared for offensive operations after the monsoon period.

This appreciation has been given at some length, as it formed the basis of Lt.-Gen. T. J. Hutton's policy throughout the period of his command, and as, unlike the previous appreciations, it was a fairly correct anticipation. It must, however, be noted that in actual operations certain changes were made. Local military considerations do not always prevail. It was essential to gain time for the arrival of reinforcements and this could hardly be furthered by abandoning large areas of difficult country without fighting. So long as Malaya held out it was desirable to maintain the aerodromes on the reinforcement route; and the effective use of such fighter aircraft as might be available in Burma was dependent on retaining the warning system established in the Tenasserim peninsula. Mergui and Tavoy in Japanese hands might present a threat to the Andamans and Nicobar islands which had also been placed under Burma Command. It would also bring Japanese aerodromes within close range to Rangoon. Burma was well placed for an air offensive into Thailand and the loss of Mergui and Tavoy would interfere with the air plan of leaning forward from Rangoon and striking at Thailand. The greatest stumbling block to Hutton's plan of concentrating superior numbers at the decisive point was the necessity of protecting Rangoon. The more Lower Burma territory was given up, the closer came the threat to Rangoon. So the troops in Lower Burma were tied to certain defensive lines until certain

---

Ibid, p. 12. "By holding the whole of the Tenasserim peninsula south to Mergui we use up troops in small pockets out of supporting distance to one another." Nor could they hold the Shan States east of the Salween as by doing so they would expose the line of communication Loimwe-Taunggyi to infiltration by forces moving north-west from Chiengrai and Chiengmai.

definite dates. This led perforce to great difficulty in breaking contact with the Japanese when the time for withdrawal came, and to close engagements in a country disadvantageous to the troops not trained in jungle warfare.

In the north it would have suited the Burma Command to withdraw behind the Salween but this would have left the Chinese regiment on the line of the Mekong unsupported on its right flank. It would also have left Yunnan open to invasion. Therefore this course would not have helped the Chinese who were themselves prepared to relieve the troops already deployed east of the Salween. Actually the withdrawal of the latter troops began early in the campaign and only a thin covering screen was left. However, shortage of transport and the long distances to be traversed made the withdrawal a tedious and protracted business. Some of the troops had to march for three weeks before being picked up by motor transport.

But no protection of the Shan States was given up nor did the forces concentrate behind the Salween in the Martaban-Bilin area. In Tenasserim, in the opening phases of the campaign, troops were used as they arrived, in small pockets. There was in fact no alternative. In the Shan States when the Japanese thrust occurred in April it did not come through Thailand, but from Karenni. But the wide disposal of Chinese VIth Army over the areas east of Salween and its inability to concentrate a striking force in the threatened sector, had a decisive bearing on the campaign.

On 20 January, Lieutenant General Hutton made yet another appreciation. He was of the opinion that the Japanese would use all possible approaches to Burma and throw in their greatest weight against Tenasserim. Experience in Malaya seemed to show that paucity of communications would not prevent the employment of very large numbers of Japanese; and these communications were being rapidly improved. Owing to lack of intelligence and difficulty of air reconnaissance over jungle, surprise attack was possible. Nor could he guarantee the safety of Burma with the forces then available. He insisted that a total of four divisions should be completed early and India should give absolute priority to Burma's needs and accelerate despatches. These and the Chinese divisions would provide reasonable degree of security and might even enable some offensive action to be taken before the monsoon.[10]

ATTACK ON TAVOY

8 January

At Sinbyudaing large-scale Japanese operations in Burma began with a drive on Tavoy by the *3rd Battalion 112th Infantry Regiment* and the *Oki Branch Unit*. These forces had advanced in the later half of December by the Kanchanaburi-Tavoy road. It was a variegated road an automobile road up to Bondei, a cart road up to Sinbyudaing a packhorse road up to Myitta and from that point an automobile road again to Tavoy. It passed through jungles and valleys running

---

[10] *Appreciations and Plans* (601/2/3/H), p. 31.

in all directions through the complicated mountainous area of the Tenasserim range.[11]

Allied forces at Tavoy

Though the Japanese had crossed the border into Sinbyudaing as early as 8 January, and were preparing a track along the southern bank of the Tenasserim river up to Myitta, 24 miles west of Sinbyudaing, this fact was reported by the police only on 13 January. The forces at Tavoy were the 6th Battalion Burma Rifles, Tavoy Company of the Tenasserim British B.A.F., aerodrome guards and two companies of the 3rd Battalion Burma Rifles which were transferred from Mergui on 17 January. These forces at Tavoy as we well as those at Mergui were mainly for the defence of aerodromes, and were therefore not adequate for an all round defence. Mergui is 300 miles from Moulmein and communications consisted of the road Ye-Tavoy-Mergui which crossed many ferries and ran for the most part through thick jungle. There were a considerable number of known tracks from the Thai border only a few miles away, by which the road could be intercepted. From Ye to Moulmein there was a railway but no road. Withdrawal from either Mergui or Tavoy was therefore difficult except by sea; and even here the total available naval forces consisted of two small motor launches; other suitable craft were manned by indigenous crews who were likely to melt away at the appearance of the Japanese. In any case there were not enough of such craft to enable the Mergui garrison to be evacuated in one lift. "In view of these circumstances and the certainty that sooner or later the Japanese would begin to work up the coast or across the border from Thailand it was decided that in the event of a serious threat the Mergui garrison would be evacuated to Tavoy which would then be capable of defence".[12]

On the day on which information of Japanese penetration to Sinbyudaing and beyond, was received, a company of the 6th Battalion Burma Rifles at Kaleinaung, a village about 23 miles north by east of Tavoy, was called back to Tavoy and sent to Myitta in order to delay and obtain information of the reported Japanese force. One platoon took position at Myitta itself (25 miles east of Tavoy) to prepare defensive positions east of Myitta near the river junction of Ban Chaung, Kamangchaung and Thwechaung with the Tenasserim river, one platoon was stationed at Seinpyon, a village 14 miles north-by-west of Kyaukmedaung, to watch the track running from the border; the reserve platoon and company headquarters were stationed at Kyaukmedaung.[13]

At Myitta—15 January

On the evening of 15 January, news was received that the Japanese estimated to be 100, were on the eastern bank of the Ban Chaung.[14]

---

[11] 'Topographical Reports—Routes Across the Burma Siam Frontier', pp. 1 and 2.
[12] *Report* by Lt.-Gen. T. J. Hutton on the Operations in BURMA, 27 December, 1941—5 March, 1942, p. 16.
[13] Capt. W. R. Andrews, *Tavoy*. (601/3/18/H), No. 11.
[14] *The Situation Reports*, Part I, gives an exaggerated account:—"Enemy commenced penetration Tenasserim river route against Tavoy and are now also reported advancing by joining tracks from south against Mergui. Following is estimated strength of the enemy. Against Tavoy 1200, against Mergui 500 to 1000", p. 46. By a curious coincidence, Burma passed under ABDA Command just at this time (1720 hours).

The reserve platoon at Kyaukmedaung was at once ordered to Myitta. The first Japanese crossing at a point south-east of Myitta at 1700 hours was foiled, but two hours later they succeeded in crossing the Chaung at a point further south. Under orders from the Battalion Headquarters two forward platoons fell back on Kyaukmedaung and along with another company which had just arrived took up a position on the hills astride the road near milestone 25 on the Kyaikmaraw-Tavoy road. Their intention was to attack the Japanese the next day.

At Kyaukmedaung—16-17 January

Next morning (16 January) these forces advanced on Kyaukmedaung only to hear that the Japanese were in possession of Myitta with outposts near milestone 32. They therefore withdrew to the old position at 2300 hours. Soon they heard that the Japanese were south of Kyaukmedaung in great strength. On 17 January, one company was sent to cover the right flank from the vicinity of Yebu Taung to the southwest of milestone 25; the other company remained on the road along with a new company of the 3rd Battalion Burma Rifles which had arrived in the afternoon. At about 2000 hours orders were received for withdrawal to Wagon, a village between milestones 21 and 22. The plan was apparently for a later attack on Kyaikmaraw in great strength.[15]

Engagement at Kyaukmedaung—Night of 17-18 January

But before the withdrawal could take place at 2300 hours, the Japanese had attacked the position at milestone 25, and the company of the 3rd Battalion Burma Rifles and a platoon of 'A' company of the 6th Battalion Burma Rifles became involved. The main attack came straight up the road, while a small force came over the hills north of the road and attacked the flank, their first objective being the detachment of headquarters. They also ambushed the transport. The company at Yebu Taung neither retreated to Wagon nor ran to the help of the attacked. The engagement stopped in the early hours the next morning when the companies including the two platoons of 'A' company which were south of the road melted away. These trekked through the jungle to the Hermyingyi tin mine and later turned up in small parties at Moulmein. Worse still, one platoon and headquarters of 'C' company of the 6th Battalion Burma Rifles missed the way to Wagon while the other two platoons bumped into the Japanese rear-guard near Wagon; the latter were led by a Karen through the jungle to Hermyingi from where they again marched through the jungle to Moulmein.

The hills and dense forest to the north and south of milestone 25, made infiltration by the Japanese easy; the noise made by them both in Myitta and Kyaukmedaung gave the defenders an impression of large numbers. Even so it must be said that the section of the three companies in the absence of definitely appointed commander "was not too well-planned or directed". Nor did they make any attempt to strike the Tavoy road and rush to Tavoy for its defence. In short the defence of Tavoy was nothing better than the forward companies of the 3rd and 6th Burma

[15] In Lt.-Gen. T. J. Hutton's *Report*, it is said that two companies of the 6th Battalion Burma Rifles came in contact with the Japanese on 16 January.

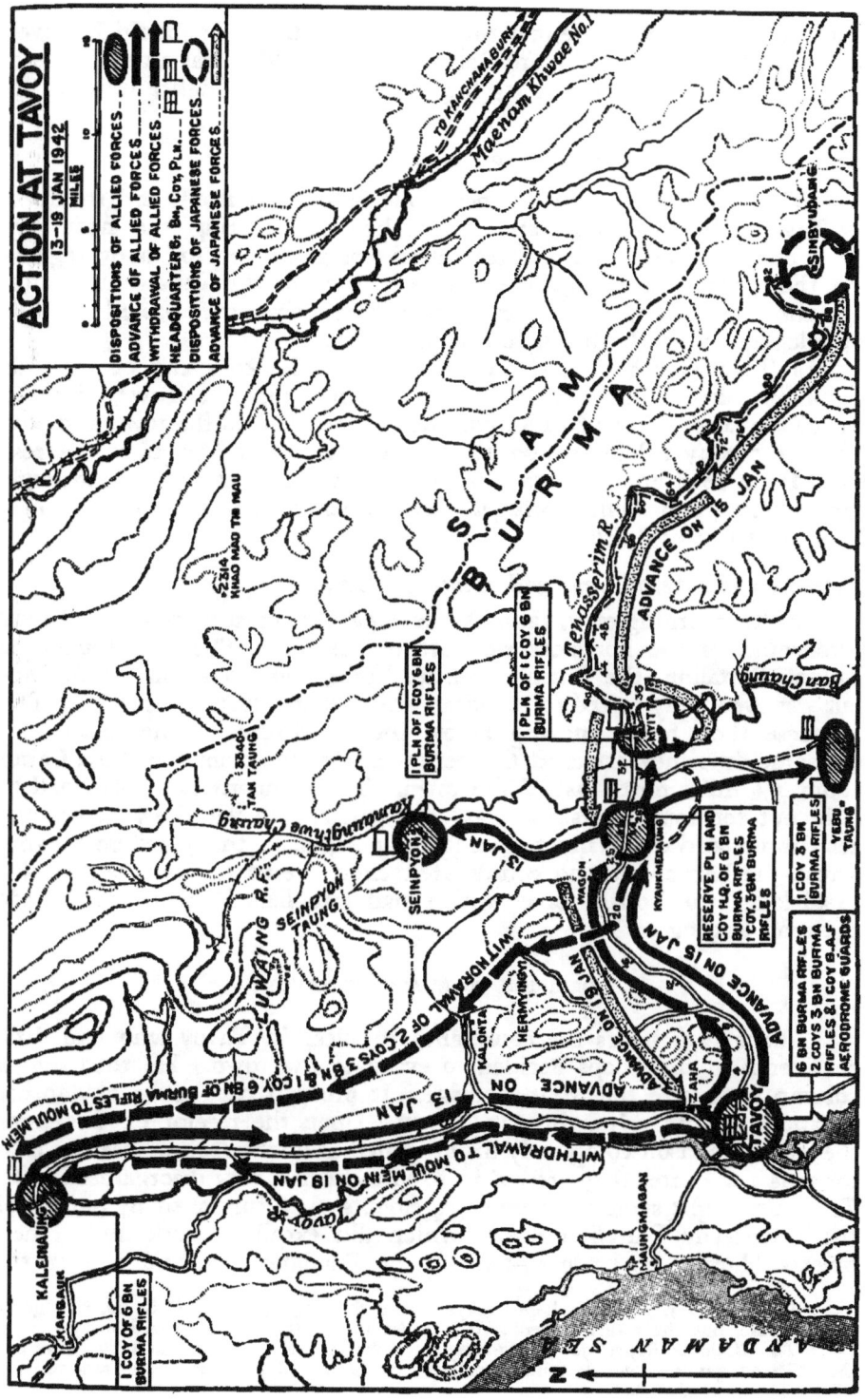

Rifles melting away at the first impact of the attack. It should however be mentioned here that the 6th Battalion Burma Rifles was a newly raised unit which had no opportunity for carrying out the higher training in any force.[16]

Japanese advance on Tavoy—18 January

With nothing to obstruct them, one battalion cut off, and the road to Tavoy left open, the Japanese pushed on. During the next day (18 January) a good deal of information was passed on to Tavoy regarding the movements of Japanese troops by men of the Tenasserim Battalion and mine managers. In some cases these reports were passed through by telephone after the Japanese had passed by.

In Tavoy itself, as early as 10 January, the company of the 6th Battalion Burma Rifles which had been sent across the Tavoy river to patrol the coast south of Maungmagan was recalled to the town and was asked to occupy a defensive position from south of the Mergui road across the Myitta road and half way to the Ye road, the line to run through the Paktaing and Myitta bridges. The other remnants in Tavoy organised a perimeter defence.

Attack on the Aerodrome and town—19 January

On the morning of 19 January the Japanese appeared near the Tavoy aerodrome, in the north-eastern part of the city. The detachment of Kokine Battalion, the Burma Frontier Force, put up a spirited defence but was eventually forced to withdraw and the aerodrome was lost.[17] The Japanese then began moving across the aerodrome to the bazar. At the same time they attacked the perimeter defence from the Zaha Camp about 1½ miles north-east of the town. The company here managed to hold out for four hours. It was then ordered to withdraw across the aerodrome, and do as much damage as possible to the Japanese moving across the bazar. But no coordinated effort seems to have been made to dislodge the hostile forces which had established themselves astride the road leading to Ye.[18]

DECISION TO EVACUATE TAVOY

About 1230 hours the commanding officer in Tavoy who had little confidence in his troops decided to evacuate the town. He then sent a column to unwire the Myitta bridge. It brought back news of another Japanese column advancing on Tavoy. Upon the receipt of this news the Tavoy garrison completely disintegrated and withdrew across the hills towards Ye. Later they arrived in Moulmein in a very disorganised state. The only bright spots in these engagements were furnished by parties of the Tenasserim Battalion B.A.F. which did excellent work under their officers, blowing up bridges—two on the Thailand road and one on the

---

[16] Lt.-Gen. T. J. Hutton's *Report* says about this engagement "It is hard to get a clear picture, but the attack failed". It is truer to say the attack melted away.

[17] *The Situation Report for 18 January* says that the situation up to 1800 hours was that "Tavoy garrison one Battalion (was) forced back and portions (were) reported cut off by Japanese advance."

[18] Capt. N. R. Watts, 'Operations in Tavoy'.

Hermyingyi road—and roads. Many of them remained behind for long periods after the other troops had left. Eventually they got back either through jungle or by boat taking with them much useful information.

The 2nd Burma Brigade Headquarters and the 4th Battalion 12th Frontier Force Regiment were sent to Ye to keep open the road from Tavoy to Moulmein and help the withdrawal from Tavoy. But the latter failed to contact the Tavoy garrison for a long time. This detachment was however withdrawn when it was learnt that the Japanese had occupied Tavoy.

EFFECTS OF THE LOSS OF TAVOY

The loss of Tavoy gave the Japanese an important port and the control of the entire coast from Malaya to Moulmein and made it possible for their forces from Victoria Point, Mergui and Tavoy to be moved up to Moulmein. It also necessitated a withdrawal from Mergui. In the light of after events it is possible to say that it might have been wiser to hold on to Mergui even if the eventual withdrawal of the garrison or part of it was thereby prejudiced. Its retention would have enabled the air forces, small as they were, to have carried out effective bombing attacks along the line of communication supplying the Japanese forces in Malaya. It should however be remembered that at the time plans were made the air forces available for this purpose were practically nil and that if the plan actually made had succeeded it might have ensured the retention of Tavoy for a considerable period.

"Another and perhaps more serious effect of the operation at Tavoy was that the units of the Burma Rifles involved suffered a serious loss of morale from which they did not entirely recover and that this infected other units also. The Japanese received a corresponding encouragement to undertake similar enterprise in future."[19]

EVACUATION OF MERGUI

Preparations to meet a Japanese Attack

From the middle of December and particularly after the Bokpyin incident, Mergui, an ill-protected and periodically bombed town, began to be on the alert. On 16 December, the mines at Karathuri, Thabawleik and Theindaw were closed in consequence of an order for the evacuation of European women-folk. In Mergui the foreshore was wired and positions which could be assaulted were defended and regularly patrolled. The RAF undertook reconnaissance of the coast south of Mergui and three motor launches, 1100, 1101 and 1104, were also continually patrolling the coast southwards from Moulmein.[20] A patrol of launches officered by evacuees from Victoria Point was also in operation. There was thus a fairly good local intelligence service. As regards denial measures, the plan to collect and destroy all boats along the Mergui coast so that they might not be of use to the Japanese moving up by sea, did not succeed as the

---

[19] General Hutton's *Despatch*, p. 19.
[20] BRNVR—*Narrrative Account*.

local population hid them away. A great part of the stocks of tin, rubber and wolfram in the district were got away to Rangoon. After the raid on 13 December the town was almost deserted; hence for want of labour and markets many smaller mines and rubber plantations were forced to close down.

Reports of Japanese thrust northwards from Victoria Point

Further south, the Japanese appeared to be infiltrating cautiously northwards. On 2 January, the Naval Office reported the presence of a Japanese patrol at Hangapru, and a few days later small parties of their force were reported between Karathuri and Victoria Point. F.F. 2, which had the area under observation, reported on 16 January, that bodies of Japanese troops were advancing along the Lenya river, and from Bengsap Anyiac, and through the Maw Daung Pass from Parachuap-Khirikhan. Hostile Burmans armed with rifles and a light machine-gun were reported near Karathuri. This was the first known instance of Burmans actively joining hands with the invaders.

Decision to Evacuate Mergui—18 January

Somewhere about 10 January, the officer commanding troops in Mergui began to be apprehensive of an attack on Tavoy from Thailand. A few days later news was received of a reconnaissance into the southern part of Tavoy district by seven Japanese. Two days after the Tavoy district was attacked, it was decided to evacuate Mergui while there was yet time and transfer the troops to Tavoy by sea in small boats and motor launches. The Japanese were also reported to be advancing by tracks from the south against Mergui. The troops in Mergui then were the 2nd Battalion Burma Rifles, two companies of the 3rd Battalion Burma Rifles, a Frontier Force detachment and aerodrome guard. On 17 January, the two companies of the 3rd Battalion Burma Rifles were transferred by road and sea to Tavoy as the situation was fast developing at the latter place.

The order as well as the arrangements for the evacuation of Mergui emanated from the Army Headquarters. The order was issued on 18 January and received the next day. By this time preparations for civilian and military evacuation were well advanced. It may however be asked whether the final decision was not taken too late. It was perhaps due to a hitch between the Army and the Air Force, and the order despatched by telegram had not been given priority. Later in the day (18 January) this order was modified to the extent that no further troops should be put into Tavoy unless communications with that place could be left open. As Tavoy was now seriously threatened the Army Headquarters directed the Mergui garrison to withdraw by sea to Rangoon.

Evacuation—20-22 January

It was only late in the evening of 20 January, that half of the total forces in Mergui district, and those civilians whose services were no longer required sailed by s.s. *Harvey Adamson* to Rangoon. The remainder of the troops, except a small demolition squad, left by the next evening for the Tenasserim Island by several launches one of which (*Curtana*) was attached to BRNVR. The rest of the civilians left on 22 January, after the last demolitions of the Power House, Burma Oil Company godown and the jetty,[21] had been carried out, and joined the main party on the Tenasserim Island. The civilians do not seem to have received proper facilities. One of the best motor launches belonging to F.F. 1 was available but had not been offered to the civil authorities.[22] Another thing to be regretted was that a few of the jailors and the Public Works Department staff who were Indians and who should have been evacuated were left behind. The Japanese could secure the services of these and the large coolie gangs working on the mines and rubber estates in the district, who would have been a welcome addition to the Rangoon labour list. The authorities had told the population that RAF would deal effectively with the Japanese air raids and that whatever might happen the authorities would stand by the civil population. On 23 January, the parties on the Tenasserim Island boarded S.S. Heinrich Jassen for Rangoon after scuttling many of their launches and after an uneventful voyage reached Rangoon on 25 January. The troops and their equipment were saved, thanks to the failure of the Japanese aircraft to attack them. Perhaps, it was partly due to secret and careful planning. But it must be noted that at Mergui as in Victoria Point, there had been no contact with the Japanese.

The motor launches 1104 and 1110 of BRNVR which had covered the evacuation, stood by for stragglers from the hinterland of Mergui. They then went about their last job of demolishing the secret fuel dumps on the islands of the Mergui Archipelago. At Port Owen some refugees from Tavoy together with a motor boat taking 50 soldiers were picked up.

---

[21] The jetty was not completely demolished.
[22] Such complaints are worth noting.

CHAPTER VIII

Action in Kawkareik Sector

THE KAWKAREIK ROUTE TO MOULMEIN

The attack on Tavoy was looked upon by the Burma Command as probably an isolated attempt and not as the beginning of a general offensive.[1] But the Japanese were not content to rest there. Their next objective was Moulmein where, by drawing the allied forces and staging a surprise attack by the *33rd Division*, they planned to "annihilate the British forces along the river south of Bilin".[2] In this advance, they were expected to follow the old trade route running from Rahaeng to Kyondo through Kawkareik. This route was a camel-track up to Mae Saut[2a] and from there a cart-track up to Myawadi, an old and once fortified town but now a village. The track ran mostly through steep mountainous regions; and along the road side grew a dense jungle of bamboos. The bridges were scarcely passable for either men or horses. As already noted the Japanese began the construction of a new motor road from Rahaeng to Mae Saut early in January and completed it in the middle of February. From Myawadi to Kyondo ran a road unmetalled for five miles. On this road stood Kawkareik, a town situated near the foot of the Dawna Range and on the banks of the Kawkareik stream. It was 39 miles from Myawadi and occupied an important position on the chief trade route to Thailand. Kyondo was connected with Moulmein by launch services up the Gyaing river. From Kyondo there also ran a maze of tracks, some of them joining the Moulmein-Kyaikmaraw road. One of them was a track motorable in the dry season and crossed the Haungtharaw river by ferry at Kyain. There was another route through the Three Pagodas Pass. The forward positions for the defence of Moulmein were therefore Myawadi, Kawkareik, and the Three Pagodas Pass.

FORCES IN THE KAWKAREIK SECTOR, NOVEMBER 1941—JANUARY 1942.

Since November 1941, the forward positions at Myawadi and the Pass over the Dawna Range were held by the 4th Battalion Burma Rifles, under the command of the 2nd Burma Brigade in Moulmein. Its strength of 540 men had been sadly depleted by malaria. The men, moreover, seemed to consider the place as a peace-time training camp; in the face of concen-

---

[1] *Burma Operational Control* (601/2/4/H), p. 9. Earlier on 19 January Burma Army Command had telegraphed to India that in view of the evacuation of Tavoy and withdrawal from Mergui the situation was serious. They also requested that one Brigade of 14th Division on lower scale of equipment be prepared for despatch to Burma as early as possible. But the Supreme Commander, South West Pacific Command took a different view. He said that he could not understand why the situation was considered serious as the Burma Command had for a long time been prepared to abandon both Tavoy and Mergui.
[2] *Japanese Operations*, (601/8255/H), p. 17.
[2a] Also spelt as Mesoht.

trated attack, this position, which was fifty miles from Moulmein as the crow flies, was isolated. Moreover, the country between Kawkareik and Mae Saut (7 miles east of Myawadi and Thailand) was very broken and densely forested. The Thaungyin river forming the boundary offered no great obstacle particularly in view of the small number of forces there to keep watch. Worst of all, the Japanese could avoid the Rahaeng-Myawadi-Kawkareik road and use minor tracks.³ One ran from the frontier village of Palu, south-east of Myawadi; another ran from Pyataung north of Myawadi. The former gave access to Ale Mekane, Aet Mekane and Kwingale and the latter to a pass through the hills at Kyawbo and to Nabu, a village on the western plain. Above all the only straight road to Moulmein across the Thai frontier through the Three Pagodas Pass, 85 miles south-by-east of Kawkareik and a very likely route for Japanese thrust, was unguarded.

As soon as he assumed command, Lt.-Gen. T. J. Hutton decided to strengthen the defences of Moulmein, Kawkareik and Tenasserim in general. The 16th Indian Infantry Brigade and one battalion in reserve were ordered to move down to the Tenasserim from Mandalay.

THE 16TH INDIAN INFANTRY BRIGADE IN COMMAND OF THE SECTOR
8 JANUARY

On 7 January, Brigade Headquarters with the 1st Royal Battalion 9th Jat Regiment and the 4th Battalion 12th Frontier Force Regiment left Mandalay under the command of Brig. J. K. Jones and arrived in Moulmein on 9 January. These battalions together with the 1st Battalion 7th Gurkha Rifles in Moulmein and the 4th Battalion Burma Rifles constituted the 16th Indian Infantry Brigade, Headquarters of which was established on the main road near milestone 23, seven miles forward of Kawkareik. About the same time the 7th Battalion Burma Rifles was also ordered to Moulmein. The Commander of the 16th Indian Infantry Brigade took over responsibility for the defence about Kawkareik with a view to meeting any potential Japanese thrust.

TROOP DISPOSITIONS—JANUARY 8-19

The new dispositions about Kawkareik consequent upon the arrival of the 16th Indian Infantry Brigade were as follows: On 8 January, the 1st Battalion 7th Gurkha Rifles less 'B', 'C', and 'D' companies, already at Kya-in-Seikkyi, 36 miles south of Kawkareik, left for Kawkareik and pitched their camp in the thick scrub jungle two miles west of Kawkareik. Here they were joined by the 1st Royal Battalion 9th Jat Regiment a week later. 'C' company was sent to a place in the Dawna Range about 10 miles east of Sukli. On 17 January, the advance party of the 1st Battalion 7th Gurkha Rifles moved off to Sukli, where was established Battalion Headquarters (milestone 36). 'B' company which had arrived from the south, was at once sent to milestone 51.5, 3 miles west of Myawadi. The Battalion thus took over the position from the 4th Battalion Burma Rifles. The latter while moving out caused a traffic jam,

---
³ They did use them much to the discomfiture of the defences.

caught the eye of a Japanese reconnaissance plane, and brought on Sukli and Misty Hollow (milestone 33) heavy bombing. On 19 January 'A' company also arrived. One company was posted at Kyungaung to cover the trans-frontier track through the Three Pagodas Pass and Kya-in-Seikkyi to Moulmein. This company was later to be relieved by a company of the 1st Royal Battalion 9th Jat Regiment which was proceeding to Kya-in-Seikkyi direct from Moulmein.

As regards the 1st Royal Battalion 9th Jat Regiment 'B' company less a platoon and a sub-section of MMGs took up a position about milestone 33, to cover set demolitions on the Kawkareik-Myawadi road. The Battalion Headquarters and two companies were stationed at Kawkareik. 'C' company went to Kwingale and Ale Mekane, all to the south of the Myawadi-Kawkareik road. Headquarters of 'C' company was at Kwingale, with a W/T set. From Ale Mekane a motor truck patrol was maintained along the cart-track which ran through dense jungle and very hilly and broken country to Palu. A company watched the frontier in the Mepale-Tichara area about four miles north of the road and covered the track running from Payataung to Mepale and from there to Thingannyinaung on the main road through the Kyaukkho pass. Another company was at Nabu where the track debouched on the plain west of the hills. The main position was near the summit of the Dawna hills about milestone 35.

It would thus be seen that the brigade was very widely dispersed. It was a triangular front extending at the base from Nabu to Kawkareik with its apex 34 miles away from Kawkareik. This state of affairs was necessitated by the dense jungle, an ideal ground for the Japanese tactics of infiltration, by the numerous tracks running north and south of the road and above all by the lack of intelligence which left local commanders guessing as to the routes of Japanese advance.

TROOP DISPOSITIONS ON 19 JANUARY

On the eve of the attack the relief of forward positions began and that night the battalions were disposed as follows:—The 1st Royal Battalion 9th Jat Regiment less two companies and one platoon was in the area of milestone 17 north of Kawkareik, At milestone 18 was the 4th Battalion Burma Rifles less three companies. At milestone 35 position there was the 1st Battalion 7th Gurkha Rifles less three companies with one Battalion Burma Rifles under command. D Company of the Battalion was holding milestone 51.5 area, while the company at Kwingale was preparing to relieve the Burma Rifles company at milestone 35 on the following day. The remaining companies of the Burma Rifles were at Nabu guarding the Nabu Pass and the Mepale area north of milestone 47. One company of the 1st Battalion 7th Gurkha Rifles was at the Three Pagodas Pass and one company of the 1st Royal Battalion 9th Jat Regiment had relieved the Gurkha Rifles Company at Kwingale. The only line of easy communication between all the units was the main road. Many of the posts were without wireless equipment, the whole Brigade having only seven sets and one battery charging set; most of the sets were miles away in a roadless country. The detachments without

W/T could make contact with the Headquarters only by runners. Above all the troops were denied time to settle down as the attack started in the early hours of the morning of 20 January.[4]

JAPANESE TROOP MOVEMENTS

To turn to the Japanese side, the movement of the *55th Division* (less *14th Infantry Regiment* and the *3rd Battalion 112 Infantry Regiment*) to Mae Saut has already been noted. It has also been mentioned that air reconnaissance in the Rahaeng—Mae Saut area in the first fortnight of January had revealed nothing of the Japanese preparations. This was so because the Japanese movements took place mostly during night, the jungle rendered reconnaissance difficult, and the Japanese were adepts in the art of camouflage. The only intelligence report available was that about 5,000 Japanese had concentrated in Mae Saut just across the Thai frontiers.[5] It is however strange that even the road construction between Rahaeng and Mae Saut went unnoticed for days together.

But the Japanese also had committed a mistake. If only they had attacked late in December or early in January they could have scattered like chaff the Burma Rifles Battalion watching the forward positions and enjoyed a walk over to Moulmein. But as already stated the poor state of communications rather than the desire to concentrate on Malaya and await the outcome there held up their advance. And Thailand had not developed her roads for fear of competition with the state owned railways. Nor was there much trade and commerce with Burma to warrant such a development.

JAPANESE STRATEGY

In the middle of January the *Fifteenth Army* advanced its Headquarters to Rahaeng in order to be able to command the operations of the *55th Division* near Moulmein, as well as to direct the penetration of the *33rd Division* to the banks of the Salween. The master plan was to attack Kawkareik and Moulmein thus drawing the Burmese forces to the vicinity of Moulmein, while the *33 Division* moved north, made a surprise crossing of the Salween at Pa-an in order to "cut off and annihilate the forces along the river south of Bilin and thus clear the way for a crossing of the Sittang at Mokpalin"—a move which would seal the fate of Rangoon. The preliminaries to this advance were to be the air raids on Moulmein and Kawkareik.[6]

AIR RAIDS UP TO 20 JANUARY

The air raids on Moulmein in the first fortnight of January have already been detailed. Moulmein was raided on 18 January by a force of 14 Japanese bombers escorted by 5 fighters.[7] The main targets were

---

[4] See *War Diary*, 16 Brigade.
[5] *Situation Reports*, Part I, pp. 42 & 43.
[6] *Japanese Operations*, p. 17.
[7] The attack lasted one hour. The aerodrome had Blenheim and two fighters on it. *War Diary*, 17th Division Signals, sheet 4.

the aerodrome and the supply depot. Though there was no damage or casualty the Burmese population as in Mergui and later in Rangoon started a steady evacuation into the surrounding country, and labour which was needed very urgently was hard to get. On the same day movement had been reported by the 1st Battalion 7th Gurkha Rifles of concentrations on the east bank of the Thaungyin river at Myawadi. On 19 January, Moulmein had another air raid and bombs set fire to a portion of the town. From the middle of January reconnaissance air-craft were also very active. The positions along the road were heavily attacked daily and already on 7 January, the landing stage at Kyondo had been attacked. The local intelligence service engaged by the Brigade Intelligence Officer, also reported "concentration by Japanese of stores and men for a general advance". It was thus evident that a large scale attack on Kawkareik and a push to Moulmein were imminent.

JAPANESE ADVANCE—20 JANUARY

Engagement at Myawadi

The Japanese advance by the *55 Division* began in the small hours of 20 January.[8] They crossed the frontier at points north of the Mepale river where it joins Thaungyin river, at Myawadi and at Palu. The first blow naturally fell on the forward company at milestone 51 i.e. on D company of the 1st Battalion 7th Gurkha Rifles. The Jemadar in charge of the platoon stationed in Myawadi itself heard rifle fire in the direction of his forward section, went forward and found the section surrounded by the Japanese. He went up to the position of the other two sections and found them also surrounded.[9] He made his way back through the jungle to the company headquarters in order to get assistance, but found it also surrounded. There was nothing for him to do except to make his way back to the main positions. Information of this attack was sent to the Battalion Headquarters and it was confirmed by three villagers from Tatmaan to the north of Myawadi who said that they had found 100 Thai troops in their village and run up to Thingannyinaung at once. Meanwhile one section of 'D' company was shot down by a burst of automatic fire. The rest of the company, attacked from the east, held out for nearly five hours under intense fire even when the telephone communication was cut off and ammunition ran short. Nothing was heard of the company for some days except for one or two stragglers who managed to get away and gave the news that the company had been cut off. It was also given out that the hostile force was a mixed Japanese and Thai force 1000 strong. This news made the spirit of the rest of the Battalion run low. In fact, the whole company of 100 men gallantly broke out the Japanese ring and got away with all mules and most of the trucks. They then marched across country by compass to the south bank of the Salween river from where they floated down to Martaban in a barge and reached it on 26

---

[8] The *55th Division* had left behind at Rahaeng all heavy equipment such as vehicles and carts. Troops carried artillery pieces and ammunition on their backs. Cows were used to carry other supplies. Divisional Commander's answer to Question 44. ATIS Interrogation Centre. 601/10111/H.

[9] *War Diary*, 1/7 Gurkha Rifles.

January. The mules had to be abandoned during march, but much useful information and some Japanese weapons and ammunition were brought back.

On receipt of the telephone communication, the Commanding Officer of the 1st Battalion 7th Gurkha Rifles with two sections of the Gurkhas and one of the Intelligence Officers went forward in order to relieve the D company. He was, however, unable to get near the company, having run into patrols. The Intelligence Officer was killed in the first encounter. The Commanding Officer rallied his men, and dislodged patrols but found the opposition to be too great and therefore returned to Thingannyinaung at 1730 hours. While retiring he encountered one platoon of the company which was guarding the Kwingale pass and which had been sent on patrol duty to Hpalu; it had encountered the Japanese and was returning to Thingannyinaung. He also encountered a party from the company which was guarding the Nabu Pass and which had also been forced to retire to Thingannyinaung. At 1900 hours he received information that the Jats had come away from their positions on the right flank between the two Kwingales and thus opened the right flank.[10]

Attack on right and left flanks—20 January

The Myawadi attack was supported by attacks on the right and left flanks at Kwingale sector. On hearing of the Myawadi attack a subaltern of the 1st Royal Battalion 9th Jat Regiment at Ale Mekane post, took about 20 men in two trucks down the track running to Palu.[11] Near milestone 10 he encountered mounted officers leading a Japanese column estimated to be two companies with elephants carrying mortars. It was later estimated as one division. The patrol opened tommy gun fire and accounted for at least three of the mounted officers. The patrol then took up defensive positions and held up the Japanese column after inflicting heavy casualties. It then withdrew and took up further defensive position near the Rest House at Ale Mekane. It then received orders to move along the main road to Kawkareik. When the main position of the 'C' company of the 1st Royal Battalion 9th Jat Regiment at Ale Mekane was surprised by the Japanese in the evening, they were given orders by the Commanding officer to disperse and withdraw via Atet Mekane and Kwingale through the Koko Chaung track running south-west from Kwingale to Kawkareik. The Brigadier had sent orders to them as well as to the left flank in the Nabu position to hold out, but as there was no reply from them he assumed that the Japanese had overwhelmed both the flanks. In fact the right flank had vanished and there was nothing left in front of the Japanese advancing by the Palu-Ale-Mekane-Kwingale-Kawkareik track.

The Brigadier had to make further plans to meet the situation. To remedy this loss on the right flank late in the evening, he issued hurried verbal orders to 'D' Company of the 1st Royal Battalion 9th Jat Regiment to take up positions in Myohaung, Kawnwe and Tadanku[12] to cover three

---

[10] M. A. Maybury, s.d.o. Kawkareik, *Personal Narratives of operations*—Narrative and comments on the same by Brig. J. K. Jones, (601/3/18/H).
[11] Statement by 2/Lt. A. Balls—*War Diary*, 1/9 Royal Jat Regiment.
[12] Not Tadangu as *War Diary*, 1/9 Jats has it.

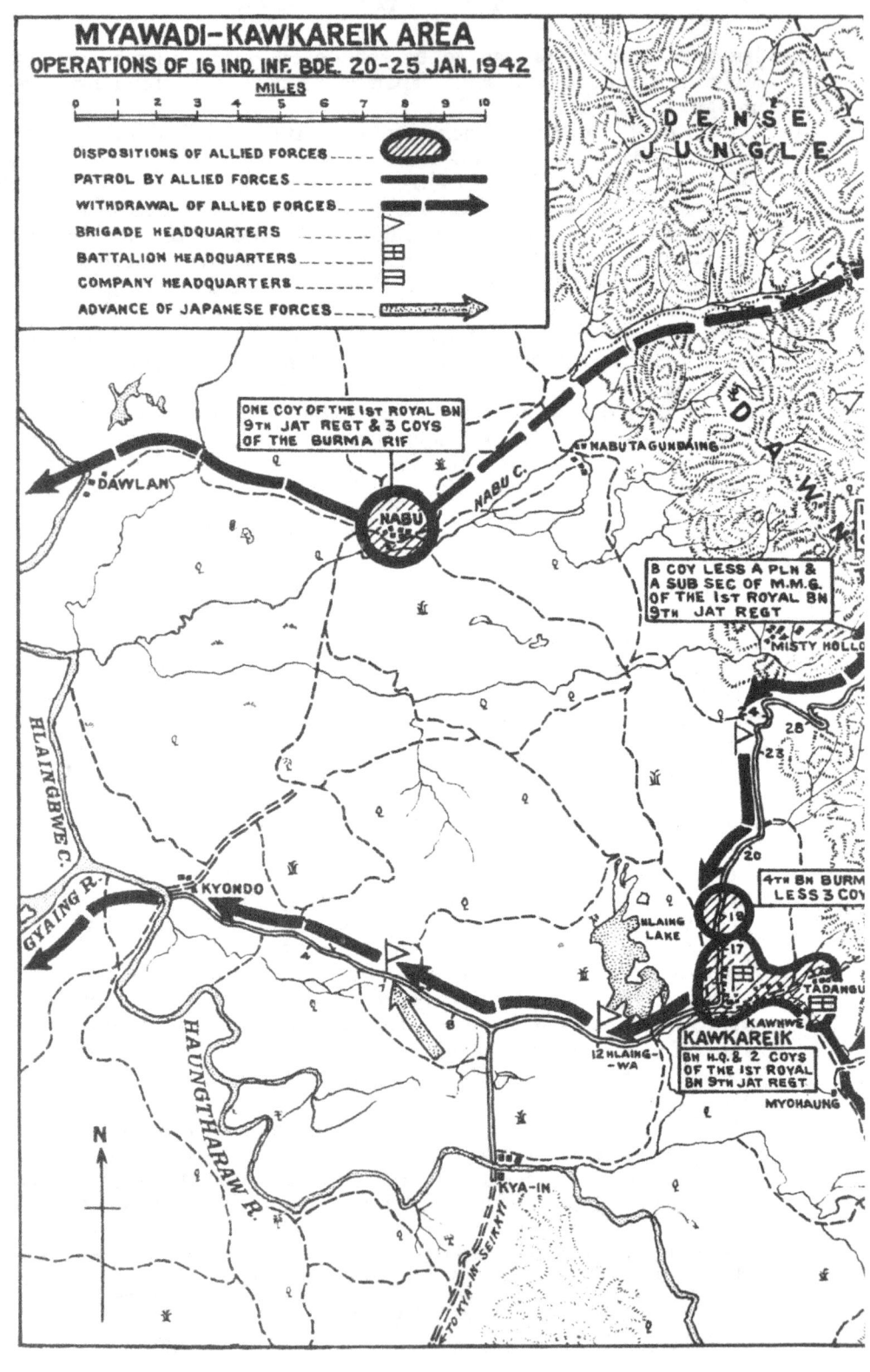

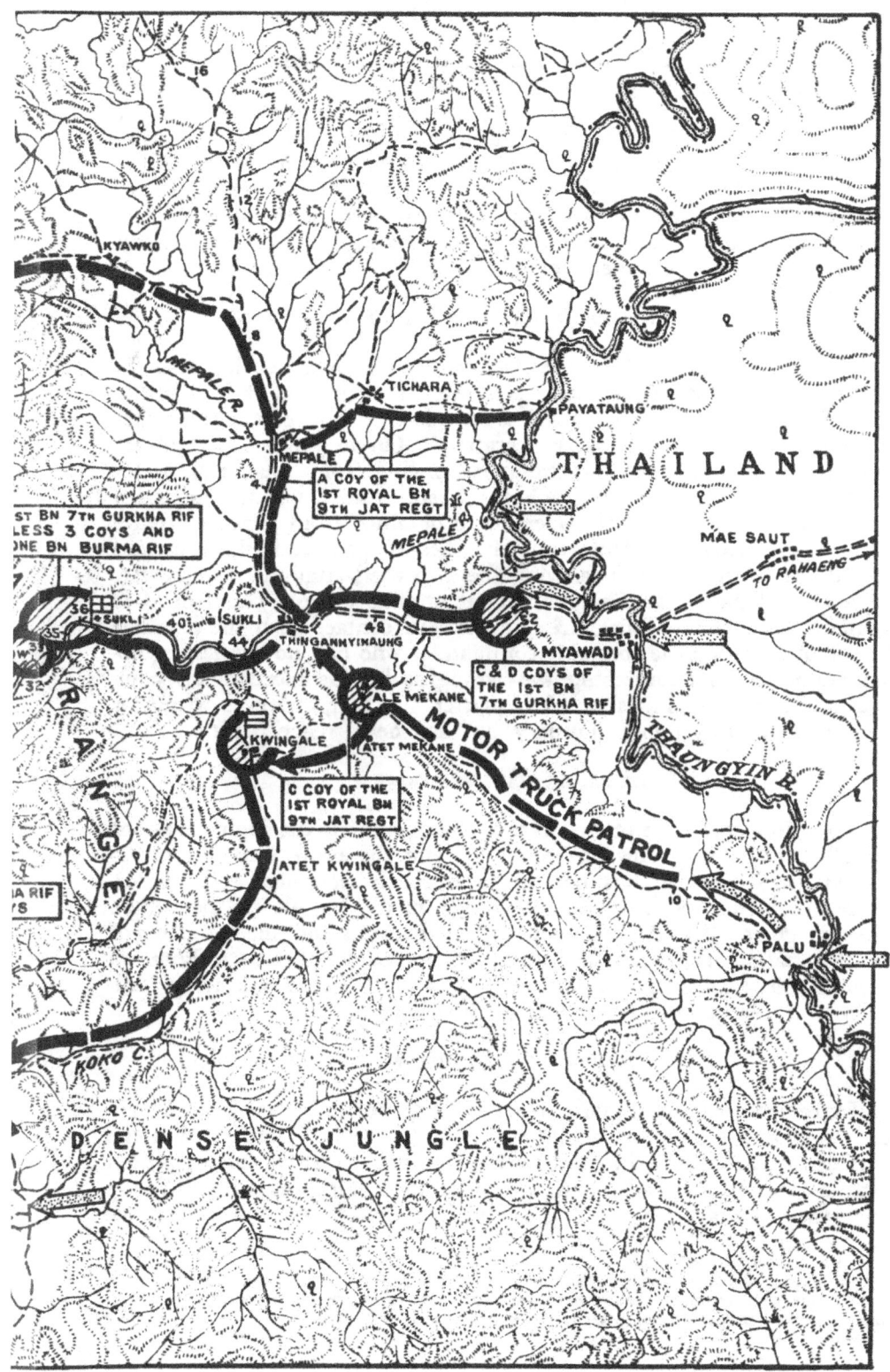

tracks, one from Kwingale to Myohaung along the Myohaung and Koko Chaungs, another from Myohaung area via Kawnwo and the third via Tadanku to Kawkareik. A little while ago they had been detailed for covering the 4th Battalion Burma Rifles at milestone 17 on the Myawadi-Kawkareik road. But as it was dark the company could not locate the position. The Brigadier also ordered the forward demolitions to be blown and asked the 1st Battalion 7th Gurkha Rifles to retire to the mountain and the 4th Battalion Burma Rifles to take up positions 4 miles to the east of Kawkareik—a last minute attempt to defend Kawkareik.[13]

NORTHERN FLANK—JANUARY 20-23

As there was no W/T in the Tichara-Mepale area nothing was for some time known of the happenings there. The exploits of the Burma Rifles company here ('D' company less one platoon) relieved the somewhat dismal picture of the Kawkareik operations. On 20 January, it had encountered a Japanese force of twenty advancing from Thailand. After a sharp engagement it drove back the hostile force. On the next day identifications and important papers were obtained from Japanese patrol which was destroyed.[14] Unfortunately these papers and identifications were all lost when the truck carrying them to the Battalion Headquarters ran into the Japanese at Thingannyinaung. The company continued to dominate the Tichara-Mepale area and was in contact with the invaders till 23 January when the company commander who had no wireless equipment, suspected that something was wrong as he was receiving no communications from the Battalion Headquarters. In fact, orders to withdraw had been sent to him on 21 January, but had never reached him.

ATTACK ON MAIN POSITIONS

Right from the time of the start of the operations the main positions at Sukli and Misty Hollow (milestone 33) and the entire line of communication to Kawkareik was bombed and machinegunned at intervals. The noise and the effect of the bombings on the morale in the jungle were very great. The day closed with Headquarters and one company of the 1st Battalion 7th Gurkha Rifles and two companies of the 4th Battalion Burma Rifles, holding the milestone 35 position. There was every indication that a large-scale attack was in the offing.

DECISION TO WITHDRAW

Extremely varying reports reached Brigade and Divisional Headquarters. On the basis of this information the AHQ concluded that the Japanese appeared to be in considerable strength;[15] It was also reported that the Japanese were advancing north up the coastal plain from Tavoy which they had taken two days ago and as no reinforcements or reserves

---

[13] *War Diary*, 16 Brigade.
[14] A patrol of 4 was destroyed by one man of this Kachin company.
[15] It was later estimated from the information available that there were about 2500 Japanese troops in the initial attack. It was actually one Infantry Regiment less one Battalion.

were available it was possible that if the 16th Indian Infantry Brigade tried to fight it out on this position near Kawkareik it might be overwhelmed. Orders were therefore issued that this Brigade was not to get so involved as to render withdrawal impossible. The Divisional Commander was also told at the same time not to give up more ground than necessary and that an intermediate position should be occupied.[16] The Divisional Commander, however, issued orders for immediate withdrawal. It appeared afterwards that the alarmist reports received at Headquarters 17 Division were not really justified by the situation. The attack was nowhere pushed home and there is little doubt that the Brigade could in fact have retained its position for the time being.

WITHDRAWAL OF BRIGADE HEADQUARTERS TO KYONDO—21 JANUARY

By the early hours of 21 January (0030 hours) Brigade Headquarters moved to Kawkareik only to move out at dawn. Brig. J. K. Jones gave the Sub-Divisional Officer, Kawkareik a summary of the previous day's events and advised him to evacuate the civil population at once at Kawkareik and Kyondo and move his headquarters at dawn in the direction of Kyondo. As there was only one hour left, the Sub-Divisional Officer had very little time to salvage either government or private property. The civilian population of Kawkareik were warned through the Home Guard and Raid Wardens to leave the town at once. Criminals were released on bail but political prisoners were sent off at once under escort to Moulmein. Though the office staff was asked to join the exodus they chose to remain with their families. The only staff the Brigadier wished to remain at Kawkareik, was the telegraph and telephone staff whom he agreed to evacuate with his troops. The Post-Master was asked to destroy the installations before leaving, as the arrangements for putting the installations underground were not complete. The Sappers were asked to blow the Treasury in addition to the three mills, the electric Power Plant and reserves of paddy. By dawn the town was quite deserted. The Brigade Headquarters moved to milestone 12 (Hlaingwa west of Kawkareik) and the Field Hospital to milestone 7. These moves happened to be wise because when at about 1100 hours Kawkareik was bombed by 22 Japanese planes there were no civilian casualties.[17] On the same day 6 RAF Blenheims bombed Mae Saut, all their bombs falling in the target area.[18]

NEED FOR WITHDRAWAL IN THE CENTRAL SECTOR—21 JANUARY

At dawn on 21 January, the Sappers had blown up the road east of Sukli. The Japanese had advanced at night up to this road-block, and demolition to clear a way through was heard by the troops at milestone 35. Contact was also made with the Japanese patrols attempting to get round the northern flank. About 1600 hours the Commanding Officer of the Gurkha Battalion informed the Brigade Commander that if he

---

[16] Lt.-Gen. T. J. Hutton's *Report*, p. 19. *The Situation Report* (p. 47) described the day's (20 January) fighting as heavy.
[17] *War Diary*, 17th Division Signals Section gives it as 1230 hours.
[18] Two Japanese aircraft were lost for the loss of AVG fighter escort.

persisted in holding the milestone 35 position he would be cut off by the next morning by Japanese troops moving on at wide front.

At about 0700 hours Headquarters of the 1st Royal Battalion 9th Jat Regiment and Headquarters Company took up position in Kawnwe. One platoon took up position at Tadanku and one in Myehaung tracks. For a long time there was no news of Myehaung patrol and the officer who had gone out with it, and all efforts to contact them were without success. The 1st Royal Battalion 9th Jat Regiment reported that the Japanese were entering the plain about three miles south of Myehaung.

ORDERS FOR WITHDRAWAL OF TROOPS TO KYONDO

The Brigadier had to take a difficult decision. He could not allow the Japanese to get on behind his demolitions. The junior officers were quite panicky and the panic spread to the lower ranks also. They were all new to jungle fighting and the first day's experience had shattered their nerves. In the open plain west of Kawkareik there was no position that could be safely maintained for long; and moving on a wide point and in superior numbers the Japanese could easily by-pass any position held by the 16th Indian Infantry Brigade. Hence at about 1800 hours on 21 January, the Brigadier issued orders for withdrawal at night to Kyondo, a straggling village situated on the Haungtharaw river at the terminus of the Public Works Department road from Myawadi.[19] It was 15 miles west of Kawkareik of which it may be said to be the port as from there one had to ferry down the river to Moulmein. The population there mainly consisted of Indians and Karens.[20] An intermediate defensive position was also to be taken at milestone 12 west of Kawkareik where some delay could be imposed on a hostile advance. Verbal orders were issued to the 1st Royal Battalion 9th Jat Regiment to cover the withdrawal of one company of the 1st Battalion 7th Gurkha Rifles and the 4th Battalion Burma Rifles and then withdraw itself.

Evacuation of MT

The mechanised transport of the Brigade was to be evacuated to Moulmein by the long round-about fair weather track via the Kya-In ferry on the Haungtharaw river eight miles south-west of Kawkareik. As the ferry was a primitive one operated by local boatmen and as the route was long and round-about, it was feared that only a small portion of the MT would be able to go across and that the rest would have to be burnt. Verbal orders were sent that kit stores which could not be loaded on unit MT were to be prepared for burning in case of necessity. The order was misunderstood and they were set fire to. There were several panics— one a totally unfounded 'gas' alarm and another when some ammunition was set on fire. These caused considerable delay in starting as the MT drivers were raw and were alarmed at the slightest sound. All MT were eventually brought into Kawkareik just before dark.[21]

[19] *War Diary*, the 16th Indian Infantry Brigade—"Reports were continually coming in reporting enemy advances along the Myawadi-Kawkareik Road towards Kawkareik, and a further withdrawal was (therefore) ordered to Kyondo about fifteen miles west of Kawkareik on the Kyondo river".
[20] *Burma Gazetteer*, Amherst Dt.
[21] *War Diary*, 1/9 Jats.

At 2000 hours the MT convoy eventually got away. But worse was to follow. Only one vehicle could be carried at a time across the river. The first, a heavy truck of the Sappers containing ammunition, slipped into water and the ferry boat was also sunk.[22] No Brigade vehicle could thereafter be got to Moulmein and orders were therefore issued to the 1st Battalion 7th Gurkha Rifles and the 1st Royal Battalion 9th Jat Regiment to destroy all their MT and kit.

Withdrawal of 1/9 Jats—21 January

At about 1800 hours on 21 January the 1st Royal Battalion 9th Jat Regiment which was to cover the withdrawal of one company of the 1st Battalion 7th Gurkha Rifles and the 4th Battalion Burma Rifles and then withdraw itself to Kawkareik, received the news through a patrol of local police, that the Japanese were advancing on the Tadanku-Myehaung tracks. This was followed by a rumour that the invaders were using gas. These reports were wrong.[23] The firing of dumps and kit at the camp of the 1st Royal Battalion 9th Jat Regiment at milestone 17, had been mistaken for hostile fire. Though there was no signal from Kawkareik that the 1st Battalion 7th Gurkha Rifles and the 4th Battalion Burma Rifles had completed their withdrawal the commanding officer of the Jat Battalion acted in a hasty manner and decided to withdraw the Battalion at 2200 hours into a more concentrated position at Kawkareik. By this action he spread wild panic and confusion through the ranks.[24]

Withdrawal from milestone 35—21 January

The withdrawal from milestone 35 of one company, the 1st Battalion 7th Gurkha Rifles and the 4th Battalion Burma Rifles to Kyondo via Kawkareik, began at dusk. According to the Brigadier's orders the demolitions were blown before the withdrawal. The Japanese did not follow up the retreating troops; the latter after marching to milestone 25 at the foot of the hill were taken in MT to the dump one mile west of Kawkareik where they arrived at midnight.[25] When these had passed through the position at milestone 18 the force there proceeded to carry out as many demolitions of bridges as possible and blow up dumps. The mules which had left Misty Hollow (milestone 33) at 1300 hours on 21 January arrived near Kawkareik at about 0100 hours. One company of the 1st Battalion 7th Gurkha Rifles and the 4th Battalion Burma Rifles had already arrived. As the mules entered the town they were fired on by the 4th Battalion Burma Rifles.[26] The majority of the mules with their loads of Bren guns,

---

[22] The accounts in different *War Diaries* slightly differ from one another.
"The first lorry which was loaded with ammunition was so heavy that it sank the ferry on the Oijaing river so preventing any MT from getting out at all." *War Diary* 1/7 G. R. p. 3.
"A heavy truck of the Sappers had been driven on to the ferry at Kya-In carelessly thus blocking the route", *War Diary*, 1/9 Jats.
"Part of the confusion and losses in transport was due to the ferry boat being sunk—which rendered impracticable a withdrawal by road and necessitated a move across country by a track unpassable to vehicles". Lt.-Gen. T. J. Hutton's *Report*, pp. 19-20.
"The ferry boat was not properly tied up and when the first truck drove off the moorings gave way". Lt.-Col. Foucar's *Narrative*, p. 54.
[23] *War Diary*, 1/9 Jats.
[24] *Ibid.*
[25] *War Diary*, 1/7 G. R.
[26] *War Diary*, 1/7 G. R.

mortars and other equipment stampeded into the jungle and were lost. However, the drivers continued the march and rejoined the Battalion at Kawkareik itself.

The incident was reported to the Commanding Officer of the 4th Battalion Burma Rifles who had halted his motor transport short of the town. The firing in the town continued and also broke out from the direction of milestone 12 (Hlaing-Wa village). No contact could be made with the 1st Royal Battalion 9th Jat Regiment. Hence the motor transport was taken some way back along the road, the troops debussed, destroyed vehicles and stores that could not be carried and moved across country towards Kyondo. Elements of the 1st Battalion 7th Gurkha Rifles took over the local defence of the dump area which they held until 1300 hours on 22 January. The covering troops then fell back after blowing up the bridge nearby while the 1st Battalion 7th Gurkha Rifles and the 4th Battalion Burma Rifles were ferried down the Kawkareik Chaung and Haungtharaw river to Kyondo.

1/9 Jats—22 January

As regards the withdrawal of the 1st Royal Battalion 9th Jat Regiment the War Diary says, 'No clear picture can be painted as it was nothing short of a panic.' At about 0530 hours on 22 January Headquarters company embussed for Kyondo. Two platoons of 'D' company and one platoon of 'C' company withdrew through the Tadanku position. Next came two platoons of 'C' company. They all collected at Hlaing-Wa and left for Kyondo. At the bridge the Commanding Officers received orders to form a bridgehead at Kyondo at the meeting of the three rivers, Haungtharaw, Hlaing-Wa and Gyaing. On arrival at Kyondo it seemed no arrangements had been made and it was some time before the bridgehead area could be found. The War Diary says, "Each officer of the Bridge Headquarters, from the Commander downwards was completely lost and on his own. They had no idea of each other's whereabouts and it was obvious that no clear orders had been given or any proper reconnaissance made."[27]

Plan to form a bridgehead at Kyondo

But the Diary of the Sub-Divisional Officer, Kawkareik clears up the mystery.[28] On reaching Kyondo (21 January) he requisitioned all river craft that could be found and ordered them to go to the junction of the Haungtharaw and Gyaing rivers from where the evacuation was to take place. He then crossed the river to the village of Gyaing where after making enquiries about tracks he drew up a scheme for evacuation. The country craft were to assemble after dusk at the promontory opposite Gyaing village and await there the coming of the troops. Another ferry was also arranged on the Thaton side of the river opposite Kyaukton village two miles to the south of Gyaing. All troops were to march southwards from Gyaing village. When they reached the second ferry half their number was to continue marching southwards to Martaban. The other half was to cross the river to Kyaukton and to march southwards to

[27] *War Diary*, 1/9 Jats, p. 4.
[28] Diary of M.A. Maybury s.d.o. Kawkareik—*Personal Narrative of Operations* (3/18).

Moulmein, using the bullock carts for transport if they were needed. The last body of the troops was to use the boats and float down to Moulmein. At Kyondo a dozen Karen guides were found to lead the troops to the first embarkation point. The Sub-Divisional Officer then telephoned to Brigade Headquarters but got no reply. He could not himself go as his motor-car had been rendered unusable. While waiting for a reply he warned the villagers to leave at once, scatter themselves, hide their supply of grains in the jungle and also dismantle their bullock carts.

DISINTEGRATION OF BRIGADE HEADQUARTERS—21 JANUARY

Meanwhile at Brigade Headquarters at milestone 7, at about 2000 hours, the noise caused by crackers or bamboos was taken for Japanese rifle fire. In spite of the efforts of the Brigadier and Brigade-Major to stop the disintegration the greater part of the Headquarters made their way to Kyondo. The Brigadier then went to milestone 12 to meet the Gurkhas who were to take up a position to cover the withdrawal of the Jats from Kawkareik.

Its effect on the bridgehead

The Staff Captain and those of the Brigade Headquarters who had fled to Kyondo told the Sub-Divisional Officer and also phoned up Divisional Headquarters that the 16th Indian Infantry Brigade Headquarters had been attacked and that the Brigadier had been killed. Thus the Sub-Divisional Officer was led to presume that the main body of the troops had been cut off. The Staff Captain had left the Sappers building a road block a few miles to the east of Kyondo and proposed, with the few men at his disposal, to form a line round Kyondo which would be held until dawn. When informed of the Sub-Divisional Officer's plans of evacuation he asked the Sub-Divisional Officer to evacuate the non-combatant troops. This was done at night. At dawn the Staff Captain and his troops left. These arrangements had been confirmed by the Divisional Commander. These troops which consisted of some Jats who had left their positions at Kwingale, details of Brigade Headquarters Field Ambulance, Brigade Signal Section and other Ranks crossed the river and set out in their march southwards to Martaban.

1/7 Gurkha Rifles and 4th Burma Rifles at Kyondo—22 January

When the 1st Battalion 7th Gurkha Rifles, the 4th Battalion Burma Rifles and Headquarters and two companies of the Jat Battalion reached the river on the morning of 22 January, there were therefore no guides, no Sub-Divisional Officer and no craft. There was a considerable confusion due to lack of organisation of transport and crossing place. After the destruction of ammunition and transport as far as possible, the troops got across the river by country boats and craft; they were then welded into their units. Later they received orders to march to Kare about four miles to the south-west. While marching through the trackless country in the evening they lost their way and landed on an island."[19]

---

[19] *War Diary*, 1/7th Gurkha Rifles.

As the men were hungry and tired they halted for the night and recrossed to the mainland at dawn on 23 January. From there they marched to Kare where they rejoined Brigade Headquarters. As there were no boats at Kare, they marched to Tarana, a steamer station and a village 19 miles to the south-west, via Kawbein by cart track. At one place it took the Brigade six hours to cross a flimsy bridge. Here, after a long period of waiting, they embarked at 0400 hours on 24 January on three paddle steamers, set off down the stream and reached Martaban at 0930 hours. Exhaustion was common as no food had been available for any one during the previous three days.

FAILURE OF 1/9 JAT TO FORM A BRIDGEHEAD AT KYONDO—22 JANUARY

The 1st Royal Battalion 9th Regiment which had been detailed to form a bridgehead, signally failed in the task, having arrived at Kyondo later than the Gurkhas and Burma Rifles Battalion. As there were no guides, it took them some time to find the bridgehead area. The sight of other units crossing the river, 'shots fired in Kyondo' (very probably sound of Japanese bombing of the Kyondo ferry), and the setting fire to ammunition and lorries, drove many into a panic and into a hurried crossing of the river. They were called back; and after Jemadar Jug Lal had recovered the machine-guns and mortars which the staff captain had thrown into the river, they began the march to Kare. Soon they also lost the way and lay up for the night. Early next morning (23 January) they contacted Brigade Headquarters, reached Tarana at 0400 hours on 24 January only just to miss the rest of the Brigade and to wait for the steamer till 2200 hours; eventually they arrived at Martaban at 0500 hours on 25 January; from where they were moved by rail to the rest camp at Kywegyan.

Scattered elements of the 16th Brigade

To sum up the position of the rest of the scattered and tattered 16th Indian Infantry Brigade, the Kya-in-Seikkyi company of the 1st Battalion 7th Gurkha Rifles was contacted on 29 January near Mardan south of Moulmein,[30] the Myawadi company arrived in the rest camp at Kywegyan on 26 January. Stragglers also kept coming in. On 25 January it was decided to open the Rear Brigade Headquarters at Kywegyan. Administrative Headquarters and a part of the 1st Royal Battalion 9th Jat Regiment remained in Martaban and were later joined there by the rest of the Battalion which had been taken to the rest camp at Kywegyan. On 27 January the 1st Battalion 7th Gurkha Rifles left for Thaton and from there via Duyinzeik to Kuzeik, a village opposite to Pa-an. The 4th Battalion 12th Frontier Force Regiment was left to defend Moulmein.

According to a previously arranged plan the Burma Rifles company in the Tichara-Mepale area, fell back slowly to Kyawko where it remained on 24 January covering the pass through the hills. Next day it retired on Nabu and found that village unoccupied and burnt by hostile Burmans. The Company commander was informed by the villagers that the forces had left the area and that the Japanese were ahead of him. It had then

---

[30] *War Diary*, 4/12th Frontier Force Rifles.

two engagements with guerilla bands. The company then marched to Pa-an on the Salween across two unbridged rivers. It eventually rejoined the 16th Indian Infantry Brigade with mules, equipment and reserve ammunition complete after having killed thirty Japanese without loss to itself.[31]

CONCLUSION

The withdrawal from Kawkareik over a distance of 53 miles for some and 80 for others has been described at length as it brings into bold relief the mistakes committed by the officers and their units. The net result was loss of all transport and equipment including complete Signal Section. Somehow, orders were passed to destroy arms and equipment. Even rifles were thrown away. However, some mortars and M.M.Gs had been saved. The men were thoroughly shaken and the Brigade thoroughly disorganised. The operation, as the small number of casualties (on either side) showed, was not very creditable to those concerned though there were isolated instances of gallantry and coolness. 'D' company of the 1st Battalion 7th Regiment Gurkha Rifles which the Japanese attacked in the first instance did specially good work and the 4th Battalion Burma Rifles did creditable service. Gen. Sir A. Wavell commented, "It is quite clear that the enemy were allowed to gain cheap initial successes through bad handling of local commanders, lack of training and in some instances lack of fighting spirit on the part of our troops. It was an unfortunate beginning to the campaign and had serious results in raising the morale of the enemy and depressing that of our own troops."[32]

It is desirable to mention here that the Commanders and units concerned wiped out any stains on their reputation resulting from this section by their subsequent achievements. The road from Myawadi to Kyondo was effectively blown, and the demolitions, in addition to the Japanese attempts to bring additional reinforcements, considerably slowed up the Japanese rate of advance. But this breathing time was not of much use to Moulmein as we shall see. Even after the Kawkareik action both ABDA and Burma Army Commands failed to appreciate that a large scale Japanese offensive had begun. In his telegram of 21 January, Gen. Sir A. Wavell said, "Large scale effort against Burma seems improbable at present. Japanese land effort also dispersed." In his telegram to Gen. Sir A. Wavell, Lt.-Gen. T. J. Hutton wrote, "Attack on Tavoy and Kawkareik may have been isolated operation and not first stage of general offensive. Acceleration minor reinforcements remain therefore of first importance but urgency is no longer so great as indicated in my telegram of 21st."[33]

[31] *War Diary*, the 4th Battalion Burma Rifles, p. 13.
[32] Gen. Sir A. Wavell's *Despatch*, p. 6.
[33] *South Burma Operations* (601/2/2/H), p. 9. On 26th January Gen. Sir A. Wavell telegraphed to Mr. Churchill as follows: "Returned this morning from Rangoon. Do not consider situation immediately serious provided certain steps outlined below are taken as early as possible. Japanese advance in Tenasserim probably made by comparatively small force (It was in fact 2/3rd of a Division). Our main force south has been withdrawn across Salween, and Japanese occupation of Moulmein is probable but have instructed Hutton to take offensive action as soon as he has organised sufficient force." 601/2/3/H, p. 33.

CHAPTER IX

Defence of Moulmein

MOULMEIN

The crumbling of the forward positions at Kawkareik left the road open to Moulmein, the headquarters of the Amherst Division. This port town, the first great defended locality in Lower Burma, lay at the mouth of the Salween on the left bank of the river below its junction with the Gyaing and the Ataran and was situated at a distance of 28 miles from the sea. Before the annexation of Burma by the British it was only a fishing village. Its subsequent history has been one of almost continuous growth owing to its being a timber port with rice mills, saw mills and timber mills.[1] It was one of the six great ports of Burma but its imports were mostly coastwise from Rangoon. In the beginning the city was a maze of tortuous streets and mat houses but by a long chain of baptisms by fire (1843, 1846, 1854, 1856, 1865, etc.) the town gradually assumed its present form.

The configuration of the city was roughly that of an inverted L, the vertical line, long and narrow, representing the course of the Salween to the west, and the horizontal line that of the river Ataran. The town itself lay among trees at the foot of a sharp ridge. Through the town and parallel with the vertical line of the inverted L ran another ridge. To the east and north-east of the town stretched vast paddy fields intersected by the courses of the Gyaing and the Ataran. North of the town lay the promontory of Martaban with its low hills stretching away north and west till they merged in the mass of Thaton hills. To the southeast stretched a long ribbon of jungle and rubber plantations and the low chain of Taungnyo hills. The ridge in Moulmein was practically a continuation of this range. The eastern side of the district was occupied by the lofty spurs of the thickly wooded Dawna Range, which is 5,500 ft. at its highest point in 16.5° North and 98.42° East. The range presents the appearance of a wooded plateau of laterite cut up into hills by drainage action. It runs south-east between the Thaungyin and the Haungtharaw rivers and throws out numerous spurs. From the point of view of defence Moulmein had very little to recommend it. It was surrounded on three sides by tidal estuaries and on the fourth side by the jungle. All these waterways could be easily crossed by raft or boat.

ALLIED FORCES ON 1 DECEMBER

The following forces were stationed in Moulmein on 1 December 1941:—Headquarters Tenasserim Area and 2 Burma Brigade, Tenasserim Battalion B.A.F., less one Company, 12 Mountain Battery I.A., the 8th

---

[1] *Burma Gazetteer.* Amherst Dt.

Battalion Burma Rifles, one Section Field Company Burma Sappers and Miners, a detachment of Kokine Battalion B.F.F., 1 Animal Transport Company less the Mechanical Transport Sections 1, 2, 4, 6 and 8, and 3 Ordnance Field Depot. On 18 January, the 1st Battalion 7th Gurkha Rifles (16 Brigade) arrived in Rangoon and was diverted to Moulmein the same night.

On 17 January 1942, 17th Indian Division Headquarters also moved forward to Moulmein and took over command from the 16th Indian Infantry Brigade. This Division was to be in action against the Japanese in Burma and Assam from January 1942, until the Japanese surrendered in 1945, with a few short breaks for reorganisation and training. It was thus to fight against the Japanese longer than other British or Indian formation. "The Division was formed in July 1941 under command of Maj. Gen. H. V. Lewis, C.B., C.I.E., D.S.O. The units were concentrated in the Ahmednagar Area. The official date of mobilisation was 1 December 1941. The Division consisted of the 44th, 45th and 46th Indian Infantry Brigades. It moved to Dhond for training in November 1941. Events in the Middle East, Persia and Russia at that time demanded the deployment of the larger part of the military resources and for this reason, the Division was organised, trained and equipped for desert warfare on a high scale of MT. At one time arrangements had been in hand to move it complete to the Middle East. In November Maj. Gen. H. V. Lewis became ill, and was succeeded in command by Maj. Gen. J. G. Smythe, V.C. In December, 44th and 45th Indian Infantry Brigades with a proportion of Divisional troops sailed for Malaya where they were soon to be wiped out. Later in December the Divisional Headquarters sailed for Rangoon, with the 46th Indian Infantry Brigade to follow early in January 1942."[2]

PLAN OF DEFENCE

Ever since his arrival there the Divisional Commander felt that the defence of Moulmein, devoid of proper communications, was a hopeless proposition.[3] Nevertheless, he was ordered to defend it. On 20 January, he gave up his policy of defending Moulmein by sections and changed it to one of battle Headquarters with Brigades closed in around Moulmein. He also issued orders for the collection of barbed wire to be used for outer defences. In a telegram of 22 January, Gen. Sir A. Wavell also stressed the necessity for holding Moulmein and added that "the nature of the country and resources must limit Japanese effort". On 23 January, the Brigadier General Staff from AHQ and the Divisional Commander inspected the defences of Moulmein and came to the conclusion that with no defences to speak of actually constructed and with the length of perimeter that must be held, it was difficult to defend the town without a far larger force than was available. At least two brigades were required to hold a secure perimeter. But "one Brigade was the most that could be spared for it and the eventual withdrawal of that Brigade might be a difficult if not an impossible proposition". The Divisional Commander, therefore, represented to the Army Headquarters that "in view of the

[2] *History of the 17th Indian Division, July 1941 to December 1949*, 60/2440/H, p. 1.
[3] *War Diary*, C.S.O., 17th Indian Division, Sheet 4.

disorganised state of the troops at his disposal and the fact that the enemy was believed to be in considerable strength . . . . he considered it desirable to move his Division right back to the area Pilin-Kyaikto—River Sittang where he could concentrate his troops in a strong position, and establish a secure base from which to deliver a counter stroke."[4] Lt.-Gen. Hutton did not consider withdrawal on that scale justifiable and desired that Moulmein be held for which, if time permitted, he proposed to move up the 2nd Battalion King's Own Yorkshire Light Infantry from the 1st Burma Division in the Shan States to reinforce the Moulmein garrison. The Divisional Commander was told that the first requirement was to regain touch with the Japanese. This had been entirely lost as a result of the withdrawal from Kawkareik and was not really regained until the Japanese attacked Moulmein on 30 January.

Lieutenant General Hutton was perfectly clear about the position of Moulmein, and had no intention of leaving "a Brigade closely invested in that place". He fully realised that "Moulmein does not necessarily defend Rangoon and there are other routes at present inadequately guarded". All that he desired to secure was "to delay enemy advance on Moulmein as much as possible with troops available but not to allow forces there to become isolated in tactically unsound position". Hence his plan was to "build up forces as they arrive in area between River Salween and River Bilin with the object of taking the offensive as soon as reinforcements" were available. He seems to have agreed with the view of the Divisional Commander that the line of River Salween should be held as it provided "better defence than the isolated position at Moulmein."[5] On 24 January, therefore, he issued orders to the 17th Indian Division to plan arrangements for withdrawal. He was to keep touch with and delay the Japanese advance while stores, animals and motor transport were evacuated from Moulmein and forces were organised west of the Salween river.[6] Owing to the poor communications across the river and the presence of considerable quantity of stores which had very unwisely been dumped in Moulmein, this was likely to take a considerable time. However, as early as 20 January, orders had been issued by the Divisional Commander that all stores and MT unnecessary for the defences were to be shipped across the Salween to Martaban and on 22 January they were back-loaded as fast as possible. On 24 January at a Brigade conference the provision of launches etc. for the evacuation of civilians was discussed and withdrawal had begun.

Nevertheless, on the night of 24/25 January Gen. Sir A. Wavell visited Rangoon and reported to the Chiefs of Staff that he did not consider the situation serious. He also instructed Lt.-Gen. T. J. Hutton to forestall the Japanese occupation of Moulmein by taking vigorous offensive action as soon as he had organised sufficient force. The 17th Indian Division was accordingly informed that Moulmein must be held at all costs though withdrawal of surplus stores was to continue, and that the

---

[4] Lt.-Gen. T. J. Hutton's *Report*, p. 20.
[5] *South Burma Operations* (601/2/2H), p. 10, Tel. 0453 dated 24-1-1942 from Burma army to Abdacom.
[6] *South Burma Operations* p. 11 Tel. No. 0481 dated 25 January 1942 from Burma army to Abdacom.

2nd Battalion King's Own Yorkshire Light Infantry would, if time permitted, be moved up to reinforce Moulmein. Plans were also to be made to send offensive patrols.

2ND BURMA BRIGADE

The defence of Moulmein was entrusted to the 2nd Burma Brigade which for this purpose consisted of the 3rd Battalion Burma Rifles less two companies, the 4th and 7th and 8th Battalions Burma Rifles, the 4th Battalion 12th Frontier Force Regiment (less one company) in reserve, 12 Mountain Battery 'C' Troops, 3rd Indian Light Anti-Aircraft Battery which had been in Moulmein from 5 January,[7] and one section of 60th Field Company Sappers and Miners and various supply and medical units. The aerodrome which was the most important point, was guarded by a detachment of four platoons of infantry and one machine-gun platoon, all from Kokine Battalion, Burma Frontier Force. The counter-attack company of the 8th Battalion Burma Rifles and the A.A. Guns were recalled for duty before the attack on the aerodrome began.[8]

The Divisional Headquarters had moved back on 24 January to Kyaikto where it was established in the local jail. Great confusion was caused by the Divisional Headquarters moving out, stragglers from Tavoy and Kawkareik moving in, and the civil population evacuating.

AIR ATTACKS ON MOULMEIN

The bombing of Moulmein up to 15 January, has already been noted. On 18 January, a force of 14 Japanese bombers escorted by 5 fighters raided the town. The attack lasted one hour. The main target was the aerodrome which had a Blenheim and two fighter planes on it. The Supply Depot was also attacked. There was, however, no damage or casualty. But the Burmese population, as in Mergui, and shortly afterwards in Rangoon, started a steady evacuation into the surrounding country, and labour which was needed urgently, became very scarce. There was another air raid on 19 January and a portion of the town was set fire to. On 21 January, the Japanese aircraft were very active over Moulmein. The aerodrome was heavily bombed. There was nothing to oppose the hostile aircraft except 4 Bofors and 2 fighters which had only arrived that day. The bombing led to a fire in the bazaar which further aggravated the evacuation of the civilian population. The aerodrome was also virtually put out of action. But the disaffected elements remained, and looters became very active. Thereupon the control of the town was assumed by the military authorities and looters were shot.[9] There was another air attack on 23 January, this time on the aerodrome, by nearly 30 bombers and fighters. Though the Japanese had not pressed forward from Kawkareik, probably because they were bringing up

[7] During the withdrawal to India one or other troops of the battery were present in every action in Burma with enemy forward troops.
[8] Later on one platoon was detailed as escort for civil prisoners being evacuated from Moulmein to Martaban.
[9] Between 3 January and 23 January Moulmein had been raided seven times. *War Diary*, 8 Burma Rifles gives the dates as 17 and 20 January.

reserves, or fanning out on a wide front it was clear from the almost daily bombing from 17 January that the Japanese forces would soon close in on Moulmein. On 26 January, a large party of pack artillery was located at Kya-in-Seikkyi. They would seem to have entered Burma through the Three Pagodas Pass and followed the company of the 1st Battalion 7th Gurkha Rifles retreating from Kya-in-Seikkyi.

FIRST CONTACT—26-29 JANUARY

The first detachment to contact the Japanese in the Moulmein area was 'A' company, the 4th Battalion 12th Frontier Force Regiment. Upon receipt of the news of the capture of Tavoy the Battalion less 'C' company had been withdrawn to Moulmein from the Tavoy-Ye sector on 26 January. 'A' company with one section MMG was then sent to carry out a patrol in the hills east of the Mudon town (15 miles south of Moulmein). It ran into heavy mortar and small arms fire and extricated itself with great difficulty, though the casualties were only four wounded. The Japanese were reported to be one battalion strong. On receipt of this news the Frontier Force Battalion less 'B' Company, was sent to join 'A' company north of Mudon, only to be ordered back the next day to the main defence of Moulmein. Meanwhile, on 27 January, a W/T detachment sent out with a company of the Frontier Force Regiment Battalion in order to locate the Gurkha Rifles company retreating from Kya-in-Seikkyi, contacted Japanese units and suffered a few casualties.

'D' company, the 4th Battalion 12th Frontier Force Regiment, had been left at Mudon with orders to help the company of the 1st Battalion 7th Gurkha Rifles withdrawing from Kya-in-Seikkyi. The former were attacked on the night of 29/30 January, and were cut off from Moulmein. It was with great difficulty that they cut their way through, crossed the Salween in country boats and rejoined the Battalion at Kyaikto on 1 February. The same night (January 29/30) the posts along the river front in Moulmein frequently fired on suspicious looking craft.

DEFENCE OF MOULMEIN PROPER

In Moulmein itself the perimeter of about eleven and a half miles was held by three battalions of Burma Rifles, the 4th Battalion 12 Frontier Force Regiment being in reserve about Point 183, near the bungalow which housed the Brigade Headquarters. The 7th Battalion Burma Rifles held the south end of the town about the railway jetty, and the whole of the west and north river fronts to a point near the Kyaikpane Jetty. Thence the line cut across country to Hmyawlin on the Ataran river, followed that river south to Ngante and turned south-west along the road to the Zegyo quarter of Moulmein. The whole of this sector from near Kyaikpane Jetty up to a point midway between Ngante village and Zegyo was held by the 3rd Battalion Burma Rifles. The gap between the 3rd Battalion Burma Rifles and the left flank of the 7th Battalion Burma Rifles at the south of the town was filled by the 8th Battalion Burma Rifles. To the south-east and outside the perimeter was the aerodrome. No efforts had been made to put Moulmein in a state of effective defence during the period before operations began. But the Army Commander after a rapid reconnaissance had given orders for defences to be put in hand. With the forces available it is doubtful if it would have been a sound policy to make arrangements for the protracted defence of Moulmein which was more suitable to act as an advanced base for mobile operations.[10] Local defences to cover the landing stages would have been invaluable, but the real line of defence in this area lay on the west bank of the Salween.[11]

The Army Commander had directed Brig. R. G. Ekin to take control of operations in Moulmein, when they began and the latter was informed of this by the Divisional Commander on 30 January. As the Brigadier had no previous knowledge of either the troops or the ground at Moulmein he decided to go there at once from Hoinpale. From Martaban he crossed the Salween and arrived at Moulmein at midday on 30 January when the attack on the town had already begun.

ATTACK ON MOULMEIN—30 JANUARY, 1942

The attack opened at about 0720 hours on 30 January with typical Japanese attempt at a surprise.[12] Four of the Burma Army lorries with drivers in civilian clothes approached Zegyo along the road from Mudon. They were travelling fast and were packed with Japanese soldiers. At that moment 'D' company and one platoon of 'A' company of the 8th Battalion Burma Rifles had just begun to move down the road to deal with a Japanese force of 50 to 100 reported to be in a village east of the aerodrome. The road-block in the perimeter defence line was opened to allow the 'D' company to pass through. Had it not been for the quick and correct appreciation of the situation by No. 1 of the LMG Section, L/NK Jwala Singh, covering the road, the surprise attack might have been carried right into the heart of Moulmein and created untold confusion. As it was, the first lorry was stopped by the burst of the L/NK's Bren Gun fire and thirteen Japanese were killed. The Japanese also opened automatic fire on 'D' company. Heavy toll was taken of the Japanese as they debussed by the above-mentioned Bren Gun and another in the rear. The lorries behind had time to pull up, the Japanese debussed and took to ground action. Meanwhile, the two rear platoons of 'D' company and the platoon of 'A' Company managed to get back behind the other companies of the Battalion north of the cross-roads.

A heavy attack on the 8th Battalion Burma Rifles, 'B' and 'C' companies and on the left flank of the 7th Battalion Burma Rifles now rapidly developed. The Japanese from the lorries had joined up with others who were on the road to the aerodrome and attempted to work round the left

---

[10] The opinion has been expressed by senior staff officers that a force of at least one division was required to defend Moulmein. Appendix A to Brig. R. G. Ekin's *Account of the Defence and Evacuation of Moulmein*, Microfilm No. D/167/390.

[11] The troops in Moulmein had to fight with their backs to the swiftly flowing Salween. It was doubtful whether the civilian crews of river steamers would stick to their posts of duty in a difficult situation—*Ibid*.

[12] The troops of the *55th Division* which attacked Moulmein were five Infantry Battalions, five Batteries of field artillery, with a total of twenty 75 mm mountain guns, two companies of cavalry troops, two companies of engineer troops, totalling 7000 to 8000— the Divisional Commander's answer to Ques. 44, ATIS Interrogation centre, 601/1011/H.

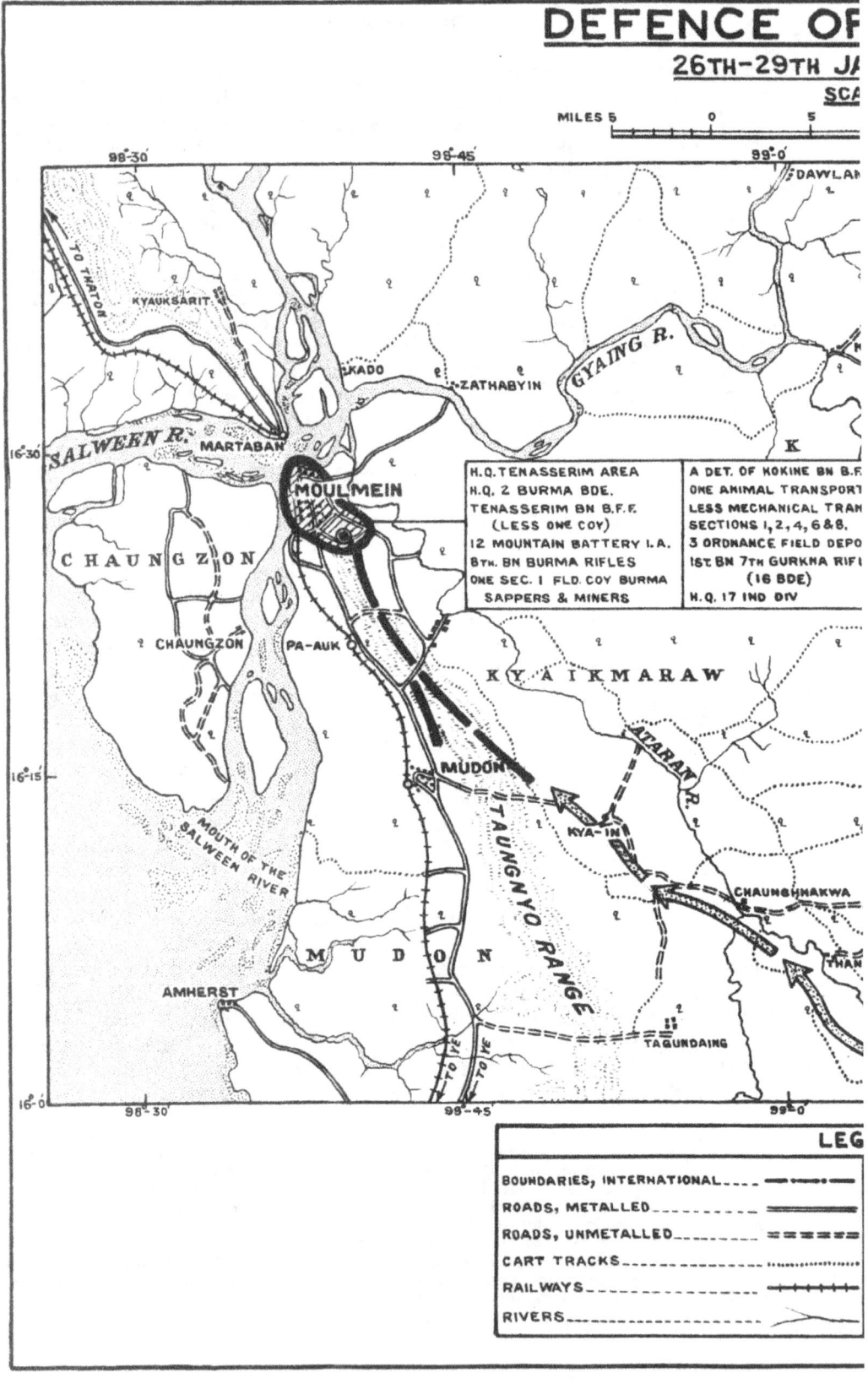

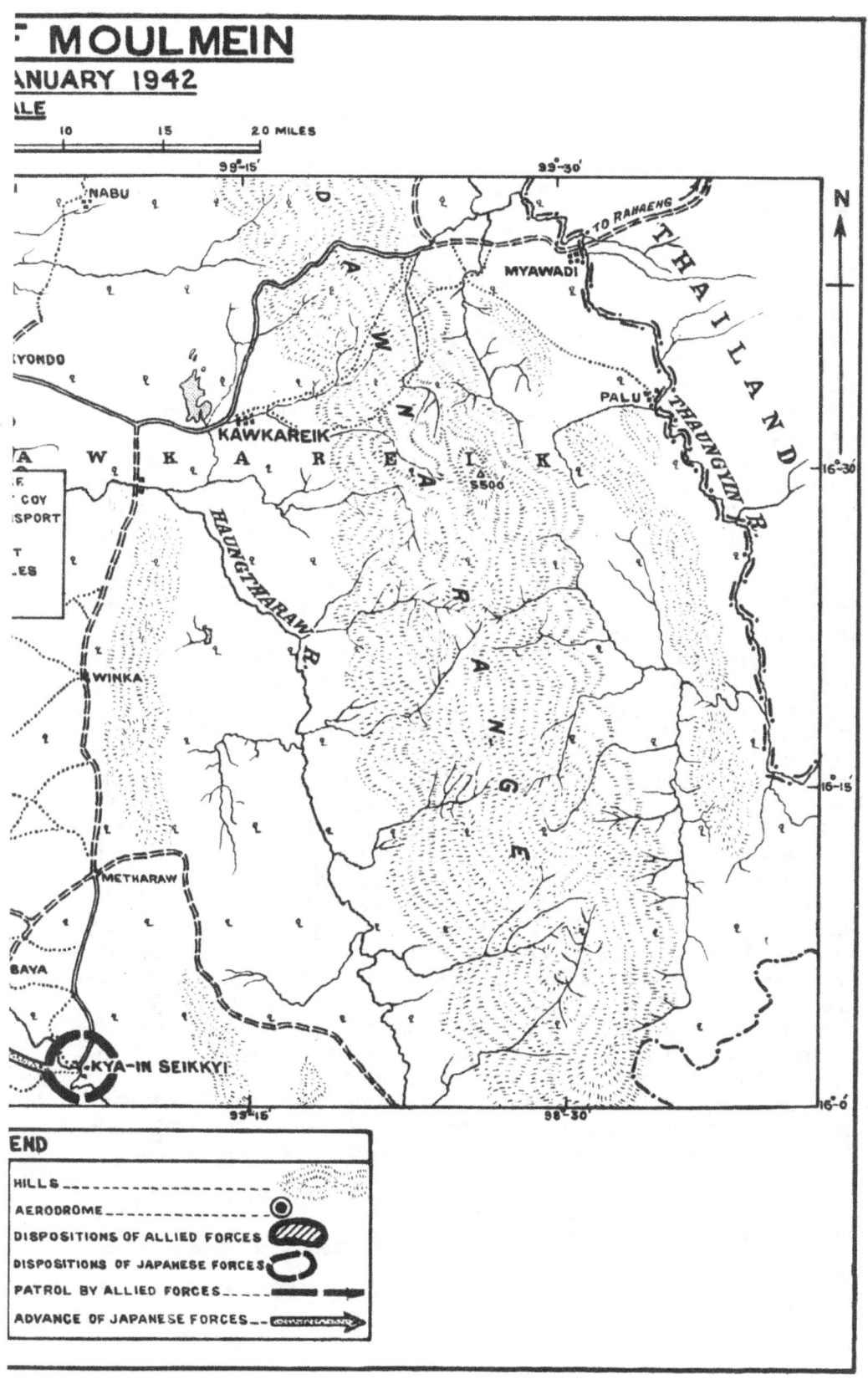

flank of the 8th Battalion Burma Rifles. At first the Japanese attacked 'B' Company which was to the left of 'C' company. When this failed, they attacked 'C' company's position. But here again the attack was firmly held. The Japanese then turned to 'B' company. Its forward sections began to suffer considerable casualties from the Japanese grenades and small arms fire. Two sections of the Brigade employment platoon were sent forward to fill the gaps in the company. 'B' company put up a good show and repulsed all Japanese attacks. A section of 12 Mountain Battery gave them excellent support and inflicted many losses on the Japanese. Late in the afternoon the attack died away, but sniping of defence positions in this sector continued.[13]

On the east, the Japanese crossed the Ataran during the morning and penetrated the positions of the 3rd Battalion Burma Rifles to occupy both Hmyawlin and Ngante.[14] Again the Mountain Battery did good work by engaging a Japanese battery near Ngante. At least one gun was destroyed and the battery silenced. At 1300 hours, on receiving the impression that the Battalion was badly rattled Brig. R. G. Ekin ordered the 3rd Battalion Burma Rifles to withdraw to a shortened line east of, and covering, the Ridge and Zegyo. At the same time he ordered the 4th Battalion, 12th Frontier Force Regiment (less one company in Brigade reserve) to occupy the Ridge which dominated and was tactically the key to Moulmein. Later that day when the situation on the Ridge was serious the reserve company rejoined the Battalion.

The detachment of the Kokine Battalion on the aerodrome was fighting an isolated action. It was first attacked by a small party of the Japanese at about 0730 hours from the north. This attack was beaten off easily. While this action was in progress the telephonic communication between the aerodrome and the Brigade Headquarters failed and it was presumed that the Japanese had cut it. Later, a heavier attack developed from the same direction. The detachment was in communication with the Brigade Headquarters and asked for artillery support. This was accurately given by the Mountain Battery. Thus assisted the detachment put up a splendid resistance against the superior forces throughout the day although at about 1630 hours a hill feature[15] dominating the aerodrome was captured by the Japanese. From that moment the situation at the aerodrome itself became serious as the hill which was only 1000 yards from the centre of the aerodrome commanded the whole field. From this hill heavy mortar and gun fire supported further attacks. As darkness fell the Japanese began to close in round the aerodrome. The troops on finding the situation hopeless withdrew at 2030 hours and made their way to Martaban.[16]

About 1730 hours the posts along the Ridge were heavily engaged by the Japanese at close quarters. During the day they had brought up their light artillery. There was no sign of the 3rd Battalion Burma

---

[13] Capt. N. A. P. Rannard, *Diary of Events*, Appendix I, *War Diary*, 8 Burif.
[14] The Battalion of two companies was not up to strength in men and arms and had no equipment for carrying 3″ mortars.
[15] Hill No. 895 which was guarded by a platoon of 8 Burif under command of the aerodrome detachment. The platoon was overrun.
[16] Capt. N. R. Watts, *Personal Narratives of Operations—Operations on Moulmein Aerodrome.*

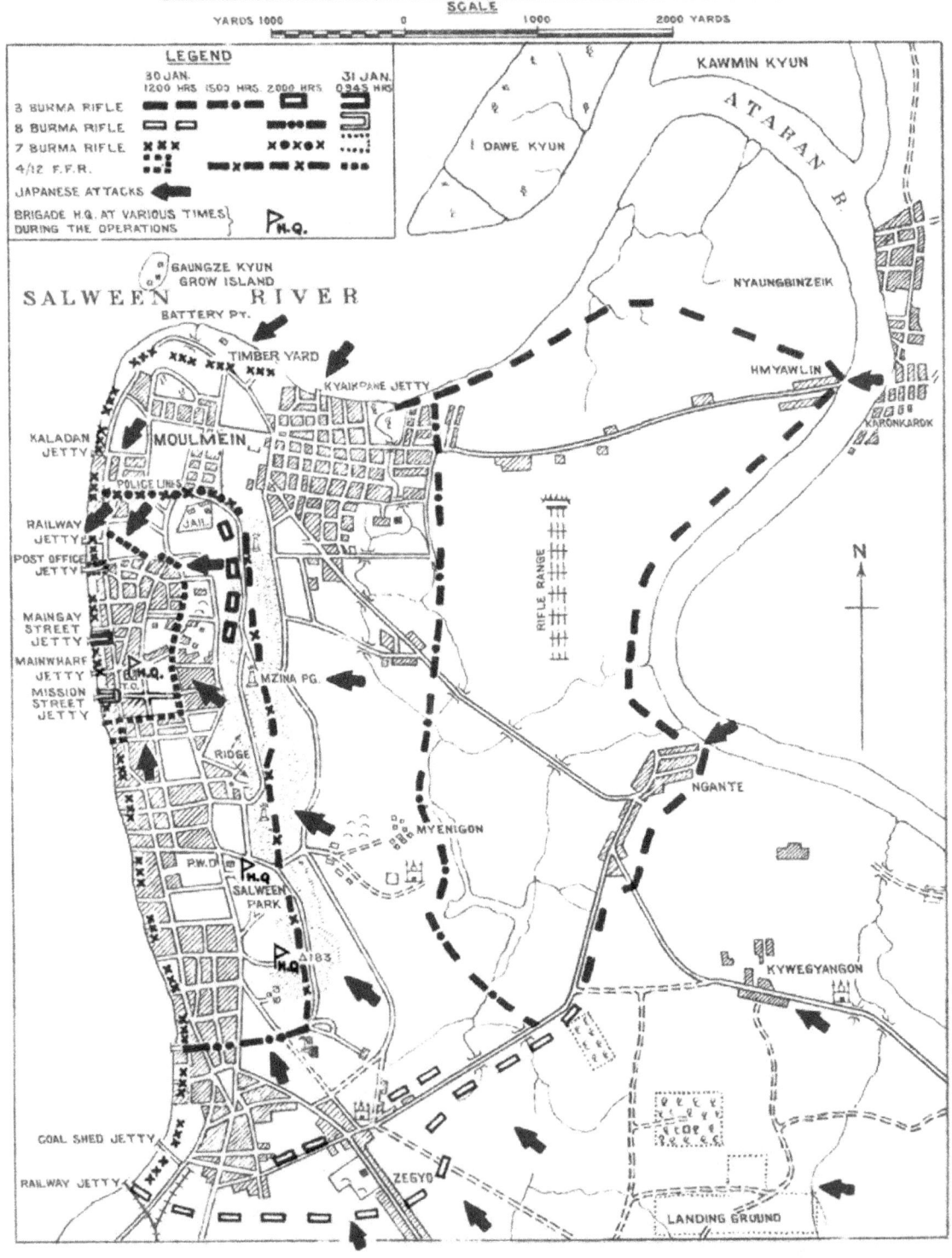

Rifles which was supposed to be holding a line east of, and covering, the Ridge. Nor could its headquarters be found. The situation appeared to the Brigadier to be critical, but the 4th Battalion 12th Frontier Force Regiment repulsed all attempts to dislodge it and was well supported by its own mortars and the guns of the Mountain Battery. There were several sharp hand-to-hand engagements. As darkness fell heavy gun and mortar fire was directed against the Ridge and the southern front of the perimeter.[17] At this time, too, the Brigade Headquarters was informed that hostile craft were coming down the Salween from the direction of Kawton, 3 miles north of Moulmein.

Headquarters of the 8th Battalion Burma Rifles had been located that day in a bungalow at the south end of the Ridge. It was in a prominent position and the considerable movement round the house must have been watched by the Japanese. As a result the bungalow was shelled with extreme accuracy at about 1830 hours, and after some casualties had been sustained Battalion Headquarters moved to a less conspicuous position.[18]

In order to shorten and strengthen the perimeter and, if possible, to counter any penetration into the town under cover of night, Brig. R. G. Ekin, withdrew the troops on the southern face of the perimeter at 2300 hours. They fell back about one thousand yards to an east and west line joining the south of the Ridge with the river front.[19] The Japanese followed up the withdrawal and on this sector the positions were engaged all night with small arms, automatic and cracker gun fire. The aerodrome detachment was ordered to make its way back as best as it could through the positions of the 8th Battalion Burma Rifles. Many of the detachment came in safely.[20]

Throughout the night the Japanese were in contact with the troops on the Ridge and frequent assaults were beaten off, the 4th Battalion 12th Frontier Force Regiment maintaining its positions intact. In the sector of its left hand company were now also the Headquarters and such men as remained of the 3rd Battalion Burma Rifles.[21] However, the 8th Battalion had not been followed up as its patrols kept touch with and held off the Japanese throughout the night.

During the evening of 30 January, Brigade Headquarters had moved from the Ridge to the Public Works Department bungalow in Salween Park. This was given particular attention by the Japanese who directed fire on it. Early next morning it was attacked by a small party of the Japanese who had infiltrated through the defences. Headquarters

---

[17] O.C. 8 Burif informed the Brigadier that his men who had fought magnificently for nearly 12 hours were exhausted.

[18] One Jemadar was killed and 2/Lt. T. C. Flack and one sepoy were wounded. Battalion HQ was moved to a large dugout near C.G.S.

[19] The defences were now in the shape of a rectangle some 3 miles from north to south and varying from 1000 to 1500 yards from east to west. Except for the Ridge it would mean street fighting but it could not be helped—46th Indian Infantry Brigade Diary Appendix "Z".

[20] This detachment had put up a splendid resistance and had guarded a Blenheim bomber and some RAF stores. However, they failed to destroy them completely before withdrawal.

[21] Contact had been made with the Battalion at 1600 hours and it withdrew to new positions at 1800 hours. It had no line for any reconnaissance, and no transport for any equipment except Bren Guns. One of its two companies had ceased to exist.

therefore moved to the Telephone Exchange near the Mission Street Jetty. No sooner had it been established there, than large fires broke out in the buildings along the river front close by. Fifth columnists appeared to have a good knowledge of the movements of Headquarters.

The Bofors guns of the Anti-Aircraft Battery had been stationed in the northern area of the town to cover the jetties and the Ridge. In the early hours of 31 January these guns were over-run by parties of the Japanese. These had landed from the river near the Timber Yard at the north end of the town. When challenged they gave the correct Password and posing as Burmans or mingling with withdrawing Burmese troops entered the gun positions. The gunners were taken by surprise and some were bayonetted. There was a fierce hand-to-hand encounter, but the survivors of the gunners were compelled to withdraw abandoning their guns. However, they were able to remove the breach locks of two guns.

The Divisional Headquarters at Kyaikto was in continuous telephonic touch with Moulmein and was kept closely informed of the events. Early on 31 January Brig. R. G. Ekin gave Maj. Gen. J. G. Smyth an appreciation of the situation. It had been reported that a large number of men, mostly Burmans, were streaming down to the jetties. These men had been at once ordered back to their units, but the incident pointed to a break in the morale of certain units. This fact combined with the landing on the northern front and the repeated attacks against the Ridge, led Brig. R. G. Ekin to consider the situation as extremely serious. He now had no reserve, and doubted very much if the force in Moulmein could hold the town against renewed attacks from three sides during the day. Maj. Gen. J. G. Smyth replied that the Army Commander had agreed that, if necessary, Moulmein should be evacuated and that plans should be prepared for this eventuality.[22] The decision whether they were to be put into force was left to the Brigadier on the spot.

Here it is significant to note that when it was known that the 2nd Battalion King's Own Yorkshire Light Infantry was not arriving as a reinforcement there had been a general drop in the morale, particularly among the Burman troops. The Battalion was now available, but events had moved too quickly. The Battalion was weak and one of the only two British Battalions in Burma. There was no guarantee that its despatch across the Salween would enable Moulmein to be held, and the possibility of withdrawing it after it was committed was equally remote.

DECISION TO WITHDRAW—31 JANUARY

The situation did not improve and the Brigadier was satisfied that the town could not be held much longer. He decided to withdraw his troops across the river and telephoned this decision to the Divisional Commander who concurred. He asked for air support during the withdrawal operations. Maj. Gen. J. G. Smyth said that he would endeavour to obtain support from the RAF. Orders for a withdrawal to begin at 0800 hours were then issued.

[22] Brigadier R. C. Ekin's account of the *Defence and Evacuation of Moulmein, War Diary*, 46th Indian Infantry Brigade, p. 2.

Meanwhile at about 0600 hours the Japanese had attacked from the Timber Yard area. The 7th Battalion Burma Rifles in spite of a counter-attack was forced back to a line about the jail and Police Lines.[23] Other Japanese troops were infiltrating across the Ridge through the environs of the pagoda above the jail. Here a dawn attack penetrated the defences of the 3rd Battalion Burma Rifles at one point, a machine-gun post being overrun after heavy fighting. The first contact was made in a sunken road cutting through the Ridge. The Commander, A. A. platoon, Subedar Maru Gam, although wounded, accounted for four of the Japanese with his *dah*. On the south, at the other extremity of the perimeter, also at about 0600 hours[24] an attack was made along the whole front. At 0700 hours some of the Japanese suddenly appeared in Salween Park, but an immediate bayonet charge by the Headquarters company of the 8th Battalion Burma Rifles was entirely successful and cleared the Park of the Japanese.

Plan of Withdrawal

The plan for withdrawal was simple. The 'box' of the diminishing perimeter was to be kept closed, units maintaining touch as they fell back on the jetties. The 12th Mountain Battery and the 4th Battalion 12th Frontier Force Regiment were to form a bridge-head covering the Post Office, Maingay Street, and Mission Street jetties at each of which five river steamers had been berthed to take off the troops.

Each unit was detailed to withdraw on a particular jetty or jetties, and embarkation was controlled by specially appointed officers. The wounded, together with medical and supply units, had been evacuated as soon as the decision to withdraw was made.

Withdrawal

At 0800 hours 31 January, the troops holding the perimeter began to fall back.[25] Rear parties were followed up by the Japanese, not at first in great strength. Street fighting took place both in the north and south quarters of the town, but the Japanese were held off and suffered many casualties. Then, however, they began to close in on the Post Office Jetty and embarkation there was seriously held up. Counter-attacks to clear the approaches were launched by parties of 60 Field Company and the 7th Battalion Burma Rifles.

Of the many acts of gallantry carried out that morning two deserve special mention. Major J. G. L. Hume, R. A., commanding 12th Mountain Battery, on arrival at his embarkation jetty was informed that one section of the Battery was missing. At once he set out with a small party of his own men and some of the 4th Battalion 12th Frontier Force Regiment, forced his way through the Japanese to the gun position, and brought both guns back. The Battery thus saved all its guns.

2/Lt. Mehar Dass of the Anti-Aircraft Battery learnt that the Japanese had left no sentries on the Bofors guns they had captured.

---

[23] *War Diary* of 7 Burma Rifles is silent on this point.
[24] *War Diary*, 8 Burif makes it 0630 hours.
[25] Lt.-Gen. T J. Hutton's *Report* gives the embarkation time as 0730 hours. This is wrong.

Organising a party from Troops Headquarters he succeeded in bringing to the Post Office Jetty the gun that had not been disabled by its crew. Here he made every endeavour to load the gun on a steamer but was unable to do so. Then under fire he went ashore from the last vessel at the jetty to disable the gun and assist the survivors. He was not seen again, but long after the close of the campaign was reported to be a prisoner of war.

By 1000 hours the 4th Battalion 12th Frontier Force Regiment had withdrawn to within a few yards of the Maingay Street and Mission Street jetties. The Power House and the Telephone Exchange had been destroyed, and all vehicles used to bring arms and vital equipment to the steamers had been put out of action. Brig. R. G. Ekin then ordered the final evacuation, the Brigade Headquarters together with the rearguard leaving by the last steamer from Mission Street Jetty. As the vessel left, the Japanese gained the jetty and a brisk exchange of fire took place. It was shelled most of the way to Martaban from Moulmein shore. But in spite of several near misses it managed to reach Martaban safely. The forces had destroyed their MT, and abandoned their A.T. and the majority of the signals stores.

Fighting still continued round the Post Office jetty. Embarkation was interfered with here by the Japanese at close quarters and parties of 60 Field Company and the 7th Battalion Burma Rifles had to counterattack in order to clear the approaches to the quayside. Many who could not embark on the steamers had to leave on improvised rafts or by swimming, and eventually nearly all who had been left behind escaped in this manner.

The Japanese were now in position on the Ridge. Their artillery and machine-guns opened accurate fire on the steamers going up the river, and one of the smaller vessels was sunk by shell fire. Large formations of hostile bombing aircraft had been overhead during the period of evacuation but, fortunately, they persisted in bombing Martaban and not Moulmein.[26] No RAF cover had been provided.

On the arrival of the steamers at Martaban every encouragement and threat was used to induce their local civilian crew to return to the Post Office Jetty to take off personnel still remaining there. It was also known that a party of the troops was isolated at the Kaladan Jetty north of the embarkation area. However, the crew refused to take their ships back to Moulmein. They had been highly tried and were, of course, not subject to military discipline.

The casualties during the operations on 30 and 31 January amounted to 617, a considerable proportion being missing; approximately three-fourths of the Moulmein force had been evacuated. It was several days, however, before all the stragglers eventually came in from these and the previous operations. The four Bofors guns were lost, but all the mortars and mountain guns were saved. On the other side of the balance sheet were the heavy casualties inflicted on the Japanese at Zegyo, on the Ridge, and during the final withdrawal. Before the action was over it was found

[26] Each time this happened the civilian crew in spite of their armed guards took their boats off to midstream leaving the anxious defenders wondering whether they would return at all.

that a whole Japanese division had been engaged.[27] This was identified as the *55th Division* which had also been at Kawkareik and at Bokpyin and Tavoy.

With the capture of Moulmein the Japanese considered that the first phase of their operations in Burma had come to an end.[28] For the other side it meant the loss of an important port, an important base for counter-offensive into Thailand and an advance fighter air base; it also meant the withdrawal of its troops west of the River Salween. "That the bulk of the forces was withdrawn safely by broad daylight under every sort of difficulty reflects the greatest credit on the commanders and troops concerned".[29] There were, of course, left behind small parties of men who could not get ships or who had been separated from the units. Many of these later on managed to cross the river in country boats or on crafts. For some days after the evacuation of Moulmein they came singly or in parties; some were dressed in Burmese clothes. One had swam across from island to island.

The question has been asked whether it was necessary to evacuate Moulmein. Gen. Sir A. Wavell was for a long time of opinion that Moulmein should be held for a counter-offensive into Thailand even though later on he approved the evacuation of Moulmein as the only course open. But Lt.-General Hutton opines that the problem of Moulmein had not been easy. Once the Japanese had reached its outskirts in force it was really indefensible with less than two brigades, and no prepared defences existed. With the Japanese established to the north and south of the town and, probably, on the island of Chaungzon to the west, no communication with the town would have been possible; and in the absence of any naval or military boat crew, operations for relief, even if troops had been available, would probably have been impossible. Moreover, these craft could be brought under close-range fire from outside the perimeter.

It is also said that the retention of Moulmein would not have blocked the Japanese advance; that there was another route via Pa-an which, for an invader not dependent on motor transport, was in many ways preferable; and that if, of the small Allied forces available, the greater part had been isolated in Moulmein it is probable that they would have been cut off and destroyed. In such a case the occupation of Rangoon by the Japanese would have been carried out considerably earlier than it was.

---

[27] In fact, it was *55th Division* less the South Seas Detachment.
[28] The Japanese account of their operations in Burma (Dec. 41—Aug. 45) edited by 12th Army, 601/8255/H, p. 17.
[29] *USI Journal*, July 1942, p. 211.

CHAPTER X

Salween Line—Martaban and Pa-an

THE PLAN

With the loss of Moulmein, the Burma Army was thrown behind the line of the Salween river. According to the appreciation of Lt.-Gen. T. J. Hutton on 10 January, it was behind this line that the real defence of Burma was to be organised. The vital areas in this sector were considered to be Martaban-Bilin,[1] Ywathit-Bawlake, Mongpan and Takaw—the main road and track junctions leading to Rangoon. After the loss of Moulmein, however, the Divisional Commander was still anxious to withdraw to the Bilin river and give up Martaban. But the General Officer Commanding, Burma Army issued orders that the Division must fight hard to hold the line of the river Salween and that it should give no ground. It was accordingly to be spread as far as possible in depth so as to be able to deal with hostile infiltration across the Salween. The general plan was as follows:—The road and railhead at Martaban was to be held securely. All Japanese attempts to cross the river Salween or to land troops from the Gulf of Martaban were to be dealt with by immediate counter-attacks.

Martaban, Thaton, Bilin, Kyaikto, Papun and Pa-an were to be strongly held, and the main road and railway from Martaban to the Sittang bridge, the gateway of Rangoon, were to be patrolled under Brigade arrangements.[2]

DISPOSITION OF THE FORCES ON 1 FEBRUARY

16th Indian Infantry Brigade

On 1 February, the position was as follows[3]:—The 16th Indian Infantry Brigade was composed at first of the 2nd Battalion, King's Own Yorkshire Light Infantry, 1st Battalion 7th Gurkha Rifles Regiment, the 1st Royal Battalion 9th Jat Regiment, the 4th Battalion Burma Rifles, the 8th Battalion Burma Rifles and 5th Mountain Battery. Until the 8th Battalion Burma Rifles came into the Brigade, the 3rd Battalion 7th Gurkha Rifles less 2 companies was to remain under the command of the 16th Brigade. Brigade Headquarters was at Thaton.[4] The area of responsibility was to be Kamamaung, Pa-an, Martaban, Thaton and Duyinzeik (nearly a thousand square miles). The main task was to hold

---

[1] *War Diary*, 17th Indian Division, General Branch, Appendix I.
[2] The Divisional and 46th Brigade Commanders felt that Martaban was too isolated from Thaton and Pa-an to be defended. Brig. R. G. Ekin, *Actions at Martaban and Pa-an, Narrative*, Microfilm D/167/391 ff.
[3] See sketch map accompanying Divisional Operation Instructions, *War Diary*, General Branch, 17th Indian Division.
[4] 'Here Liaison was established with the District Commander and local rubber planters who, incidentally afforded great help...'. *War Diary*, 16th Indian Infantry Brigade.

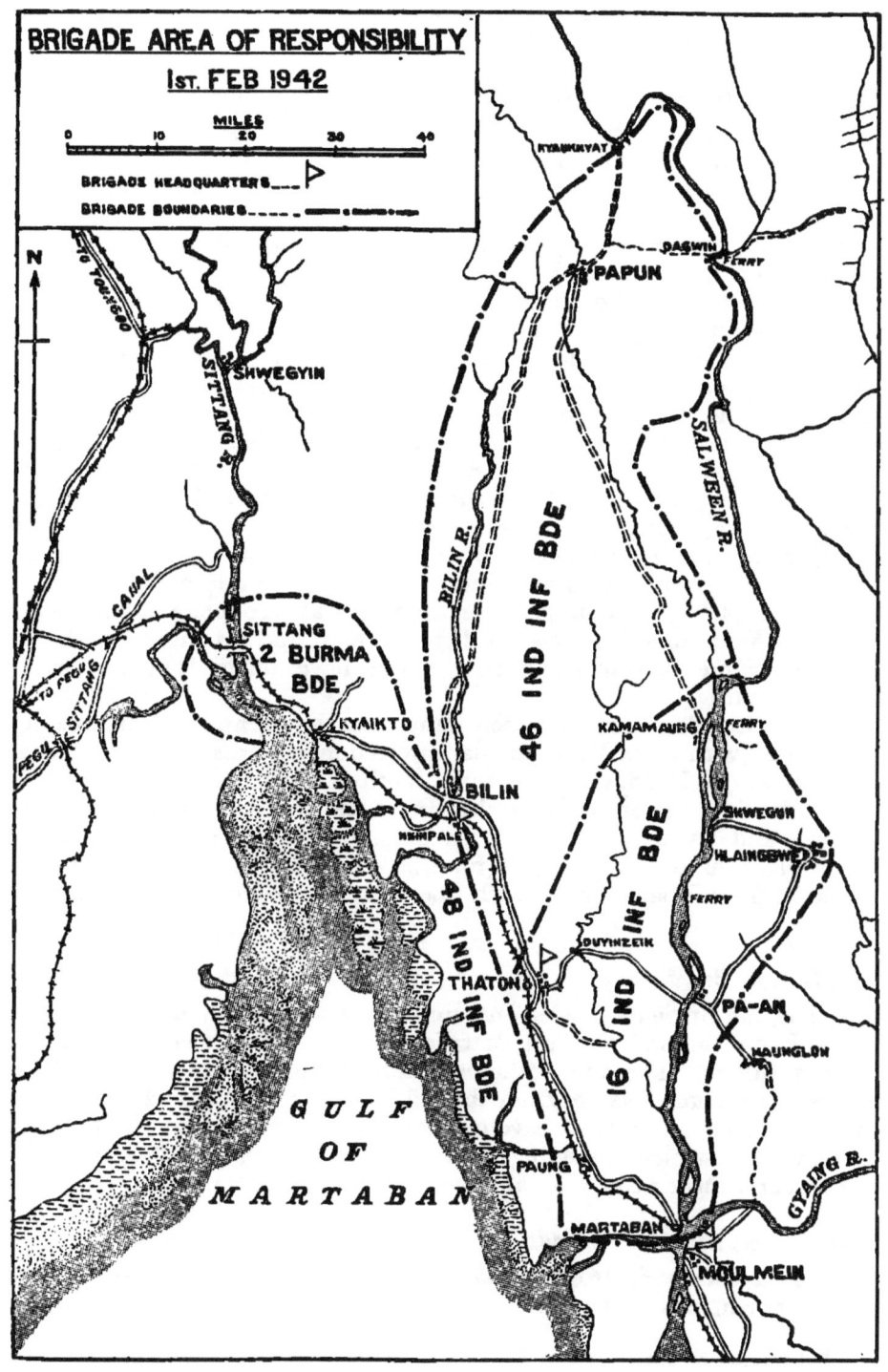

Martaban strongly, watch and guard the ferries at Shwegun and Kamamaung and patrol the Thaton-Martaban road.

46th Indian Infantry Brigade

The 46th Indian Infantry Brigade was disposed behind or north of the 16th Indian Infantry Brigade. It was one of the Division's oldest brigades and was the first reinforcement to arrive in Burma towards the end of January. It consisted of three battalions, the 7th Battalion 10th Baluch Regiment, the 5th Battalion 17th Dogra Regiment and the 3rd Battalion 7th Gurkha Rifles Regiment. The first and third disembarked from India without transport, which did not arrive till 30 January. On 16 January, they were moved by rail from Rangoon and joined the 17th Indian Division. They were then ordered to the area about Bilin where they were joined by the 2nd Battalion King's Own Yorkshire Light Infantry. The 5th Battalion 17th Dogra Regiment arrived on 31 January, and on the next day joined Headquarters 46th Indian Infantry Brigade in the Hninpale area. Its M.T. was also left behind. The Brigade consisted of young troops, milked as it had been often and heavily. Individual training was not up to standard. An influx of new officers and quick promotions had thrown additional burden on the more experienced officers. Moreover, it had been meant for Iraq where it was intended it should complete its training. The training was also on a higher scale of M.T. With all this it was excellent material and six more months of training before it reached Burma would have made it a far better fighting unit.

This Brigade's area of responsibility was Kyaukhnyat, Kamamaung and Bilin, with a small triangular projection towards Thaton. Headquarters was at Hninpale, three miles south of Bilin. The Brigade's task was to hold Papun strongly as also the ferries over the Salween river at Degwin and Kyaukhnyat. The 7th Battalion Burma Rifles was temporarily placed under the Brigade for this purpose.[5] It was also to patrol the road Bilin-Thaton and watch the approaches from the sea in that area.

2nd Burma Brigade

The 2nd Burma Brigade consisting of the 4th Battalion 12th Frontier Force Regiment and the 3rd Battalion Burma Rifles was to guard the Sittang Bridge. The 2nd Battalion Burma Rifles was to take over local protection around Kyaikto from the 3rd Battalion 7th Gurkha Rifles with two companies. It was to have one company watching the Sittang river estuary for possible sea landings and keep a reserve of one company. On 2 February, these tasks were allotted to the 2nd Burma Brigade.

48th Indian Infantry Brigade

The coastal strip from Martaban in the south to the Sittang bridge in the north, was to be watched by the 48th Indian Infantry Brigade.

---

[5] The object of mixing Burma Rifles Battalions in each Indian Infantry Brigade was to whip up the former's fighting spirit as also to get interpreters and guides to the Indian battalions.

This Brigade had arrived from India in Rangoon on 31 January.[6] It consisted of three regular Gurkha Battalions, the 1st Battalion 3rd Q.A.O. Gurkha Rifles, the 1st Battalion 4th P.W.O. Gurkha Rifles, and the 2nd Battalion 5th Gurkha Rifles, all withdrawn from the North-West Frontier and equipped on a lower scale for service overseas. It had received only three months' training in M.T. and modern weapons (Brens, 3" and 2" mortars, Thompson Sub-machine guns). It went to Burma on a special scale of transport consisting of mixed M.T. and mules. But it arrived without its transport and was therefore held in Army reserve. It was later ordered up to the Bilin river to join the 17th Indian Division which it did on 17 February. The Divisional Commander was, however, asked to keep this Brigade concentrated and not use it until there was a real necessity to do so.[7]

REORGANISATION—5 FEBRUARY

On 5 February the following moves and reorganisations were ordered. They were to be completed between 6 and 8 February. The object was "to reduce troops in the 16th Indian Infantry Brigade area, to rest tired units and to make the defence more mobile and more offensive".[8] The 46th Indian Infantry Brigade was to take over from the 16th Indian Infantry Brigade. The former's area of responsibility was lessened by more than half to a line running from Tilon, a village 13 miles north-east of Pa-an, to Naungala, a Railway Station three miles north by west of Thaton. North of the line it was the responsibility of the 16th Indian Infantry Brigade with Headquarters at Hninpale. The 46th Indian Infantry Brigade was to consist of 5th Mountain Battery, the 2nd Battalion King's Own Yorkshire Light Infantry, the 3rd Battalion 7th Gurkha Rifles, the 5th Battalion 17th Dogra Regiment, the 7th Battalion 10th Baluch Regiment and the 4th Battalion Burma Rifles less one company. Headquarters was at Thaton. The 16th Indian Infantry Brigade was to consist of the 1st Battalion 9th Royal Jat Regiment, the 1st Battalion 7th Gurkha Rifles and 8th Battalion Burma Rifles (less one company) in the area Hninpale-Bilin, one company of the 8th Battalion Burma Rifles to be at Kamamaung, the 2nd Battalion Burma Rifles at Papun and one company of the 4th Battalion Burma Rifles at Shwegun. Thus the actors were to change as fast as the scenes. On 7 February the relief move began and was completed by 9 February. The plan remained the same as that on 1 February, except that Martaban was to be held "by mobile and offensive action rather than by static defence".[9] The invader was to be contacted boldly, watched continuously and attacked vigorously. He was to be allowed no further advance.

[6] This Brigade is in some records erroneously called a Brigade Group. It had no artillery or Field Company R.E., or C.M.P. Shortage of these three arms was a contributory cause to the loss of Burma.
[7] On the day on which the Brigade moved up to the Bilin river, the 1st Battalion 4th P.W.O. Gurkha Rifles was in action at 1630 hours and on the next day the 2nd Battalion 5th Gurkha Rifles was engaged with the Japanese who had landed on the coast—*War Diary*, 48th Indian Infantry Brigade.
[8] *War Diary*, 17th Indian Division, General Branch, Appendix No. 7.
[9] This change of strategy was greatly responsible for the abandonment of the strong Salween line.

The points made out by Gen. Sir. A. Wavell during his visit to Kyaikto from Java on 6 February were:

"We must allow the enemy no further advance. Offence is the best means of defence. We must eventually get back that part of the Tenasserim we have lost." And the Divisional Commander's instructions on operation and mobility stressed the need for holding to, and counter-attacking if lost, certain key-points of which Martaban and Pa-an were the most important, for watching the line of the Salween and for patrolling the main Martaban-Thaton, Kyaikto-Sittang road. Strong road-blocks were to be established at suitable places. As regards the offensive, information of Japanese troops numbers and concentrations was to be obtained from local agents, patrols were to push out and gain contact with the invader. Both the 46th and 16th Brigades were to start mobile columns consisting of one company from each battalion. These columns were to move very light with a radius of action of about three days. Such a course would give them control over the no-man's land between the Burma Army and the Japanese and would also give the former troops the much needed training in jungle warfare.[10]

FURTHER RE-ORGANISATION—9 FEBRUARY

On 9 February, a further re-organisation was made. The 16th Indian Infantry Brigade got the 2nd Battalion King's Own Yorkshire Light Infantry, but lost the 8th Battalion Burma Rifles and one company of the 4th Battalion Burma Rifles. The 46th Indian Infantry Brigade lost both the 5th Mountain Battery and the 2nd Battalion King's Own Yorkshire Light Infantry.[11] The 48th Indian Infantry Brigade came to consist of the 1st Battalion 3rd Q.A.O. Gurkha Rifles, the 1st Battalion 4th P.W.O. Gurkha Rifles, the 2nd Battalion 5th Gurkha Rifles and the 3rd Battalion Burma Rifles. The 2nd Burma Brigade consisted of the 1st Battalion the Cameronians, the 4th Battalion 12th Frontier Force Regiment, the 7th Battalion Burma Rifles and the 8th Battalion Burma Rifles. Though this was to be the permanent composition of Brigades in the 17th Division it was also stated that "operational requirements will inevitably cause Battalions to be placed temporarily under command of Brigades which are not their own".[12]

On 9 February, the 46th Indian Infantry Brigade took over the forward area from the 16th Indian Infantry Brigade. The troops under it were disposed as follows:—

(a) MARTABAN: 3/7 Gurkha Rifles and one company Koyli.
(b) THATON: HQ 46th Brigade and Signals, 12th Mountain Battery, 60th Field Company Sappers and Miners (less detachment), Koyli (less one company), 2 companies 1/9 Jat, the 4th Battalion Burma Rifles.
(c) DUYINZEIK: 5/17th Dogra Detachment, 60th Field Company.

---

[10] *War Diary*, 17th Indian Division 'G' Branch, Appendix 8.
[11] *Ibid.* Appendix 'A' for Appendix No. 9.
[12] *War Diary*, 17th Indian Division, General Branch, Appendix 9.

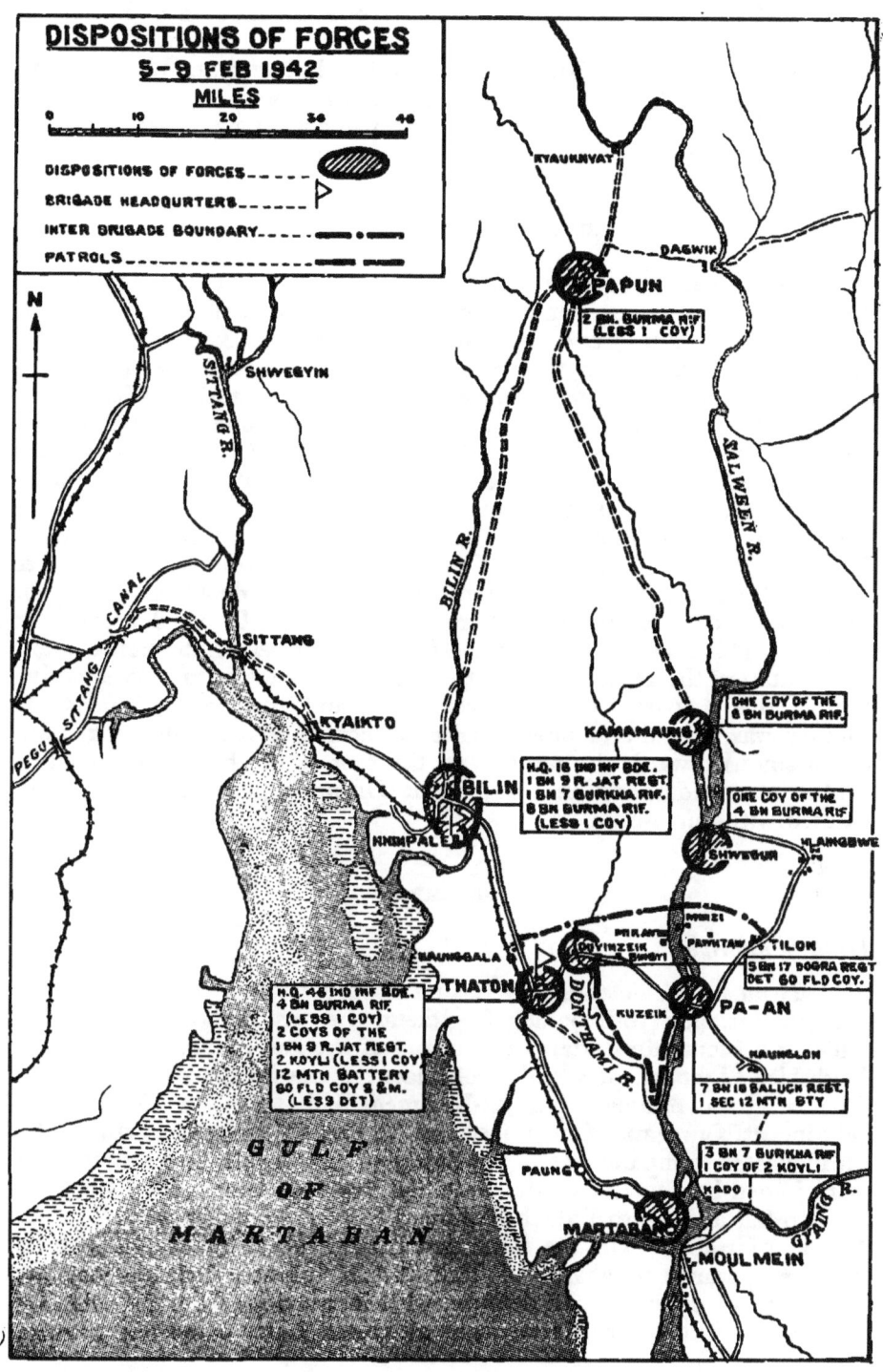

(d) PA-AN: 7/10th Baluch, one section 12th Mountain Battery.

(e) Two launches patrolled the Donthami river from Duyinzeik to the south and up the river Salween to Pa-an.

Thus it will be seen that the Brigade was covering an area, 40 miles from north to south and 23 miles from west to east.

THE DIFFICULTIES OF DEFENCE

In spite of these reinforcements, reorganisations and ambitious plans, the situation was serious. Information of the Japanese plan, strength and dispositions was scanty and they could cross and attack anywhere across the Salween, or the coast to Martaban Bay. No air support for troops was possible, there being only a total of eight fighters and six Blenheims; the A.V.G. was threatening to leave Burma any time. Above all the Burma Army had to face a second Japanese division.[13] The 17th Division was required to cover a most extensive and difficult tract of country extending from the Salween north-east of Papun to the Sittang river in the west and the coastline in the south. Martaban in a direct line is more than fifty-five miles distant from Kamamaung. The country, very broken and jungle-clad as it was, increased the problems of defence. Along the coast was a flat and narrow belt much intersected by tidal creeks and streams. This area and some of the flat lands bordering the Salween and its tributaries, the Donthami and the Yanzalin, were given to the cultivation of rice. Apart from the coastal belt and the riverine tracts, the country was rugged and jungle-clad and became increasingly broken and mountainous towards the north. At the foot of the hills were extensive rubber plantations and in 1942, about Hninpale, large areas were also planted with sugar-cane.

MARTABAN

Upto 7 February

Martaban was defended by the 1st Royal Battalion 9th Jat Regiment, the 7th Battalion 10th Baluch Regiment, the 3rd Battalion 7th Gurkha Rifles, 5th Mountain Battery, a company of the 2nd Battalion King's Own Yorkshire Light Infantry and a contingent of the Burma Auxiliary Force. The 1st Royal Battalion 9th Jat Regiment had moved in after rest and refitting at Kywegan. On 31 January, 'C' and 'D' companies and half of Headquarters company of the 3rd Battalion 7th Gurkha Rifles arrived and were joined by the rest of the Battalion five days later. On 1 February, the 7th Battalion 10th Baluch Regiment less 'D' company went into position at Martaban. On the same day Lt.-Col. H. R. Stevenson who had been temporarily in charge of 46th Indian Infantry Brigade took over command of the Martaban defence, with instructions from Brigade Commander to hang on to Martaban at all costs. Later came one company

---

[13] *33rd Division.*

of the 2nd Battalion King's Own Yorkshire Light Infantry (without artillery) and a Mountain Battery.[14]

Even with these forces the defence of Martaban was not easy. They had a big front, eight miles along the north bank of the Salween, to about eight miles up the coast from the estuary. They had also to watch the jungle-covered ranges or hills behind them in the north, to the west of which ran the main road and railway. The water-front was not wired. The river being tidal, at low tide mud flats and shallow water between some small islands on the mainland, gave the strung out forces still more area to be watched.

Before the arrival of Lt.-Col. H. R. Stevenson and the additional troops, the commanding officer of the 1st Royal Battalion 9th Jat Regiment, thinking that he was in an isolated position, had ordered a withdrawal; but his orders were countermanded by the Divisional Headquarters.

Even after the troop reinforcements had come the Jats had a very big front, eight miles up along the north bank of the Salween with the wharves and ware-houses and the railway station all to be held in detail. Two companies of the 7th Battalion 10th Baluch Regiment were, one, to the right and, the other, to the left of the Jats and a company of the 3rd Battalion 7th Gurkha Rifles was also on the left. 4MM Guns were sent to Martaban Point to bloster up point defences. A mortar detachment was also placed on river bank west of the railway station with instructions to bomb any movement.

On 1 February, RAF bombed Kado opposite Martaban across the Salween. The coast about eight miles from the estuary was patrolled by the 3rd Battalion 7th Gurkha Rifles, in reserve about three miles north of Martaban. From the first day of the defence the troops sustained casualties from air action and there was regular and heavy shelling from Moulmein, and mortar fire from an island in the middle of the Salween river. On 2 February, seven boats each capable of carrying 50 men were observed reaching Kawkami Kyun, an island east of Martaban; 5th Mountain Battery engaged the target. The Japanese were also reported moving down in dark hours (0100) between Katpali Kyun island and the mainland. 'B' company the 7th Battalion 10th Baluch Regiment opened fire and later sent a fighting patrol across. Next day 'A' and 'B' companies crossed over to Katpali and took positions there. On 4 February, RAF bombed the island of Kawkami Kyun and caused considerable confusion among the Japanese there. A Japanese attempt to land from 50 small craft with tommy guns and grenades was also repulsed. The next day (5 February) also boats were seen moving up stream from Moulmein. All these probings were intended to test the defences of Martaban.

---

[14] *A brief account of Our First Action with the enemy* by Lt.-Col. H. R. Stevenson with a rough sketch. Also a *Revised Account, War Diary*, the 3rd Battalion 7th Gurkha Rifles. *Notes on the Defence of Martaban February 1942* by Lt.-Col. S. F. Harvey Williams, *War Diary*, 3/7th G.R. *War Diary* of 3/7th G.R. and Lt.-Col. A. F. Harvey's account give the date. Lt.-Col. A. F. Harvey's account says that one or two sections of artillery and one company of the Koyli arrived at Martaban with Lt.-Col. A. R. Stevenson. The order to hang on to Martaban at all costs was dictated by a desire to hold the Salween line and not by the desire "to give reinforcements expected in Rangoon time to land there". Lt.-Col. S. F. Harvey William's *Account*, p. 2.

Jats withdrawn—7 February

The force for the defence of Martaban was not strong. It was further thinned when the 1st Royal Battalion 9th Jat Regiment and 7/10th Baluch were withdrawn to Bilin. The 3rd Battalion 7th Gurkha Rifles took up the positions from them. On the night of 6-7 February, the Jats had carried out certain demolitions in Martaban prior to the move to Bilin and had marched a company down the road. These troops were observed by the Japanese in the light of the flames and believing that Martaban was being evacuated they sent a landing party across in boats. 'A' company of the Jats engaged them with machine-gun fire and sank them.[15] The Battalion then withdrew to Bilin on 7 February. On the same day the 7th Battalion 10th Baluch Regiment positions were also taken over by the 3rd Battalion 7th Gurkha Rifles. Even the artillery was taken away from Martaban. The only troops left in Martaban were 3/7th Gurkha Rifles and one company of 2nd Koyli.

New Dispositions of 3/7th G. R.

The new dispositions of the 3rd Battalion 7th Gurkha Rifles were as follows:—On the right were 'C' company and one company of the 2nd Battalion King's Own Yorkshire Light Infantry; 'A' company was at Martaban Point; 'B' company was to the left and 'D' company was in reserve with the main Battalion Headquarters. Advanced Battalion Headquarters was just behind Martaban Point. There were no other troops between Martaban and Thaton, 36 miles away. Martaban was as good as abandoned.

PA-AN

We must now turn to another and more important theatre, Pa-an. Pa-an was a village in the Thaton district but, there, as at Shwegun and Kamamaung, was a ferry to cross the river Salween. Two tracks from Kawkareik led one to Pa-an and the other through Hlaingwabe to Shwegun. From the west bank of the Salween, ran an all weather motor-road to Thaton, Bilin and Kyaikto. There was also a track leading to Bilin and Kamamaung.

The Japanese 33rd Division

The Japanese force which had made its appearance in the Pa-an area during the last week of January consisted of units of the crack *33rd Division* fully blooded in China.[16] It was a more seasoned formation than the *55th Division*. It had been organised one year earlier than the latter. Its troops had been drawn from earlier formations (*2nd* and *19th Divisions*) and it had seen service in China for nearly two years. When organised in Sendai in March 1939, it consisted of *Divisional Headquarters. Headquarters Infantry Group, 213th, 214th and 215th Infantry Regiments* and

---

[15] Statement by 2/Lt. A. Balls, *War Diary 1/9th Jats.*
[16] History of the Japanese *Fifteenth Army*-SEATIC Bulletin No. 245 (601/7785/H), pp. 22 ff. History of Japanese *33rd Division* HQ, ALF, SIAM, 601/7725/H. History of the Japanese *Fifteenth Army*, ALF, SIAM, Weekly Intelligence Summary No. 7, (601/7720/H).

a full complement of *Transport Reconnaissance, Engineering, Ordnance Signal, Medical,* and *Artillery* units. Landing in China three months later, it saw there almost continuous service. Early in 1941 Lt.-Gen. Sakurai Shoso assumed command and in December 1941, the Division concentrated in Nanking.

When war broke out, the *33rd Division* was incorporated into the *Fifteenth Army* and transferred to Thailand in three groups. The first group to leave was the main force of the Division including *215th Infantry Regiment* which had been located separately; it disembarked at Bangkok on 10 January 1942. The second group known as the *Araki Detached Force* consisting of *33rd Infantry Group, 213th Infantry Regiment* (less the 2nd Battalion) and the *Mountain Artillery Regiment* landed at Bangkok on 26 February; the third group consisting of *2nd Battalion 213 Infantry Regiment* and *6th company* of the *Mountain Artillery Regiment* landed at Bangkok.

From Bangkok the main force took the route which the *55th Division* had taken and concentrated in the Sawankhalok-Phitsanulok-Rahaeng area. Here it undertook the reconstruction of the Rahaeng-Mae Saut road and for this purpose despatched *33rd Engineering Regiment.* The Division marched from Phitsanulok to Rahaeng, on foot, and from there the Division's spearhead, *215th Infantry Regiment,* dashed to Pa-an through Mae Saut and Kawkareik. The task of the *33rd Division* was to advance parallel to the *55th Division* so as to be able to cut off and annihilate the Burma Army retreating before the *55th Division* and thus prepare the way for the crossing of the Sittang at Mokpalin.

Brushes in the Pa-an Area upto 7 February, 1942

On 31 January, the 1st Battalion 7th Gurkha Rifles had taken positions along the western bank of the Salween opposite Pa-an with the object of preventing a crossing of the river. During the first week of February there was much activity in this area. In spite of inferiority in numbers and trained units of the Japanese they opposed, the Gurkhas acquitted themselves well. On 1 February, the 4th Battalion Burma Rifles was despatched to watch the ferries at Shwegun and Kamamaung with the special task of "reporting Japanese movements, engaging small parties and if possible gaining identifications." On the same day, the 7th Battalion 10th Baluch Regiment took over the defence of the Duyinzeik ferry; it was a vulnerable bamboo-raft ferry across the Donthami river, and was the sole link between Thaton and Pa-an. Sappers and Miners did excellent work in repairing and keeping the ferry in action.

The Gurkha Battalion maintained a standing patrol of one platoon of 'A' company on the east bank of the Salween in Pa-an itself. On 1 February, eight Japanese drove into Pa-an, hoisted a flag on a building, but soon got away. The next day at 0630 hours a Gurkha patrol was attacked first by the Japanese patrol and then by the Japanese cavalry. The patrols gave a good account of themselves and were supported by M.M.G. and L.M.G. fire from the opposite shore. The Japanese also replied with machine-gun and mortar fire. But as they were heavily out-numbered the Gurkhas made their way back to the Battalion lines and the Japanese occupied Pa-an. The Gurkha officer, a Jemadar, with two men held off the invaders while the patrol got away. In the evening the Battalion positions were heavily shelled by Japanese heavy mortars and light artillery.[17]

On 3 February, there was a brisk exchange of fire across the stream. On 4 February, a company patrol had a brush with the Japanese at Pa-an; for the first time close air support was given when three Blenheims escorted by fighters thrice bombed the Japanese positions in Pa-an. In view of the increasing activity in this sector, one company of the 2nd Battalion Burma Rifles was despatched to Pa-an (on 4 February) to guard the ferry and also report hostile movements. On the report of a police officer that a party of the Japanese had crossed the Salween at Dagwin, east of Papun, the Gurkhas sent strong patrols but the latter did not contact any Japanese.[18] On 7 February, there was a combined air raid and shelling on the 1st Battalion 7th Gurkha Rifles positions at Pa-an, as also an air raid on Thaton. Information was also received that a police officer had shot three Japanese Intelligence Officers in Udaung, a village 13 miles north of Pa-an. The maps in their possession showed the crossing places and the 17th Indian Division positions in detail and also indicated the Japanese plan of attack. The Gurkha Battalion therefore sent a patrol some miles north to one of the crossing places indicated but found no signs of activity. On 8 February, the Gurkha Battalion was relieved by the 7th Battalion 10th Baluch Regiment and as the change over was taking place, Japanese aircraft noticed it; the Battalion positions then came in for heavy bombing and mortar fire.

MARTABAN

7-8 February

To turn to Martaban, upto 7 February, the Japanese had been nibbling at its defences. On 7 February, some boats were seen moving up the river, a landing from the river side was anticipated and 'C' company of the 3rd Battalion 7th Gurkha Rifles was brought to the left flank in order to extend the line there.[19] As the lines were continually broken by shell fire and bombing, communication between companies and with Brigade Headquarters was difficult.[20] One platoon was detached and established in the pass across the range of hills ten miles north of Martaban to give warning of movements around the flanks of the Martaban garrison. M.T., patrol was maintained seven miles up the road leading north on the east side of the range and daily establishment there of an intelligence group was arranged.

Road-block and counter attack—9 February

On 8 February, Martaban was bombed. RAF Blenheims retaliating bombed Moulmein and Mutpun. On the morning of 9 February, a patrol was located for the first time, a small party of the Japanese trying

---

[17] *War Diary*, 1/7th G.R.
[18] *Situation Reports*, Part I, p. 50.
[19] *War Diary*, 3/7th G.R.
[20] The wireless set was always giving trouble and so they had to use the existing telephone line which was, with fifth columnists trying to cut it, a very unreliable means of communication.

to infiltrate around the east flank. The patrol, thereupon, opened fire and dispersed the invader. At this time the telephone line to the Brigade Headquarters at Thaton was cut and no wireless communication could be established. A party of signallers who moved up the main road to the west of the range to investigate the break, bumped on a strong Japanese road-block at milestone 8.[21] Two British officers and their orderlies who went up the east-side road on reconnaissance brought back news of a party of the Japanese 70 to 100 strong obviously preparing a road-block about five miles north of the left flank. Meanwhile, Observation Posts were reporting barges and boats crossing form Bilugyun and landing men on the seaward side. It seemed to the Officer Commanding that the defenders were being surrounded. He therefore gave orders at about 1400 hours for the two left flank companies[22] to attack the Japanese on the east road and moved the company of the 2nd Battalion King's Own Yorkshire Light Infantry to a position three miles up and astride the main road (west side) to face north for an all round defence. A water-front defence has thus changed into a land-front defence. The two companies sent north met and engaged the Japanese, and after a successful encounter they dislodged the latter off the road into the jungle towards the central hills and also removed the road-block. In this encounter occurred the first bayonet charge in the Burma Campaign. The men also brought back with them a truck load of small arms, uniforms, an infantry gun and a 3" mortar.[23]

Withdrawal—9-10 February

At about 1400 hours the Officer commanding observed a considerable number of Japanese (estimated by him to be one or two thousand) landing from the coast westward and moving north-west.[24] To him it looked as though they were moving to the road-block at milestone 8 on the Thaton road north of Martaban from where they could attack the city the next day. It was clear that the Japanese had by-passed Martaban and were in a position to attack it from the northwest. No good purpose could be served by holding the town any longer. Therefore, he decided to withdraw his force at night. A route to the east of the range was decided upon. As soon as darkness fell he detached 'D' company to cover the Thaton Road and a pass through the hills, and destroying all M.T. commenced withdrawal along the road to Thabyegon. He was determined to fight the way through. Fortunately they met no opposition and slipping through the Japanese positions in the jungle-covered hills, marched as much distance as they could. Late in the evening of the next day (10 February) they hit the Pa-an-Thaton road and arrived at Thaton on 11 February after a march of over fifty miles through marshes, muddy fields and waterless hilly jungles. 'D' company had been ordered to rejoin the main body by way of the pass. But it misinterpreted the orders and

---

[21] Only one man returned at about 1530 hours, Lt.-Col. A. R. Stevenson's account.
[22] *War Diary*, 3/7th G. R. has it as—'B' company supported by a platoon of 'C' company.
[23] *War Diary*, 3/7th G.R. Subsequent reports in papers attributed this success to the Koyli Company.
[24] In Lt.-Col. A. R. Stevenson's account the time given is 1800 hours. *War Diary*, 3/7th gives it as 1400 hours.

made direct for Thaton. It had to fight its way through a cordon put by the Japanese and reached Thaton after a few days. On the very day Martaban was evacuated, the Divisional Headquarters had decided to withdraw the force and had sent a Liaison Officer to communicate the message, but he was shot at the road-block at milestone 8 and the message was never delivered.

PA-AN

8-11 February

In the Pa-an area, on 8 February,[25] the 7th Battalion 10th Baluch Regiment was at Kuzeik, a village opposite Pa-an, across the Salween, and the 5th Battalion 17th Dogra Regiment was at Duyinzeik, while the 2nd Battalion King's Own Yorkshire Light Infantry less one company was at Thaton.[26] One Section of 16th Mountain Battery arrived on 9 February and went under command of the 7th Battalion 10th Baluch Regiment. The 2nd Battalion King's Own Yorkshire Light Infantry and the 5th Battalion 17th Dogra Regiment were to act as brigade reserve for a counter-attack role. The latter was to patrol daily up to the Baluch positions. The Baluch Battalion was to prevent the Japanese crossing into the area of Pa-an. It was also to maintain a twenty-four hour patrol up to Mikayin, ten miles north, and Pagat, three miles south of Kuzeik, in order to harass and delay Japanese advance. The patrols were, if necessary, to split into platoons, sections and even half sections. The country around Pa-an was thickly wooded which made patrolling difficult and loose.[27]

The telephone line between the Battalion Headquarters and the Brigade Headquarters was often cut by either Burmans or Japanese in Burmese dress. On 9 and 10 February, Thaton was bombed. There was considerable hostile reconnaissance of Kuzeik but there was no bombing. On 10 February, it was reported that the Japanese had struck out from Minzi, ten miles north of Pa-an, crossed the Salween at Mikayin and were heading for the Pa-an-Duyinzeik road to the south west. Orders were then issued by the Divisional Headquarters to open out and piquet the road.

The beginning of the engagement near Pa-an—Night 10-11 February

On the night of 10-11 February platoons of A and B companies patrolling south of Kuzeik were attacked and overrun. Another patrol

---

[25] *Situation Reports*, Part I, p. 55—"3/7th Gurkhas withdrew during night 10/11 after being heavily involved with enemy and carrying out bayonet charge, previously attributed to Koyli". Lt.-Col. A. R. Stevenson's *Account* gives 2015 hours as the time when the withdrawal commenced. Lt.-Col. S. F. Harvey Williams thinks this an error and gives 1915 hours as the time.

[26] Considering the importance of Pa-an the force kept there (one Baluch Battalion) was too small. A plan had been made by the Brigade Commander to reinforce it by the Dogra Battalion at Duyinzeik and two companies of Koyli from Thaton. The Divisional commander however could not construct a bridge across the Donthami river and the ferry which consisted of bamboo rafts could take only 2 lorries at a time and they took ten minutes to negotiate it. As a second best the Dogra Battalion had been asked to keep half their mules and some vehicles on the east bank of the river so that they might be able to move to Pa-an in an instant.

[27] *The War Diary* of 7/10th Baluch gives a detailed and pathetic account of the action at Pa-an.

(C company) which went to their help met a Japanese section and routed it. On finding that the Japanese had also landed in the rear, the patrol withdrew from the river side at 0230 hours but not before driving back with their light machine-guns and rapid fire, a company of the Japanese. The new positions were also heavily attacked but the patrol succeeded in withdrawing to the Battalion position after defeating Japanese attempts to surround it. An attack on the main Battalion position at 0400 hours was also beaten off by C company against whose sector it was launched. But the Japanese did not appear to have been in appreciable strength. Earlier the artillery had shelled Pa-an and possible Japanese-forming-up places on the west bank of the Salween, south of the ferry.

Japanese cross the Donthami river in small parties—11 February

In the morning (11 February) both Duyinzeik and Pa-an were continuously dive-bombed but only one casualty occurred owing to the excellent protection afforded by slit trenches. During the day from 1130 hours small parties of the Japanese were seen crossing Pa-an in dug-outs. Artillery and Machine-gun opened fire. The dug-outs beached on sands 100 yards up the river and the Japanese could be seen jumping out of their boats and making for the west bank.

Baluch dispositions on the eve of the main attack

In the evening the officer commanding of the Baluch Battalion sent a written report to 5/17 Dogras, in which he stated that the Japanese might attack them in strength that night (11-12 February) and that the Dogras would do well to take position along side the 7th Battalion 10th Baluch Regiment during the night itself. As communications with the Brigade Headquarters had ceased, the Dogras were asked to inform the former of the situation. At dusk patrols reported strong Japanese forces advancing from Pagat in the south. The Baluch Battalion positions in the wooded country north of the road running in a curve from the ferry to Duyinzeik were as follows:—'A' company less two platoons was just north of the ferry, 'D' company less one platoon was 350 yards to the north-west, 'B' company less two platoons was 425 yards to the west and 'C' company 425 yards to the south-west of 'A' company. Battalion Headquarters was in the centre of this ring and mortars were just west of 'A' company. It should be noted that the strength of 'A' and 'B' companies had been greatly reduced by casualties. The other platoons were on patrol. In the evening a party of the Japanese attacked a position, near the ferry. 'C' company counter-attacked and the Japanese broke contact and withdrew.

Attack on the Kuzeik positions—Night 11-12 February

During the night of 11-12 February a major action developed. The Japanese threw in a whole Regiment (*215th Infantry Regiment*). Two Battalions attacked while the third in reserve formed an outer cordon and also protected the Japanese from a counter-attack in the west. The initial attack came from the west. At about 0045 hours a section of 'C' Company on the Duyinzeik road was attacked and driven back with heavy losses. Soon came the attack on 'C' company itself. Using cat calls and chattering, the Japanese infiltered between 'C' and 'D' companies and at 0230 hours attacked the former from the rear. They also employed tracer ammunition (green, white and red) and Chinese crackers to draw fire and locate the positions of automatic weapons. Pressure on 'C' company became greater each half an hour. At the same time an attack in waves also developed from the north-west at the junction of 'B' and 'D' companies. Each wave contained several parties attacking at various sectors and each party consisting of ten to fifteen men armed with swords, bayonets, and grenades and supported by automatic weapons. These parties attacked in short rushes of 10-12 paces, lying flat on the stomach at the end of each rush. As the Japanese got close, the companies counter-attacked with the bayonet and *'dahs'*, killing or driving back the invader.

Between 0200 hours and 0700 hours 'C' company counter-attacked with bayonet every half an hour. Capt. Siri Kanth Korla, commanding 'C' company, fought with exemplary gallantry and inspired his men all the night. He himself led six bayonet attacks and his company fought magnificently. For his gallantry and leadership during these operations Capt. Siri Kanth Korla was made a Companion of the Distinguished Service Order.

At 0330 hours 'B' company which was reduced to 35 men was attacked in strength, surrounded and isolated. Soon 'D' company was also heavily engaged. Having driven a wedge between 'B' and 'D' companies the Japanese attacked Battalion Headquarters in small parties but these were mopped up. Now the Pioneer Platoon detailed as Battalion counter-attack reserve, forced the invader back in the second attempt, and established itself on the slopes between 'C' and 'B' companies. At 0450 hours breaking through 'D' company left flank the Japanese attacked the Battalion Headquarters, but after hand-to-hand fighting they were again beaten off. All this time 'A' company on Pagoda Hill was preventing the Japanese from breaking through from the east.

At this stage it was thought that though the situation was serious, the Battalion positions could be held if the Dogras arrived. Repeated attempts to establish communication with the Brigade Headquarters and the Dogras failed. On the morning of 11 February the Brigade Commander had heard by wireless of the situation at Kuzeik and had ordered the Dogras, less Headquarters Company and 'C' company at 1100 hours to counter-attack from the Duyinzeik direction. The Koyli companies at Thaton were also put in readiness to move. Unfortunately communication between the Baluch and Brigade Headquarters had by this time broken down.[28]

At 0550 hours 'C' company had been surrounded and 'B' company overrun. A Naik of the latter company though short of ammunition clubbed three Japanese to death with his tommy gun before he himself

---

[28] At approximately 1400 hours a wireless message was received at Brigade Headquarters. It purported to come from the Baluch Regiment. Using our code calls and signal procedure it informed the Brigade Headquarters that Japanese attacks had been beaten off and that all was well. It can now be safely assumed that this message was sent by the Japanese—11 February.

was killed. Capt. Siri Kanth Korla fought his way through to 'A' company and returned with the much needed ammunition. Soon 'D' company and the northern portion of 'A' company were also overrun. Japanese mortars now opened up with accuracy and effect. Infantry guns from Pa-an shelled 'A' company on the river front. The silence in the 'C' company direction was construed as its having been overwhelmed and overrun. With the platoons on patrol also cut off, the remainder of the Battalion (Battalion Headquarters and 'A' company personnel) formed near Pagoda Hill for a counter-attack on 'C' company position. They reached the objective at 0730 hours, the Japanese withdrawing in the immediate vicinity of the attack, but failed in their ultimate object, being beaten back by Japanese automatic fire.

Failure of the Dogra Battalion to counter-attack

The failure of the Dogras to counter-attack was a serious and costly mistake. True, they had been dive-bombed heavily by a large number of hostile aircraft at Duyinzeik at 0930 and 1230 hours, (11 February). Several casualties were sustained due to the men not occupying slit trenches. Later the Battalion advanced nine miles along the road when it met stragglers who said that all was well. Moreover, the spurious message from the Baluch Battalion had been repeated to the Dogras. The Battalion consequently returned to Duyinzeik and the counter-attack could not take place.[20]

Conclusion

Organised resistance was no longer possible and the Baluch Battalion position was completely overrun. Soon Japanese patrols could be seen mopping up isolated pockets of resistance. The casualties suffered were very high, and only a few remnants, presumably five officers, three V.C.Os and sixty-five I.O.Rs withdrew to Thaton through Duyinzeik. Among these several were wounded and a number including Capt. Siri Kanth Korla escaped after having been captured by the Japanese. The casualties on the Japanese side were also heavy. The tattered but glorious Battalion was at Thaton on 13 February and at Kyaikto on 14 where it had three days for reorganisation and refitting. It was then sent to guard a ration dump just outside the village of Mokpalin.

It was a young Battalion with very few old soldiers and a number of very young officers, but it had fought like veterans. Even when the Officer Commanding was killed the companies fought on under their own officers, as long as any organised resistance was possible. Although the Battalion had suffered terribly it had also exacted a heavy toll on the Japanese. "There is no doubt that this Battalion fought most gallantly whilst completely surrounded by superior numbers and it was only after all ammunition was exhausted that a small remnant was forced to surrender. Had the 5th Dogras carried out the counter-attack as ordered

---

[20] *The War Diary* of the Dogra Battalion merely states that "the Battalion returned to position at Duyinzeik without gaining contact with the enemy." Lt.-Gen. T. J. Hutton's report also simply says, "for various reasons the counter-attack did not take place".

there is little doubt that the Battalion would have been extricated and a considerable defeat inflicted on the enemy".[30]

MEASURES TO MEET THE THREAT TO DUYINZEIK

The crossing of the Salween in strength by the Japanese and the extinction of the force at Kuzeik necessitated the reorganisation of the defences. To replace the 7th Battalion 10th Baluch Regiment and to meet the new threat to Duyinzeik, the 1st Battalion 7th Gurkha Rifles was sent forward on 12 February from Bilin to assist in covering the Donthami river about the ferry area. To the right of this force the 4th Battalion Burma Rifles continued the line through Singyon, Zemathwe and south-west to the pass through the hills, about three miles from that village. One company of the 2nd Battalion King's Own Yorkshire Light Infantry held the area about Yinnyein. The remainder of this Battalion with the 3rd Battalion 7th Gurkha Rifles defended Thaton where it took up perimeter defence, whilst the two companies of the 1st Royal Battalion 9th Jat Regiment rejoined their Battalion at Bilin.[31]

ATTACKS ON THATON AND DUYINZEIK

During this period Thaton and Duyinzeik were subjected to frequent air bombing attacks. The former had been heavily bombed on 7, 9 and 10 Ferbuary. Heavy bombs were dropped; roads and telephones were damaged and a greater part of the town was destroyed by fire. Fifth columnists, usually in the guise of Buddhist priests, were most active. They signalled to the Japanese from the wooded heights above Thaton and also started fires in various parts of the town. The King's Own Yorkshire Light Infantry effectively cleared areas of the town of these priests, but all efforts to capture the signallers failed. It is of interest to note that the fifth columnists employed the same tactics in several other places later in the campaign.

In Duyinzeik everybody's nerves were in a bad state as they did not know from where and when the next attack would come. In spite of negative reports from the patrols, working in the enclosed country east of the Donthami, the Japanese opened a sudden and heavy bombardment of Duyinzeik and the ferry on the afternoon of 13 February. This lasted about forty-five minutes but was not followed by any infantry attack. It boiled to a *denouement* and it was obvious that the Japanese were testing the flanks of the defence. This bombardment and the previous aerial bombings had much disorganised the 5th Battalion 17th Dogra Regiment.

At the same time the detached company of the King's Own Yorkshire Light Infantry at Yinnyein was attacked by a small force on which numerous casualties were inflicted. Subsequently, after blowing up the

---

[30] Lt.-Gen. T. J. Hutton's *Report*, p. 23. The Report is wrong in saying that the Baluch Battalion fought for 48 hours. Actually the action near Pa-an lasted from 0045 hours to 0900 hours. The casualties suffered by 7/10 Baluch were 15 officers and some 400 men.

[31] Brig. R. G. Ekin's Narrative of *Actions at Martaban and Pa-an*.

road and railway bridges across the Yinnyein river the company withdrew to Thaton. It was not followed up. All patrols were actively patrolling.

Hutton's appreciation on 13 February

On 13 February the General Officer Commanding sent the following appreciation to the Commander-in-Chief, India:—Though they had every intention of fighting it out east of the river Sittang it was possible that exhaustion of troops available and continued infiltration might eventually drive them back to the river Sittang. Even there withdrawal of transport across the river would be difficult as, except for the vulnerable rail-road bridge, communications consisted of ferries of which one only had road connection, which also was under construction; but the large area west of the river Sittang consisted, before the monsoon, of open paddy fields, ideal for tanks and A.F.Vs. For this type of fighting however, more infantry was necessary. So the situation, until more infantry arrived and the Chinese Vth Army began to be available in Lower Burma, was bound to be critical.

The General Officer Commanding also prepared the world for the loss of Rangoon. "We shall exert every effort to defend Rangoon but if Pegu were lost, its fate would be more or less certain. In this event remnants of our forces would withdraw northwards towards Prome, covering the bases now being stocked in Central Burma and the road to India, with a view to subsequent counter-offensive. Toungoo and the upper reaches of the river Sittang would be covered by 1st Burma Division and Chinese Vth Army".[32]

The Commander of the 46th Indian Infantry Brigade then reported to the Divisional Headquarters that there appeared to be no substantial Japanese threat from the south and that the attack on Duyinzeik was probably a feint to distract attention whilst a crossing of the Donthami was made further north with a view to cutting the Brigade line of withdrawal. However, the Brigade was ordered to fight on the line Thaton-Duyinzeik.

Permission to withdraw from Duyinzeik—14 February

The Divisional Commander reported that, while he still had the 48th Indian Infantry Brigade intact and in hand, in the 16th and 46th Indian Infantry Brigades there was only one Battalion, the 2nd Battalion King's Own Yorkshire Light Infantry, in a fit state to fight. In view of the extent of his front and the condition of his troops he wished to withdraw to a better defensive position with a less extended front. While pointing out the necessity for fighting as far forward as possible the General Officer Commanding, Burma Army gave him permission to withdraw if and when he considered such a course essential.[33]

Next day, 14 February, the Army Commander was at the Divisional Headquarters and the situation was reviewed. In reply to a telephonic enquiry from Maj. Gen. J. G. Smyth, Brig. R. G. Ekin replied that he

---
[32] *Ibid.* Appendix 'A'.
[33] Lt.-Gen. T. J. Hutton's *Report*, p. 23.

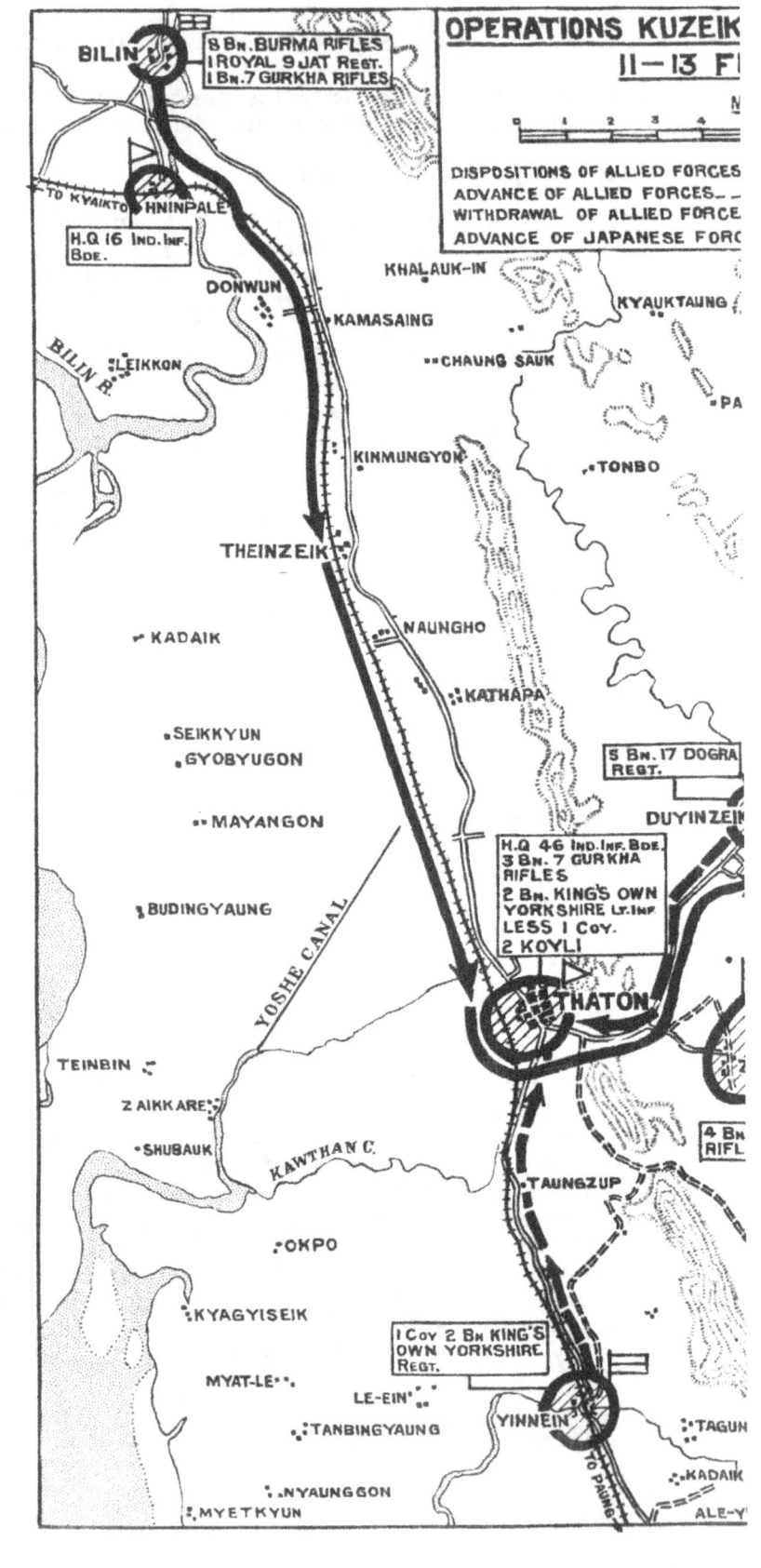

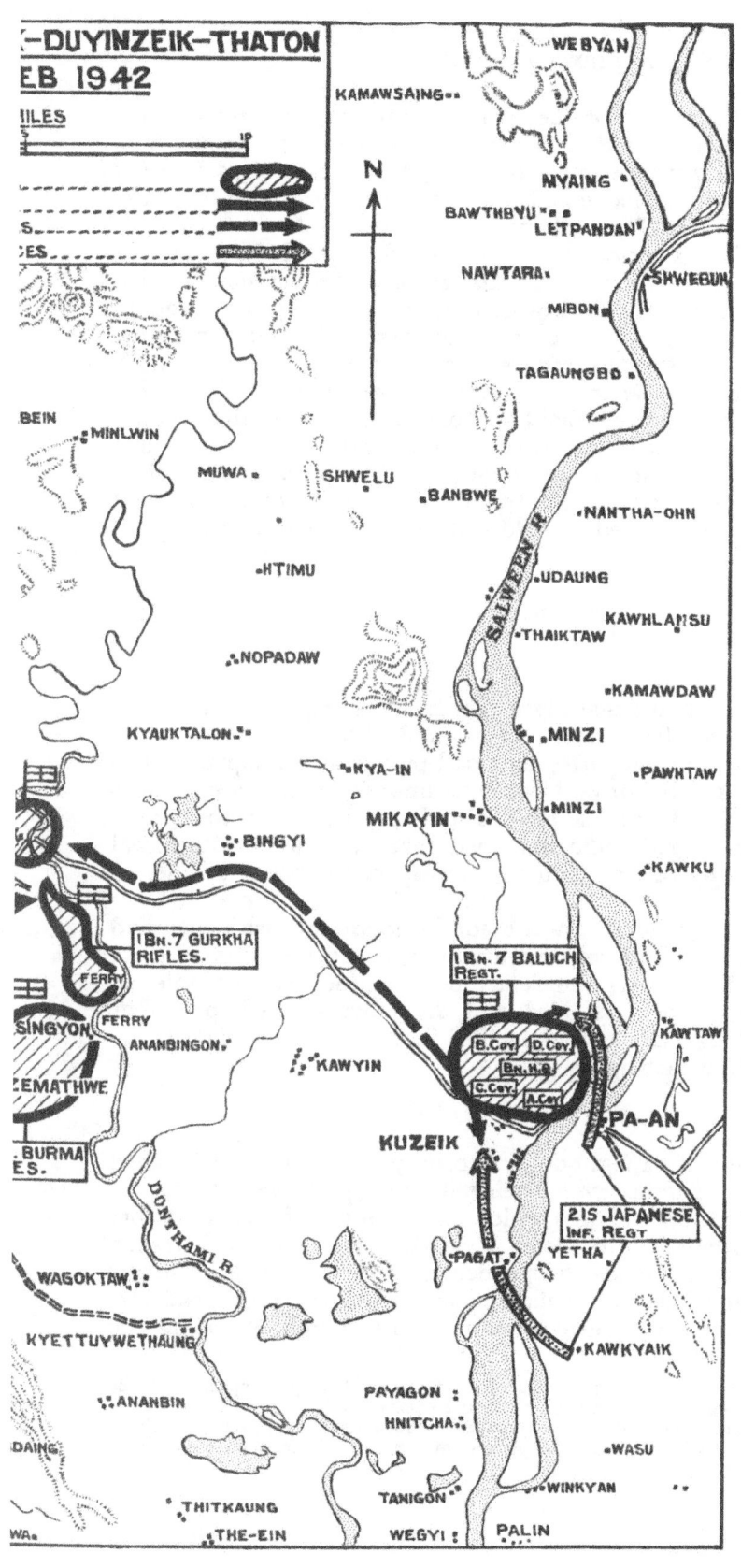

was more strongly than ever of the opinion that the Japanese had by-passed the Thaton position and were moving round his left flank. Subsequent events proved this view to be correct as the Japanese *33rd Division* had crossed the Salween at Pa-an and was advancing north-west on tracks east of the line Martaban-Thaton-Kyaikto.

The same day it was decided to concentrate the 17th Indian Division behind the Bilin river. At 1730 hours that evening the Divisional Headquarters issued orders to the 46th Brigade to withdraw to Kyaikto at once; Thaton was to be completely evacuated by first light next morning. Demolition of as many wooden bridges as possible along the road south of the Bilin river was to be carried out. At the same time the 16th Indian Infantry Brigade was ordered to hold a strong defensive position behind the Bilin river from approximately Leikkon to Payaseik. This was a line that the Divisional Commander was confident he could maintain against the Japanese. The 48th Indian Infantry Brigade was to act as divisional reserve and was to be prepared to hold a defensive line from Taungzun behind the Thebyu river.

WITHDRAWAL

14 February

Shortly after 2000 hours that night very heavy firing broke out round Thaton on the west, north and east. It was undoubtedly the work of the fifth columnists, probably supported by small parties of the Japanese who had infiltrated through the forward positions since coloured tracer ammunition was employed. It had a most disquieting effect on the young soldiers of the 46th Brigade who imagined that the line of withdrawal had been cut.[34] Many drivers of motor transport temporarily deserted their vehicles.[35]

Nevertheless, the withdrawal was made in accordance with plan and its arrangement, within the brief time available, constituted a good piece of staff work. Scattered units and detachments spread over ten miles of jungle country had to be assembled and the movement of some four hundred vehicles along a single road detailed in time to ensure the evacuation of Thaton before first light.

15 February

During the hours of daylight on 15 February the Thaton force halted under cover in the Kinmungzon-Theinzeik area protected by the 1st Battalion 3rd Q.A.O. Gurkha Rifles which had been sent forward for that duty. The 5th Battalion 17th Dogra Regiment and the 1st Battalion 7th Gurkha Rifles, withdrawing independently from Duyinzeik by jungle paths via Methawabo-Thegon-Chaungsauk and so to the main road also halted. That evening the Brigade continued its march, dropping the

---

[34] *War Diary* of the 3rd Battalion 7th Gurkha Rifles says, "everyone appeared to be firing in different directions with no idea of where the enemy was".
[35] It is to these operations that the Japanese Account of the *Fifteenth Army* (601/7785/H, p. 23) refers when it speaks of pockets of resistance it brushed aside on its march to the Bilin river.

5th Battalion 17th Dogra Regiment at milestone 58 on the main road to provide a forward outpost line and patrols to cover the main Bilin position of the 16th Indian Infantry Brigade. On crossing the Bilin river the 2nd Battalion King's Own Yorkshire Light Infantry and the 1st Battalion 7th Gurkha Rifles also joined the 16th Indian Infantry Brigade, whilst the remainder of the 46th Indian Infantry Brigade continued to Kyaikto to man the defences of that place. Troops forming part of the Kyaikto defences were to come under the command of Brigadier Ekin who was to be responsible for road protection from excluding the Sittang bridge to including the landing ground at about milestone 75.[36]

Comments

The withdrawal behind the Bilin River pushed back the line of defence further west and the untenable line of the Salween was given up. Opinions will differ as to the wisdom of this step. There were some who considered the Salween with its numerous ferries across as a sufficiently strong obstacle to hold back the invader. This opinion regarded the Bilin as no obstacle owing to its shallow stream and felt that by this course the Japanese were brought very much nearer the Sittang bridge, a keypoint for the advance on Rangoon. There were others who believed that the sound strategic plan was to withdraw to the defensive area of the Sittang river and there prepare to fight on the ground of their own choosing. According to this view, the dispositions at Martaban, Thaton-Pa-an and the Bilin River were for political reasons and against the best military judgment of the Divisional Commander. There is no doubt that once the Salween was pierced and the Japanese forces had infiltrated across, with their strategy of infiltration and encirclement, a continued resistance in the Salween sector by the 17th Indian Division would have been a dangerous adventure which would have involved its complete annihilation. Effective reinforcements with considerable air support alone could have retrieved the situation, but the British resources at the moment seriously limited the scope of these measures. A vigorous counter-attack was of course indicated, but with exhausted troops and some ill-trained raw units and the declining morale of some Burmese units, this step was impracticable.

The task of the Divisional Commander was extremely arduous and

---

[36] The Japanese account of the operations in the Pa-an area is quite different from that given in 17th Division and 7/10th Baluch *War Diaries*. About the first engagement in Pa-an the Japanese accounts say: "In the early part of February 1942 *33rd Division vanguard (215th Inf. Regt.)* made a surprise attack on a force of about 400 of 17th Indian Division in the Pa-an area, (here is a reference to the engagement of 2 February). The enemy was routed and it fled to the west bank of the Salween river". The action actually took place on the west bank and the Burma Army unit engaged in it was only a Battalion patrol of one platoon.

The Japanese account goes on: "The Division (33rd) halted along the line of the Salween river, re-organised and prepared for the crossing after about ten days of preparation. The vanguard crossed the river in a native craft and defeated the enemy force of about 3,000 at Duyinzeik (here is obviously a reference to the engagement at Kuzeik with the 7th Battalion 10th Baluch Regiment). The battles round (around) Pa-an Duyinzeik were the first encounters with the British and Indian troops and the Victory raised the morale of the Division considerably". As a matter of fact Duyinzeik was only bombarded on 13 February. This was not followed by an infantry attack..... SEATIC BULLETIN No. 245, *History of the Japanese Fifteenth Army*, p. 23.

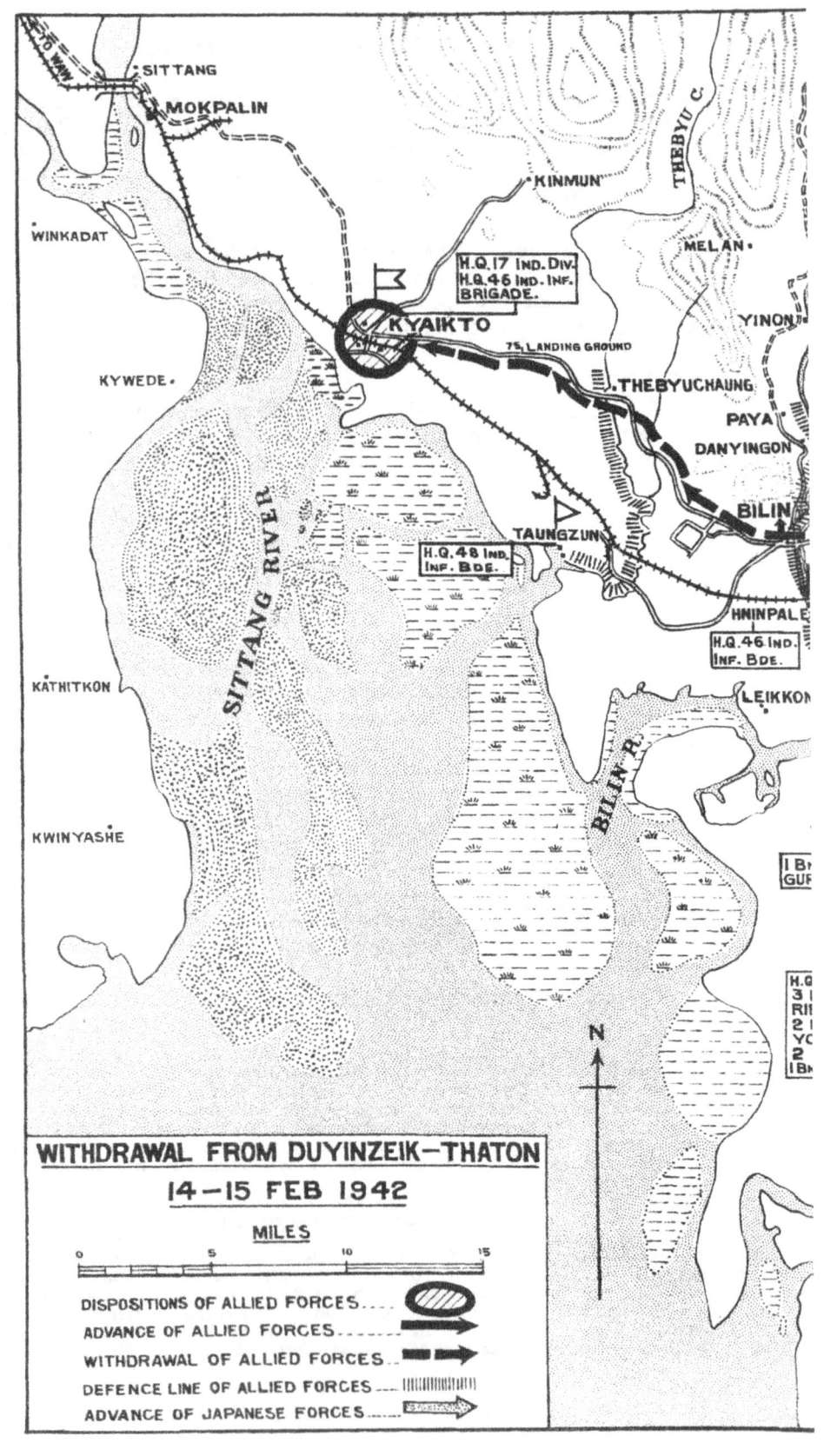

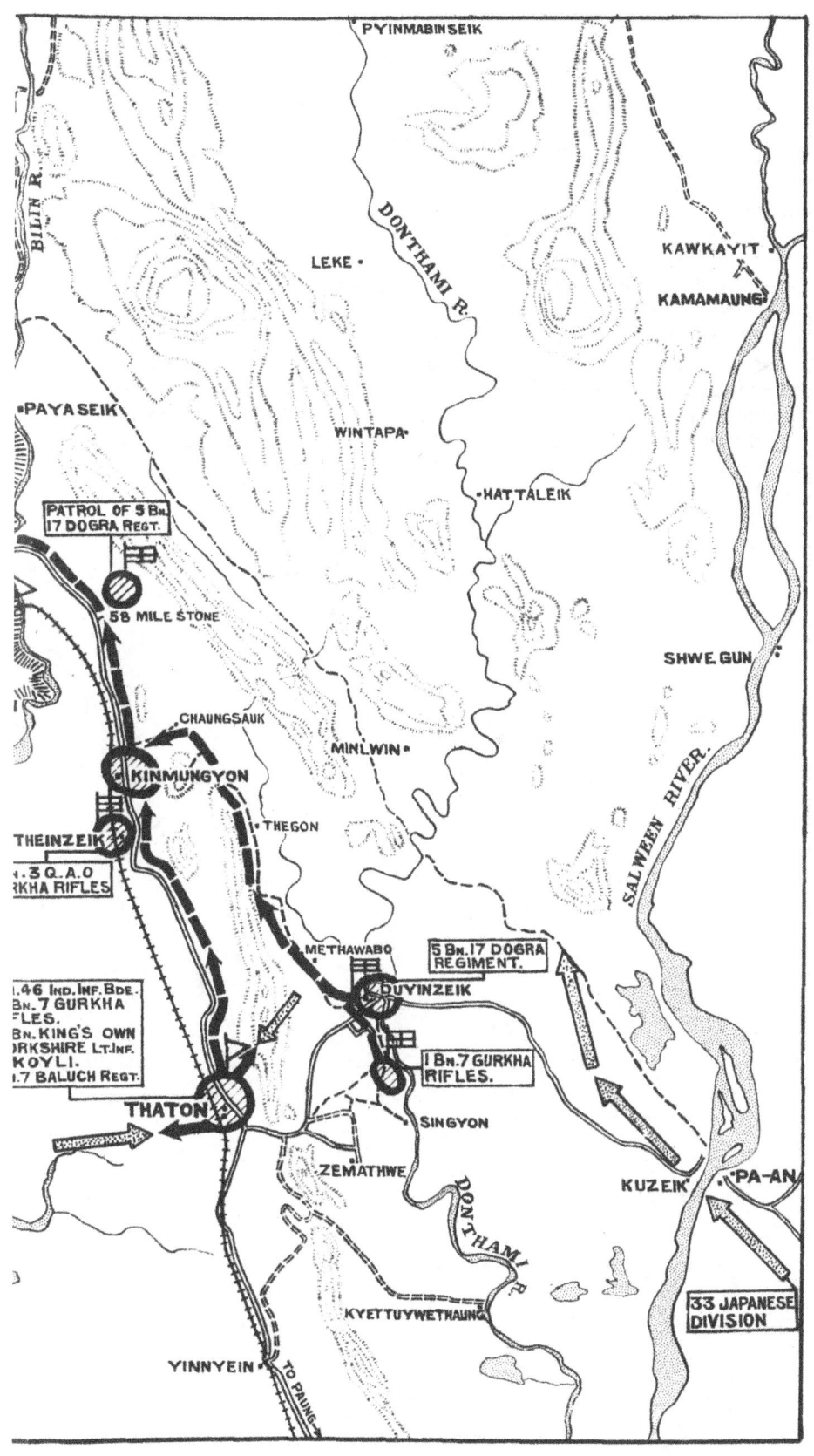

was made more difficult by reason of inadequate forces and half-trained troops. The Army Commander was in Rangoon and could not easily control the operations in detail particularly when the events moved so rapidly. This circumstance led to the demand for the appointment of a Corps Commander. But all that came was the posting of Brigadier D.T. Cowan to the 17th Division to work unofficially as Brigadier General Staff, before assuming command of the Division.

The loss of the Salween line of defence was a severe blow which raised the morale of the Japanese divisions considerably and placed the invader in a favourable position to race for the Sittang bridge and pound the British-Indian defences in that area. Lack of appreciation of Japanese strategy, the rawness of some units and the hostile attitude of the Burmese population along with the thickly wooded terrain affording facilities for infiltration and the highly trained Japanese forces, all these factors were responsible for one more set-back and withdrawal westwards.

CHAPTER XI

Bilin Line

THE BILIN LINE—ITS WEAK LINKS

As soon as it was complete Maj.-Gen. J. G. Smyth reported to the Army Headquarters his withdrawal to the Bilin river. He was confident that he could hold this line and check a further advance by the Japanese. He was also aware that any withdrawal west of the Bilin would inevitably endanger the communications between Rangoon and the north of Burma since the Sittang river, the next defensible line of importance, was at no great distance from the road and rail links between Rangoon and Mandalay.

The Bilin river ran through the Salween and Thaton districts. It presented no formidable obstacle, for except in the monsoon the river is nowwhere more than knee deep and is thus fordable throughout its length. The country in and around the Bilin line also presented few difficulties. Save for the coastal belt it was hilly and covered with considerable patches of jungle. There were also extensive rubber plantations.

Most units of the Burma Rifles and certain Indian Army Battalions were no longer fit for further fighting without rest and reorganisation. If the invader could be halted, it was hoped, as soon as reinforcements were available, to withdraw these tired units west of the Sittang.

Moves to protect the north of the line

Whilst the main Bilin position was being manned, certain moves were carried out to protect the area to the north of the 17th Indian Division. The 2nd Battalion Burma Rifles still covered Papun, and was controlled directly by the Divisional Headquarters. It was to be prepared to withdraw if necessary either on to Shwegyin or Toungoo. One company of the 8th Battalion Burma Rifles at Kamamaung was to remain at that place but was to come under the orders of the 2nd Battalion Burma Rifles and to be withdrawn if necessary. The company of the 4th Battalion Burma Rifles at Shwegyin was to remain in its old position and if forced to withdraw was to join the company of the 8th Battalion Burma Rifles. The 2nd Burma Brigade which was to consist of units that had become disorganised and required time to refit, was ordered on 16 February, to Nyaunglebin to ensure that the line of the Sittang should be patrolled and, if possible, prepared for defence. River crossings were to be watched, and the important railway bridge across the Sittang near Mokpalin, now boarded over to take road traffic, was to be safeguarded. At this time the 2nd Burma Brigade comprised the weakened 3rd and 7th Battalions Burma Rifles. The former of these was stationed at Mokpalin.[1]

---

[1] *War Diary*, 17th Indian Division 'G' Branch, *Operation Instruction* No. 10.

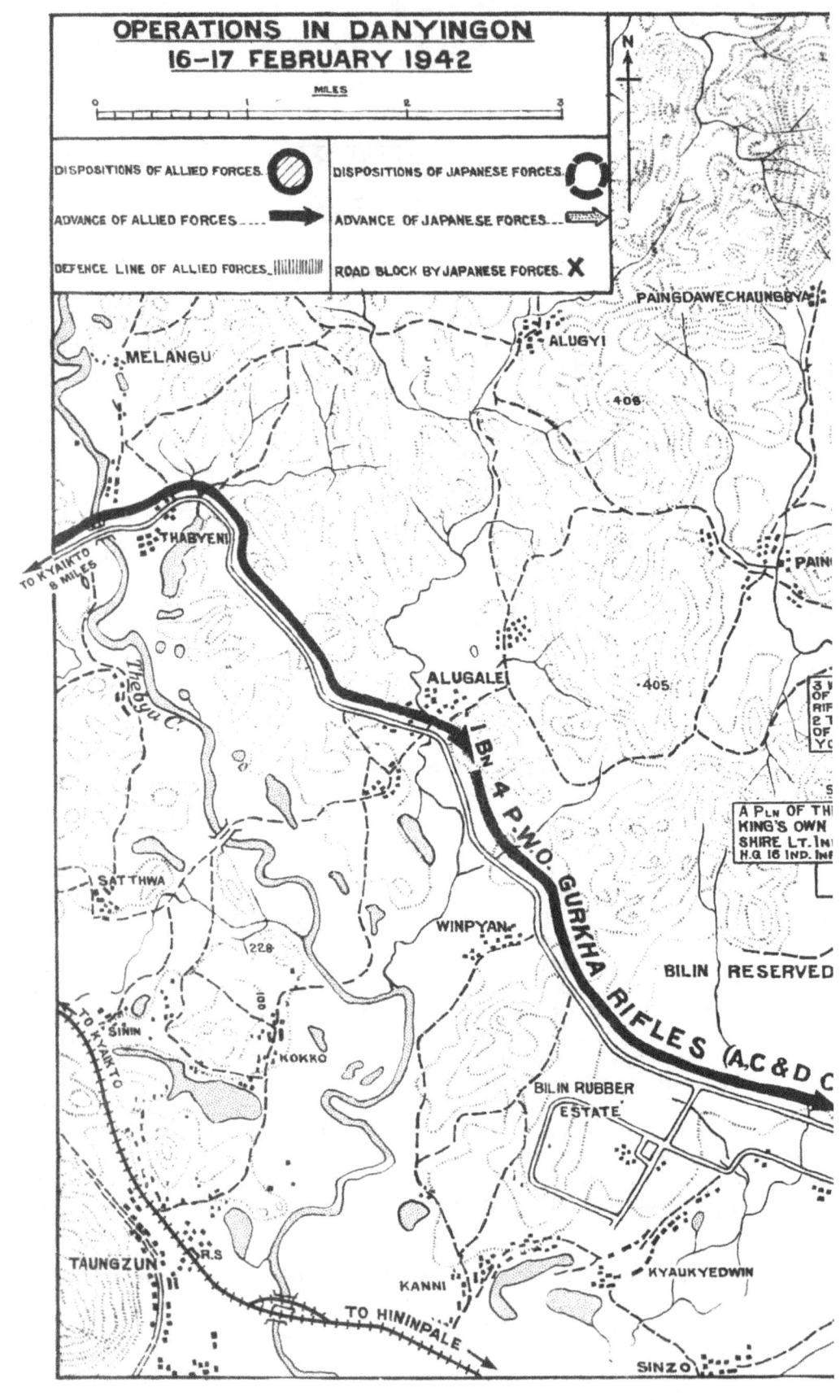

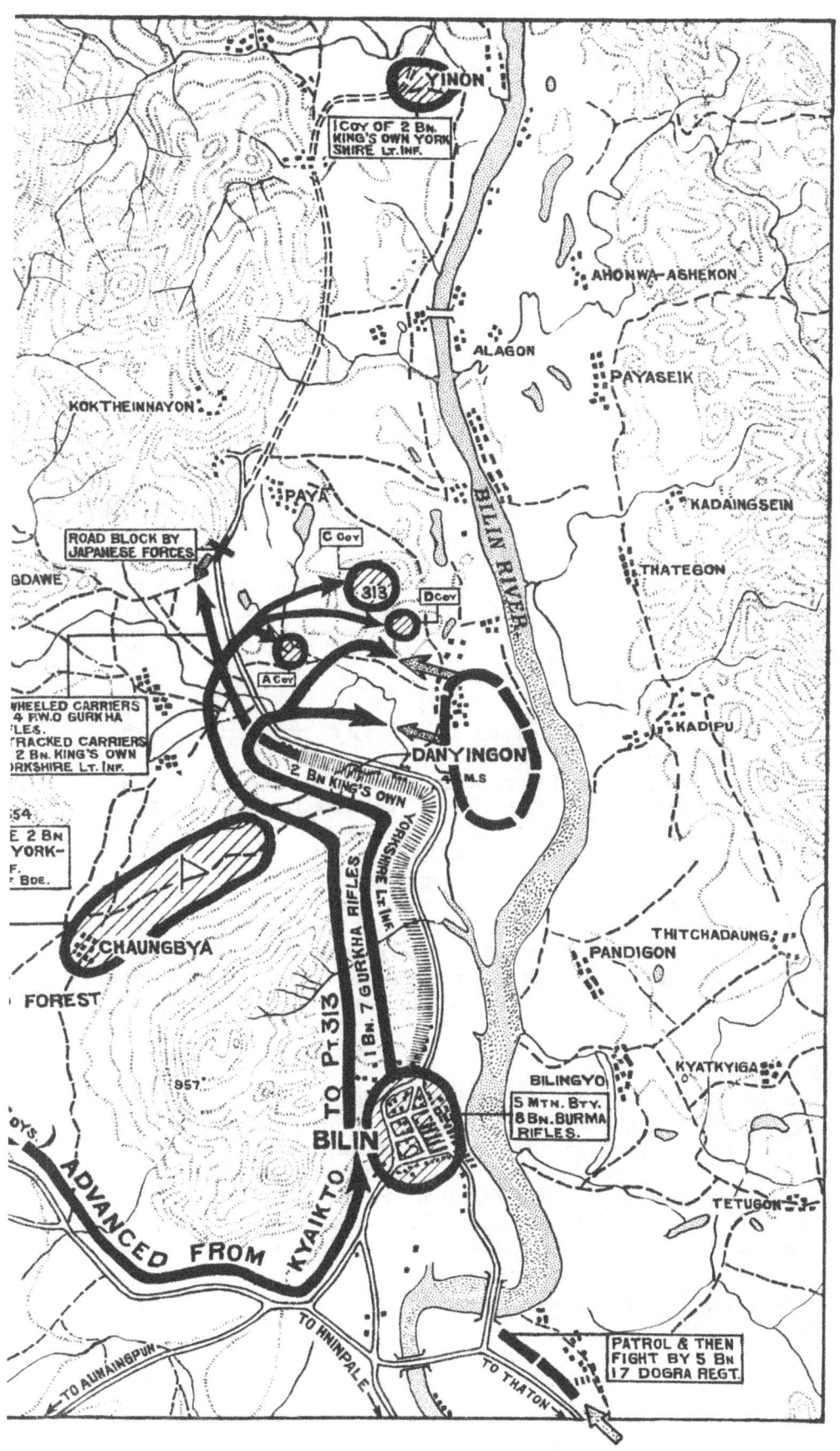

That these steps were necessary was indicated by a report on 16 February that a large Japanese force had crossed the Salween at Yinbaing, 8 miles north east of Kamamaung.[2] The company of the 8th Battalion Burma Rifles at Kamamaung sent out a patrol and established contact with the invaders (later identified as Thais) whose strength was estimated at eight hundred. They had been endeavouring to collect bullock carts near Mepli, west of the Salween and 12 miles north-west of Tinbaing. Effort was made to prevent this as it amounted to a threat to the left flank of the Bilin line.[3]

FORCES DEFENDING THE BILIN LINE

The 16th Indian Infantry Brigade under Brig. J. K. Jones was entrusted with the defence of the Bilin line, and was ordered to take up a strong defensive position behind the Bilin river from approximately Leikkon on the river estuary to Payaseik in the north with a detached company further north at Yinon. The line of the river near Payaseik was found to be unsuitable, and it was decided to prolong the position from Bilin to include the village of Danyingon, Point 313, and Paya. Menegontha was to be watched and particular attention was to be paid to demolitions and anti-tank defence. Patrols were to work well forward to watch all approaches. For this operation the Brigade had under its command the following units:—

    5th Mountain Battery,
    12th Mountain Battery,
    One Section 5th Field Brigade, B.A.F. (2 × 18 pounders in an anti-tank role),
    One Section Armoured Cars, Rangoon Battalion B.A.F.,
    The 2nd Battalion the King's Own Yorkshire Light Infantry,
    The 1st Royal Battalion 9th Jat Regiment,
    The 1st Battalion 7th Gurkha Rifles,
    The 5th Battalion 17th Dogra Regiment,
    The 8th Battalion Burma Rifles—less one company at Kamamaung.

The first five units had been transferred from the 46th Indian Infantry Brigade on arrival at Bilin. No. 1 column of F.F. 2 was to continue to operate on the coast as far as the Bilin river. No. 2 column was to be based on Melan and watch all approaches to the west flank of the area.[4]

Their dispositions

On the right the 1st Royal Battalion 9th Jat Regiment held a three mile front from Shwele up to and including the road bridge across the river just south of the Bilin village. 'A' company was on the right, an open flank, 'B' company in the centre, 'D' company on the left. 'C' company was in reserve. The Battalion Headquarters was north of Hninpale to the right of 'D' company. 'A' company was to patrol deep on the open right flank up to Leikkon and across the river. The defences

---
[2] *Ibid.* Sheet for 16 March.
[3] *War Diary*, 17th Indian Division 'G' Branch.
[4] *Ibid*, Appendix 16.

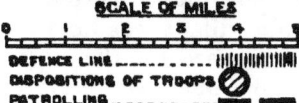

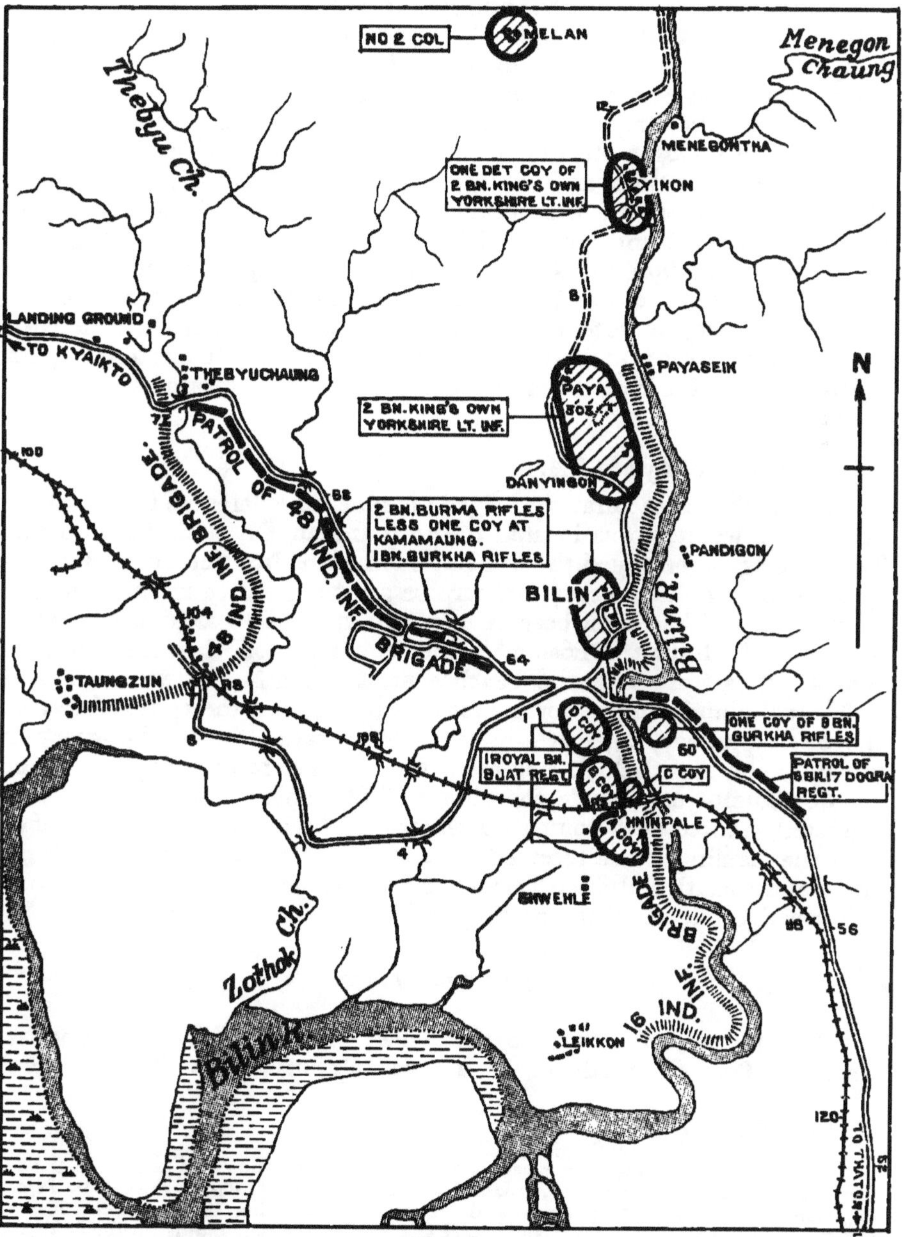

of the Jats were only weapon pits there being no wire or communication trenches with alternative positions dug out. There was no signalling equipment whatever.⁵ Bilin village was held by the 8th Battalion Burma Rifles with one company forward on the high ground east of the river astride the main road where a block was established. North of Bilin, the line was to be continued by the 2nd Battalion King's Own Yorkshire Light Infantry covering the villages of Danyington and Paya. A detached company of the Battalion was to be further north of Yinon. The whole front from Shwele to Yinon was eleven miles long.

To cover the preparations of the main defensive positions the 5th Battalion 17th Dogra Regiment occupied outpost positions three miles east of the river Bilin and maintained patrols down the Thaton road. These outpost positions were occupied early on 16 February when the Battalion arrived from Thaton with the 46th Indian Infantry Brigade.

The 1st Battalion 7th Gurkha Rifles acted as brigade reserve. Behind the main position the 48th Indian Infantry Brigade was to act as divisional reserve and carry on reconnaissance and be prepared to hold a defensive position from Taungzun behind the river to Thebyu. It was also to patrol during the day the road from excluding the landing ground to excluding Bilin.

Defences in the Kyaikto Area

The 46th Indian Infantry Brigade manned the defences in the vicinity of Kyaikto wherein was located the 17th Indian Divisions Headquarters. To this Brigade belonged the 4th Battalion 12th Frontier Force Regiment which had lost all its heavy kit, surplus arms and stores in the defence of Moulmein, and had later been reorganised at Kyaikto as divisional troops to the 17th Indian Division.⁶ One company of this Battalion ('B' company) was guarding the beaches at Kyaikkatha (a few miles south of Mokpalin and 7 miles north-west of Kyaikto) and the approaches along the Sittang estuary against a possible sea attack. On 18 February the 7th Battalion 10th Baluch Regiment went on a nominal duty of guarding a ration dump just outside the village of Mokpalin. As already noted it consisted of three weak companies which had been reorganised and refitted after the mauling it had received at Pa-an. The 3rd Battalion 7th Gurkha Rifles and the 4th Battalion Burma Rifles (less one company) were also not fit for active role requiring as they did reorganization and rest.

JAPANESE MOVES

The Japanese followed up the Allied withdrawal from Thaton very closely.⁷ They were advancing in two columns; *55th Division* by the

---

⁵ *War Diary*, 1/9 Jats.
⁶ *War Diary*, 4/12 F.F.R.
⁷ All the Japanese accounts except two do not even mention the action on the Bilin Line. In one account they say, "After the engagement in Pa-an the *215th Infantry Regiment* began its advance towards the Bilin river brushing aside pockets of enemy resistance. On arrival at Bilin it was found that the enemy had blown up the bridge and withdrawn". *History of Japanese 15th Army SEATIC Bulletin No. 245*, 601/7785/H, p. 23. "......the Division (33rd Division) traversed Phitsanulok and Raheng on foot and passed Mae Saut, the Burma-Siam frontier and then advanced to Pa-an and Bilin where

main road, and *33rd Division* by the jungle tracks north-east of it. Their intention as already noted would appear to have been to fight frontally with *55th Division* whilst *33rd Division* by-passed the 17th Indian Division position and moved directly on to the vital Sittang bridge. During the march of the 46th Indian Infantry Brigade from Thaton elements of the Japanese *33rd Division* must have been in close proximity to the Allied columns comprising the battalions of the 17th Dogra Regiment and the 7th Gurkha Rifles. The Japanese reached the Bilin river simultaneously with the 46th Indian Infantry Brigade.[8]

First contact at Danyingon—16 February

The 2nd Battalion the King's Own Yorkshire Light Infantry moving into its position on the morning of 16 February came into contact with parties of Japanese troops in Danyingon village.[9] The Japanese did not suspect that they were so near the Allied troops and one party was surprised when washing round a village well. The men fled, but there were considerable numbers of the hostiles close by and an action soon developed. That day, repeated attempts were made by the King's Own Yorkshire Light Infantry to clear the village. 'D' company of the Battalion suffered heavily in carrying out these attacks, but could not dislodge the Japanese. Eventually a line was established along the main road south and west of the Danyingon. At noon a party of 100 Japanese troops was reported in the area four miles from Bilin. They wore white *longyis* and used grenades.[10] Propaganda leaflets had also been dropped in the area by Japanese planes.

One company of the King's Own Yorkshire Light Infantry was sent to Yinon in motor transport under escort of three tracked carriers of the Battalion. These were the only carriers in the Brigade and they continued to maintain contact with the Yinon company.

In the southern sector of the front the day passed quietly. There was some firing by Dogra patrols; here the Japanese were obviously feeling their way forward.

Further attacks in the Danyingon-Paya sector by 1/7 G.R.—16 February

At 2100 hours on 16th February, the 1st Battalion 7th Gurkha Rifles was ordered to the Danyingon-Paya sector to restore the situation there. It had arrived at Bilin only a few hours earlier after a trying thirty-six

the *215th Infantry Regiment* fought against Indian troops (about one Battalion strong"). *History of the 33rd (Jap.) Div.* 601/7725/H, p. 2.

The latter account would make us believe that it was the *215th Infantry* that fought the Bilin action. But the parties of Japanese who infiltrated along the coast on 18 February certainly belonged to the *55th Division*. The fact that all Japanese accounts say that their Divisions crossed the Salween on 21 February shows that the Japanese troops engaged in the Bilin fighting (16-20 February) were the spearheads of the two Divisions.

[8] *55th Division* crossed the Bilin river with the help of motor-power floats and a couple of native boats. The troops engaged Allied troops as fast as the fording was accomplished. The Division was therefore strung out in a long column after it crossed the river—FEC, GHQ, ATIS. Answer to ques. 46 by the Commander *55th Division*.

[9] War Diary of the 17th Division has it as Papun, War Diary 1/7 Gurkha Rifles gives it as Paya and War Diary 3/7 speaks of a village 4 miles north-east of Bilin.

[10] The Japanese say that except in rare cases and that too for want of uniform, they did not disguise themselves in civilian clothes, *Japanese Operation in South East Asia, 1941-1945*—Operations of 18th Division, Hukaung & Mugaung Area, 601/10111/H.

hour cross-country march from Duyinzeik. It was thus by no means fresh. Yet in this, its first attack in jungle country, the Battalion went forward with great determination. At 0820 hours on 17 February the Battalion attacked the village of Danyingon,[11] just north of the bend at milestone 4. One company attacked from the north of the village while the other two attacked from the west. Half an hour later heavy hand to hand fighting developed and both sides rushed forth with terrific war cries. The companies to the west then moved to the eastern side, leaving behind only a few pockets of resistance. To help the company attacking from the north the officer commanding sent another strong company. But as the Japanese were established in much greater strength than had been estimated the attack on the village was in the end unsuccessful. On the Allied side casualties were fairly heavy.[12]

It therefore became necessary to cover the tracks running south of the main road between Paya and Danyingon. A platoon of the King's Own Yorkshire Light Infantry was brought into brigade reserve and together with the Brigade Headquarters protected the track leading to Chaungbya through a gap in the hills.

Point 313—17 February

In order to stabilise the situation in the northern sector the Divisional Commander whose aim it was to fight hard to hold the Bilin line, ordered the 48th Indian Infantry Brigade to send forward the 1st Battalion 4th P.W.O. Gurkha Rifles. This Battalion had not been in action before. It was at once hurried forward in motor transport and at 1730 hours carried out an attack on Danyingon and Point 313 and the bamboo jungle to the south of it. 'D' and 'A' companies were detailed for the jungle while 'C' company moved against point 313. Fire support was given by a section of 5th Mountain Battery and mortars of the 2nd Battalion King's Own Yorkshire Light Infantry, the 1st Battalion 7th Gurkha Rifles and the 1st Battalion 4th P.W.O. Gurkha Rifles. 'C' company reached its objective without firing a shot and the dense jungle with which the hill was covered showed no sign of its having been penetrated by Japanese troops.[13] For the next two days it continued to hold this hill. A Forward Observation Officer was posted on it. Good observation from this position made possible accurate artillery and air bombardment of Japanese concentrations on the eastern bank and Japanese columns by-passing the divisional position to the north.

Meanwhile 'D' company had lost direction but 'A' company encountered the Japanese and in the brush that followed sustained some casualties, one killed, eight wounded and three missing. Later it dug in the very dense jungle about 60 yards forward of the road for the night.[14] At the same time 'D' company dug itself in the ditches in the open fields.

---

[11] *War Diary*, 17th Indian Division 'G' Branch gives a detailed account.
[12] 2 Officers and 17 other ranks were killed, 25 were wounded and 30 were missing.
[13] *War Diary*, 1/7 Gurkha Rifles gives 18 February as the date. Though *War Diary*, 1/4 Gurkha Rifles is a reconstructed one the date therein given has been accepted.
[14] *War Diary*, 17th Division 'G' Branch refers to it as 'hard fighting leaving reserves very light'.

Road-block north of Bilin

About 1800 hours (17 February) report was received that the Japanese had established a road-block (that acebogey of Japanese strategy) at mile 6¼ from Bilin between the detached company, the 2nd Battalion King's Own Yorkshire Light Infantry in the north (Yinon) and the rest of the 16th Indian Infantry Brigade. Three wheeled carriers of the 1st Battalion 4th P.W.O. Gurkha Rifles and two tracked carries of the 2nd Battalion King's Own Yorkshire Light Infantry went up the road to investigate.[15] The latter came under heavy Japanese fire and returned because "their company was cut off". The three Gurkha Battalion carriers also came under heavy small arms and grenade fire and returned a little later unable to clear the road-block.

Withdrawal of Dogra Battalion to west bank

With the 1st Battalion 4th P.W.O. Gurkha Rifles established on Point 310 and in the southern part of Danyingon, the 1st Battalion 7th Gurkha Rifles was withdrawn to the west of the main road with forward companies holding the hills astride the road north-west of Point 310 and maintaining contact with the troops there. The heavy fighting in the Danyingon sector had left the Brigade without reserves and at 1300 hours (17 February) the 16th Indian Infantry Brigade Headquarters ordered the 5th Battalion 17th Dogra Regiment to cross to the west bank of the river as soon as possible and occupy positions behind the 1st Royal Battalion 9th Jat Regiment.

In the morning patrols of the 8th Battalion Burma Rifles had reported a force of 800 troops in long trousers at Yinbaing a few miles north-east of Bilin. But tactical reconnaissance of Yinbaing showed no activity. Hence "the withdrawal of the Dogra Battalion commenced at 1415 hours. Japanese parties approaching from north got astride the road between Battalion position and the bridge and captured five trucks. The Battalion line of withdrawal was now altered to the railway bridge* south of the road bridge and the ford farther east. The withdrawal was however closely followed by the Japanese who opened up accurate mortar fire from high ground to the north-west of the Battalion position. Though very few casualties were sustained owing to the small danger area of the Japanese mortar bomb",[16] the Battalion is reported to have withdrawn "in complete disorder, without rifles, automatic weapons and in some cases boots".[17] By 1530 hours, however, the crossing was completed and half an hour later the Battalion moved to a defensive position in support of the 1st Royal Battalion 9th Jat Regiment at the junction of the Bilin and Thaton cross-roads. The forward company of the 8th Burma Rifles was meanwhile overrun by the Japanese. Though the 1st Royal Battalion 9th Jat Regiment had been ordered to blow up the road bridge, after the Dogras had withdrawn, Headquarters 48th Indian Infantry Brigade (to which the Battalion was now temporarily attached) left it to

---

[15] Lt.-Col. C. Foucar gives the date as 18 February. See *War Diary 1/4 G.R.* for 17 February.
* The bridge was later demolished at about 1700 hours.
[16] *War Diary 5th Dogras* (February—p. 3).
[17] *War Diary 1/9 Jats.*

the Battalion Commanding Officer's "discretion whether the bridge was to be blown or not, an extraordinary and quite incorrect transference of responsibility".[18] However the bridge was finally blown up at about 1700 hours, all the Dogras having crossed by then.[19]

Jat positions attacked—February 17

In spite of the blowing of the road bridge the Japanese followed up in small numbers. At first the left flank of the Jat Battalion came under rifle fire, making movement to and form their weapon pits impossible. A little later the mortars of the 'B' company in the centre came under Japanese mortar fire, but were saved from destruction by being moved to a previously prepared alternative position. During the evening and night the Japanese were probing for weak spots all along the river front. About 2100 hours a section of 'B' company got panic-stricken and gave the Battalion Headquarters false information that the Japanese had broken through the centre. It was now felt that a single Brigade Headquarters could not control the jungle-broken and partly pierced front. Heavier thrusts were also anticipated.

Separate Command for the right sector

Brig. Hugh Jones (48th Indian Infantry Brigade) was therefore ordered to go forward to Bilin to assume command of the right sector. As the 1st Battalion 4th P.W.O. Gurkha Rifles had already moved to Bilin and the 1st Battalion 3rd Q.A.O. Gurkha Rifles was defending the dumps in Abaing Harbour, only the 2nd Battalion 5th Royal Gurkha Rifles went with him. They reached the Bilin Rubber Estate at midnight. The 48th Indian Infantry Brigade was now composed of the 1st Royal Battalion 9th Jat Regiment, the 2nd Battalion 5th Royal Gurkha Rifles and the 8th Battalion King's Own Yorkshire Light Infantry. The 1st Battalion 7th Gurkha Rifles and the 1st Battalion 4th P.W.O. Gurkha Rifles continued to be under the 16th Indian Infantry Brigade in the left sector. Brigade Headquarters moved out of the Bilin Rubber Estate a few miles due east.

Soon after darkness, the Japanese crossed the river opposite Bilin and pressed on the 8th Battalion Burma Rifles in and around the village. Later a message was received from 'D' company of the 1st Royal Battalion 9th Jat Regiment that the 8th Burma Rifles in the Bilin village had withdrawn thus leaving the company's left flank open. Of the Burma Rifles there remained Battalion Headquarters and three platoons in rear positions. At 0300 hours the 2nd Battalion 5th Royal Gurkha Rifles was ordered to go into reserve behind the Burma Rifles. 'D' company of the Jats was however told to hang on at all costs and this dangerous situation was reported to the Brigade Headquarters. Throughout the day 'A' company patrolled deep on its right and rear towards the sea but made no contact with the invader.

[18] *War Diary*, 1/9 Jat Regiment.
[19] Though the forward company of the Burma Rifles Battalion had been overrun 5/17 Dogra Regiment *War Diary* speaks Burma Rifles men also as having crossed the river. Perhaps, the reference here is to stragglers.

1/3rd G. R. in lay-back position

On 16 February the 1st Battalion 3rd Q.A.O. Gurkha Rifles, which had now become the divisional reserve, was ordered to take up a position on the Thebyuchaung to cover the river bridge. On the next day, one company was ordered to watch tracks from the left of the Bilin positions and took up position at Alugale. One company was to patrol to the south of the road up to the railway line to watch for and attack Japanese working round the right flank of the Bilin position. It thus formed a good lay-back for the 16th Indian Infantry Brigade with an important role.

Throughout the day (17 February) there was considerable aircraft activity on both sides. Blenheims and Lysanders bombed Moulmein.

Northern and southern flanks—18 February

On 18 February also there was heavy fighting west of Bilin; the northern flank being again the scene of great activity. The carriers which had failed to clear the road-block the previous day were again sent up with a platoon of the King's Own Yorkshire Light Infantry. An engagement lasting a couple of hours ensued. Both sides sustained casualties but the small Allied force was unable to overcome the resistance around the block. Though the 1st Battalion 7th Gurkha Rifles was fresh, it was not put in for a large scale attack and the company at Yinon was allowed to be cut off.[20]

The Japanese succeeded in crossing the river south of the Bilin village.[21] Whilst 'A' and 'C' companies of the 1st Battalion 4th P.W.O. Gurkha Rifles consolidated their positions, 'D' company worked forward towards the river to Pogon and got into position to snipe the invader on the eastern bank. 'C' company from its hill reported about Japanese positions and movements on the eastern bank and the artillery put up a successful fire and two flights of Blenheim bombers carried out an effective bombing.[22] During the day upwards of 80 Japanese casualties were seen being carried on stretchers. This bombing was very opportune as the Japanese were deterred from carrying out their counter-attack plan at 1430 hours. About 1730 hours 'D' company came under heavy mortar and L.M.G. fire from the Japanese posts dug in the rear of Pogon. It therefore withdrew to take up a position farther back.

Counter-attack by 2/5 R. G. R. in the Jat sector—18 February

In the morning of 18 February two companies of the 2nd Battalion 5th Royal Gurkha Rifles were ordered to counter-attack the Japanese detachments which had opened the left flank of the 1st Royal Battalion 9th Jat Regiment. 'A' company had earlier at dawn established itself in and around the village of Bilin. 'C' company moved forward at 1100 hours followed by 'D' company echeloned to the left rear of 'C' company. The attack was supported by 12th Mountain Battery and 3" mortars but no opposition was encountered. Thus the gap in the left flank of the 1st Royal Battalion 9th Jat Regiment was closed. Soon news was received

---

[20] *War Diary*, 17th Indian Division, 'G' Branch.
[21] Lt.-Gen. T. J. Hutton's *Report* p. 25.
[22] In the forenoon itself a large party of the enemy was reported advancing from Paya. *War Diary*, 17th Indian Division.

of the Japanese infiltration west of the Bilin hill. So 'A' and 'B' companies were ordered into Brigade reserve at the Brigade Headquarters. 'A' company sent one platoon behind the hill but the latter contacted no Japanese troops.

That night, however, Japanese patrols were active on the west bank of the river and the Allied troops were introduced for the first time to Japanese faked battle, battle-noises, crackers, and cracker firing automatics, representing rifle and automatic fire. These novelties must have had some effect on the untried riflemen for the latter's expenditure of ammunition was heavy.[23] But the lesson was quickly learnt and at Sittang there was no reply to these faked noises and long before the campaign was over the Japanese had ceased to use crackers against the 48th Brigade. A company of the 1st Royal Battalion 9th Jat Regiment while moving to rejoin the Battalion mistook 'C' company for the Japanese and fired on them. 'C' company thought that it was the Japanese who had infiltrated behind the lines and also thought that it was ambushed. It lost five killed, eight wounded and two missing. The rest were somehow kept together and rejoined the Battalion next morning. The 8th Battalion Burma Rifles was also concentrated in an area in front of, and north of, Bilin.

JAPANESE IN THE COASTAL AREA—18 FEBRUARY

On the morning of 18 February the Japanese were reported on the coast south-west of Bilin in the area Kali-Tawgyi-Taungoy.[24] At dusk a company of the 2nd Battalion 5th Gurkha Rifles was ordered to this area. In the north also strong Japanese patrols had attacked 'A' company of the 1st Battalion 4th P.W.O. Gurkha Rifles at night, using tracer ammunition, grenades, Chinese crackers and mortars.[25] The mortars exploded behind the forward lines. There was panic and the whole Brigade (the 1st Battalion 4th P.W.O. Gurkha Rifles, the 1st Battalion 7th Gurkha Rifles and the 2nd Battalion King's Own Yorkshire Light Infantry) opened up heavy L.M.G. and rifle fire—the rounds fired being about 15,000. It was not only unnecessary but also dangerous, for to reply to Japanese fire at night was to disclose the Brigade positions; and so the next day new forward lines had to be established. Quite a number of the Allied troops were injured by their own fire. In the confusion created by the Japanese "cracker battle" the Brigade Provost mistook one of his armourers for a Japanese and shot him.[26]

DIVISIONAL COMMANDER'S SUMMING UP OF THE SITUATION ON 18 FEBRUARY

In spite of the tough fighting in the north the Japanese were working round the flank of the 16th Indian Infantry Brigade. The 48th Indian Infantry Brigade could only hold up the Japanese advance, and not push them back across the river. The Divisional Commander summed up the position at 1500 hours as follows: The 48th Indian Infantry and 16th

---

[23] Brig. R. T. Cameron's 'Start of the War in Burma', *War Diary*, 2/5 Gurkha Rifles.
[24] *War Diary*, 17th Indian Division, 'G' Branch.
[25] Red tracer ammunition was certainly alarming at night until one got used to it.
[26] *War Diary*, 1/4 Gurkha Rifles.

Indian Infantry Brigades were in close contact with the Japanese on the western bank of the Bilin river. But of the 48th Indian Infantry Brigade which had the counter-attack role the 5th Battalion 17th Dogra Regiment had almost disintegrated while the 8th Battalion Burma Rifles was reduced to four platoons and had been very shaky. The 16th Indian Infantry Brigade had done most of the fighting but had only fought to a standstill. The ranks of the 2nd Battalion King's Own Yorkshire Light Infantry and the 1st Battalion 7th Gurkha Rifles had thinned, to 350 and 400 respectively.[27]

G.O.C'S APPRECIATION ON 18 FEBRUARY

In his appreciation of 18 February to ABDACOM, the General Officer Commanding, Burma Army had expressed the view that though the 17th Indian Division was holding the line of Bilin river and had inflicted heavy casualties on the Japanese, he could not be certain of holding the Bilin line,[28] the reason being that the battalions of the 17th Indian Division were most tired while the Japanese appeared to be bringing fresh reinforcements. He added, "if this battle should go badly enemy might penetrate line of River Sittang without much difficulty and evacuation of Rangoon would become imminent possibility".[29]

LAST BID TO HOLD THE BILIN LINE—COUNTER-ATTACK BY 4/12 F.F.R. IN THE LEFT FLANK ON 19 FEBRUARY

As the Divisional Commander had received definite orders to fight it out on the Bilin line and not withdraw without the permission of Army Headquarters he decided during the day (18 February), to risk coast landings and the defence of Kyaikto and throw in the only reserve, the 4th Battalion 12th Frontier Force Regiment, in a last bid to hold the Bilin line. It was to be used to prevent further infiltration on the left flank of the 16th Indian Infantry Brigade, and counter Japanese advance from Paya. There was also, of course, the 1st Battalion the 3rd Q.A.O. Gurkha Rifles at Thebyuchaung forming a strong lay-back for troops on the northern front.

The 4th Battalion 12th Frontier Force Regiment had arrived back in Kyaikto with the 2nd Burma Brigade after the evacuation of Moulmein. It was kept there as the divisional reserve with 'B' company guarding the beaches at Kyaikkatha about 7 miles north of Kyaikto. On 18 February it received orders to counter-attack the right flank of the Japanese in the northern sector by a wide turning movement. It was to proceed round the left flank of the 16th Indian Infantry Brigade, attack the Japanese trying to come round that flank, and create a diversion; but it was to get heavily involved and was later to go into the 16th Indian Infantry Brigade as a reserve. Since it was going without mortar and M.M.G. platoons, the 16th Indian Infantry Brigade was to support the attack with artillery fire.

---

[27] *War Diary*, 17th Indian Division, 'G' Branch.
[28] It is perhaps because of the heavy casualties that they sustained in the four-day action at Bilin that all but two of the Japanese accounts are silent about it.
[29] Lt.-Gen. T. J. Hutton's *Report*, Appendix 'D'.

The Battalion left at night (18-19 February) and proceeded by lorry to Alugale and from there by footpath north-east and reached Paingdawe at first light of 19 February. It then turned south-east sweeping the hills on both sides of the track to Paya in the area north of the 1st Battalion 7th Gurkha Rifles positions. In the afternoon it put in a two-company attack on a heavily wooded hill to the north-east, but did not get the promised artillery support as the W/T could not contact the Brigade Headquarters. In spite of heavy and sudden mortar barrage from the Japanese, the companies pressed home the attack with great determination; using bayonet and firing from the hip, they inflicted heavy casualties on the Japanese, drove them off the hill and captured it. But they failed to pierce the latter's main position in the hills around. Heavy and persistent mortar fire from there followed by repeated Japanese counter-attacks forced the Battalion to withdraw to the Brigade Headquarters, to the south-west with about 70 casualties. There it was put in reserve to cover certain tracks to the south-west of the Brigade Headquarters. The operation had achieved some success but left the Division without any reserves and weak along the coast.[30]

Coastal defence

To turn to the coastal region in the rear, as early as 12 February extensive Japanese landings had been anticipated there.[31] Burma Military Police posts were established at Kadaik, Zothok, Taungzun (one platoon each), Kyaikkatha and Mokkam (one section each) as also at Mayangon, Okpo, Thegon and Tatmugyaung. The forces were to watch these places and the intervening coast to the best advantage. All posts were to patrol day and night the specified areas and pass on all important information they might gather. If the Japanese landed, messages were to be sent off, and they were to be engaged and held up till reinforcements arrived. Three platoons of F.F. 2 (a Divisional Reconnaissance Unit) known as Column 1, were to support the coast watching platoons.

JAPANESE PENETRATION ALONG THE COAST

'B' Company 2/5 G.R's patrolling—18-19 February

Though the Japanese were well established along the line south of Bilin on 19 February, the danger developed on the coast to the south west of Bilin and in the rear of the Jat and the 2nd Battalion 5th Royal Gurkha Rifles positions. The orders to the 'B' company of the latter were to contact the F.F. 2 patrols who were holding isolated posts along the road, to discover the position of the Japanese and if possible to contact them. They moved out at 2200 hours (18 February) along the road running through Taungale to Taungzun and patrolled down towards the coastline but found the post at Zothok had been vacated;[32] nor could they contact the Japanese. They returned to Taungale and waited at

---

[30] Lt.-Gen. T. J. Hutton's *Report* speaks of it as "Considerable Success", p. 25. W/D 4/12 gives the casualties as 55.
[31] *War Diary*, 17th Indian Division, General Branch, Appendix 13.
[32] The C.O. of F.F. 2 informed the Divisional Headquarters that he had failed to make contact with 'B' company during the night of 18-19 February.

the road and rail crossing near the village for the carrier patrol which had been sent at first light along Taungale-Taungzun road to join them. But they missed each other.

The company then moved off westwards along the railway towards Taungzun. While they were approaching the railway station fire was opened on the leading platoon from the jungle to the north. The Japanese were engaged with light automatic fire and eight of them who ventured out into the open were all shot down; the remainder made off into the jungle. These would seem to have been the advance elements. After a futile search for the rest the company reported to the Brigade Headquarters at 1900 hours. Its casualties in the encounter were two killed and four wounded. The second-in-command who arrived on the scene half an hour after the fight had taken place contacted the F.F. 2 detachment of Pauktaw. The latter reported the Japanese approaching from the coast and within half a mile of the post, but during his return to the main road he did not contact any Japanese detachments. On the return journey the carrier patrol was fired on by some Japanese dressed as Burmans, just south of Taungale.

On receipt of this information, 'A' company in reserve at the Brigade Headquarters was ordered to collect the platoon on road-block at road junction at Point 51, patrol the road Taungale-Taungzun, contact the Japanese units said to be moving up and also link up finally with 'B' company.

Engagement at Anaingpun—18 February

'A' company which left at dawn encountered the Japanese at the village of Taungale where it met a road-block. The forward platoon and company headquarters which moved up to the block were forced back by close automatic fire from all sides and lost the company second-in-command. A 3" mortar detachment and two LMG. teams were now got from the Battalion Headquarters; this mortar fire quickly silenced the Japanese machine-guns near the road-block. The second platoon then advanced by the left of the road with a view to drive the Japanese off the road-block; and force the latter to give ground. The young section commanders Lance Naik Jaisora Rana, Padambahadur Gurung, and Kumbhasing Gurung "each played away with their Tommy Guns and set a magnificent example of fearless leadership to which their young soldiers were quick to respond".[33] Leaving the other platoon to hold the ground gained, No. 9 platoon moved up on the right of the road but could not, on account of the volume of hostile fire, show itself on the road on the Japanese side of the first block. So it made another advance by the left and here forced the Japanese still further back and made good the line of the second road-block on the left. There it came under heavy fire, but Naik Harkabahadur Gurung with his L.M.G. subdued the hostile automatic fire. His first burst of tracer struck a Japanese officer. No. 9 platoon now made good to the right of the second road-block; it just failed to cut off a large Japanese party making off through the shops near the road to the left.

[33] *War Diary 2/5 Gurkha Rifles, Account of 'A' company's action* by Brig. R. T. Cameron.

The road or main street was cleared of the Japanese but it was 1600 hours and the men were tired as they had attacked for four hours without a pause. And the Japanese were still strongly posted in the village. It was later learnt that the coastal party was 200 strong.[34] There was no hope of getting fresh troops to continue the work and there was no sign of 'B' company. So the brave platoons were ordered to fall back and rejoined the Battalion at night. This was the opening engagement of the Battalion at close range with the Japanese in the jungle as it was the first time that "blitz" fire tactics had been used and with good results.

DECISION TO ATTACK THE COASTAL PARTY ON 20 FEBRUARY

At 0800 hours (19 February) the Divisional Headquarters received news of two Japanese sections at Kittokyun in the rear of Jat positions and ordered one company of the Jats (less one platoon) to pursue them. 'A' company's action at Taungale had established the fact that there was a Japanese stronghold on a hill south of that village. But Brig. N. Hugh Jones (48th Indian Infantry Brigade) ruled out covering fire by M.M.Gs and mortars, as the 2nd Battalion 5th Royal Gurkha Rifles companies were also fighting nearby in the Taungale sector. Later it was decided at a conference in the Brigade Headquarters to put in an attack on this area at 0800 hours next day with 'A' and 'B' companies of the 2nd Battalion 5th Royal Gurkha Rifles and artillery and air support.

G.O.C.'S PERMISSION FOR WITHDRAWAL

On the morning of 19 February, Lt.-General Hutton visited the Divisional Headquarters. The Divisional Commander had only the previous day represented that the 48th and 16th Indian Infantry Brigades had either thinned out or disintegrated. The counter-attack by the 2nd Battalion 5th Royal Gurkha Rifles had not altogether succeeded in driving away the coastal parties of the Japanese in the rear of the right flank. The Japanese were also well established in the centre of the position and there was every indication that they were bringing up strong forces against the left flank. "The situation was, therefore, such that there appeared to be grave risk of not being able to disengage the troops unless a further withdrawal was ordered".[35] In view of the strong position on the river Sittang in the rear and the anticipated arrival of reinforcements especially tanks (7th Armoured Brigade which could be operated to advantage in the open country west of the Sittang), a decision to fight it out on the Bilin, the General Officer Commanding thought, had little to recommend it. He therefore told the Divisional Commander to make all necessary preparations for withdrawal and to judge for himself when the necessity for doing so had arrived. "In view of the subsequent events there is little doubt," wrote Lt.-Gen. T. J. Hutton, "that if the withdrawal had been further deferred, the Division would have been practically destroyed and Rangoon left open to the enemy".[36]

[34] *War Diary*, 17th Division, 'G' Branch.
[35] Lt.-Gen, T. J. Hutton's *Report*, p. 25.
[36] *Ibid.*

Night of 19-20 February

During the night of 19 February 'A' and 'D' companies of the 1st Battalion 4th P.W.O. Gurkha Rifles withdrew to new positions 200 yards behind the old positions and in low ground. A few minutes after this change over (2330 hours) the Japanese attacked 'A' company's old positions. The latter's forward troops silhouetted on rising ground offered a good target and were shot by two L.M.Gs while Japanese mortars plastered 'A' company's old positions. Shortly after midnight there was the sound of firing behind the Jat positions thus revealing that the Japanese were strong there.[37]

Japanese patrols were also active over the west bank of the river from nightfall but caused no damage to the 2nd Battalion 5th Royal Gurkha Rifles. For communications between the Divisional Headquarters and Brigades reliance had to be placed on permanent lines owing to the shortage of cable and here each evening cable spurs were cut and considerable lengths removed. Moreover, it was too much to expect the operators with less than one year's service and no practical experience, to maintain communications at top efficiency. To sum up the results of three days' fighting, the Japanese attacks had been held up, heavy casualties had been inflicted on them all along the front, but they could not be dislodged. Some of their parties had crossed the river in the centre, the northern sector was much threatened and a large party threatened the rear from the coast. There were also indications that they had been reinforced.[38]

WITHDRAWAL

Hence on the evening of 19 February orders were issued by the Divisional Commander that there was to be a withdrawal in case Japanese pressure and flanking movements increased. The time of withdrawal was to be announced later. In case a sudden situation should arise or communications with the Divisional Headquarters break down it was left to the Brigades acting in conjunction to determine it. Headquarters 16th Indian Infantry Brigade was to move as soon as practicable to the 48th Indian Infantry Brigade Headquarters in order to form a joint Headquarters. The 48th Indian Infantry Brigade was to cover the withdrawal of the 16th Indian Infantry Brigade to the Thebyu Chaung river. The rearguard on the Thebyu Chaung river was to consist of 12th Mountain Battery, the 1st Battalion 3rd Q.A.O Gurkha Rifles, the 1st Battalion 4th P.W.O. Gurkha Rifles and the 2nd Battalion 5th Royal Gurkha Rifles. It was to be under the command of Brig. N. Hugh Jones. All other troops with the 16th and 48th Indian Infantry Brigades were to be withdrawn under the orders of Brig. J. K. Jones to Kadat Chaung just west of Kyaikto. Here the 16th and 46th Indian Infantry Brigades were to take up positions. When all the troops had passed through the Thebyu-Chaung position, the 48th Indian Infantry Brigade was to withdraw into

---

[37] *War Diary*, 17th Division, 'G' Branch speaks of two local counter-attacks by 1/4 and 1/7 Gurkha Rifles, on 19th February, but the Battalion *War Diaries* are silent on this point.

[38] This information was given by the Chief Intelligence Officer of 17th Division. Later on he gave accurate information about Japanese moves on the Sittang sector.

divisional reserve behind Kadat Chaung. Brigadier Hugh-Jones was to be responsible for blowing the road bridge across the Thebyu Chaung; all other bridges up to Kadat Chaung were to be prepared for demolition.

At night the Japanese penetrated the front of the 48th Indian Infantry Brigade south of Bilin and it became apparent that if the 16th and 48th Indian Infantry Brigades were not withdrawn within a few hours it might become impossible to extricate them at all. The withdrawal was therefore to be at first light and was to be co-ordinated by the commanders of the two Brigades. As the withdrawal was to be rapid some equipment and much stores had to be abandoned; and with the invader around both the flanks and in the centre the withdrawal was expected to be an arduous and difficult task.

Withdrawal of the 16th Indian Infantry Brigade

The 16th Indian Infantry Brigade got away well under cover of darkness. The withdrawal was effected in the following order: the 2nd Battalion King's Own Yorkshire Light Infantry, Brigade Headquarters, the 1st Battalion 7th Gurkha Rifles and the 1st Battalion 4th P.W.O. Gurkha Rifles. At the time that the withdrawal orders were received, the Brigade Commander was attending a Conference at 48 Brigade Headquarters, in the South. The senior battalion commander being diffident of taking over, the withdrawal plans were therefore drawn up jointly by all the battalion commanders—a plan which worked very smoothly indeed. Transport left at about 0200 hours down the road to Bilin. The troops withdrew from 0430 hours via Channgby where they passed through the 4th Battalion 12th Frontier Force Regiment. Great difficulty was experienced in getting orders of withdrawal to 'C' company, the 1st Battalion 4th P.W.O. Gurkha Rifles, still on the isolated hill. Ultimately it withdrew behind 'A' and 'D' companies. There was, however, no interference from the Japanese. On reaching the Bilin rubber estate the 1st Battalion 4th P.W.O. Gurkha Rifles reverted to the 48th Indian Infantry Brigade. The rest of the Brigade rested for some time there and then resumed its march to Kyaikto, 18 miles away, where it arrived late in the night after stopping for rest in the Boyagyi Rubber Estate north of Kyaikto. There it was joined by the 4th Battalion 12th Frontier Force Regiment. The 1st Battalion 7th Gurkha Rifles which had acted as rearguard also left at 1200 hours. Soon after, the Japanese planes attacked the road and the positions left behind.

In the morning of 20 February at 0630 hours the 8th Battalion Burma Rifles was withdrawn from the Bilin village through the 2nd Battalion 5th Royal Gurkha Rifles who acted as rearguard.

It was not, however, all well with the 1st Royal Battalion 9th Jat Regiment. Shortly after midnight (19 February) Japanese patrols were active to the left of the Battalion positions. 'B' company in the centre was attacked by Japanese parties which had crossed the river by the demolished river bridge. They were also known to be operating on the right rear. As the Battalion's W/T had broken down, the orders for general withdrawal could not be received by it and the Battalion was completely in the dark as to what was happening to the rest of the front. The Battalion Commanding Officer therefore withdrew his companies from the river line into a closely defensive area under cover of darkness. At about 0900 hours, 'B' company's mortar and automatic fire at close range drove back a party of the invader. An hour later the W/T set was got to work again. Then the Brigade Headquarters asked them whether they could carry out the counter-attack which had been planned the previous day. But at 1130 hours it ordered the Battalion to withdraw to the Brigade Headquarters. When the Battalion was making preparations for the withdrawal 9 Blenheim bombers and 3 Hurricanes appeared, as arranged previously, and accurately bombed the jungle area in the Battalion's rear where, the previous day, the 2nd Battalion 5th Royal Gurkha Rifles had been at grips with the Japanese. Later, they machine-gunned 'B' company by mistake but fortunately there were no casualties. The Battalion then jettisoned all its kits, surplus ammunition etc., withdrew across country and rejoined the Brigade near the Bilin Rubber Estate and marched along with it to Kyaikto.

Withdrawal of the 48th Indian Infantry Brigade

The Jats had held up the withdrawal of the 48th Indian Infantry Brigade by many hours, which finally left at 1500 hours and was ferried by Kyaikto by M.T. arriving there at about 0200 hours. One company of the 1st Battalion 4th P.W.O. Gurkha Rifles which withdrew, on its own, reported later at Kyaikto that it had seen several Japanese patrols *enroute*.

The Koyli company at Yinon

As regards the Yinon detachment, orders to withdraw were dropped by aircraft on the detached company of the King's Own Yorkshire Light Infantry on the afternoon of 18 February. The company had not been worried save for a brief attack by a solitary Japanese aeroplane. Proceeding cross-country towards Kyaikto the company encountered a small force of Japanese on the morning of 19 February. In the engagement that followed both sides suffered casualties, but the Japanese withdrew hurriedly. Continuing towards the Thebyu Chaung the company found numerous indications that Japanese troops had already passed along the jungle tracks ahead of it.

All troops that had fought on the Bilin river were very much tired, and some units had had fairly severe casualties. There is no doubt that they were in urgent need of a period of rest. Yet at Kyaikto the 17th Indian Division was still in a precarious position such as would not permit it to enjoy even the moderate protection afforded by the Bilin river.

1/3 G. R.

Meanwhile, the 1st Battalion 3rd Q.A.O. Gurkha Rifles patrols had exchanged fire with the Japanese patrols north of Thebyu Chaung on 18 February, and later they reported to the Divisional Headquarters movement of the Japanese on the northern flank. On 20 February one of its companies patrolling south reported large numbers of Japanese troops towards the railway line, and in the afternoon Japanese planes bombed and machine-gunned the bridge over Thebyu Chaung. When all the troops of the 16th and 48th Indian Infantry Brigades had passed, the

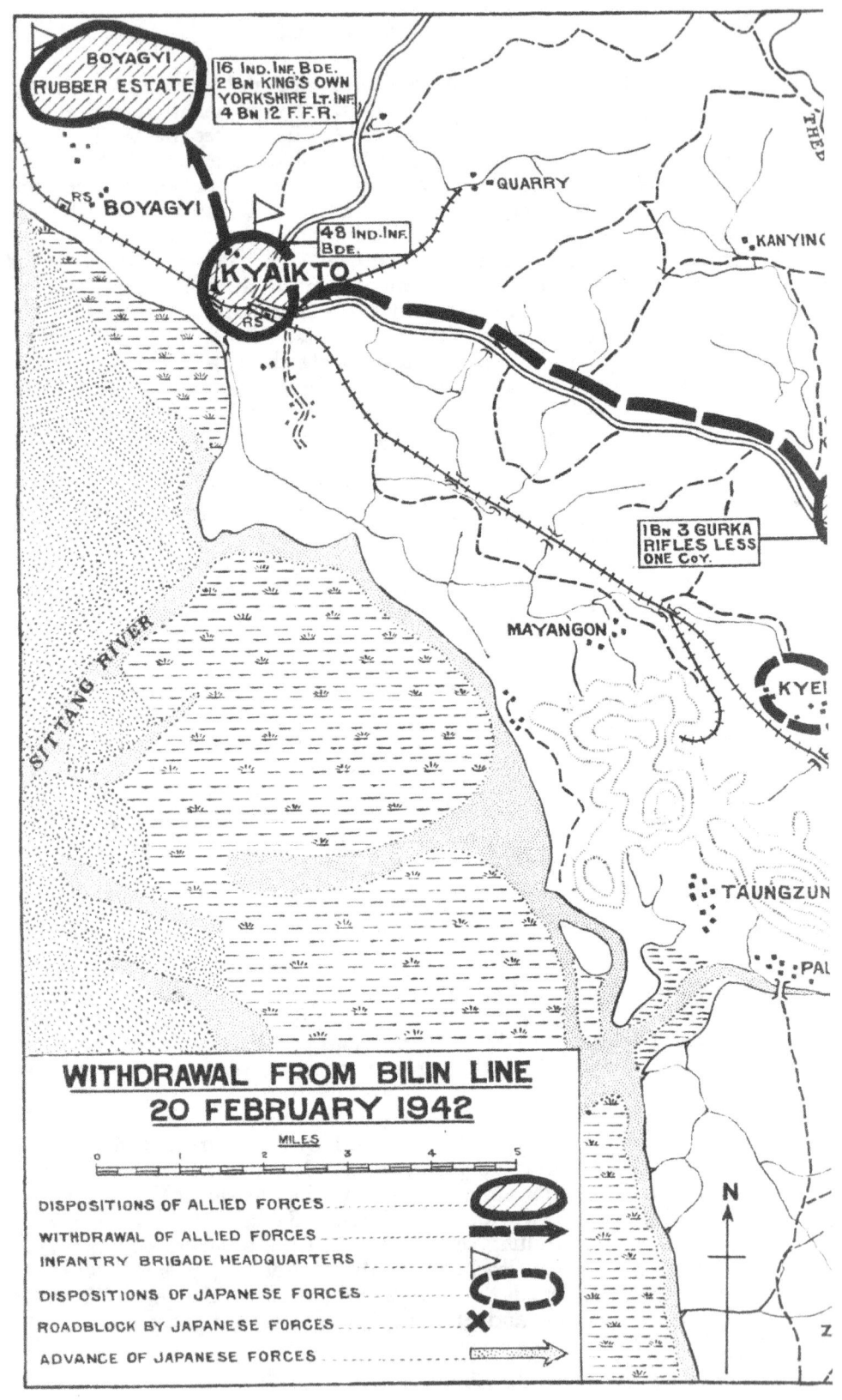

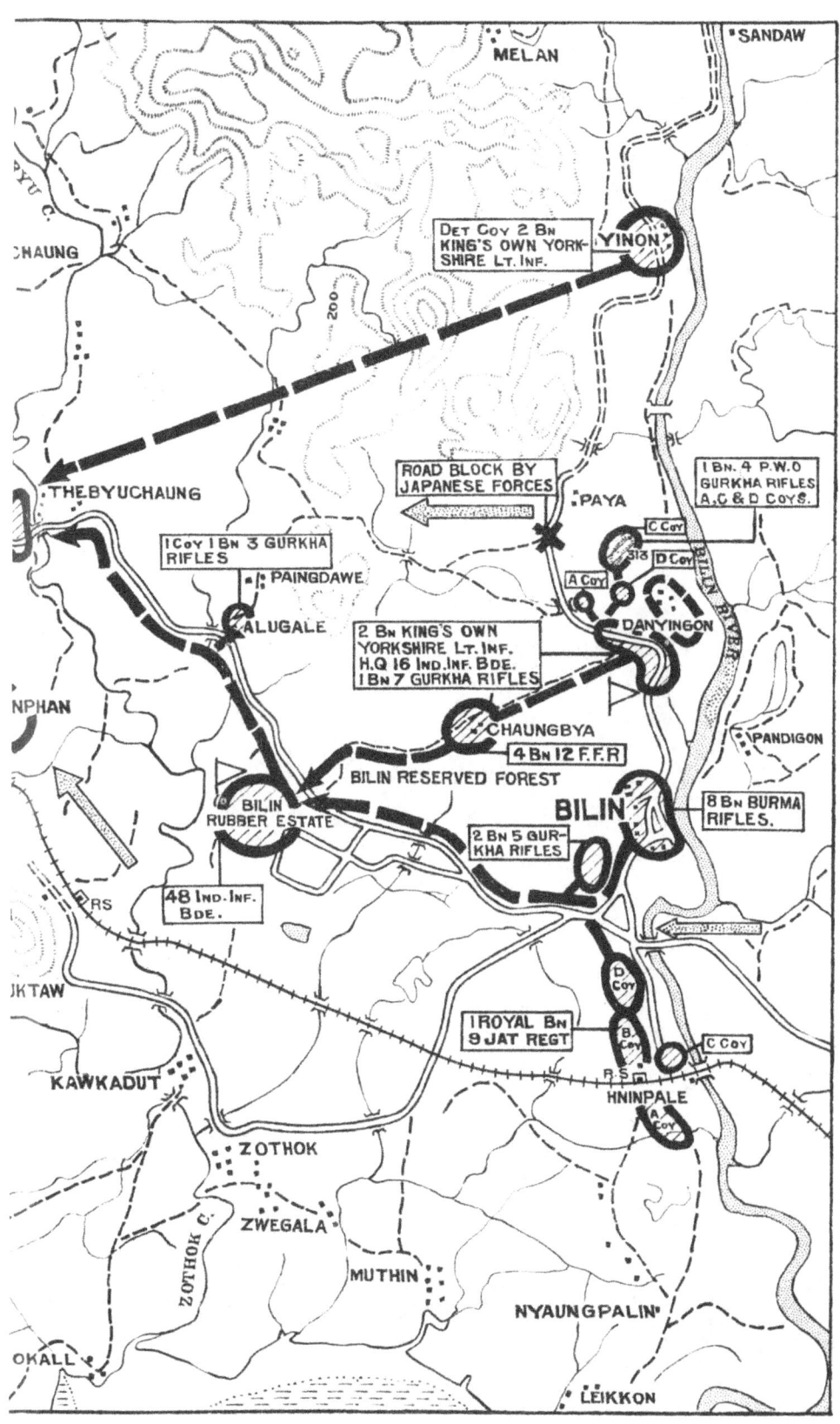

bridge was blown up at 1900 hours and the Battalion then marched to Kyaikto as rearguard.

On 20 February at about 0400 hours a large Japanese coastal column with elephants reached Kyeinphan, three miles north west of Taungzun. On their way at Kaukadut and Taungzun, they had been welcomed by villagers with flags and rejoicing.[39]

---

[39] The action at Bilin was a four-day one of well co-ordinated but vain fighting. The Japanese had by the time of the withdrawal by-passed allied positions and dashed north-west to the Sittang. The commander of the *53rd Division* refers to it as a series of skirmishes—*Japanese Operations in South East Asia, 1941-1945*. Operations of *18th Division*, Hukaung & Mugaung Area. FEX, GHQ, ATIS 601/10111/H.

CHAPTER XII

Battle of the Sittang River

DIFFICULTIES PRESENTED BY THE SITTANG LINE

Forces inadequate

The withdrawal from the Bilin line had been made so that the 17th Indian Division could form a strong line on the west bank of the River Sittang, where, it was thought, the expected reinforcements[1] particularly the 7th Armoured Brigade, would make the country west of the River Sittang ideal for strong defence. This withdrawal had been envisaged in the message from Lt.-Gen. T. J. Hutton to the Commander-in-Chief, India, as early as 13 February.[2] Not only the withdrawal but also the difficulties attending it were then stressed. Without solid infantry reinforcements, Divisional Reconnaissance Regiment and an Armoured Car Regiment the defence of the new line, it was said, was not an easy proposition. The single railway bridge and the few ferries made the withdrawal of transport across the river difficult. Hence the necessity of fighting hard to retain bridgeheads on the east bank was emphasised.

Five days later in an appreciation sent to the Supreme Commander, South-West Pacific Command, Lt.-Gen. T. J. Hutton struck a more pessimistic note. It would not be possible, he said, to hold the Bilin line in the face of a fresh Japanese offensive in the near future. But it was fully appreciated that "if this battle should go badly enemy might penetrate line of River Sittang without much difficulty and evacuation of Rangoon would become imminent possibility." The prospect, however, was gloomy for the existing forces were not adequate for the task and reinforcements were not expected immediately. Two divisions were required for holding the Sittang line permanently or undertaking offensives, but only one was available. He concluded "*probably* the best that can be hoped for is that we shall be able to hold the line of River Sittang *possibly* with bridgeheads on east bank." He added, fighting on the new line would "interrupt or seriously interfere with use of railway to Mandalay through Pegu which is the main route of supply to China. Alternative route beyond Prome depends on the use of road and river and will be most seriously congested if evacuation of troops, R.A.F. stores and H.Q. from Rangoon are carried out by this route".[3]

17th Indian Division disorganized

When the 17th Indian Division was ordered to fall back on the Sittang, the situation was grave. "Danger of complete collapse" was present

---

[1] 7 Armoured Brigade, the 1st Battalion the Cameronians and two East African Brigades.
[2] Lt.-Gen. T. J. Hutton's *Report*, Appendix A.
[3] *Ibid*. Appendix B. In the body of his Report, (p. 25) he calls it a 'strong' line.

as Frontier Force and Burma Rifles had not been fighting well and troops were very much tired.⁴ The 7th Battalion 10th Baluch Regiment and the 5th Battalion 17th Dogra Regiment were rendered non-effective as fighting units owing to heavy casualties. The 1st Battalion 7th Gurkha Rifles was only 400 strong and the 1st Royal Battalion 9th Jat Regiment was in a 'doubtful condition.' Only the 4th Battalion 12th Frontier Force Regiment and 48 Indian Infantry Brigade were fit for operations and even these had been engaged on a counter-attack role to a point of exhaustion. The British battalions were also weak and few reinforcements were available. The only division available was therefore of doubtful fighting value unless rested, refitted and reorganized. Frontier Force and Burma Rifles Battalions were not fighting well and of these five were totally valueless; and the armed police had deserted without warning, thus making the Japanese coastal landing parties a menace to the rear. In the absence of solid infantry support, even the 7th Armoured Brigade which was then available, could not be expected to do anything more than temporarily stabilize the situation. Its area of operation was limited by the water courses and the keeping in tact of bridges.⁵

Communications

The withdrawal to the River Sittang was rendered difficult by the poor communications. The road from Martaban stopped at Kyaikto. Between the latter place and the Sittang bridge, a distance of sixteen miles, there was only a dusty and rough track with sides badly built up. It had been demarcated but the construction had not begun. The track skirted the eastern boundary of the extensive Boyagyi Rubber Estate and ran north-west through dense jungle country to Mokpalin village and the Sittang railway bridge. To the west of the river there was a road only as far as Waw, a town 10 miles west of the Sittang bridge. The railway running to the west of the Kyaikto-Mokpalin track afforded the second means of communication. It ran along the estuary of the Sittang when it met the track near Mokpalin railway station and continued north in close proximity. The railway line then turned westward while the road proceeded northwards and approached the river in a wide sweep from the north-east. The bridge itself was over 500 yards long and decked over with planks to take road traffic. But the railway bridge, the only life line for the retreating army, was very vulnerable to air attack. Of the ferries only one had road connection but that too was under construction. Hence the transport of M.T. across the river was a very difficult proposition. However, a ferry service of three power-driven vessels had been placed in position immediately north of the bridge as an alternative to it and had been provided with landing stages of elaborate construction. "It may be added that the River Sittang at this place is nearly 500 (yards) wide and very swift. The rapidity of the current, the enormous rise and fall of the tide (40 feet) and the existence of a bore, were considered to

⁴ Tel No. 801A Nov Group to AHO India 20.2.1942. Also Burma Army Tel No. 0792 dated 20.2.1942 File 5262 MO 5 *South Burma Operations* 601/2/2/H.
⁵ Tel 0764 and 0792. *Ibid.*

render it unsafe for navigation. It was difficult even for a very strong swimmer."[6]

Nature of the country

Between the bridge and the quarries east of Mokpalin, the country was hilly and covered with jungle and scrubbed with a few small patches of paddy land. However, south of Mokpalin where the land adjoining the river was flat there were large stretches of paddy fields. Between the road and the railway near the bridge there was high ground. That part of the ridge near the river was known as Pagoda Hill, whilst its eastern extremity was called Buddha Hill. A prominent pagoda and a great image of Buddha on the ridge gave rise to these names.

IMPORTANCE OF THE SITTANG LINE

The Sittang line was the 'key point,' of the bottle-neck of Rangoon. Once the line was pierced, the fate of Rangoon was sealed and once Rangoon was lost, nothing was left but to extricate the forces from Burma as there was no other route for supplies and reinforcements. The fate of the First Burma Campaign therefore hung by the Sittang bridge, a slender thread of steel and stone. To the Japanese it was the only road to Rangoon ; to the retreating army the only way of escape or else a more terrible and perhaps final road-block.

The campaign had now reached a critical stage for any further Japanese advance was bound to threaten not only the security of Rangoon but also the very existence of the Allied forces in Burma. Lieutenant General Hutton was fully conscious of the danger even before the withdrawal from the Bilin line, for he telegraphed to the South West Pacific Command on 18 February that in case of failure to despatch reinforcements, which would be justified by the prospects of holding Rangoon and denying the oilfields to the Japanese, "the risk of losing Rangoon within the next few weeks is considerable, especially in the event of seaborne attack."[7] Yet the retention of Rangoon was very important for the Imperial strategy. The Chief of Staff emphasised the object as being "to maintain a front in Burma with particular object of keeping open a supply route to China preferably through Rangoon but failing that through Assam." But they were doubtful if Rangoon could long be used as a base for convoys for China owing to air and naval threat to it. Yet they advised that Rangoon port should "be held as long as its retention can contribute to the achievement of our main object," failing which the port was to be blocked. At the same time the Chief of Staff, while eager to cling to Rangoon, did not consider justifiable the loss of the forces in Rangoon when it had been isolated and desired plans to be prepared for the defence of Northern Burma in case of withdrawal from Rangoon.[8]

On the receipt of the above appreciation Sir A. Wavell indicated his views regarding the immediate strategy. He believed that neither

---

[6] Lt.-Gen. T. J. Hutton's *Report*, p. 26. See also Chapter I. q. v. Sittang River. But the Japanese crossed it with ease in country and portable and collapsible boats *A short history of 55 Japanese Division* (601/7247/H), p. 1.
[7] Tel No. Mo. 0749 dated 18. 2. 42 File 4704 MO 5. 10920 2/3.
[8] Tel No. 72178 M.O. 10. (C.O.S. SWP 25) dated 21/2, *Ibid.*

Rangoon nor Burma could "be held by defensive methods and maintaining a front," but that prospects of success lay in early vigorous counter-offensive for which the 7th Australian Division and 7th Armoured Brigade were required. He did not agree with the view that Rangoon port could be closed by naval or air action and held the view that combined air action by RAF and the American air forces could turn the tide. Concluding, Wavell said, "If Rangoon is lost we can maintain few troops in Burma and do little to help China. We have got to fight these Japs some time somewhere. Burma is not ideal geographically but represents almost our last chance to show the Japs and the world that we do mean to fight."[9]

On this basis Sir A. Wavell directed Lt.-Gen. T. J. Hutton to draw up plans for counter-offensive, possibly to the east of the Sittang river, and to hit the Japanese hard if they succeeded in crossing it.[10] His own plan of subsequent operations was to fight "the battle for Rangoon .... somewhere in area between river (Sittang) and railway Pegu-Nyaunglebin. It must be offensive battle on our part to drive enemy back into river with heavy loss if he succeeds in crossing it." For this purpose, early reconnaissance of the country and setting up of Advanced Base at Pegu were to be undertaken. The method of operation in this wide area was to be by "widely separated Mobile Brigade Groups or even smaller columns operating from railway as base and converging rapidly on any body of enemy between railway and river" and not by divisions. The advantage in the suggested method was that "wide area can be covered offensively and enemy infiltration tactics defeated by immediate attack from several directions. Use can be made of natural obstacles to protect flanks and to drive enemy against. We have advantage of Railway Base and better communications."

It was evident that if the Sittang line was broken Rangoon would be exposed and the battle for South Burma would be lost. The danger was real and the Burma Army Command decided to initiate schemes of evacuation for, as Lt.-General Hutton put it, "prospects of holding it (Rangoon) are not good."[11]

WITHDRAWAL TO THE SITTANG

Time was of the essence of the factor in the formation of the defence line for there was a race for the bridge and the crossing of the river. But while the Japanese forces, particularly the right flank of *33rd Division* moved fast, the retreating forces moved very slowly. The Burma Army Headquarters had issued orders "that all transport should be got across the river Sittang, at an early stage of the withdrawal and that the 1st Battalion Duke of Wellington's Regiment should be sent back to guard the bridgehead as early as possible."[12] The Divisional Commander's plan of withdrawal was for the 48th Indian Infantry Brigade to move back first and establish a secure bridgehead through which the rest of the Division could pass. But as it was to pass through the 46th

---

[9] Tel No. 02083 dated 22/2 from Abdacom to Troopers, *Ibid*.
[10] Tel No. 01934 dated 21/2 from Abdacom to Burma army, *Ibid*.
[11] Tel No. 8336 dated 22/2 for Burma army to Abdacom-South Burma Operations 2/2.
[12] Lt.-Gen. T. J. Hutton's *Report*, p. 25.

Indian Infantry Brigade which was already at Kyaikto, the latter could have reached the bridgehead much earlier if it had been detailed for this task.[13] Even then only one battalion of the 48th Indian Infantry Brigade was to go right through to the Quarries, two miles east of Mokpalin, while the rest were to halt at camps (Inkabo-Auk and Sain Saw) which were 4 and 7 miles respectively to the south of it. The scattering of the Bridge was due to water shortage. The whole Division was to cross the bridge on 22 February. On 21 February, the 16th and 46th Indian Infantry Brigades were to march no further than the Boyagyi Rubber Estate about three miles north-west of Kyaikto. The 46th Indian Infantry Brigade as rearguard would hold defensive positions on the line of the Kadat Chaung just east of the Rubber Estate.

The vital north flank of the Division was covered by two columns of F.F. 2. On 21 February, these were on a line from Kyaikto through Kinmun Sakan to a point some five miles north of the latter place. Their orders were to remain on this line until 1430 hours on 22 February and then to withdraw towards Mokpalin covering the area to the north of it.[14]

The order of withdrawal for the rest of the Division was the 16th Indian Infantry Brigade M.T., the 46th Indian Infantry Brigade M.T. and then the 16th Indian Infantry Brigade followed by the 46th Indian Infantry Brigade. All but one battalion of the 46th Indian Infantry Brigade were to be moved by road and track. The use of the railway line and of tracks near it for infantry does not appear to have been considered except as a route for the flank guard. Furthermore, the 1st Battalion Duke of Wellington's Regiment (less one company detached for duty at the Sittang bridge by the order of Army Headquarters) was attached to the 46th Indian Infantry Brigade from 20 February and no action was taken to carry out the special instructions issued as to its early withdrawal, to hold the bridgehead. No action was also taken to move back all M.T. behind the river and it was decided to leave it with the units. The matter had been raised at a divisional conference held at Kyaikto on 20 February, when the withdrawal was discussed. The Brigade Commanders present strongly supported the suggestion that all unwanted transport numbering hundreds of vehicles should be sent across the river as early as possible and that Brigades should only retain the minimum of transport for first line requirements. The suggestion was not accepted and thus the Army Headquarter's order was ignored.[15]

No wonder that Gen. Sir A. Wavell remarks, "From reports of this operation which I have studied, I have no doubt that the withdrawal from the Bilin River, to west of the Sittang was badly mismanaged by the

[13] The Divisional Commander's defence is that 48 Indian Infantry Brigade was better. It must be noted however that Brig. R. G. Ekin concluded from the fact that the Japanese had not followed them along the Bilin-Kyaikto road, that the Japanese were working round the flank through the jungle. He, therefore, asked the Divisional Commander to consider sending a part or the whole of 46 Indian Infantry Brigade to form at once a strong bridgehead to cover the approaches to the Sittang Brigade. The Divisional Commander did not agree to this proposal.

[14] F. C. Simpson, *Personal Narratives of Operations* (601/3/18/H). Also Capt. E. W. Booker's '*Short History of the original F.F. 2*'.

[15] The withdrawal was as badly managed as contact at Bilin had been broken splendidly.

Headquarters of the 17th Indian Division, and that the disaster which resulted in the loss of almost two complete Brigades ought never to have occurred."[16]

Just during the most fateful period of the Burma Campaign the General Officer Commanding, Burma Army, was away at Lashio. As the withdrawal of the 17th Indian Division on 20 February had been successfully begun, on 21 February he felt able to fly up to Lashio to meet Generalissimo Chiang Kai Shek on his way back to China. His object was to hasten as far as possible the arrival of the Chinese troops in Burma. Unfortunately, the Generalissimo decided at the last moment not to land and flew straight to Chungking and Lt.-Gen. T. J. Hutton returned to Rangoon by air on 22 February only to find himself faced with a serious situation.

JAPANESE ATTACK ON KYAIKTO—21 FEBRUARY

Division Rear Headquarters left Kyaikto on the afternoon of 20 February. Advance Divisional Headquarters and the Divisional Commander were to move at 0930 hours on the next day to an area some two miles west of Mokpalin Quarries. As early as 18 February the weak 7th Battalion 10th Baluch Regiment had been moved to this place to guard a ration dump. A Battle Headquarters remained at Kyaikto. Information about the Japanese was even then scanty. That they were pressing forward fast was shown by the attack on Advance Divisional Headquarters at 0500 hours on 21 February,[17] when a small nuisance party infiltrated into the middle of the Divisional harbour. They fired automatics with red and white tracer ammunition and crackers and also uttered war cries. Perimeter posts and many units opened fire with Tommy guns, Bren guns and rifles, but as no liaison between the units in defensive position had been made, no unit knew well the location of the other. There was, therefore, a lot of indiscriminate firing in all directions and nothing could be done to get organised fire power. There was considerable confusion and a few casualties were caused on their own troops by the uncontrolled fire. The Japanese drew off at dawn but their light raid proved to be effective in creating much confusion.

THE BRIDGEHEAD—3 BURIF AND 4/12 F.F.R.—21 FEBRUARY

The same day the 4th Battalion 12th Frontier Force Regiment was ordered to strengthen the bridgehead which was held by one company of the 3rd Battalion Burma Rifles and one company of the 2nd Battalion Duk of Wellington's Regiment. Unfortunately on its way from Kyaikto to the bridgehead the Battalion got badly bombed from the air like the other Battalions and arrived at the bridgehead only as it was getting dark. Hence it was decided to readjust the positions the next day. The troops already in position seemed to have done little to prepare the bridgehead

---

[16] *Despatch*, p. 7, para 18.
[17] *War Diary*, 17 Indian Division, has it as 0600 hours. *War Diary*, 2nd Battalion 5th Gurkha Rifles has it as 0500 hours.

for defence. Of course the ground was jungle covered and difficult, but something could have been done to build up the defences.[18]

WITHDRAWAL OF 48TH INDIAN INFANTRY BRIGADE—21 FEBRUARY

Most of the units of the 48th Indian Infantry Brigade had arrived after dark the previous evening. No units had sent advance parties ahead and the areas to be occupied were given by the Divisional Staff. The 2nd Battalion 5th Royal Gurkha Rifles took up position at Kyaikto at midnight 20/21 February, a very tired battalion after the endless days at Bilin and on the hot, dusty and confused line of march from there to Kyaikto.[19]

On the outskirts of Kyaikto the columns were bombed and machine-gunned by four Japanese aircraft, Later Hurricanes and Blenheims with British markings and AVG Tomahawks appeared and bombed the Boyagyi Estate and the columns moving to Mokpalin. Believing the planes to be British ones in the Thai air force, or those captured in Singapore, the columns returned the fire with all available weapons and some planes were also believed to have been brought down. This continued up to 1700 hours, Japanese and British planes coming alternately. The bombing of the road and machine-gunning and strafing of vehicles was in both cases most accurate. Many craters were created. All transport mules stampeded into the jungle. Wireless sets were all lost except one. Casualties were very heavy. The effect on the morale of the troops was most serious. On the whole these bombing attacks had much influence on the next day's happenings. The Rubber Estate also suffered heavy strafing. Vehicles were destroyed by bombs and machine-gun fire. Nearly 200 men of the 8th Battalion Burma Rifles deserted. Fortunately before these air attacks developed, the majority of the Divisional Headquarters and the Divisional Signal Unit had reached their destination and dispersed under cover.

There is no clear explanation of the tragedy, but the facts seem to be as follows: On 21 February reconnaissance machines had reported a very long column of Japanese transport estimated at 300 vehicles moving through Kyaikto to Kinmun Sakan. The total available strength of the RAF and AVG on the Rangoon aerodromes was employed to deal with this column. But by error the crew had been given the Kyaikto-Mokpalin road instead of the Kyaikto-Kinmun Sakan road as the western limit of their operational area[20] which might have accounted for the unfortunate tragedy.

[18] The 3rd Battalion Burma Rifles was now not over 200 strong. A company had been reduced to a section. Battalion H. Qrs. had lost many men who had been cut off on the wrong side of the Salween for lack of transport—*War Diary*, 3 Burif, p. 8.

[19] 1/4 G.R. has it as 1130 hours on 21 February. 2/5 G.R. has it as 1100 hours on 21 February. 17 Ind. Div. *Diary* has it as after 1000. Brigadier Cameron has pointed out in his comments that the units of the 48th Indian Infantry Brigade arrived late in the evening of 20 February.

[20] In his *Despatch* Air Vice Marshal D. F. Stevenson says that even after an exhaustive enquiry, he had failed to reach a firm conclusion that our aircraft bombed our own troops at this time and place. He ends it all by saying it is not improbable that some crews may have bombed the wrong objectives. His arguments against the latter conclusion are that whereas the attacking aircraft are said to have had roundels on the under side of their wings, our Blenheims had roundels only on the upper side of the wing. More-

The 1st Battalion 4th P.W.O. Gurkha Rifles reached Mokpalin Quarries in the evening of 21 February and while approaching it was repeatedly machine-gunned from low altitude by 3 S.S. fighters with AVG markings. 'C' company which had been escort to transport had been heavily bombed on the outskirts of Kyaikto and had lost touch with the battalions. It rejoined the battalion at about 1200 hours on 22 February at the bridge, working its way through the jungle and along the river bank. The 2nd Battalion 5th Gurkha Rifles and the 1st Battalion 3rd Q.A.O. Gurkha Rifles reached their destinations, a little later. Communications between units in the Brigade in their various camps did not exist as there was no W/T.

At 0010 hours the commanding officer of the 1st Battalion 4th P.W.O. Gurkha Rifles was called to the Divisional Headquarters. Here he was informed of a communication from Army Headquarters that the Japanese might try and land troops by parachute in the open ground west of the Sittang and take the bridge from that side. The battalion was to march to the west bank of the Sittang at 0400 hours, contact the company of the 2nd Battalion Duke of Wellington's Regiment which was already there, take them under command and then watch for paratroops from first light.

FAILURE OF F.F. 2 TO GUARD THE LEFT FLANK OF THE RETREATING FORCES—21-22 FEBRUARY

On withdrawal from the line of Bilin river, F.F. 2 was ordered to take up a position along the line Kyaikto-Kinmun Sakan, which is about five miles north-east of Kyaikto. It was to act as tactical left flank guard for the retreating 17th Indian Division and protect it from Japanese infiltration from the north. This was what it exactly failed to do both by not giving the information of, and by not resisting, the thrust. The Battalion reached this line during the afternoon of 20 February, one column covering the area between Kyaikto and Kinmun Sakan and the other the area from Kinmun-Sakan to about six miles to the north. Their orders were to remain on this line until 1430 hours on 22 February and then to withdraw on Mokpalin and Sittang and cover the area from there to the north. About 1430 hours on 21 February the southern column of F.F. 2 became heavily engaged with a force of the Japanese. The northern column was also engaged. From the sound of the battle, the latter conjectured that the other column must have been surrounded. Therefore, it disengaged itself and made for the Sittang river just north of Mokpalin using jungle tracks north of the road. The southern column though heavily engaged broke off engagement and made for the same place by the same routes, but actually withdrew ahead of the northern

---

over there, he says, is a great similarity in the plane silhouette of the Japanese Army 97 Medium bomber and our Blenheim. But it must be noted that there were also British markings on bomb fragments. Later one of the squadron leaders "acknowledged", to Brig. R. G. Ekin that he had wrongly attacked our own troops having been given wrongly the Kyaikto-Mokpalin road as the western limit of their operational area—Brig. R. G. Ekin's Narrative (*War Diary*, 46 Ind Inf Bde) and letter D.O. No. E 9/7 of January 7, 1943.

War Diary, 17 Ind Div and Lt.-Gen. T. J. Hutton's Report admit that the casualties were very heavy. But *War Diaries* of 215 and 1/3 G.R. whitewash it all by saying that "Casualties were very few and bombing was ineffective".

column; and there was no contact between them till they reached Pegu. Both columns in turn ran into the Japanese forces, when they got near Mokpalin on 22 February. So they sheared off to the north and crossed the river Sittang by means of country boats some seven miles north of the bridge and eventually rejoined what was left of the Division at Pegu. The failure of F.F. 2 to inform the Divisional Headquarters about the Japanese thrust from the north flank of the Division was attended by the most disastrous consequences.[21]

Commander of the 16th Indian Infantry Brigade was responsible for the withdrawal of his and the 46th Indian Infantry Brigade as the Divisional Headquarters had left Kyaikto on the evening of 21 February. The Commanders of the two rear Brigades agreed upon the necessity of withdrawing from the Boyagyi Estate area towards Sittang as speedily as the situation permitted, on the road ahead of them. They had received no definite marching times and were bound to conform to the movements of the 48th Brigade. A night march was therefore out of the question, though the battalion commanders and the Commander of the 46th Brigade suggested it.[22] However, it was arranged that save for essential vehicles, the motor transport of both the Brigades should be sent on ahead, escorted by carriers. Machine-guns, mortars, and reserve small arms ammunition would be in these vehicles. Motor transport was to be clear of the starting point by 0500 hours next morning, the 16th Indian Infantry Brigade was to march at 0515 hours, and the 46th Indian Infantry Brigade was to follow immediately. In the 46th Indian Infantry Brigade it was arranged that units were to march with no tactical gaps between Battalions or companies. This formation was adopted to ensure mutual support in the event of an attack on the column in the thick jungle country.

At about 0100 hours on 22 February the two rear Brigades received an 'immediate' cipher message from the Divisional Headquarters warning them that a strong Japanese force was probably moving round the northern flank, and suggesting that the Brigades should move towards the river as early as possible.[23] It was then too late to alter the timings. Meanwhile, some of their out-posts on the line of the Kadat Chaung were in contact with the Japanese patrols.

The Divisional plan was for the motor transport to move across the bridge at 2330 hours and proceed to Abya, seven or eight miles westward. The Divisional Headquarters was to march in M.T. at 0400 hours from the Mokpalin Quarries to Abya. The 48th Indian Infantry Brigade Headquarters marched a little later.[24]

Suddenly at 0300 hours there occurred a road-block in the central span of the bridge. A three-ton lorry crashed through the temporary decking on the bridge blocking movement either way. There was no recovery apparatus and it being a girder bridge the lorry could not be thrown over the side. By the light of flames and the moon the Sappers

---

[21] RAF had reported on 21 February strong enemy MT column on the Kyaikto-Kunmun Sakan road with the head about Inwa.
[22] *War Diary*, 1/9 Jats.
[23] This outflanking move from the north had been reported at the conference at Brigade Headquarters on 21 February at 1830 hours.
[24] 0430 hours according to 1/4 G.R.

toiled hard and three and a half hours passed before the flow of traffic could be resumed at 0630 hours. The approach to the bridge and the road through Mokpalin and beyond it were now packed with a long line of halted vehicles. To add to the congestion the transport of the two rear Brigades was also arriving, and the block extended far east of Mokpalin. North of the bridge the ferry was being employed for the transport of mules across the river.

There appears to have been no traffic control along the road.[25] Vehicles forced their way into the column in any order. Shortage of motor transport owing to previous losses resulted in overloading. This caused delays whilst articles that had fallen off the lorries were picked up. The road itself was pitted with bomb craters—dangerous traps in the dark. An unfinished embankment across a water course had not been blocked nor the diversion marked, and here, too, much delay ensued. Vehicles that had driven on to the embankment had to be packed into the crowded stream of traffic. There were many ditched vehicles. Amongst these were ambulance vans still carrying casualties. Parties were detailed to render unusable, vehicles that could not be extricated.

To return to the bridgehead area on 22 February, the 1st Battalion 4th P.W.O. Gurkha Rifles got through the congested road with difficulty to the Sittang bridge and crossed by a cat-walk on the upstream side of the bridge. On the west bank it contacted one company of the 1st Battalion Duke of Wellington's Regiment which had bivouacked in the wood about one mile north-west of the bridge. The Section 3.7" Battery, crossed in a barge. It was followed by the Divisional Headquarters. The 48th Indian Infantry Brigade Headquarters crossed at 0800 hours and established command post on west bank of the river about one mile from the bridge. The same morning, a detachment of the 7th Battalion 10th Baluch Regiment which was just astride the village of Mokpalin and had received orders to cross the bridge and take up positions on the western side, moved along the railway line through Mokpalin. Just as it was moving along the railway cutting east of the bridge, at about 0830 hours, it came under heavy mortar fire from the direction of the bridge. It now swung over to the left and made its way under fire by the river bank on to the bridgehead.

The Japanese forces from concealed jungle positions to the north-east of the bridge were trying to rush the bridge and put in an attack on the bridgehead defences, just east of the bridge, both north and south of the railway line. The Allied positions here were dangerously weak as they were held by the 3rd Battalion Burma Rifles less one company. North of the bridge were one and a half companies holding the Buddha and Pagoda Hills, and positions further north. Headquarters was near the bridge. A company and a half held positions south of the line. It was arranged that at first light on 22 February, the 4th Battalion 12th Frontier Force Regiment would take over north of the railway, 'A' company to hold Pagoda Hill and Buddha hill positions, 'B' company to

---

[25] An Officer who was present describes the traffic situation east of Mokpalin thus: "Vehicles of all sorts including carriers and of many different units were all mixed up together. They were head to tail in a defile and in many cases had double banked on the road."

the north of it, 'C' company to the west of the latter whilst Battalion Headquarters with the reserve company would be near the bridge. Thus 4 FFR was to take over north of the railway and small knots south of it. The 3rd Battalion Burma Rifles was to take over the rest of the bridgehead south of the railway line including the Bungalow Hill.

As 'A' and 'B' companies of the 4th Battalion 12th Frontier force Regiment were ready to advance and take over positions the Japanese attacked the Pagoda Hill, the key hill of the bridgehead defence and positions to the north of it. The Company and a half of the 3rd Battalion Burma Rifles there broke almost at once. 'A' and 'B' companies of the 4th Battalion 12th Frontier Force Regiment with 3" mortar support were then ordered to retake the hills which they did after good fighting and severe casualties.[26] Capt. S. H. F. J. Manekshaw, commanding officer of 'A' Company, who was severely wounded, received an immediate award of the Military Cross for his gallantry and leadership. In this engagement many Japanese were killed and identifications obtained.[27] The remainder of the 3rd Battalion Burma Rifles south of the 4th Battalion 12th Frontier Force Regiment hung on and did well. Subsequently, the 7th Battalion 10th Baluch Regiment came to the support of the 4th Battalion 12th Frontier Force Regiment at the bridgehead.[28]

The Japanese advancing from the south of Mokpalin surrounded from three sides the Advanced Dressing Section of 39 Field Ambulance, situated south-east of the railway station, and took all the medical personnel prisoners including the Assistant and Deputy Assistant Directors, Medical Service. Motor transport drivers, men standing with mules and some of the bridgehead troops panicked and made a rush for the bridge.

At about 1000 hours the Commander of the 48th Indian Infantry Brigade, Brig. N. Hugh-Jones, took command of all troops holding the bridgehead.[29] 'D' company of the 2nd Battalion Duke of Wellington's Regiment, then on the west bank, was ordered across the river and took up a position on Bungalow Hill on the south-east of the bridgehead perimeter. This hill was already held by the remnants of a company of the 3rd Battalion Burma Rifles, who then joined their Battalion in the centre.

In view of the situation at the bridgehead the CRE, 17th Indian Division, gave orders for the destruction of about three hundred sampans collected on the west bank of the river. He further ordered the destruction of the power-driven ferry vessels, if they could not be manned. Accordingly, all these craft were destroyed by the engineers in the course of the day.

Simultaneously with their assault on the bridgehead, the Japanese attacked the column of transport massed along the road through Mokpalin. When they first appeared there, the only troops to oppose them were the small baggage guards with the vehicles. At this stage vigorous action by the Japanese might well have secured for them the whole area

---

[26] 'A' Company 35% 'B' Company 19%.
War Diary, 4/12 FFR gives killed as 11 and wounded as 40.
[27] *War Diary*, 1/4 G.R.—W.D. Edward's *Narrative—4/12 Frontier Force Regiment*.
[28] W. D. Edward's *Narrative with sketch map—War Diary*, 4/12 FFR. The Japanese made several attempts to retake the Pagoda Hill which was the key to the bridgehead position.
[29] *War Diary*, 4/12 FFR makes it to be 1230 hours.

of Mokpalin, and the eastern approaches along the main road and railway.

The 2nd Battalion 5th Royal Gurkha Rifles F.F. were without rations, hence the Quartermaster was sent at midnight with two lorries to the 48th Indian Infantry Brigade Headquarters to collect some. There he was given verbal orders for his battalion and the 1st Battalion 3rd QAO Gurkha Rifles to withdraw to the bridge at once, whilst the motor transport was to cross the bridge without fail at 0600 hours. Consequently on the arrival of the Quarter Master at 0215 hours on 22 February the 2nd Battalion started to move at 0300 hours while its motor transport moved at 0500 hours and got across the bridge safely after the carrier escorts had brushed aside Japanese opposition in Mokpalin village.[30]

When the Battalion had reached a point on the road just east of Mokpalin at about 0815 hours, it was held up by the troops in front who were under heavy fire. Therefore the Commanding Officer decided to sweep the right flank of the road and to picquet it until his transport had crossed the bridge, without knowing that it had got across much earlier. As soon as the Battalion had deployed, it came under fire at close range from a temple on the Knoll on the eastern outskirts of the village. This led to a stampede of the mules of the mortar platoon, leaving only a single 3" mortar with the battalion. Notwithstanding, two attacks were made on the Japanese positions which were halted with heavy casualties. The third assault, however, overcame hostile resistance, and the Battalion continued its advance to the area of the Railway Station. In the Goods Yard snipers had established themselves, but they hurriedly withdrew when a further advance was made.

Without artillery support and with but the single mortar which was without sights, two companies of the Battalion proceeded to advance along the east of the main road against Buddha Hill. The ground was covered with thick scrub jungle and contact was difficult to maintain. The two companies soon lost touch with each other.[31] It is, however, considered that had this attack been put in with greater resolution, they could have got through to the bridgehead at this juncture; it is worth remembering that the Japanese had only just arrived, completely tired after a long march, including the previous night, and were completely ignorant of the situation.

In the low ground south of Buddha Hill the left company came under intense mortar fire, suffered heavily, and was therefore withdrawn to the higher ground further south. The right company was out of contact with the Battalion.

It had been thought that the 7th Battalion 10th Baluch Regiment was on the west of the main road. But when this flank was found to be devoid of troops, a third company was moved forward to prolong the line astride the road and to the west of it. The Battalion had been in action without any support against superior hostile forces for about three hours, but by its determination it had cleared the Japanese from Mokpalin.

[30] Brig. Cameron's *Account*.
[31] R. T. Cameron's *Account of the Sittang Battle*. *War Diary*, 48th Indian Infantry Brigade.

At this juncture the leading company (B company) of the 1st Battalion 3rd Q.A.O. Gurkha Rifles arrived at the railway station; and artillery also began to enter the village. The Battalion had received orders for marching to Sittang at 0400 hours and was on the move at 0500 hours.[32] At 0530 hours it was overtaken by the mechanised transport of the 46th and 16th Indian Infantry Brigades and much confusion was caused by closely packed transport moving past troops on the dusty road. 'C' company were therefore separated from the Battalion. The rest of the Battalion advanced along the railway line. While doing so it discovered some Japanese in the jungle between the railway line and the road, and attacked them with 'A' and 'B' companies. On this and the following day all units in Mokpalin were severely tried by the bitter fighting that continued incessantly, but a special tribute must be paid to these two Gurkha Battalions, the first to be engaged, the 2nd Battalion 5th Royal Gurkha Rifles and the 1st Battalion 3rd Q.A.O. Gurkha Rifles. The latter Battalion when it mustered west of the Sittang two days later numbered just over a hundred of all ranks.

The Commanding Officers of the two Battalions conferred. It was agreed that the 1st Battalion 3rd Q.A.O. Gurkha Rifles should attack the Buddha and Pagoda Hills, on both of which the Japanese were believed to be in position. The attack was to be supported by guns in the village. The 2nd Battalion 5th Royal Gurkha Rifles, now reorganising, would, it was planned, hold the eastern outskirts of Mokpalin, the left forward company remaining in position west of the main road and facing Buddha Hill.

This plan was drawn up without any knowledge of the situation at the bridgehead with which there was no communication. The whole area being covered with thick jungle very little could be seen. The Japanese were on and forward of Buddha Hill. It was not unreasonable to suppose that they also held the whole of Pagoda Hill, more particularly as there was a report that they had secured the bridge. If that were so, the plan proposed was proper. On the other hand, if the true state of affairs had been known it would have been a comparatively easy matter to establish contact with the bridgehead troops on Bungalow Hill and to co-ordinate an attack that would have cleared the way to the river. It might have been necessary to abandon the transport, but the troops could certainly have crossed the Sittang by the bridge.

At about 1400 hours[33] the Mountain Batteries grouped near the Mokpalin railway station and sent down a heavy and accurate barrage on the bridgehead positions north of the railway line for about twenty-five minutes. At the same time these Allied posts came under mortar fire from the Japanese. Had there been any inter-communication between the bridgehead and the Batteries, this deplorable thing would not have happened. Brig. N. Hugh-Jones therefore had to order the troops on the bridgehead position to withdraw to the west bank of the river. They were to hold the bridge by fire from the west.

---

[32] According to Brig. Cameron the orders were communicated by 2/5 G.R. and the Battalion had no direct orders from the Brigade.

[33] *War Diary*, 4/12 FFR, gives it as 1100 hours. W. D. Edward's account makes it to be 1230 hours. See *War Diary*, 1/3 G.R.

'B' and 'C' companies of the 1st Battalion 3rd Q.A.O. Gurkha Rifles advanced on the left and right respectively of the road supported by fire from 'D' company. They crossed the bottom of the valley and swarmed up the opposite slope, blitzing as they went, and killing many of the Japanese in their positions on the forward slopes. They rapidly reached the top of the ridge where much stronger opposition was encountered; but after some confused fighting they drove back the Japanese and the two companies then got into position on the top of the ridge. During the attack, 'B' company had swung rather far left and one platoon was held up by a strong Japanese post on the lower slopes and lost itself in the jungle. Eventually two platoons gained the deserted bridgehead, manned the Pagoda Hill area and reorganised themselves for meeting a counter-attack.

Parties of the Japanese troops who had been overrun by 'B' and 'C' companies were reinforced and soon reappeared from the flanks. They tried to prevent a breakthrough to the bridge. They, however, succeeded in separating the two forward companies from each other and from the Battalion Headquarters. Runners from 'B' company were all killed and no report was received from the company that it had taken the Pagoda Hill. As spasmodic fighting still continued on the ridge, 'D' company was ordered to advance and clear up the situation between 'B' and 'C' companies. 'D' company attacked, killed many more Japanese and reached the ridge where 'C' company was in position.[34]

With 'C' company commander wounded and sent to the Battalion Headquarters and 'D' company commander killed during the attack, these were now commanded by their Gurkha Subadars. Throughout the hard fighting and Japanese counter-attacks they encouraged and inspired their men by their cool and resolute conduct and held their position despite all Japanese efforts to dislodge them. 'C' and 'D' companies were heavily engaged and cut off from the Battalion Headquarters. Two platoons of 'B' company were in occupation of Pagoda Hill but were still out of touch with the rest of the Battalion.

The battalion reserve consisted of the Headquarters Company and a single platoon of 'A' company, the other platoons having been sent forward. This small reserve was in position covering the main road on the outskirts of Mokpalin, north of the railway station. Contact with the forward companies had been lost, and as evening approached they became heavily engaged with the Japanese.

At the bridgehead, after taking up position, the two platoons of 'B' company were trying to get into touch with the rest of the Battalion. In the small actions that went on in this area, Jemadar Gangansing and Havildar Sulbahadur Rana were particularly outstanding for their cool behaviour.

At 1600 hours the Commander of the 48th Indian Infantry Brigade under whose command the bridge was, received orders from Advance Divisional Headquarters to reoccupy the original bridgehead position. As the original garrison had suffered considerable casualties, the 4th Battalion 12th Frontier Force Regiment, the 1st Battalion 4th P.W.O. Gurkha Rifles

---

[34] *War Diary*, 1/3 Gurkha Rifles.

and one company of the 2nd Battalion Duke of Wellington's Regiment were detailed for this task. The 4th Battalion 12th Frontier Force Regiment occupied the same position as before (less Pagoda and Buddha Hills). The 1st Battalion 4th P.W.O. Gurkha Rifles (less 'C' company which had reported at 1200 hours) occupied Pagoda and Buddha Hills and the position previously occupied by the 3rd Battalion Burma Rifles, and the company of the 2nd Battalion Duke of Wellington's Regiment occupied Bungalow Hill without opposition. The two platoons of 'B' company, the 1st Battalion 3rd Q.A.O. Gurkha Rifles, which had occupied Pagoda Hill just a little before, came directly under command of Brig. N. Hugh-Jones, who expected the rest of the Battalion to arrive soon. They were pulled in for a close defence of the bridge. The morale of the men was high, though they were tired and hungry.

To turn to the events farther south, the 16th Indian Infantry Brigade left Boyagyi Rubber Estate at dawn (22 February) followed by the 46th Indian Infantry Brigade.[35] The 8th Battalion Burma Rifles moved first, followed by the 1st Royal Battalion 9th Jat Regiment and Koyli, with the 1st Battalion 7th Gurkha Rifles doing rearguard. When it was four miles south of Mokpalin the 1st Royal Battalion 9th Jat Regiment heard firing in the area and ahead of it. The 8th Battalion Burma Rifles had gone on ahead, and the Brigade Headquarters was much in the rear. Hence the Officer Commanding, the 1st Royal Battalion 9th Jat Regiment collected his troops and piquetted the road for one and a half miles. In the afternoon the 16th Indian Infantry Brigade and remnants of the 46th Indian Infantry Brigade which had been ambushed and badly cut up passed through the piquetting block. Small parties of Japanese troops who attacked these forces were thrown back by the Jat fire. The piquetting of the road, the abandoned vehicles *en route* and their destruction made progress very slow. Yet the piquetting was continued between Mokpalin Quarries and the village; and when the 16th Indian Infantry Brigade reached the village it found a confused fighting and roads choked with the vehicles.

The 16th Indian Infantry Brigade was closely followed by the 46th Indian Infantry Brigade.[36] The 3rd Battalion 7th Gurkha Rifles led the vanguard and was followed by the Brigade Headquarters, the 5th Battalion 17th Dogra Regiment (less about 2 companies) and the 2nd Battalion Duke of Wellington's Regiment less one company. The 4th Battalion Burma Rifles acting as a flank guard was to march to Mokpalin along the railway. The vanguard had been instructed to keep contact with the 1st Battalion 7th Gurkha Rifles, the rearguard of the 16th Indian Infantry Brigade. Motor Transport including 'A' echelon carrying machine-guns, mortars and reserve small arms ammunition marched earlier accompanied by all seconds-in-command and administrative

---

[35] Abandoned vehicles were destroyed *en route* and when 16 Indian Infantry Brigade reached Mokpalin quarries it heard LMG fire in the rear. It was the attack on 46 Ind. Inf. Bde.

[36] 16 Indian Infantry Brigade consisted of the 8th Battalion Burma Rifles, the 1st Battalion 7th Gurkha Rifles, the 1st Royal Battalion 9th Jat Regiment and KOYLI. 46 Ind. Inf. Bde. marching behind it consisted of the 3rd Battalion 7th Gurkha Rifles, the 5th Battalion 17th Dogra Regiment and the 7th Battalion 10th Baluch Regiment.

personnel who were sent ahead to reconnoitre a defence position, west of the Sittang river.[37]

Progress was very slow as at intervals of about half a mile or less were found broken down vehicles which had been set on fire by a party detailed from the preceding Brigade; and there were also regular rests. After going for an hour and a half the 3rd Battalion 7th Gurkha Rifles received orders to halt as the 2nd Battalion Duke of Wellington's Regiment had started late due to the non-arrival of one of its companies which had lost its way. The Gurkha Battalion waited for an hour without the 16th Infantry Brigade contacting it which caused a gap of ¾ mile between the brigades.[38]

The Japanese who were concealed in the dense jungle on the eastern flank seized this opportunity to take up positions astride the road and erect a block.[39] The track had been cut right through the jungle which was thick on either side. At 1000 hours[40] the 3rd Battalion 7th Gurkha Rifles encountered the road-block. The leading companies 'A' and 'C' were held up and soon the whole Battalion came under heavy fire from small arms and mortar astride the road slightly west of Meyon Chaung. After reconnaissance, the Battalion commander ordered 'D' and 'B' companies to pass through the jungle on the left flank; the former was to gain a position behind and beyond the road-block while the latter was to attack the road-block from the south side. The signals platoon and a runner party were sent to support the hard pressed forward 'C' company on the right. These troops on the right flank aided by a company of the 5th Battalion 17th Dogra Regiment sent by the Brigade Headquarters succeeded in clearing the Japanese 300 yards beyond and north of the road. At this point additional help was given on the right flank by a company of the 2nd Battalion Duke of Wellington's Regiment.[41] 'B' company was able to annihilate a small force of the Japanese on the left of the road. 'A' and 'D' companies circumvented the road-block by a detour to the left and made for the bridge. But the road-block position could not be captured and the Japanese rallied on its right flank. At 1100 hours the battalion commander made his way to the Bridge Command Post to ask for further support to effect a break through particularly on the left flank which appeared to meet with less Japanese resistance. But soon the troops withdrew across the road from the right flank.

Arrangements were then made by the Brigade Headquarters to move forward. At this juncture the Japanese who were in considerable force charged across the road between the Gurkhas and the Brigade Headquarters. The battalion commander covered by forward Dogras was forced off the road side and failed to rejoin his forward troops.

Fresh attacks also developed on the 46th Indian Infantry Brigade Headquarters and the 5th Battalion 17th Dogra Regiment. Finally, the 2nd Battalion Duke of Wellington's Regiment also came under short-

---

[37] Brig. R. G. Ekin's 'account of the Withdrawal from Kyaikto and the Battle of the Sittang', War Diary, 46 Indian Infantry Brigade.
[38] Brig. R. K. Ekin's Report gives time of halt as 15 minutes during which 2 D.W.R. had arrived. This halt occurred near Seinkalet C525. Ibid.
[39] Ibid. The road-block was opposite Seinkalet.
[40] Brig. Ekin gives the time as 0830 hours. Ibid.
[41] Brigadier Ekin's account gives brief details of the engagement. Ibid.

range heavy fire, the Japanese employing a number of light automatics and small mortars. The latter were used against many targets on the road itself. Fighting was at close quarters and most confused and both sides suffered very severe casualties. Direction was difficult to maintain in the thick jungle; companies and smaller units rapidly separated, and men of all the three Battalions became mixed up. The Brigade, however, maintained its hold on the road although Japanese attacks came right through on to it. But little progress towards Mokpalin could be made.[42] After about three quarters of an hour of this confused fighting Brig. R. G. Ekin decided to sweep the jungle on the west of the road.[43] A column of about four hundred men was collected and under his command advanced through the jungle, making as much noise as possible and clearing it of the invader. The remnants of the Brigade followed a carrier on the road covering the right flank.

After moving forward for some two miles the column became split in the dense jungle and contact was lost between its various parts. Eventually, Brig. R. G. Ekin with some three hundred men after nightfall of 22 February, reached the railway at Tawgon, south of Mokpalin.[44] The main body continued along the road. The 2nd Battalion Duke of Wellington's Regiment and the remnants of the 3rd Battalion 7th Gurkha Rifles forced through the block, marched down the road and after an hour met a party of the Dogras. Shortly after, they joined the 16th Indian Infantry Brigade which, as already stated, had halted near the Quarries and close piquetted the road.

The 4th Battalion Burma Rifles had marched in along the railway without incident.[45] But on this route, too, the Japanese were advancing. A body of twelve hundred Japanese was seen marching down the railway by 'B' company of the 2nd Battalion Duke of Wellington's Regiment. This company, after failing to make contact with the Battalion, had sought to enter Mokpalin along the railway. It found the Japanese ahead of it. Turning east it then made a detour out of the battle area, and late on the night of 24 February crossed the Sittang at a ferry several miles above the bridge.

When Brig. J. K. Jones (16 Indian Infantry Brigade) entered Mokpalin late in the afternoon he found the 2nd Battalion 5th Royal Gurkha Rifles, engaged at 1730 hours with the Japanese who were trying to break through on the east, out of the jungle, to the main road just south of the railway station. Contact had been lost with the greater part of the 1st Battalion 3rd Q.A.O. Gurkha Rifles, though the remnants were in position astride the main road north of the Station. The troops were encountering heavy fire from small arms, mortar and artillery. The defence of southern outskirts of the village, where the Japanese were advancing along the line of

[42] The engagement, mostly hand-to-hand fighting, swayed backwards and forwards. The Japanese would succeed in breaking through to the road only to be hurled back by bayonet and fire. There were severe casualties on both sides.
[43] 46 Indian Infantry Brigade had successfully prevented the Japanese from taking the road, but the block ahead on both sides of the road was still there and prevented a further advance.
[44] On the way they had been joined by 100 men of 3/7 G.R.
[45] It arrived at Mokpalin at 1300 hours. It went in search of its Brigade (46 Indian Infantry Brigade) but found the Commander 16 Ind. Inf. Bde.; the latter took it under his command.

the railway was manned by the 8th Battalion Burma Rifles (16 Indian Infantry Brigade).

Brig. J. K. Jones ascertained the situation and assumed command of all troops in the area. Less than an hour of day-light then remained. With no knowledge of the Japanese strength and dispositions as also the situation at the bridgehead, he decided that crossing of the bridge that evening was not possible. Accordingly, he decided to form a rough perimeter for the night, around Mokpalin, the positions on the east and south being maintained. In some places there were gaps, and not all adjoining units were in contact. Astride the main road and railway, some four hundred yards south of the station, the 8th Battalion Burma Rifles held the line. On its right the 2nd Battalion King's Own Yorkshire Light Infantry continued the defence along the bund and towards the river. Next in line along the river face was the 4th Battalion Burma Rifles. The 1st Royal Battalion 9th Jat Regiment held the high ground south-east of Bungalow Hill, and the remnants of the 1st Battalion 3rd Q.A.O. Gurkha Rifles were across the main road and railway north of the station. On the east of the main road the perimeter was maintained by the 2nd Battalion 5th Royal Gurkha Rifles. Along the railway, near the station, the 1st Battalion 7th Gurkha Rifles was in local reserve. In Brigade reserve were the two companies of the Duke of Wellington's Regiment. These were near the Brigade Headquarters which had been established in a building close to the bund at a point almost due west of the station. Stragglers, parties that had lost touch with the main bodies of their units, and the remnants of the 5th Battalion 17th Dogra Regiment and the 3rd Battalion 7th Gurkha Rifles were also within the perimeter. The last named units were in position in the southern sector held by the 8th Battalion Burma Rifles, and under its command.

Brig. J. K. Jones had ordered the remnants of the 1st Battalion 3rd Q.A.O. Gurkha Rifles to hold on to its position at all costs and had sent over two platoons of the 2nd Battalion 5th Royal Gurkha Rifles, to help them. All around a defensive position was quickly organized. All Japanese attacks which extended far into the night were beaten off with grenades and artillery fire. When ammunition ran short, sorties were made to the abandoned transport outside the perimeter. Here a 3" mortar was also found and used with much effect. The Japanese mortars directed by red tracer never secured a direct hit; but the Allied gunners in the village, mistaking the tracer for their Battalion distress signals, brought effective harassing fire on the area on several occasions. Throughout this time the Battalion was isolated from the village.

At dusk the Japanese from the jungle east of the village put up mortar and artillery concentration near the 1st Battalion 7th Gurkha Rifles position.[46] These and subsequent attacks throughout the night were beaten off, but the supply and ammunition situation was serious.[47] Meanwhile the Brigade Headquarters was heavily mortared and forced to find an alternative position further back behind the bund. A party of the 8th Battalion Burma Rifles was mortared out of their position but gallantly

---

[46] *War Diary*, 16 Brigade, p. 4.
[47] *War Diary*, 1/7 G.R.

went back after an hour.⁴⁸ The Koyli were also being attacked on the right flank by troops hidden in the jungle bordering on the railway line south of Mokpalin.

The 2nd Battalion 5th Royal Gurkha Rifles had formed a perimeter round the railway station with piquets on R.A.P. Hill, Solar Hill and Red House Hill. The patrol that had been sent during the day remained out all the night as there was no means of recalling it. These isolated troops did gallant work during the night 22-23 February in driving off the Japanese trying to advance on the perimeter. The main Battalion also had launched five counter-attacks, the last at 1700 hours before the 16th Indian Infantry Brigade arrived. The troops were without food or water.

As already noted the Jats had been ordered in the evening by the commander 16th Indian Infantry Brigade to occupy the long ridge south-east of Bungalow Hill and west of the railway station. They occupied it easily as no opposition was encountered there. But the panicky rush of stragglers at the burst of the Japanese shell fire made their 'advance' slow. Throughout the night they failed to gain touch with the units to the right as well as to the left and were much disturbed by stragglers.

Japanese artillery and mortar fire from time to time set alight vehicles in the long line of transport. The Allied guns grouped to the south and west of the station were continuously in action, often engaging targets at short ranges and over open sights, probably causing heavy losses to the invader. The artillery units in action were 5 Field Battery R.A., B.A.F. and 5, 12, (one section), 15 and 28 Mountain Batteries of 28 Mountain Regiment, I.A.

Brig. J. K. Jones had not been able to make a detailed reconnaissance before dark, but during the night and after a further examination of the ground another attack towards the bridge was planned. The Brigade reserve with the 1st Battalion 7th Gurkha Rifles (less one company) was to assault Buddha and Pagoda Hills as soon as possible after first light. The advance was to be covered by the Jats from their position on the high ground south-east of Bungalow Hill. Having made contact with the bridgehead and cleared the main road and railway, the assaulting troops were to maintain their positions until casualties were evacuated and such transport as could be moved had crossed the bridge. There was still no wireless communication with the force about the bridge or on the west bank of the river, and in consequence no information of this plan could be sent to the Headquarters 17th Indian Division.

As regards the 1st Battalion 3rd Q.A.O. Gurkha Rifles, throughout the night, 'C' and 'D' companies were heavily engaged on Buddha Hill and ran out of ammunition in the early hours of the morning. Just before the bridge was blown at 0530 hours on 23 February, 'C' and 'D' companies were overrun and only a few men succeeded in fighting their way back to the Battalion Headquarters. The others were either killed, captured or fought on in small pockets.⁴⁹

Meanwhile at the Bridgehead itself the situation was fast deteriorating. In the night of 22 February the Japanese closed in on the bridgehead

⁴⁸ *War Diary*, 3/7 G.R.
⁴⁹ *War Diary*, 1/3 G.R. Sheet 5.

defences in great numbers. They made several attempts to infiltrate to the bridge but the Indian troops generally held their ground except for the 3rd Battalion Burma Rifles which left its positions and ran back in disorder over the bridge. This withdrawal jeopardised the inner flanks of the 1st Battalion 4th Gurkha Rifles on the left, and a company of the Duke of Wellington's Regiment on the right, which formed the outer cordon of the defences, 4/12th Frontier Force Regiment being in depth. The reserve company of 1/4 G.R. tried to fill the gap caused by the withdrawal of the 3rd Battalion Burma Rifles but owing to darkness, it could not stop it completely. Consequently, before 0330 hours Japanese L.MG. infiltrated on to the railway line and brought fire to bear on the entire length of the bridge. Part of the defences here were wired. There was a lot of firing from both sides but fire discipline on the Allied side was not good. A company of the 1st Battalion 4th P.W.O. Gurkha Rifles and detachment of the 1st Battalion 3rd Q.A.O. Gurkha Rifles endeavoured to dislodge the Japanese L.MG. but failed owing to intense darkness and thick jungle. As time passed hostile pressure increased.

Moreover from the intense and continuous firing from the direction of Mokpalin, coupled with the non-coming of the rest of the Division, Brig. N. Hugh-Jones concluded that his two Battalions (the 2nd Battalion 5th Royal Gurkha Rifles and the 1st Battalion 3rd Q.A.O. Gurkha Rifles) and the 16th and 46th Indian Infantry Brigades were being overwhelmed. He could not, unfortunately, get into touch with either. Stragglers coming along the river bank from the south arrived with stories of troops ambushed, cut up and scattered. It seemed as if not one unit of the Division had remained in tact.

Brig. N. Hugh-Jones to whom the responsibility for blowing the bridge had been delegated was faced with a very difficult situation. With hostile pressure increasing, it seemed certain that the Japanese would attack the bridgehead in the morning in great strength. If the bridge fell, with practically no opposing troops on the other side, the Japanese would have passed two divisions straight into Rangoon. In the dash they might overwhelm the 7th Armoured Brigade, concentrating west of the Sittang, and with both banks of the Sittang in their possession the chances of getting the rest of the Division across were very small. On the other hand, to destroy the bridge meant leaving the greater part of the Division on the eastern side in a very precarious position and converting its only line of retreat into a first rate road-block. There was at the bridgehead a great hubbub of people trying to get into touch with the troops cut off. Horns were blown, signals made on whistles, battle cries and singing were resorted to, but all to no effect.

At 0400 hours, Brig. N. Hugh-Jones reported by telephone to the Divisional Commander that Japanese pressure had increased and that he could not guarantee to hold the bridge for more than an hour. Moreover, it was problematical whether the men could blow charges by daylight, as the bridge was now under observed by L.M.G. and mortar fire. The Divisional Commander had to make a difficult and quick decision. But he felt that blowing the bridge was the lesser of the two evils and told the Brigadier to blow it. The covering troops began to withdraw at 0430 hours. They took off their boots and fled over the bridgehead to a timed programme. Two platoons of 'B' company of the 1st Battalion 3rd Q.A.O. Gurkha Rifles acted as rearguard and with four minutes to go even these less two sections guarding the sand bagged emplacements on the bridge, were withdrawn. Just at the time a telephone message came to say that the Sapper officer was not ready and that the two sections must hang on. With the Japanese moving in the jungle and probing about, the two sections pushed a few men forward to keep up the fire that had been going on all the night. Fortunately the Japanese did not know that for five minutes only two sections stood between them and the bridge! The Officer Commanding the 1st Battalion 3rd Q.A.O. Gurkha Rifles and one rifleman with L.M.G. covered the Sappers as they blew the bridge which went up at 0530 hours.[50] One span collapsed.[51]

The terrific explosion caught the ears of all the scattered elements of the Division on the wrong side of the river. It soon dawned on them that it was the bridge that had been blown. They were worn out by incessant fighting and were suffering from lack of food, water and sleep. Their feelings on their only line of withdrawal having been cut, can easily be imagined. Even the Japanese were stunned for a while. All firing on their side ceased and for a brief period a deathly hush reigned over the battlefield. Soon the Japanese broke into excited shouts and chatter.

On the west bank the 1st Battalion 4th P.W.O. Gurkha Rifles took up a defensive position from the bridge northwards. The 4th Battalion 12th Frontier Force Regiment held the river front to the south of the bridge. These positions were raided by Japanese bombers

To return to the troops on the eastern side, half an hour after the destruction of the bridge a wireless message, the first since the beginning of the action, was received from Headquarters 17th Indian Division. It was from 'Punch' to 'Jonah', i.e. from Brig. D. T. Cowan B.G.S. 17th Indian Division to Brig. J. K. Jones. The message in clear referred to, 'friends waiting to welcome you at the east gate.' Obviously sent off before the blowing of the bridge the message was heartening as it indicated that the force on the west bank of the river was ready to give whatever co-operation was possible.

At about 0900 hours Brig. J. K. Jones saw the bridge and took stock of the situation. He decided to maintain his positions round Mokpalin during the day of 23 February. Orders were issued to units to hold their positions until the following day. Casualties were to be evacuated by raft, and troops thinned out. Complete withdrawal would be effected before first light on 24 February. All men who could be spared would be employed in building rafts. No men were to cross the river until ordered to do so. The plan was communicated to unit commanders at 0930 hours.

---

[50] *War Diaries* of 48 Indian Infantry Brigade and 1/3 G.R.—0530 hours.
War Diary, 17 Indian Division—0830 hours.
War Diary, 4/12 FFR—about 0520 hours.
War Diary, Edward's account, *War Diary*, 4/12 FFR—about 0400 hours.
Situation Reports I—first light on 23 February Brig. R. G. Ekin says that he heard a violent explosion at 0300 hours—*W. D.*, 46 Indian Infantry Brigade.
[51] *War Diary*, 1/4 G.R.—one span.
War Diary, 17 Indian Division—two spans and one piece.

A Subedar of the 1st Royal Battalion 9th Jat Regiment volunteered to swim across the river carrying details of this plan to the Divisional Headquarters as also a request for air support. He got across in a small boat, and delivered the message.

At 0730 hours a platoon of the Japanese marching along the railway line appeared before the 1st Battalion 3rd Q.A.O. Gurkha Rifles positions north of Mokpalin, carrying a flag, shouting and singing. L. M. Gs opened fire killing most of them and driving the rest down the river back into the jungle. Immediately thereafter a strong attack was made on the flank, but this too was flung back with heavy losses. The two mortars produced very accurate fire indeed, and "this was the hardest single blow the Battalion gave the Japanese at the Sittang."[52]

A small single engined Japanese aircraft, audaciously flying at a height of only fifty feet or so, carried out a reconnaissance of Mokpalin. On repeating its reconnaissance flight from west to east the small Japanese aircraft, for the appearance of which the troops were prepared, was shot down. Its fall was greeted with loud cheers. Immediately afterwards, at 1000 hours, infantry guns and mortars shelled the main artillery positions near the railway station. Brigade Headquarters was subjected to heavy attack for two hours. Later it moved further back to a hill overlooking railway line and river. Fighting flared up on the east and south. But with the exception of the 4th Battalion Burma Rifles, which broke, all troops in position on the perimeter held their ground. The attempts of the Japanese infantry to advance were repulsed. Soon after, however, the attacks died away.

As many men as could be spared from the defence were set to work on building rafts from the bamboos and timbers of huts and buildings, and in collecting petrol tins, water bottles, and other buoyant articles. A matter that caused grave anxiety to all commanders was the evacuation of the wounded which began at once. Walking wounded were sent down the river bank by a previously reconnoitred route, but came under accurate Japanese mortar fire. Many of the slightly wounded swam the river, more serious cases were taken across on rafts. But in spite of every effort of the doctors and others it is feared that a large number had to be left on the battlefield. Many men had already taken flight and were crossing the river contrary to orders that no withdrawal should take place before 1600 hours. Stragglers were another problem.

At 1115 hours a formation of about twenty-seven Japanese bombing aircraft made an attack on the Allied positions and on the massed transport along the main road. The bombing caused considerable damage. More gun ammunition and vehicles were set alight, houses and the surrounding jungle began to burn, and there were a number of casualties. Hostile mortar fire also increased. Sniping and small arms fire continued against the Allied troops south of the railway station.

Brig. J. K. Jones visited units and was satisfied that some troops were in no condition to hold out much longer and an attempt to maintain the positions until nightfall might lead to disintegration. Under the circums-

---

[52] *War Diary*, 1/3 G.R.

tances orders for a general withdrawal at about 1430 hours⁶³ were issued. These orders did not reach some posts with which it was impossible to get into touch. Before the withdrawal took place two bombing attacks were made on Brigade positions causing casualties and loss.

Defensive positions were withdrawn towards the river bank, but fighting still continued from isolated posts south of the railway station and east of the main road. The Japanese did not follow up the withdrawal, and it is probable that after the severe casualties they had sustained they were in no mood to do so. Moreover, many isolated detachments were still gallantly carrying on the fight.

The remains of Mokpalin village and other buildings were set on fire. So, too, were the vehicles. These conflagrations and the burning ammunition dumps made a protective barrier for the retiring troops. Guns were dismantled, and the breach mechanisms and sights were thrown into wells or the river. Machine-guns and mortars were similarly treated.

The river-beach soon became a seething mass of men and equipment. All available rafts were seized hurriedly. Groups of men could also be seen hastily making rafts out of whatever they could lay their hands on. The Battalions (the 1st Royal Battalion 9th Jat Regiment and the 2nd Battalion 5th Royal Gurkha Rifles) that came last found all the improvised rafts gone and had no other alternative but to swim. Once these Battalions had reached the river they were told that each man was to fend for himself. The violent current below the bridge made it difficult for swimmers. Worse still, the tide had come in and made the river 1½ miles wide. Japanese mortars machine-gunned the men on and in water; also

---

⁶³ *War Diary*, 16 Indian Infantry Brigade gives it as 1600 hours. But this account was written from memory.
  War Diary, 4 Burif says that the Battalion received orders to withdraw at 1430 hours.
  War Diary, 2/5 G.R. says that it received orders to withdraw at 1500 hours and reached the river last.
Brigadier Cameron writes:—
  "I am quite certain the order was for 1430 hours."
  The original order was for 2030 hours, under cover of darkness. Brigadier Jones changed this to 1430 hours after the bombing and mortar fire at midday, which had caused great demoralisation. After this bombing there was no further communication with 16 Brigade Headquarters. Some units to the south up the railway station had abandoned their positions, and O.C. 1st Battalion 7th Gurkha Rifles on the right of the 2/5th decided to withdraw at 1200 hours. Before doing so he expended all his 3" mortar ammunition. The 2/5 just east of the railway station, however, decided to stay on according to the order for 1430 hours. It was feared that the casualties had not had sufficient time for a chance of getting across the river.
  But 15 minutes before this zero hours, the exploding artillery and other ammunition and the burning bazaar of the village threatened to cut off the 2/5th from the beach and they thus withdrew at 1415 hours. A small volunteer party, under the C.O. remained behind till 1600 hours, to continue to set fire to lorries, the village and the jungle, thus forming an effective barrage of exploding shells and a wall of fire through which the Japanese could not advance. This gave a greater chance for the seething mass of leaderless men at the river beach to build rafts or to take their chance of swimming across. To many at the beach the only material now available was sodden green bamboo, and with rafts made of this the crossing was a desperate affair for the wounded and the non-swimmers, not lessened by a strong outward current for the tide had turned and was now going out, bearing into the hostile bank of the river below the beach; and, in any case, calling for a swim of two hours or more before the west bank was reached. Many of the swimmers, were carried miles down the widening estuary before reaching the west bank. Those more feeble in the water could not defeat the current and were again swept into the East bank to meet an unknown fate.

Japanese planes which were conspicuous by their absence on 22 February came quite low and machine-gunned them.[54]

Certain units maintained their cohesion to the last until the men received the order to cross. The Sittang being a nasty river to swim, all those who had to swim had to divest themselves of most of their clothes and certainly of their boots. Many men in their attempt to swim the river were drowned. Those who found it impossible to negotiate the current drifted back to where they came from or were carried down stream a few miles on to the opposite bank. Swimmers assisted non-swimmers. Many swam the river again and again under fire bringing over parties of wounded, and the whole episode, disastrous as it was, was a magnificent example of heroism on the part of all ranks of the forces engaged. Those who could not swim made their way up north and crossed in boats assisted by the Burmese or were killed or captured. The fact that a large proportion of men eventually rejoined their units shows that at no time was there any disposition to surrender to the Japanese.[55] Brig. R. G. Ekin swam the river at about 1500 hours and Brig. J. K. Jones about an hour later. The guns on the west bank of the Sittang rendered what support was possible and succeeded in keeping down Japanese machine-gun fire.

The scene on the river bank which was protected by a cliff has been described by a senior officer. "Here there was chaos and confusion; hundreds of men throwing down their arms, equipment and clothing and taking to the water. In describing this scene it is only fair to emphasise the conditions under which these men had been fighting. 17th Division had now been fighting almost day and night for five weeks continuously in most difficult country against a superior and far better trained enemy. They were exhausted after their non-stop efforts since the recent battle of Bilin river, and now on 23 February they were attacked as we know by two Japanese Divisions, and their only line of withdrawal, the Sittang bridge, had been destroyed.... As we crossed, the river was a mass of bobbing heads. We were attacked from the air and sniped at continuously from the east bank. Although it was a disastrous situation there were many stout hearts and parties shouted to each other egging on others to swim faster with jokes about the boat race!"[56]

To go back to units to which it had not been possible to communicate the withdrawal order. At about 1630 hours the 1st Battalion 3rd Q.A.O. Gurkha Rifles learnt that withdrawal had been made and decided to make for the river. At 1730 hours it formed a column, struck due west through the jungle and reached the river, some 800 yards below the bridge where many wounded were found.[57]

Japanese opposition on the bridgehead was encountered, and the platoons had to retire with casualties. In the meantime, the Battalion had started to ferry men across the river in rafts. After many men had been drowned it was stopped and the Adjutant with two others swam across in the dark to contact the Brigade Headquarters and organise boats to ferry

[54] *War Diary*, 1/9 Jats.—2/5 G.R. 23 February, 1942.
[55] Lieut.-Gen. T. J. Hutton's *Report*, pp. 28-29.
[56] Brig. R. G. Ekin's *Account, War Diary*, 46 Indian Infantry Brigade, p. 7.
[57] But all other troops except for a few stragglers seemed to have crossed the river.

men across. They returned without contacting the troops on the western bank but with a large boat. Many loads of wounded were taken across. At dawn on 24 February the rest of the Battalion moved south to be ferried that night. But they were later in the day surrounded by a strong Japanese force and after some fighting were forced to surrender. Those across reached Waw at 2230 hours after a 15 miles cross-country march and rejoined the Battalion the next day (25 February).

In spite of hostile attempts to liquidate them and in face of heavy mortar and L.M.G. fire, the 8th Battalion Burma Rifles, Koyli, remnants of the 3rd Battalion 7th Gurkha Rifles and the 5th Battalion 17th Dogra Regiment held their own positions, and their gallant defence undoubtedly assisted the general evacuation of the force. At 1930 hours when it was evident that a general withdrawal had been effected they were ordered to retire to the river. This was not followed up by the Japanese. Of this phase of the action the Commander, 16th Indian Infantry Brigade has said, "The 2nd Battalion King's Own Yorkshire Light Infantry and the 8th Battalion Burma Rifles in particular fought stubbornly to the last and .... enabled many of their comrades to cross the river successfully."

At 1900 hours 23 February, the 5th Battalion 17th Dogra Regiment learnt that the withdrawal of the Brigade had been, and was, taking place. Half an hour later it also moved to the river bank, without being followed up by the Japanese. It arrived at the river bank at 2000 hours, and there contacted the 1st Battalion 3rd Gurkha Q.A.O. Rifles. On learning from the latter that numerous men of that unit had already been drowned in attempting to cross, it was decided not to attempt the crossing at night. Therefore the Battalion attempted to cross the railway and moved up the river but finding numerous hostile patrols eventually returned to the beach at 0600 hours. It then moved to a place about 1 mile south of the bridge where it joined a force of 200 Gurkhas of the 1st Battalion 3rd Q.A.O. Gurkha Rifles. They decided to remain in hiding all day and also make rafts. At 1130 hours their position was located by a Japanese reconnaissance patrol which gave the alarm. Subsequently, small parties started swimming across the river. The remainder (60. I.O.Rs, 3 officers and 2 Jemadars) were surrounded along with the 1st Battalion 3rd Q.A.O. Gurkha Rifles and taken prisoners.

Along with the Dogras some men of the 3rd Battalion 7th Gurkha Rifles had also swum across.[58] Men of the 1st Battalion 7th Gurkha Rifles had got across the river during the night of 23/24 February and on the morning of 24 February, some in boats and some on rafts; some swam with the help of bamboo or petrol tins and many without any aid.

Remnants of the 7th Battalion 10th Baluch Regiment had crossed the Sittang on 22 February in the evening, some on rafts, some by swimming and a few by the bridge which had only a gap of 20 yards. To bridge this short-gap, ropes were used, and most men got through by this means after dark.

In short, many were able to make good their escape; a good many were drowned and only a few surrendered. But those who reached the west bank mostly arrived without arms and even clothing. Quite a good

---

[58] The Battalion lost more than 250 in the Sittang Battle.

number got back to their lines days afterwards and some, weeks later. Even so, nearly half the number of officers and more than half of other ranks had been lost. The 46th Indian Infantry Brigade had been badly knocked about and broken up. Other units were very much depleted. More serious was the almost complete loss of all equipment,—rifles, Brens and machine-guns, ammunition and transport. However, many of the transport mules which had to be turned loose were made to swim the river and later joined up with other units which had mules. In short, the 17th Indian Division was completely disorganised and had lost nearly two Brigades and ceased to exist as a fighting force for some time. The table in Appendix "C" shows the state of infantry of the 17th Indian Division on the evening of 24 February.

The commander of the 17th Indian Division later wrote that 'the Sittang battle is a fitting climax to the first phase of the operations'.[59] It was nothing less than a total disaster with far reaching results. A Division was knocked out, the holding of the Sittang line was rendered impossible and the fate of Rangoon was sealed; and when Rangoon was lost the campaign reduced itself merely to an orderly retreat. The force had to fight against a superior adversary which made the task of holding the Sittang line extremely difficult. But the disaster which overtook the Division culminating in its utter disorganisation and the almost total annihilation of two brigades, was aggravated by mistakes which in the circumstances were perhaps unavoidable, and arose, in some cases, owing to the neglect of the instructions of the Army Headquarters. Yet, it must be admitted that the units acquitted themselves well and fought bravely a hostile force which was both numerically strong and better trained. The breach of the Sittang line exposed Rangoon and made the defence of South Burma an impossible task.

Two Japanese Divisions were engaged in this momentous battle.[60] The *55th Division* followed up the retiring forces, along the main road and railway. Two Regiments of the *33rd Division, 214th and 215th*, moving from Pa-an along jungle tracks north-east of Thaton, Bilin and Kyaikto were no doubt intended to cut off and annihilate the Allied forces east of the Sittang and thus prepare the way for the crossing of the river. The right flank of the *33rd Division* reached Sittang on the dawn of 22 February and moved west, south-west and south and attacked the bridgehead and the 16th Indian Infantry Brigade and ambushed the 46th Indian Infantry Brigade. Here even the Japanese command nodded. They did not carry out an outflanking move across the river early by way of the Makkamaw ferry, six miles north of the bridge, though they did cross the river here a few days later. An early additional crossing here might well nigh have destroyed the 17th Indian Division.

The Japanese had the assistance of local guides. Many of the stragglers reported that they had found the tracks used by the Japanese to be carefully marked by paper arrows. This is only one instance of the

---

[59] *U.S.I. Journal*, July 1942, p. 217.
[60] Of the Sittang Battle Japanese accounts say the following: "On February 23 it (*33rd Division*) gained the banks of the Sittang and gave a decisive blow to the British forces numbering about 10,000 with the British 17th Division at Bilin as nucleus near the Sittang bridge". *The Japanese Account of their operations in Burma* (Dec. 41 to Aug. 45) edited by H.Q. 12th Army (601/8255/H), p. 17.

thorough methods employed by the Japanese in jungle fighting. Against their divisions specially trained in this particular form of warfare the Burma Army had been compelled to employ troops inferior in numbers, without any specialised training, in many cases even with their general training incomplete."[41]

[41] Lieut.-Gen. T. J. Hutton's *Report*, p. 29.

CHAPTER XIII

Operations in the Pegu Area

CHANGES IN COMMAND

Just before and during the battle of the Sittang river there occurred three changes of importance in the control of operations in Burma. On 21 February, Burma came under the Commander-in-Chief, India, and the War Cabinet appointed Lt.-Gen. Sir H. Alexander to succeed Lt.-Gen. T. J. Hutton in command of the troops in Burma. The latter was to remain as Chief of the General Staff after the former's arrival. As early as 18 February, the Chiefs of Staff had telegraphed to the Commander-in-Chief ABDACOM asking his views on the desirability, in view of the loss of Singapore and Sumatra, of Burma reverting to the control of the Commander-in-Chief, India. The former replied that he had never varied in his recommendation that Burma should be under the Commander-in-Chief, India for defence. On 23 February, that fateful day for the Burma Army, the Commander-in-Chief ABDACOM was ordered to close down ABDA Headquarters and to resume his appointment as the Commander-in-Chief, India.

REORGANISATION OF THE 17TH DIVISION IN PEGU AREA

At the same time, the General Officer Commanding, Burma Army met the Divisional Commander, 17th Indian Division, near Pegu on 23 February, in order to know the state of the Division. It was decided to reorganise it in the Pegu area, as one squadron of tanks of the 7th Armoured Brigade, then available for operations, could not get across the Sittang-Rangoon River canal at Waw.[1] None of the Division's Infantry Brigades could be regarded as more than mere remnants, ready to defend themselves doggedly but otherwise unfit for any of the normal operations of war. If they could have been pulled out for a few weeks to rest and refit and if it had been possible to provide their deficiencies in personnel, equipment and transport, no doubt they would have recovered. Under the existing circumstances this was of course impossible, and after only a short pause they were again engaged in the severe fighting at Pegu.

The troops were moved by train to Waw and from there to Pegu. Japanese planes did not interfere with this evacuation. On 24 February, the Divisional Headquarters was established at Pegu where the 7th Armoured Brigade was to protect the Division while it was resting, reorganising and reequipping for a short time. All except two battalions

---

[1] These 150 tanks did great service in the rest of the Burma Campaign; they conveyed or carried thousands of troops out of encirclement, broke sometimes the Japanese road-blocks, held at bay the Japanese armour, and acted as the artillery of the rear guard all the way northward to the frontier of India. Gen. Sir A. Wavell says that these tanks 'played a very important part in all the fighting in Burma after their arrival about 21 February'—*Despatch* p. 7.

of the Division had suffered heavy casualties; the Division had also lost practically all its equipment, transport, guns and ammunition. Many had lost even their rifles, others had, in addition, to discard some of their uniform including boots. The morale was low and most of the troops were exhausted. A large number of men who were unarmed had to be evacuated to reinforcement camps upcountry where they could be rested, rearmed and reequipped. However, owing to the transportation difficulties many of them could not rejoin their units until after the loss of Prome. The very little available transport, arms, clothing and equipment was distributed amongst the rest.

On 25 February it was decided to reorganise the Division into two Brigades—the 16th and 48th Brigades had been practically broken up. The three battalions of the 16th Brigade were to be (A) the 2nd Battalion King's Own Yorkshire Light Infantry and the 2nd Battalion Duke of Wellington's Regiment amalgamated (B) the 1st Royal Battalion 9th Jat Regiment and (C) the remnants of the 4th Battalion 12th Frontier Force Regiment, the 7th Battalion 10th Baluch Regiment, the 5th Battalion 17th Dogra Regiment, the 3rd, 4th and 8th Battalions Burma Rifles, all amalgamated into one. The 48th Indian Infantry Brigade was to consist of (A) the 1st Battalion 4th P.W.O. Gurkha Rifles, (B) the 2nd Battalion 5th Royal Gurkha Rifles and the 1st Battalion 3rd Q.A.O. Gurkha Rifles amalgamated to form the 5th Battalion 3rd Gurkha Rifles and (C) the 1st Battalion 7th Gurkha Rifles and the 3rd Battalion 7th Gurkha Rifles forming the 7th Gurkha Rifles.[2]

REINFORCEMENTS

The 7th Armoured Brigade with the 1st Battalion the Cameronians arrived in Rangoon on 21 February, and in spite of insufficient dock labour disembarked quickly. One squadron of the Armoured Brigade reached Pegu on that date, and came under command of the 17th Indian Division.[3] The remainder moved on 23 February. The Cameronians were attached to it as a motorised regiment. It had originally been intended to use the Armoured Brigade in a counter offensive role in Malaya, but the withdrawal to Singapore island precluded the possibility, and Java was unsuitable for armoured operations. During his visit to the Salween on 5 and 6 February Gen. Sir A. Wavell, Commander-in-Chief, ABDA, was impressed by the possibility of the use of armoured troops in that area and so decided to direct the 7th Armoured Brigade to Burma which was then on its way from the Middleast to the ABDA Command. In anticipation of its arrival every effort had been made to strengthen the bridges, and to convert railway bridges for the passage of tanks in order to give them as large an area to operate as possible. In Burma it

---

[2] *War Diary*, 17th Indian Division 'G' Branch for 25 February.
Even with this amalgamation numbers were not sufficient to create full battalions. All specialist establishments had to be reduced. The wireless sets provided after the Sittang battle did not function properly and were abandoned at Pegu. No helios or lamps were issued to many battalions and it is a remarkable fact that a whole Brigade worked and fought with no internal means of communication other than an occasional telephone supplied by the Brigade Signal Section right up to the final evacuation of Burma.
[3] *Situation Report*, Part I, p. 57.

played an invaluable role from the third week of February up to the withdrawal into India three months later. It was, however, too late to take part in the operations east of the Sittang. But it did impose considerable delay on the Japanese west of the Sittang and relieved pressure on the tired troops in the Pegu area.

PEGU FORCE—18 FEBRUARY

Meanwhile, on 18 February the Pegu Force had been formed to counter possible Japanese attempts to cross the estuary of the Sittang by boat and cut off the allied communications with Pegu or to land near the Rangoon river.[4] Initially this task had been assigned to small detachments of Burma Frontier Force and Burma Military Police. But the arrival of reinforcements, the 1st Battalion the West Yorkshire Regiment and the 1st Battalion the Cameronians, made eventually the formation of a strong Pegu force possible. This force consisted of the 1st Battalion the West Yorkshire Regiment, F.F. 6 and detachments of the Burma Military Police. It was given the role of protecting Pegu from the southeast and linking up with the 17th Indian Division at the Sittang bridge. In co-operation with the force an armoured train was maintained on the Pegu-Thongwa branch of the railway. Further east, another force made up of a company of the 1st Battalion, the Gloucestershire Regiment, F.F. 7 and some Burma Military Police was responsible for the approaches to Syriam from the sea.

THE ROLE OF REINFORCEMENTS

After the withdrawal from Sittang a protective screen for the 17th Indian Division was provided by the Armoured Brigade (composed of the 7th Queen's Own Hussars, the 2nd Battalion Royal Tank Regiment and 414 R.H.A. Battery) and Pegu Force while the Burma Military Police were watching the coast.[5] The 7th Armoured Brigade had detachments at Payagyi, Waw and Tamatake while motor patrols based on Pegu were sent out for considerable distances. The 1st Battalion the Cameronians, which was the support Battalion to the Armoured Brigade, was to carry out local counter-attacks and offensive action as far as possible on the line Payagyi-Waw. Further-south similar duties were performed by the 1st Battalion the West Yorkshire Regiment. With Headquarters and two companies at Thanatpin it maintained patrols in Kamase and Yitkan areas and one company at Minywa was patrolling north-east towards Waw and Nyaunggaing. Coast watching was done by Burma Military Police. The crossings of the Sittang from Shewegyin to Kunzeik were watched by the 2nd Brigade of 1 Burma Division at Nayaunglebin. But the force was not enough to cover such a long front of three miles; moreover many of the Burma Rifles were deserting with arms. The 1st Burma Division on relief by the Chinese VI Army had moved out of the Shan States and was concentrating to cover Karenni and the Sittang Valley sector south of Toungoo.

[4] Lt.-Gen. T. J. Hutton's *Report*, p. 24.
[5] 17th Indian Division *War Diary, Operation Instruction No. 15*, dated 25 Feb., 1942.

For some days after the withdrawal across the Sittang the main duty devolving upon the forward Battalions was the protection of the stragglers and the vast number of Indian refugees streaming north out of the battle zone. Hostile Burmans were active and many were armed with British weapons. They attacked unarmed stragglers, robbed and murdered Indian refugees, spied upon the movements and dispositions of the troops, and indulged in promiscuous sniping. The 1st Battalion the Cameronians dealt with many of these disaffected elements. The civil administration had ceased to function in the district and the almost complete absence of civil liaison officers made it difficult to deal adequately with the suspects.

FIGHTING IN FRONT OF PEGU

On 26 February and succeeding days there had been considerable fighting about Waw, where Lieutenant General Hutton believed that the Burmese forces took an active part in the operations on the side of the invaders. The Japanese tactics were "to work across the plains by night with the object of infiltrating into the jungle to the west of the main road from Pegu to Toungoo". They had cut the road at Pyinbon on 25 February, but the position was restored by the Armoured Brigade. It was impracticable to prevent the Japanese infiltration through the Pegu Yomas and the Jungle, as the lack of forces had left a gap of about 30 miles between the 17th Indian Division and the Burma Brigade at Nyamglabin.

DETACHMENTS SENT TO THARRAWADDY—27 FEBRUARY

There were reports of Japanese infiltration through the Pegu Yomas to Tharrawaddy (on the Rangoon-Prome Road) with the object of cutting the Prome road, and of causing deterioration in the internal situation in that area. Hence on 27 February, a squadron of tanks and one company of the 1st Battalion the West Yorkshire Regiment were sent back to Tharrawaddy. The company commander was to take command of all the troops in Tharrawaddy. His task was fourfold: to guard the very important dump of supplies and petrol which at that time was quite unguarded (a fortunate move in view of subsequent events), watch north and south of Tharrawaddy to prevent interference with road traffic, watch tracks leading to Tharrawaddy from the east and organise the civil administration with the help of local civil authorities. The company commander was to communicate direct with the Headquarters Burma Army.[6]

In an appreciation despatched on 27 February, the General Officer Commanding indicated the probable line of Japanese action, which was to infiltrate across the open country west of the Sittang by night into the close jungle of Pegu Yomas and eventually cut the Rangoon-Prome road. In view of these developments, fear was expressed as regards the successful defence of Rangoon, especially owing to the non-arrival of the 7th Australian Division. This brought to a head the question of carrying out the demolition and evacuation of Rangoon, particularly because with

---

[6] Lt.-Gen. T. J. Hutton's *Report*, p. 31. Also 17th Indian Division *War Diary*, 'G' Branch for 27 February.

the withdrawal of 1 West Yorks from Syriam, the coastline was undefended and the oil refineries were completely exposed. It was clearly mentioned by the Burma Army Command that the 17th Indian Division was in no position to resist further Japanese attacks and would have to be withdrawn by mechanised transport to "selected rear lines covered by the 7th Armoured Brigade". This could merely impose some delay but eventual loss of South Burma appeared inevitable. The Japanese would, it was believed, occupy the oilfields and if they decided on an offensive into Upper Burma, the only course open to the Burma Army would be to retire on the Assam road. As regards Rangoon, blowing up the demolitions and evacuating it seemed to be the inevitable course unless effective reinforcements were available.[7]

DEMOLITIONS IN RANGOON

The General Officer Commanding was, at the same time, of the opinion that with the forces available, the line of withdrawal from Rangoon could not be covered for more than a brief period in the event of Japanese attack. The problem was, therefore, whether it was desirable to prejudice the work of demolition and the evacuation of essential civil personnel, administrative units, etc., by hanging on sufficiently long to enable 63rd Indian Infantry Brigade, a young and only partially trained formation, to arrive. He was of the view that it was not, and both the Air and Naval opinion was against it especially in view of the risks involved in bringing a convoy into Rangoon at that stage. While, therefore, this recommendation was referred to India, all preparations were proceeded with for the demolitions.[8]

Gen. Sir A. Wavell arrived at Magwe in Upper Burma on the morning of 1 March. He had a conference with the Governor, Lt.-Gen. T. J. Hutton and Air Vice Marshal D. F. Stevenson. On the information available to him he considered the decision to evacuate Rangoon as premature. He was fortified in this view by the possibility of reinforcements, and ordered the convoys which had been turned back from Rangoon to be diverted to that port. In his opinion there was 'no reason why Rangoon should not continue to be held at least long enough to enable the reinforcements on the way (the 63rd Indian Infantry Brigade, and a Field Regiment) to be landed.' He was led to this opinion by the fact that at that stage there was no evidence of any great hostile strength west of the Sittang, while "the 7th Armoured Brigade was still in tact, and Chinese troops were moving down towards Toungoo". He "therefore countermanded orders for evacuation of Rangoon and directed that all ships with stores or troops for Burma should proceed."[9]

DIVISIONAL COMMANDER'S PLANS TO EVACUATE PEGU—COUNTER-MANDED BY GEN. SIR A. WAVELL

Meanwhile the Headquarters, 17th Indian Division had been located at Hlegu where the 16th Indian Infantry Brigade was also withdrawn

[7] Tel No. 0932 dated 27 February, 1942 Burmarmy to Armindia File *Appreciations.*
[8] Telegrams dated 27 and 28 Feb. *Ibid.*
[9] Wavell's *Despatch,* p. 8.

owing to its weak state.[10] The Divisional Commander had taken alarm at the mounting infiltration of the Japanese, and the report that they were converging on Myitkyo, Shwegyin and Pyinbon. On 28 February, he had recommended the immediate evacuation of Pegu. Gen. Sir A. Wavell visited the Divisional Headquarters at Hlegu on 1 March and found that the report on which the Divisional Commander's recommendation was based had proved a false one. The Commander-in-Chief found the Divisional Commander to be a 'sick man' and replaced him by Brig. D. T. Cowan 'who commanded the 17th Division with success for the remainder of the campaign'. On 2 March, Gen. Sir A. Wavell visited the troops of the 17th Indian Division and the 7th Armoured Brigade on the Pegu front and then flew to Lashio where he had two satisfactory interviews with Marshal Chiang-Kai-Shek.[11]

In view of Gen. Sir A. Wavell's orders, the 48th Brigade was retained in Pegu, troops in Payagyi and Waw which had fallen back on Pegu on 28 February in anticipation of a general withdrawal were pushed forward again on 1 March. But Waw had been meanwhile occupied by the Japanese.

JAPANESE MOVES

We may now turn to the Japanese side. After the victorious battle of the Sittang the *Fifteenth Army* concentrated its forces on the east bank of the Sittang in preparation for a strike at Rangoon. At that time they learnt that there was a strong Allied force in the vicinity of Pegu and Waw and in Toungoo and that the Chinese Armies also were moving down. The Japanese therefore split their forces in two. The main body of the *33rd Division* was to cross the Sittang six miles north of Mokpalin and advance on Hlegu and Hmawbi. The *Kawashima Detached Unit (55th Cavalry Regiment, the 1st Infantry Battalion 55th Division, and one company of Mountain Artillery)* was sent to the area north of Daiku in order to guard the rear against the Allied forces around Toungoo.[12] The main body of the *55th Division (less the Kawashima Unit)* was ordered to advance to the area south of Pegu. The *3rd Battalion 143rd Regiment* with one *Battery of Mountain Artillery* was sent to capture Syriam with the oil refineries intact.[13] It was known as the *Syriam Force* and was commanded by Lieutenant Colonel Hasegawa. The Japanese accounts however differ as regards the date of the crossing of the Sittang, the margin of difference being four days, end of February to 4 March.[14]

[10] *War Diary*, 17 Ind. Div. G.
[11] Wavell's *Despatch*.
[12] *Japanese Account of their Operations in Burma*—December 1941—August 1945, 601/8255/H, pp. 18-19.
[13] *A short history of Japanese 55th Division*, 601/7247/H, p. 2.
[14] 2 March, 601/7785/H, p. 1. *History of the Japanese 15th Army*. SEATIC Bulletin 245, for Fifteenth Army. End of February, 601/7247/H, p. 1. *A short History of 55 Jap Div.* for 55th Division. Night of 3/4 March 601/7735/H, p. 23. *History of the Japanese 15th Army* for 33rd Division. Night of 2-3 March 601/8255/H, p. 18. Japanese account of their ops in Burma (Dec. 41 to Aug. 45) for both Divisions. Night of March 2-3 601/7720/H, p. 1. *History of the Japanese 15th Army* for both Divisions.

FIRST CLASH PAYAGYI AREA—27 FEBRUARY

Meanwhile, in the Pegu area, in the early hours of 27 February, a patrol of the Cameronians was attacked by a Japanese force some miles north of Payagyi. The attack was made whilst the patrol was talking to an apparently friendly Burman. The same day Japanese cyclists were observed, but it was not possible to establish contact with them. On the same day, too, 'A' Squadron of the 2nd Battalion Royal Tank Regiment supported by a company of the Cameronians entered Tazon, twelve miles north of Payagyi, and cleared it of a force of hostile Burmans. Fourteen were killed and six captured. It was then firmly established that the Japanese had raised, armed and organised a Burmese force known as the Burma Independent Army. The tanks then went on to clear the village of Sinchidaing, eight miles south-east of Tazon, of Burmans.

FIGHTING AT WAW AND PYINBON—1-3 MARCH

On 1 March a detachment of the 2nd Battalion Royal Tank Regiment contacted a detachment of hostile troops (a mixed force) from Waw but only skirmishes occurred there. The next day a squadron of the same Regiment patrolling on the bank of the canal north of Waw came under anti-tank fire. Three tanks were hit. That afternoon an attack by a company of the Cameronians supported by artillery was made on Waw, but the Japanese were in considerable strength there and could not therefore be dislodged. Two tanks were hit by anti-tank fire. At 1645 hours RAF aircraft bombed Waw and left it in flames.[15]

On 3 March there was further fighting near Waw and at Pyinbon where the Japanese had put down a road-block. As was so often the case this block was erected to protect the flank of a force by-passing the 17th Indian Division positions. On 4 March another block was established just south of Pyuntaza, where elements of the 2nd Burma Brigade were in action. Between these two blocks the Japanese were moving across the Rangoon-Mandalay road into the Pegu Yomas with the object of outflanking Pegu. Through the gap between Pyuntaza and Pyinbon went columns with tanks and guns. They marched by night.

The block at Pyinbon was first encountered by a carrier patrol of the Cameronians. Subsequently, when a Squadron of the 2nd Battalion Royal Tank Regiment reconnoitred Pyinbon, two tanks were damaged by shell fire. The Japanese then began to advance south towards Payagale and Payagyi.

FIGHTING NEAR NAUNGYPATTAYA—3-4 MARCH

From Waw the Japanese also pushed forward south-west along the railway to Kyaikhla, and on the morning of 3 March were established in a patch of jungle near that village. A company of the Cameronians attacked from the direction of Naungpattaya. It was supported by artillery and a Squadron of the 2nd Battalion Royal Tank Regiment. The

---

[15] On 1 March an aircraft attacked concentrations of small boats near the Sittang bridge.

only covered approach to the Japanese position was by way of a nullah. This was found to be filled with water and covered by Japanese machine-guns. The Cameronians could make no progress and were extricated with some difficulty.

Next day the Japanese and Thakins infiltrated round two companies of the Cameronians at Naungpattaya and heavily attacked them. The latter were therefore withdrawn to Shanywagyi. At Payagyi the Japanese attacked at first light. Although repulsed by the Cameronian company there, they succeeded in establishing themselves in the town. It was decided to eject them by means of an attack supported by bombing aircraft, artillery, and a squadron of tanks.

FIGHTING AROUND PAYAGYI—4-5 MARCH

The bombing aircraft failed to appear and accordingly the attack was cancelled, but a troop of the 7th Queen's Own Hussars went through the town without opposition. Patrols of the Cameronians followed and encountered Japanese parties, which were dealt with in hand to hand fighting. Considerable casualties were inflicted and a gun and mortar were captured. But the force available was insufficient to prevent further penetration in the area. Meanwhile, the Japanese had occupied Tandawgyi close to Payagyi.

On 5 March the Japanese held the road from Waw to Payagyi, and it seemed that an out-flanking movement on Pegu from the north-west was in progress. At 0130 hours a patrol of the 1st Battalion the West Yorkshire Regiment which had relieved the 1st Battalion the Cameronians was ambushed south of Payagyi, and it was later found that a road-block had been set up in Payagyi itself. A patrol of the 2nd Battalion Royal Tank Regiment moving north of Pegu on the west bank of the Pegu river came under fire from an anti-tank gun and it was forced to turn back. During the morning vehicles on the road between Pegu and Rangoon were fired at from several positions. Later the Japanese established a block on this road, but this was cleared with little difficulty by the tanks of the Royal Tank Regiment. The Japanese had passed these troops in darkness. This was, however, a clear indication that the Japanese were now well behind the Allied forces in Pegu.

It was on this day that a Japanese tank was encountered for the first time.[16] The existence of many water courses and small bunds surrounding rice fields had proved unexpectedly serious obstacles to the British tanks and restricted their operations. Coming however, within range of a troop of the 7th Queen's Own Hussars near Shanywagyi the Japanese tank was at once destroyed. It was a small two man tank and appeared to be similar to the Italian C V/43 model. Supported by a company of Cameronians the tanks then cleared the Japanese from the vicinity of Shanwagyi, and patrolled the area immediately south of Payagyi. In the afternoon the RAF bombed Waw and left it in flames.

On the morning of 5 March, Lt.-Gen. T. J. Hutton proceeded to the Headquarters of the 17th Indian Division at Hlegu with the intention of

---

[16] As early as 4 March, air reconnaissance had reported their existence.

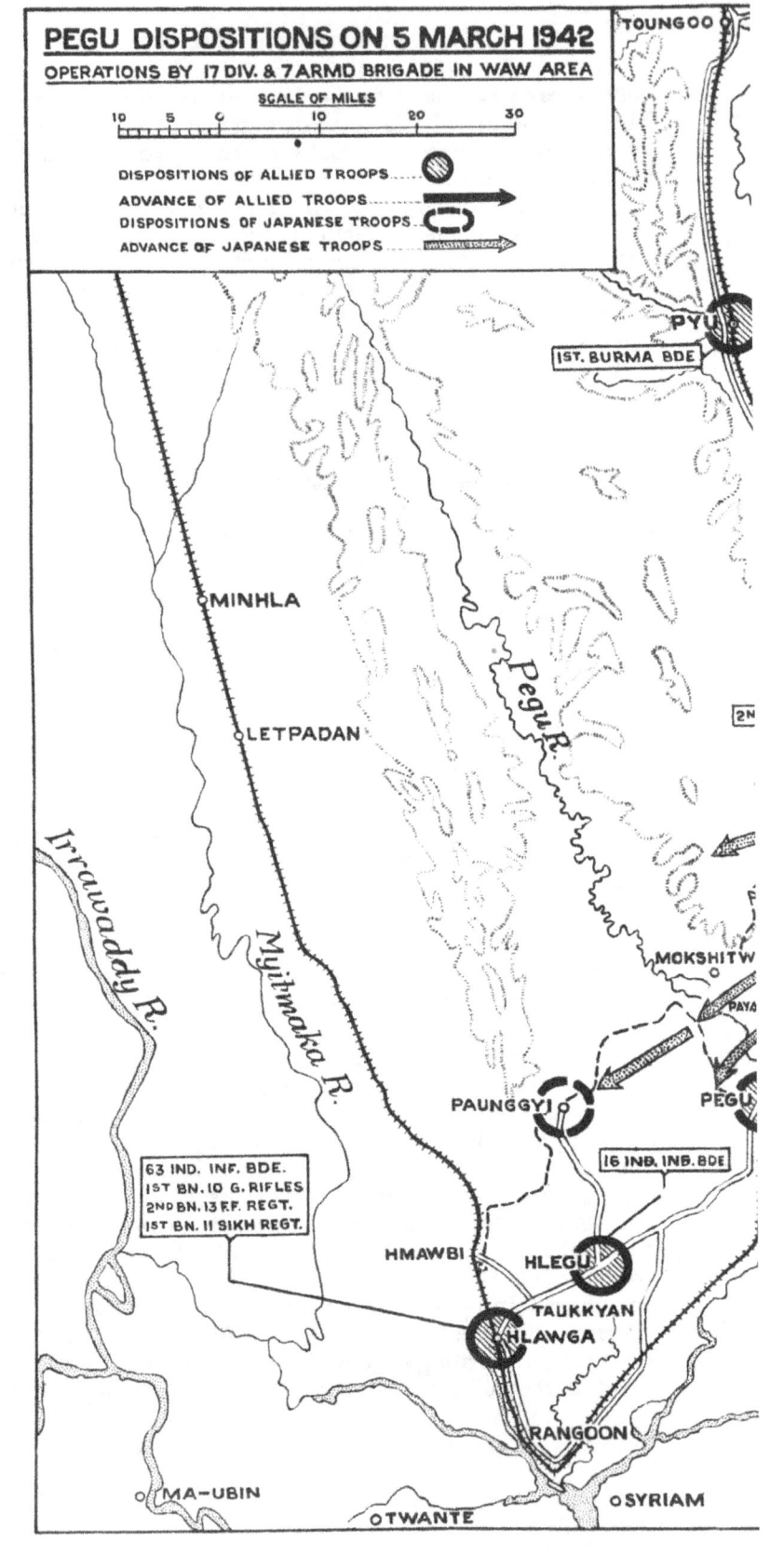

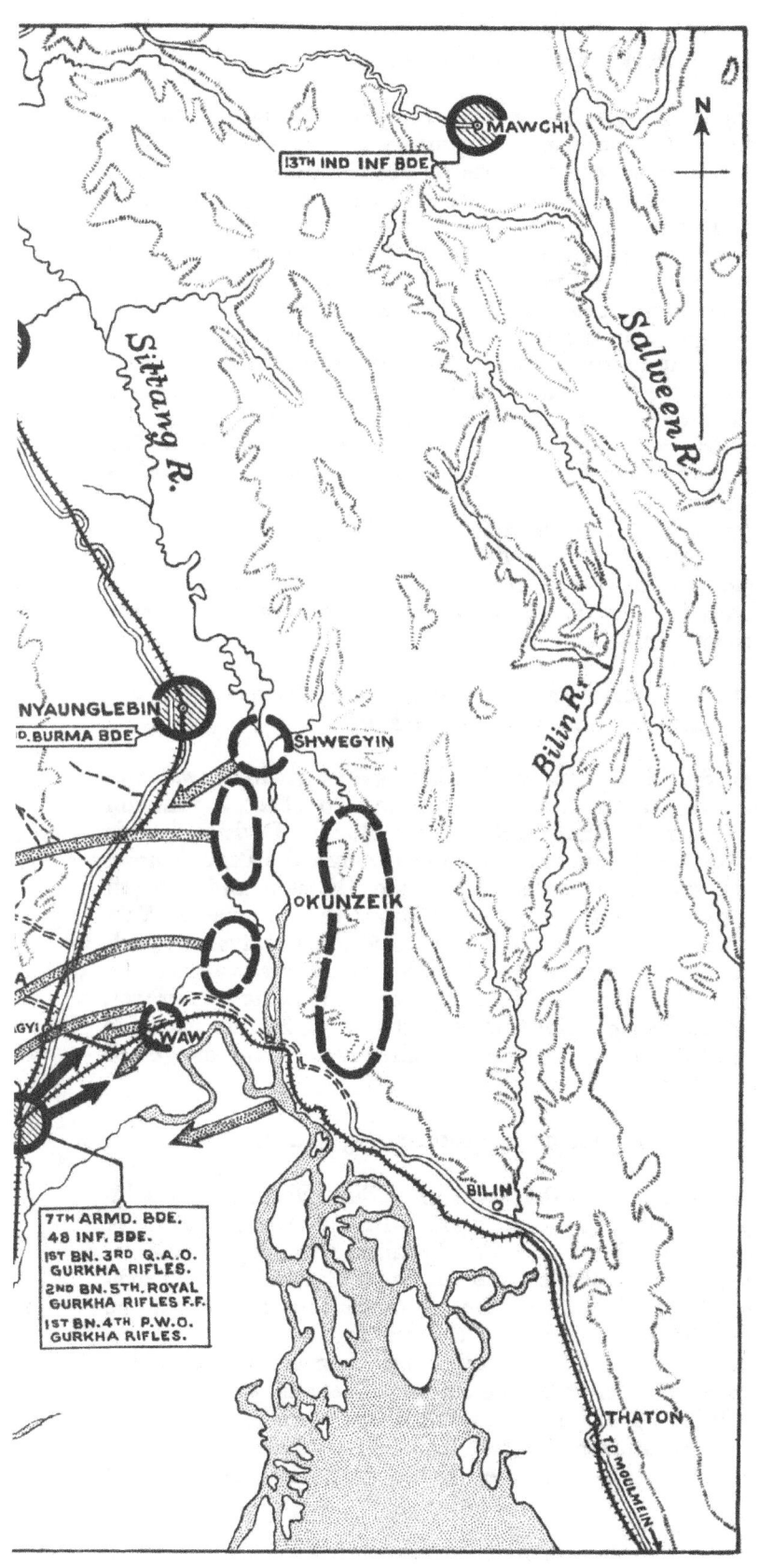

visiting the troops holding Pegu, but by that time the road was cut and he was unable to proceed. The position at the time was that the 48th Indian Infantry Brigade was holding the outskirts of Pegu while the Armoured Brigade with the Cameronians and West Yorkshires was acting in a mobile role in the open country to the east. After consultations with Maj. Gen. D. T. Cowan, who had just assumed command of the Division, he issued orders to clear the road and withdraw the 48th Brigade to Hlegu and the 16th Brigade to the Taukkyan cross roads. This was necessitated as much by the situation at Pegu as by the fact that a hostile column, believed to be with tanks, had already passed through Paunggyi, north of Hlegu, and was making for the Prome road which might, it appeared, be cut in the near future. The withdrawal of the force in a fit state to continue the defence of the oil-fields, and the evacuation of the administrative units, demolition parties, and essential civilians from Rangoon were both obviously seriously threatened.

However, while Lt.-Gen. T. J. Hutton was still at Hlegu Gen. Sir H. Alexander arrived in Rangoon on 5 March to assume command of the Army in Burma and at once visited the Headquarters of the 17th Indian Division there and met Lt.-Gen. T. J. Hutton who was to remain in Burma as Chief of the General Staff.

GEN. SIR H. ALEXANDER'S PLANS TO CHECK INFILTRATION ACROSS PEGU YOMA—5 MARCH

As related later, Sir. H. Alexander decided against a withdrawal and was of the opinion that it might still be possible to effect a junction between the 17th Indian Division and the 1st Burma Division. This would prevent any further Japanese infiltration through the Pegu Yomas. Consequently, Sir H. Alexander ordered the 17th Division and the 7th Armoured Brigade to carry out offensive operations in the area of Waw and at the same time directed the 1st Burma Division to advance south from Nyaunglebin. To support the 17th Division there was available the 63rd Brigade which had just arrived in Rangoon from India. However, events were moving too fast to permit of any attempt at further offensive action in this area. The force in Pegu was already in great danger of being cut off.

SITUATION ON HIS ASSUMING COMMAND—5 MARCH

The situation at the time was that the 17th Indian Division was holding the area at Pegu—Hlegu; the 48th Infantry Brigade was in defensive positions about the town. The composite Battalion made up of the 1st Battalion 3rd Q.A.O. Gurkha Rifles and the 2nd Battalion 5th Royal Gurkha Rifles, held the north face of the perimeter eastwards from the railway bridge across the Pegu river. On the east face was the 1st Battalion 4th P.W.O. Gurkha Rifles. The defence was then continued on the south of the town back to the river by the combined 1st and 3rd Battalions of the 7th Gurkha Rifles. The 7th Armoured Brigade was operating east of Pegu. The 6th Indian Infantry Brigade (the 1st Battalion 10th Gurkha Rifles, the 2nd Battalion 13th Frontier Force Regiment and the 1st

Battalion 11th Sikh Regiment) had disembarked on 3 March and was at Hlawga, 16 miles north of Rangoon. It was in a position to support the 17th Indian Division but its transport was still on board ship and was not expected to arrive before two or three days. A reconnaissance party consisting of the Brigade Commander (Brig. J. Wickham) and Battalion Commanders arrived in Pegu on the evening of 5 March but it was too late to carry out reconnaissance. The intention was that the Brigade would come to Pegu to help the 48th Indian Infantry Brigade in the defence of the town for a limited period.[17] The 1st Burma Division was located as follows:—the 13th Indian Infantry Brigade was at Mawchi, the 1st Burma Brigade was at Pyu and the 2nd Burma Brigade was at Nyaunglebin. There was a gap of 30 miles between the forward elements of the 1st Burma Division and the 17th Indian Division.

Japanese forces were in Waw and the neighbouring villages and the north-east of Pegu; in addition from 3 March, Japanese columns (*33rd Division*) had been infiltrating across the Sittang river between Pegu and Nyaunglebin under cover of darkness. Their objective, as we know from the Japanese accounts was not only to cut the Rangoon-Prome road as it was thought then, but also to move on Hmawbi, Hlegu, and Rangoon.[18] These sources also say that this force met with no resistance. It had taken advantage of the small gap between Kunzeik and the Sittang Bridge.

Though the situation appeared to be serious, Gen. Sir H. Alexander thought that the only course of action which could save the situation was to effect a junction between the 1st Burma Division and the 17th Indian Division with the object of preventing any further Japanese infiltration into the Yomas. But we know from Japanese account that it was all too late as the *33rd Division* had already passed through the gap.

DEFENCE OF PEGU

5 March

The offensive carried out on 5 March by the 17th Indian Division and part of the Armoured Brigade from Pegu was locally successful, but while this operation was on, the Japanese attacked from the wooded country bordering Pegu on the west and succeeded in capturing a part of the town. With the depleted numbers in the Brigade and with a big town to defend, it was not possible for the 48th Indian Infantry Brigade to throw a complete harbour ring around it; hence the defensive position prepared by it could be nothing more than a semi-circle on the east bank of the Pegu river with the 5th Battalion 3rd Gurkha Rifles on the north, the 1st Battalion 4th P.W.O. Gurkha Rifles in the centre, and the 7th Gurkha Rifles in the south. There was an open back door on the west of the river including the railway station; and the main Japanese advance next day came through this gap. There was no field artillery under command of the 48th Indian Infantry Brigade.[19]

---

[17] The 63rd Indian Infantry Brigade was originally intended to take Hlegu-Taukkyan position from the 16th Indian Infantry Brigade which was then to move to Syriam Tharrawaddy-Prome-Magwe area.
[18] *History of the Japanese 15th Army*, 601/7785/H, p. SEATIC Bulletin No. 245.
[19] Brig. R. T. Cameron's *Pegu War Diary* 2/5 G.R.

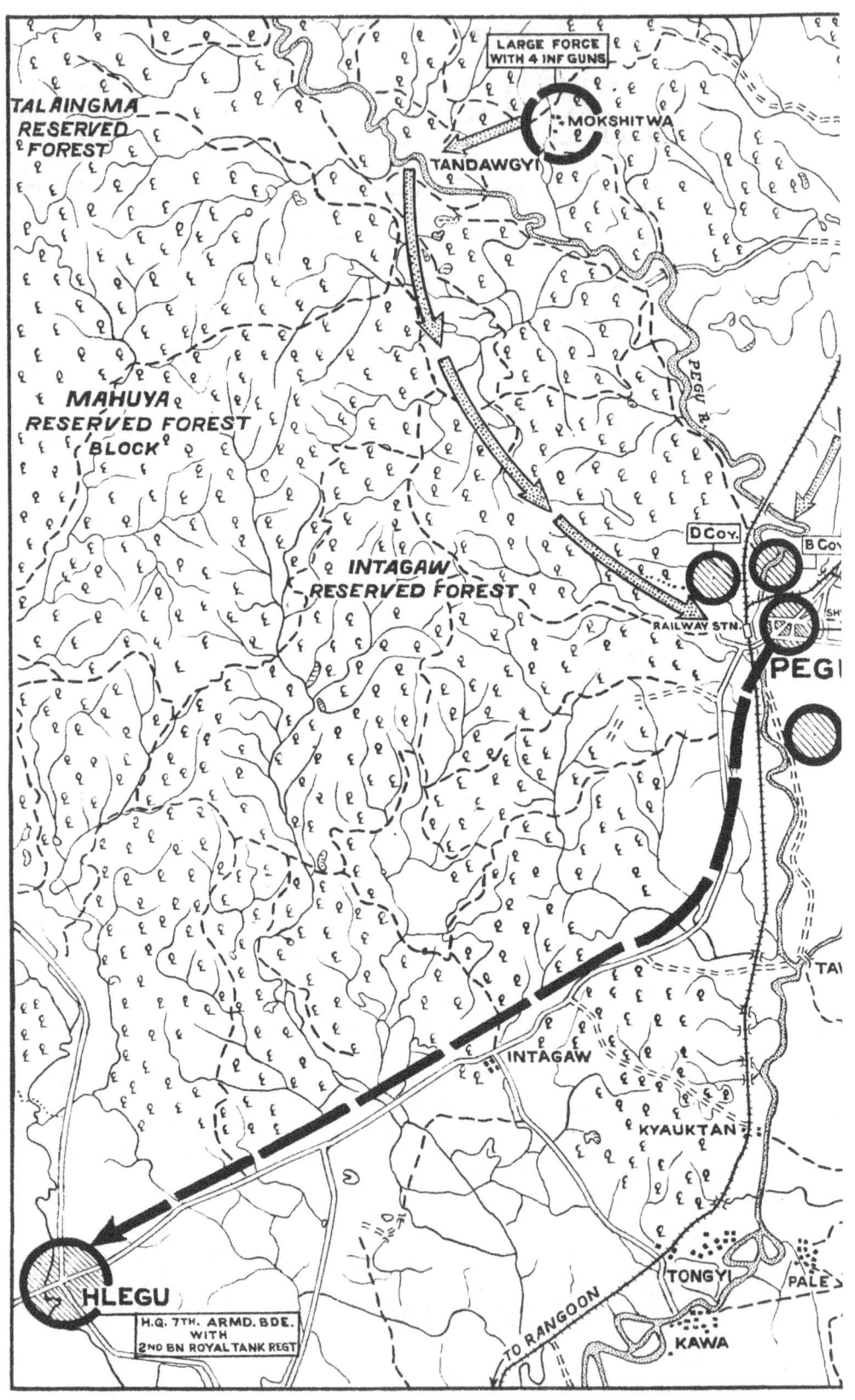

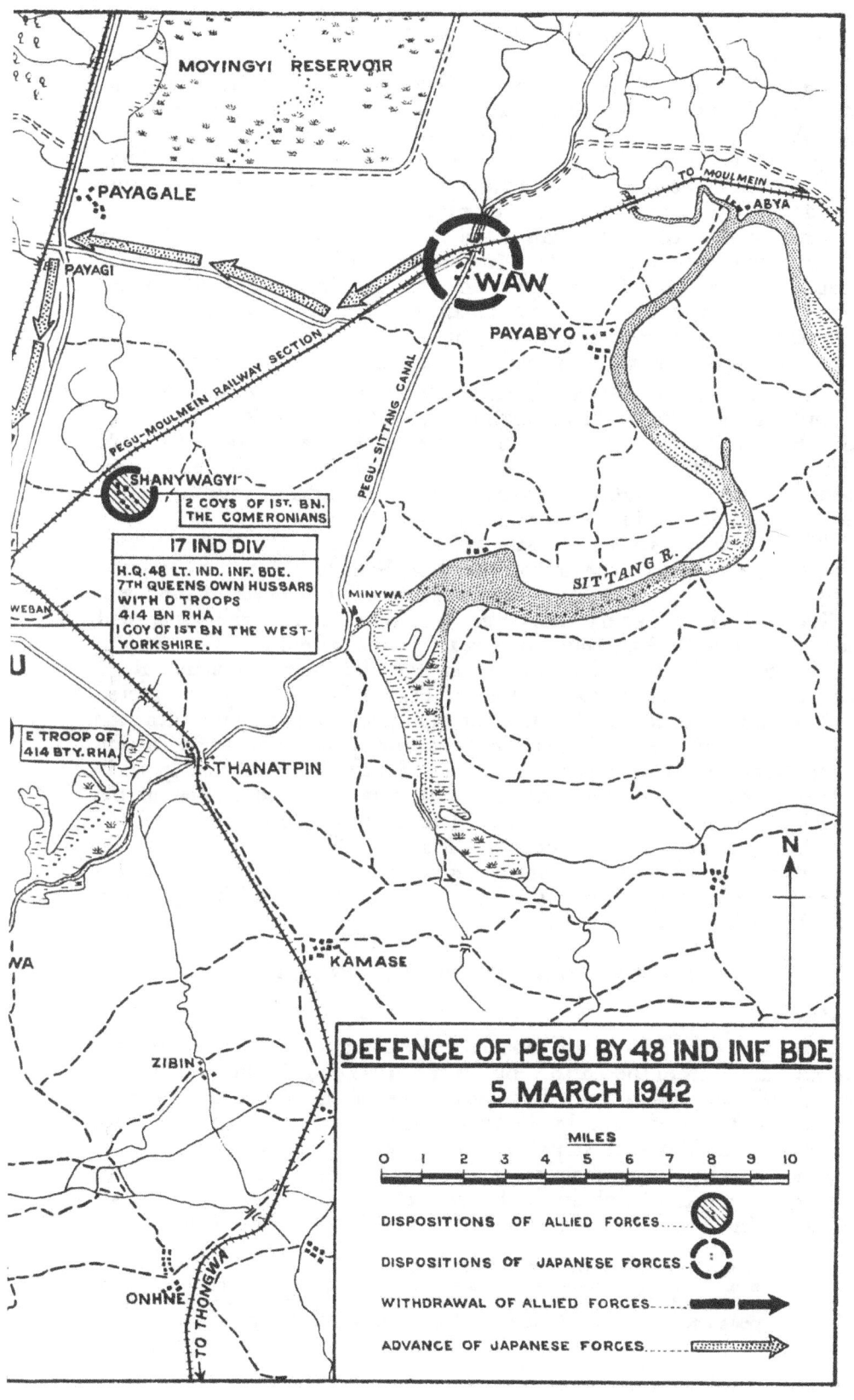

Pegu had been air bombed on 27 February and 3 March. In the latter raid the supply depot and main road were hit. At 1530 hours on 5 March the Japanese bombed the road bridges over the railway and river in Pegu. This did no damage to the bridges but started large fires which raged over half the town till mid-night before the main road was again passable. It was reported in the evening that the hostile forces were approaching the railway line from the north. A large force with four Infantry guns was reported at Mokshitwa, north-west of Pegu, with advanced elements at Tandawgyi.[20] In fact the Japanese were moving from Waw through the cross-roads village of Payagyi.[21] An early attack in strength was expected, and that night many boats were built one mile down the Pegu river, and left ready for use in case of withdrawal.

In the evening of 5 March, Headquarters 7th Armoured Brigade with the 2nd Battalion Royal Tank Regiment withdrew from Pegu to Hlegu. The 7th Queen's Own Hussars, 414th Battery R.H.A., and attached British Infantry were left in support of the 48th Indian Infantry Brigade. These troops were directly under command of the 17th Indian Division. They were disposed in the following manner :—

The 7th Queen's Own Hussars with 'D' Troop, 414th Battery RHA and a company of the 1st Battalion the West Yorkshire Regiment leaguered for the night east of the Pegu river and immediately north of the town. 'E' Troop of 414th Battery RHA was in harbour astride the main road about a mile and a half south of Pegu. Headquarters and the remaining two companies (B and D) of the 1st Battalion West Yorkshire Regiment covered the north-western area of Pegu. 'B' company was posted north of and astride the junction of the main railway line with the Moulmein branch line. These railways afforded possible lines of approach to the Japanese. 'D' company was disposed in the area of the gigantic reclining image of Buddha west of the railway. The companies of the 1st Battalion the Cameronians were in Shanwagyi These were ordered to withdraw to Pegu at 0700 hours on 6 March. The other two companies were in Pegu west of the river, one of them covering the road bridge across the river, the other protecting the long and important road bridge across the railway just south of the station.

JAPANESE OCCUPATION OF THE RAILWAY STATION

6 March

At dawn on 6 March the Japanese were found to be approaching the railway station from the north. But as the advancing Japanese converged on the railway station, their left flank came within range of the static defences and was engaged by Vickers gun fire at a range of 1500 yards and dispersed. Battalion snipers further disrupted the left fringe of the Japanese advance. But their main force was further moving out in the scrub and could not be observed clearly. This Japanese movement was a threat behind the defence lay-out on the east bank of the river. There

---

[20] *War Diary*, 17th Indian Division. 'G' Branch.
[21] "The main force passed through Waw and occupied Pegu on 7 March 1942, passing through the cross-roads village of Payagyi in rather higher spirits than they did three and a half years later". *A short History of 55th Japanese Division*, 601/7247/H, p. 2.

was a heavy mist. Advancing, the Japanese occupied the railway station and the jungle fringing the western outskirts of the town.

Road-block—6 March

At 0930 hours on 6 March, it was learnt that the main road from Pegu to Rangoon was cut by the Japanese who had established a road-block five miles south of Pegu, and 3/4 mile south of the village of Payathonzu where the road takes a bend to the left.[22] The road had been under sniper fire the previous day, when a Royal Artillery convoy had also been shot up north of Intagaw.

On the previous day (5 March) the 63rd Indian Infantry Brigade less Field Ambulance and SIS had been ordered to Pegu for limited operations. Escorted by one squadron of the 2nd Battalion Royal Tank Regiment they marched to Taukkyan and from there to Intagaw, and arrived at Banbwegon at the Tawa road junction at about 1200 hours on 6 March.[23] At about 1130 hours the reconnaissance party at Pegu received information that the 63rd Indian Infantry Brigade had embussed and was on its way up the road Taukkyan-Pegu. Two hours earlier they had received reports of the road-block and waited for this to be cleared. Tanks of the 2nd Battalion Royal Tank Regiment forced their way through the block and went on to Pegu to bring back Brig. J. Wickham and unit commanders of the 63rd Brigade. They reported that the road-block was not manned by the Japanese. The reconnaissance party was ordered back to the Brigade, it being apparent that the Japanese had vacated the road-block. The party set off in three wheeled carriers and one tank. One carrier each was provided by 5/3 G.R., 1/4 G.R. and 7 G.R. At 1215 hours the party was hopelessly ambushed and badly shot up by Japanese snipers, perched on trees overlooking the road. The 5/3 G.R. and 7 G.R. carriers were destroyed and all their occupants killed. The only survivors were those in the 1/4 G.R. carrier. But here too, every occupant was killed or wounded except the Bren gunner who was standing up. By continuous bren gun fire and a shower of grenades, the Japanese were held off while the driver, though wounded in one eye was able to back and turn the carrier. The tank, carrying the Adjutant of 1/11 Sikh as passenger, passed through the block, unscathed. The whole nerve centre of the 63rd Indian Infantry Brigade was thus destroyed before the Brigade had been properly in action, "an appalling blow for any formation to receive". The survivors were rushed back to Pegu in the only carrier left.[24] A section of the carriers of the 1st Battalion the Cameronians was also ambushed at the road-block and further casualties were sustained. In the afternoon four attempts were made to break the road-block but these failed as the Japanese were strongly entrenched there.

The 63rd Indian Infantry Brigade was thereupon ordered to march to Pegu on the right of the main road between the road and the railway. The order was subsequently changed to hold an outpost from astride

---

[22] *War Diary*, 63rd Indian Infantry Brigade has it as 6 miles south of Pegu, *War Diary*, 17th Indian Division 5 miles south of Pegu, *War Diary*, 1/4 G.R. gives its location in detail, *War Diary*, 48th Indian Infantry Brigade gives it as 2 miles down below the Pegu-Rangoon road from the 7th Armoured Brigade's harbour.

[23] *War Diary*, 17th Indian Division 'G' Branch gives it as 1000 hours.

[24] This left the Brigade with very junior Commanders.

the road junction Tawa-Pegu as a layback to the 48th Indian Infantry Brigade which was withdrawing from Pegu the next day.

Japanese streaming out of Pegu in the north

Many refugees could be seen streaming back to the north of Pegu and as the day wore on Japanese columns well to the north were spotted by the dust they raised. The officer commanding the 5th Battalion 3rd Gurkha Rifles reported these movements to the Brigade Headquarters and asked permission to attack the railway station from the rear of the Japanese. This was not agreed to. In the course of the day the jungle strip immediately north of 'C' company's (the 5th Battalion 3rd Gurkha Rifles) forward platoon was set on fire by fifth columnists but the fire was beaten off before it could jeopardise the security of the defensive positions.

Attack on Railway Station

At about 1200 hours an attack was launched from the main road northwards to clear the railway station of the Japanese. It was carried out by three companies. On the right a company of the 7th Gurkha Rifles moved up the west bank of the river, in the centre was a company of the Cameronians, and on the left a company of the West Yorkshire Regiment. The attack was supported by mortars and 'E' Troop, 414th Battery, RHA. The station and its northern outskirts were captured, but a further advance was held up.

Attacking the parties of Japanese moving out of Pegu in the north

In the late afternoon parties of Japanese troops streaming out of the town north-west and then west were clearly seen, by 'C' company of the 5th Battalion 3rd Gurkha Rifles near North Bridge; its machine-guns and mortars opened fire at once. But as the targets were out of range of the infantry weapons an urgent request was sent to the Armoured Brigade 25 Pounder Battery that an Observation Post might be sent to engage these targets. The Observation Post arrived shortly after 1700 hours and North Railway Bridge was used as gunner Observation Post. Then the guns of 414th RHA Battery opened fire. The actual results could not be seen on account of the scrub; as night quickly fell firing had to be stopped.

Establishment of an all round defence

It was then decided to consolidate the positions gained by establishing an all round defence. 'B' company of the 1st Battalion 4th PWO Gurkha Rifles relieved the company of the 7th Gurkha Rifles which had been fighting all day and was exhausted. West of the company of the 4th Gurkha Rifles was the West Yorkshire Regiment under whose command 'B' commany was. To their left the Cameronians faced west and then continued the line south of the river. The rear of 'C' company (the 5th Battalion 3rd Gurkha Rifles) strongpoint was linked up with the right of the 1st Battalion 4th PWO Gurkha Rifles on the other bank of the Pegu river by a series of posts down the left bank. These were formed from Headquarters Company. The cover, where they were, was very dense and communication among the posts extremely difficult.

Late in the afternoon of 6 March the Japanese aircraft bombed Headquarters 48th Brigade and scored a direct hit on the Mess building causing casualties. Heavy hand to hand fighting continued all day in the western portion of Pegu, and on its outskirts. All ranks displayed great gallantry, and maintained the positions that had been gained.[25]

Attacks near Payagyi—6 March

North of Pegu the force under command of the 7th Queen's Own Hussars got engaged in a separate action. At first light the tanks had advanced towards Payagyi but soon came under shell fire from anti-tank guns. Two tanks were hit. The Japanese guns appear to have been manhandled into forward positions as neither mules nor motor transport was visible. In the early morning when the mist cleared, the guns of 'D' Troop 414th Battery, RHA speedily engaged them, and the company of the West Yorkshire Regiment held the position whilst the tanks withdrew. Under cover of an artillery concentration this company then made a bayonet charge. Some Japanese were killed, and four guns were captured. With the co-operation from the tanks, the infantry then went on to clear the Japanese from a patch of jungle. It was estimated that sixty casualties were inflicted on the Japanese without any loss to the company.

Later in the day three Japanese tanks were sighted. These were attacked by the 7th Queen's Hussars and were destroyed by 37 mm. gun fire at a range of twelve hundred yards. At 1540 hours the 7th Queen's Own Hussars were ordered to concentrate in the northern part of Pegu and then to rejoin the 7th Armoured Brigade at Hlegu.

Pegu force ordered to cut through the block—2000 hours, 6 March

In spite of these local successes particularly in the railway station area the situation was really grave. The road-block was there. The 7th Armoured Brigade less the 7th Queen's Own Hussars was on the Rangoon side of the road-block. The Japanese were well established in the rear and northern flank of the 49th Indian Infantry Brigade. Also it had been decided to evacuate Rangoon. Hence orders were issued at 2000 hours to the 48th Indian Infantry Brigade to withdraw.

Immediately after the receipt of the order a conference of all unit commanders was called at the Brigade Headquarters. At first it was intended to carry out the evacuation of the town that night, and the 7th Queen's Own Hussars moved out at about 2030 hours. Immediately south of the town the road was impassable owing to an enormous forest fire, but the tanks found a diversion and regained the road about a mile north of the road-block. This was covered by a gun and machine-guns, and the tanks were unable to force it. The 7th Queen's Own Hussars and attached troops subsequently leagured in open paddy fields on the east of the road. Here 'D' Troop of 414th Battery RHA was rejoined by 'E' Troop of the Battery.[26]

The conference went on throughout the night. A reconnaissance

---

[25] The night was comparatively peaceful all over the front, the only difficulty experienced being by 5/3 G.R. from 2 or 3 snipers but these were silenced by turning the carriers loose at them.

[26] *War Diary*, 17th Indian Division 'G' Branch speaks also of an attempt at night to break the road-block.

party had been sent to report on the crossing of the river to the south at Tawa. It reported that there was only a flimsy bamboo bridge there which would not stand up to use by heavy MT and tanks. Thus it was not possible to bypass the road-block. All sorts of plans were examined and discussed. From these it became apparent that only two feasible courses lay open to the 48 Brigade either (a) to abandon MT and withdraw down the railway line or (b) to force the road-block for a passage by the MT at the same time fighting a rearguard action with the Japanese still at close range in the Pegu railway station area and elsewhere in the town.

Plan of withdrawal—7 March

At about 0500 hours on 7 March the final decision was made.[27] The plan adopted was that troops to the east of the river would withdraw across the Pegu town bridge by 0600 hours. The 7th Queen's Own Hussars in harbour about three miles to the south-west supported by 25 pounders and the infantry was to break the road-block at first light. After this all MT was to be evacuated by the main Pegu-Hlegu road. The bridges were to be blown up soon after withdrawal. The order of withdrawal was to be the 7th Gurkha Rifles, the 1st Battalion 4th PWO Gurkha Rifles, Brigade Headquarters, 5th Battalion 3rd Gurkha Rifles. The Cameronians and the West Yorkshire Battalion (with 'B' company, the 1st Battalion 4th PWO Gurkha Rifles under command) already in touch with the Japanese on the right flank of the railway station were to be the rearguard. Troops were to march on both sides of the road leaving the centre clear for MT. Head of the 7th Gurkha Rifles column was to halt level with the 7th Queen's Own Hussars harbour and the Brigade was to close. When mist had cleared, the 7th Queen's Own Hussars was to clear the road-block. They were to be followed by MT with infantry in the rear.

The withdrawal

Initially the withdrawal went according to plan with no Japanese interference and the bridge was blown up in time. The line of march was however, considerably held up by the mechanical transport having to use a long diversion over rough country so that by 0730 hours the 5th Battalion 3rd Gurkha Rifles had moved only three miles away from Pegu. Already sounds of firing could be heard from the direction of the railway station in the rear. This clearly indicated that the rearguard was heavily engaged. The columns halted about 1½ miles away from the block. The 7th Gurkha Rifles, the leading infantry, was probing for the Japanese covering the road-block. The 1st Battalion 4th PWO Gurkha Rifles and the 5th Battalion 3rd Gurkha Rifles halted on both sides of the road in rice fields. The mist was too thick for guns to open fire and there was lull in forward movement. It had been understood that the West Yorkshire Battalion or part of it would be level with the 5th Battalion 3rd Gurkha Rifles on the other side of the road.[28]

[27] *War Diary*, 17th Indian Division 'G' Branch makes it 0200 hours. *War Diary*, 5/3 GR as 0600 hours.
[28] The West Yorkshire Battalion was heavily engaged near the Railway Station.

Tanks break through the Block—7 March, 0830 hours

As day broke and the morning mist cleared slightly, the Japanese began firing on the 1/7 G.R., 1/4 G.R. and Brigade Headquarters with mortars and light machine-guns, their infantry being located in large numbers in the jungle and gardens on the west side of the road, and to the north of the actual road-block. On the east of the road there were open paddy-fields on which the tanks had been harboured during the night. Very soon afterwards the 25 pounder of the Armoured Brigade without reference to the 48th Infantry Brigade opened fire on to the actual road-block, and the tanks advanced along the road in a line. Soon they broke through losing two of their number at the block. Their 'B' Echelon followed close behind after which the transport of 48th Infantry Brigade also trailed in; but many vehicles had been damaged by the Japanese fire or abandoned by their drivers so that the road which was on a low embankment soon became blocked. The tanks with the 25 pounders and a proportion of soft vehicles in their rear pushed straight on and did not wait for the slower moving infantry.[29] Many of these soft vehicles were hit and destroyed during the next two miles as they ran the gauntlet of the Japanese, concealed on both sides of the road, which in the actual area of the road-block was closed in on both sides by thick jungle. The 1/7 G.R. attempted to follow the tanks, and in fact Headquarter Company actually reached the road-block, where unfortunately the Commanding Officer, Lieut-Colonel B. J. White, was killed. The two leading companies diverged and finding that the Japanese were only holding a narrow front some 200 yards astride the road, passed round the flanks of the Japanese position and went on to Hlegu. Headquarter Company and one of the reserve companies did likewise, leaving only B Company under its commander on the Pegu side of the block.

5/3 G.R. and 1/4 G.R. in action north-west of the block—7 March

While tanks were smashing their way through the road-block the fire on the 1/7 G.R. and 1/4 G.R. spread further north and snipers opened fire on the 5th Battalion 3rd Gurkha Rifles positions from a garden to the west of the other side of the road and from a house to the south. 'B' company which was sent in to attack could make little progress against the Japanese automatic fire. 'C' company then moved across the road to the south and west of the garden and thus pinned the Japanese to the garden. 'A' company cleared the house on the south but 'B' company could not make any impression on the Japanese in the garden. At this stage officer commanding the 5th Battalion 3rd Gurkha Rifles, was wounded by a sniper from the culvert to the north. There were also a lot of Gurkha casualties in the 'B' Company.

A local counter-attack was launched by one company of the 1st Battalion 4th Gurkha Rifles which cleared the garden of the hostile elements. This local success combined with the losses inflicted on the Japanese in the fighting near the railway station had a profound effect on the events of the day. It effectively prevented any reinforcements by the Japanese from Pegu towards the road-block throughout the rest of the day.

---

[29] This was a costly mistake.

Fighting in the Railway Station area

Meanwhile bitter fighting ensued around the railway station, where Cameronians and the West Yorkshire Battalion met with stout opposition while getting away from their positions there. 'B' company 1/4 PWO Gurkha Rifles held the sector north of and between the railway station and the railway bridge over the river. It came under heavy fire from all directions as soon as it started to withdraw southwards towards the railway station according to plan, and in the process lost touch with the West Yorkshires, who withdrew southwards towards Hlegu, and with 48 Brigade. The Company suffered heavy casualties and was unable to move along the road to Hlegu. It therefore followed the line of the railway and rejoined the battalion on 8 March at Tankkan road-fork, having moved via Tawa and Hlegu. A party of Cameronians were similarly cut off but were able to rejoin their unit at a later date, by much the same route.

Encircling movement against the road-block

To return to the road-block, when it was found that the Japanese were again manning the road-block and that MT had been stopped, the Officer Commanding the 7th Gurkha Rifles with Headquarters Company went forward to clear the road-block. He succeeded in the attempt but was himself killed by a sniper from a tree. The rest of the Brigade was now divided into two echelons and as no artillery support was available encircling movement was directed against the road-block; also piquets were posted on the right in the jungle at intervals of 50 yards thus ensuring that the Japanese did not filter in again.

The break-through

Moving at high speed the MT convoy got through successfully without serious casualties. By 1730 hours all resistance at the road-block was at an end but not before the Japanese MM Guns had fired along the road from the direction of Pegu. As the transport had all gone, the Brigade now moved south-west in hollow square across rice fields, then struck south across country to the railway line, clear of the jungle, followed it and approached Tawa at 2100 hours. There it halted for an hour. The Brigade marched again at 2200 hours, and at 0430 hours reached Intagaw where a three-hour halt was made. The men were much exhausted and the Brigade Commander was anxious that at Hlegu food should be ready and transport available to lift those most exhausted. There was, however, no means of communicating with the Divisional Headquarters, except to send a messenger, a risk which was taken in spite of the possibility of a large number of Japanese troops being found in the Intagaw—Hlegu area. The message was safely communicated and cooked meal and transport awaited the 48th Infantry Brigade when it entered Hlegu on 8 March.

Meanwhile, as will be stated in the next chapter, Rangoon had been evacuated and the whole British force was withdrawing north. This withdrawal, begun on the previous day, was temporarily delayed by a road-block put down by the Japanese across the Prome road just north of Taukkyan. When the 48th Indian Infantry Brigade arrived in Hlegu the road had been cleared and the Brigade, less transport troops required for rearguard duties, was moved in motor transport to Taikkyi.

Conclusion

Two squadrons of tanks had by 1630 hours been ordered to move back towards Pegu and assist in the final get-away of the remnants of the 48th Indian Infantry Brigade. But not finding the Brigade on the road they retired again towards Hlegu. But all this long hold-up and loss of men and MT at the road-block might have been avoided if the first tanks to get through had halted and held the block for the MT and infantry to pass through. It had been severe fighting, and the Japanese also admit that they were severely resisted in and around Pegu.

CHAPTER XIV

Fall of Rangoon

IMPORTANCE OF RANGOON

The ultimate objective of the Japanese operations in Lower Burma was Rangoon. Its capture would not only virtually close the Burma Road, but also cut off the reinforcement line for the Allied armies. The Japanese tried to reach their objective by establishing air superiority over Rangoon and by a land drive. They failed in the former as much as they succeeded in the latter. It has been aptly said that with the fall of Rangoon fell the rest of Burma; from a defensive battle the action deteriorated into a rearguard action. From that time the campaign became a retreat, a retreat in which the pursuing Japanese forces were able to occupy the country from Rangoon to Myitkyina in a month. For the Allied troops it was one long story of hardship, not the hardship of trenches and a vegetating existence therein, but the hardship of trekking, hunger, cold, fever, dysentery, and worst of all uncertainty. No one could be trusted, and no news could be accepted as authentic. One lived in an atmosphere of suspicion and doubt. Never were conditions worse for the British-Indian Army and better for the other side. The loss of Rangoon also completely changed the air situation. Not only did it mean a rude check to the building up of the air force up to 16 squadrons—Rangoon was the only point through which maintenance for an air force could pass—it also meant the loss of organised airfields in the vicinity of Rangoon and the loss of warning system, with its disastrous results on airfields and forces in North Burma.

To the Japanese, Rangoon was a great asset. They could abandon their long overland routes and bring the supplies and reinforcements by sea. With the considerable number of airfields prepared in the Rangoon area, heavy reinforcements of Japanese aircraft could also be flown in, at will, to Burma.

AIR RAIDS ON RANGOON

24-25 December

The original Japanese plan was to attack air bases near Rangoon with the object of destroying the growing British fighter force, and achieving air superiority over Rangoon to the point where it would be possible for them to undertake unrestricted day bombing operations on a destructive scale.[1] This would have enabled them not only to close the Burma Road, and prevent supplies and reinforcements to the Indian-British troops,

---

[1] According to Sato Shochoi, Chief of Staff with the *5th Air Division*, the Japanese object of bombing Rangoon "was to destroy British air power at Rangoon, to destroy all planes and personnel, if possible, so that the British force would not be a threat to the Japanese forces." FEG, GHQ, ATIS Interrogation Report. Answer to Question 69.

but would also have given them 'the best chance of surrounding and destroying the army'.

The two air raids on Rangoon in December had more than achieved the Japanese object of dislocating life and essential services. Although labour returned in considerable number during the first week of January, and sufficient labour was available for immediate purposes, and docks were cleared, life never became normal. There was also the danger that with further raids, labour might once more disintegrate. In fact, with the advance of the Japanese armies on and from Moulmein, labour once again disintegrated by the middle of February.

1-14 January 1942

But the two raids were not without some effect on the Japanese also.[2] Their losses in day-light raids were so heavy that during the first fortnight of January the Japanese took to night bombing, their scale of effort varying between one to sixteen heavy bombers. Their night bombing was somewhat effective as Rangoon was clearly defined by river junction and adjacent lakes, and there were no facilities for night interception. On the arrival of Hurricanes trained in night fighting, however, some check could be offered. Nor did the Japanese send many aircraft or risk ground strafing. Most of these raids were directed, as already seen, against the Mingaladon aerodrome. The other targets were Hlegu 30 miles north of Rangoon railway station and the alternative aerodrome. But these raids caused neither great material damage nor great loss of morale of the civil population.

Air Vice-Marshal's plan

On 1 January 1942 Air Vice-Marshal D. F. Stevenson took over command of the small air force in Burma. He found his main task to be "to defend the base facilities at Rangoon, the docks, the convoys arriving and departing and the air bases at Mingaladon and Zayatkwin." So his general plan was to keep his "fighter force concentrated in the Rangoon area, to accept such enemy bombing attacks as might be made on any other objectives in Northern Burma, to fight the enemy in the defence of the base and lean forward to hit the enemy wherever and whenever I could with my small but total air force."

"To achieve this against a numerically superior and constantly growing air force," he had to do all that he could "to reduce the scale of air attack on the Rangoon area," and yet be "able to meet attacks on the bases in sufficient force to inflict a high casualty rate proportional to the scale of attack thus making such attacks in this area abortive and wasteful" for the Japanese.[3]

By day bombing of widely separated points like Chiengmai, Mehohngsohn, Lampang, Rahaeng, Parachuab, Khirikhan, Jumbhorn, Kanchanabur, and also using advanced air bases like Moulmein, Tavoy and Mergui Japanese aircraft were to be attacked wherever found. By this means it

---

[2] Not less than 36 Japanese first line bombers and fighters were claimed as destroyed during these two days. Stevenson's *Despatch* on Air Operations in Burma and the Bay of Bengal 1942, para 63, F 9555.

[3] *Ibid*, paras 63, 64, 65.

was hoped to weaken the Japanese force in the centre by compelling them to disperse their fighters.[4]

The small force of one Squadron of P. 40's of the A.V.G., half a Squadron of Buffaloes, and the equivalent of two Squadrons of Hurricanes commencing to arrive in January and continuing to halfway through February, maintained air superiority over Rangoon and gave it a long period of rest up to 23 January.[5]

23-29 January

Between 23 and 29 January the Japanese made a second attempt to overwhelm the small fighter force, putting in a total of 218 planes, mostly fighters. In the air battle of these days the British fighter forces destroyed nearly 50 Japanese bombers and fighters. The latter thereupon at once reverted to night operations and continued these until their third and last atempt to achieve air superiority over Rangoon, on 24 February and 25 February.[6]

24-25 February

The reverses in February deprived the RAF of its advanced bases and warning system of the observer corps. It was therefore certain that further operations could be possible by having base landing grounds in India, and operational landing grounds in Akyab. Only advanced landing grounds could be possible in the Rangoon area. In Rangoon itself, the telephone system had ceased to function on 21 February, and the only RDF Set was worn out. In the circumstances only limited warning arrangements could be practicable.

It was against this background that the Japanese put in on 24 and 25 February the third and last of their efforts to secure air superiority over Rangoon.[7] The scale of the attack was 166 bombers and fighters. They sustained the heavy loss of 37 fighters and bombers which were claimed destroyed with 7 probably destroyed. On the second day, the P.40's of the A.V.G. claimed no less than 24 aircraft shot down. "Such a wastage had been inflicted on the enemy that thereafter he never attempted to enter our warning zone round Rangoon, until the city was captured and the air bases in his hands."[8] "This had a critical influence on the course of our land operations and on the security of our convoys bringing in final reinforcements. These and the demolition of our oil and other interests in the port and the final evacuation by land or sea were completed without interference from enemy bomber and fighter escort."[9] Soon after the air force was shifted to a *kutcha* strip called Highland

---

[4] *Ibid*, para 66.
[5] One of the reasons for the pause in attacks, as given by the Japanese, was lack of fuel and bombs. They received limited supplies on or about 20 Jan. 1942, and this enabled them to re-commence aerial operations three days later. FEC, GHQ, ATIS Interrogation Report.
[6] Stevenson's *Despatch*, para 73.
[7] The reasons for the absence of major air offensive against Rangoon between 29 January and 23 February is given by the Japanese as follows:—
"The air force was giving aerial support to ground troops that were attacking Moulmein." ATIS Answer to Question No. 73.
[8] *Despatch* by Air Vice Marshal D. F. Stevenson, paras 73-74.
[9] *Ibid*, para 75.

Queen. But there too it was not free from danger. On 6 March a Japanese formation of about 20 aircraft flying over Japanese troops advancing through the jungle towards the Prome Road and Rangoon overshot its mark and discovered the *kutcha* strip over Highland Queen where the British fighters, some bombers and some General Reconnaissance aircraft were on the ground. It was fortunate that the Japanese shooting was bad and some of the Hurricanes were able to take off. Only two of the RAF aircraft were destroyed on the ground. Also the anti-aircraft defence of the aerodrome went into action and did satisfactory work. "This was a raid which might well have been a decisive end to our small air force. Orders were at once issued for all aircraft to fly in from Highland Queen to Mingaladon whence our last sorties were carried out."

Effects of these raids

It was vital to keep the port open and working. Reinforcements and military stores were coming in, and there was also a vast accumulation of Lease/Lend material awaiting transport to China. The flight of labour seriously interfered with the handling of much of this material. Although it was, in fact to a large extent, dispersed by the time of the evacuation of the port, the working of transportation services for military purposes was most precarious up to the fall of Rangoon. Military units for essential work of this kind were only available on a very limited scale.

It was necessary, too, to maintain in action as long as possible the Syriam and other oil refineries near Rangoon, although the removal of certain plant from the refineries to the Yenangyaung oil fields had ensured the continued output of a very considerable quantity of petrol in the event of the loss of Rangoon.[10]

EVACUATION OF RANGOON

Plan

But in view of the turn land operations were taking it became necessary to carry out the evacuation of Rangoon in time before the Japanese could interefere with it. The policy of His Majesty's Government was also clear. Their main aim was to maintain a front in Burma with the particular object of keeping open a supply route to China, preferably through Rangoon, but failing that through Assam. There was no use holding the port if it was virtually blocked by the Japanese naval and air threat. They did not consider that the delay which could be imposed on the Japanese by an attempt to hold Rangoon, after it had been isolated, would justify the loss of the forces in the attempt.[11] If it proved impossible to hold Rangoon it was essential that the demolition of oil refineries, oil storage and other important installations should be as complete as possible.

[10] Protection of Syriam oil refinery, 1941. F. 948.
[11] The Chiefs of Staff wrote: "It therefore seems to us that port should be held as long as its retention can contribute to the achievement of our main object. But rather than continue to hold it after this stage has passed you should consider the possibility of blocking the port preferably for establishing all forces on a port to the north." Troopers to Abdacom No. 721178 dated 21 February.

At the same time the port had to be used as long as possible, particularly in view of the expected reinforcements. Hence the evacuation was to be carried out in three stages. During the first or warning stage all non-essential personnel would be encouraged to depart leaving only those required to run essential services. In the second stage the final arrangements for demolition etc. would be completed and all civilians not required in connection with this work would be evacuated. The third was the demolition stage, on completion of which all personnel concerned and the military for guarding them were to depart in transports for which special arrangements had been made.[12]

Voluntary Evacuation

Voluntary evacuation began after the bombing of Rangoon, and many essential workers then left the city. There was no effective method of preventing this. At the same time large numbers of other persons left by road, rail and ship, and military transports returning to India were also utilized for evacuation purposes. Many thousands of Indians set out on foot for Prome, and thence across the waterless Arakan Yoma to Taungup intending to proceed to Chittagong by country craft. Others went to Upper Burma, preferring to follow the Chindwin routes to Assam. On the Taungup route lack of food, water and medical attention soon caused suffering and many deaths occurred, mostly from cholera and exhaustion. Cholera also appeared south of Prome, and a serious epidemic was anticipated.

First Stage—20 February

The first stage of evacuation was put into effect on 20 February. In an appreciation sent on 18 February, Lieutenant General Hutton favoured an early commencement of the first stage, as operations near the Sittang would seriously interfere with the use of the railway to Mandalay and might necessitate the use of the Rangoon-Prome-Mandalay route for supplies to China and thus lead to congestion.[13] Two days later after consultation with the Governor and the combined commanders he reached the decision to start the first stage of evacuation.[14] Orders were issued to remove within 72 hours all motor transport not marked with an 'E' label. The route of evacuation for the majority of the population was inevitably the main Mandalay road and railway. The proximity of the Japanese to this line after the battle of the Sittang and the small forces available to cover the evacuation rendered it a little risky. Also owing to defections amongst the subordinate staff, the railway had almost ceased to function. "It was only by the closest margins that the last few trains succeeded in getting away. Evacuation by the Prome route was of course possible, but the fact that the railway ended at that point, and the presence of cholera and serious unrest made it undesirable to use it more than necessary. Another factor was the importance of avoiding serious congestion on either route both of which were of course essential for military purposes. A further difficulty arose from the fact that Rangoon

---

[12] Hutton's *Report*, para 60.
[13] Tel 0749 Burmarmy to Abdacom 18 Feb. 1942.
[14] Tel 0792 Burmarmy to Abdacom dated 20 Feb. *Situation Reports*, Part I, page 57.

was only 80 miles south-west of Pegu, and the Pegu road joined the Prome road 21 miles north of Rangoon".[15]

It was also decided to send back to India all ships which contained units not likely to affect the outcome of the military operations. Production in Syriam and other connected refineries was also to be closed, firstly to ensure removal of skilled personnel from the danger of being captured and secondly, to ensure preparation for comprehensive demolition as early as possible.[16] Thus, within a day or two of the evacuation order, Rangoon became almost a deserted city though essential services were maintained. All these, however, were only precautionary measures reducing in no way the prospect of holding Rangoon, which was to be abandoned "only in the face of overwhelming attack on the outskirts of the city".[17]

Rangoon Garrison—February-March 1942

At that time the Rangoon Garrison carried out a multiplicity of duties over a very widespread area. These duties included internal security, aerodrome and anti-aircraft defence, manning of the Examination Battery at Dry Tree Point, protection of Syriam and other refineries, and the guarding of the approaches from the coast. Brig. R. B. Leslie was in command of Rangoon Fortress and the garrison then comprised:—

    1 Heavy Anti-Aircraft Regiment, B.A.F. (With one Light Anti-Aircraft Battery).
Rangoon Field Brigade, R.A., B.A.F.
Detachment Royal Engineers.
Detachment Burma Sappers and Miners.
Detachment Royal Marines (Force 'Viper').
The 1st Battalion the Gloucestershire Regiment.
The 12th Battalion Burma Rifles.
One Company the 1st Royal Battalion 9th Jat Regiment.
Headquarters, 2 Garrison Battalion.
4 Garrison Company.
23 Garrison Company.
One Company Kokine Battalion, Burma Frontier Force.
F.F. 4 and
Burma Military Police.

The Royal Marine Detachment had recently arrived from Ceylon. It acquired a small fleet of launches and was employed on river patrol work. Later in the campaign it was destined to carry out similar duties on the Irrawaddy. It consisted of five officers and one hundred and two other ranks. All had volunteered for special service.

Conditions of Rangoon after 20 February

Even before the general evacuation there had been a certain amount of looting, and after 20 February both looting and arson increased. The general evacuation left property unprotected in every part of the city. This attracted such of the local population as remained and the Burmans from surrounding villages. The position was aggravated by the action

---
[15] Lt.-Gen. Hutton's *Report*, Para 61 Page 15.
[16] Lt.-Gen. T. J. Hutton's *Report*, Tel 0792 dated 20 Feb & Abdacom, Appendix C.
[17] *Ibid.* Appendix C.

of the civil authorities in opening the doors of the jails and the lunatic asylum and releasing the inmates. This was due mainly to the defection of the staff.[18] The inmates made use of their freedom in a manner to be expected. On the water-front, werehouses were being rifled by soldiers, sailors and coolies.

Town handed over to the military

The majority of the Rangoon Police had been evacuated; so, too, had the greater part of the Burma Military Police and the Fire Brigade. To cope with the general lawlessness five hundred of the Military Police and part of the Fire Brigade were brought back to the city and Major Walton, of the Gloucestershire Regiment, was appointed Military Commandant. There was still no desire to impose Martial law partly owing to the lack of clear definition of what it meant and partly owing to its association in the minds of the people with the civil rebellions in former years. It was, however, decided to hand over the town to the military. A system of patrols by troops and Burma Military Police was instituted. The 12th Battalion Burma Rifles first employed on this duty proved extremely weak in dealing with the looters. In some instances, too, men of the Burma Rifles were themselves looters. Later, detachments of the 1st Battalion the Gloucestershire Regiment restored order. In many cases looters were shot. Others, both soldiers and civilians, were punished by caning and being set to work at the docks where labour was scarce. Disorder was thus put down in the centre of the city, but it continued in the suburbs. Plans to take over Water and Power Stations and maintenance of public services by military were also prepared.

On 21 February, Rear Headquarters of the Army (mainly administrative echelon) left for Maymyo where it opened at 2400 hours on 23 February. Thereafter only an Advanced Headquarters, reduced to a minimum strength, remained in Rangoon.

Second Stage of Evacuation

The interval between the first and second stages was longer than anticipated, partly owing to the lack of pressure on the part of the Japanese after the battle of the Sittang and partly owing to the anticipated arrival of reinforcements which made it possible, even up to the last moment, to believe that the position could be retrieved. During this period a certain number of people evacuated under the first stage were brought back to keep essential services and transportation services going till the last moment. During this period large quantities of stores and personnel were also disembarked and moved up-country to Prome and Mandalay. As has been stated earlier, the orders for the evacuation of Rangoon (2nd stage) were issued on 27 February but were later countermanded by General Sir A. Wavell.[19]

Fear of a Seaborne Attack on Rangoon

The greatest bogey of the Burma Command was the possibility of

---

[18] It is believed that these men were released on the evacuation of Rangoon as it was difficult to transfer them to Upper Burma.
[19] General Sir A. Wavell's *Despatch*, para 8, para 21.

Japanese landings in the Delta area which was virtually undefended and where fighter cover also could be available for the Japanese from aerodromes on the Tenasserim coast. It was estimated that for defence against seaborne attack alone, one division was required. After the Sittang battle it was anticipated that small hostile parties would move across the Gulf of Martaban between the Sittang and Rangoon rivers and along the shores of the China Bakir river mouth. Motor launches of the Burma R.N.V.R. patrolled in a rough triangle from Rangoon to the east coast of the Sittang estuary and then down to Tenasserim coast up to Amherst and Moulmein and back to Rangoon. In addition ships of the R.I.N. the "Hindustan", "Ratnagiri" and "Indus" patrolled the immediate seaward approaches to the south. That the apprehension was not unjustified was demonstrated by the infiltration of small hostile parties which were detected by the patrols. On the afternoon of 4 March, R.A.F. reconnaissance aircraft observed eight river type boats steaming west from the Salween mouth.[20] On 5 March one of these, a power driven sampan, was sighted by the M.Ls 1100 and 1103 on patrol off the Elephant Point at the mouth of the Rangoon River. On investigation it was found to contain 55 men of the Burma Independent Army mostly deserters from the Burma Rifles and Frontier Forces, under a Japanese officer. The Burmese promptly hoisted the white flag and surrendered. They were taken prisoners and brought to Rangoon for interrogation where they stated that they were the first flight of a seaborne expedition. Meanwhile ML. 1100 noticed more masts in the distance and racing towards them saw that they were also small power driven country boats. The M.L. signalled the facts of the situation to the "Hindustan" which was then patrolling out at sea. The former was unable to catch these boats which had meanwhile reached shoal water and had passed out of range up into the China Bakir river. Later R.A.F. units attempted to contact them, but succeeded in machine-gunning merely the empty sampans.

GEN. SIR A. WAVELL'S DIRECTIVE—5 MARCH

On his way to Burma Gen. Sir H. Alexander had met Gen. Sir A. Wavell in Calcutta. The Commander-in-Chief having just returned from a visit to Rangoon and the Sittang front, gave General Alexander a résumé of the position in Burma and a directive to the following effect:—

"The retention of Rangoon was a matter of vital importance to our position in the Far East, and every effort must be made to hold it. If, however, that was not possible the British force must not be allowed to be cut off but must be withdrawn from the Rangoon area for the defence of Upper Burma. This must be held as long as possible in order to safeguard the oilfields at Yenangyaung, keep contact with the Chinese, and protect the construction of the road from Assam to Burma."[21]

Gen. Sir H. Alexander's Plans

As has been already stated in the previous chapter, after a survey of

---
[20] *Situation Reports 1800 hours, 4 March.*
[21] General Alexander's *Despatch*, page 1, para 2.

the military situation Gen. Sir H. Alexander was "not satisfied that Rangoon could not be held". He thought that the situation might be saved if Japanese infiltration through the Pegu Yoma could be prevented by a junction of the 1st Burma Division with the 17th Indian Division, thus closing the gap between Nyaunglebin and the Sittang bridge.[22] But it was all too late as the main body of the Japanese 33rd Division had already pushed through this gap and was nearing Rangoon.[23] With a view to relieving pressure on its immediate front Gen. Sir H. Alexander also ordered the 17th Indian Division, which had come under the command of Maj.-Gen. D. T. Cowan on 1 March, to carry out offensive operations at Waw and in the neighbouring villages. But this also did not prove to be effective as the Japanese were closing on Pegu from the wooded country to the west and the fighting on 6 March did not succeed in ejecting them from the town. Meanwhile by a wider encircling movement the Japanese had cut the Rangoon-Pegu road. There was a further confirmation from R.A.F. of reports by B.F.F. patrols that 2000 Japanese had passed through Paunggyi about 30 miles north of Hlegu and were moving in a south-westerly direction. A number of Burmans of the Independent Burma Army under Japanese officers had landed at the mouth of the Rangoon river threatening the Syriam oil refineries, held by only a small garrison.[24] There was also the danger of a flank attack from Bassein. This port had been bombed on 21 February and immediately evacuated, much to the annoyance of the military authorities in Rangoon. Transportation agencies were closed down, power house destroyed, and post, telegraph and telephone staff evacuated. The General Officer Commanding requested Rear Army Headquarters to get into touch with the Secretary to the Governor in order that he might use influence to calm the people of Bassein and induce the officials to return to their posts. But all efforts were in vain. Matters had reached a stage where nothing could stop the frantic abandonment of what appeared to be untenable positions. In short, with Rangoon threatened from north, south and west, and with the Pegu Force almost cut off, it was high time that the evacuation of Rangoon was ordered. If the Japanese succeeded in cutting the road north of Rangoon, even the secondary objects of denying the oilfields to them, and keeping contact with the Chinese in the north could not be realised. The last hope of holding Rangoon vanished when the Australian Government decided not to send to Burma the Australian Corps which was on its way to Java from the Middle East.

In this situation, Gen. Sir H. Alexander decided late on 6 March that the retention of Rangoon was quite impossible and that the right course was to carry out demolitions, evacuate the city, and regroup his forces in the Irrawaddy valley further north. The order to put the Denial Scheme into operation was issued at 2359 hours that night. All demolitions were to be begun simultaneously the next day at 1400 hours.[25]

[22] *Ibid*, para 5.
[23] *History of the Japanese Fifteenth Army*. 601/7785/H. pp. 1 and 23.
[24] Gen. Alexander's *Despatch*, page 2, paras 5-6.
[25] Alexander's *Despatch*, p. 2, para 6.

Evacuation of the City—7 March

On the morning of 7 March, Advanced Army Headquarters, administrative units and troops, not required to cover the demolitions in the Rangoon area, moved out of Rangoon in M.T. and proceeded along the Prome road. With them was also a small party of airmen and officers who were previously left behind to complete demolitions of the operations room, the facilities at North Group Headquarters and the Mingaladon aerodrome. Advanced Army Headquarters was to proceed to Maymyo and there rejoin Rear Headquarters. Near Taukkyan, twenty-one miles north of the city, this force was compelled to halt. Ahead of it the Japanese had established a road-block. News of this development was received by the demolition parties in Rangoon but this in no way interfered with their plans.

DEMOLITION SCHEME

The Demolition scheme had been drawn up long before and rehearsals were carried out. As for oil denials, as early as December 1941, a scheme was started for the complete destruction of the three refineries at Syriam, Seikkyi and Thailawa. It was later revised to a scheme of maximum denial in the time available. For this purpose, Mr. W. L. Forster (Production Manager of Shell Mex Ltd.) was flown to Burma from Cairo and he laid down the following policy:—

'All tanks and stocks, pumps and plants, which could not be evacuated were to be destroyed. Personnel were also to be evacuated.' The preparations for demolitions were made by one section of the Burma Sappers and Miners. The actual demolitions were carried out by three European Engineer Officers, eleven Royal Marines, fifteen Sappers (Burma Sappers and Miners) and three members of the Burma Oil Company's staff and one Burma Officer. Fire parties were entirely made up of personnel of the Companies' Staff. The denial work on or before 7 March included destruction of all tanks holding 10,000 gallons or more and half the number of smaller tanks by means of explosives or organised fire. All stocks of crude oil and products excepting a few dozen isolated drums of lubricants and a few thousand gallons of spirit in the refinery pipe lines were burnt; there was also positive immobilisation of all pumps, as well as machine shops, oxygen plant, electric plants, drum and tin plants. The pipe-line river crossing from Rangoon was effectively plugged with cement. But large scale demolition of massive refinery plant could not be undertaken.[20]

A large number of vehicles and other supplies imported for China under Lease/Lend arrangements had already been destroyed by orders of a senior United States Army Officer without reference to Army Headquarters. The loss of the vehicles was seriously felt later in the campaign.

The Power Station was also blown up. All the fire generating sets and four of the seven boilers were wrecked beyond repair. The distribution system was left in tact, as also 28,000 tons of coal and all stores and

---

[20] Lt.-Gen. T. J. Hutton's *Report*, Appendix H, and *Report on the Effect of Denial and Demolition Schemes in Burma*, pp. 14, 15 and 16.

spares. Thus soon after their occupation of Rangoon, the Japanese could restore the town's electric supply. Demolitions were also carried out at the Telegraph Office, Wireless Stations and Telephone Exchange; the Headquarters of the Rangoon Police were burnt.[27]

From the Railway Workshops at Insein much machinery had been earlier moved up-country. The remainder was now destroyed. Locomotives were immobilised, but the important railway bridge over the Oazundaung Creek was not very successfully blown up. It was soon repaired by the Japanese.[28]

Next in importance to the oil demolitions was the denial of the port to the Japanese but any measures taken could only be partially effective. It was impracticable to block the channels. Jetties and warehouses, many of them privately owned, extended over several miles of water front. But ten berths with storage sheds etc., which would have been of the greatest value to the Japanese were completely wrecked above deck level by explosive charges and by fire. It was, however, deemed impossible to try to destroy the modern concrete pile foundations. Screw pile posts were badly damaged. Three vessels were sunk along side the three most useful berths. The wharf equipment including all cranes was smashed or otherwise destroyed. The Hydraulic Power Station was rendered useless. Warehouses and in general all godowns containing stocks in the Port Commissioner's custody were destroyed. All mooring buoys were perforated by machinegun fire and sunk. No vessel belonging to the Port Commissioners was left in Rangoon. They were either sent to Calcutta or up-river or scuttled.[29]

As regards Government dockyards, all machines, pumps, lathes etc., were completely immobilised by the removal of all chucks, tools, gear and essential parts. These were sent to Mandalay. Vessels under construction were moved to India. Moreover, from the Irrawaddy Flotilla Company dockyards, even before 7 March, vital parts were removed from most of the prime-movers and the machine tools and these were sunk in the river. The remaining prime-movers were destroyed on 7 March.

But these steps could not serve by themselves to close the port altogether. Many warehouses, wharves and jetties remained functioning. There were still available thousands of river craft ranging from paddy gigs, barges and small launches to sampans. Numerous undamaged workshops were to be found in rice and timber mills and elsewhere. In the absence of the destroyed shore installations, the most serious limitation was that of maximum lift dictated by the capacity of a ship's gear. Heavy motor transport, tanks, locomotives, and rolling stock could only be unloaded by ships specially fitted for the work. But the port still sufficed for the maintenance of eight divisions, a force larger than the Japanese were likely to require in Burma. It is known that the Japanese were using the port shortly afterwards. All road and rail bridges leading out of Rangoon were also demolished.

In spite of the large quantities of valuable goods despatched to India by sea during January and February and the strenuous efforts to evacuate

[27] *Ibid*, p. 37.
[28] *Ibid*, p. 35.
[29] *Ibid*, pp. 24-25.

all military stores and Lease-Lend material for China to places in Northern Burma, the authorities were compelled to abandon very large stocks of various kinds including timbers, coal, steel, rails and bridging materials in Rangoon.

All demolitions having been successfully carried out Garrison Headquarters with troops and civilian personnel concerned made their way to jetties and the railway where river steamers and trains were in readiness. Further down-stream a sea-going convoy was waiting to sail for Calcutta with the parties evacuated by river.

Rangoon on Fire

The deserted city and oil refineries and shattered storage tanks along the river presented an awe-inspiring spectacle as huge columns of flame leapt skyward beneath a vast canopy of smoke. The last train drew out of Rangoon at 1930 hours on 7 March, and the river steamers moved off from the jetties. Before dawn the first Japanese patrols entered the empty streets.

JAPANESE 33RD DIVISION MOVEMENTS AFTER 23 FEBRUARY

As stated earlier, *33rd Division*, less one infantry brigade, had been allotted the task of capturing Rangoon. It crossed the Sittang 6 miles north of Mokpalin and began its advance towards Hlegu and Hnawbi.[30] Although the *55th Division* was severely resisted in the Pegu area, the advance of *33rd Division* was unopposed and through Paunggyi it reached the area of Wanetchaung, north of Rangoon. As there seemed to be only a small defence force in Rangoon, the Divisional Command decided to launch the attack. The left flank consisting of the main force of *214th Infantry Regiment* advanced along the Rangoon-Mandalay road and encountered resistance at Mingaladon from the Allied forces retreating from Rangoon. *215th Infantry Regiment*, on the right flank, advanced along the Rangoon-Prome road and entered Rangoon with no loss at dawn on 8 March.

The *55th Division* then took up positions to guard against any possible counter-attacks from the Pegu sector and at the same time despatched a large force to secure the Syriam oilfields and to mop up remnants of the Indo-British forces in the triangle area. The detachment of *55th Division* sent to Syriam to occupy the place with its oil refineries, captured it but great destruction had already been done."[31] The capture of Syriam facilitated the unopposed occupation of Rangoon.

THE ROAD-BLOCK NEAR TAUKKYAN CROSS ROADS

The Japanese right flank from Wanetchaung area set up a road-block at milestone 27 north of Taukkyan near the village of Mithwephok. It was as usual on a stretch of road bordered by jungle on either side.[32] It

---

[30] *History of the Japanese Fifteenth Army*, 601/7785/H, p. 23. (c).,
[31] *A Short History of 55 Japanese Division*, 601/7247/H, p. 2.
[32] A detailed account of this road-block is given by Lt.-Col. G. T. Wheeler. 601/318/H. There is a difference in the statements about the exact place at which the

consisted of only two tar barrels presumably full of stones on the road-way with one anti-tank gun immediately behind it.

THE RETREAT FROM RANGOON—7 MARCH

On the evening of 6 March an advance guard for the move of the Rangoon Garrison had been formed at Taukkyab, north of Rangoon. This force was made up as follows:—

1 Field Battery, 1 Indian Field Regiment, I.A. (4 guns).
One Squadron the 7th Queen's Own Hussars (already at Tharrawaddy).
One Company the 2nd Battalion King's Own Yorkshire Light Infantry.

It was divided into an advance party which was to proceed to Prome at first light on 7 March, and a rear party consisting of tanks to move just ahead of the Rangoon Garrison. A detachment of the advance party was to be posted at Wanetchaung railway station and to rejoin the main body subsequently.

The advance party moved out at first light without incident and reached Tharrawaddy. The Rangoon Garrison, less troops covering demolitions in Rangoon, led by Advanced Headquarters passed through Taukkyan at about 1100 hours. About a mile beyond that village it halted with the rear party of the advance guard at the fork made by the main road with the road running south-west to Hlawga railway station. There informaion was received that the Japanese were astride the Prome road some five miles further north. At that point a carrier patrol had been destroyed by fire from an anti-tank gun placed behind the block at milestone 27.

Meanwhile, this information had also been given to the Headquarters 17th Indian Division by a Baluch carrier patrol which gave the number of the Japanese covering the block as 150. The Divisional Headquarters at once ordered the 7th Armoured Brigade to deal with the situation.[33] A squadron of the 2nd Battalion Royal Tank Regiment was detailed for this duty, but the 7th Queens Own Hussars arrived there first. They were already on their way from Hlegu to Taukkyan where they were to leaguer. Two tanks of 'B' Squadron at once went up the road to the block. One of these tanks received a direct hit from a shell which did not penetrate but put its guns out of action and the crew were concussed.

The object of the Japanese in establishing the road-block was twofold, to cut the Indo-British forces retreating north and to secure their own flanks in their drive on Rangoon from Wanetchaung along Rangoon-Prome Road.[34] When it became apparent that the road-block was held

---

block was established. *War Diary*, 63 Indian Infantry Brigade locates it 2 miles north of Taukkyan at milestone 23. This is wrong. Air Vice Marshal D. F. Stevenson's *Report* makes it to be near milestone 22. *The situation Report* Part I make it to be milestone 26.

[33] *War Diary*, 17 Indian Division 'G' Branch. Also *War Diary*, 7 Armoured Brigade.
[34] That the object was not only to protest their flanks but also to cut the Allied forces retreating north is shown by the admission of Lieutenant General Sakurai Shozo, Commander of 33rd Division that 'The road-block placed by the Japs at Taukkyan in March 1942 to prevent our Army Headquarters and troops getting out of Rangoon, was removed prematurely and in error." Conference between British and Japanese Commanders Burma Command Intelligence Summary No. 7, 601/7273/H, p. 1.

in strength by one battalion group with an additional force moving up, the retreating Rangoon Garrison put the area into a state of all round defence with such troops as were then available. Few combatant troops were available, and the defence could not have been in a position to withstand any serious assault. However, the 63rd Indian Infantry Brigade near Hlegu had been ordered to Taukkyan by the 17th Indian Division which afforded strength to attack the road-block.

ATTACK ON THE ROAD-BLOCK—7 MARCH

At 1500 hours on 7 March an attack was launched against the road-block. The available force then was:—
7th Queen's Own Hussars, less one Squadron and two troops.
One troop, 2nd Battalion Royal Tank Regiment.
One Company, 1st Battalion the Gloucestershire Regiment (from Rangoon).
One Battery, 1 Indian Field Regiment, I.A.
One Section, 12 Mountain Battery.

The block was infested with snipers many of whom were perched on trees. The snipers were very active and conveyed the probably false impression that the position was held by a large Japanese force. The block was shelled, then attacked through the jungle by two platoons of the Gloucestershire Regiment supported by two carriers. The carriers were knocked out by mortar and anti-tank gun fire, and the infantry advance was held up by snipers and machine-guns. However, working its way forward, and dislodging the Japanese with grenades, a patrol came within sixty yards of the anti-tank gun covering the block. A Japanese counter-attack then drove it back. By 1600 hours the attack had failed.

A Second Attack also Failed

Meanwhile Headquarters company and two rifle companies of the 2nd Battalion 13th F.F. Rifles and the 63rd Indian Infantry Brigade had been ordered forward and directed by Army Headquarters to report to the officer commanding the company of the 1st Battalion Gloucestershire Regiment and assist him to clear the road-block. They were first stationed some distance back in the Taukkyan village where they were shortly joined by the remainder of the Battalion from Hlegu. When the attack by the company of the 1st Batalion Gloucestershire Regiment had failed, the two companies and part of the Headquarters company of the 63rd Indian Infantry Brigade were ordered to put in an attack supported by a Mortar platoon and 12 Mountain Battery. One company attacked frontally moving through the jungle on the east of the road, and the other company echeloned behind it was to pass east of the former and attack the block from the rear. The first company advanced to within 200 yards of the road-block but was held up by intense LMG fire and by snipers well concealed in trees and trenches. The second company passed to the east of the first company, and emerged into the open country on the right flank. Here it was caught by long range LMG and mortar fire from the north-east. At this point the Headquarters Company held in reserve was also put in. This attempt, too, proved abortive and casualties were heavy. Hence, the two companies had to be withdrawn to the road and it was decided to put in the attack up the road.

This was put in with the object of locating and destroying the Japanese A/Tk Gun covering the road-block. Two companies advanced right up to the road-block but while doing so met with no opposition. On reaching the block, however, they came under intense fire from both sides of the road. The companies then went east and located the A/Tk gun; but as dusk was falling it was decided to withdraw the Battalion into leaguer for the night about 500 yards south of the road-block.[35] It was about 1730 hours and was growing dark. Further offensive action had therefore to be postponed until the morning.

Night of 7-8 March

Advanced Army Headquarters, the Rangoon Garrison, and all other troops in the vicinity were packed into the rubber plantation just north of milestone 22 at the road fork already mentioned. The perimeter was guarded by such infantry as was available (about 300 stragglers) and the tanks, which were placed at approximately 50 yards interval all around the plantation. The plantation contained the usual strange crowd which makes up the rear of an army: every type of line of communication unit, and office staff, civil police with their wives and children, civilian clerks, motor vehicles of every type besides one full General, one Lieutenant-General, and one Major-General with their staffs.

Plan for Attack on Road-Block—8 March

"After nightfall (7 March) Gen. Sir H. Alexander issued orders for the road-block to be opened at any cost by tanks at first light the next morning".[36]

At 2300 hours orders were accordingly issued to the Battalion Commander. The 1st Battalion 11th Sikh Regiment was to reach an assembly position approximately 1500 yards north-east of the road-block, the 1st Battalion 10th Gurkha Rifles was to reach an assembly position 1500 yards south-east of the road-block, all by 0730 hours. The artillery (2 Batteries of Field Artillery and one of Mountain) were to put a concentration on to the road-block area 400 yards north and south of the block for 10 minutes from 0835 hours. This was to be followed by a dash on to the block itself by tanks. The 1st Battalion 11th Sikh Regiment and the 1st Battalion 10 Gurkha Rifles were to close in on both sides. The 2nd Battalion 13th F.F.R. was to move as reserve behind the tanks of the 17th Queen's Own Hussars. The 63rd Brigade Headquarters was to proceed along the road Taukkyan-Prome.

It has been mentioned that the advance party of the Rangoon Garrison advance guard had proceeded to Tharrawaddy without incident. There the officer commanding heard that the road behind him was cut. He then went back towards the block in the evening of 7 March to make

---

[35] In the night (7-8 March) the 2nd Battalion 13th F. F. Rifles was attacked in force by the Japanese twice, first with tommy guns and later with intense mortar fire. But both attacks were beaten off. The remainder of the night passed off without incident—*War Diary*, 63 Brigade.
[36]*Personal Narrative of Operations.*

an attack in the rear and in carrying out this duty was mortally wounded by a mortar shell but the attack failed.[37]

Detachment of Wanetchaung—7 March

Meanwhile the detachment at Wanetchaung remained in position. Before dawn it withdrew north-west after encounters with hostile elements, especially armed Burmans. Later that night there arrived at Wanetchaung the last train to leave Rangoon. This train was wrecked by hostile action at a bridge near Wanetchaung station. The troops, Military Police, and civil personnel in the train were attacked by the Japanese and hostile Burmans. They drove off the attackers, killing twenty of them, and during the morning of 8 March joined the main body of the retreating troops.

The Attack on Road-Block—8 March

At about 0730 hours, members of the Brigade staff observed hostile elements to the west of the road leading mules and artillery on pack, about 100 yards away moving south. Fire was opened on both sides and they disappeared behind the rubber plantations in a south-westerly direction. This was reported to Army Headquarters and the Brigade Command.

The 1st Battalion 10th Gurkha Rifles had carried out a night march to the railway line which was its starting point for the attack. During the march it passed within two hundred yards of a line of bullock carts and animals proceeding along jungle track in the opposite direction. This was believed to be part of a Japanese force moving south towards Rangoon. The Battalion advanced at first light through dense jungle towards the main road. A thick mist also hampered it from keeping the direction, and the Battalion could never reach its objective. It got dispersed in the jungle. A great part of it did not rejoin the main body of the force for several days. Many of the men who did rejoin had been deprived of their arms by the hostile Burmans.[38]

The 1st Battalion 11th Sikh Regiment made a night march across country and arrived at the assembly point in open country at the appointed time and awaited the Zero hour, 0845. At 0800 hours they disclosed their position by firing at two Japanese on horse back who rode across its front at close range, but both of them escaped. Half-an-hour later seventeen Japanese bombers appeared. They first attacked artillery positions and then the 2nd Battalion 13th Frontier Force Rifles position. Two tanks were put out of action, the aircraft then flew back to the forward positions of the Japanese.[39] It seems that they had obtained information about the 1st Battalion 11th Sikh Regiment positions from the escaped Japanese for the planes came and searched for them. Their dive bombing combined with the ground machine-gun fire and

---

[37] Lt.-Col. Tynte was killed. Lieutenant Colonel Wheeler, *Prome Road-Block*, p. 4.
[38] The account in *War Diary*, 63 Brigade makes it that the 1st Battalion 10th G. Rifles reached the assembly position and then marched to a point north of the road-block. Here this met some men of 1/11 Sikhs who said that their Battalion was split. So the C.O. of 1/10 Gurkha Rifles withdrew to the railway with the object of collecting the Battalion and with a portion of his Battalion struck north-west.
[39] The road was jammed with artillery and tanks.

accurate mortar fire put terror into the hearts of the young soldiers, most of whom had not more than one year's service. Officers of 'C' and 'D' companies set a bad example. Artillery had not opened up.[40] But 'B' company, which was also badly disorganized by the air attack, went forward and reached the objective without further losses.

Shortly before the 7th Queen's Own Hussars began their advance it was found that the block was undefended. The tanks then went down the road and through the block without opposition. The infantry then cleared the area of the few remaining snipers.

THE FORCE MOVES NORTH—8-10 MARCH

At about 1030 hours the whole force began moving north, but a good deal of sniping made piqueting necessary. The road as far as Tharrawaddy was continuously patrolled by tanks whilst the 16th Indian Infantry Brigade close-piquetted the stretch in the immediate area of the block from Tharrawaddy to Hmawbi. The only opposition along the road itself was from the air, Japanese bombing aircraft maintaining almost continuous activity. Headquarters of the 17th Indian Division which had moved to Taukkyan from Hlegu in the morning as rearguard, suffered heavily. Almost the entire strength of the British light and heavy anti-aircraft guns in Burma was in the Taukkyan area and these kept the Japanese bombers at great height. One Japanese aircraft was brought down by a direct hit and other aircraft were probably disabled.

With the depleted 'B' company and elements of 'A' company which had joined in on their own initiative the 1st Battalion 11th Sikh Regiment continued to advance north, up the road to the junction of the main and Wanetchaung roads. There they held a position against continuous hostile fire and air attack for the rest of the day during the course of which they captured from the Japanese important code books and War Diaries giving their plan of action. It was only then known that the retreating force had been in action against the Japanese *33rd Division*.

At 1530 hours another Japanese force moving in from the west endeavoured to place machine-guns in position near the road fork at milestone 22. A troop of Hussars drove them off and the road was kept open. Similar attempts by hostile mortar detachments to shell the road from the direction of Hlawga were dealt with by the 1st Battalion the Gloucestershire Regiment. On the evening of 7 March, the situation was quite desperate. The Japanese were in a strong position and there were virtually no troops to hit against them. The 17th Indian Division was on its way from Hlegu, but it was tired and still very short of men and arms. But thanks to the Japanese mistake of removing the road-block early, it was able to escape.

Throughout the day and into the following night the force moved north from Taukkyan and Hlegu, one Squadron of the 2nd Battalion Royal Tank Regiment acting as rear-guard. Shortly after 2300 hours the last of the marching infantry had passed through Hmawbi, and the majority of the infantry battalions of the 17th Indian Division were

---

[40] Lieutenant-Colonel Wheeler's *account* has it that it opened up.

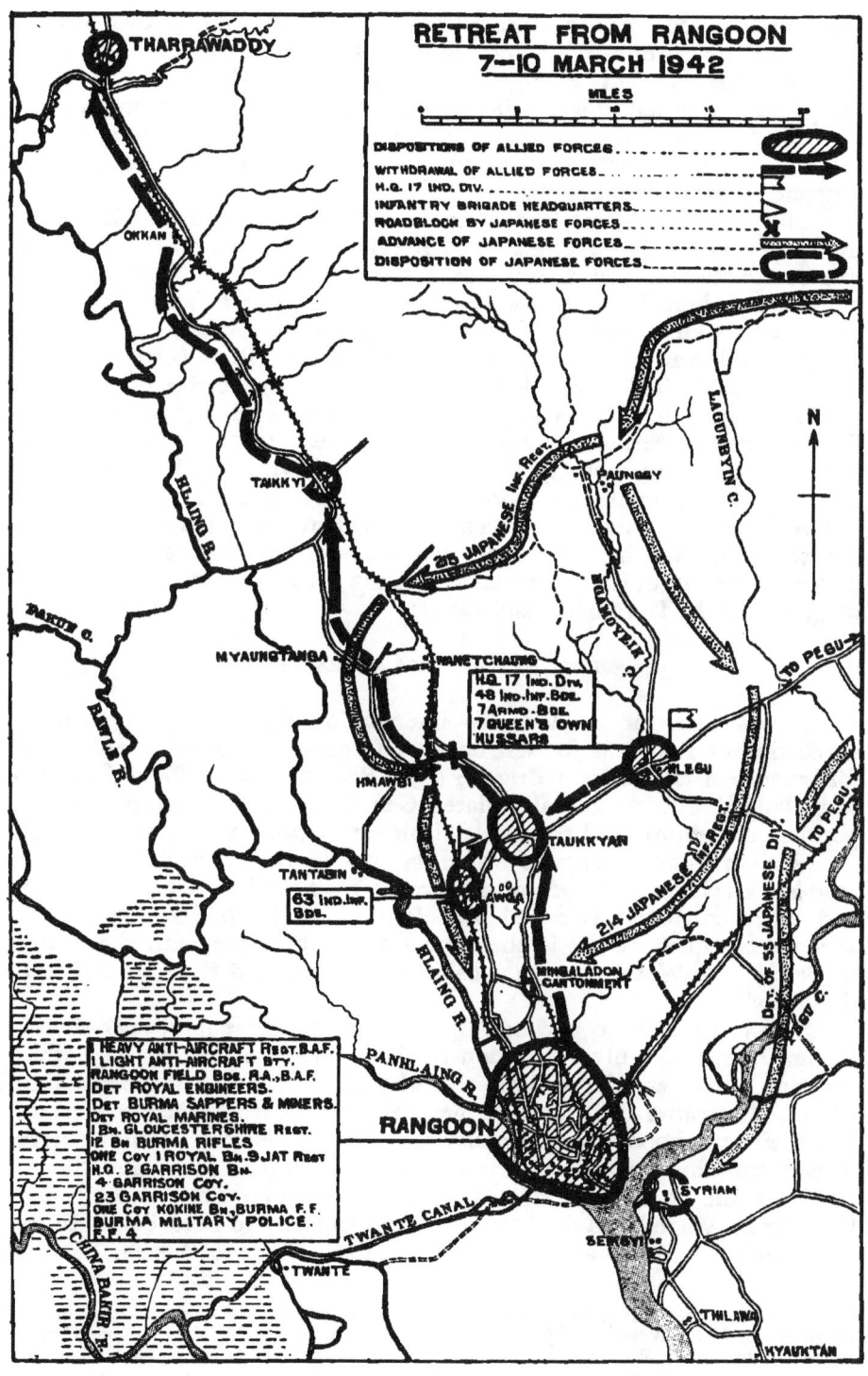

assembled in open paddy land west of the village. They then carried out a further withdrawal across country towards Thaikkyi, halting at dawn to disperse. Only emergency rations were available. Many of these troops had marched thirty miles in the last twenty-four hours, an outstanding feat under the trying conditions to which they had already been subjected. The rear-guard then consisted of the 7th Armoured Brigade leaguered near Myaungtanga.

On 9 and 10 March the force continued its withdrawal by motor transport and rail from Thaikkyi to the Tharrawaddy area, where intensive reorganisation and re-equipment were carried out. First reinforcements left behind by Brigades together with stragglers from the Sittang and more recent operations helped to swell the numbers.

At Taukkyan the Japanese had made one of their costly mistakes. The road-block had been placed not only to protect the flank of the Japanese forces (*33rd Division*) moving towards Rangoon along the Rangoon-Prome Road but also to prevent the Army Headquarters and troops in Rangoon from getting out. In its hurried rush for the city, *33rd Division* ignored the more important operation of cutting off the retreating force. Possibly the Japanese acted in the belief that a general British withdrawal by sea was in progress. The retreating force offered an admirable target for the Japanese aircraft with a column some 40 miles long, mostly M.T. vehicles and tanks.[41]

EFFECT OF THE LOSS OF RANGOON

It was Gen. Sir A. Wavell's intervention that had postponed the evacuation of Rangoon for ten days. Of course the delay enabled reinforcements of an Infantry Brigade (63rd Brigade) and a Field Regiment to be landed, but it eventually placed Gen. Sir H. Alexander in a difficult position and almost had the result of his forces being nearly cut off. The 63rd Indian Infantry Brigade which had lost its nerve centre in the Pegu road-block split on the rock of the Prome road-block and if the Japanese had not prematurely removed the block, there would have been more serious consequences. It is therefore difficult to agree with the remark of Gen. Sir A. Wavell that "on balance I am satisfied that we gained by the delay".

The loss of Rangoon which the previous Japanese land operations in Burma had made only a question of time, was in every respect nothing short of a disaster. It changed the whole face of the first Burma Campaign. Thereafter the Allied armies were cut off from outside assistance and their only hope was an orderly retreat with delaying tactics in order to gain time for the construction of the Assam-Burma Road and the outbreak of the monsoon. In a general appreciation sent on 7 March, Gen. Sir A. Wavell had doubted the Allied capacity to hold Upper Burma indefinitely.[42] In the absence of a road from India to Burma, Rangoon

---

[41] The Japanese reason for the absence of air attack on the Rangoon Garrison as it retreated northward is 'that the Japanese air force did not know that the Rangoon Garrison retreated northward,' FEC, GHQ, ATIS, 601/10111/H. Answer to Q. 74 by Shoichi Sato.

[42] Gen. Sir A. Wavell was of opinion that "with Rangoon in their possession the Japanese can abandon long and difficult line of communication through Thailand and

was the only point of entry into Burma through which personnel and supplies could be moved in large numbers. With its loss, very little reinforcement of personnel and stores could be sent by air as the number of transport aircraft in India was extremely limited. The Army was thus compelled to fight, facing its former base and with no line of communication behind it.

Much depended upon how quickly the process of driving a road from India to Burma could be achieved. "The project of a road between Assam and Upper Burma had been the subject of a discussion for some years previous to the war, but no action had been taken. As a military necessity, it began to take shape in the late autumn of 1941; the actual orders to begin work at all speed were issued in the middle of December. India was to widen the metalled road already existing from Dimapur to Imphal in Manipur State (135 miles) and to make a road from Imphal to Tamu (65 miles) where only a bridle track existed. Burma Government was to make an all weather road from Tamu to Kalewa (100 miles) between which places only a fair weather cart track existed".[43] Up to February work inside India had proceeded somewhat slowly but thenceforward was pushed on with all possible speed. Even then there was no prospect of its being finished for some months to come. A motor road not metalled reached Tamu just in time for the withdrawal of the Burma Army, but maintenance of this road during the wet season would have been impossible. Work on the Burma side had progressed very little. Very difficult country had to be traversed, there was shortage of material of all kinds, and the difficulty of retaining a labour force; above all there was the passage of innumerable refugees.

Base and Line of Communication installations and reserves of various commodities had already been moved north of Rangoon, and as this backloading had to continue throughout the withdrawal this placed an enormous strain on the administrative machine and on the transportation agencies. On the river steamers it was difficult to persuade indigenous civilian crews to operate in forward areas. Civil heavy repair installations in the Rangoon area which could not be removed were lost altogether, and the maintenance of mechanical transport and equipment became a matter of great difficulty.

The destruction of the refineries, where the refining of all crude oil from the oilfields had been carried out, very much reduced the output of motor and aviation spirit and lubricating oils and rendered the Allied forces in Burma dependent on such spirit as could be produced by improvised methods in the oilfields themselves, when reserve stocks had been consumed.

The air situation was also completely changed with the loss of Rangoon which involved the loss of considerable number of aerodromes with an efficient warning system. The dislocation of this warning system was to have disastrous results on the remnants of the air force in Burma.

Tenasserim and supply and reinforce by sea. They can increase their forces up to 7 or 8 Division, if necessary, while we shall be hard put to supply the comparatively small forces we have in Burma." Tel. No. 5084/G dated 7 March from Gen. Wavell for C.O.S. *Appreciations & Plans.* 601/2/3/H, p. 58.

[43] Gen. Sir A. Wavell's *Despatch*, pp. 13-14.

Magwe was the only airfield left in Burma with any degree of warning. There was one R.D.F. set and Magwe lay behind two lines of Observer Corps telephone lines, one down the valley of the Salween, towards Rangoon and the other down the valley of the Irrawaddy. The loss of Rangoon also stopped the flow of R.A.F. personnel and equipment planned by the Air Ministry when these were actually in passage from the United Kingdom and the Middle East. Once Rangoon had gone the maximum force that could be maintained in Upper Burma from the resources available was one Bomber Squadron, one Fighter Squadron and one Army Co-operation Flight, in addition to one A.V.G. Squadron.[44]

On the contrary, the Japanese, after the fall of Singapore on 15 February, were able to release considerable ground and air forces for a more vigorous assault on the Allied forces in Burma. The fall of Rangoon further afforded to them all the advantages in communications which had previously been available to the Indo-British forces. Instead of having to supply their army by difficult mountain roads the Japanese were now able, after effecting repairs to the port, to move very large forces into Burma. Two more divisions and ancillary units were soon to make their appearance.[45] With the considerable number of airfields prepared in the Rangoon area, heavy reinforcements of Japanese aircraft could be flown in at will into Burma.

In short "until such time as the road from Assam to Burma was completed the retention of Upper Burma by the Allies was dependent on the amount of force which the Japanese decided to employ in that theatre. The task of the Allies therefore, was to impose the maximum delay on the enemy and make him expend resources, which he might have employed elsewhere".[46]

---

[44] Air Vice Marshal D.F. Stevenson's *Despatch* paras 124-25.
[45] 56 and 18 Divisions.
[46] Gen. Sir H. Alexander's *Despatch* p. 4.

CHAPTER XV

Operations in the Shan and Karenni State

OPERATIONS IN JANUARY AND FEBRUARY 1942

Early in January the Chinese 227 Regiment had taken over the defence of the Mekong river east of the road Kengtung-Mongpayak. This reduced considerably the very long sector held by the 1 Burma Division in the Shan States.[1] Nevertheless the distance from the Chinese positions on the Indo-China border to the mouth of the river Salween was some three hundred miles "to guard which there was only one division consisting of two infantry brigades and a few of the Frontier Force Detachments". Apart from the 17th Indian Division concentrated in Tenasserim, there were only two Brigades of the 1st Burma Division and a few Frontier Force units to cover this extensive front.

Although the Japanese were not very active in the Shan States and Karenni during January and February 1942 the position then was not free from anxiety. There were known to be numbers of Japanese as well as Thai troops in northern Thailand, and there were persistent reports of large hostile concentrations at Chiengmai and Chiengrai and indications of an early invasion.[2] The road from Kemapyu on the Salween in Karenni to Toungoo was practically unguarded. Yet, to meet the more threatening situation in Tenasserim troops had to be constantly withdrawn from the Shan States. Thus the 1st Burma Division lost the 2nd Battalion King's Own Yorkshire Light Infantry, 5 Field Brigade, R.A., B.A.F., the Malerkotla Sappers and Miners and later, the 1st Battalion Burma Rifles.[3]

Relief of 1 Burma Division by Chinese Sixth Army

On 19 January the remainder of the Chinese 93 Division was ordered to move into Keng Tung, and later in the month General Sir A. Wavell sanctioned the entry of 49 Division. Shortly afterwards it was agreed that the Chinese 55 Division should also be employed. These three Divisions comprised the Chinese Sixth Army.

CONCENTRATION OF 1 BURMA DIVISION SOUTH OF TOUNGOO

It was Lieutenant General T. J. Hutton's policy to concentrate, as early as possible, the whole of the available Indo-British forces in the south of Burma with the object of holding up the Japanese advance in the area where it presented the greatest threat to Rangoon and the communica-

---

[1] 1 Burma Brigade was reinforced by the arrival of F.F.I. which moved into the area east of the Salween and south of the main road to watch tracks leading northwards from Thailand into the Shan States—*War Diary*, 1 Burma Brigade.
[2] Lieutenant General T. J. Hutton's *Report*, para 63.
[3] This situation caused the G.O.C. no little anxiety.

tions with China. Accordingly, as the Chinese Sixth Army deployed, the remaining units of the 1st Burma Division in the Shan States withdrew southwards. The 1st Burma Brigade moved south during February and early March. Additional units of the 13th Indian Infantry Brigade moved into Karenni in February and there 23 Mountain Battery, the 5th Battalion Burma Rifles, and the 5th Battalion 1st Punjab Regiment joined the 1st Battalion 18th Royal Garhwal Rifles.

The withdrawal of these units from remote areas was not easy. Maintenance had been by mule and elephant transport, and when the Chinese forces took over, there was the added difficulty of finding for them the correct items of supply. The line of communication which had previously been considered incapable of maintaining more than two brigades was now compelled to provide for two Chinese divisions.

Both in the Shan States and Karenni operations had been confined to minor encounters on the frontier, particularly in the neighbourhood of the Keng-Tung—Chiangrai road. These actions were fought by Frontier Force Columns, the opposition being provided by Thai troops led by Japanese officers. On 17 February F.F. 4 carried out a most successful surprise raid on the Thai outposts south of Pung Pahkyem. A Japanese officer and sixty troops were killed without loss to the Frontier Force. During this period a large patrol of the 1st Battalion 18th Royal Garhwal Rifles had also entered Thailand and reconnoitred the area of the Mehongsohn airfield.

By the end of February the 1st Burma Division was covering the Sittang valley south of Nyaunglebin with the very weak 2nd Burma Brigade. This Brigade, after the defence of Moulmein, had been withdrawn to Kyaikto and in the middle of February became, for a brief period, a line of communication formation. With Headquarters at Nyaunglebin it was then responsible for the protection of the Sittang river crossings from Shwegyin southwards. The 4th Battalion 12th Frontier Force Regiment had by that time reverted to the 16th Indian Infantry Brigade. When the 1st Burma Division moved south the 2nd Burma Brigade rejoined it, having covered the concentration of the Division.

During this period the 1st Battalion Burma Rifles had furnished the forward screen for the 2nd Burma Brigade. Covering Nyaunglebin it had maintained contact by motor patrol with the 7th Armoured Brigade to the south about Pegu.

It should here be noted that the 1st Burma Division had only one carrier platoon. This was made up of a few old tracked carriers originally issued for instructional purposes. This small unit had a mixed British, Indian and Burman personnel and did valuable reconnaissance work until its carriers wore out and had to be abandoned. It also fought a very successful minor action when two Japanese machine-guns and a mortar were destroyed.

North of the 2nd Burma Brigade on the main Rangoon-Mandalay road was the 1st Burma Brigade in position about Pyu and Kyauktaga. The 13th Indian Infantry Brigade remained for the time being in Karenni covering Kemapyu and the important tin mines at Mawchi; but the 5th Battalion Burma Rifles and the 5th Battalion 1st Punjab Regiment were withdrawn for duty on the Sittang valley front. This left the 13th Indian Infantry Brigade with only one Battalion and one Frontier Force column.

East of the 2nd Burma Brigade, at Papun on the upper Yunzalin river the 2nd Battalion Burma Rifles was watching the trans-frontier tracks converging at that point. On 23 February, following upon the Sittang Bridge battle, it received orders to retire from Papun and to join the 1st Burma Division.

UNRELIABLE ELEMENTS IN BURMA RIFLES BATTALION

Events on the Tenasserim front were not without effect on the Burma troops in the 1st Burma Division. On 26 February Brig. A. J. H. Bourke reported to the 17th Indian Division that men were deserting at the rate of twenty or so every night from each Battalion of the 2nd Burma Brigade. In some cases arms and equipment were also taken away by the deserters. Morale was so low even in units that had never fired a shot that he could no longer count on his Brigade to check an attack. At that time the Brigade consisted of the 1st and 7th Battalions of the Burma Rifles and the remnants of the 3rd Battalion. The first named Battalion had recently joined the Brigade but soon reverted to the 1st Burma Brigade.

It is only fair to note here that officers who served with the Burma Rifles do not agree with Brig. A. J. H. Bourke's views and regard the estimate of twenty desertions each night from the Battalions in the Brigade as incorrect. They claim that the strength returns will support them in this and that numbers were fairly well maintained. Whilst agreeing that there were some desertions and that the men were depressed by lack of success and by the streams of dejected troops of all classes and refugees passing through the covering positions, they also state that morale was still good, that the Brigade was keen to meet the Japanese again, and that a successful action would have removed any depression. Certainly all units were to prove in subsequent actions that there was plenty of fight left in them.

The above-mentioned report together with earlier events in the campaign led the Army Commander to authorise the release from the Burma Rifles battalions of all men considered unreliable. This and the shortage of trained recruits to replace battle casualties necessitated a re-organisation of the battalions. The 3rd Battalion was broken up. The 9th and 10th Battalions were to be wasted out. The 6th Battalion became a Garrison Company of Karens.

It should also be noted that the Shans of the 13th and 14th Battalions Burma Rifles proved most unreliable, deserting in large numbers and often taking with them arms and ammunition. On one occasion officers went with the deserters. These Battalions, however, were never actively engaged. They were recently raised to Territorial Battalions. The majority of their officers were Shan Sawbwas (Chiefs).

Subsequently when the 1st Burma Division had withdrawn to Toungoo, the Karens of the 1st Battalion Burma Rifles consisting of a formed rifles company and a portion of the Headquarters company, were sent to strengthen the Karen Levies operating in their own hill country east of Toungoo. Early in April these Karens fought most gallantly against the very superior Japanese force advancing from Toungoo on Mawchi.

ATTACKS ON PYUNTAZA AND SHWEGYIN

Pyuntaza

Whilst the Sittang bridge battle was being fought, other Japanese forces were feeling their way north along the east bank of the river. They were a few miles south of Donzayit on 23 February. Two days later they were at Kunzeik. Next day a mixed force of Japanese and hostile Burmans was in Shwegyin from which the Allied forces had previously withdrawn.[4] They then crossed the river, and on 27 February Burma Brigade patrols encountered a party of about one hundred on the Rangoon-Mandalay road about mid-way between the towns of Daiku and Pegu. On the same day another Japanese force was astride the road and railway at Pyinbon, sixteen miles north of Pegu.

The wide gap between the 2nd Burma Brigade and the 17th Indian Division around Pegu was only covered by patrols which could not prevent Japanese infiltration. Taking full advantage of this state of affairs and moving under cover of darkness Japanese tanks and columns crossed the main road. During the night of 3/4 March one such column passed through Daiku. Next morning the road was cut about one mile south of Pyuntaza at the Yenwe Chaung bridge where a patrol of the 1st Battalion Burma Rifles encountered a road-block.[5]

"A" Company[6] of the Battalion succeeded in taking the block and the adjacent railway bridge, but was then forced to retire under heavy fire from machine-guns and mortars. The hostile force was a mixed one of Japanese and Burmans. Following this engagement during the early hours of 5 March a large body of the Japanese troops with light guns and with a long column of transport including mules, carts, and elephants, passed through Pyuntaza travelling west. Touch between the two Indo-Burman divisions along the main road had now been lost.

The 1st Battalion Burma Rifles sent out patrols to reconnoitre the Japanese positions near Pyuntaza. Great enterprise was shown by a Burman Havildar who disguised himself as a villager and thus entered the Japanese lines where he helped to dig trenches. Having obtained valuable information he returned to his Battalion.[7]

Meanwhile Japanese infiltration westwards had led to the fall of Rangoon on 8 March. However, only the previous day the 1st Burma Division had received orders to attack Shewegyin and Daiku, and to exploit any success southwards with the object of impeding infiltration round the north flank of the 17th Indian Division. The attack was launched on 11 March. The 1st Burma Brigade on the right was to secure Pyuntaza and the large village of Daiku, whilst the 2nd Burma

[4] *War Diary*, 17 Indian Division, 'G' Br. for Feb. 26.
[5] *War Diary*, 1 Burma Rifles gives it as 1½ miles.
[6] Chin Company with one section Support Platoon and one detachment of Mortar Platoon.
[7] Havildar Myaung Kyan; *War Diary*, 1 Burma Rifles (Reconstructed) p. 2.

Brigade (less one Battalion) was to take Madauk and Shwegyin. The 27th Mountain Regiment was to support the 1st Burma Brigade.

To ensure secrecy all forward movements of troops were made by night, the two Brigades concerned moving forward from Nyaunglebin to their starting points for the attack during the hours of darkness on the night of 10/11 March. By reason of the considerable fifth column activity in the district the Divisional Commander ordered that:—

"Ranks will only be told what they need to know when they need know it, in order to carry out their tasks."

On the 1st Burma Brigade front it was intended that the 2nd Battalion 7th Rajput Regiment[8] should take Pyuntaza and the road-block south of the town. The 1st and 5th Battalions Burma Rifles were then to pass through to Daiku, the final objective.

The Rajputs moved out of Wingabaw village, where they had arrived earlier that night, at 0400 hours on 11 March. At first light 'C' and 'D' companies advanced on Pyuntaza across the flat paddy lands. 'D' Company on the left was assisted by a section of carriers. Meanwhile, 'B' company on the right flank advanced on the road-block on the Yenwe Chaung bridge. The infantry was supported by the 2nd Mountain Battery from Eywa village, the area south of the road-block being shelled.

'C' and 'D' companies secured Pyuntaza and then continued their advance towards the road-block. But the attack was then held up by extremely heavy machine-gun, mortar and shell fire. The officer commanding the Battalion, decided to throw in his reserve, 'A' company. The left section of the Mountain Battery had moved forward two thousand yards to support the second phase of the attack.

The Japanese position round the road-block was entered by 'A' company, but an immediate counter-attack by a much superior force compelled the company to fall back in some confusion. Information was received at Advanced Battalion Headquarters that the hostile force was advancing round the left flank, and when it became obvious that the attack could not succeed without additional support the Battalion was ordered to withdraw from Pyuntaza.[9]

During this withdrawal the right section of the Mountain Battery was attacked by a Japanese party making much noise and armed with light machine-guns. At that time the Battery was without infantry protection, a Burmese Platoon of the 5th Battalion Burma Rifles acting as escort to the guns, having deserted. There was a certain amount of disorder in the wagon lines but the guns were got away. The Battery casualties were one officer and over forty other ranks missing. Many of the latter appear to have deserted.

The 2nd Battalion 7th Rajput Regiment withdrew through the Battalions of Burma Rifles to concentrate at Tawpathi. The Battalion had suffered heavily, particularly 'D' company. Its commander was lost. Total casualties were killed eleven, wounded fourteen, and missing seventy-nine.

[8] Assisted by Divisional Bren Carriers supported by 2nd Mountain Battery.
[9] *War Diary*, 1st Burma Rifles says, "The Brigade Command decided not to press the attack and 1 and 5 Bimp remained in position astride the Rangoon-Mandalay road 1 mile north of Pyuntaza."

At the end of the day a line had been established on the Aleywa Chaung held by the two Battalions of Burma Rifles. These were in contact with the Japanese patrols and were not affected by the failure of the attack. On the other side, the Japanese reconnaissance aircraft had been active throughout the day.

Shwegyin

The operations carried out by the 2nd Burma Brigade against Shwegyin and Madauk were intended for the crossing of the Sittang river at Waing by the 5th Battalion 1st Punjab Regiment. The Battalion was then to be joined by F.F.3, already on the east bank of the river, for the attack on Shwegyin. The 7th Battalion Burma Rifles was to secure Madauk. Both Shwegyin and Madauk were to be bombed by the RAF for a period of half an hour immediately before the attacks were launched.

On 10 March the 7th Battalion Burma Rifles established a bridgehead at Waing, and at 0300 hours next morning the 5th Battalion 1st Punjab Regiment[10] crossed the river on rafts constructed by the Divisional Engineers. The Battalion then marched five miles across rough country to the Shwegyin-Papun road where it was joined by F.F.3. Turning south the force moved slowly on Shwegyin, halting near the town at milestone 2 at 0700 hours. It then waited for the air-bombing of the town.[11] But no aircraft appeared. Nevertheless, it was decided to proceed with the attack.[12]

The Japanese were in position astride the road outside Shwegyin. The 5th Battalion 1st Punjab Regiment attacked with one company on each side of the road and drove the Japanese before it into the town. Strong resistance was encountered there, and two mortar detachments went into action to support the advance. At the same time the officer commanding the Battalion ordered one column of F.F.3 to work round the right flank. The advance soon continued, the troops keeping excellent communication during the street fighting by their cries of "Sat Sri Akal" and "Ya Ali". Finally the hostile force fled across the Shwegyin Chaung at the south end of the town, many being killed in the stream by light machine-gun fire. By 1000 hours the town was free. Forty hostile Burmans were captured and at least fifty had been killed. They were dressed in civilian clothes, and were well armed with light machine-guns, Thompson Sub-machine carbines, rifles, and grenades. The casualties on this side were four killed and seventeen wounded.[13]

Madauk, to the west of Shwegyin, lay on both banks of the Sittang river. That portion of the village on the west bank was occupied by a company of the 7th Battalion Burma Rifles without opposition.[14] It was

---

[10] Less M.T.
[11] The R.A.F. was scheduled to carry out half an hour's bombing of selected targets.
[12] At 0730 hours.
[13] The enemy killed numbered 50. A building in the centre of the Bazaar was searched and large quantities of rifles, shotguns, ammunition and rations were collected. While the search was going on a Burman set fire to the premises and attempted to escape, but was shot. *War Diary—5/1 P.R.*
[14] 'D' Company—But like 5/1 Punjab Regiment, it had no air support—*War Diary, 7 Burma Rifles.*

then found that all boats had been removed to the opposite bank of the river. Major Kyadoe, (a Karen) the Company Commander, swam the river under hostile fire, secured a boat, and returned with it. Then, under strong covering fire, two platoons of the company were ferried across the Sittang, who dispersed the foe on the east bank. Contact with the 5th Battalion 1st Punjab Regiment was then established.

Subsequently, the 2nd Burma Brigade took up a line south of Madauk and the Shwegyin Chaung, and extensive forward patrolling was carried out. Next day the 1st Burma Division issued an order that this line, and that of the Aleywa Chaung on the west, should be consolidated. But the Division was not to hold this position for long.

DECISION TO WITHDRAW 1 BURMA DIVISION TO THE IRRAWADDY FRONT

The Chinese Fifth Army was at the time entering Burma to take over the Sittang valley sector. Gen. Sir H. Alexander was concentrating the Indo-British Forces in the Irrawaddy valley where he considered it necessary to have greater strength. This involved the transfer of the 1st Burma Division from the Sittang sector as soon as its relief by the Chinese Fifth Army could be arranged.

Although they could have done so, the Chinese were unwilling to take up a line south of Toungoo. It therefore became necessary to give up the extensive area held south of that town or alternatively, to abandon the concentration along the Irrawaddy. This latter, Gen. Sir H. Alexander felt he could not afford to do. As a result the 1st Burma Division was ordered to fall back towards Toungoo whilst the Chinese Fifth Army moved into position.

The first stage of the withdrawal was to the area Pyu-Bawgata-Myogyaung-Udo and the movement was completed without incident by the evening of 15 March. The front held by the Division was designed to cover the valley from the forest-clad hills of the Pegu Yoma on the west to those of Karenni, east of the Sittang. Forward detachments continued to hold the Aleywa-Chaung-Shwegyin line thinly until the afternoon when Japanese infiltration compelled their withdrawal.

Brigades were then warned that there would be a further withdrawal to the Toungoo area and thence to Prome where the newly formed Burcorps was to concentrate. The 13th Indian Infantry Brigade in Karenni would fall back by stages to Toungoo, leaving the Karen Levies to hold the area in front of the Chinese.

The withdrawal along the main road itself was followed up closely by the Japanese, and on 17 March an attack was launched against the 5th Battalion Burma Rifles in the centre of the 1st Burma Brigade front. The Battalion was in the position astride and to the east of the main road and railway just south of Kyauktaga.

At 1840 hours on the previous night, 15 March, seven Japanese lorries had driven along the main road to within two hundred yards of the Battalion posts. They were engaged by every Bren gun that could be brought to bear. Five lorries were disabled and heavy casualties inflicted. During the night the Japanese attempted further to infiltrate through the 2nd Battalion 7th Rajput Regiment on the right of the line.

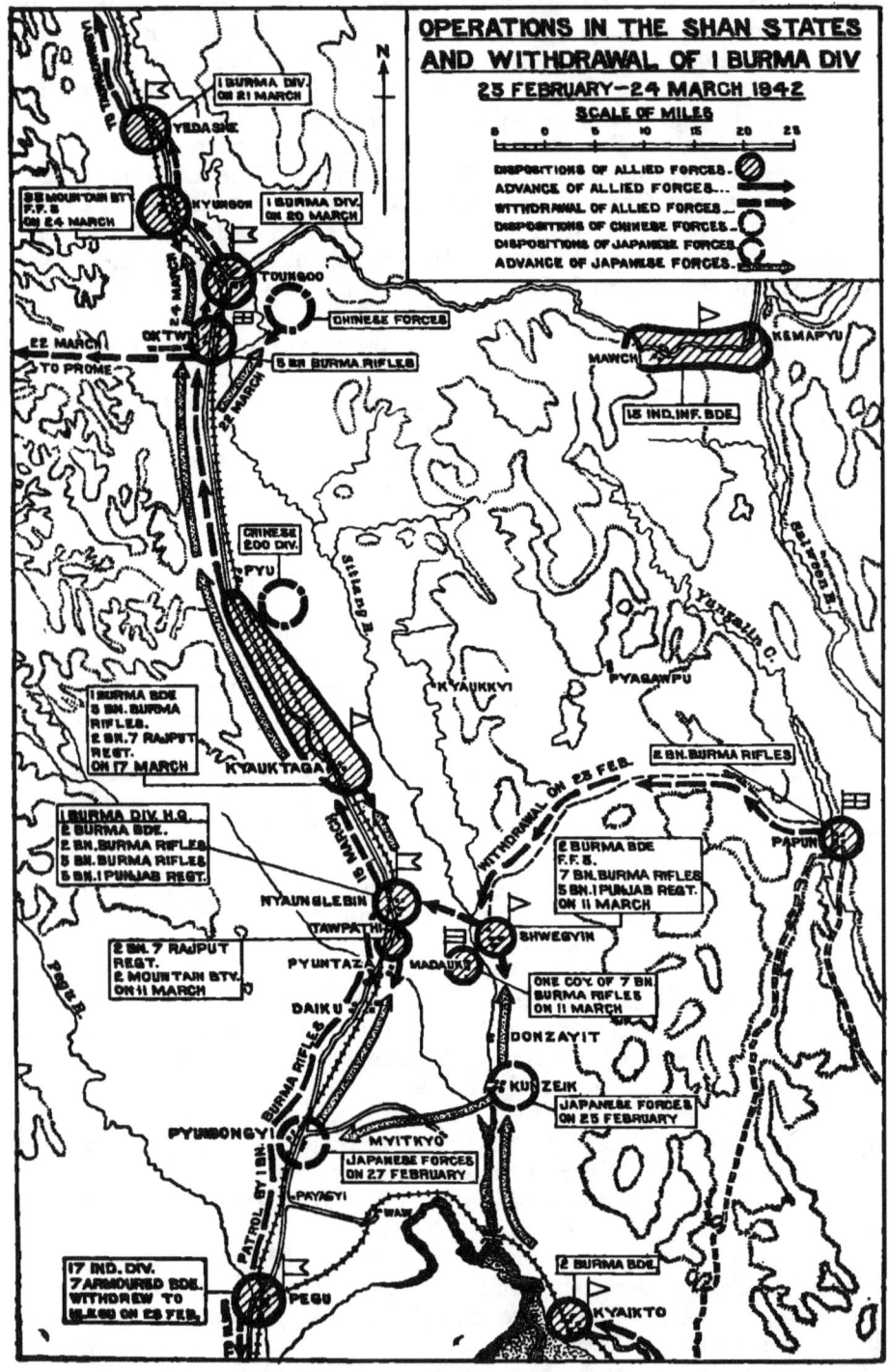

There were occasional bursts of uncontrolled fire in the dark. Nothing further happened until 0630 hours next morning, 17 March, when there was a brief attack on the right company of the 5th Battalion Burma Rifles. Soon that died away, but at 1150 hours there began heavy and accurate shelling of the centre company and Battalion Headquarters of the 5th Battalion Burma Rifles located on the southern outskirts of Kyauktaga town. It was estimated that mortars and two Mountain Batteries were employed, and the shelling continued intermittently all day.

About 1500 hours a large mixed force of Japanese and Burmans advanced against the centre forward company on the sector immediately to the left of the railway, whilst a smaller force of infantry and cavalry moved against the left company. The invaders did not press the attack seriously, but the centre company gave ground.

Behind the centre company, in a village was the Burmese company of the Battalion in support. Before this date it had become much depleted in numbers. The company commander soon found that one of his platoons had deserted *en masse* leaving him with only twenty-six men.

At 1700 hours the Japanese attack developed again and they infiltrated through the centre company to within a hundred yards of the Battalion Headquarters. On the left they had surrounded the remnants of the Burmese company. This handful of men however fought well and cut their way through the Japanese.

At 1745 hours the Battalion began to withdraw on orders from the Brigade Headquarters. The Burmese company lost two Governor's Commissioned Officers and fourteen other ranks killed, and a considerable number of men throughout the Battalion were missing.

Early next morning (18 March) the 1st Burma Brigade passed through the defensive position taken up behind it by the 2nd Burma Brigade. This position crossed the main road just south of Gonde, the central sector along the Kung Chaung being held by the 7th Battalion Burma Rifles. On the west, the line was continued by the 2nd Battalion Burma Rifles whilst on the east was stationed the 5th Battalion 1st Punjab Regiment.

The last elements of the 1st Burma Brigade had withdrawn at 0700 hours. At 1030 hours a Japanese column was observed marching up the main road. It was allowed to approach to within two hundred yards when 'C' company of the 7th Battalion Burma Rifles opened fire. The guns and mortars followed suit at once and very heavy casualties were inflicted on the Japanese. The remnants of the column took cover in a piece of jungle to the east of the road. They were then shelled intermittently by mortars and artillery.[15]

The Japanese further endeavoured to work round the east flank of the centre Battalion and in the afternoon began to shell Gonde village. This was countered by the guns and mortars which replied on each occasion when hostile artillery and mortar fire was opened. Meanwhile, the Japanese attempt to advance on the east was met by counter-attack by the 7th Battalion Burma Rifles which maintained all its positions intact.

---

[15] *War Diary*, 7 Burma Rifles.

On the west of the main road the 2nd Battalion Burma Rifles observed two Japanese tanks, but these appear to have taken no part in the operations. At 2000 hours the Brigade withdrew, and during this operation the 7th Battalion Burma Rifles was heavily shelled. Casualties were, however, light owing to dispersion.

The units of the 1st Burma Division then passed through the advanced posts of the Chinese 200 Division, south of Pyu and along the Pyu river where the Chinese Divisional Cavalry was maintaining forward patrols. These were in contact with the Japanese on 19 March.

Night marching combined with extensive patrolling and the reconnaissance and preparation of positions by day caused much exhaustion to the troops in the 1st Burma Division during its withdrawal. Men fell asleep on their feet, and at halts during the night marches, it became necessary to keep a proportion of officers and men standing. Scanty hours of rest were often lost through preparation of positions which were soon abandoned. By the time that orders to withdraw had reached the Battalions, it was sometimes too late to recall distant patrols which were necessary in the absence of mobile troops or motor transport.

On 20 March, the Chinese in Toungoo set fire to a large area of the town with the object of preparing a defensive position. The fire threatened the railway station and also the Rear Headquarters of the 1st Burma Division and the Supply Depot. Working parties were sent into the town by the Division and their strenuous efforts averted the danger. Surplus stores were cleared and the move of the Divisional Rear Headquarters to Yedashe was expedited.

The 1st Burma Division withdrew to the area Yedashe-Kyungon preparatory to the move to the Irrawaddy front. This assembly was carried out on 21 March and next day units began to entrain for Taungdwingyi. The 5th Battalion Burma Rifles had been detailed to proceed to Prome by march route through the Pegu Yoma. With certain attached units the Battalion marched from Oktwin along the track to Paukkaung on 22 March. Its orders were to deal with any hostiles encountered in the Pegu-Yoma where F.F.1 was acting as a covering force. F.F.1 had been operating independently for about three weeks and had shown considerable resource in living off the country, as owing to the failure of communications it had not been possible for the 1st Burma Division to supply it.

On 22 March twenty minutes after the 5th Battalion Burma Rifles had left Oktwin, a Japanese attack on the Chinese force developed. Two days later whilst 33 Mounain Battery and F.F.3 were still at Kyungon the Japanese carried out an outflanking movement round Toungoo and made an attack on the Kyungon landing ground. The Mountain Battery and F.F.3 became involved in the fight and put up a stubborn resistance. Eventually they were extricated and entrained next day for Taungdwingyi.

Meanwhile the 1st Burma Division had received a modification of its original order to concentrate in the Prome area. Burcorps altered this to the area Dayindabo-Kyaukpadaung-All-Wenmyo-Theyetmyo immediately behind the 17th Division.[16]

---

[16] *War Diary*, Burcorps. G Branch Microfilm No. D/166/278-395.

CHAPTER XVI

Regrouping of Force after the Fall of Rangoon

Having failed in his primary task to hold Rangoon Gen. Sir H. Alexander set himself to his secondary task of retaining upper Burma. But until the Assam-Burma road was completed this was dependent on the amount of force which the Japanese decided to employ in this theatre. The task of the Allied forces was therefore "to impose the maximum delay on the enemy and make him expend resources which he might have employed elsewhere."[1]

Since a double advance along the Rangoon-Prome and Rangoon-Mandalay roads was expected, it was decided to maintain two fronts, the Irrawaddy front and the Toungoo front. The arrival of the Chinese forces and the shattered condition of the 17th Indian Division necessitated a thorough regrouping of forces. The period of respite which followed the fall of Rangoon was very useful. The Japanese were obviously resting, refitting and reinforcing in the Rangoon and Pegu area and waiting for the Chinese Armies to move in, while their propaganda machine exploited to the full the fall of Rangoon.[2]

In reorganising the forces it was necessary to have more strength in the Irrawaddy valley. Gen. Sir H. Alexander therefore arranged for the Chinese Fifth Army to relieve the 1st Burma Division on the Toungoo front so that this Division could be brought across into the Irrawaddy valley and concentrated there with the 17th Indian Division. The date on which this could take place was dependent on the moves of the Chinese Army and it was not until the third week of March that the relief of the 1st Burma Division could be effected. The original intention was to concentrate the 17th Indian Division in the area of Thonze-Tharrawaddy-Letpadan and to hold the line -Henzada-Sanywe Ferry-Thonze-Thonze Chaung. The Chinese Army was to operate south of Toungoo. But the Chinese were unwilling to go south of Toungoo and as a common front with the Chinese was necessary it became important to give up the area south of Prome and Toungoo. A position around and south of Prome was finally chosen with the intention to fight on the general line Prome-Toungoo-Mongpan-Keng-Tung. This resulted in the loss of an area more than 80 miles in depth in which there were large quantities of food, particularly rice. Endeavours were made to move these supplies which would be required by the Chinese. In Upper Burma there was little or no surplus production of rice.[3]

To keep in touch with the events on the Toungoo front, columns from

---

[1] Gen. Sir H. Alexander's *Despatch*, para 12. p. 4.
[2] It may be so owing to their change of the original plan to capture only South Burma initially.
[3] As much as possible of the enormous quantities of rice south of the line Prome-Toungoo was moved, but owing to the withdrawal on both fronts large quantities had to be abandoned. There was a fair amount of food and water between Toungoo and Mandalay, but little north of Prome.

Frontier Force Units were stationed in the Pegu Yoma to give warning of, and prevent, any Japanese infiltration through the area. Light forces were also stationed west of the Irrawaddy to intercept hostile penetration on that bank of the river.

The concentration of the forces and the additional responsibilities placed on the Army Command by the nominal command of the Chinese Expeditionary Force necessitated the immediate formation of a small Corps Headquarters (Burcorps). The General Headquarters in India was therefore requested to supply a Corps Commander and a skeleton Corps Headquarters. Lt.-Gen. W. J. Slim M.C., who was appointed the Corps Commander, arrived on March 19; but owing to limitation of air transport a skeleton Corps Headquarters could not be provided from India and the staff and Signals had to be found from the Burma Army resources.[4]

Meanwhile, the 17th Indian Division was reforming, resting and taking defensive positions in the area Thonze-Tharrawaddy-Letpadan with the idea of denying the line Henzada-Sanywe-Thonze river and reorganising it also. The 1st Battalion West Yorkshire Regiment came under the 7th Armoured Brigade, the 1st Battalion Duke of Wellington's Regiment under the 16th Indian Infantry Brigade, the 1st Battalion the Cameronians under the 48th Brigade, the 1st Battalion Royal Inniskilling Fusiliers under the 63rd Brigade. The last named arrived in Burma on March 19 having been flown from India. The 1st Battalion Gloucestershire Regiment became Divisional Reconnaissance Regiment. Fully motorised and provided with some light armoured vehicles, it was employed as a mobile screen well forward of the Division.[5] The organization of the defensive zone was in the form of Brigade Group areas acting as bases from which mobile groups could operate, the whole being covered by a screen of irregular forces and patrols. In the forward zone the right was held by the 63rd Indian Infantry Brigade under the command of which was also one Troop Anti-tank Battery, and in support 1 Indian Field Regiment less one Battery. The centre (Thonze) was held by the 1st Battalion Gloucestershire Regiment with under command one column Frontier Force Group. It was to patrol on a twenty-four hour basis deep towards Okhan. The left (north of Thonze Chaung) was held by the 16th Brigade. The rear zone (Letpadan) was held by the 48th Indian Infantry Brigade with the support of one Battery 1 Indian Field Regiment. It was to do close patrolling east, west and north-east. The 1st Battalion the Cameronians was to protect and maintain law and order in Tharrawaddy. The outer screen was provided by Frontier Force Group, Burma Military Police Battalion, the forest-watchers. The Tharrawaddy river patrol by the Royal Marines River patrol was also to come under the 17th Indian Division.

The country chosen consisted mostly of wide expanses of flat paddy lands surrounded by small patches of jungle and minor hill features. Although it appeared to offer excellent opportunities for tank operations, small earth bunds surrounding each field compelled tanks to slow down while crossing them, and thus rendered them vulnerable to hostile fire.

During this period the forward elements of Burcorps kept the Japa-

---

[4] See *War Diary*, Burcorps 'G' Branch, p. 1, for the Skeleton Staff.
[5] *War Diary*, 17 Indian Division, 'G' Br, Appendix 'C'.

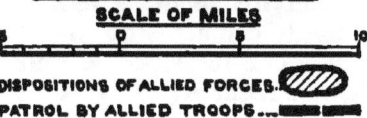

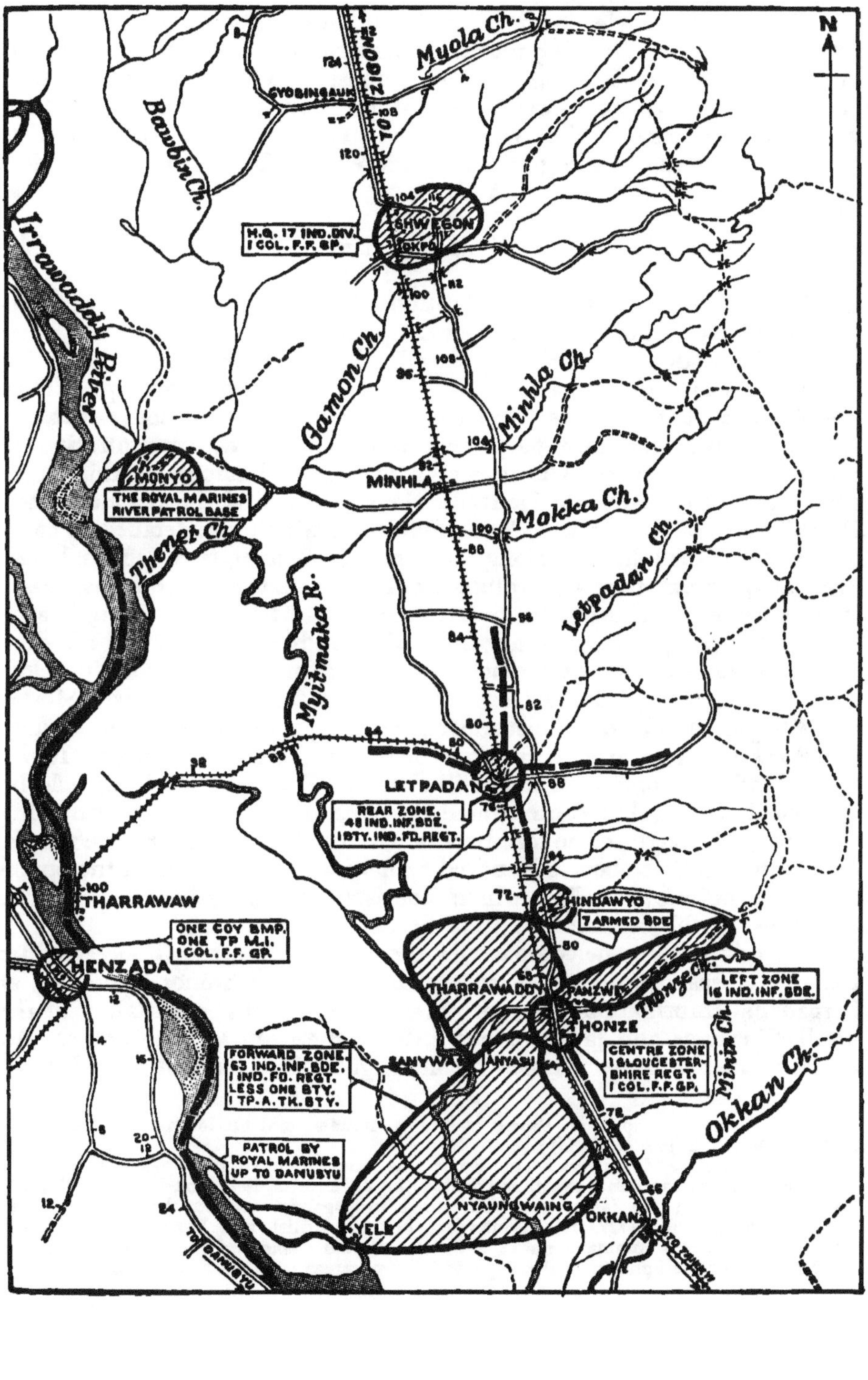

nese under observation, but for about a week there was little activity.⁶ It was difficult to establish contact with the Japanese who were well served with information. The local people were friendly to them, and the Allied withdrawals were regularly signalled by the lighting of bonfires in the villages evacuated.

The Divisional Headquarters, 17th Indian Division which had moved to Tharrawaddy on March 9 moved to Shwegon on 13 March. During 14 and 15th March the Division took new defensive positions in Okpo (2 miles south-west of Shwegon) area, from where counter-offensive operations could be undertaken. This was the first step in a gradual withdrawal to Prome conforming to the gradual withdrawal of the 1st Burma Division.

JAPANESE ACTION

On 14 March there were indications that the Japanese were contemplating a pincer movement, one arm up the Pegu Yoma and the other up the Irrawaddy. Hence, the Royal Marines River patrol based on Monyo was ordered to patrol down the river as far as Danubyu. They were also to close the river north of Henzada removing and destroying all large boats, and take offensive action against any concentration of hostile boats met with. On 17 March one of the launches of this patrol escorted a river steamer to Henzada, then well behind the Japanese lines. On this steamer there was a Commando force which was detailed to carry out certain demolitions along the river.⁷ These were effected. At Myanaung locomotives and rolling stock were destroyed. So, too, was a railway bridge. Boats on the river were sunk. At Henzada on 19 March the landing party was surrounded, called upon to surrender, and attacked by a large force armed with machine-guns. A brisk engagement developed, heavy fire being directed on the Japanese from the vessels. Mortar shells began to fall near the steamers, but the greater part of the landing party was taken off after it had fought its way back to the river. It was then found that some men were still ashore. The river bank was held by the hostile forces, but concentrated covering fire enabled the remaining party to get through to the foreshore where it was taken aboard the vessels. It is estimated that about a hundred casualties were inflicted on the opposing force of one battalion which consisted mainly of Burmese. The casualties on the commandos were five.⁸

Two days later one company of the 1st Battalion the Gloucestershire Regiment, was concerned in an equally successful minor operation at Letpadan. Information was received from F.F. 2 that a battalion of the hostile Burmans and Japanese had entered the town at 0430 hours. An attack was accordingly planned for first light. One platoon moved down

---

⁶ The Japanese advance on Prome in two columns started on 16 March. *History of 33 (Jap) Div.*, p. 2, (601/7725/H).

⁷ Under Maj. J. M. Calvert. This Force was from Maymyo Bush Warfare School.

⁸ The Japanese accounts say that "during the advance of 1942, the Burma Independence Army, helped the Japanese by spreading propaganda and not by actual contact with the enemy." (601/7273/H). Conference between British and Japanese Commanders held at H. Q. Burma command on 12 Feb. '46. *Burma Command Intelligence Summary No. 7* p. 1. But the fighting in the Pegu and Prome areas tells a different tale.

the road in motor transport from the north-east to attract the attention of the hostile force. Debussing, it demonstrated against the eastern side of the town. Mortar fire was put down on the town, later shifting to cover the east and south exits. The remainder of the company attacked from the west. The Japanese were taken completely by surprise by this attack. A party occupying the school was annihilated by grenades and automatic gun fire. There was panic and the Japanese fled from the town. Their casualties were very heavy, while those of the British were nine missing and one wounded. But the next day there was a strong battalion of the Japanese in Letpadan.

REORGANISING THE DEFENCE OF IRRAWADDY

The move of the 1st Burma Division, on relief by the 200 Chinese Division, to the Irrawaddy front commenced on the night of 21/22 March.[9] Owing to the difficulties of communication between the Toungoo and Irrawaddy valleys, the bulk of the 1st Burma Division was despatched by rail and road via Pyinmana and Taungdwingyi. The 5th Battalion Burma Rifles[10] proceeded by march-route from Toungoo to Prome touring over the Pegu Yoma. On 25 March the newly formed 1 Burcorps issued orders for the concentration of the Corps in the area Allanmyo-Prome with the 1st Burma Division in the area Dayindabo-Kyaukpadaung-Allanmyo-Theyetmyo, the 17th Indian Division in the area Wettigan-Prome-Shwedaung-Sinde, the 7th Armoured Brigade in the area Tamagauk in Corps reserve. The 63rd Indian Infantry Brigade was in Prome, the 16th Indian Infantry Brigade in the area of Sinmizwe-Hmawaza and the 48th Indian Infantry Brigade about Wettigan. The 1st Battalion Gloucestershire Regiment was based on Paungde, covering the Divisional front. The left flank was protected by Frontier Force units whilst the Royal Marines River Patrol and a Commando watched the right.[11] The Yomas Intelligence Service was also functioning along the whole front.

Gen. Sir. H. Alexander intended that the defence of the Irrawaddy valley should be based on the Brigade Groups in Prome and Allanmyo. These towns were to be made defended localities and stocked with supplies and ammunition for twenty-one days. If the Japanese got round these places, as they obviously would, the garrisons were to remain and fight on. Part of Burcorps was to be mobile and be prepared to act offensively. The 17th Indian Division was divided into two parts. A force comprising the 7th Armoured Brigade less one squadron, the 1st Battalion Gloucestershire Regiment, the 1st Battalion the Cameronians, the 1st Battalion 4 P.W.O. Gurkha Rifles and the 7th Battalion 10th Baluch Regiment were allotted the task of occupying Paungde and driving back the Japanese as far as

---

[9] Started at 1900 hours. At 2330 hours the rear guard met Chinese road-block at milestone 166. After a frantic discussion the road-block was lifted for troops and A.T. to pass through. *War Diary*, 1 Burma Infantry Brigade.

[10] Also detachments of Malerkotla Sappers and Miners and 57 Field Ambulance. The column was only just clear of the starting point when Japanese attack on Toungoo commenced.

[11] They had earlier covered the demolitions in Syriam.

Okpo.[12] The remainder of the force was to form a defensive ring around Prome.[13]

There were, at the time, frequent reports that the Japanese were being reinforced by substantial numbers of organised Thakins who had been formed into units of the Burma Independent Army. This particular district of Burma was then a centre of disaffection and it was estimated that the Japanese there had a Burmese force of three or four thousand men co-operating with them. Recruiting for this force was proceeding briskly

DISASTER TO THE AIR FORCE

On the air side the loss of Rangoon produced serious consequences. The two raids on Magwe on 21 and 22 March resulted in the complete elimination of the small Royal Air Force in Burma. After the loss of Rangoon there were only four aerodromes in Burma fit for operational use—Magwe, Akyab, Lashio and Loiwing (in China). None of the above with the exception of Loiwing had any efficient warning system. This was due partly to the lack of essential equipment and W/T personnel and partly to the hills which acted as a screen to the approach of hostile aircraft. Thus the operational advantages were with the Japanese who could also land supplies through Rangoon. The events at Magwe and Akyab had already proved this.

On 20 March reconnaissance carried out by Burwing disclosed a concentration of hostile force in progress in the Rangoon area.[14] It was therefore decided to attack Mingaladon the next morning with 10 Hurricanes and 9 Blenheims of 45 Squadron. The Blenheims were intercepted by the Japanese Naval "O" fighters, 40 miles north of Rangoon, but they fought their way into Mingaladon. A bomb lift of 9000 lbs. with stick adaptors was dropped on the runways among the Japanese aircraft, and the formation fought its way back to Tharrawaddy. During this gallant engagement in which 18 Japanese fighters were encountered the Blenheims shot two and claimed as probably destroyed two and damaged two. Most of these aircraft were shot up but none was shot down.

The Hurricanes carried out a low flying attack on Mingaladon. Nine Japanese fighters were claimed as destroyed in the air combat while sixteen Japanese bombers and fighters were destroyed or damaged on the ground. This was a magnificent air action. Some Hurricanes were badly shot up, and one crashed on the Allied side of the line through lack of petrol following the combat. Burwing had planned to repeat the attack in the afternoon but while final preparations were being made for this sortie the Japanese commenced their retaliatory attack on Magwe.

On 21 and 22 March over a period of 25 hours the hostile aircraft in great force made five devastating attacks on the Magwe aerodrome and virtually put an end to the Allied air support in Burma. The first attack was at 1330 hours by 21 bombers escorted by 10 fighters, which bombed

---

[12] Also one tp 1 Indian Field Regiment, one tp 77 mm and 1 tp Light Anti-Aircraft Battery.
[13] It was to be based on static areas as pivots and as mobile reserves for local operations—*War Diary*, 17 Indian Division 'G' Branch, Appendix 'G'.
[14] Despatch on "Air Operations in Burma and Bay of Bengal, Jan. 1 to May 22, 1942," by Air Vice Marshal D. F. Stevenson, para 183, (601/9255A/H).

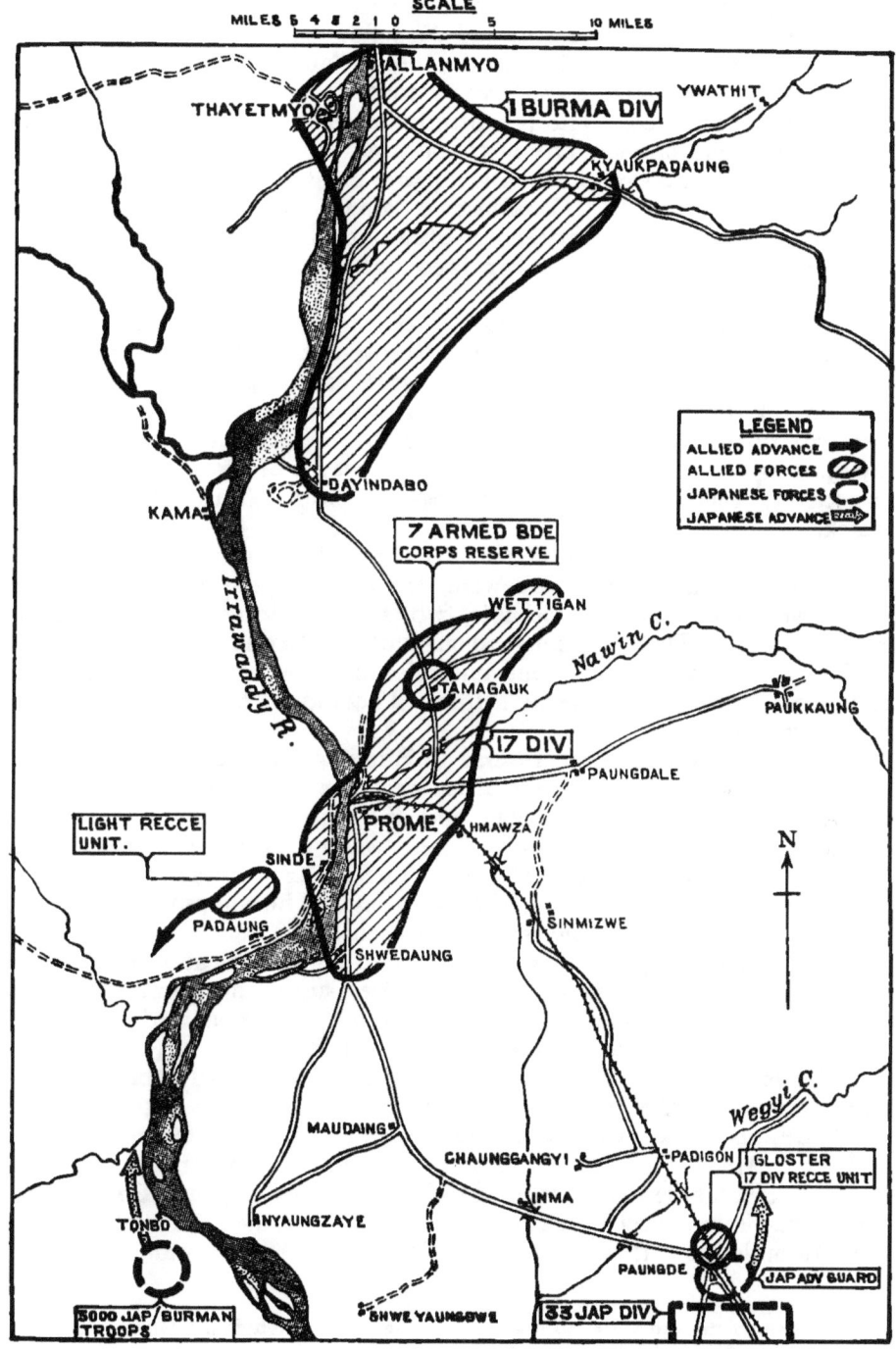

and machine-gunned the airfield. The available Hurricanes and Blenheims had been engaged in the early morning against Japanese concentration of aircraft at Mingaladon. Thus when they retaliated only 10 of the British fighters[15] were serviceable and were able to take off. These fighters, however, intercepted and destroyed 4 hostile aircraft but the weight of the attack was considerable and great damage resulted in which communications were destroyed. The Japanese followed this up with further raids at 1410 and 1430 hours. The next morning there was an attack in two waves at 0847 and 0900 hours. Owing to a breakdown of W/T no warning had been received.[16] "Considerable damage was sustained. The runways were rendered unserviceable, communications broke down and a number of aircraft, both bombers and fighters, were destroyed on the ground."[17]

In the afternoon the commander of the Second Pursuit Squadron A.V.G. withdrew his three remaining flyable aircraft to Loiwing to refit. At 1330 hours reconnaissance aircraft were again reported approaching and two of the three remaining Hurricanes were sent up but failed to intercept them. While they were returning to land at 1430 hours the Japanese again commenced attacks in two waves of 26 and 27 bombers respectively each accompanied by fighter escort. This was the final attack.

Great damage had been done by the second day's raids also. 9 Blenheims and at least three P.40's were destroyed on the ground. 5 Blenheims were rendered unserviceable, while 3 Hurricanes were destroyed in air combat. The remaining 20 aircraft (6 Blenheims 3 P. 40's and 11 Hurricanes) were flyable but unserviceable due to normal unserviceability or damage from hostile action. These aircraft except the P. 40's were flown out to Akyab.

The cause of this grave reverse to Burwing (the R.A.F. detachment in Upper Burma) was the result of its weakness in fighters, the weakness of the warning system at Magwe and the complete absence of aircraft pens and dispersal arrangements. There was no Observer Corps system to the west and north-east of Magwe. The R.D.F. set was of the wrong type. Its arc observation was to the south-east. . The equipment had given three months' service and no spares had been available.

On March 23, 24 and 27 a small force at Akyab was attacked and the Akwing (R.A.F. detachment in Akyab) after sustaining great losses was withdrawn to Chittagong. These two actions at Magwe and Akyab in effect terminated the R.A.F. activities based on Burma.

The loss of these aircraft which constituted practically the only airforce available at the time and the somewhat premature withdrawal of the R.A.F. made the air support of the Burma Army an extremely difficult problem. Aircraft were only reaching India in small numbers and it was essential to organize the defence of Calcutta and of Ceylon. Gen. Sir A. Wavell had reluctantly to decide that he must use the air force reaching India to build up a defence in that country and that he could not afford

---

[15] Four Hurricanes and 6 P.40's.
[16] So beyond the two Hurricanes sent off to intercept a high flying Japanese aircraft, no fighters could be sent to engage the raiders.
[17] Stevenson's *Despatch*, para 193 *op. cit.*

heavy losses that the Japanese numerical superiority, the lack of training of British Air Squadrons, the absence of a warning system and the difficult flying conditions in Upper Burma were bound to cause in the attempt to render air support to the forces in Burma.[18] All this had an adverse effect on the morale of both the Army and the civil population; thus the Japanese air force had almost a free hand in the later stages of the Burma Campaign "and it was fortunate for us that they failed to take full advantage of their opportunity".[19]

SITUATION AT THE END OF MARCH

"At the end of March and the beginning of April, the Japanese commenced heavy bombing raids on centres of communication in central and upper Burma, raids being made on such places as Prome, Meiktila, Mandalay, Thazi, Pyinmana, Maymyo, Lashio and Taunggyi. Except for the damage to house property, the material effect of these raids was not very great but the moral effect amongst the civil population was enormous. After a heavy raid on a town the life of the community came practically to a standstill, the population moving into the jungle. From the military aspect, the effect on the working of the public utility services was the most serious. Many railway employees and Inland Water Transport workers in the employment of the Irrawaddy Flotilla Company left their jobs. The police force disintegrated and the power supply broke down; but the Post and Telegraph service, to which a tribute should be paid for the manner in which a large number of personnel stuck to their jobs, was affected to a lesser degree."[20]

In an appreciation dated 26 March Lieut.-Gen. T. J. Hutton set out the position in the following words:—

"Many of the essential services of Burma have practically collapsed. Even at several hundred miles from the front, services have already ceased to function, personnel have disappeared and orders are disobeyed or ignored. This applies to both superior as well as subordinate personnel, and even those who are permanently enrolled do not seem under any obligation to perform their duties. In the absence of any effective police forces, looting of trains, stations, and dumps is very prevalent. Cholera and other diseases are prevalent and likely to increase owing to the failure of the Medical and Hospital Services. The Civil A.R.P. organisation has almost entirely dispersed."[21]

Towards the end of March Gen. Sir H. Alexander visited Chungking to discuss the military situation with the Generalissimo "and to ensure that he was satisfied with the administrative arrangements which had been made for his troops."[22] The Chinese Vth Army was then heavily engaged

---

[18] Gen. Sir A. Wavell's *Despatch*, para 22.
[19] Burwing was withdrawn to Lashio and Loiwing for refitting. It was the intention of the authorities concerned to make good the deficiencies of warning at Magwe, and make it fit in every way for Burwing to return there for operations. Till such time as it returned however limited support could be given to the Army by the use of advanced landing grounds.
[20] Gen. Alexander's *Despatch* para 26.
[21] *Burma Army Appreciation* (601/2/9/H), p. 2.
[22] General Alexander's *Despatch*, para 21. He left Maymyo on 24 March.

around Toungoo and the Generalissimo therefore represented that to relieve pressure on it offensive operations be initiated on the Irrawaddy front. A telegram ordering these operations was received by 1 Burcorps from Gen. Sir H. Alexander early on the morning of 27 March. But a day earlier *i.e.* on 26 March the Japanese had commenced operations against the positions held by 1 Burcorps in the Irrawaddy valley; Prome was bombed on the same day and three quarters of the town was burnt.

ATTEMPTS AT COUNTER-OFFENSIVE

The 17th Indian Division was directed to carry out a local offensive. For this purpose additional troops were placed at its disposal by 1 Burcorps and the tasks of the striking force were defined to be:—

(a) To secure Okpo, establishing a lay-back at Zigon to watch the east flank.
(b) To destroy all enemy detachments encountered during the advance and to exploit any local success.
(c) To protect the west flank by securing Nyaungzave.

The danger to the west flank was very real, reports having been received on 27 March of a large mixed force of Burmans and Japanese with an estimated strength of four or five thousand advancing up the west bank of the river from Henzada to Tonbo. This force had twenty rubber boats. It was expected to reach Tonbo on March 28. A Commando force was detailed to deal with it and moved by steamer. Co-operating with the Commando was the Royal Marines River Patrol and a Burma Military Police detachment. This latter was already on the west bank of the river.

On 28 March the Japanese advance-guard on the east bank of the Irrawaddy occupied Paungde. On receiving this information the 17th Indian Division reconnaissance unit, the 1st Battalion Gloucestershire Regiment, moved forward from its position just north of the town to the attack. Supported by mortars and machine-guns, the advance made good progress, and very shortly there was fighting in the streets. Japanese snipers were, however, active from houses and trees and Burmans actively supported them. Clearing houses with grenades or burning them, the British troops pushed through the town. An infantry gun attempting to come into action was at once knocked out by a mortar. Japanese mortars were similarly silenced. The fighting lasted only two hours, but the Japanese casualties were heavy while on the other side there were only 2 British Officers killed, 3 wounded and fifteen British other Ranks killed and 9 wounded. At least one Japanese battalion and two hundred armed Burmans were in the town. The Gloucesters were far ahead of the 17th Indian Division and could not expect support. Consequently they were withdrawn before becoming too heavily involved.

Commander Burcorps decided that this was a good opportunity for offensive operations. These were to be carried out in two phases—the attack on Paungde on 29 March, and the advance on Okpo on 30 March. For the first phase the troops near Paungde were to be augmented by the striking force. Brigadier Anstice of the 7th Armoured Brigade was placed in command of this striking force. His orders were to attack Paungde on 29 March and to advance on Okpo the following day.[23]

For the first phase (Paungde) the following troops were detailed:—
414 Battery, R.H.A.
7th Queen's Own Hussars.
The 1st Battalion Gloucestershire Regiment.
The 2nd Battalion Duke of Wellington's Regiment.
The 1st Battalion the Cameronians.
One Company the 1st Battalion West Yorkshire Regiment.
24 Field Company Sappers and Miners.

For the advance on Okpo which was never carried out the troops detailed were:—

7 Armoured Brigade Group (less one squadron).
One Troop 1 Indian Field Regiment.
One Troop 15 Mountain Battery (77 mm).
One Troop Light Anti-Aircraft Battery (Bofors)
24 Field Company Sappers and Miners.
The 1st Battalion Gloucestershire Regiment.
The 1st Battalion the Cameronians.
The 7th Battalion 10th Baluch Regiment.
The 1st Battalion 4th P.W.O. Gurkha Rifles.
One Company of the 1st Battalion West Yorkshire Regiment.

The Duke of Wellington and the Baluch Battalions were to remain at Paungde and two Battalions and 1 Troop of the Mountain Battery were to be at Zigon as a strong rear layback. They were to patrol forward on the flanks and protect the line of communication.

The 4th Battalion 12th Frontier Force Regiment and one company of the 1st Battalion Royal Inniskilling Fusiliers together with Burma Military Police units were intended to provide protection at Shwedaung, Maudiang, Inma, and Nyaungzaye on the river flank. The 4th Battalion 12th Frontier Force Regiment was to be posted in Shwedaung. As will be noted later it never entered that town. One company of the 1st Battalion Royal Inniskilling Fusiliers watched the hill section of the road southeast of the village of Maudiang.

There was a shortage of motor transport; so the forward movement of troops was carried out by a shuttle service of vehicles. This considerably delayed operations.

Action at Padigon

On the evening of 28 March the 1st Battalion Gloucestershire Regiment with a strength of only two companies and a Headquarters Company was holding positions forward of Inma village which was at milestone 154 on the Rangoon-Prome road. One company was at Wetpok (milestone 148) whilst another was at Padigon on the railway line 7 miles north-west of Paungde. Padigon and Wetpok were connected by a road branching north-east from the main road. The Battalion Headquarters was at Inma. There arrived that evening the 2nd Battalion

[23] *War Diary*, 17 Indian Division, 'G' Branch, Appendix 24.

I BURCORPS COUNTER OFFENSIVE PLAN (1st PHASE)
29 MARCH 1942

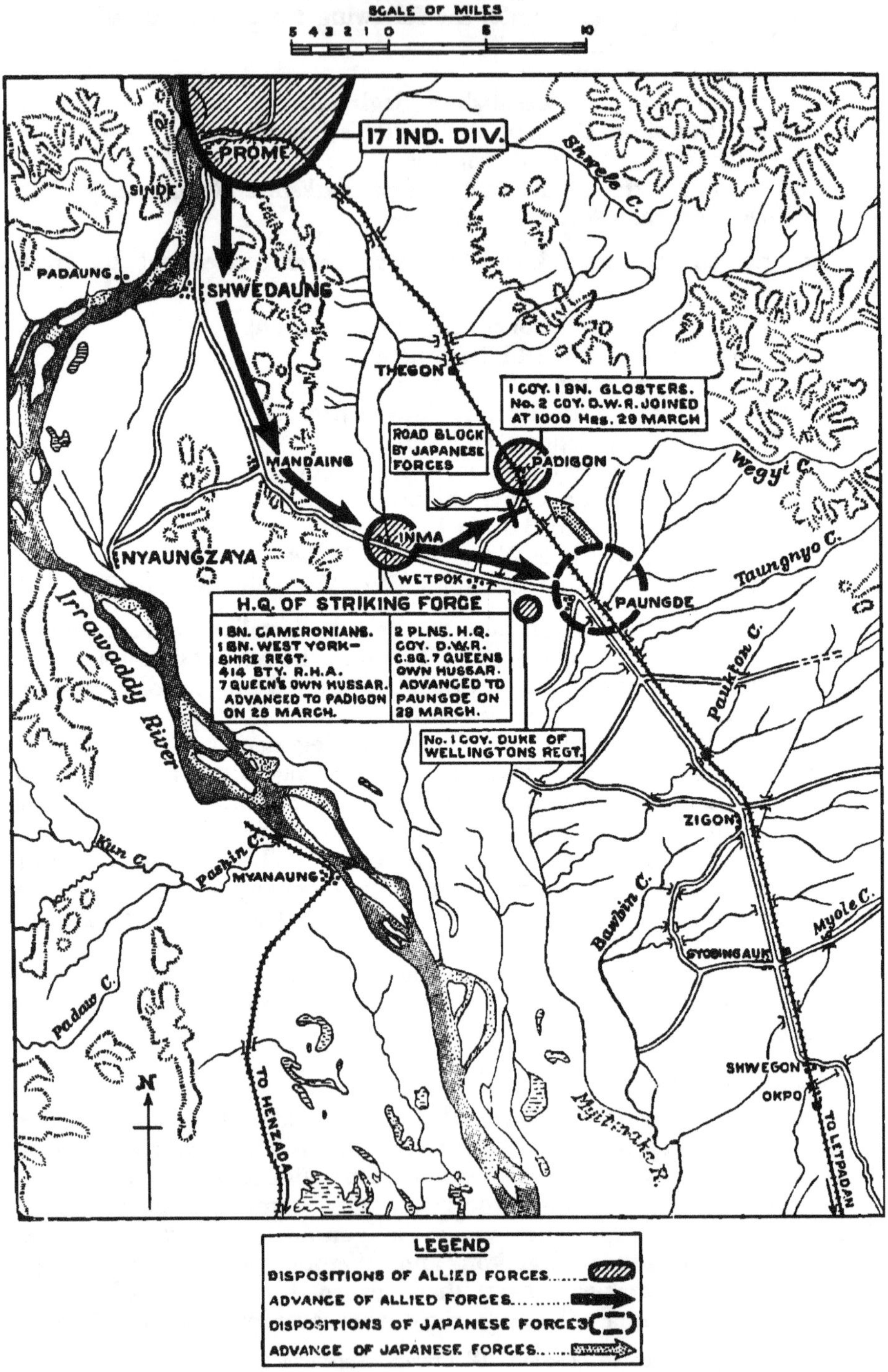

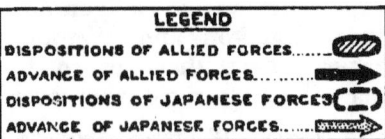

Duke of Wellington's Regiment, the leading unit of the striking force. This Battalion too, was much below srength. It consisted of two companies and a Headquarters Company. It proceeded to send out two fighting and reconnaissance patrols. No. 2 Company was to operate south from Pàdigon towards Paungde; No. 1 Company was to patrol south-east from Wetpok to a point on the main road some two miles south of Paungde. These companies were to make contact with the Japanese. If possible they were to drive them out of Paungde, but were to withdraw if opposed by much superior forces.

It was a moonlit night. No. 2 Company reconnoitring from Padigon had a successful encounter with a Japanese patrol near the railway bridge over the Wegyi Chaung. It then observed large bodies of Japanese troops north of Paungde, one of them marching along the railway towards Padigon. A warning message was sent back to Padigon. Finding the Japanese on the outskirts of Paungde to be too strong to be dealt with, the company made a detour north-east with the object of returning to Padigon. The other company reached the main road south of Paungde without incident before first light on 29 March. It was not far from the southern outskirts of the town.

Early that morning two distinct actions developed round Paungde and Padigon. The company of the 1st Battalion Gloucestershire Regiment at Padigon was attacked from the east of the village by a battalion of the Japanese force. They appeared to be carrying out an outflanking movement northwards. Brigadier Anstice who had established his Headquarters at Inma ordered one squadron of the 7th Queen's Own Hussars to move immediately to Padigon to contact the force there, and then to go on to Thegon to cut off the outflanking hostile column.

Three miles south of Padigon two tanks were knocked out by antitank guns on the road. Assisted by 414 Battery R.H.A. the 7th Queen's Own Hussars overcame the Japanese resistance and then went forward. However, closer to Padigon a road-block was encountered and the antitank guns again opened heavy fire. The block was about one and a half miles south of Padigon where a long line of jungle-enclosed villages stretched east and west across the road.

Brigadier Anstice soon ordered the 1st Battalion the Cameronians supported by a company of the 1st Battalion West Yorkshire Regiment, one troop of 414 Battery R.H.A., and a squadron of the 7th Queen's Own Hussars to attack the block.

After a fifteen minute artillery bombardment the Cameronians fought their way through the villages south of Padigon and cleared the roadblock. They then came under fire from snipers who had concealed themselves in the village buildings. Many of these snipers were destroyed by burning the villages. A party of Japanese troops disguised as Burmans endeavoured to move round the left flank, but the Battalion machine-guns from a rear position dealt effectively with this group.

The tanks continued their advance. They met further road-blocks and also came under artillery fire from Padigon, which appeared to be held by the Japanese, and from positions south-east of it; this fire was ineffective and the Japanese guns were silenced by the troop of 414 Battery R.H.A.

At 1720 hours the Burcorps force south of Padigon was ordered to withdraw on Inma.

In Padigon itself the company of the Gloucestershire Regiment withstood a heavy attack early in the morning. At about 1000 hours it had been joined by No. 2 Company of the Duke of Wellington's Regiment.

The village was now being attacked on the south-east, south, and south-west. The troops were subjected to small arms and mortar fire, and the Japanese began to work round further to the west.

Shortly after 1100 hours the force in Padigon withdrew north along a track on the western bridge of the railway embarkment. It then struck west with the object of gaining the main road some ten miles north-west of Inma. Arriving on the road at dusk it made contact with the main body of the striking force then withdrawing towards Shwedaung.[24]

The operations round Padigon had interfered very largely with the attack on Paungde, the first objective of the striking force. Although, on paper, three infantry battalions were available, their actual strength did not exceed that of one and a half normal battalions. The greater part of this force was employed about Padigon.

Paungde

No. 1 Company of the Duke of Wellington's Regiment south of Paungde was in position in a patch of jungle west of the main road and on the southern outskirts of the town. At about 0600 hours a body of about three hundred Japanese alighted from a column of motor vehicles and began to advance on the position. Fire was held until the Japanese had approached to within two hundred yards or so. It was then opened with excellent effect. Flanking movements from north and south were begun by the Japanese, but the company had no difficulty in maintaining its position. It reported the situation to the Battalion Headquarters, asking for rations and further supplies of ammunition.

Tanks of the 7th Queen's Own Hussars made contact with the company and as Paungde itself did not appear to be heavily held by the Japanese it was decided to attack the town with two platoons of the Headquarters Company of the 1st Battalion Duke of Wellington's Regiment. 'C' squadron of the 7th Queen's Own Hussars would be in support.

The attack made progress through the north-western part of the town but was then held up. The tanks destroyed some Japanese transport and infantry, but the opposition was heavy. The Japanese were also largely reinforced by troops coming up the road from the south. Two of the tanks were hit, and the infantry sustained a number of casualties.

The troops in Paungde and No. 1 company of the Duke of Wellington's Regiment to the south of it had received orders that they were not to become so heavily involved as to render themselves liable to be cut off. Consequently, at 1530 hours when hostile pressure increased, No. 1

---

[24] The operations in the Padigon area are, in Japanese accounts, referred to as action at Zigon about 5 miles west of Padigon. One of them says, 'Reinforced by the recently arrived Arakai Detached force, and the Artillery unit of 24 IMB the Division met and defeated a formidable enemy force with tanks at Sigon (Zigon)" (601/7785/H), p. 24. S.E.A.T.I.C. Bulletin No. 245 *History of the Japanese 15th Army*.

company began to withdraw. By that time Paungde was burning. The troops in the town shortly afterwards began to fall back. The Duke of Wellington's Regiment had suffered some thirty casualties.

Action at Shwedaung

Meanwhile, the Divisional Liaison Officer on his way back to Prome, had found Shwedaung held by the Japanese in considerable strength, by *214th Infantry Regiment*.[25] He was compelled to return to Inma where he reported the situation to Brigadier Anstice who then, by wireless, asked the Divisional Headquarters for orders. He was instructed to break out either by way of Shwedaung or Padigon, whichever was the easier.[26] Since efforts to take Padigon, had been unsuccessful Brigadier Anstice decided to fall back on Prome through Shwedaung. He therefore broke off the actions at Padigon and Paungde and concentrated his troops at Inma. At 1815 hours a force consisting of one troop of 414 Battery R.H.A., one troop of the 7th Queen's Own Hussars, and two companies of the 1st Battalion Gloucestershire Regiment were sent on ahead to clear the road-block at Shwedaung.

At that time the Allied forces were already engaged with the Japanese at Shwedaung. The 4th Battalion 12th Frontier Force Regiment and the 2nd Battalion 13th Frontier Force Rifles had been detailed by the 17th Indian Division to retake the town from the North. These Battalions were supported by a Battery of the 1st Indian Field Regiment I.A. Attacking along both sides of the road the 4th Battalion 12th Frontier Force Regiment found itself strongly opposed. It gained the outskirts of the town but could get no further. About seventy prisoners, mostly members of the Burma Independent Army, a machine-gun, and several automatic weapons were taken. The Battalion was then reinforced by the 2nd Battalion 13th Frontier Force Rifles, but the hostile force in Shwedaung held out. The Frontier Force eventually withdrew to a harbour about two miles to the north, and a further attack was planned for the following morning.

Shwedaung was a small town on the east bank of the Irrawaddy. Together with its adjoining villages it extended towards the east for more than two miles inland from the river. It also flanked the main road on both sides for more than a mile. Its southern outskirts were well fringed with trees and jungle growth. It was therefore an excellent position for the establishment of a block to prevent the passage of transport, and one was laid two miles south of Shwedaung.

The armoured force despatched at 1815 hours to clear the block encountered it at 1900 hours. This was only lightly held and was cleared by the tanks after it had been bombarded. A second block was then encountered just south of the town. This was strongly held with guns, mortars, and machine-guns. Fire was again opened by the troops of 414 Battery R.H.A., after which the tanks went forward to investigate. The Japanese remained active with machine-guns and mortars from the jungle on both sides of the road. The infantry endevoured to clear this. Tanks succeeded in passing through the block with difficulty, but the infantry

[25] *History of the Japanese Fifteenth Army*, p. 24, (601/7785/H).
[26] *War Diary*, 17th Indian Division, 'G' Branch, Sheet for 29 March.

strength was not sufficient to sweep the hostile force from the flanking jungle.

By that time Brigadier Anstice and the main body of the striking force had arrived. It was decided to attack the block again with one company of Gloucestershire Regiment and one company of the West Yorkshire Regiment.

The attack, preceded by a bombardment by the whole of 414 Battery R.H.A., was made at 0200 hours on 30 March. Once again the infantry could make no progress. Operations were then suspended until dawn.

At 0700 hours the attack on the block was resumed by the striking force. It was delayed for a short time by a heavy ground mist. There was then a fifteen-minute artillery concentration on the area of the block, 414 Battery R.H.A. being in action on the west of the road, one thousand yards south of the block. The bombardment was followed by an infantry advance with the object of sweeping through Shwedaung and clearing away all opposition and thus enabling the transport to pass through.

The Cameronians encountered considerable opposition near the road, but the company on the right flank entered the village with some difficulty. On the west of the road the advance was at once held up. The company of the West Yorkshire Regiment on the outer flank came under fire from the left rear where the Japanese were concealed in tree-girt villages. These were dealt with by the tanks and a company of the 1st Battalion Duke of Wellington's Regiment went in to sweep a patch of jungle, five hundred yards west of the road. From this point fire had been directed on the British guns. Close range and confused fighting ensued there. Japanese snipers, posted on trees harassed the advancing company with mortar and machine gun fire. Nevertheless, it cleared the jungle, inflicting heavy casualties on the Japanese and destroying two machine guns. The attack on the extreme west flank then went forward, and a part of the company of the West Yorkshire Regiment fought its way through the town to its northern outskirts.

Round the road-block there was very bitter fighting in which tanks and troops of all the three leading Battalions took part. The Japanese had a strong point in a rice mill on the western side of the road close to the block. From there heavy machine-gun fire was directed on the force which was now at close range. Grenades were freely employed.

Anti-tank guns, mortars, and Molotov cocktail bombs were used against the British tanks, but by 1030 hours the road-block was overcome. The Japanese had fallen back towards the centre of the town followed by the Indo-British troops, but the main road was not close-picquetted.

The transport column then began to move forward and to pass through the site of the block. It was however soon brought to a halt as a second block had been established towards the north of the town. Mortar fire wrecked some of the vehicles and set others on fire. In places vehicles were nose to tail and double banked on the road, and this added to the difficulty of extricating the transport. Diversions down the side roads were found, but here, too, blocks were created by burning or overturned vehicles. Close fighting continued.

On the south of the town a rearguard composed of the Duke of Wellington's Regiment (less one company) and a squadron of the 7th

Queen's Own Hussars held covering positions. During the afternoon they were joined by a body of about two hundred Burma Military Police which had marched in from the south, but some of these men disappeared in the course of the action.

Japanese reconnaissance aircraft were overhead all the morning and indulged in some fruitless machine-gunning of the transport. In the afternoon, at about 1500 hours, Japanese bomber aircraft began a series of heavy and accurate attacks on the massed columns of vehicles and also on the rear-guard south of Shwedaung. These attacks continued at intervals for a couple of hours and resulted in casualties and the destruction of much transport. Shwedaung was soon on fire.

The tanks, with considerable loss, were able to force a passage for themselves and for 414 Battery R.H.A. which succeeded in getting through the town with the loss of two guns. It had become evident, however, that there was little prospect of the unarmoured vehicles passing through the hostile force safely.

Meanwhile, the rear-guard squadron of tanks reported to Brigadier Anstice that it was in contact with a Japanese column advancing from the south. All the available troops were then engaged.

The 4th Battalion 12th Frontier Force Regiment, the 2nd Battalion 13th Frontier Force Rifles and one Squadron of the 2nd Battalion Royal Tank Regiment had attacked Shwedaung from the north during the day, but again could not progress beyond the edge of the town. The Battery of the 1st Indian Field Regiment supporting this attack fired on parties of the Japanese troops crossing the river from the west bank, from where substantial reinforcements during the action had been received by them.

A further attempt was made to extricate the transport in the town. Tanks found a new diversion and some vehicles were taken out on this route, but the greater part of the unarmoured vehicles could not be saved. Opposition continued to be heavy and grenades and machine-gun fire were still employed by the Japanese.

At about 1800 hours orders were issued to abandon the transport. All troops remaining in Shwedaung were to proceed north on foot. The remnants from all infantry units then withdrew under fire, though a few more vehicles were taken out of the town.

That night the striking force retired towards the area of Prome where units concerned reorganised.

Next morning the 1st Indian Field Regiment from north of Shwedaung subjected the town to harassing fire and also put out of action an infantry gun on the west bank of the river. The fire on Shwedaung was most effective, direct hits being obtained on motor vehicles in which Japanese troops were embussing.

During the operations of March 29/30 a force consisting of one squadron of the 2nd Battalion Royal Tank Regiment, one Company of the 1st Battalion West Yorkshire Regiment, and the 1st Battalion 4th P.W.O. Gurkha Rifles occupied Sinmiswe on the railway south-east of Prome to counter any Japanese thrust from Padigon. But no action developed there.

Although the Japanese had been hard hit, the striking force lost heavily in transport equipment and personnel. Accurate casualty lists

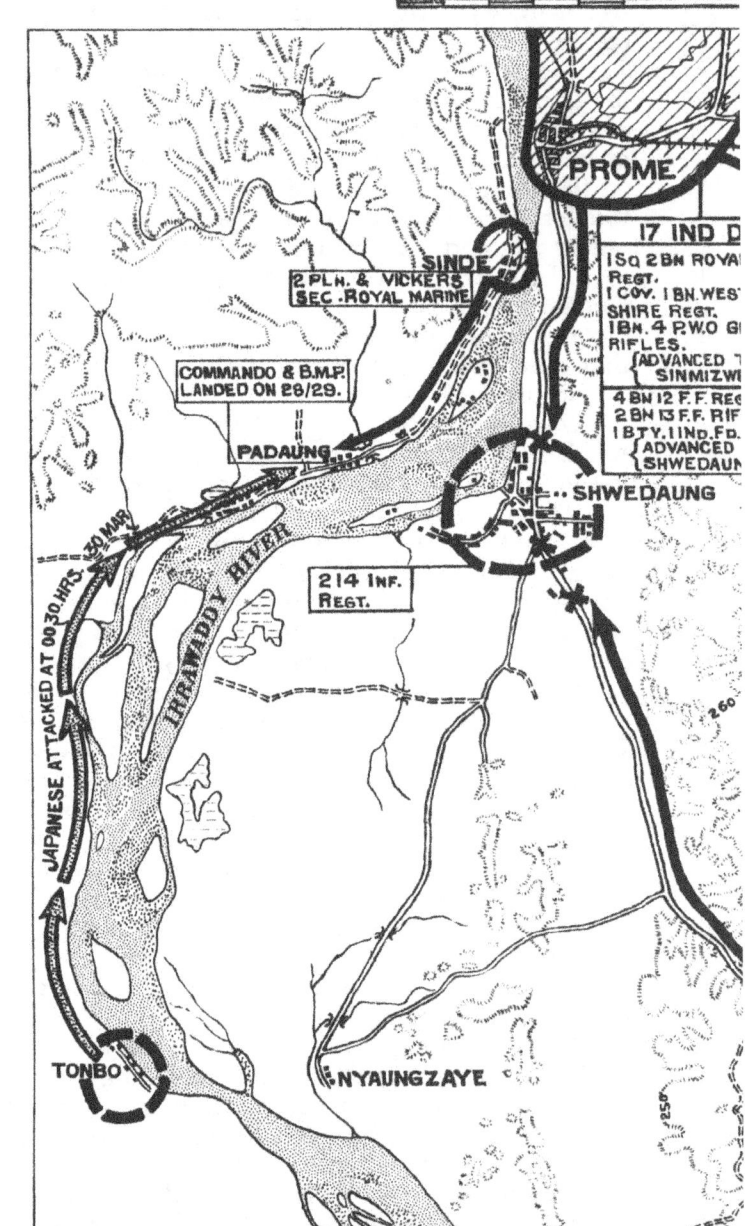

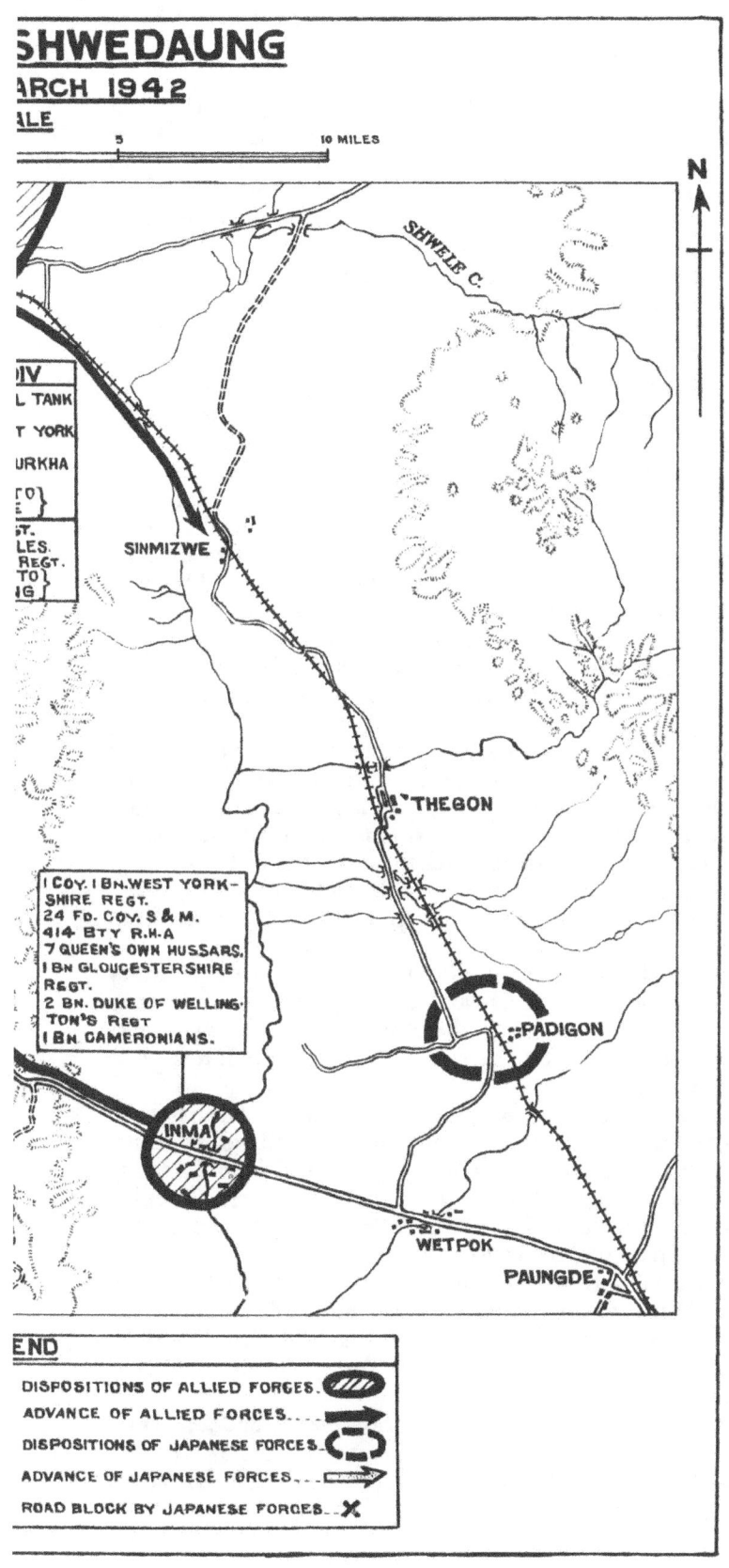

for the Burma Campaign have been difficult to compile, but it is possible to form a reasonable estimate of the losses in the actions on these two days.

The 7th Queen's Own Hussars had many men wounded on its unarmoured vehicles. It lost ten tanks, eight of them on March 30. 414 Battery R.H.A. had ten other ranks killed and six wounded. The 2nd Battalion Duke of Wellington's Regiment lost five officers (three killed, one wounded and one missing) and one hundred and seventeen other ranks. The 1st Battalion the Royal Inniskilling Fusiliers had thirteen other ranks killed and four wounded. The 1st Battalion the Cameronians lost five officers (two killed) and sixty-four other ranks (twenty-six killed). The 1st Battalion West Yorkshire Regiment had one officer and eight other ranks killed and thirteen other ranks wounded or missing. The 1st Battalion the Gloucestershire Regiment lost two officers wounded and thirty-four other ranks killed, wounded or missing. The 4th Battalion 12th Frontier Force Regiment lost in killed one officer, two Viceroy's Commissioned Officers, and fifteen other ranks; in wounded two officers, three Viceroy's Commissioned Officers and forty other ranks. The 2nd Battalion 13th Frontier Force Rifles had one officer wounded, one other rank killed and twenty-three wounded. No figures for other units are available. Having regard to the fact that nearly every unit was by that time much below its proper strength the figures indicate a high percentage of losses.

During these operations the Burcorps was engaged with the Japanese *33rd Division* of which *315th Regiment* was encountered at Shwedaung. Here, units of the Burma Independent Army took a prominent part, and in particular, opposed the Allied attacks on the town from the north. They are reported to have fought with fanaticism and were killed in large numbers. These Burmese units had crossed the Irrawaddy having formed part of the hostile force marching up the west bank of the river from Henzada.

On the night of March 28/29 the Commando and Burma Military Police had been landed from the river near Padaung, and the following day were ordered to defend Padaung with the object of preventing a crossing by the Japanese to Shwedaung on the east bank. At this latter place fighting had already begun.

Two platoons and a Vickers gun section of the Royal Marines then accompanied the Commandos to Padaung from Sinde, a village five miles higher up the west bank of the river. This force moved into Padaung at dusk and was received by the villagers in friendly manner. Supplies were sold to the troops and the Sub-assistant Surgeon stationed in the village took a prominent part in greeting the force.

A defensive position was taken up round the compound of a bungalow near the river bank. Some patrols were already south of Padaung but additional partols were sent out. A Commando detachment, eight miles to the south, reported that there were no hostile forces north of Tonbo, eighteen miles down the river.

At 0030 hours on the morning of March 30, however, a sudden attack was made on the positions round the bungalow, and in a short time a number of Japanese troops had entered the compound. Isolated parties of the Commandos put up a stout resistance, but the attack was too heavy and too sudden to permit of any organised defence.

About half of the Commando force eventually made its way back to the lines and so, too, did the greater part of the Burma Military Police. The Royal Marines' losses were one officer and thirty other ranks missing.

Apparently the Japanese had arrived in Padaung ahead of the Commandos and had then been hidden in the houses of the villagers who gave the troops not the slightest hint of this fact.

As a result of this operation the Japanese found it possible during March 30 to reinforce, from the west bank of the Irrawaddy, their hard pressed force in Shwedaung.

As a result of this action, the 17th Indian Division was compelled to retire to Prome which it did by the evening of March 30.

CHAPTER XVII

Entry of the Chinese Expeditionary Force

ENTRY INTO BURMA OF THE CHINESE EXPEDITIONARY FORCE

When war with Japan became probable there was established in Burma a Supply Base with the object of maintaining British forces in China; for it was anticipated that in the event of war the Allies would be in active conflict with the Japanese in China. Later, however, when the possibility of a Japanese invasion of Burma became apparent, arrangements were made for assistance to be rendered by the Chinese in the conflict there. The size of the Chinese force to be employed in Burma was conservatively fixed at one Regiment (227 Regiment of 93 Division). The Chinese were always ready and willing to send a much larger force into Burma for its defence. It was of course a case of helping others to help themselves.

About 23 December 1941, Gen. Sir A. Wavell flew to Chungking in order "to discuss the war situation with Marshal Chiang-Kai-Shek". The former's request for a Squadron of the A.V.G. and temporary use of some of the Lease and Lend materials for China was met by the offer of the Chinese Fifth and Sixth Armies for the defence of Burma.[1] The Generalissimo made it perfectly clear that as a condition of the acceptance of this offer a separate line of communication should be available for his troops and that they should not in any way be mixed up with British troops. However, all Chinese troops were put under the command of the General Officer Commanding, Burma Army, though breaches of discipline were to be reported to the Generalissimo personally. The Burma Army Command was also to be responsible for the supply of rice and any other requirements that could be spared, including, if possible, medical stores and mosquito nets.[2]

Gen. Wavell accepted at once the 93rd Division (Sixth Army) part of which was already approaching the Burmese border at Puerh and the 49th Division as a reserve on the northern frontier of Burma at Wanting. Another division, the 55th Division was so scattered that it was thought that it would take some time to collect. Fifth Army, which was of good quality, was collecting round Kunming. Gen. Sir Archibald Wavell asked that it should not be moved at once into Burma but should be held in reserve in the Kunming area. He considered "that it would be well placed here either to move into Burma if required or for the defence of Yunnan if the Japanese made an advance north from Indo-China against the Burmese road... or for offensive operations into Indo-China in co-operation with an advance from Burma if all went well."[3]

[1] "It should be noted that a Chinese 'Army' was approximately the equivalent in numbers of a British division but with a much lower scale of equipment." Gen. Sir. A. Wavell's *Despatch*, pp. 4-5.
[2] Lt.-Gen. T. J. Hutton's *Report*, p. 6, para 21.
[3] General Wavell's *Despatch*, p. 4.

Before the end of December 1941 one Regiment of the 93rd Division (227th Regiment) was moving towards the Southern Shan States with the object of taking over the defence of the Mekong River sector east of the Kengtung-Chiengrai road, with headquarters at Mogyawng. Subsequently, the Regiment was engaged with the Japanese in patrol encounters on the frontier.

At the same time the 49th and 55th Divisions were stationed near Poshan but by 14 January 1942, the 49th Division was approaching Wanting, a frontier town on the Burma Road to be held in reserve. The Chinese anticipated that additional forces would be required to assist in the defence of Burma. They were anxious to render substantial aid, particularly in view of the importance to themselves of Rangoon and the Burma Road.

About 15 January, Lt.-Gen. Hutton visited Keng Tung and discussed the possible move of the remainder of the 93rd Division from China to the Keng Tung area.[4] On 19 January, when the situation in Tenasserim area became serious, the rest of the 93rd Division located about Puerh in China was ordered to the Keng Tung area which it took over by the middle of February; the 1st Burma Brigade gradually withdrew from its positions south-east of Keng Tung.

When Lt.-Gen. T. J. Hutton assumed command of the Burma Army at the end of December, it was laid down in his directive that no additional Chinese troops were to be brought into Burma without reference to the Supreme Commander, South-West Pacific Command. On 21 January, he obtained the latter's consent for bringing in the 49th Division. On 29 January, it was decided that this Division should come into the Southern Shan States via Lashio and take over the area east of the Salween about Takaw and that 55th Division, which was in a poor state, should move forward to Wanting on the Chinese frontier to complete training and equipment. But the orders for their movement were issued on 3 February by the Chinese Minister of War and they came in by Regiments, commenced taking over from 15 February and completed it by the end of February.

On 31 January, Lt.-Gen. T. J. Hutton sent a personal cable to the Supreme Commander, South-West Pacific Command, seeking permission to move the fifth Army to Lashio where they would be readily available either for the defence of Burma as far south as Toungoo or for offensive operations against Thailand passing through the Sixth Army which was not well-equipped for such a role.[5] He pointed out that such an arrangement would enable the Burma Army to concentrate all its forces for the defence of Burma. And there was ample rice in Burma for the Chinese troops. This proposal was agreed to immediately and the Chinese Fifth Army started moving to the Toungoo area about

---

[4] Lt.-Gen. T. J. Hutton's *Report*, p. 5. On the same day he sent a telegram to ABDACOM for more Chinese troops. On 20 January Lt.-Gen. Hutton telegraphed to ABDACOM "investigation shows it to be practicable, request authorities to bring in 49th Chinese Division of 6th Army in addition to 93rd and for these he became responsible for the whole N. W. frontier of Thailand" *Situation Report* I, p. 30.

[5] "When I was satisfied that the V Army were worth having and that one could collect sufficient M.T. to feed them, asked that they might come in and General Wavell immediately agreed." Hutton's letter to Foucar, Chinese Armies. 601/3/8/H.

29 February but only the 200th Division could arrive in Burma before the fall of Rangoon.

This qualified, belated and piecemeal acceptance of the Chinese offer was criticized in China and the United States. Gen. Sir A. Wavell's justification was that he could not foresee an immediate threat to Burma, that he had reason to suppose that he would get ample British, Indian and African troops; that he believed that "a country of the British Empire should be defended by Imperial Troops rather than by foreign"[6] and that he feared that the Chinese who had no administrative services of their own would have complicated the already difficult administrative problem in Burma. He wrote later, "from subsequent experience of the slowness of Chinese troop moves I think that even if I had accepted the whole of the Fifth and Sixth Armies at once, they would actually have reached Burma very little, if any, sooner than they eventually did. I do not think that it would have made any difference in the end to the defence of Burma."[7]

No doubt the movement of the Chinese Armies was slow but if the Sixth Army had been accepted at once and had moved immediately, the transport used for its movement later could have brought in the Fifth Army much earlier than it did arrive. Secondly, if the Sixth Army had been brought in all at once and concentrated in the Southern Shan States, the Burma Army troops in that area could have been moved into the Tenasserim area which badly needed reinforcements. This is fully borne out by the statement of Lt.-Gen. T. J. Hutton that "throughout the operations (in North Tenasserim) leading up to the battle of the Sittang I had constantly in mind the necessity for fighting as far forward as possible between the enemy and Rangoon so as to have room in which to deploy expected reinforcements. I therefore took every unit I could from elsewhere."[8] The Chinese Armies would have released more troops from the Southern Shan States. The Commander of the 17th Indian Division voiced the same opinion, "it was obvious that another two divisions between Moulmein and Toungoo would have made Japanese infiltration impossibly difficult and that the Chinese forces gradually moving down from the north would have held off indefinitely the threat to Rangoon."[9] In other words, the early acceptance of the Chinese Armies would have released more troops of the Burma Army for operations in the Tenasserim area and might have, to some extent, changed the course of the operations in that vital area.[10]

Lt.-Gen. T. J. Hutton flew to Lashio on 2 February to meet the Generalissimo. Unfortunately his aircraft crashed at night on the way, and he did not escape without injury. However, next day he was able to confer with the Generalissimo then on his way to India. A most satisfactory discussion ensued and the Generalissimo accepted all proposals placed before him, and in particular agreed to take over the Toungoo front with his Fifth Army, then in readiness to enter Burma. This Army

[6] Gen. Sir A. Wavell's *Despatch*, p. 5.
[7] *Ibid.*
[8] *Report*, p. 19.
[9] *USI Journal*, July 1942.
[10] Lt.-Gen. Hutton also admits, "If the latter (Sixth Army) had moved earlier the whole situation would have been different." The Fifth Army could not be moved earlier.

commanded by General Tu Yu Ming, consisted of the 22nd, 96th and 200th Divisions. These three divisions were all partly mechanised. This Army had a number of lorries for the transport of personnel, some guns of the 105 mm howitzer type, anti-tank guns, some tanks of various kinds, a few old armoured cars, and about one hundred motor cycle combinations. It also had a small cavalry force. It was one of the best equipped and was regarded as one of the finest fighting formations in China.

On 11 February Lt.-Gen. T. J. Hutton visited Taunggyi and met the Chinese representative there. At that meeting it was decided that the 55th Division would go to area Lawlake and not remain in reserve in Loilem. Thus the Sixth Army was to take over the Karenni front and free the whole of the 1st Burma Division for operations south of Toungoo. The two stronger divisions of the Army would cover the routes from Thailand through Kengtung and Mongpan respectively. These were regarded as the danger points. The Mongpan area was assigned to the 49th Division, whilst the 93rd Division held the left of the line covering the road Chiengrai-Tachilek-Kengtung and the Mekong river front. The General Officer Commanding the Sixth Army was reluctant to accept responsibility for Karenni. This extension of his front greatly dispersed his force and he decided to hold Karenni with one Regiment of the 55th Division retaining the other two Regiments in Army Reserve.

It was not until the end of February that the Fifth Army began its advance into Burma. This had been delayed by the movement of the last elements of the Sixth Army and by the fact that a force entering Burma by Lashio could only proceed along the Burma Road, the capacity of which was limited. It had been estimated that the concentration of the Fifth Army at Wanting would take a minimum of twenty days. Consequently, when Rangoon fell early in March, only 200th Division of the Fifth Army had arrived in the country.

The position at the time was that the Chinese forces had taken over all sectors in the Shan States, were taking over in Karenni, and had also agreed to take over the Sittang valley sectors about Toungoo. On the Shan States and Karenni fronts the months of February and March passed with little incidents, and in consequence the relief of the Indo-British forces was completed without interference by the Japanese. There were occasional patrol encounters and engagements along the frontier and in one of them in mid-March, south of Mongpan, the Chinese inflicted one hundred casualties on the Thai troops. At the end of the same month two companies attacked a mixed Japanese and Thai force of three hundred at Wan-Maklang on the frontier north-west of Chiengrai. Heavy casualties were inflicted on the hostile force and a mortar and heavy machine guns were captured. The Chinese had only five casualties.

The general policy as regards the employment of troops was that all Indo-British forces available were to be concentrated in South Burma with the object of holding up the Japanese advance in the area where they had the best communications and presented the greatest threat to Rangoon and the communications with China. Sooner or later it was hoped to develop an offensive into Thailand based on Moulmein.

At the same time it was hoped that the Chinese forces would advance into northern Thailand and keep occupied a considerable number of the

Japanese forces. Although communications were poor, the fact that there was abundance of rice in north Thailand made this region particularly suitable for an offensive by the Chinese. Unfortunately this offensive though practicable never took place. The Generalissimo did not consider the Sixth Army by itself strong enough to undertake it and the course of the operations rendered it more important to use the Fifth Army to relieve the 1st Burma Division towards Toungoo than to deploy it further north on the chance that an offensive would be undertaken in time to relieve the situation.

OPERATIONS UNTIL THE END OF MARCH 1942

The Chinese were not prepared to stand on a line south of Toungoo although the taking up of a defensive position about the town itself had obvious disadvantages. It meant giving up considerable ground, and also that the airfield just north of Toungoo at Kyungon could not be used. In addition, it endangered the Toungoo-Mawchi-Bawlake road which, if uncovered, gave the Japanese a good and direct line of approach to Karenni and the Shan States.

The Chinese 55th Division had begun its advance from Hlegu on 11 March. The troops of the 200th Division were entrenched in Toungoo with the Divisional cavalry unit holding the river line to the south. The 22nd Division was no further forward than Lashio whilst the 96th Division was still in China. On 18 March the Japanese vanguard estimated to be about 450 with armoured cars advanced to the long bridge about 12 miles south of Pyu.[11] There they came into contact with the Chinese patrols which held them up for two days and inflicted heavy casualties and destroyed three armoured cars. On the morning of 20 March the Japanese detailed 500 to 600 infantrymen and cavalry to attack Pyu. Met by one company of Chinese infantry and part of cavalry regiment they, however, retreated in a hurry leaving 200 killed. The Chinese lost only 30. In the afternoon the Japanese returned with reinforcements in infantry and artillery. The fighting continued all through the night. The next day they brought in more artillery. The Chinese troops therefore retired to the first defensive line at Oktwin in accordance with a pre-arranged plan but not before inflicting on the Japanese a heavy loss of 300 men; the main body of the Division was engaged in placing the area of Toungoo in a state of defence. On the morning of 22 March the Japanese further attacked the advanced position at Oktwin but failed in the endeavour. Part of their forces then attempted to outflank the Chinese left wing. But when threatened from the area by one column of Chinese troops, they retired. At daybreak on 23 March the Japanese made a fresh combined infantry, artillery and air attack on the positions on Oktwin. Their gun fire was fierce and aircraft bombed the positions six times. After nine hours of severe fighting they brought in reinforcements of infantry, armoured vehicles and tanks and made repeated charges. Of these two armoured cars and two tanks were destroyed. The remaining then retreated south only to return and attack the flanks of the Chinese

---

[11] *Official Account of the Chinese Army in Burma.* 601/3, pp. 4 ff.

positions. Part of the Japanese columns penetrated into the Chinese lines and fierce hand-to-hand fighting ensued which lasted the whole night. Both sides sustained heavy casualties.

LOSS OF TOUNGOO

On 24 March the Japanese made a fierce attack on Toungoo. One column made a wide detour through the mountainous regions to the west to cut off the rear communications at a place 20 miles north of Toungoo. Another column about 600 strong with several small guns slipped into the Toungoo airfield. The rear of the 1st Burma Division including the 23rd Mountain Battery and Frontier Force columns 1 and 4 were still at Kyungon pending their transfer by rail to the Irrawaddy front, and they also became involved in the fighting for the aerodrome and put up a stout resistance. The 200th Division was cut off in Toungoo. The Fifth Army troops were in Pyawbwe with certain units forward under command of 200th Division. The leading Regiment of the 22nd Division was arriving at Pyinmana with rear formation at Lashio. The 96th Division was approaching the frontier. By the evening of 26 March the whole of the Chinese 22nd Division had been concentrated in the area Pyinmana-Yedashe and the leading troops of the 96th Division were approaching Pyinmana.

The force in Toungoo held on stubbornly, but the position was serious. The Fifth Army then instructed the Sixth Army to send what was available of the 55th Division to the rescue of the Toungoo garrison. Only one Regiment (3rd Regiment) was sent and even this was retained in Thazi. This of course further weakened the 55th Division in the Karenni area. Its Commander thought that it was unnecessary for the 55th Division to proceed to the Toungoo front as the two divisions of the Fifth Army were fast moving towards Toungoo.

In Toungoo itself on 24 March two battalions of the reserve Regiment of the Fifth Army were surrounded by the hostile force and fighting raged north, south and east of the city. After 1700 hours the Japanese at the airfield were largely reinforecd and the fighting became very violent. General Tu, Commander of the Fifth Army, ordered General Tai, Commander of the 200th Division, to hold out and detailed one Regiment of infantry and one company of cavalry of the 22nd Division to attack south from Yedashe to relieve the Toungoo garrison.

At 2000 hours the Japanese finally occupied the airfield. On the next day Toungoo was again attacked by them from three sides and violent fighting ensued throughout the day and night. General Tai continued to hold out. On the morning of 26 March, the Japanese main force launched a fierce attack on the north western corner of the city and entered it. Fierce street fighting ensued. But when they were no longer able to hold out, the main body of the 200th Division cut their way to the rail-road in the eastern part of the city. The next day the Japanese changed direction and launched a severe attack on the left wing. On the morning of 28 March the Japanese brought in more reinforcements, bombed Chinese positions all the time, used gas and violently attacked the centre and left wing. Chinese officers and men fought gallantly, killed many and desperately held to their positions. Fighter support was given to the Chinese by six Tomahawk aircraft of the A.V.G., the only force available in this sector. The recent heavy air attacks by the Japanese on the Magwe airfield had destroyed the greater part of the British air force in Burma. This was particularly unfortunate since the Chinese expected in Burma a reversal of the conditions prevailing in China where Japanese aircraft enjoyed complete mastery.

At nightfall the Japanese employed part of their troops to raid General Tai's Headquarters and also sent a powerful detachment to threaten the rear. On 28 March, the 22nd Division launched a fierce counter attack on the advancing Japanese, occupied one half of Nangyun station, killed over 200 of the Japanese and seized numerous weapons and documents. This halted the hostile advance but no further progress could be made. On 29 March there was no prospect of any reinforcements for the 200th Division which was unable to withstand the strong hostile pressure. Hence it cut its way out of Taungoo, where it had been besieged for a week, in a northernly direction and left Toungoo to be occupied by the Japanese.

On 30 March, the 200th Division established contact with the 22nd Division which by a surprise attack from the west took the Kyungon landing ground. The 200th Division passed into reserve at Yezin, north of Pyinmana, whilst the line was re-established by the 22nd Division south of Yedashe. The Chinese estimated their own casualties at three thousand, but the Japanese had not escaped lightly in the heavy fighting.

Before retiring from Toungoo the Chinese did not destroy the important bridge across the Sittang. Its demolition would have delayed a hostile advance on Mawchi and Bawlake.

There was a Chinese detachment at Mawchi. Between that place and Toungoo there were only some Karen Levies strengthened by the Karen personnel of the 1st Battalion Burma Rifles. The Japanese at once began an advance on Mawchi. On the road west of that town were some favourable defensive positions, but General Liang, Vice Commander 55th Division and commanding troops in Karenni, refused to move beyond Mawchi. His reasons were that Mawchi was his western boundary, and that he could not move into the Fifth Army area without instructions; furthermore, his force was too small to hold both the Mawchi and Salween fronts. He maintained that any Japanese advance across the Salween would cut off his force and leave open, behind him, the road to the Shan States.

THE EFFECT OF THE LOSS OF TOUNGOO

The loss of Toungoo was a disaster. It ultimately led to the loss of Prome as the forces in the Irrawaddy valley had to keep in line with the Chinese. It must, however, be noted that the Japanese thrust to Shwedaung was equally responsible for the evacuation of Prome. Moreover, at a conference which took place at Allanmyo between the Commander-in-Chief, India and Gen. Sir H. Alexander, it was "agreed that in view of the difficulties of the country and the fatigue of the troops in 17th Division, a withdrawal from Prome to the Allanmyo area should commence forthwith and that this withdrawal might have to be continued even further north into the dry zone south of Taungdwingyi where the country was more open and more suitable for the employment of tanks." As long as Toungoo was held Karenni was in little danger since the approaches to it from the south or from Thailand across the Salween were very difficult. However, with the loss of Toungoo and with it of the important bridge across the Sittang, Karenni was open to attack either from Mawchi or by a track leading north-east across the hills. The withdrawal of part of the 55th Division to Thazi when Toungoo was threatened was disastrous and it weakened the Karenni front.

The Toungoo disaster might have been averted and the course of the campaign altered if the rest of the Fifth Army had been thrown into Toungoo. This was made impossible by many factors. Great objection had been taken by the Generalissimo to their moving south of Mandalay. But they did move, only they were too late. This was due to the delay in getting the Generalissimo's consent, as also to distance and delay in transport. This again delayed the transfer of the 1st Burma Division to the Irrawaddy and thus contributed partly to the loss of Prome. But it must again be stressed here that if Gen. Sir A. Wavell had not deferred acceptance of Chinese help and the Sixth Army had moved earlier than it did, the Fifth Army's movement would not have been delayed by lack of transport.

But for the decision of the Chinese not to stand on a line south of Toungoo vast quantities of rice available in the Sittang valley could have been removed. Their loss, like the loss of much of the rice in the Irrawaddy valley from the areas below Prome greatly prejudiced the supply position of the Chinese Armies.

CHAPTER XVIII

Withdrawal from Prome

DECISION TO WITHDRAW FROM PROME

Following upon the action at Shwedaung and the loss of Toungoo by the Chinese Fifth Army on 29 March, it was felt that continued occupation of Prome must be attended by considerable danger, and it was reported by the Corps Commander that the morale of the troops, subsequent to those actions, had left a great deal to be desired. At the same time it was very necessary that the large dumps of petrol, ammunition, and supplies in the town should be evacuated. On 29 March, the Army Headquarters informed Burcorps that it was essential for the continuance of operations in Burma that no stores should be abandoned in Prome.

Yet the back-loading of these stores was a matter of much difficulty. After the devastating attack on the Magwe airfield Japanese aircraft had made frequent raids on the road and river traffic between Prome and Allanmyo. Despite possible danger from the fifth column activities and infiltration by the Japanese the Burcorps was forced into running night convoys on the road. But the same could not be done on the river which was abnormally low, thus making night navigation dangerous.

Prome town was not easy to defend by one Brigade Group. It straggled for more than two miles along the east bank of the Irrawaddy and its outskirts were surrounded by dense scrub jungle. Particularly on the south it was dominated by similarly overgrown hill features. There were, however, certain areas which could have been defended in strength by concentrated battalions, and from where vigorous steps could have been taken against the Japanese forces by-passing them. The main road to Allanmyo left the town towards its southern extremity and ran nearly due east for over three miles before turning north. From the northern end of the town a subsidiary unmetalled road traversed jungle and reserved forest to join the main road at Dayindabo, seventeen miles distant from Prome. A boom had been put across the Irrawaddy below Prome. This prevented any direct approach by river, but of course did not hinder the Japanese from crossing the Irrawaddy from the west bank above the town.

On 1 April Gen. Sir A. Wavell and Gen. Sir H. Alexander were at Burcorps Headquarters at Allanmyo where a conference took place that afternoon. They agreed that, in view of the difficulties of the terrain and the fatigue of the troops in the 17th Indian Division consequent on the local offensive ending with the operations at Shwedaung, a withdrawal from Prome to the Allanmyo area should begin forthwith. This withdrawal might have to be continued even further north where the country was more open and more suitable for operation by tanks.

A warning order was at once sent to the 17th Indian Division stating that a decision had been taken to regroup Burcorps in the general area

Allanmyo-Kyaukpadaung-Bwetkyi-Chaung-Thayetmyo. All possible stocks were to be back-loaded at once. When this order was received the force was in touch with the Japanese immediately south of Prome.

FIRST ATTACKS

After the striking force had disengaged itself at Shwedaung the Japanese took no immediate steps to follow up in strength, although small parties advanced towards Prome and Sinmizwe. Patrols were active and occasionally fired on the 17th Division forward positions. On the west bank of the river, the Japanese were opposite Prome on the night of 30/31 March. The duty of preventing any advance in strength up the west bank of the Irrawaddy had now devolved on the 2nd Burma Brigade of the 1st Burma Division. The 2nd Battalion Burma Rifles with a Garrison Company was stationed at Thayetmyo with orders to patrol to the south.

During the night of 30/31 March, the Japanese managed to get a gun of large calibre on the west bank of the river just opposite Prome. Soon after dawn they shelled the flotilla of the Royal Marine patrol and obtained hits on some of its craft. The patrol moved up the river out of range, while 17th Division artillery silenced the gun, which was finally removed during the night. On 1 April, British tank patrols south-east of Hmawza were in contact with small parties of the Japanese troops, some of whom were successfully engaged by the artillery.

DISPOSITION OF ALLIED TROOPS IN THE PROME AREA

The 63rd Indian Infantry Brigade for the defence of Prome

The 63rd Indian Infantry Brigade was detailed for the actual defence of Prome and occupied an extensive perimeter to cover the main road from the south through Shwedaung, as also the tracks approaching parallel to the main road and the main exit to the north. The perimeter was held as follows:—the 5th Battalion 17th Dogra Regiment with one company of the 2nd Battalion 13th Frontier Force Rifles and the 12th Mountain Battery under command, protected the river bank astride War-Shwedaung-Prome and the southern approaches to the town. It was also responsible for the defence of the block erected across the main road from Shwedaung. It had dug its position which was wired. On the left the 1st Battalion 10th Gurkha Rifles continued the eastern defences from War-Shwedaung-Prome to inclusive of the railway. The 1st Battalion 11th Sikh Regiment held the line from a point north of the railway to the river north of Prome. The 2nd Battalion 13th Frontier Force Rifles was in brigade reserve in Prome itself. It had taken part in the operation at Shwedaung in support of the 4th Battalion 12th Frontier Force Regiment of the 16th Indian Infantry Brigade. There was also available a force of some four hundred of the Rangoon Battalion Burma Military Police. This Battalion was disposed in platoon posts guarding the foreshore, dumps, and the 63rd Indian Infantry Brigade Headquarters which was in a building on the river bank. The remaining men were in defensive positions round the Police Lines in the north-east quarter of the town.

1 Field Battery of the 1st Indian Field Regiment and one section of the 12th Mountain Battery were also stationed in Prome.

The perimeter was extensive; the front of the 1st Battalion 10th Gurkha Rifles alone was some 1800 yards. The sector held by the 5th Battalion 17th Dogra Regiment was full of broken hillocks which rendered observation impossible and Japanese approach to the position easy. It was overlooked by thick high scrub with patches of jungle. So was the centre. The area, immediately behind the Battalion was closely built up. Consequently any Japanese infiltration at that point would enormously increase the task of defence and open the town itself to an attacking force. Of course the left was clear.

The main portion of Prome had been bombed and burnt out but a considerable portion still remained as also a number of inhabitants, particularly the Pongyi element. Efforts were made to clear the civil population, but as the area was considerable they were not successful. It was difficult to check all movement in front of the area, which made it possible for the Japanese to get accurate information about these positions.

The 16th Indian Infantry Brigade east of Prome

The 16th Indian Infantry Brigade which had been moved from Zigon on 25 March took up a defensive position east of Prome in the triangle Sinmizwe-Hmawza-Paungdale. It comprised the 2nd Battalion Duke of Wellington's Regiment, the 1st Royal Battalion 9th Jat Regiment, the 4th Battalion 12th Frontier Force Regiment and the 7th Battalion 10th Baluch Regiment. The 1st Royal Battalion 9th Jat Regiment was at first at Sinmizwe but later, on 31 March, it was ordered to take over just south of the road Prome-Paungdale linking up on its right with the 1st Battalion 11th Sikh Regiment on the eastern perimeter of Prome. The line was continued to the east by the 7th Battalion 10th Baluch Regiment and the 4th Battalion 12th Frontier Force Regiment. The 2nd Battalion Duke of Wellington's Regiment was in the area of the Divisional Headquarters at the village of Nattalin. With the Brigade was 15 Mountain Battery. On the night of April 1/2 the 1st Battalion Gloucestershire Regiment took up a position on the left of the 7th Battalion 10th Baluch Regiment.

The 48th Indian Infantry Brigade to the east of the 16th Indian Infantry Brigade

To the left and somewhat forward of the 16th Indian Infantry Brigade was placed the 48th Brigade about Hmawza. This Brigade then under the command of Brig. R. T. Cameron held the area demarcated by the ruined walls of the ancient city that once existed on the site. On the extreme left, the 1st Battalion 4th P.W.O. Gurkha Rifles faced east astride the Prome-Paungdale road. On its right, facing south, was the combined Battalion 7th Gurkha Rifles; whilst further to the right the line was held by the 2nd Battalion 5th Royal Gurkha Rifles. The 1st Battalion Royal Inniskilling Fusiliers was in reserve, but later it left the area on the night of 1 April to join the 1st Burma Division. 2 Field Battery of the 1st Indian Field Regiment was in the Brigade area. The very weak 1st Battalion 3rd Q.A.O. Gurkha Rifles, just reformed, was not with

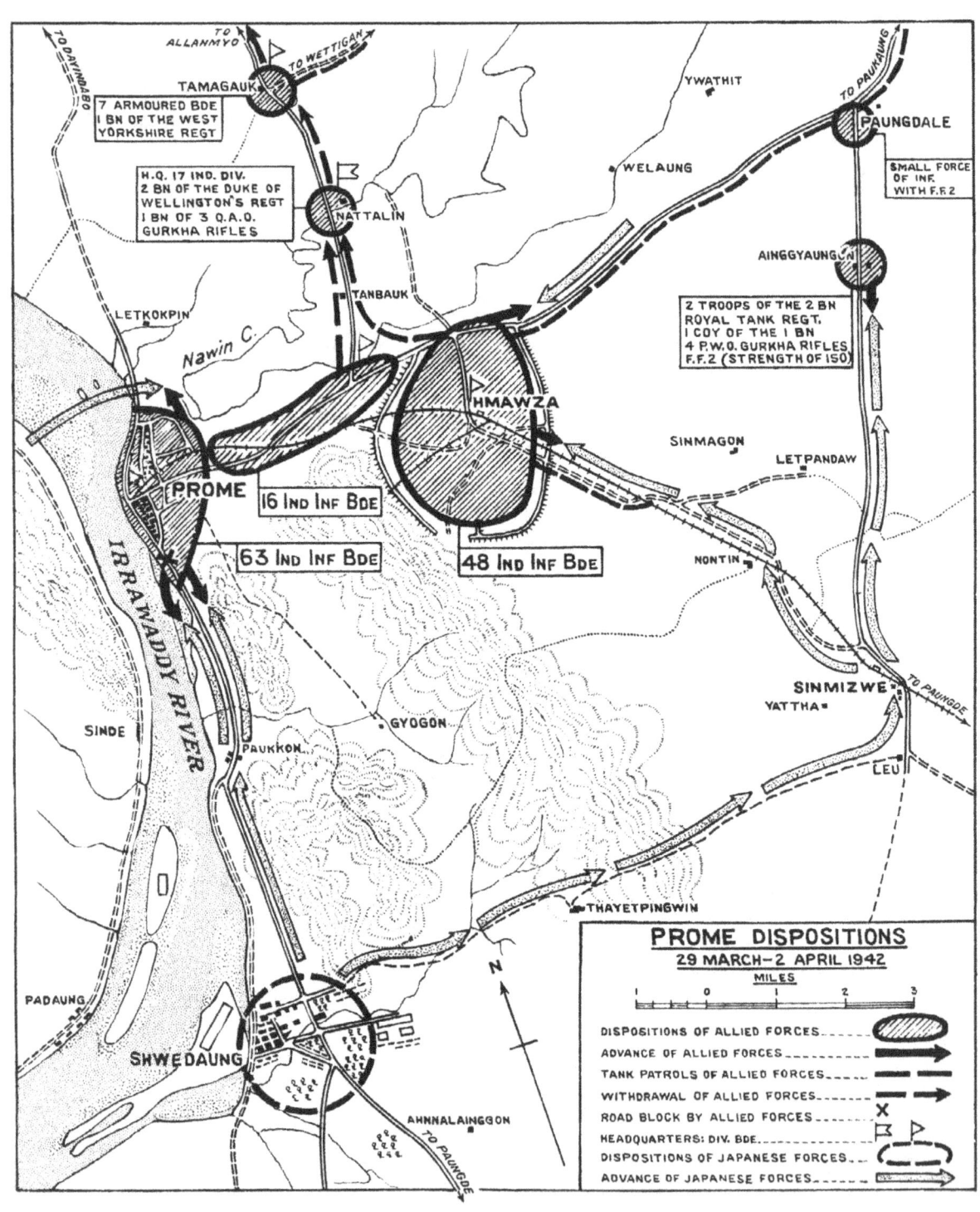

the Brigade, but at the Divisional Headquarters, employed as its Defence Battalion.

At Tamagauk, not far from the Divisional Headquarters, was the 7th Armoured Brigade with the 1st Battalion West Yorkshire Regiment. Tanks were maintaining patrols to the south-east of the frontier towards Sinmizwe, and also towards Wettigan. Near Paungdale there was a Company of 1/4 Gurkha Rifles with F.F. 2.

JAPANESE MOVES

Coming to the Japanese forces, we find that in the middle of March, the *Fifteenth Army* had received orders from the Southern Region Army for an advance into North Burma along two axes, the Rangoon-Prome and Rangoon-Mandalay roads. The immediate objective was to secure a line Loikaw-Yamethin-Yenangyaung. The ultimate objectives were to be the annihilation of the Chinese Expeditionary and Indo-British Forces and the capture of the oil-fields. The *55th Division* at Pegu was therefore to change direction and advance along the Rangoon-Mandalay road with the Chinese Fifth and Sixth Armies and Lashio as operational objectives. Later the *18th* and *56th Divisions* were to mass on the right flank with the object of cutting the retreat of the Chinese Armies and squeezing Allied forces westwards on to the Irrawaddy. The *33rd Division* was to advance along the Rangoon-Prome Road and the line of the Irrawaddy river, cross to the west bank of the river, and trap and nail the whole Burma Army on the left flank in the area of Monywa or Shwebo. The *215th Infantry Regiment* was sent along the Irrawaddy river, northward to the Prome area, while the main force advanced north to Prome along the Rangoon-Prome road. This advance had begun on 16th March.

Attack on Dogra positions—1 April

On 29 and 30 March Japanese patrols were active in front of the positions held by the 5th Battalion 17th Dogra Regiment. They were ambushed by a company on patrol and driven off. On 1 April at 1830 hours a large party of 400 Japanese troops was reported moving across the Battalion front from the direction of the main road, which approached the right of the Dogra positions to within 600 yards of the forward lines. Another party stronger than the first was reported moving down the main road in the direction of the road-block held by the 'B' company. They had all been brought in from Shwedaung by mechanised transport.

Further to the east where the line was held by the 16th Indian Infantry Brigade there was some firing, perhaps by reserves. The 17th Division mortars shelled the areas where the Japanese had been observed at dusk, but they made no attempt to advance against its positions.

The Indian artillery in Prome fired on the attacking Japanese infantry and their transport. In some cases the targets were so close to the observation post that it was possible to observe fire by moon-light. The mortars of the 1st Battalion 10th Gurkha Rifles also engaged them to the south of the town.

The attack on the road-block began at 1900 hours. The platoon of 'B' company on the road-block was driven back and parties of the Japanese troops began infiltrating round the right flank of the Battalion. At 1915 hours they established a post in a Pagoda, south of 'B' company's position and were seen digging in. At that time arrived reports of Japanese movement on the road from Shwedaung. These Japanese were engaged by the 25 Pounder Battery from the observation post in the Battalion area.

Between 1915 and 2000 hours the Japanese attacked all along the Battalion front, but all of them except those on the road-block were driven off and numerous casualties inflicted. For the next half an hour there was slight hostile activity except for infiltration through the 'B' company front where the block had been overrun. But at 2100 hours a large Japanese party overran the Battalion Headquarters. Communication by telephone to the Brigade Headquarters ceased. The river front had crumbled and infiltration into the town through the gap in the defences continued. The company of the 2nd Battalion 13th Frontier Force Rifles (less one platoon) held in reserve was sent to restore the situation which was rather obscure. But the counter-attack could make no headway owing to darkness and the impossibility of maintaining any cohesion in the thickly built up area in the rear of the Dogra position.

At 2115 hours the Battalion Headquarters was moved to 'A' company area and 'A' and 'C' companies were withdrawn to cover approaches down the track leading to Prome. There they remained till 0300 hours the next day. At about midnight the 12th Mountain Battery, the 2nd Field Battery and the 1st Indian Field Regiment were ordered to withdraw from the town and the guns were safely got away. Later, after the withdrawal of the 63rd Indian Infantry Brigade, 2nd Field Battery shelled the Japanese in Prome from positions north-east of it. The previous battalion area then held by them was shelled by 25 Pounders from the area of the railway line, inflicting casualties on the Japanese.

In the darkness and confusion it appeared impossible to restore the situation on the Dogra front. The Brigade Headquarters in the rear of the Dogra position was nearly overrun. After consultations with the Divisional Command the Brigade Commander on 30 March at 0105 hours ordered the Dogras to withdraw to the road and rail crossing at the north-eastern exit of the town, which was held by the 1st Battalion 11th Sikh Regiment. His plan was to withdraw from Prome and take up a position generally along the line of the road and railway on the east side of the town and in the area of the 16th Indian Infantry Brigade.

Attack on 1/11 Sikh Regiment

At 2200 hours on 1 April an attack on the 1st Battalion 11 Sikh Regiment positions developed. The Japanese would seem to have crossed the river from the west bank at a point north of Prome. They first fired on 'D' company, north-east of Prome, with the idea of making the company fire and disclose its position. Throughout the night the company waited in its wired weapon pits watching for a sure target. At one period the Japanese reached the wire in front of the Battalion but did not press home an attack and eventually withdrew. At 2300 hours the Battalion Headquarters, south of 'D' company position, was subjected to steady and accurate mortar fire. 70 Field Company, Indian Engineers, in the battalion area suffered casualties. Evidently the positions had been disclosed by the Burmans. At 0105 hours even though the Battalion positions were in tact, 'C' and 'D' companies were ordered by the Brigade Commander to withdraw to the level crossing to the east of the Rear Headquarters and A and B companies. This was on account of the fact that the 5th Battalion 17th Dogra Regiment had fallen back towards the east and the area previously occupied by it was now in the hands of the Japanese who were working north along the river bank and through the centre of the town.

It is not known what casualties the 5th Battalion 17th Dogra Regiment had suffered, but the other Battalions of the Brigade had not been heavily engaged and their total casualties appear to have been one other rank wounded.

Burma Military Police

The order to withdraw did not reach either the town platoons of the Burma Military Police at the north end of the foreshore, or the party in the Police Lines. The two platoons on the river bank were overrun by the Japanese during the night, but the majority of the men fought their way north and rejoined the main force later. The party in the Police Lines remained in position until first light. Then, finding the town in hostile occupation and all the other troops withdrawn, these men also retired through the eastern outskirts of the town and went north, making contact with the main body some three hours later.

After the withdrawal of the 63rd Indian Infantry Brigade the passage of the Japanese troops and transport through Prome to the north had been observed by the Burma Military Police. This movement had not been interfered with as at that time it was believed that both troops and transport belonged to the 17th Division. But the mistake was soon realised and the fact was reported to the Division on 2 April.

Japanese Pincer Movements to Encircle Prome

A Japanese column was believed to be heading for the unmetalled road to Dayindabo as the left prong of the pincer movement intended to encircle the forces around Prome. The Japanese troops comprising the right flank of their advance were in action very early on 2 April about Hmawza and at Ainggyaungon about six miles to the east. The latter village was on the road from Sinmizwe to Paungdale where two troops of the 2nd Battalion Royal Tank Regiment with one company of the 1st Battalion 4th P.W.O. Gurkha Rifles had been posted to watch the left flank. There, too, was F.F. 2 at a strength of about one hundred and fifty.

On the night of 1/2 April the tanks were in Paungdale, but the remainder of the small flankguard was in position facing south-west astride the road near Ainggyaungon. At about 0300 hours a Japanese column in very close formation approached from Sinmizwe. When it was one hundred yards away fire was opened on it which continued for some minutes. The Japanese were thrown into great confusion and suffered heavily. Later, when they began to mortar the flankguard positions, the Allied troops withdrew. At first light patrols observed seventy or eighty bullock carts being employed in the area of the action to evacuate Japanese dead and wounded.

THE 48TH INDIAN INFANTRY BRIGADE AT AMBUSH—31 MARCH

On the 48th Indian Infantry Brigade front, a company of the 1st Battalion 7th Gurkha Rifles was pushed out 4 miles on the left flank of the 1st Battalion 4th Gurkha Rifles and carriers and tanks patrolled still further out for another 15 miles along the Prome-Paukkaung road to ensure that any encirclement from the east would be known. At 1430 hours on 31 March a Frontier Force Group Officer arrived south with word that the Japanese were pressing down the road from Paungdale with a considerable train of bullock carts and elephants with them. As there appeared to be a good chance of surprising them orders were issued for an ambush to be laid. A company of the 1st Battalion 4th P.W.O. Gurkha Rifles moved left at 1700 hours on a south-easterly course across country for a point some seven miles distant. Down the road went a supporting troop of the 2nd Royal Tank Regiment and a Forward Observation Officer from the section of the 2nd Indian Field Battery then under command of the 48th Indian Infantry Brigade. Avoiding all contact with the Burmans the company got to its destination that night. There it lay up on 1 April, whilst the artillery engaged some Japanese movement to the east. This artillery fire from a range of 8500 yards must have been an unpleasant surprise to the Japanese.

That night the main Japanese force came straight into the ambush. It was shot up at point-blank range while marching in close formation. The L.M.Gs massed for the opening fire took a heavy toll and before the troops withdrew they had inflicted 200 casualties on the Japanese. The latter were taken so completely by surprise, and thrown into such utter confusion, that not a shot could they fire for twenty minutes, but, by then, of course, the Gurkhas had flitted away from the area.

As mentioned later, that night the rest of the Brigade had withdrawn from their sector of the Prome defences before this company of the 1st Battalion 4th P.W.O. Gurkha Rifles could link up again.[1]

1/4 GURKHA RIFLE'S SUCCESSFUL ATTACK—2 APRIL

At 0030 hours on 2 April, the Japanese column approached the 1st Battalion 4th Gurkha Rifles position along the road from Paungdale. It was moonlight and they could be seen in close formation, talking and singing. Fire was held till they were within 50 yards range. 'B' and 'C' companies then opened with L.M.Gs and 2" mortars. The two medium machine-guns fired the seven bolts which were all they possessed in a swinging traverse at 50 yards range and scattered the Japanese over the rice stubble. 'D' company joined in as they got clear of the shadow of trees along the road. Then 3" mortars also came into action. The Japanese suffered heavy casualties. The Gurkhas in the forward lines near the road frequently worked forward in the ditches and shadows and bombed hostile parties taking cover in road ditches and bushes to the north.

---

[1] Cameron's comments, p. 5.

Fifteen minutes later, the Japanese rallied and their mortars and infantry guns opened fire; but it was wild shooting as the positions had been concealed. Their bombs and shells were very ineffective, killing only one and wounding three in the Battalion Headquarters. The 7th Gurkha Rifles to the right of that position also came under shell fire but the Japanese made no attempt to advance.

THE 48TH INDIAN INFANTRY BRIGADE ORDERED TO BREAK CONTACT—2 APRIL

At about 0300 hours, following the withdrawal of the 63rd Indian Infantry Brigade from Prome, the 48th Indian Infantry Brigade was ordered to break contact with the hostile force and to withdraw to a position south of Tamagauk to cover the main road. The Japanese did not immediately follow up this movement.[2]

No sooner was this under way than a large body of the Japanese troops was reported to be moving across the front of the 1st Battalion 7th Gurkha Rifles in close formation. But more than half the Brigade was on the move backwards. The orders from the Division had to be obeyed and there was nothing left but to carry on with the withdrawal. But it was a moment of great disappointment, especially because the tanks had suitable country to move over for a counter-attack, a very rare opportunity in the First Burma Campaign.

At the time the Divisional Commander considered it possible that the Japanese having broken into Prome would swing right on to the position to the east, and his dispositions were accordingly made to prevent an enveloping attack of that nature. Hence there was the general withdrawal towards Tamagauk. The possibility of a counter-attack by his own forces to regain Prome was not ruled out, but the launching of such an attack could not be carried out before the evening.[3]

THE WITHDRAWAL FROM PROME—2 APRIL

The initial stage of the withdrawal was covered by the 7th Armoured Brigade and the 16th Indian Infantry Brigade and through these there began to pass, before first light, the elements of the 63rd Indian Infantry Brigade and the 48th Indian Infantry Brigade. At about 0630 hours the 16th Indian Infantry Brigade also began to withdraw. The order to

---

[2] The reason for the withdrawal was the break up of the Dogra front. The 17th Indian Division *War Diary* is vague when it says that "for various reasons it was decided to withdraw from Prome". "This was carried out in good order, despite being heavily mortared and subjected to M.G. fire by close following enemy". *War Diary*, 'G' Branch 17 Indian Division.

[3] Of the action in and around Prome a Japanese account says, "Prome was captured without much opposition, and after a surprise attack on enemy position at Allanmyo the Division broke through the enemy line and captured the town. In order to prepare for the next phase the Division (33) concentrated at Allanmyo in the early part of April for three days to re-equip and reorganize. The Division was reinforced by infantry under the command of an Infantry Group Command and a Light-Tank Company." *History of the Japanese 15th Army*. 601/7785/H, p. 24.

Another account says, "On March 16 the main body of the Division (33) advanced for Prome making two columns and occupied Shwedaung and Prome." *History of the 33rd (Jap.) Div.* 601/7725/H, p. 2.

One column marched along the Irrawaddy (*215 Infantry Regiment*) and the main force marched along the Rangoon-Prome road.

retire was not communicated to the 4th Battalion 12th Frontier Force Regiment until 1000 hours. This Battalion was in position north of the Hmawza ruins and had been under mortar fire for a couple of hours.

A defensive position was taken up south of the bridge across the Nawin Chaung. The line west of, and astride, the road was held by the 48th Indian Infantry Brigade and was continued further east by the 1st Royal Battalion 9th Jat Regiment. Three miles east of Tamagauk on the road to Wettigan was the 2nd Battalion Royal Tank Regiment with attached troops. It patrolled eastward from this point and the tanks were in contact with a column of Japanese cavalry.

On the east there was considerable hostile activity. The sector of the Nawin Chaung position was shelled. They did not, however, at once attempt to follow up the Indian troops along the main road. But later they began to shell the road, but no further action developed.

DIVISIONAL COMMANDER'S ORDERS FOR A FURTHER WITHDRAWAL TO DAYINDABO—2 APRIL

It was at about 1000 hours on 2 April that Maj.-Gen. D. T. Cowan received the report that a strong Japanese column had moved north through Prome during the previous night. It was feared that if this column was marching on Dayindabo with the object of cutting off the 17th Indian Division the position would become serious.

The main road along which the Division must fall back on Allanmyo passed through some fifteen miles of reserved forest, ideal terrain for Japanese road-block tactics. Caught between a block and a strong force following up behind it the 17th Indian Infantry Division might well have been destroyed. This would have left the 1st Burma Division, then comprising two weak brigades and with practically no artillery, between the Japanese and the oilfields. These latter were not yet ready for destruction. The Divisional Commander therefore considered that it would be unwise to risk everything on a major battle when the Japanese were between his own force and the 1st Burma Division, and that an immediate further withdrawal should take place. Lieutenant General Slim agreed that the proper course was for the 17th Indian Division to march at once for Dayindabo. The hurried withdrawal of the 17th Division inevitably caused some confusion, but by 1130 hours the whole force was marching north with the object of harbouring round Dayindabo that night.

The 63rd Indian Infantry Brigade led, the 16th Indian Infantry Brigade marched on the east of the road, the 48th Indian Infantry Brigade to its west. The road itself was close picquetted to prevent the establishment of road-blocks. One squadron of the 2nd Battalion Royal Tank Regiment acted as rearguard, whilst the remaining tanks of the Battalion were interspersed between guns and vehicles and moved continuously up and down the road. On their northward journeys they ferried infantry.

HARDSHIPS OF THE TROOPS

April in Burma is the hottest month of the year and the 17th Indian Division was then entering the most arid region of the country. The heat was intense, the route was dusty, and the march was a severe trial to the troops. Many men began the march exhausted and had had no water since the previous evening. Some battalions were very short of water bottles, and north of Tamagauk was a stretch of waterless country where the road traversed teak-covered forest lands. In certain units, but by no means in all, march discipline was not well maintained. The infrequent water-holes that were encountered on the line of march were surrounded by numerous stragglers who persisted in drinking from what were probably contaminated sources. Cholera was prevalent in the Prome area, having been spread by the numerous Indian refugees passing through it on their way to India. There was no air support, and towards evening bomber aircraft attacked the long column of troops. Considerable casualties were caused particularly in the 63rd Indian Infantry Brigade.

JAPANESE MISTAKE OF NOT FOLLOWING UP THE 17TH INDIAN DIVISION

That night the 17th Division was in the Dayindabo area. Contact with the hostile force had been broken, and no attempt was made by the Japanese to engage this Division. The Japanese column that had advanced through Prome the previous night had certainly not struck for Dayindabo. Once again the Japanese had allowed the 17th Division to get out of a tight corner without a follow-up which would have been extremely difficult to contend with. It was once more the old story of brilliant mobility by the Japanese which allowed them to make contact; but after that there was a lack of initiative which always, right to the end, robbed them of the full gains of victory which could have led to the elimination of the 17th Indian Division from war. Beyond following up the Division for a few miles no atempt was made by them to chase the Indian forces. It may be that the Japanese had exhausted their troops by long approach marches to the battlefield in the hope that by surprise encircling movements they would achieve their aim.

The concentration of the 1st Burma Division was still not entirely complete although it was accomplished very shortly afterwards. By the evening of 2 April, the 1st Burma Brigade which, less the 5th Battalion Burma Rifles, had been in Shwebandaw was in position at Dayindabo and to the north of it. Next day the 17th Division passed through this Brigade and marched on to the area of Allanmyo-Ywataung-Kyaukpadaung. But it was again heavily attacked from the air on the line of march.

BURCORPS' PLAN TO FIGHT ON THE LINE OF YIN CHAUNG

An Operation Instruction outlining the plan of further operations was issued by Burcorps on 3 April.[4] The intention was to deny to the

---

[4] Burcorps 'G' Branch. Appendices 17, 18 and 19.

Japanese the main oilfields of Yenangyaung and Chauk, to cover Upper Burma, and to maintain touch with the Chinese Fifth Army to the east. Delaying positions were to be taken up on the Bwetkyi Chaung south of Allanmyo, on the Linban Chaung south of Sinbaungwe, and on the line Minhla-Taungdwingyi. The Corps would fight on the line of the Yin Chaung south of Magwe.

The defence of the river sector was entrusted to the 1st Burma Division which would retain a brigade group on the west bank of the Irrawaddy. The 2nd Burma Brigade already at Thayetmyo continued to carry out this role.

The defence of the Bwetkyi Chaung line was to be undertaken by the 1st Burma Division; and the pause there was to be sufficient to cover the demolition of the small oilfields in the Thayetmyo area, and to allow for the back-loading of stores and the resting of the troops. The successful evacuation of stores was vital since the premature withdrawal from Prome had resulted in the loss of a substantial quantity of supplies.

The 17th Indian Division would then hold the Linban Chaung whilst the 1st Burma Division passed through it.

At Allanmyo the road turned north-east to Taungdwingyi away from the Irrawaddy. From Taungdwingyi it swung westward to rejoin the river at Magwe. It was necessary, therefore, for the 3rd Brigade of the 1st Burma Division covering the east bank of the river to withdraw north of Migyaunge on a pack basis, whilst all wheeled transport of the Division together with the remaining brigade made the long detour through Taungdwingyi. The Division would then be reunited on the Yin Chaung position about Tamo as the 17th Indian Division fell back towards Taungdwingyi.

Only such motor transport as was tactically required was to be retained in forward areas, and some brigades were to be placed entirely on a pack or bullock cart basis.

On 4 April the 17th Indian Division remained on the general line Ywathaung-Kyaukpadaung and the troops obtained a much needed rest. They were still very much fatigued and it was considered desirable, therefore, to accelerate the withdrawal of the Division.[5] Back-loading of stores and administrative units continued whilst the line of the Bwetkyi Chaung was held by the 1st Burma Division. South of it, at Nyaungbinzeik, a strong hostile column had been located. The 48th Indian Infantry Brigade and the 7th Armoured Brigade, less one regiment, were formed into a Corps reserve.

Burcorps now proceeded to fall back rapidly to the north. On the night of 5/6 April Allanmyo and Thayetmyo were evacuated. All stores and ammunition were got away and both towns were destroyed by fire. Demolitions on the oilfields had been carried out.

On the night of 7/8 April they retired from the Linban Chaung position then held by the 16th Indian Infantry Brigade and the 2nd Battalion Royal Tank Regiment. Three vehicles alleged to be hostile tanks were encountered on the road near Nyaungbintha. These dispersed

---

[5] 17th Indian Division *War Diary*, 'G' Branch, Appendix 1.

on being engaged by the British tanks, and the withdrawal continued without further incident.

By 8 April Burcorps was on the general line Minhla-Taungdwingyi. Japanese aircraft were active and carried out much bombing and machine-gunning of the forward areas. There was, however, no contact with hostile ground forces.[6]

---

[6] "During the withdrawal the 17th Division was subjected to heavy air attacks which caused considerable casualties. We had no air cover or support.
   The withdrawal was originally to be to Allanmyo. In view of the tired nature of the troops a further withdrawal to Minhla-Taungdwingyi was ordered." Gen. Sir H. Alexander's *Despatch*, p. 9.

CHAPTER XIX

Race for the Oilfields—Minhla-Taungdwingyi Line

GEN. SIR H. ALEXANDER'S REQUEST FOR A CHINESE DIVISION

The stretch of front from Minhla to Taungdwingyi held by Burcorps was over forty miles in length. In consequence, the defence was without depth. With this fact in mind Gen. Sir H. Alexander had, on April 4, requested General Tu, commanding the Chinese Fifth Army, to send one regiment to hold Taungdwingyi and thus enable Burcorps to form a reserve.[1] General Tu informed Sir H. Alexander that he had already ordered one battalion to Taungdwingyi. But as the fire power of a Chinese battalion was, however, no more than that of a company of Indian troops, a regiment was promised.

After further consideration Gen. Sir H. Alexander decided that at least one Chinese division was required if the line was to be maintained. When the Generalissimo was in Maymyo on April 6 he undertook to make a division available for this purpose. In fact, only one Chinese battalion ever reached the Taungdwingyi area and the failure to provide a division for the defence of Taungdwingyi had the most serious consequences.

NATURE OF THE COUNTRY

The Indo-British forces were henceforth to operate in the thinly populated dry zone of Burma. The country was very undulating, in places almost rugged. Water-courses bit sharply into hill features and, save for the main tributaries of the Irrawaddy, were dry in April. The country presented a dusty, waterless appearance. Its thin vegetation and scanty patches of jungle were generally parched. Village cart tracks were rough, and at that season were heavy with loose sand or dust. Roads were even fewer than in Lower Burma. The entire country between Taungdwingyi and the Irrawaddy was of this nature. Many of the bare hills were steep. The Yin Chaung, much shrunken, flowed between banks dropping sharply to the stream-bed along which the vegetation was greener. The courses of feeder streams were marked by deep nullahs.

In an endeavour to improve communications Burcorps ordered the railway track between Taungdwingyi and Natmauk to be dismantled as the permanent way was to be employed as a motor road. Working day and night the Sappers effected this conversion. Intensive work was also done on the track from Natmauk to Ywamun, and along the two tracks

---

[1] Gen. Sir H. Alexander's *Despatch*, p. 9.

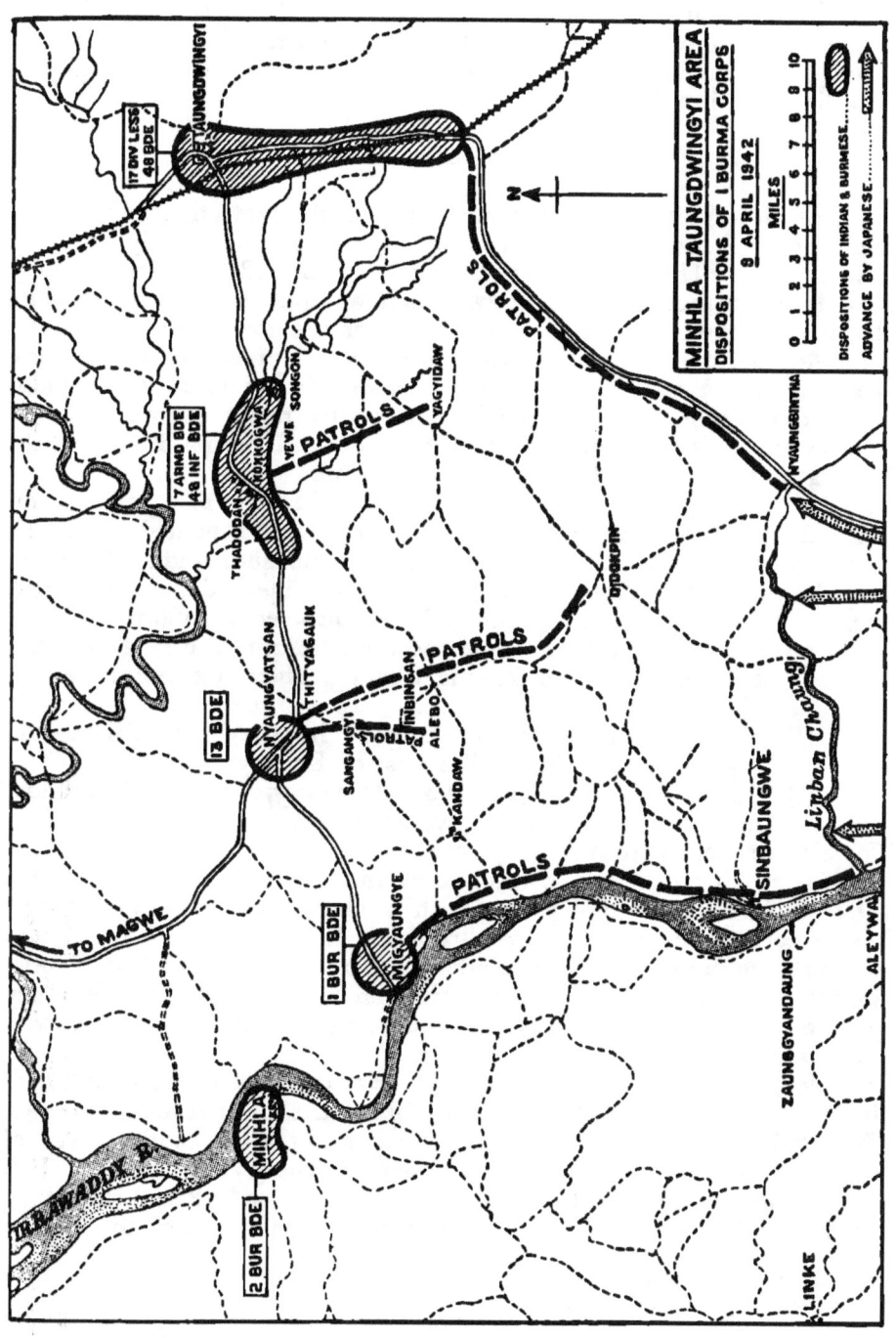

linking the latter place with Zayetkon and Pyawbwe. They were made fit for heavy transport. East of Taungdwingyi the forest-covered Pegu Yoma still separated the Burcorps from the Chinese Fifth Army which in mid-April was withdrawing upon Pyinmana,[2] with intention of fighting on a line covering that town.

DISPOSITION OF BURCORPS

The disposition of Burcorps was based on the protection of both the flanks and the formation of a striking force to deal offensively with the hostile forces. The 17th Indian Division, less the 48th Indian Infantry Brigade was to hold Taungdwingyi which was put into a state of close all-round defence. For this purpose parts of the town were cleared by controlled burning, a necessary precaution as was proved later when the Japanese aircraft carried out bombing attacks. Elaborate works were also constructed, barbed wire was put up, and booby-traps prepared.

On the west bank of the Irrawaddy the 2nd Burma Brigade held Minhla and came directly under Corps control.

The centre of the line was held by the Corps striking force commanded by Major-General Bruce Scott. This force consisted of the 1st Burma Division (less 2nd Burma Brigade), the 48th Indian Infantry Brigade, and the 7th Armoured Brigade. Water supply dictated the areas to be occupied by the striking force. It was disposed as follows:—

(a) the 48th Infantry Brigade and the 7th Armoured Brigade about Kokkogwa on the Yaume Chaung, about ten miles west of Taungdwingyi.

(b) the 13 Indian Infantry Brigade in the area Thityagauk-Nyaungyatsan, eight miles west of Kokkogwa.

(c) the 1st Burma Brigade about Migaungye on the Irrawaddy,[4] ten miles south-west of Nyaungyatsan.

These three areas were linked by road.

The striking force was to reconnoitre the tracks leading into the area Inbingan-Alebo-Sanmagyi-Kandaw with a view to concentrating against hostile columns moving in that direction. It was also to be prepared to attack the flanks of any force advancing by the main road on Taungdwingyi or by the east bank of the river on Migyaungye. The infantry brigade could, if necessary, operate along country tracks and move on a pack basis.[3]

Along the whole corps front an observation screen was established, the line for this being some eighteen miles to the south through Aleywa, Nyaungbintha, and along the Linban Chaung to the Irrawaddy. West of the river it continued through Zaunggyandaung and Linke.[4] F.F. columns were allotted to formations for this purpose.[5] Patrol vessels on the Irrawaddy covered the river as far south as the mouth of the Linban

---

[2] See Chapter, "Chinese Front".
[3] *War Diary*, Burcorps 'G' Br. App. 17.
[4] By 17 Div.—road Aleywa—Gwedankkon Thikkokkwin excluding Nyaungbintha By striking force—Including Nyaungbintha and line of Linban Chaung to Irrawaddy. By 2 Burma Brigade Zanggyandaung and Sinke.
[5] To 17 Div. B, Sqn. M.I. (F.F. 3) and F.F. 6. To striking Force A Sqn. M.I. (F.F. 1) and F.F. 5. To 2 Bur. Bde. 2 cols of F.F. 8.

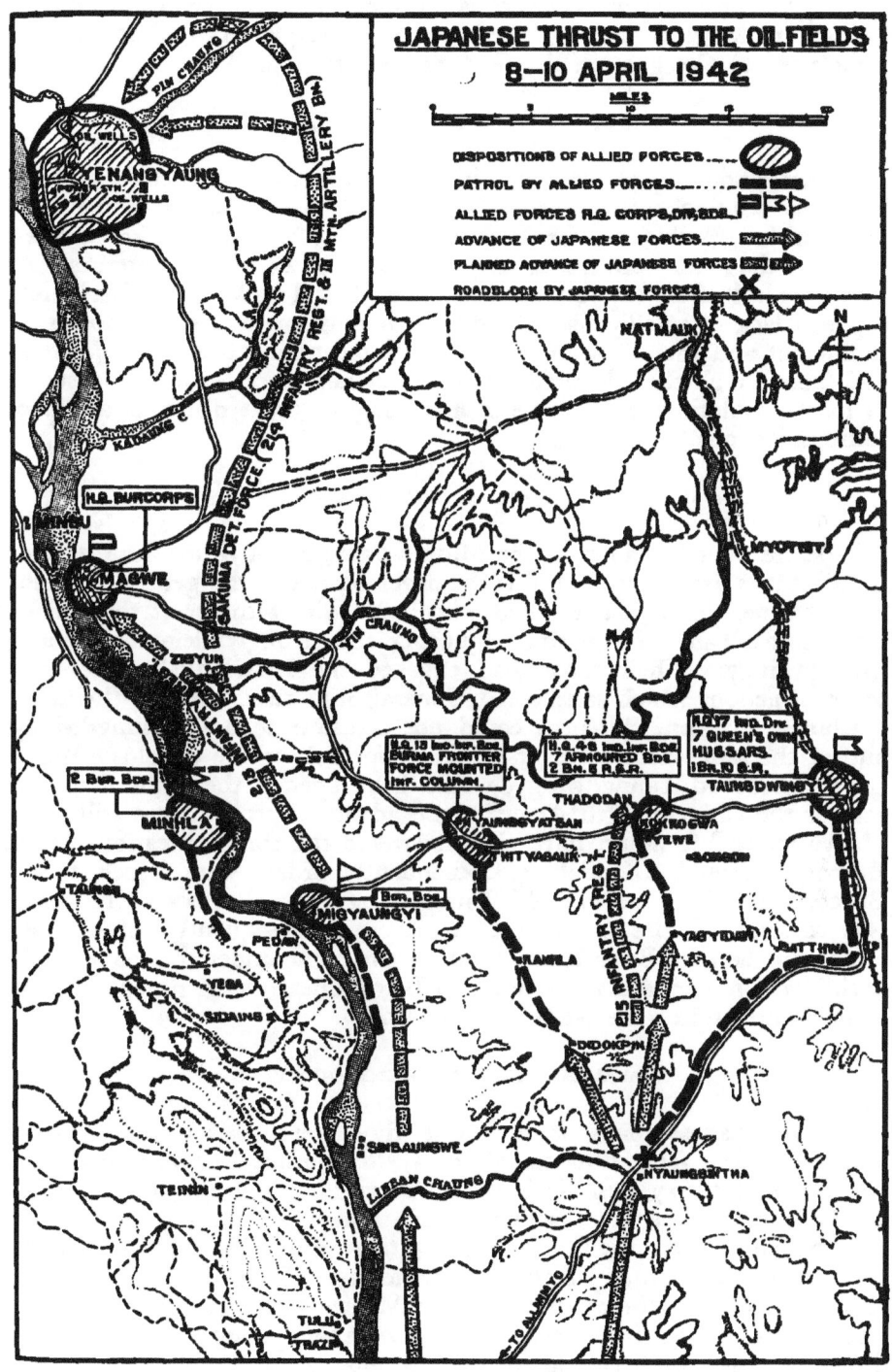

Chaung.[8] On 8 April, the Corps Headquarters moved from Taungdwingyi to Magwe. But by April 15 the Headquarters had again been transferred to Gwegyo, on the road Yenangyaung-Meiktila.

LACK OF AIR SUPPORT AND INTELLIGENCE

Throughout April Japanese aircraft continued to be active, and the Burcorps positions were frequently subjected to bombing and machine-gun attacks. Both Gen. Sir H. Alexander and the Corps Commander, when on the road, were frequently involved in some of these attacks. At that time lack of air support was keenly felt by all ranks. Another handicap was lack of intelligence. The local population was either hostile or indifferent and there was total lack of air reconnaissance. The Japanese had therefore all the advantages which a trained force, with the assistance of local population, could have in a country of great distances and poor communications.

GENERAL SITUATION

Before the operations on the Minhla-Taungdwingyi line are discussed in detail it is necessary to outline the development of the general situation at that time. The Japanese had launched a direct thrust at the oilfields up the east bank of the river, ignoring the strongly defended area of Taungdwingyi. Their forces had engaged the Indo-British forces in a series of actions which satisfied Lt.-General Slim that, without the aid of a Chinese division, Burcorps could not continue to hold Taungdwingyi and at the same time cover the direct approach to the oilfields. But to have abandoned Taungdwingyi would have opened the right flank and rear of the Chinese Fifth Army whose advanced troops were still south of Pyinmana. It would have also uncovered the communications of the Burcorps through Mandalay. Consequently orders were issued to the Burcorps on April 12 to hold Taungdwingyi at all costs. This order was received on the morning of April 13. Subsequently, orders were issued for the 48th Brigade and 7 Hussars to come under command of the 17th Division, and the 7th Armoured Brigade less one regiment to come under command of the 1st Burma Division.[7]

JAPANESE THRUST TO THE OILFIELDS

The Japanese plans at the same time were as follows: *Sakuma Detached Force (consisting mainly of 214th Infantry Regiment and IIIrd Mountain Artillery Battalion)* was to move ahead of the main column, outflank the Magwe positions and make a surprise attack on Yenangyaung from the north-east. *213th Infantry Regiment,* supported by 1 *Mountain Artillery Battalion* was to attack Magwe from the south. The occupation of the main position at Magwe was scheduled to coincide with the entry of *Sakuma Force* into Yenangyaung. *215th Infantry Regiment,* the Artillery unit of *24 MB* and the light-tank unit were to

---

[6] They were to be based at Minhla under command 2 Bur. Bde.
[7] General Alexander's *Despatch*, paras 30-32.

hold the Allied forces at Kokkogwa to protect the Division's flank. On April 13 a Japanese force of about two thousand, having passed through the Allied line, crossed the Pyin Chaung. It marched towards the oilfields. At the same time their pressure on the 1st Burma Division, south of Magwe, continued, and a wide gap was caused between the two Divisions. Through this gap further hostile forces struck north.[8]

Orders for the Destruction of Oilfields—April 14

Orders for the destruction of the Yenangyaung oilfields were issued by Lt.-General Alexander on the night of April 14. The necessary demolitions were extensive, requiring forty-eight hours for completion. They ended with the destruction of the power house which was carried out when the Japanese were on the northern outskirts of Yenangyaung,[9] and when the 1st Burma Division was still several miles south of that place.

With this general picture in mind it is easier to follow the particular operations carried out by Burcorps during this phase of the campaign.

Patrol Clashes—April 10

On April 10 a Burma Frontier Force mounted infantry column made contact with the Japanese at Didokpin about twelve miles south of Thityagauk. The patrol was ambushed and followed up to the vicinity of Kanhla. The strength of the hostile force was estimated at two companies.

The same day a patrol of the 7th Queen's Own Hussars with carriers of the 1st Battalion 10th Gurkha Rifles, moving south from Taungdwingyi to make contact with the observation screen found a block near Nyaungbintha at milestone 23 on the main road.[10] This indicated that the Japanese were thrusting north by tracks to the west of Taungdwingyi, the block being intended to prevent an outflanking movement down the road.

Later on the same day, three patrols of the 2nd Battalion 5th Royal Gurkha Rifles, sent out from the Kokkogwa position converged on Yagyidaw village, some seven miles to the south. In each case these patrols found in Yagyidaw a large number of troops who were taken by our men to be part of the Chinese force expected in the area. Officers speaking English greeted the Frontier Force Officers in seemingly friendly fashion. The result was that the whole of one patrol and part of another were captured by the Japanese.[11]

On the evening of April 11 patrols of the 48th Indian Infantry Brigade located, and were in contact with, the Japanese at Yewe and Songon about two miles south of the Kokkogwa position. The tanks burnt several villages to deny their use to the opposite force. Further west, units of the 13th Brigade had also been in action.

---

[8] In order to prepare for the next phase Japanese *33rd Division* concentrated at Allanmyo, in the early part of April for three days to re-equip and reorganise. The Division was reinforced by infantry under the command of an Infantry Group Command and a Light Tank Company (601/7785/H), p. 24.
[9] General Alexander's *Despatch*, para 32.
[10] Two tanks.
[11] Estimated at one Battalion—*War Diary*, 7 Armoured Brigade Group.

ACTION AT KOKKOGWA

Disposition of the 48th Indian Infantry Brigade

That night (April 11) the Japanese began an attack on 48th Indian Infantry Brigade which was heavily engaged for almost two days.[12] The Brigade position was astride the main road and based on the adjoining villages of Yakaingzu-Kokkogwa, south of the road. It also cut through the village of Thadodan, north of the road. This latter village was too large to be held entirely. Between the two villages, in the centre of the position, the ground rose in a small plateau where was located 2 Field Battery, less one troop, of the 1st Indian Field Regiment. The southwest corner of the position was entered by a bend of the Yaume Chaung. The stream bed was sandy and winding, covered with grass in places.

The western face of the perimeter was held by the combind Battalion 7th Gurkha Rifles with one detached company in a post on the road two miles to the west of Thadodan; the north by the 1st Battalion 4th P.W.O. Gurkha Rifles; and the south and east by the 2nd Battalion 5th Royal Gurkha Rifles, with an attached company of the 1st Battalion 3rd Q.A.O. Gurkha Rifles. The remainder of this last Battalion (Headquarters and one company) was in Taungdwingyi. The attached company of the 3rd Q.A.O. Gurkha Rifles held a post in Sonzu village, a mile south of the main position round Kokkogwa. A troop of the 2nd Battalion Royal Tank Regiment leaguered inside the perimeter, the remainder of the 7th Armoured Brigade being in harbour at Wetchangan, two miles to the east. Throughout the 48th Indian Infantry Brigade there was a general lack of signalling equipment which handicapped inter-communication and thus hampered the defence.

Shortly after dark hostile patrols worked up to the listening posts on the south side of the perimeter, and there was another movement, further to the west. Firing intensified at about midnight.

The Attack—April 12

By 0130 hours on April 12 an attack in considerable strength had developed, the main effort being down the Yaume Chaung. It started with automatic weapons and mortar fire duel. But soon after the forward elements of the 48th Brigade were driven back along the banks of the Chaung, hand grenades being freely used by both sides. The 2nd Battalion 5th Gurkha Rifles soon exhausted all its reserves, and the Japanese armed with light automatic weapons penetrated Kokkogwa village as far as the Brigade Headquarters area. The only reinforcements available were the Brigade Employment Platoon, one platoon of the 7th Gurkha Rifles, and another of the 1st Battalion 4th P.W.O. Gurkha Rifles. These were rushed up.

Shortly before 0300 hours one company of the 2nd Battalion 5th Royal Gurkha Rifles, counter-attacked and partly restored the position.[13]

---

[12] Brig. R. T. Cameron's account of the action at Kokkogwa. App. to the 48th Indian Infantry Brigade *War Diary*.

[13] *War Diary*, 2/5 G. G. Burcorps. 'G' Br. War Diary says, "the enemy was put to flight with heavy casualties. Captured enemy documents, gave order of Battle."

But the Japanese soon launched another violent attack on Thadodan village, held by one platoon of the 7th Gurkha Rifles. The detached company on the road to the west was recalled, but at the bridge across the Yaume Chaung it was heavily shelled and dispersed. The remnants of this company then counter-attacked Thadodan. They were met by light machine-gun fire and a shower of hand grenades from the eastern edge of the village. The fire was returned with effect, but the counter-attack failed with considerable loss. Advancing across the plateau east of Thadodan the Japanese reached the 1st Indian Field Regiment gun positions. They were flung back at the point of the bayonet. The guns were then swung round, Thadodan was shelled at point blank range, and the 7th Gurkha Rifles, reorganising, took up a new position on the western edge of the plateau.

By 0500 hours the situation had eased. It had been critical for some hours, and at the Brigade Headquarters all officers stood by as a bombing squad ready to fight on any sector. They had been busy detonating bombs from the brigade reserve.

Whilst the Japanese attack was in progress large numbers of motor vehicles were heard moving from east to west through Yewe village. A force was evidently by-passing the 48th Indian Infantry Brigade. Possibly it was the force afterwards reported to have crossed the Yin Chaung on April 13 and which appeared north of Yenangyaung on the evening of April 16.

The company of 3 Gurkha Rifles at Sonzu held out all night against a superior force, but at dawn it was attacked by Japanese tanks and infantry. Without anti-tank rifles or 'Molotov cocktail' bombs it was overrun and dispersed. Some stragglers regained the main position.

At first light on 13 April, the 1st Battalion 4th P.W.O. Gurkha Rifles dealt with the remaining snipers in Kokkogwa. The tanks with fighting patrols of the 2nd Battalion 5th Gurkha Rifles, moved up the Yaume Chaung. They caught several parties of the Japanese troops and found many of their dead lying scattered.

The Japanese were still in Thadodan, and a company of the 1st Battalion 4th P.W.O. Gurkha Rifles was commissioned to repulse them. But before the company could launch the attack, a scratch company or the combined battalion 7th Gurkha Rifles had successfully counter-attacked shortly after dawn and had cleared the village and inflicted heavy casualties on the Japanese. But it ran out of ammunition and was withdrawn by its commanding officer. Another move of the Japanese troops soon re-occupied the village and against this a company of the 1st Battalion 4th P.W.O. Gurkha Rifles was put into the attack with a Squadron of the 2nd Battalion Royal Tank Regiment. This attack was launched at 1300 hours. At least two Japanese companies broke out of Thadodan. One company was trapped in a nullah running into the Yaume Chaung. It was wiped out by the infantry and tanks. The other company scattered to the north and then came under fire from the tanks. Unfortunately the Gurkha casualties were not light, and two tanks were hit by artillery fire.

West of Thadodan near milestone 294, the Japanese had put down a road-block. It was cleared without difficulty by the 2nd Battalion

Royal Tank Regiment which then maintained a patrol up to the 13th Indian Infantry Brigade position at Thityagauk.

By 1500 hours the situation had been fully restored. The perimeter was shortened as units had sustained severe casualties, but the troops felt that they could continue to hold their own. That evening the Commander of the 48th Indian Infantry Brigade reported that he had only seven infantry companies and asked for reinforcements.

April 13

The Japanese still held positions north of Thadodan. At about 0100 hours that night they again attacked the southern sector. Firing became intense, but nowhere was the line breached and by 0030 hours the engagement was broken off by the Japanese.

On the morning of April 13 the fighting patrols were active. A patrol of 2nd Battalion 5th Royal Gurkha Rifles came upon some Japanese in Yewe village and opened fire with automatic weapons, scattering them in great confusion. Later the village was burnt. A 3" mortar, manned by a volunteer detachment, moved out 1200 yards into the "no man's land" in broad daylight and stalked a Japanese gun, an unusual and daring feat. A direct hit was made. It then stalked a hostile platoon in Tewa, its opening mortar landing fairly amongst it. This episode greatly heartened the troops. At Songon the Japanese were kept subdued by a patrol of the 1st Battalion 4th P.W.O. Gurkha Rifles.

Hostile aircraft made three attacks on the Brigade positions that day. Incendiary bombs set Kokkogwa alight, much mortar and other ammunition being destroyed. Casualties amongst men in the slit trenches were however, negligible.

The 1st Battalion 10th Gurkha Rifles arrived as a reinforcement just before dusk. One rifle company went into immediate reserve in each of the three perimeter sectors, the fourth company being held as brigade reserve. The night passed quietly. Activity was shifting west and north.

ACTION IN THE 1ST BURMA DIVISION SECTOR

We may now turn to the 1st Burma Brigade and the 13th Indian Brigade which had also been fully engaged from April 11 to 13. These two Brigades had been directed by the 1st Burma Division to destroy a hostile force in the area Kanhla-Alebo. For this purpose the 1st Burma Brigade was to concentrate about Kandan by first light on 11 April and to advance on Alebo. One of its battalions was to hold the high ground about Kunon Taung. At the same time the 13th Brigade with its headquarters at Thityagauk was to maintain an observation line about Inbingan while one battalion was concentrated about Nyaungbingyi to attack south-west towards Alebo.

The 1st Burma Brigade had arrived in Migyaungyi on 9 April. Its disposition was as follows: the 2nd Battalion 7th Rajput Regiment remained south of Migyaungyi with its "C" Company at Sinbaungive, fourteen miles down the river. Leaving this company of the Rajputs and FF5 to watch the river area, the Brigade concentrated at Kandan on 11 April at 1730 hours. The 1st Battalion Burma Rifles had moved in position at Kunon Taung, while the 5th Battalion Burma Rifles and the 2nd Battalion 7th Rajput Regiment (less "C" Company) had moved close to Alebo by the evening.

The 13th Indian Brigade was in contact with the Japanese north of Alebo. The 1st Battalion 18th Royal Garhwal Rifles held a perimeter at Point 558 east of Powe and was supported by 2 Mountain Battery. The 1st Battalion Royal Inniskilling Fusiliers was in position to the west of the Garhwalis south of milestone 300 on the main road. On the evening of 11 April, "C" squadron of the 2nd Battalion Royal Tank Regiment had also joined it.

On 11 April, the Garhwalis had located a large force of the Japanese in a village one and half miles south of their position, but a projected attack on it was cancelled by the Brigade Headquarters. Meanwhile, the patrols of the Inniskilling Fusiliers were in contact with the forward Japanese elements and several skirmishes occurred in which the Battalion suffered severe casualties. It had also observed a large hostile force moving west through Latpanwy. At 1930 hours the 5th Battalion Burma Rifles was ordered to clear Alebo which it did in the dark of the night. The Japanese had taken to hurried flight leaving considerable equipment and important papers.

The same night the Japanese also attacked the southern sector of the perimeter held by the Garhwalis. They had used light automatic and rifle fire, but could not penetrate the sector. Later, they worked round to the western and northern sides of the position, but had to abandon their efforts at 0330 hours. No contact could be made with them by the dawn patrols, though later in the day a Japanese force was observed in a position overlooking the main road. One company of the 1st Battalion 18th Royal Garhwal Rifles was moved out in the afternoon and posted west of Powe to cover the road.

The continued advance of the Japanese to the east bank of the river led to the shifting of the 1st Burma Brigade from the Alebo area. It was evident on 12 April that a considerable hostile force was concentrated in the valleys north of Alebo, and it was likely that portions of this force were by-passing the 1st Burma Division positions by night and moving further north across the main road. At the same time threat to Migyaungyi had made it necessary to protect that area, as it was covered only by C Company of the 2nd Battalion 7th Rajput Regiment and F.F.S. Consequently, the 1st Burma Brigade was ordered to move to Kunon Taung, the 1st Battalion Burma Rifles being ordered to shift to Migyaungyi, for which orders had been sent direct from the Divisional Headquarters. These orders had been miscarried and it was not before 0300 hours on 13 April that the Battalion could carry out the move.

On the same day, the 2nd Battalion King's Own Yorkshire Light Infantry which had been protecting the oilfields at Yenangyaung was ordered to move to milestone 300 on the main road to reinforce the 13th Brigade leaving the oilfields to the depleted 1st Battalion the Gloucestershire Regiment.

On the night of 12/13 April the Japanese occupied Migyaungyi as a result of a surprise attack on the outposts. Posing as men of the Burma Rifles they secured entry and soon overran the defences. In the morning

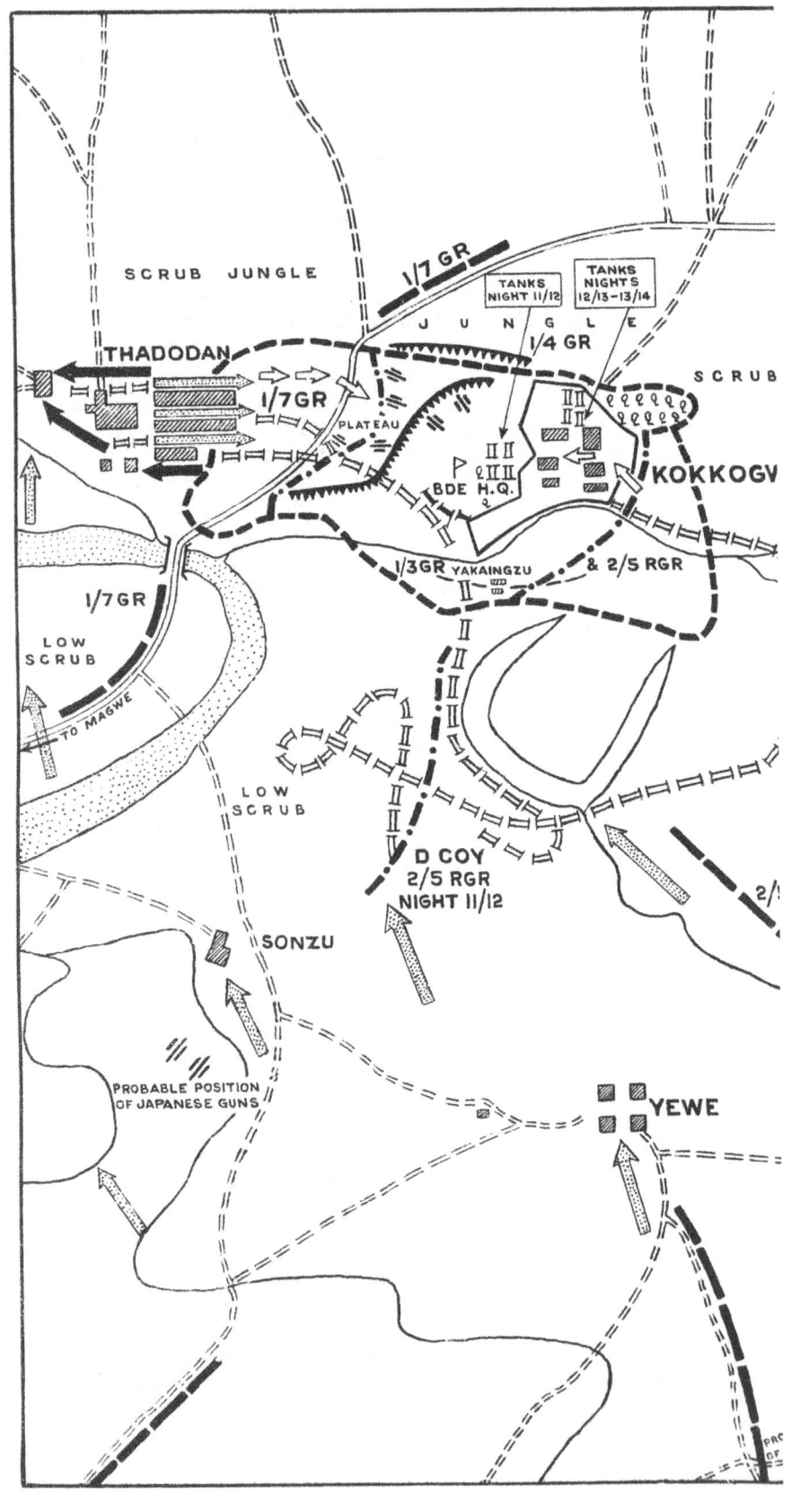

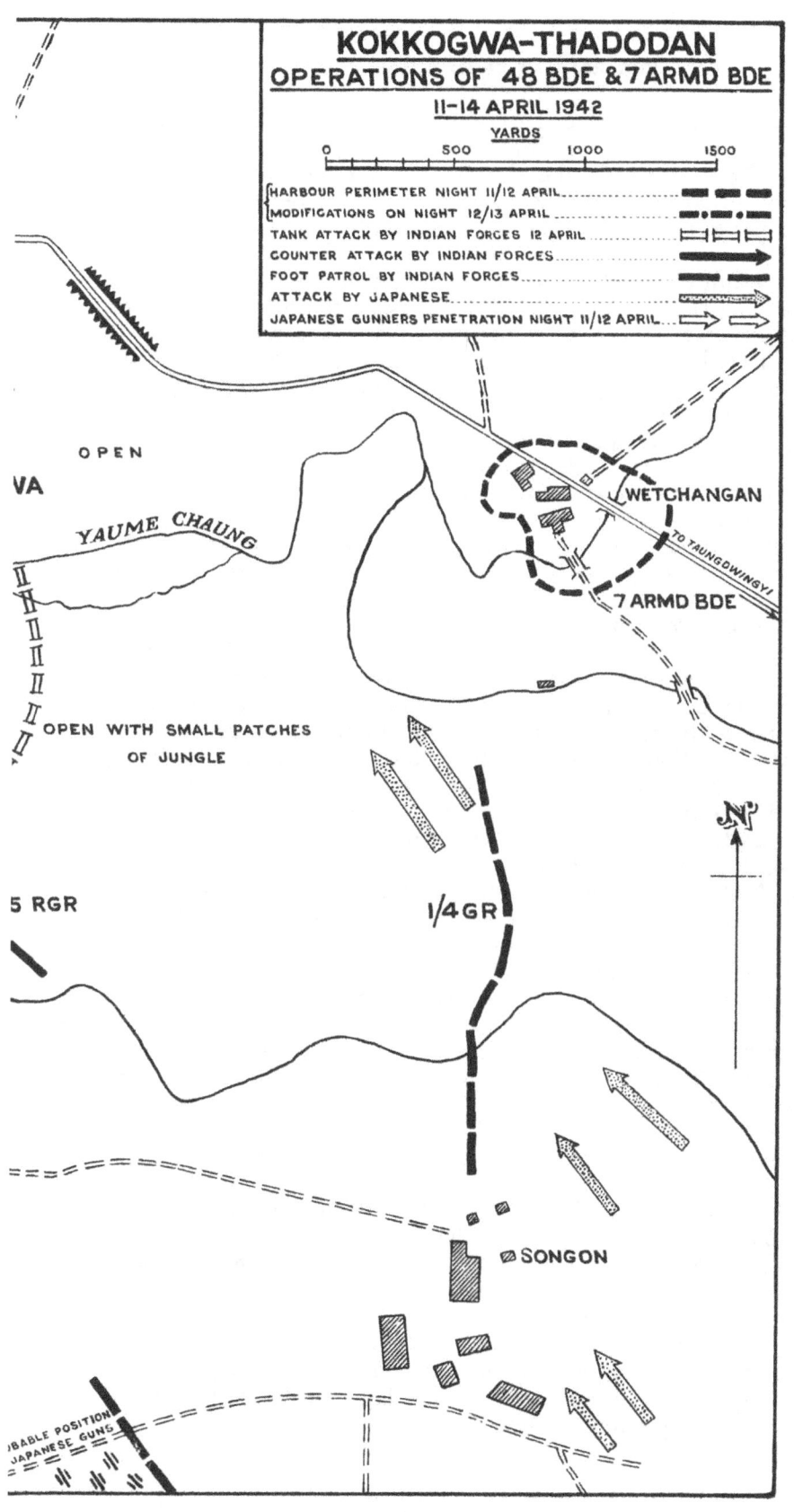

of 13 April, when the 1st Battalion Burma Rifles approached the outskirts of the town at 0600 hours, the Commanding Officer went to the Headquarters of F.F.5 to ascertain the situation. No sooner had he arrived there than he was attacked by the Japanese and captured. But later he escaped. At the same time, the Japanese attacked the Battalion forces to the south of the town, which were split up. A Company was cut off from the main body and eventually fought its way north. The main body of the Battalion however, assembled in a hollow square north of the road, but it came under heavy fire as it became light. A counter-attack was organised by it which was successful in dislodging the Japanese from the F.F.5 headquarters and the recapture of some equipment including a 3" mortar. But the ammunition was running low, the Battalion had been considerably disorganised and the hostile force was moving round the east flank and to the north. Hence the Battalion withdrew to the northeast at about 1100 hours and the movement was carried out in small parties under heavy mortar and machine-gun fire.

At the same time, the 5th Battalion Burma Rifles was attacked at Kunon Taung by small parties of Japanese troops, but no serious effort was made to press the advance, although firing continued till 1100 hours. These events compelled the 1st Burma Brigade to withdraw north to Tebingan and later to milestone 309 on the Taungdwingyi-Magwe road.

These reverses at Migyaungye completely exposed the flank on the east bank of the Irrawady. Hence the Corps Commander decided to bring, from across the river, the 7th Battalion Burma Rifles and to move down the 1st Battalion the Cameronians and the Mounted Infantry Detachment of the Burma Frontier Force from Magwe to Myingun, which was to be immediately occupied by the very weak 2nd Battalion Koyli. Eventually the sector was to be covered by the 1st Burma Brigade. The other troops could not advance to Myingun and its initial defence devolved on Koyli alone. Simultaneously, the 13th Brigade was to move back to Yin Chaung after occupying a lay-back about Saingyya to assist the movement of the 1st Burma Brigade. The 7th Armoured Brigade less 7th Queen's Own Hussars had also been ordered to the Yin Chaung area. The 13th Brigade commenced withdrawal at about 1900 hours on 13 April.

It was then perfectly clear that the Japanese were advancing direct upon the oilfields, and it was necessary to concentrate additional strength to meet this thrust.

THE NEW DISPOSITION TO MEET THE THREAT TO THE OILFIELDS

By 14 April a wide gap had developed between the two Divisions, the 17th Indian Division and the 1st Burma Division. To ensure the defence of Taungdwingyi area, the 48th Brigade withdrew to that place from Kokkogwa, and the 16th Brigade was moved to Natmauk. The 17th Indian Division was, henceforth, to be supplied by the route Kyaukpandaung-Natmauk-Taungdwingyi. The distance between Taungdwingyi and the 13th Brigade position was some twenty-five miles and the road leading to Magwe was cut by the Japanese troops. Some of these parties had also penetrated further north.

On 14 April, the 1st Burma Division issued an operation order for the occupation, the same day, of a defensive area about Magwe and Pado, but excluding the high ground about the two villages of Minywa. The 1st Burma Brigade was to hold the Yin Chaung about Pado with the 13th Brigade on its left. The 7th Armoured Brigade (less 7th Q.O.H.) was to form part of the divisional reserve, being stationed west of milestone 322 on the main road. The remainder of the reserve (Magforce) stationed in Magwe comprised 5 Mountain Battery the 1st Battalion the Cameronians, and the 7th and 12th Battalions Burma Rifles.

It was intended by Burcorps to hold the Yin Chaung position as long as possible and to withdraw only under pressure. A halt there had been made extremely desirable by the exhaustion of troops. The next defensive line could be only on the Pin Chaung, north of Yenangyaung over forty miles by road, as water was not available elsewhere.

Throughout 14 April, the 2nd Battalion Koyli was engaged with the Japanese and the Divisional Headquarters were unable to send any help. Ultimately the Commanding officer knowing of the decision to hold the Yin Chaung, moved north, under-crossed the Chaung and the battalion re-assembled near the 1st Burma Brigade Headquarters at milestone 324. Later it moved to Magwe for rest.

Yin Chaung position

On the Yin Chaung position the right sector of the 1st Burma Brigade was held by the 5th Battalion Burma Rifles disposed about Pado village. On the left, the 2nd Battalion 7th Rajput Regiment was in position covering the village of Zigyun. The 1st Battalion Burma Rifles was in reserve. Further to the norh-east the line was continued by the 13th Brigade, covering the road into Magwe; the brigade had been joined by the 5th Battalion 1st Punjab Regiment from the 2nd Burma Brigade, and it occupied the sector adjoining the 1st Burma Brigade.

At about 0100 hours on 16 April an attack along the whole front of the 1st Burma Brigade began. The Japanese employed their usual night tactics and sought, by the use of tracer ammunition and cracker gun fire, to disorganise the defence and to compel it to disclose its position. Two ambushes were laid by the 5th Battalion Burma Rifles in the Yin Chaung and the Japanese walked into both of them and suffered severely. This made them cautious and later they worked round the right flank of the Battalion where the Karen Company was in position. This company soon gave way and before it could be reformed the Japanese had infiltrated up to the position of the battalion reserve. At the same time on the front of the left company of the Battaltion the Japanese had put in three bayonet charges two of which were thrown back but the third penetrated the position. These attacks disintegrated the 5th Battalion Burma Rifles.

About the same time, an attack was launched on the 2nd Battalion 7th Rajput Regiment, the forward company of which was quickly overrun. The Battalion had to withdraw at 0145 hours and the Japanese were in occupation of Zigyun village, thus causing a gap between that Battalion and the 5th Battalion Burma Rifles positions. The Japanese soon pressed round the left flank of the 2nd Battalion 7th Rajput Regiment which was

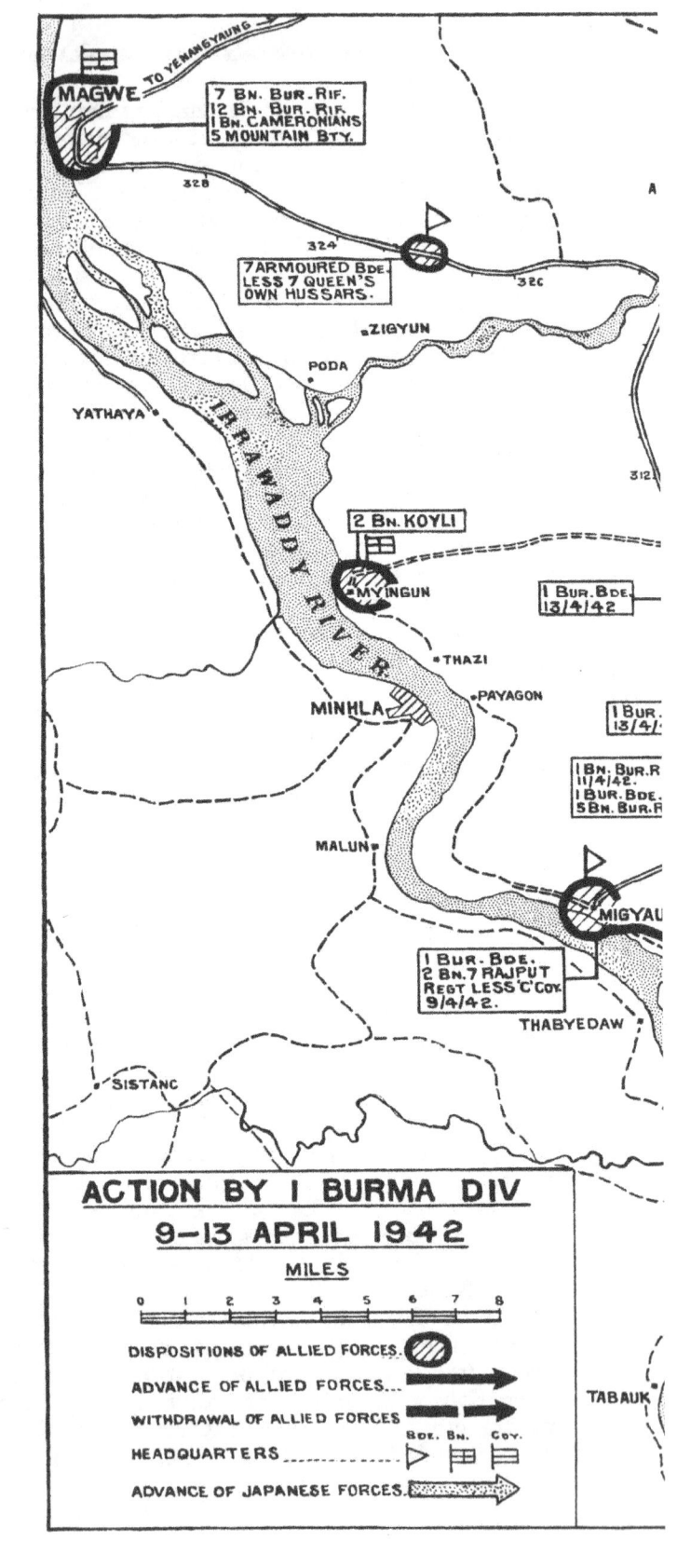

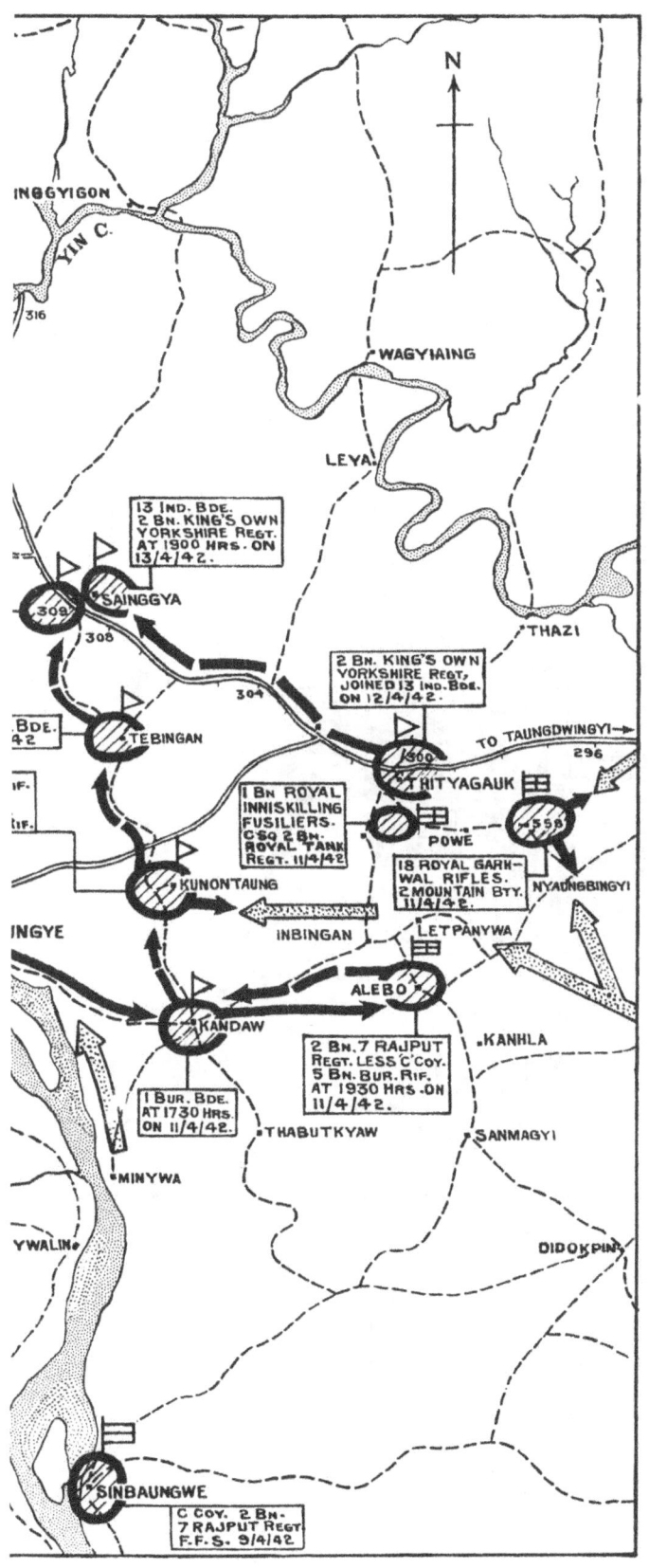

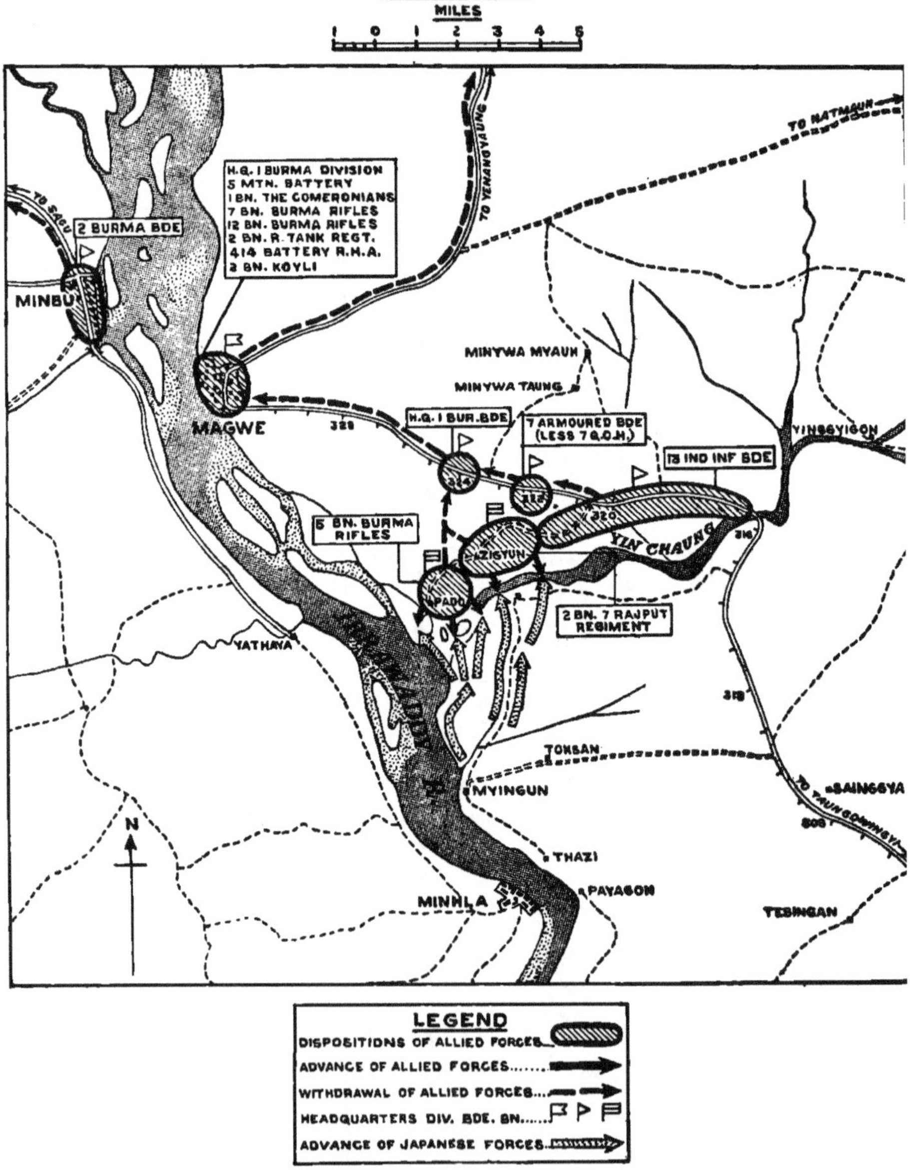

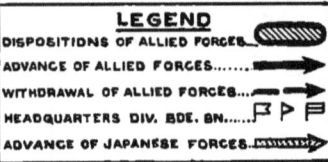

surrounded by about 0600 hours, and soon heavy mortar and machine gun fire was directed on it from all sides. This compelled the Commanding Officer to withdraw his men towards the main road.

Withdrawal

The 5th Battalion Burma Rifles had already been withdrawn at 0600 hours and the 1st Battalion Burma Rifles formed the rear-guard to cover the considerably disorganised Brigade. It was joined by the 2nd Battalion Koyli which had been hurriedly brougt from Magwe. It took up a position south of milestone 324 to cover the road and the Brigade Headquarters and to permit the passage of the motor transport through Magwe on the road for Yenangyaung. The transport had come under brisk mortar fire from the Japanese south of the road but the road was held until the transport had been secured out of the danger zone.

Subsequently, the 1st Burma Brigade and the 13th Brigade were ordered to withdraw across country to the Magwe-Yenangyaung road, the movement being initiated about 0930 hours on 16 April. Their withdrawal was not closely followed up. The Headquarters of the 1st Burma Division had also moved out of Magwe at mid-day immediately afterwards.

The 2nd Battalion Royal Tank Regiment supported by 414 Battery RHA had spent a busy day in covering Magwe and the withdrawal of the two brigades to the Yenangyaung road. They had lost 2 tanks but had inflicted considerable casualties on the Japanese. Eventually at 1800 hours when the evacuation of Magwe was completed and the troops had gained the Yenangyaung road elements of the 7th Armoured Brigade began their withdrawal to an area some 5 miles north of the Pin Chaung. One squadron of the 2nd Battalion Royal Tank Regiment remained to protect the 1st Burma Division.

The withdrawal of the brigades had been harassed by low-flying hostile aircraft which subjected the troops to machine-gun and bombing attacks. In the evening the 13th Brigade halted 2 miles south of the Kadaung Chaung whilst the 1st Burma Brigade was 2 miles north of the Chaung. Magforce acting as rear guard covered the road junction near milestone 348.

To meet the growing threat to the oilfields it had been intended to withdraw the whole of the 2nd Burma Brigade to the east bank of the Irrawaddy. The 5th Battalion 1st Punjab Regiment and the 7th Battalion Burma Rifles did in fact cross the river but the hurried evacuation of Magwe led to a cancellation of further moves. This Brigade in withdrawing up to the west bank did not seriously contact the Japanese forces. On 16 April the Brigade withdrew from Minbu opposite Magwe and on the night of 16/17 April it was in the Saqu area. At that time it was composed of the 2nd and 8th Battalions Burma Rifles and F.F.8.

On the night of April 16, the 17th Indian Division with the 7th Queen's Own Hussars, one troop of 414 Battery RHA and the 1st Battalion West Yorkshire Regiment remained disposed about Taungdwingyi (the 48th and 63rd Brigades) and Natmauk (16th Brigade). It was ordered by Lieut.-General Slim to operate strongly from both these places against the right flank of the Japanese following the 1st Burma Division.

Lieut.-General Slim had been offered assistance by General Stilwell, and the Chinese 30th Division then in Mandalay was to co-operate in relieving hostile pressure.

The Indo-British forces were opposed by the Japanese *33rd Division* which was assisted by a considerable number of the Burmans. The Japanese had, during the month of April, received considerable seaborne reinforcements through the port of Rangoon which made it possible for them to add weight to their attacks on the Chinese Fifth Army, and to initiate a thrust through Karenni and then north of Maweli against the widely dispersed Chinese Sixth Army. The Japanese were largely assisted by the local population and had accurate information of the disposition of the Allied forces. The Indo-British forces, on the other hand, were faced with a populace either hostile or persuaded into a policy of non-co-operation by fear of the advancing Japanese. Combined with the total lack of air reconnaisance this made the obtaining of information by them most difficult.

Of this phase of the campaign General Alexander in his despatch remarked that the operations "illustrate clearly the advantage which the initiative confers on a highly trained force which has assistance of the local population in a country of great distances and poor communications. The successes which the Japanese gained cannot all be ascribed to their superior training and, at this time, superior morale."[14]

---

[14] General Alexander's *Despatch*, para 31.

CHAPTER XX

Race for the Oilfields

FIGHTING IN THE YENANGYAUNG AREA

Denial Schemes

Yenangyaung which is situated on the east bank of the Irrawaddy is the main oilfield of Burma containing nearly 5,000 wells in an area of seven by two miles. It contained also three gasoline plants which, prior to their destruction, were producing one half of Burma's supply of petrol. It also had the largest power station in Burma, and a vast quantity of stores of all natures.[1]

The heavy requirements of the Allied forces and essential services demanded the continued production of petrol until the last possible moment. At the same time it was imperative that the use of the Yenangyaung, Chauk and adjacent oilfields and their very elaborate plant be denied to the Japanese. The denial schemes were carried out by Mr. W. L. Forster who had so thoroughly planned the destruction of the oil refineries in the neighbourhood of Rangoon. With Mr. Forster were again associated the staffs of the companies concerned, and in the work to be caried out the paramount object was the demolition of all vital installations. Private interests were in no way permitted to come into conflict with the larger issue.

As oil was necessary, production of petrol continued even while and after demolition work was carried out on 9 April on wells and plant not actually required. At this stage the denial schemes could not be kept an absolute secret, the consequent problem of keeping labour which was largely Indian was solved by providing for organised evacuation. The non-essential population was removed as early as 12 March. This and the definite assurance of evacuation to India had the excellent effect of stabilizing Indian labour. Thanks to this arrangement, the production of petrol until the 'E' (Evacuation) signal was given was at no time seriously affected.[2] At the same time all preparations for final demolition were made. Owing to the extensive nature of these final demolitions it was considered that at least 48 hours were required for their completion.

Demolitions Carried out—April 15

At 1800 hours on 13 April the evacuation signal was received. On 15 April at 1300 hours the Warden of the oilfields received from the Commander of the Burcorps the 'D' (Demolition) signal for Yenangyaung, the 'E' signal having been received previously. The power station was excluded from the operation of the order. By that time a very

---

[1] *Report on the Effect of Denial and Demolition Schemes in Burma*, 601/3/10/H, p. 20.
[2] On the 'E' signal, production was to cease, and all labour was to be evacuated leaving behind only those Europeans and Anglo-Indians who were required for demolition. On the 'D' signal demolition was to be carried out.

considerable amount of denial work had already been completed on the instructions and responsibility of Mr. Forster who felt himself justified in taking this step by the implications of a conversation which he had held with the Corps Commander on his way through Yenangyaung the day before. This act was justified by later events. Therefore, little work remained to be done. The demolition parties were able to leave for Chauk by boat or car at 1400 hours. Mr. Forster and one or two of his assistants remained behind for the demolition of the Power Station. As the parties left for Chauk the field resounded with the sound of explosions, the whole of the tank farm with millions of gallons of crude oil was set on fire with flames shooting up well over 500 feet. Wells, plant and vital installations were burning everywhere and the sky was darkened by a vast pall of smoke. The sight was most awe-inspiring and gave a fitting proof of the completeness of the denial.[3]

On the evening of 16 April a message was sent to the Commander, Central Area Yenangyaung to destroy the Power Station.[4] This was begun at 2359 hours. Next morning it was found that the damage was satisfactory except that the boiler house had failed to flood satisfactorily. During the night the Japanese infiltrated into Twingon, north of Yenangyaung, and occupied Thonzechauk village on the other side of the Pin Chaung and established road-blocks on the way north to Gwegyo. The Power Station had thus been destroyed just in time.

Japanese Air Attacks—11 and 12 April

In this destruction the Japanese had no hand. There were of course two raids on the environs of Yenangyaung, one on 11 April over Twingon village at the north end of the oilfields. High explosives and incendiaries were dropped and the whole of the village was devastated. The village, however, contained nothing of military importance. The raid might have been made in order to bomb the junction where the various roads through and around the oilfield converged on to the road to the Pin Chaung crossing, the main road leading from the field, or it might have been because the day before it had been decided to fire the stock tanks at Sadaing at the south end. On 12 April there was another raid, this time aimed at the steamer ghats at Nyaunghla. About a dozen anti-personnel bombs were dropped. A number of steamers were hit by splinters and three people were killed. As regards the bombing of Twingon, it has been suggested that Japanese aircraft undertook 'directional' bombing and that the fires so caused guided columns striking across country. This may account for the bombing of Twingon.

Saboteurs

Another feature of this period in Yenangyaung was the burning of the town and village areas by saboteurs. It is significant, however, that

---

[3] The two Thakins who came out from Burma in July 1942 stated that at Yenangyaung the Japanese were endeavouring to effect repairs by clearing away the wreckage of oil wells but the head of the Japanese Intelligence Hira Oka had been heard to say that there was no possibility of obtaining oil from Yenangyaung for the next six months.

[4] *Report on the Effect of Denial and Demolition Schemes in Burma*, 601/3/10/H, p. 21.

no barrack buildings for oilfield employees were destroyed. This fact would seem to indicate that these fires were inspired by the Japanese.

Forces at Yenangyaung

In Yenangyaung itself there still remained, as oilfield guard, headquarters and one company of the depleted 1st Battalion the Gloucestershire Regiment. The Battalion was without automatic weapons or mortars. Its rifle company was at Chauk. Beyond the Pin Chaung were certain Burma Frontier Force units and 8 Heavy Anti-Aircraft Battery, R.A. During the work of demolition the garrison in the area was therefore small, and by what a narrow margin of time the complete destruction of the oilfield had been safely effected was now to be proved.

Engagement North of Pin Chaung—16 April

On the evening of 16 April when men of the Anti-Aircraft Battery were bathing in the Pin Chaung the gunner acting as their armed sentry was set upon by what was believed at that time to be a gang of dacoits. The gunner was killed. Local villagers were then rounded up by the Gloucestershire troops. There was no suspicion that any Japanese were concerned in the incident, although there is now little doubt that they were responsible for the attack.

During the day the Rear Headquarters of the 1st Burma Division together with all motor transport that could be spared had crossed the Pin Chaung and come safely to its new area at Gwegyo. That night the 7th Armoured Brigade also passed north through the flaming desolation of Yenangyaung. Crossing the Pin Chaung its leading elements halted at 2300 hours to harbour for the night beside the main road some five miles beyond the Chaung. The greater part of the 2nd Battalion Royal Tank Regiment was then still on the road just north of the ford. Traffic was proceeding normally. Without warning, fire from a light automatic weapon was opened on a station-wagon at a point about two miles beyond the Pin Chaung. The vehicle was set alight. A tank went forward to investigate, and as it approached the burning wagon it was hit by a shell or grenade and was disabled. At the same time machine-gun fire opened on the rear of the column. F.Fs 1, 3, and 4 were stationed close by, and F.F. 4 was ordered to sweep the ground east of the road, the direction from which the hostile fire had come. Meanwhile, the Japanese had set fire to the damaged tank. Some distance south of the obstruction there was forming a long line of stationary traffic. Throughout the night there were bursts of hostile light automatic and cracker fire. F.F. 4 failed to establish contact with the hostile force.

A section of 8 Heavy Anti-Aircraft Battery, R.A., in position near the ford, was surrounded by the Japanese. Most of the gunners were unarmed, there being only a few rifles with the Battery, and were unable to offer any effective resistance. Later the majority of those captured made their escape and the guns were brought out by tanks.

Twingon Road-block—16 April

During the night other hostile parties were operating south of the Pin Chaung. Their patrols penetrated the northern portion of

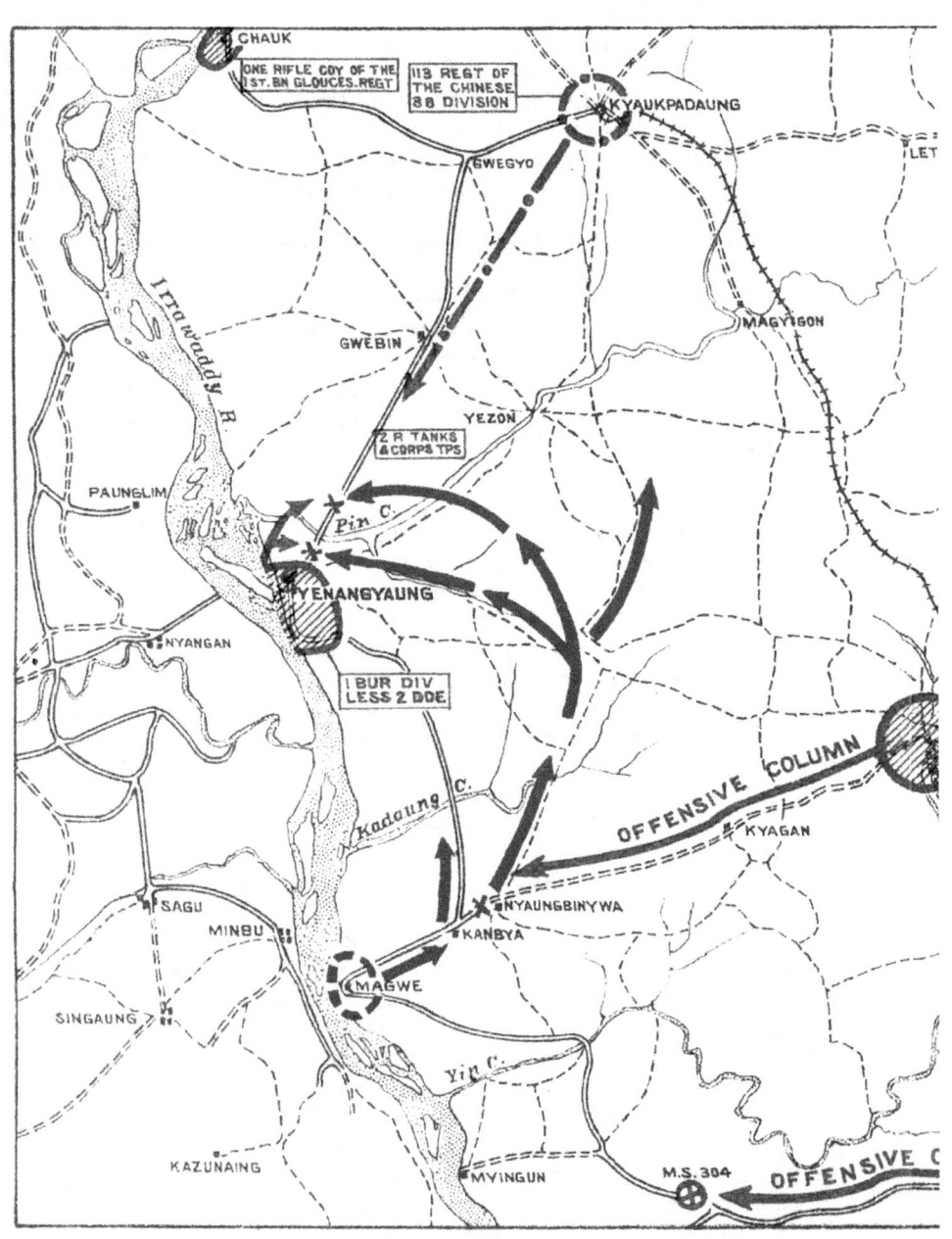

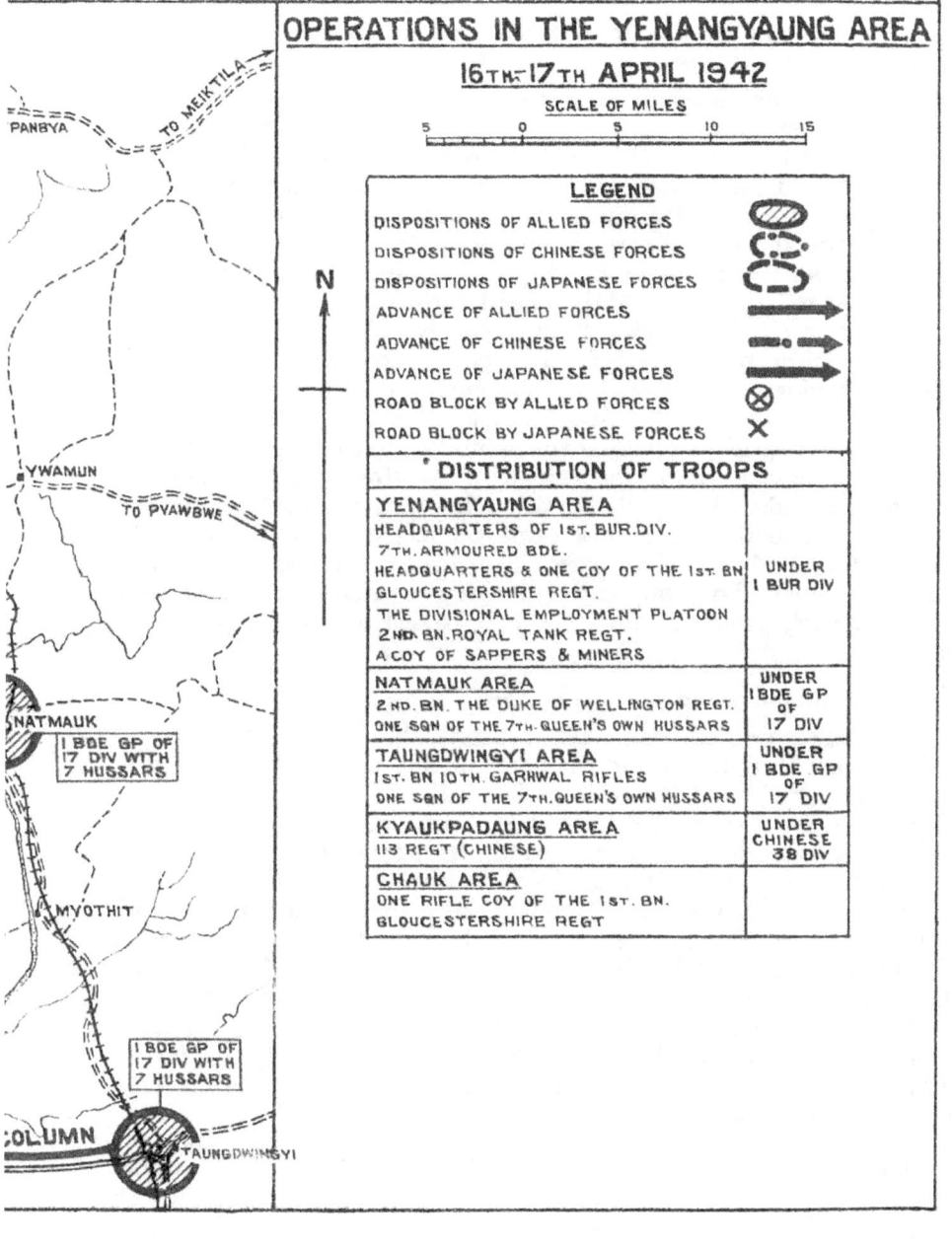

Yenangyaung itself, whilst a second road-block was put down in Twingon village. Here, south of the Pin Chaung, upon the few men of the Gloucestershire Regiment fell the whole task of meeting the Japanese thrust. They were attacked and compelled to fall back through the town.

Headquarters of the 1st Burma Division on the Southern Outskirts of Yenangyaung—17 April

A report of the situation at Yenangyaung first reached the Headquarters of 1st Burma Division near the Kadaung Chaung at 0200 hours on 17 April. Order for the following morning's march to Yenangyaung had already been issued, Magforce being detailed as advance guard. The time of departure for the Headquarters was now put forward, and at first light Maj.-General Bruce Scott left for the oilfields. Arriving there he was informed of the situation by Brigadier Roughton, Commander of the Central Area. At first Maj.-General Bruce Scott established his Headquarters at the Nyaunghla Stud Farm, but shortly moved to the road junction near milestone 358. The only troops then available, the Divisional Employment Platoon and a company of Sappers and Miners, were put in to reinforce the weak company of the 1st Battalion the Gloucestershire Regiment covering the south of Yenangyaung. Nothing further could be done until the arrival of Magforce, and no offensive action could be taken before the Division had concentrated in the area that night. As soon as Magforce came up it took over the defensive line. The Royal Marine river patrol had arrived the previous evening. It was subjected to bombing and machine-gun attacks and had come under mortar fire from the town. But it passed out of range without damage.

Attack on Twingon Road-block—17 April

Meanwhile steps had been taken to attack the Japanese north of the Pin Chaung at first light. From the north of the road-block the company of the West Yorkshire Regiment together with the half squadron of the 2nd Battalion Royal Tank Regiment then with the Headquarters of the 7th Armoured Brigade were to strike south, whilst the tanks and F.F. units on the other side of the block attacked from the other direction. The attack went on from both sides of the block as planned, and was supported from the north by 'E' Troop 414 Battery, R.H.A. One gun of 8 Heavy Anti-Aircraft Battery, R.A. also fired over open sights at hostile parties as they appeared. Advancing south astride the road the company of the West Yorkshire Regiment cleared its way with grenades, and supported by mortar fire reached its objective. This was a ridge through which the road ran in a cutting. Owing to the unsuitability of the ground the tanks had been unable to take part in this advance.

Road-block Cleared

From the south F.F. 1 met opposition on both sides of the road. On the west a platoon of F.F. 3 and tanks dealt with the Japanese post, and an attack with tanks was then put in from the west across the road. The Japanese fell back. F.F. units followed up to a line about eight hundred yards to the east of the road. Here they were under mortar and small arms fire, but the block had been cleared.⁵ By 1030 hours traffic on the road began to move north, but about one hundred vehicles had been abandoned by their drivers who had made them unserviceable. Subsequently many of these vehicles were destroyed in a bombing attack by hostile aircraft.⁶

Road-blocks Re-established—Night 17/18 April

The road-block at Twingon had been cleared, but this by no means put an end to Japanese activity. Attempts were made by them to turn the eastern flank of the Burcorps position on the ridge in the road-block area, whilst other parties remained along the banks of the Pin Chaung where they busily consolidated their positions. They concentrated round the ford. In the evening a column of about one thousand men was observed moving south from the ford and was effectively shelled by 414 Battery, R.H.A. In the night, however, the road-blocks were re-established.

Decision to Employ Chinese Troops to Break the Northern Road-block

"Meanwhile 113th Regiment of the Chinese 38th Division had been moved from Mandalay to Kyaukpadaung and placed under command of Burcorps."⁷ In view of the situation it had been decided to employ two Regiments of the 38th Division there, and these Regiments were being hurried forward. As they had no artillery the services of 414 Battery, R.H.A. were placed at the disposal of Maj.-General Sun. It was arranged that the Chinese with a squadron of the 2nd Battalion Royal Tank Regiment should attack the line of the Pin Chaung on the morning of 18 April.⁸

March of 1st Burma Division to Yenangyaung

Throughout the day (17 April) the fatigued units of the 1st Burma Division had been marching north towards Yenangyaung under most exhausting conditions. The heat was intense, there was no water, and the road was shadeless and very dusty. The men knew that ahead of them the Japanese held the Pin Chaung crossing. Hostile aircraft kept the force under constant observation and carried out frequent bombing and machine-gun attacks. The sight of burnt-out vehicles and the complete lack of any support by the British air forces was disheartening.⁹ However, the Japanese air arm did not escape without loss during this period. For the four days ending 19 April, 'B' Section of 3 Indian Light Anti-Aircraft Battery alone claimed to have hit seven aircraft. Several of these were seen falling.

The 1st Burma Brigade with a Squadron of the 2nd Battalion Royal

---

⁵ The Japanese moved East.
⁶ "2 Royal Tank Regiment left one Squadron on the ridge where the Japanese had been patrolling to south and east. The problem was how best to assist 1st Burma Division to break through with their transport. A wireless set had been sent back to Burcorps to keep them informed of the situation and this set with our 7th Armoured Brigade Group's links at Burma Division and our own rear link were the only communications existing between Burcorps and Burdiv. Without these wireless sets the situation would have been quite impossible." *War Diary*, 7th Armoured Brigade Group for 17 April.
⁷ General Alexander's *Despatch*, para 34.
⁸ *War Diary*, 7th Armoured Brigade Group, for 17 March.
⁹ So the Burdiv were too tired to make an attempt at break-through that day.

Tank Regiment and its attached company of the West Yorkshire Regiment formed the rear-guard. The last elements of this did not arrive south of Yenangyaung until after midnight. These troops had not been followed up by the Japanese even though *33rd Division's* main forces had entered Magwe on 17th April. It was only on 19 April that the divisional headquarters advanced to Magwe and *213th Infantry Regiment* was ordered to proceed to Yenangyaung where it assisted in the transportation of the *Harada Detailed Force* to Yenangyaung.

DISPOSITION OF 1ST BURMA DIVISION ON 17 APRIL

The rations of the 1st Burma Division were scarce, and it was absolutely essential that men and transport animals should have water. Consequently the force was concentrated south of Yenangyaung as near the river as possible. The 13th Indian Infantry Brigade was in the area around milestone 360. South of it between Sadaing and Yonzeik was Magforce, whilst the 1st Burma Brigade was south of the road junction at milestone 358.

PLANS FOR A CO-ORDINATED ATTACK FROM NORTH AND SOUTH—18 APRIL

A Signals detachment of the 17th Armoured Brigade was with the Headquarters of the 1st Burma Division and this furnished Maj.-General Bruce Scott with his only wireless link with the Burcorps. By this means he was able to speak with Lieut.-General Slim, and late on the night of 17 April plans were made to co-ordinate an attack with that to be carried out north of the Pin Chaung by the Chinese.[10] These latter were to be halted on the Chaung to avoid the possibility of their being confused with the Japanese troops. That this was a very real danger was demonstracted more than once during the next two days when the Japanese seized every opportunity of passing themselves off as Chinese. In spite of the fact that special recognition signals had been arranged with the Chinese and orders on this point issued to all troops, the Japanese on several occasions succeeded in their ruse.

Magforce was to attack Yenangyaung at dawn, the ridge north of Nyaunghla North being its first objective. It was then to exploit forward with a view to covering the main advance of the Division along the by-pass road from milestone 358. At the same time the 13th Indian Infantry Brigade would attack astride the by-pass road with its first objective as the ridge running east and west through Point 510. Then it was to move on Point 501 in Twingon, force the block there, and exploit towards the Pin Chaung. The rear of the Division would be covered by the 1st Burma Brigade. The 5th Mountain Battery was to support Magforce, and the remaining guns and the squadron of tanks were placed under command of the 13th Indian Infantry Brigade.

The country around Yenangyaung is barren and exceedingly broken. It is cut by many deep watercourses, always dry except in the monsoon

[10] *War Diary*, Burcorps 'G' Branch.

season. In this shadeless, arid region the heat in April is very great and is exceedingly trying even when proper protection from the sun is to be had. The Allied troops were to fight for two days under the blazing sun with a shade temperature of about 114°. Many of them were entirely without water or rations. The background to the battle was provided by the burning ruins of the town and the installations on the oilfields east of it.

THE ATTACK BY THE 1ST BURMA DIVISION—18 APRIL

At 0630 hours on 18 April the general attack of the 1st Burma Division began. Advanced Divisional Headquarters moved to the Nyaunghla Stud Farm. On the left the 1st Battalion the Cameronians (Magforce) reached its objective astride the Mani road meeting little opposition. The 13th Indian Infantry Brigade launched its attack at 0730 hours. The 1st Battalion 18th Royal Garhwal Rifles was on the right and the 5th Battalion 1st Punjab Regiment (less A Coy) on the left. The first objective was taken without any opposition at 0800 hours, the 5th Battalion 1st Punjab Regiment arriving first. The Brigade Commander then ordered an advance due north to the next objective, the Twingon ridge on which was situated Point 501. The Brigade advanced at 0900 hours, the 5th Battalion 1st Punjab Regiment leading with the 1st Battalion 18th Garhwal Rifles and the 1st Battalion Royal Inniskilling Fusiliers in reserve. As the first Battalion left Point 510 heavy firing broke out in the town of Yenangyaung where the 1st Brigade was attacking. But the Battalion advance proceeded without opposition.

On Magforce front it was intended that the 7th Battalion Burma Rifles should continue the advance beyond the first objective, the attainment of which had secured the by-pass road leading north-east from Nyaunghla. No sooner had the Burma Rifles moved forward than the left-hand company sighted a pack column advancing south through Yenangyaung, some fifteen hundred yards distant. The company opened long range rifle fire, disclosed itself, and at once came under fire from a small bluff near the river. The Company Commander and several men were killed and the company fell back in confusion.

The right company of the Burma Rifles had moved into line on the east of the right Company of the Cameronians. These two companies then advanced to the next ridge and, in doing so, came under considerable light machine-gun fire from another ridge to the north-east.

The third rifle company of the 7th Battalion Burma Rifles was ordered to outflank this ridge and work forward on to it. Throughout the engagement this company showed great enterprise and, although unable to clear snipers from the upper storeys of buildings, it effectively prevented the by-pass road from coming under small arms fire.

Commander Magforce ordered a company of the 12th Battalion Burma Rifles to clear the bluff near the river, working up to it by a good covered approach. This company consisted of Gurkha reinforcements for the 48th Indian Infantry Brigade which had been temporarily attached to the 12th Battalion Burma Rifles. But coming under desultory mortar fire it broke and dispersed. The officer commanding the Battalion then established some of his troops on the rear edge of the bluff, though he could not clear it.

During these operations the forward observation officer of the 5th Mountain Battery was with the forward troops, the guns being about three hundred yards further back. Targets were engaged at ranges between six hundred and fourteen hundred yards. Mortars were silenced, and houses containing snipers and observation posts shelled. Three hostile guns were successively engaged and put out of action after their smoke had been observed. The gunners sustained some casualties and owing to the shortage of ammunition which could not be replenished all targets were engaged with only one gun.

At 1000 hours a small column of divisional transport passed along the Nyaunghla by-pass road. It was followed later by another small column. This by-pass road was safe except for possible long range mortar fire. At that stage the Japanese attempted to work south along the river bank and a platoon of the Cameronians was moved further west to deal with the threat. The platoon successfully held them up until about 1515 hours when it was almost wiped out by mortar fire. The bluff remained as the only threatening pocket of resistance and appeared to be held by a post of about ten men with two light machine-guns and continued to function despite brave attempts by parties of the 7th Battalion Burma Rifles to capture the position.

At 1315 hours 'A' Squadron of the 2nd Battalion Royal Tank Regiment, previously operating with the 13th Indian Infantry Brigade near Twingon, broke through to Nyaunghla from Obozu to assist the advance north. The squadron commander took his tank into the compound of a house where snipers were located and engaged them at short range, but the ground was unsuitable for tanks and the squadron had shortly to return to the 13th Brigade. On their withdrawal, the morale of some men of the Burma Rifles was shaken, but stern action kept them in position. The snipers were well entrenched in the buildings so that efforts to dislodge them could not succeed. All this time the 13th Indian Infantry Brigade was fighting near Twingon. Consequently at 1530 hours Magforce was withdrawn by the Nyaunghla by-pass road. It rejoined the main body of the Division south of Twingon and then ceased to exist as a separate formation.

As regards the advance to Twingon, at 1000 hours the 5th Battalion 1st Punjab Regiment was between 500 yards of its objective—Point 501. Just then the hostile rifle and L.M.G., mortar and Infantry guns opened fire from the ridge. The Battalion was advancing on a wide front and each company found itself confronted by the Japanese in prepared positions on the ridge. In the first attack on the ridge fairly heavy casualties were sustained. Several officers were either killed or wounded. The 1st Battalion 18th Royal Garhwal Rifles had gone to the wrong meeting place and so arrived too late to attack simultaneously with the Punjab Battalion. Subsequent attacks by the latter were more successful and by 1100 hours each company had gained a footing on the ridge but with great difficulty. As the Commanding Officer was doubtful whether his Battalion could hold the position he sent a message to the Brigade Headquarters reporting the capture of the ridge with difficulty and asking that fresh troops might be sent to pass through the position. The Battalion hung on to the position on the ridge all through the very hot afternoon without relief and about 1600 hours its Headquarters which was forward on the ridge received a direct hit from a mortar which wounded the commanding officer. Japanese counter-attack forced the Punjab Battalion to give ground with heavy casualties. The 1st Battalion Royal Inniskilling Fusiliers was then ordered to restore the situation by attacking and holding the ground with the 5th Battalion 1st Punjab Regiment. Later the 1st Battalion 18 Garhwal Rifles was ordered to pass through the 5th Battalion 1st Punjab Regiment and attack hostile positions forward of Twingon village.

Round Twingon village the Japanese were in considerable strength. The 1st Battalion Royal Inniskiling Fusiliers gained some ground but could not get into the built up area of the village. There the fighting was very close. Two companies of the Battalion made their way round the village and pushed on to the Pin Chaung which they crossed with the object of establishing a bridgehead. They made contact with what they thought were the advanced elements of the Chinese. The recognition signal had been correctly replied to and the troops began to fraternise with the strangers who were in reality Japanese. The Allied troops were surrounded and disarmed. Imprisoned in a neighbouring village they, with the exception of two officers, escaped next day in the course of a counter-attack carried out by the Chinese and the British tanks.

To the right of the Royal Inniskilling Fusiliers A and C companies of the 1st Battalion 18th Royal Garhwal Rifles continued the attack. With the Japanese well established in the village it was thought that a frontal attack was not likely to succeed. So a flank attack from the east of the by-pass road was made. The advance was covered by M.M.G. and supported by gun fire. As the attacking companies were moving, a message was received from the Brigade Headquarters to the effect that tanks had been sent and that the companies should wait for them. As the time of their arrival was not known the attack was pushed in at 1520 hours. There were no signs of the Punjab Battalion except for 30 men who were holding a position approximately 200 yards east of the village. The rest had retired to a hill south of the ridge. The former were trying to persuade a Japanese officer and 16 men to surrender. When 'C' Company arrived they attempted to disarm this party but on their showing resistance they shot them. 'A' company charged the village but was held up for a short time by a high wire fence and suffered heavy casualties. 'B' company was then pushed forward along the line of the road with orders to engage any Japanese troops attempting to retire west from that area. At 1700 hours orders were received from the Brigade Headquarters to attack the village from the west of the road. 'D' and 'B' companies advanced into the village after it had been shelled for five minutes by the 2nd and 23rd Mountain Batteries which were supporting the 13th Indian Infantry Brigade, and burnt it. During this action orders were received from the Brigade that the Garhwal Battalion was to hold a perimeter with the Royal Inniskilling Fusiliers to allow the transport to pass through next morning. The situation had been stabilised and patrols went well forward to the river.

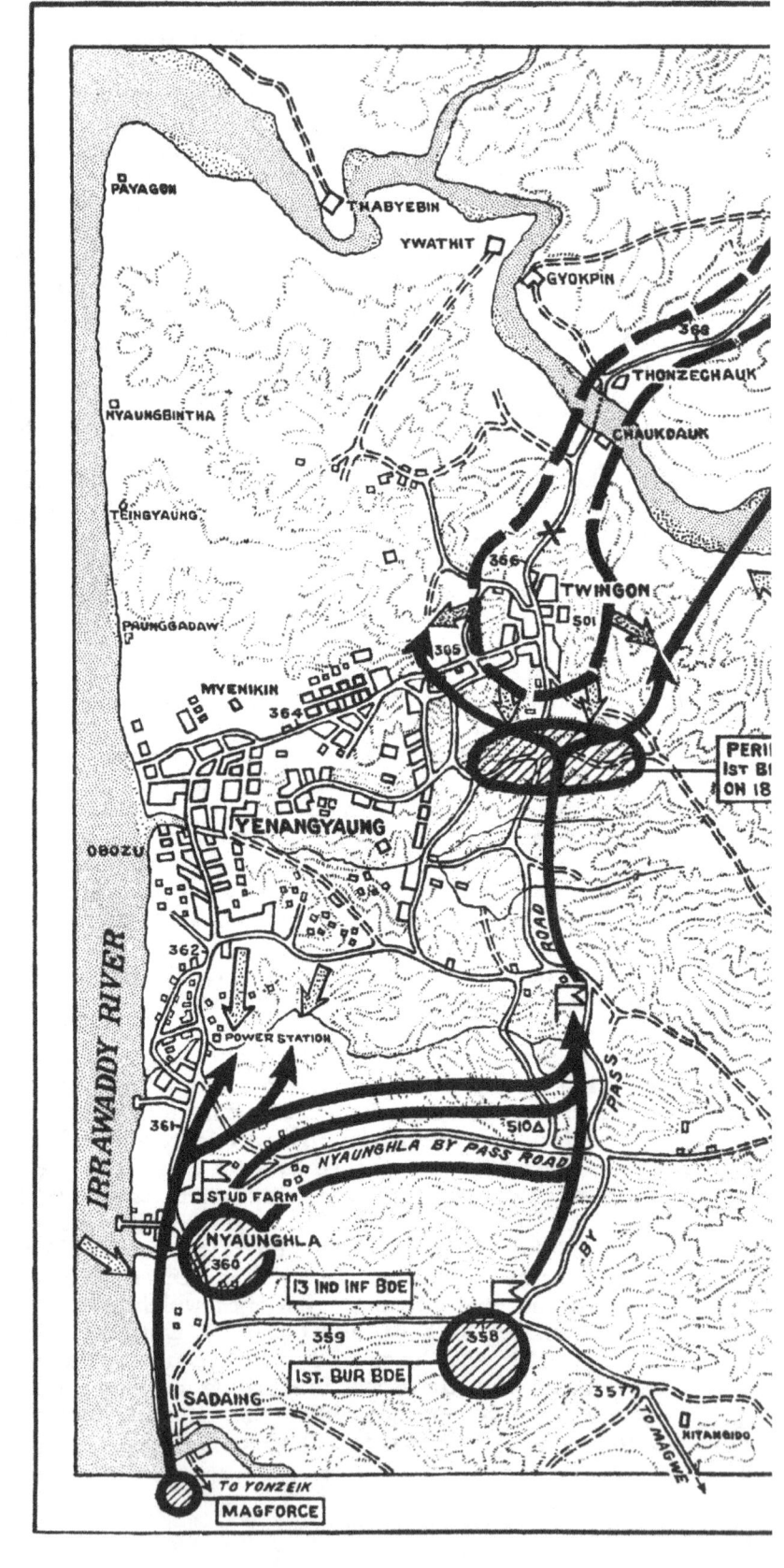

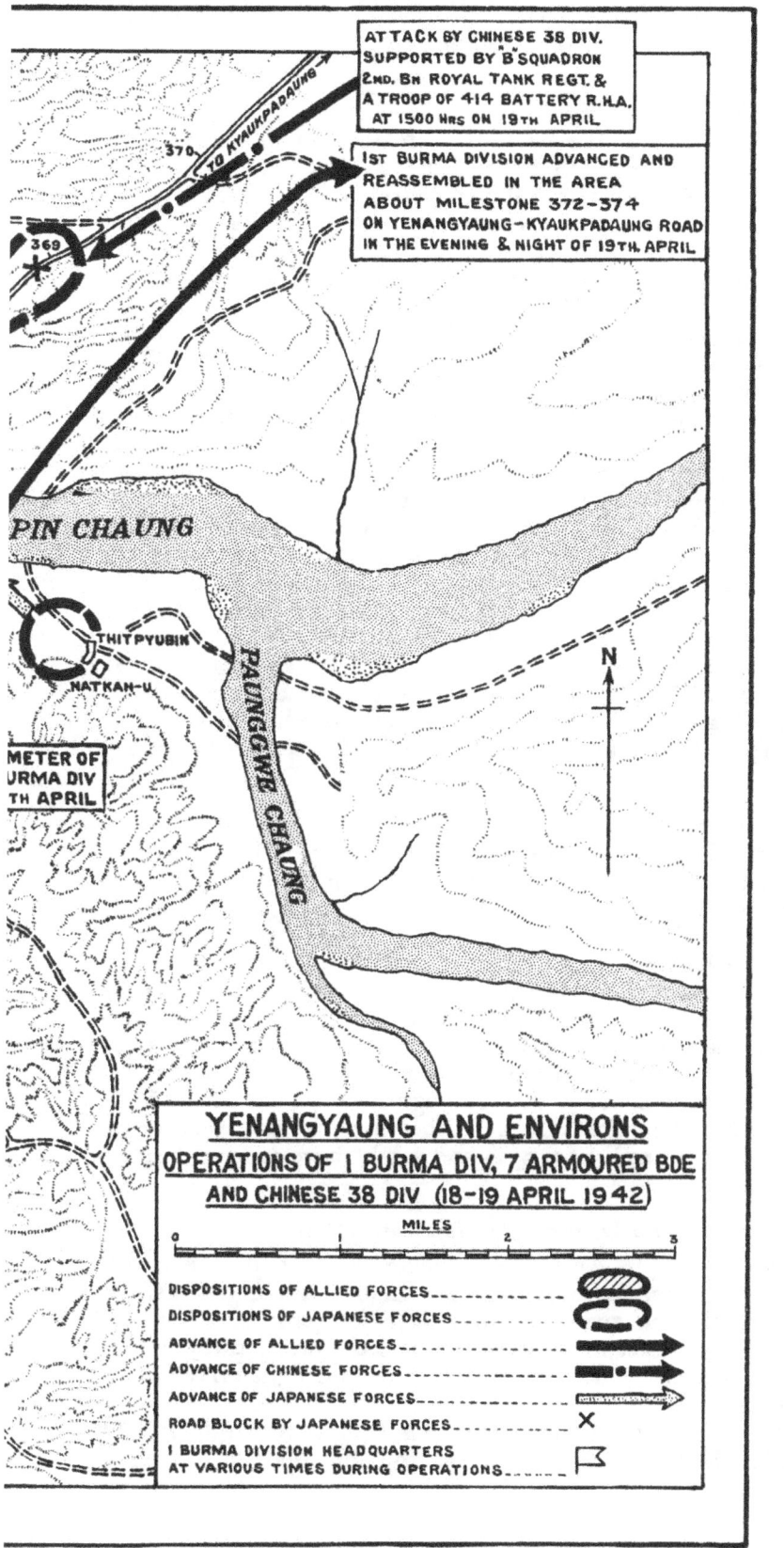

Road-block South of Pin Chaung

The road-block south of the ford still remained to be cleared and 'A' Squadron of the 2nd Battalion Royal Tank Regiment was unable to break through this. The Japanese still had a firm hold on both sides of the Pin Chaung ford. During the afternoon of 18 April, all transport began to move up the by-pass road from milestone 358, but the head of the column was halted about a mile north of Point 510 where the Divisional Headquarters was then established. At about 1630 hours the Divisional Commander proposed to Lt.-General Slim that he should abandon his motor transport and fight his way out across country. The position was grave. Troops and animals were without water and had suffered much exhaustion. Nevertheless Lt.-General Slim ordered the Division to hold on. It was arranged that the Chinese 38th Division would carry out a further attack on the following morning at first light and would cross the Pin Chaung west of the main road.

The attacks already carried out by the Chinese during that day had taken them to the north bank of the Pin Chaung except in the immediate vicinity of the main road and ford where they were unable to penetrate the Japanese defence. They had been assisted by the 2nd Battalion Royal Tank Regiment and 414 Battery, R.H.A.

Ordered to maintain his position Maj.-General Bruce Scott formed a perimeter on the high ground astride the by-pass road just south of Twingon. There his whole force was concentrated together with a mass of transport. The force was exhausted and had been considerably thinned.

The 1st Burma Brigade

The 1st Burma Brigade was little more than a brigade in name since its Battalions had lost heavily; the 1st Battalion Burma Rifles at Migyaungye, the 2nd Battalion King's own Yorkshire Light Infantry at Myingun, and the remaining battalions at the action on the Yin Chaung. This Brigade had not been engaged during the day and was employed in covering the movement of the transport behind the 13th Indian Infantry Brigade. As the main transport column moved up the by-pass road from milestone 358, Japanese troops were observed to be landing from the river about Nyaunghla. Fortunately, hostile aircraft had not been very active. The broken nature of the country, the close fighting, and the smoke from demolitions no doubt hampered them. Otherwise the congested transport would have offered excellant targets and might have suffered heavily from aerial attack.

Japanese Attack the Burma Division Positions—19 April

During the night of 18 April the Japanese closed in on the north, west, and south of the 1st Burma Division. On the east of the position the ground was precipitous and quite impassable for vehicles. However, the night passed quietly except for occasional jackal cries by the Japanese at many points. But about half an hour before first light on 19 April hostile activity began.

The northern sector of the perimeter was held by the 13th Indian Infantry Brigade which was attacked from the direction of Twingon village. At dawn on 19 April its rear and right flank came under heavy machine-gun and mortar fire. In a moment firing broke out in all directions. The attack was accompanied by the usual screams. But after some time the attack died down. A body of Japanese cavalry was then seen working round the ridge on Point 501 but it was out of range. The attack had, however, a bad effect on some men of the Burma Rifles, some units of which were in a nervous state. There was a certain amount of panic, and considerable useless firing by the troops. At 0700 hours hostile light artillery and mortar fire was again opened on the 13th Brigade positions, the massed motor transport on the main road from Yenangyaung as far as Twingon being the favourite target. The Brigade mortars and machine-guns retaliated, but during the course of the morning a number of casaulties had occurred within the perimeter.

Attempt to Force the Northern Road-block—19 April

Soon the attempt to force the road through Twingon was resumed. The main task was the clearing of the road-block 500 yards north of the ridge. Gen. H. Alexander had told the Corps Commander that the 1st Burma Division must fight its way out, and that if necessary it would have to abandon its wheeled transport. Soon after 0700 hours on 19 April the 1st Battalion Royal Inniskilling Fusiliers and 'B' company of the 1st Battalion 18th Royal Garhwal Rifles were sent forward. The latter occupied the northern edge of the Twingon village after overcoming slight opposition. But not much progress could be made. At about 0900 hours, on orders from the Brigade Headquarters, 'B' company set fire to the Japanese stores in the village. At 0730 hours the 5th Battalion 1st Punjab Regiment was ordered to move to the ridge and on its arrival the third Brigade Commander issued orders for the Battalion to advance along both sides of the road, and make a frontal attack on the block. But the orders were cancelled at the last minute. At 1000 hours the Battalion was given orders by the Brigade Commander to clear the road-block, this time by an advance along the east side of the road but these orders were also cancelled. At about 1145 hours the three tired Battalions (the 5th Battalion 1st Punjab Regiment, the 1st Battalion 18th Royal Garhwal Rifles and the 2nd Battalion Royal Innskilling Fusiliers) were moved off north to the Pin Chaung by tracks.

Meanwhile, the 2nd Battalion Koyli and the 2nd Battalion 7th Rajput Regiment, which were at Point 501, received orders to attack and break the road-block. They were to make a wide detour to the east of Twingon, and assemble on the south of the Pin Chaung from where they were to attack Twingon from the north-east. They were to advance from the Chaung at 1145 hours, a fifteen minute barrage being put down on the village at 1200 hours. Just as the Rajput Battalion was ready to move at 1000 hours, it came under heavy mortar and L.M.G. fire and only a few men could make contact with the 2nd Battalion Koyli. The planned artillery preparations never materialised and eventually it was learnt that the attack had been cancelled by Burcorps. It was feared that the attack would clash with that of the Chinese who were to advance south along the west of the main road at 1230 hours. Crossing the Pin Chaung, the Chinese would then attack Twingon from the north-west.

The Rajput Battalion remained in small units in the area of the Chaung until the general order was received that the troops were to withdraw on to the road behind the Chinese troops which were attacking from the north.

During the morning requests had been passed by Maj.-General Bruce Scott through the Armoured Brigade wireless to the Chinese asking them to attack on the east side of the main road to help to clear the block. This attack had been promised for 1230 hours, but it was postponed to 1400 hours, and again to 1600 hours. In fact, the Chinese did attack at last from the north of the Pin Chaung at 1500 hours. In the morning, however, the 2nd Battalion Royal Tank Regiment had attempted to cross the Chaung and break through to the south. 'B' Squadron with 'D' Company of the West Yorkshire Regiment actually crossed at 1150 hours but it was then engaged by infantry with petrol bombs. Having disposed of this opposition it found itself confronted by a gun covering the road. Progress was halted, but contact was made with the 2nd Battalion King's Own Yorkshire Light Infantry on the east. At this point the West Yorkshire Company was recalled as all available infantry and tanks, not already committed, were required by Burcorps to proceed north to Gwegyo to hold the road junction there. The Japanese were reported to have occupied Kyaukpadaung, thirty-seven miles to the north-east. The occupying force later turned out to be the Chinese, but the erroneous report had a most unfortunate effect at a critical period of the Yenangyaung action. It prevented 'B' Squadron of the 2nd Battalion Royal Tank Regiment from continuing its forward move.

In the perimeter the position was precarious. The withdrawal of the 2nd Battalion King's Own Yorkshire Light Infantry and the 2nd Battalion 7th Rajput Regiment involved the taking over of additional sectors by other units. The remaining companies of the 1st Battalion Royal Inniskilling Fusiliers were also employed on offensive tasks. A period of heavy, accurate shell and mortar fire resulted in the disintegration, for the time, of the 12th Battalion Burma Rifles and detachments of the Sappers and Miners. For a brief period the 5th Battalion Burma Rifles was also out of control, but later the Battalion took over the sector vacated by the Sappers and Miners. The heat of the blazing sun was again intense, and the lack of water and the scarcity of rations further exhausted the troops. During the day some men died of exhaustion. These conditions might have led to some desertions but they were easily prevented.

Attempt to By-pass the Road-block—19 April

At 1200 hours the Commander of the 1st Burma Brigade reported to Maj.-General Bruce Scott that he could not rely on his troops for further resistance. He was ordered to hold on until 1400 hours and then withdraw. At 1300 hours a somewhat similar report was received through the tanks from the 13th Indian Infantry Brigade. Men were moving down to the Pin Chaung. The tanks further reported that there was a by-pass track to the east along which vehicles might be got away if handled by really determined drivers. It was evident that this was the last and only chance of saving the transport. Accordingly the transport was formed up with guns in front and the wounded in lorries next. The drivers of many vehicles could not be found. Hence orders were given for the destruction or immobilisation of all non-essential vehicles. But these orders could be carried out only in parts owing to the exhaustion of the whole force and the lack of trained personnel to perform the work.

1400 hours arrived, and as there was still no sign of the Chinese counter-attack, Maj.-General Bruce Scott confirmed the orders for withdrawal. The 13th Indian Infantry Brigade and the 1st Burma Brigade were to cover the movement of the guns and transport. The motor transport started, then halted as the turnoff to the by-pass track could not be found. Two tanks then acted as guides, and led by the Divisional Commander the transport moved out under mortar and gun fire. On the by-pass track one of the tanks was hit by a mortar shell, some other vehicles were knocked out, and finally, the loose sand of the track brought the whole column to a halt. The transport had to be abandoned. However, vehicles had travelled far enough to permit many of the wounded to be evacuated by tanks. The guns of the 5th Mountain Battery, carried on lorries, were also destroyed. The two guns of 'B' Section, 3rd Indian Light Anti-Aircraft Battery were lost. Mortar fire knocked out one gun, the lorry towing the other. The section then endeavoured to extricate the gun, but it was surrounded. It put up a fight against heavy odds until only two men remained unwounded. The five survivors then surrendered, but escaped when later in the day the Chinese with the British tanks entered Twingon.

The 1st Burma Division Crossed Pin Chaung—19 April

The Pin Chaung at a point some two miles north-east of Twingon was eventually reached by the main body. Near this point the village of Thitpyubin was held by the Japanese, and some of the retreating units came under light machine-gun fire. The Japanese again posed as Chinese troops, and a platoon of the 1st Battalion Burma Rifles was deceived by the ruse and captured. The Chaung was, however, crossed at 1600 hours. Some further machine-gun fire was encountered north of the Chaung, and the Division then reassembled that evening and night in the area about milestone 372-74 on the Yenangyaung-Kyaukpadaung road.[11]

The State of the Division

For three days the Division had been subjected to great

---

[11] The bitter fighting around Yenangyaung is best described in the following words; "For two days the battle raged in the oilfields, under a blazing sun and against the background of smoke rising from the demolitions as riflemen and tanks strove to break through the two road-blocks the Japanese had established across the road to the north of the oilfields in an effort to encircle 1st Burma Division moving with all its transport. From the north the troops of Gen. Sunli Jen's 38th Chinese Division attacked towards the Pin Chaung which the Japanese had seized across the line of retreat. Neither 7th Armoured Brigade nor Chinese troops nor 1st Burma Division could open the jaws of the trap. But Maj.-General Bruce Scott managed to find a hole in it and led his Division across the front towards it. The screams of mules hit by bullets mingled with the volleys and explosions while soldiers dragged them down the lanes of fire. Most of the remaining transport had to be abandoned but thousands of Allied troops could pour through this gap and rejoin the main body of the army."

strain and had undergone excessive physical hardships. There had been many casualties. Yet wounded British, Indian, and Burman troops all bore their sufferings without complaint and with heroism. Their only shelter from the sun had been the shade afforded by lorries, and in their case the deprivation of water had been felt even more acutely. As an indication of how severe had been the lack of water it is stated that when transport animals smelt the water of the Pin Chaung during the withdrawal on 19 April they became quite uncontrollable. As a fighting formation the 1st Burma Division was of little value until it had rested and reorganised. Much valuable motor transport and equipment had been lost, and the campaign had reached a stage when many of these losses were irreplaceable. Two Bofors guns, four 3.7 howitzers, four 25 pdrs, most of the 3" mortars, nearly all its mechanised transport, were left behind; also four tanks had been destroyed. The Division had suffered casualties to the extent of about twenty per cent of its personnel.

Chinese Attack on Road-block from the North—19 April

At 1500 hours on 19 April the Chinese supported by 'B' Squadron of the 2nd Battalion Royal Tank Regiment and a troop of 414 Battery, R.H.A. attacked south across the Chaung. The attack was well executed, but of course it was too late to assist the 1st Burma Division. The Chinese progressed slowly, and late that evening had gained Twingon. The capture of Twingon resulted in the release of about two hundred British prisoners. Of this action the Japanese account says: "Although Sakuma Force entered Yenangyaung on 19 April, enemy forces (13th Brigade) were still offering stubborn resistance around the town. A strong enemy force with tanks counter-attacked from the direction of Kyaukpadaung (Chinese forces) and a fierce battle developed in the hill area north of the town. Both sides suffered heavy casualties.[12]"

How the Japanese Established the two Road-blocks

The thrust at Yenangyaung by the Sakuma Detached Force (consisting mainly of 214th Infantry Regiment and II Mountain Artillery Battalion) was a bold thrust far behind the Burcorps rear. Helped by a diversionary attack on Magwe which was entered on 17 April, the Sakuma Force moved across country well east of the Magwe-Yenangyaung road along probably the dry bed of the Paunggwe Chaung. Stragglers from the 1st Burma Division, on withdrawing from Yenangyaung on 19 April, crossed this Chaung and observed that the stream bed was scored with the tracks of motor transport. When it was due east of Yenangyaung, the force split into two sections, one attacking south of Pin Chaung and the other north of it. Both forces established road-blocks and the southern one entered Yenangyaung on 19 April. This bold move was facilitated by the inability of Burcorps to watch the whole length of the Taungdwingyi-Minhla line. Chinese assistance would have been invaluable in stopping the gaps. Without this assistance it had not been difficult for Japanese columns to pass between widely spaced positions. Once

[12] *History of the Japanese 15th Army*, 601/7785/H, p. 24.

through these, a forward move by unfrequented tracks and under cover of the bed of the stream was easy.

Burcorps Counter-Attack from Natamuk and Taungdwingyi—17-19 April

Whilst the battle of Yenangyaung was being fought the remainder of Burcorps had not been inactive. Strong columns were sent out from Taungdwingyi and Natmauk where the 17th Indian Division and the 7th Queen's Own Hussars had not been molested by the Japanese. Each consisted of one battalion and a squadron of the 7th Queen's Own Hussars. Their tasks were to demonstrate against the flank or rear of the hostile forces pressing the 1st Burma Division and, if possible, to draw off part of those forces. Unfortunately, they missed the opportunity to attack effectively the flank and rear of the Japanese forces which were then engaged in attacking Magwe and Yenangyaung. On the morning of 17 April the Natmauk column comprising the 2nd Battalion the Duke of Wellington's Regiment with a squadron of the 7th Queen's Own Hussars, moved out along the Magwe road. Thus they missed the Sakuma force. On 18 April, however, the patrols reported hostile force at Kanbya, 8 miles east of Magwe, and engaged it. It is perhaps to this action that the Japanese account refers when it says: "When an enemy force with tanks closed in at a point 7 miles north of Magwe an Infantry Battalion, a Heavy Field Artillery unit and a Light tank unit were sent to reinforce the one Infantry Company and Mountain Battery which were already there".[13] Gas is alleged to have been used by the Japanese against tanks but there were only three casualties and these also recovered quickly. While exploiting towards Magwe the column met also a strong hostile road-block at Nyaungbinwya. The battle lasted all day. Two tanks were hit by anti-tank gun, but were not knocked out. Considerable casualties are reported to have been inflicted on the Japanese. But this force stopped short of Magwe which by that time was in Japanese hands.

The Taungdwingyi column consisting of the 1st Battalion 10th Gurkha Rifles and 7th Hussars patrol also began its operations on 17 April. It was too late to attack the Japanese forces moving to Magwe. No wonder therefore, that it encountered no substantial hostile force. It missed even the *215th Infantry Regiment, the Artillery Unit of 24 IMB* and *the Light tank unit* at Thadodan. On 18 April, it captured a Japanese propaganda party consisting of one Japanese civilian and Burmans and recovered from them valuable documents and marked maps. It also destroyed a large hostile staff car and petrol lorry, killing the occupants. The next day this column established a road-block at milestone 304. Like the northern column this was also twice dive-bombed by the Japanese. On 19 April the columns were withdrawn to Taungdwingyi and Natmauk respectively because when information was received about the Yenangyaung battle the Divisional Command (17th Division) thought "that further demonstration on enemy right flank will not influence the northern battle any longer." In fact the columns had moved out too

[13] *Ibid.*

late and thus had failed either to save Magwe or relieve the pressure on the 1st Burma Division at Yenangyaung.

Nor could the Japanese realise their objective of capturing the oilfields intact. By a narrow margin of three days these oilfields had been denied to them.[14]

---

[14] The Japanese accounts testify to the bitter fighting. *History of the Japanese 15th Army.*

CHAPTER XXI

The Beginning of the End—Retreat North of Mandalay

GENERAL ALEXANDER'S PLANS IN THE EVENT OF LOSS OF
MANDALAY—MARCH 1942.

Towards the end of March it had become necessary to consider future plans as regards the defence of Upper Burma in the event of the loss of Mandalay. Two principal factors influenced Gen. Sir H. Alexander in his policy at this time : the need to give the Chinese Armies every possible assistance with a view to keeping China in the war, and the need of gaining time to allow India to build up her defences and to complete the roads from Assam to Burma, and from India to China via the Hukawng Valley.[1] At his instance an appreciation was prepared by Lt.-Gen. T. J. Hutton, Chief of the General Staff Army in Burma. Its stress on the need to hold on to the oilfields and the line Prome-Toungoo need not concern us here as they were closed chapters. In the event of Mandalay being occupied there were three lines of withdrawal, the Mandalay-Lashio road, Mandalay-Ye-U and Menywa-Kalewa via the Chindwin. The first route had the full advantage of retaining close touch with the Chinese, and the military advantage of being the only route by which mechanised transport and tanks could be withdrawn. But on it there were no supplies of food or ammunition stores. The second line would enable them to cover the completion of the Assam-Burma Road and the arrival of reinforcements and supplies from India as Ye-U was ultimately to be connected with the Kabaw valley road to India.

The Outline Plan contemplated the following disposition of the Allied forces. The Chinese troops of the Sixth Army which were to the east of the river Salween (93 Division VI Army) were to withdraw on Puerh in China, while those to the west of the river Salween were to move from Loikaw and Mongpan to Loilem and thence north to Hsipaw and Lashio. Chinese Fifth Army was to move by the main Burma-China road (Mandalay-Lashio) and be responsible for the defence of the territory between Mandalay in the east and river Panlaung in the west. Out of the Indo-British forces, the 7th Armoured Brigade, and one Indian infantry brigade of the 17th Indian Division were to accompany the Chinese Fifth Army as far as Lashio and thence withdraw if necessary on Bhamo. This was with the object of maintaining touch with the Chinese. The 17th Indian Division less one infantry brigade, plus one infantry brigade of the 1st Burma Division, was to withdraw astride the Mandalay-Shewbo-Katha Road, covering the projected route to China via the Hukawng valley. Thence it was to move to Kalewa or Bhamo. The 1st Burma

---

[1] General Alexander's *Despatch*, para 40.

Division less one infantry brigade was to cover the withdrawal of the administrative units and to undertake the defence of the Chindwin valley. One infantry brigade was to move via Pakokku-Monywa and one infantry brigade via Myinmu-Monywa and thus cover the approaches to India through Kalewa. Army Headquarters was to move to Shwebo and thence to Katha. During all this movement the utmost possible resistance was to be offered to the Japanese advance. This appreciation and plan were approved by the Commander-in-Chief of India during his visit to Burma on 31 March and 1 April.[2] A draft directive dated 4 April was issued to the Burcorps on 6 April which was subsequently confirmed in an Operation Instruction. Administrative arrangements were also put in hand to implement the plan.

In the Directive further details of the plan were worked out. A small column was to move north from Pakokku via Pauk on Kalemyo. It was to cover the right flank of the Burcorps, hold up the Japanese advance on the Assam road with the assistance of China irregulars and threaten the flank of any Japanese troops that endeavoured to work up the west bank of the river Chindwin. One column was to move from Pakokku on the west bank of the Chindwin to cover the movement of shipping on it and also cover the Allied installations at Monywa. One column was to move via Myingyan-Myotha-Tadau and Ngazun to cover territory to the west of the Panlaung river. It was later to operate west of the river Mu to cover the withdrawal of non-essential units and personnel via river Chindwin or Kalewa. One column was to move on the axis, Meiktila-Kyaukse, to assist the Chinese in the defence of Mandalay. Subsequently a part of it, the 7th Armoured Brigade and one infantry brigade of the 17th Indian Division, was to co-operate with the Chinese in opposing the hostile advance up the Lashio road. The rest of the 17th Indian Division was to cover the Shwebo-Ye-U road and later move to Katha.

CHINESE IN THE PLAN

During the first half of April it became clear that the above plan could not be implemented. With the gradual loss of the rice producing areas in Burma, the closing of rice mills, the difficulties of collecting sufficient grain, the disintegration of railways and the famine in Yunnan, it was impossible to accumulate in Lashio or beyond sufficient stocks of rice to feed the Chinese Armies for more than a few weeks. Therefore, a withdrawal of the Chinese and Indian troops towards Lashio would have probably meant starvation of the former unless supplies could be sent from China which seemed highly improbable. Hence Gen. H. Alexander decided to invite the Chinese to withdraw some of their forces via Shwebo as there was a better chance of their obtaining rice in that area.

At the beginning of April, Lt.-Gen. T. J. Hutton was replaced by Major-General Winterton as Chief of Staff of the Burma Army. The former then came on a special mission to the General Headquarters, India and returned on 18 April. While in India Lt.-Gen. T. J. Hutton had

---

[2] *Ibid*, para 41 ; Tel No. 8090/C Armindia to Troopers dated 4 April, 1942.

discussed with Gen. Sir. A. Wavell the question of the Indo-British forces accompanying the Chinese in a withdrawal. The latter was prepared to agree to a change in this part of the plan if Gen. Sir H. Alexander so desired. General Alexander was, however, so impressed with the political consideration that he determined to give the Chinese the opportunity of accepting or refusing the assistance of British forces, on the axis Mandalay-Lashio. He also desired to have some Chinese forces withdrawn north via Shwebo.

Accordingly Gen. Sir. H. Alexander arranged to meet the Generalissimo's principal Liaison Officer, General Lin Wei, at Maymyo on 21 April, and explained his plans. The latter agreed that the bulk of the Chinese army should withdraw north via Shwebo. He also thought that it would be better that no Indo-British forces should withdraw towards Lashio and explained his plans. The latter agreed that the bulk of the Chinese bend towards Shwebo.[3]

Events in the Shan States soon necessitated a change in the original plan. The Chinese 55th Division covering the Mawchi-Loikaw-Taungsyi road had been destroyed south of Loikaw on the night of 18/19 April. Since it had not been possible to effect any strong concentration of the widely dispersed Chinese Sixth Army behind the 55th Division there was only a small force available to oppose the hostile motorised column driving north. By the afternoon of 20 April the Japanese had crossed the To Saihka and the Chinese were retiring on Hopong to take up a line east of that town. Taunggyi and the road through it to Thazi and Meiktila were open to the Japanese. This constituted a grave and immediate threat to the Chinese and Indo-British forces in the area south of Mandalay. There the Chinese Fifth Army had been forced out of Pyinmana on 20 April, and the 96th Division was very heavily engaged. The proposed counter-offensive by Burcorps and the Chinese 200th Division would have relieved this pressure, but it was essential to stop the gap at Taunggyi. Consequently the 200th Division was diverted east from Meiktila on 21 April. It was accompanied by one Regiment of the 22nd Division. On 23 April it attacked the Japanese force holding Taunggyi.

ABANDONMENT OF THE PLAN OF OFFENSIVE IN YENANGYAUNG AREA

In these circumstances the projected offensive in the Yenangyaung area was abandoned and the Chinese 200th Division was ordered by General J. Stilwell to move to Kalaw and the 22nd Division to concentrate in the Thazi area. Further, it became a matter of supreme importance to hold securely the centres of communication south of Mandalay. Accordingly on 21 April the following moves were ordered by the Burcorps:—

    38 Chinese Division to concentrate at Kyaukpadaung.
    1 Burma Division to be prepared to move to Taungtha.
    17 Indian Division to withdraw from Taungdwingyi and later from Natmauk to positions N. W. and West of Meiktila at Mahlaing and Zayetkon.

---
[3] General Alexander's *Despatch*, paras 42-44.

7 Armoured Brigade to Meiktila under command of General Lou, who now took over command of the Chinese forces on the Pyawbwe front, General Tu having moved with 200 Division to Kalaw.⁴

The withdrawal plan also underwent a change. The new plan formulated by Gen. Sir H. Alexander envisaged the following dispositions north and west of the Irrawaddy bend:—

"(a) *West of the River Mu*
  1 Burcorps, less 7 Armoured Brigade with the 1 Burma Division astride the river Chindwin and a strong detachment covering the approach to Kalewa via the Myittha valley.
(b) *Between the R. Mu and the northern reach of the Irrawaddy*
  38 Chinese Division and the 7 Armoured Brigade.
(c) *In and south of Mandalay and holding the crossings over river Myitnge*
  22, 28 and 96 Chinese Divisions".

General Alexander "realised that a withdrawal from the Meiktila area would uncover the communications with Mandalay of any Chinese forces about Kalaw-Taunggyi and would prevent their withdrawal through Mandalay. The plan therefore contemplated that all Chinese forces east of the railway Mandalay-Pyawbwe would move towards Lashio. The situation was very delicate at the moment and it was impossible to issue a hard and fast plan for any further withdrawal since no decision could be made in the existing situation as to whether 22, 28 and 96 Chinese Divisions would withdraw to the north or whether they would fall back on Lashio".⁵ On 22 April an outline of the new plan was sent by the Liaison Officer to the Headquarters of the Burcorps. On 23 April the Operation Instruction No. 46 embodying this new plan was issued to the Burcorps. The contents of this Operation Instruction had been agreed to by Gen. J. Stilwell's staff at Maymyo.

THE PROBLEM OF THE AVA BRIDGE

Gen. Sir H. Alexander had one more problem to consider. The Ava bridge, the approaches to which ran through the bottleneck of Mandalay, was the only bridge over the Irrawaddy. Moreover, the approaches were very vulnerable to air attack. The situation to be avoided was, therefore, undue congestion in its approaches and the forces being pushed back to the loop of the Irrawaddy below Mandalay and thus forced to fight with their backs to the river which would be a repetition of the Sittang disaster. Gen. Sir H. Alexander therefore decided that the moment to order the withdrawal would be when the advanced forces had to leave Meiktila. Moreover, earlier in the month, he had ordered preparations to be put in hand for the construction of ferries over both the Irrawaddy and Myitunge rivers and of the approaches thereto in order to eliminate the bottleneck as far as possible.⁶

⁴ *Ibid*, para 46.
⁵ *Ibid*, para 47.
⁶ *Ibid*, para 48.

PLANS FOR RESISTANCE SOUTH OF MANDALAY

It must also be emphasised that though he had made plans for a withdrawal, Gen. Sir H. Alexander had no intention of withdrawing north of the Irrawaddy unless forced to give up Kyaukpadang and Meiktila, the two centres of communication to Mandalay. For the defence of these areas he had grouped his forces as follows:—Chinese 22nd and 96th Divisions and the 7th Armoured Brigade under General Lou, the Chinese Commander-in-Chief, were assigned the defence of the area Meiktila-Thazi-Pyawbwe. The Burcorps under the command of Lieutenant-General Slim (17 Division, 1 Burma Division and 28 and 38 Chinese Divisions) were to prepare the defences of Mandalay.[7]

The events in the Shan States however, compelled an early withdrawal. The Japanese thrust through the Shan States progressed rapidly. The operations connected with this move are detailed in a later chapter. Loilem fell to them on the evening of 23 April, and although the Chinese 200th Division recaptured Taunggyi on 24 April, this could not hold up the Japanese drive on Lashio. It was not possible to discover the exact strength of the Japanese armoured forces and motorised infantry; but of the weakness of the Chinese forces between them and Lashio there could be no doubt. A good deal of damage had been done by panic in the rear areas, especially at Lashio. Hence Gen. Sir H. Alexander sent Brigadier Martin his chief Liaison Officer with the Chinese forces to attempt to restore order and confidence in Lashio. The latter succeeded to a great extent in doing so.

Under the orders of Gen. J. Stilwell the 28th Chinese Division, less the regiment, was moved to Hsipaw but the disorganisation of the railways made this movement very slow. To protect the rear of his army Gen. Sir H. Alexander therefore sent a detachment to the British Infantry Depot at Maymyo to hold the Gokteik Gorge. He also moved his Rear Headquarters from Maymyo to Shwebo on 23 April.

Even though the Chinese 200th Division had captured Taunggyi on 24 April and advanced towards Hopang, it could not halt the Japanese drive to Lashio. On 24 April Gen. Sir H. Alexander asked Gen. J. Stilwell to meet him at Maymyo. But as the situation did not permit the latter to leave his Headquarters on 25 April, Gen. H. Alexander himself went to Kyanksa, where he met Lieutenant General Slim, Commander 1 Burcorps, also. There he learnt that the Japanese were exerting great pressure on the Pyinmana front and were advancing to Pyawbwe and that the Chinese 96th Division holding the front was breaking up. One regiment of the Chinese 22nd Division which had been taken from Thazi into the Shan States and subsequently to Meiktila which Gen. Sir H. Alexander had always been insisting on being held strongly, was left without any infantry. Gen. J. Stilwell was not sanguine about the operations in the Shan States and Gen. Sir H. Alexander considered that the Chinese resistance on the Pyawbwe front might collapse any moment.

[7] *Ibid*, para 48.

ORDER FOR WITHDRAWAL NORTH OF MANDALAY—25 APRIL

Hence Gen. Sir H. Alexander decided upon putting the plan of a withdrawal north of Mandalay into operation on the night of 25/26 April. He also ordered "The Burcorps to take over rear guard from the Chinese on the axis Meiktila-Mandalay and to cover the withdrawal of the Chinese 22 and 96 Divisions north of Meiktila." During the day on 25 April evacuation of units and installations in Maymyo was begun.[8]

DECISION ABOUT THE FUTURE ROLL OF THE INDO-BRITISH FORCES

The events on the Chinese front not only made Gen. Sir H. Alexander decide upon the withdrawal north of Mandalay but also on the future role of the Indo-British forces. The capture of Lashio by the Japanese was only a matter of time and there was nothing to stop them from moving from Lashio to Bhamo, from where they could cut the communications with Myitkyina. But it was not possible to disengage any part of the forces to send them to Bhamo. Moreover, the condition of the Chinese and the Indo-British forces, wrote, General Alexander, "precluded the possibility of being able to hold Mandalay and the Irrawaddy line for very long. In these circumstances I decided that the main object was the defence of India, but I had two subsidiary objects:—(a) to maintain touch with the Chinese and (b) to get as much as possible of the Imperial force back to India so that it could be reorganized".[9]

On 26 April Gen. Sir H. Alexander issued a letter to the Commander, Burcorps embodying the new plan which was to be adopted after the Mandalay-Irrawaddy line was given up. "This was as follows:—(a) For the defence of India there were to be two infantry brigades astride the Chindwin to delay the enemy as far south as possible, (b) A strong detachment in the Myittha valley, (c) The remainder of the force to move via Ye-U on Kalewa leaving a detachment to cover this route, (d) to hang on to the Chinese and take them back to India if possible, particularly the 38 Division which was fighting so well under the command of 1 Burcorps". Even this plan had to be modified later.[10] On 26 April, Gen. Sir H. Alexander moved his Headquarters to Shwebo.

PROBLEM OF MAINTENANCE FOR THE RETREATING FORCES

The question of maintenance was one of great difficulty. Preparations were put in hand for making the rough jungle track from Ye-U to Shwegyin on the Chindwin river fit for motor transport. Although this track linked up with the projected road to India from Kalewa through Tamu little work had been done on it, and it still remained scarcely better than a bullock cart track. A stretch of 30 miles was waterless. The length of the track was approximately one hundred and twenty miles, or eight marches. The condition of the road between Kalewa and Tamu was also such that once the monsoon set in the movement of stores south

---

[8] General Alexander's *Despatch*, para 49.
[9] *Ibid*, para 50.
[10] *Ibid*, para 51.

of Tamu would have to be via the Chindwin river and its tributary, the Yu. The maintenance capacity of this route was not known in any detail at the Burma Army Headquarters, and therefore it was not known what force could be maintained south of Tamu.

On 26 April arrangements were put in hand for making the Ye-U-Kalewa road fit for mechanised transport as far as possible and for stocking the road with supplies and water. Major-General Wakely, Commander Line of Communication Area, was placed in charge of all work on the road. It was estimated that the stocking of the track from Ye-U to Shwegying would take seven days. Gen. Sir H. Alexander was accordingly anxious to hold the Mandalay-Irrawaddy position for this period, although he was very doubtful of the possibility of doing so. He urged his administrative staff to accelerate arrangements as much as possible. The acute shortage of transport made it necessary to withdraw vehicles from all possible sources including the 7th Armoured Brigade and other units of Burcorps. Drastic steps were taken to effect this, the dumping of kit and all stores not having an immediate fighting value being enforced.[11] Fortunately supplies already accumulated in the Shwebo-Ye-U area by the foresight of the 'Q' staff were ample for requirements. The administrative services rose to the occasion nobly, and the problem of distributing supplies and water along the track was tackled with vigour. Throughout the administrative build-up, General Goddard, whose work at the head of the 'Q' Staff was invaluable, was the moving force and inspiration behind the Services. Dumps of rations, water, and petrol were established at likely staging camps. Further supplies were pushed forward to Shwegyin, the crossing place on the Chindwin, a few miles south of Kalewa.

During this period of the operations, Burcorps had to contend with considerable activity on the part of rebel Burmans and hostile agents. It was learnt that the Japanese were employing Indian troops captured in Malaya, the Indian National Army, for espionage and fifth column purposes. They had also induced captured men of the Burma Rifles to act as spies and a party of these was taken by the Chinese 38th Division. All units were in consequence warned of the necessity of exercising extreme vigilance when stragglers or escaped prisoners entered the lines. In the Taungdwingyi-Natmauk area the 17th Indian Division had been much troubled by the activities of Burman malcontents, and there was frequent sabotage of telephone lines. A 'Peace' party of the Burmans including a Buddhist monk with a Japanese leader had been intercepted. At Mahlaing, north of Meiktila, no sooner had the 17th Indian Division Headquarters been established than fires were started in the town. Drastic action was taken against looters and fire-raisers who were shot.

BURCORPS IN ACTION SOUTH OF MANDALAY

While these plans and arrangements for withdrawal were going forward, Burcorps was in action south of Mandalay. The execution of the amended plan of withdrawal was most expeditiously put into effect on

[11] *Ibid*, paras 52-56.

the night of 25 April. But during the day, Burcorps was on the general line Chauk-Kyaukpadaung-Thabyegon-Meiktila. This was held by the Chinese 38th Division on the east, the dividing line being east of Kyatkon. The 1st Burma Division was in reserve in the area Taungtha-Myingyan with the 2nd Burma Brigade on the west bank of the Irrawaddy about Yenangyat. The 7th Armoured Brigade had rejoined Burcorps. At Pyabwe to the south of Meiktila the Chinese 22nd Division was being encircled by superior Japanese forces.

That day (25 April) the 7th Queen's Own Hussars operating on the road between Meiktila and Pyawbwe were in contact with the hostile force. At 1200 hours a scout car met three Japanese tanks of the cruiser class about one mile north of Pyawbwe out of which place Chinese troops were then streaming. On receipt of this information a patrol of a troop of tanks was sent forward, and in the evening a Japanese motorised column with guns and mortars was encountered on the road thirteen miles south of Meiktila. The column was engaged at point blank range, the tanks running down its length. Many casualties were inflicted and several lorries were knocked out without any loss to the tanks. As it was growing dark the action could not be continued long enough to be decisive. There being no Chinese troops in Meiktila to meet the Japanese advance from Pyawbwe, Gen. Sir H. Alexander that evening ordered Burcorps to move a brigade of the 17th Indian Division to Meiktila forthwith. The 63rd Indian Infantry Brigade at once marched for that place, and the 7th Armoured Brigade from its harbour five miles north sent the 1st Battalion West Yorkshire regiment into that town. Orders were also issued to the 7th Armoured Brigade to continue to hold the area until the night of 26 April to enable the Chinese to withdraw to Wundwin where they would entrain.

WITHDRAWAL FROM KYAUKPADAUNG-MEIKTILA LINE —NIGHT 25-26 APRIL

The general withdrawal from the Kyaukpadaung-Meiktila line began on the night of 25/26 April. The Chinese 38th Division was ordered to withdraw by the road Pupaywa-Taungtha to Tada-U, south-west of the Ava Bridge, this movement being covered by the 1st Burma Division which in turn would fall back on the Sameikkon ferry. Behind its covering force at Meiktila the 17th Indian Division would retire to Ondaw across the Ava Bridge. It was intended to take up strong lay-back positions at Myittha (south of Kyaukse) and at Kyaukse.

2ND BURMA BRIGADE'S MOVEMENTS

The 2nd Burma Brigade was originally intended to fall back from Pakokku on Monywa, detaching a column to withdraw on Kalemyo by a route west of the Chindwin, thus denying the Myittha valley to a hostile force known to be advancing up the west bank of the Irrawaddy. On 27 April it was reported that this force was in Salin, sixteen miles north-west of Yenangyaung, and that it was moving north of the Myittha valley with the intention of cutting the Assam-Kalewa-Tamu road at

Kalemyo. An advance party of the Thakins was then at Sinbyugyun, and the country west of Pakokku was in a disturbed state.

ALTERATIONS IN THE PLAN TO MEET A JAPANESE THREAT TO KALEWA

In view of this information General Alexander visited the Burcorps Headquarters on 28 April and there made the following alterations to the plan for a further withdrawal in case the Mandalay-Irrawaddy position had to be abandoned. In addition to the 2nd Burma Brigade moving up the Myittha valley, one Infantry brigade of the 1st Burma Division was to be sent by river to Kalewa and thence to Kalemyo. "As a result of these alterations the force astride the Chindwin would consist of one infantry brigade of the 1 Burma Division and one brigade of the 17 Division, leaving only the 17 Division, less one infantry brigade, 7 Armoured Brigade and Corps and Army Troops to withdraw via Ye-U on Kalewa". This amended plan was embodied in Operation Instruction No. 47 which was issued on 28 April.[12]

The same instruction detailed the dispositions for the Burcorps:—

"(a) Having crossed the river by the Sameikkon ferry 1 Burma Division (less 2 Burma Brigade) would march on Monywa where 13 Indian Infantry Brigade would cross the Chindwin river to operate south and south-west from Salingyi. 1 Burma Brigade would move by steamers from Monywa to Kalewa to undertake the defence of that bridgehead. One brigade (62 Indian Infantry Brigade) of 17 Indian Division would come under command of 1 Burma Division to operate south from Chaung-U and also to protect the road Sagaing-Monywa.

(b) 17 Division (less one brigade) having crossed the Irrawaddy by the Ava bridge would undertake the defence of the area Myinmu-Allagappa and prevent Japanese infiltration between Allagappa and the Mu river.

(c) The Chinese 38 Division would hold the area Sagaing-Ondaw preventing crossings of the Irrawaddy at Amarapura or Tada-U.

(d) 7 Armoured Brigade would support the Chinese 38 Division, detaching one squadron for operations in the Chaung-U area."

The 2nd Burma Brigade marched out of Pakokku at 1830 hours on 28 April. The following night it was at Pyinchaung.

Unopposed, the remainder of the 1st Burma Division and the Chinese 38th Division carried out their crossings of the Irrawaddy. The 1st Burma Division completed its crossing by the evening of 28 April, and then issued a warning order for the onward march to the Monywa area to begin on the evening of 29 April. Subsequently this move was postponed to the evening of 30 April on the representation of the Commander 13th Indian Infantry Brigade that his troops should not march before 0700 hours on that day because of their tiredness and the loss of kit by the 1st Battalion 18th Royal Garhwal Rifles and the Brigade Headquarters.

---

[12] General Alexander's *Despatch*, para 53.

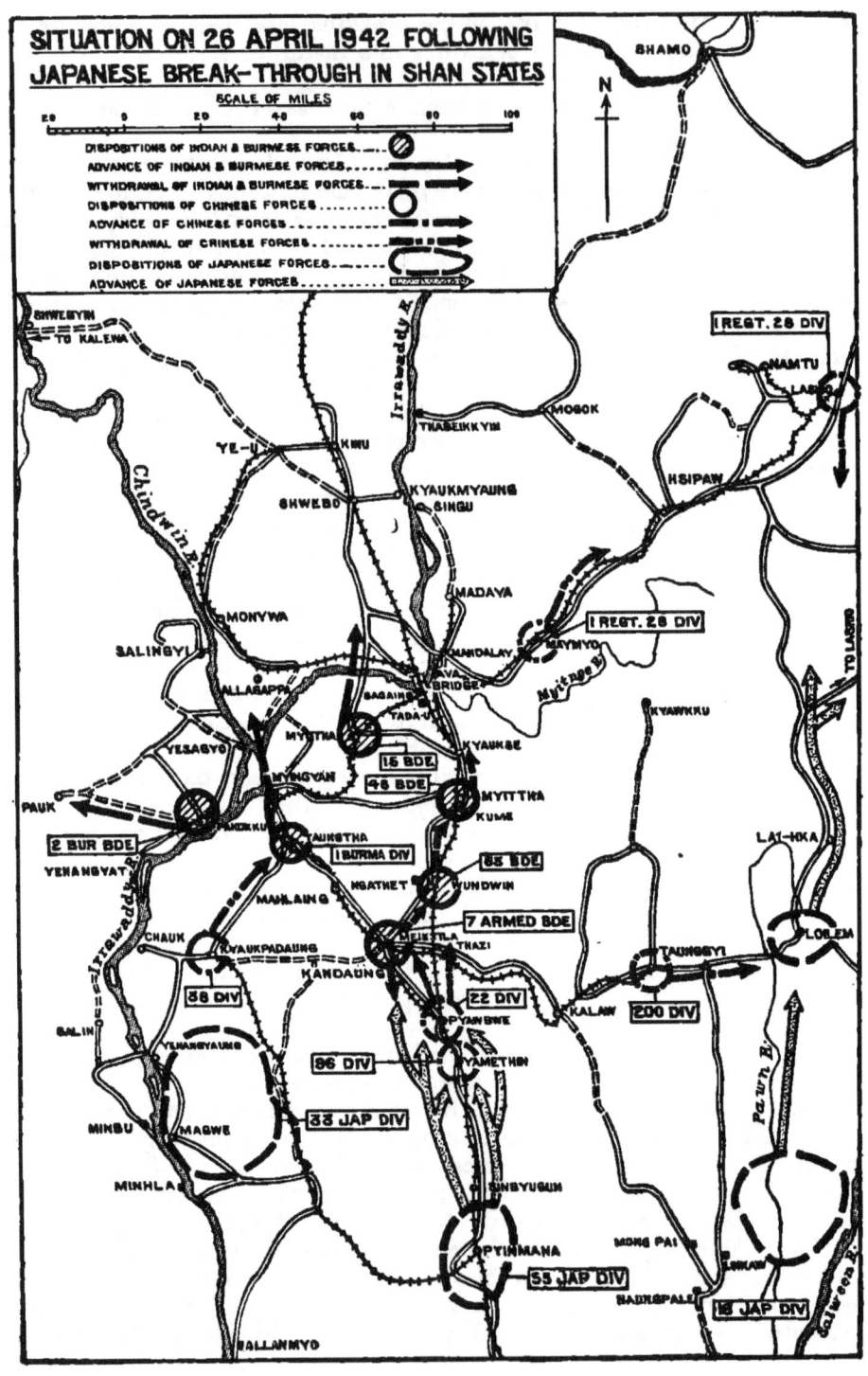

It will be noted that from the night of 28/29 April the approach from Pakokku to Monywa along the west bank of the Chindwin had been left unprotected. The delay in the march of the 1st Burma Division from the Irrawaddy opposite Sameikkon towards Monywa extended this danger period for Monywa with results that subsequently became apparent.

MEIKTILA—MANDALAY AXIS—26 APRIL

To turn to the Meiktila-Mandalay axis, on the morning of 26 April, a patrol of the 7th Queen's Own Hussars again came upon a Japanese motorised column, this time at Kadaung, 7 miles south of Meiktila. Once more the Japanese were taken by surprise. 10 to 15 of their lorries were destroyed, nearly 150 men were killed and at least one 75 mm gun was silenced. On the Allied side the losses were two tanks. A company of the 1st Battalion West Yorkshire Regiment was then sent forward from Meiktila to clear the village, but the attack was held up by Japanese aircraft which pinned the British infantry to the ground.

By this time the element of surprise had been completely lost. Eventually the attack went in at 1730 hours, the infantry being carried on tanks to within a hundred yards of the village. The advancing troops came under mortar fire but entered the village and began to clear it. It was then decided to fire the village, which was done by the guns of 'D' Troop 414 Battery, R.H.A. The Japanese then withdrew to a patch of jungle south of Kadaung and a further attack was made by the infantry company supported by tanks. Here was a much larger force of the Japanese than was expected and the attack was held up by heavy light-machine-gun and mortar fire. The company was ordered to withdraw but the two forward platoons never received the order. Held to the ground by fire, they were charged by an overwhelming force of the Japanese. The platoons split into small groups and withdrew at dusk.

The 7th Armoured Brigade and the 63rd Indian Infantry Brigade, one field battery and one A/Tk battery had to deny Meiktila to the Japanese only till the evening of 26 April and thereafter slowly move back to Kyaukse and then to Wundwin. That night the 7th Queen's Own Hussars and the 1st Battalion West Yorkshire Regiment evacuated Meiktila, withdrawing to Wundwin position. On 27 April a rear party consisting of the 7th Armoured Brigade and the 63rd Indian Infantry Brigade under the command of Brig. A. Anstice was detailed to deny the Japanese Wundwin until 1800 hours and withdraw during the night. Behind Kyaukse the 63rd Indian Infantry Brigade was to take up a position on the line of the Myitnge river, and the 7th Armoured Brigade less one squadron was to pass further north to the Ondaw area. At Kyaukse one squadron of the 7th Armoured Brigade and one battery 25 pounder were to come under the command of the 48th Indian Infantry Brigade in position at Kyaukse.

After the rough handling the Japanese had received south of Meiktila it was not expected that they would press their advance. However, at about 0700 hours on 27 April a patrol of the 2nd Battalion Royal Tank Regiment came under anti-tank fire from the village of Ngathet near milestone 350 on the main road. Two tanks were knocked out. The village was then shelled by the guns of 414 Battery, R.H.A. Subsequently four Japanese tanks were observed north-west of Ngathet and were promptly engaged by 'D' Squadron of the 2nd Battalion Royal Tank Regiment. A short but fierce action followed in which exact observation was very difficult owing to the thin scrub covering the country. Hits were obtained on at least one hostile tank whilst the British vehicles remained unscathed.

The day was an unsatisfactory one for the tanks which were employed in preventing the Japanese from engaging the 63rd Indian Infantry Brigade about Wundwin. The scrub enabled the Japanese infantry and guns to advance unseen although the movement of tanks could not be similarly concealed. The Japanese were thus in a position to bring their guns up very close, and the British tanks were subjected to constant shelling and threats of outflanking. This forced them repeatedly to withdraw for short distances throughout the day, but they succeeded in covering the 63rd Indian Infantry Brigade which had came in for considerable attention from Japanese bombing aircraft.

At 1630 hours the 17th Indian Division announced that no transport for the 63rd Indian Infantry Brigade would be available before midnight and that the Wundwin position must be held until that hour, or the resources of the 7th Armoured Brigade utilised for the withdrawal of the infantry. It was considered that once the 63rd Indian Infantry Brigade become involved it would be very difficult for it to disengage. Consequently, by utilising tanks and other vehicles, the 7th Armoured Brigade contrived to ferry all infantry to Kume where proper motor transport was found. The 2nd Battalion Royal Tank Regiment continued to act as rear-guard whilst this movement was in progress. The 7th Armoured Brigade then went on to cross the Ava Bridge for the Ondaw area. The 7th Queen's Own Hussars joined the 48th Indian Infantry Brigade at Kyaukse. The 63rd Indian Infantry Brigade took up a new position covering the road and railway bridges across the Myitnge river south of Mandalay. The 16th Indian Infantry Brigade had reached the Ondaw area on 27 April.

ACTION AT KYAUKSE—28/29 APRIL

Movement of the 48th Indian Infantry Brigade

The 48th Indian Infantry Brigade was at Myothit on 23 April, and at Mahlaing on 24 April. As the situation south of Meiktila had deteriorated, it was ordered to move swiftly and take a strong lay-back position at Kyaukse. On 26 April it passed through the 7th Armoured Brigade and arrived at Kyaukse at 1200 hours. It was under the command of Brig. R. T. Cameron. Immediate steps were taken to occupy and improvise as strong a defensive position as possible. The intention was to delay the Japanese advance up to 1800 hours on 29 April so as to permit safe passage of the Irrawaddy by all the Allied forces, and also to give the depleted Chinese 22nd and 96th Divisions ample breathing time and an opportunity of concentrating in the Mandalay area. The Brigade was then to withdraw to Ywalaing. Its final destination was to be decided later.

Behind the 48th Indian Infantry Brigade, stood the 63rd Indian Infantry Brigade, and one troop 25 pounder. The latter was to assume command of the rear party on the night of 29/30 April when the Commander of the 48th Indian Infantry Brigade reported that all his troops were over the Myitnge bridge. It was also to deny the Myitnge line to the Japanese until first light on 30 April.

Kyaukse

Kyaukse had been burnt out and devastated by hostile aircraft. Dead Burmans and cattle lay about in the streets. The country round Kyaukse was mainly a mixture of open paddy fields and banana groves, whilst the jungle was dense on the banks of the Zawgyi river. The ground near the main road was cut by numerous irrigation channels, the road itself being raised on an embankment. Adjoining the eastern outskirts of the town was a long ridge running due east. Its extent was too great to include it entirely within a brigade defensive position. On this ridge the gunners found excellent observation posts. It was known that the main bulk of the Japanese *33rd Division* was then on the front of the 1st Burma Division to the west, and consequently the roads from that direction were potential approaches for mechanised forces.

Disposition of the 48th Indian Infantry Brigade

The 48th Indian Infantry Brigade position covered the west, south, and east of the town in a wide arc. On the south-east the 1st Battalion 4th P.W.O. Gurkha Rifles held a line south of the irrigation channels which took off from the Zawgyi river. To the right of the Battalion, 'A' company, was swung back to deny encirclement, and to its left, 'D' company stopped just short of the railway line. The western end of the ridge was almost on the main road and the eastern end about one mile east of the brigade perimeter. The ridge was held by two platoons of 'A' company. One of them sent out observation posts eastwards along the ridge by day. 'B' company with three platoons covered from about 80 yards up the ridge southwards through thick scrub for some five hundred yards to the river bank. From 'B' company's right the perimeter took a bend westwards at right angle along the right bank of the river. 'C' company held this with three platoons, each with a section in reserve. The river Zawgyi, being unfordable there, afforded a good anti-tank obstacle. The area of the Battalion generally faced east. From the railway line the combined Battalion 7th Gurkha Rifles continued the defences to the river at a point some five hundred yards south of the town. The 2nd Battalion 5th Royal Gurkha Rifles, then held a line for about one thousand yards along the north bank of the river swinging back north, to cover the long ridge running due east and west on the east of Kyaukse. It held Point 816, near the centre of the ridge, a strong patrol being thrown out to protect its eastern end. 'C' company's former lines were west of the road on a low crest south of which on the left and left centre were a village and banana grove. This was cut back to give a field of fire of about 80 yards and the village was partially burnt. East of the road 'D' company's forward lines ran along the edge of a thick jungle coming right into the left centre of their position. This was as far as possible cleared of under-growth, and a field of cotton in front of the left platoon was also cleared. The 1st Battalion, 3rd Q.A.O. Gurkha Rifles (only five platoons) was in brigade reserve on the north-eastern outskirts of the town, behind the 1st Battalion 4th P.W.O. Gurkha Rifles.

The total brigade strength was about seventeen hundred, all battalions being much reduced in numbers. As in the earlier action at Kokkogwa, the available signalling resources were practically nil. There was no wireless, and only one helio and two lamps were available. This absence of signalling equipment was not peculiar to the 48th Indian Infantry Brigade, all formations being similarly situated. It naturally hampered the efficiency of the defence, as communication by runners inevitably delayed the carrying out of essentially urgent orders. Supporting the infantry were the 7th Queen's Own Hussars with one company of the 1st Battalion West Yorkshire Regiment, one troop of 414 Battery, R.H.A., one troop of 'A' Battery 95th Anti-Tank Regiment Royal Artillery and 1 Field Battery of the 1st Indian Field Regiment, Indian Army. The 70th Field Company, Bengal Sappers and Miners, provided demolition parties. The anti-tank guns were placed in pairs. One pair in depth covered the main road behind the block mentioned later, the other covered the good tank country in front of the 1st Battalion 4th P.W.O. Gurkha Rifles.

Fields of fire for the infantry were improved, banana plantations and undergrowth being cut back and thinned out. Even after this work had been carried out many covered approaches for the Japanese still existed. Therefore the area to the west of the main road in front of the positions was inundated by the opening of a water-cut. A road-block was constructed at a bend in the road near a culvert just south of the forward defence lines. In addition to the pair of anti-tank guns, mortars also covered this block. During the night of 27/28 April, the 63rd Indian Infantry Brigade passed through the position, and so, too, did the last elements of the Chinese Fifth Army.

Patrol activity—28 April

On the morning of 28 April patrols were pushed out by all the three battalions. Those of the 1st Battalion 4th P.W.O. Gurkha Rifles reported all clear on their front. An officer jeep patrol of the 2nd Battalion 5th Gurkha Rifles sent out to the foot-hills, ten miles east, returned at 1500 hours to report that on entering the village of Pyankseikpin they had learnt from the headman that a party of armed Burmans or Japanese had entered the village earlier in the morning and demanded food and rice. Tanks and a partol of the 7th Gurkha Rifles went south searching between the main road and the river. At 1800 hours tanks reported Japanese mechanised transport ten miles south of Kyaukse on the road. They engaged it but it came under anti-tank fire which necessitated a slight withdrawal. A troop of the tanks was then heavily bombed from a low altitude by hostile aircraft. One tank was destroyed.

Tank trap at milestone 399

On receipt of the news about the Japanese mechanised transport a tank trap which had been planned at milestone 399 (1½ miles south of

Kyaukse) was ordered to be manned (1700 hours). Two lorries bearing anti-tank guns of the 2nd Brigade went out with escorts of one N.C.O. and six riflemen for each lorry. Shortly after the lorries with anti-tank guns had taken position, five Japanese tanks appeared. The anti-tank guns opened fire and knocked out the leading tank but as infantry was advancing up the road on either side of the tanks the anti-tank gun lorries had to withdraw and reach the main position at 2000 hours. The escort which had been in front of the lorries on either side of the road attacked the Japanese moving on either side of the tanks with grenades and tommy guns. The small force then withdrew on foot as the lorries had gone.

Japanese attack on the main positions—28 April

The Japanese followed up and were soon in contact with the main brigade position astride the road. At first they concentrated on the 7th Battalion Gurkha Rifles shortly after 'D' and 'C' companies had reported the advance. Japanese patrols, each about two sections strong, advanced on either side of the road towards the road-block. 'C' and 'D' companies each took them on. One of these drove the Japanese back with considerable loss, the remnants taking cover in the culvert about 150 yards south of the road-block. At about 2200 hours the Japanese moved a mortar detachment forward on 'D' company, the 1st Battalion 7th Gurkha Rifles right front, east of the road, but were dispersed. At the same time a frontal attack by about two companies developed all along 'D' company's front. The Japanese were allowed to approach within 150 yards and then fire was opened. In the bright moon-light the Japanese could be seen fleeing in confusion, they lost about 25 killed and many wounded. A few parties also penetrated to the river bank opposite 'C' company of the 2nd Battalion 5th Gurkha Rifles but were dealt with by automatic fire. 'C' company of the 2nd Battalion 5th Gurkha Rifles was able to give some assistance to the 7th Battalion Gurkha Rifles by way of 2" mortar fire. The 25 pounders also opened up and were directed on to the Japanese transport, the lights of which could be seen across the river to the south. For the next two hours the front was comparatively quiet except for small parties of Japanese troops creeping forward to recover the dead and wounded.

29 April—0030 hours

At about 0030 hours another frontal attack, again by about two companies, developed against 'D' company which had been reinforced by one platoon of 'A' company. Visibility at the time was much better and the men were full of confidence. So they let the Japanese come within 100 yards before they opened up with every available weapon and with 3" mortar. One Japanese section that came up against a Bren gun at 50 yards range was completely wiped out and the attackers were thrown back with a loss of 40 men. Again, except for occasional cries from the wounded Japanese, comparative quiet reigned. Occasionally small parties of the Japanese were heard collecting casualties and were fired on when seen. Soon, however, a cloudy sky made visibility poor.

0300 hours

At 0300 hours there were signs that the Japanese had crossed the river, and were feeling around the flank of 'B' company of the 2nd Battalion 5th Gurkha Rifles. But without telephone communications between the companies it was difficult to get an accurate picture of the whole engagement. Firing from 'A' and 'B' companies made it look as though the Japanese were trying to penetrate up the re-entrant between the two. The Commanding Officer therefore ordered the headquarters reserve platoon to strengthen this gap. 'B' company had no difficulty in keeping back the light Japanese forces on its front.

Japanese attempt to pierce the 7th Battalion Gurkha Rifles front—29 April

The Japanese then waited for the moon to go down. At 0515 hours they made the final effort to pierce the 7th Battalion Gurkha Rifles front. They came in on the right of 'D' company and through the neck of the jungle on its left centre. Even this attack in darkness failed as completely as the previous two in moonlight. They were driven back with heavy losses; and judging by the screams and shouts heard they would seem to have been thoroughly shaken. A half-hearted attempt on 'B' company of the 2nd Battalion 5th Gurkha Rifles was also beaten back. The 3" mortars had opened up on both fronts and went "well into the enemy." On the front of 'C' company the 7th Gurkha Rifles no serious attack developed during the night. Only several strong patrols had advanced but even these had been driven back without difficulty.

Dawn broke to find the brigade perimeter everywhere in tact. Patrols of tanks and infantry went forward to clear the front and flanks of the position and to ascertain if any encircling movements were in progress. To the west, the patrol of 1/4 G.R. went as far as Panan and reported a complete Japanese Infantry battalion, making an encircling movement to the west. The patrol, reinforced by a troop of tanks with an armoured artillery observation post, drove the battalion out of the village by shell fire and then decimated it by machine-gun fire from the tanks. It was chased from village to village by this method and virtually wiped out—an excellent example of cooperation of infantry, armour and artillery. On the east another patrol went round the north side of the long ridge.

Counter attack by the 7th Battalion Gurkha Rifles—29 April

At 0730 hours the Japanese began shelling the guns. At 0800 hours the 7th Battalion Gurkha Rifles planned a counter-attack on the banana groves and the hamlet of Htanaungbinla to the west of the road. Its purpose was to trap the Japanese believed to be in hiding there. 'B' company, with a force of 'C' company protecting its right flank along the railway, was assigned this task and support was also to be given by troop 25 pounders and battalion 3" mortars. The plan was briefly to mortar the culvert south of the road-block where many Japanese were known to be in hiding, as also the south and centre portions of the hamlet; then the village was to be attacked from north and north-east. There was to be an advance towards the southern edge with short bursts of controlled fire with Tommy guns, Brens, rifles and grenades into any cover suspected of holding the Japanese; and also any located or seen were to be suitably dealt with by these weapons. The plan worked well. Elated by the success during the previous night the men went forward at 0900 hours. Grenades and Tommy-guns made short work of 38 Japanese inside the culvert. A few who bolted down the nulla were dealt with by grenades. 'B' company then moved rapidly through the village. The Japanese force in the village was destroyed. The action has been characterised as "a most successful attack skilfully planned and boldly led .... it cost the enemy, at a conservative estimate, 100 killed. 'B' company's casualties were one killed and three wounded. A Japanese flag, three 2" mortars five L.M.Gs and a large number of rifles and pistols were captured besides two haversacks full of papers."

Japanese artillery activity—29 April

Throughout the day Japanese artillery which had begun shelling the gun positions from 0730 hours, was active. At intervals they concentrated on searching the long ridge for gunner observation posts. The pagoda on the ridge came in for direct hits. 'A' company of the 2nd Battalion 5th Gurkha Rifles also came in for a lot of shelling but suffered no casualties. The gunners maintained their position gallantly, searched out hostile positions and landed some timely shells into a party of the Japanese who were trying to work round the flank to the east. At about 1300 hours the Japanese guns shortened their range and directed their shells on infantry positions. They had brought up some heavier artillery and it looked as though they were about to put in an attack on the whole front. At 1400 hours there was a conference at the Brigade Headquarters which was well concealed. The news seems to have reached the Japanese through fifth columnists for no sooner the Commanding Officers had collected than the Brigade Headquarters came in for the heaviest and most concentrated shelling of the day.

Fresh attacks by the 7th Battalion Gurkha Rifles

At about 1530 hours patrols of the 7th Battalion Gurkha Rifles at the southern end of the hamlet of Htanaungbinla reported about two companies of Japanese moving forward to the village. 'C' company opened up fire and one M.M.G. opened up on the banana grove and killed a number of Japanese. As, however, they seemed to be in great strength both in the village and the banana grove, a sub-group of tanks was asked to thicken the fire in both areas. This was done from the road most effectively. Japanese attempts to advance therefore could make little headway.

ORDERS TO THE BRIGADE TO BREAK CONTACT—29 APRIL

Orders had then been received from the Divisional Headquarters that the brigade was to be withdrawn at 1800 hours or as soon as possible on 29 April. Although contact with the Japanese was close, and a withdrawal at 1800 hours involved a movement in daylight, Brig. R. T. Cameron decided to break off the action at that hour. The plan for this had been carefully worked out. It was executed speedily and with perfect timing.

At 1700 hours hostile activity again increased and Japanese aircraft began to dive-bomb and machine-gun the brigade troops. These attacks caused no damage. Two tanks of the 7th Queen's Own Hussars moved forward across the main road bridge at 1730 hours and at once had the effect of deadening hostile fire.

WITHDRAWAL—1800 HOURS

Before 1800 hours the troops in the forward defence lines began to thin out and the first line motor transport moved off. The railway bridge across the Zawgyi river had been destroyed earlier in the day, and at 1800 hours precisely the main road bridge was blown. The deafening explosion had an electrical effect. All firing ceased as though both sides had received an order to do so. There was an eerie silence. Then the Allied guns opened on the Japanese forward positions and the tanks followed suit. The infantry remaining south of the river crossed it by wading. The two forward tanks covered this movement and immediately afterwards swung west along a road skirting the river to cross it by a subsidiary bridge which was then blown. Other tanks covered the broken bridges. The guns shortened their range to shell the recently evacuated forward defence lines. The 1st Battalion 3rd Q.A.O. Gurkha Rifles had formed a layback at a hammock near the road just north of the town, and by 1815 hours the other battalions were passing through this position. Five minutes later the tanks in Kyaukse were withdrawn but continued to act as a rear-guard to the brigade which marched to an embussing point. As the last of the tanks withdrew up the main road the bridge over the Zawgyi near milestone 410 was blown. Not long afterwards the 63rd Indian Infantry Brigade demolished the road and rail bridges across the Myitnge river. The demolition of the railway bridge was not very successful.

ESTIMATE

The action at Kyaukse by the 48th Indian Infantry Brigade was a brilliant rear-guard one. Though the Japanese forces pitted against it were at least double its number, it threw back repeated hostile attacks with heavy loss of about five hundred to the latter; the losses of the 48th Indian Infantry Brigade were an incredible number of only ten killed and wounded. The majority of the Japanese casualties were inflicted by the 7th Battalion Gurkha Rifles. Mention must also be made of the exceptionally fine work done by the Troop of Battery 1st Indian Field Regiment supporting the battalion. The forward observation officer Captain Ranbir Bakshi, was in close and constant touch with the forward companies and moved his observation posts into most exposed positions to get better shots. The fire of his Troop was most accurate and effective. The brigade had also accomplished the major task of allowing the rest of the 17th Indian Division and the Chinese troops to pass north through the Ava Bridge. That the Japanese had received rough handling is shown by the fact that their long account of their advance on Mandalay is silent about the action at Kyaukse and merely says that

THE BEGINNING OF THE END—RETREAT NORTH OF MANDALAY

the *18th Division* made no attempt to follow up or force the Myitnge position.

The 48th Indian Infantry Brigade crossed the Ava Bridge and concentrated at Myinmu near the confluence of the Mu river with the Irrawaddy. During 29 April Mandalay had been cleared by Burcorps of as much of its accumulation of stores as possible. Shortage of transport made this difficult and much had to be destroyed, whilst other stores were made over to the Chinese.

FUTURE MOVEMENT OF THE CHINESE FORCES

On that day (29 April), too, the situation regarding the future movement of the Chinese forces in the Mandalay area crystallised. At a meeting at Shwebo between Generals Sir H. Alexander and J. Stilwell the latter stated that the remnants of the Chinese Fifth Army would move north on Katha when Mandalay was given up. They would probably then fall back on Bhamo, but Gen. J. Stilwell was uncertain on this point and was awaiting the Generalissimo's instructions. It was even apprehended that the capture of Lashio, then imminent, might force the withdrawal of the Chinese Fifth Army to India.

Gen. J. Stilwell further stated that their exhaustion made it impossible for the Chinese 96th Division to fight south of Mandalay. He proposed, therefore, to move this division by train to Myitkyina as soon as possible. This left only the Chinese 22nd Division to cover Mandalay and hold the crossings over the Myitnge river. Consequently only a delaying action could be fought on that line. The 22nd Division would then continue its withdrawal up the east bank of the Irrawaddy to Singu, crossing to the west bank by ferry at that point.

Gen. J. Stilwell also requested that the Chinese 38th Division should revert to his command to cover the withdrawal of the Chinese Fifth Army. Gen. Sir. H. Alexander felt obliged to agree to this request, although the withdrawal of the 38th Division must uncover the flank of Burcorps when it moved into position west of the Irrawaddy.[13]

Whilst this meeting was taking place the Japanese were on the outskirts of Lashio, and before the day closed had entered the town to get astride the main line of communication with China. Ahead of them, almost unguarded, lay the road to Bhamo and Myitkyina.

The Chinese 22nd Division was very weak. Apart from the heavy losses it had sustained, one of its regiments was with the 200th Division in the Shan States. On 30 April only one battalion was on the Myitnge position, the remainder of the division being south of Mandalay in the Amarapura-Myohaung area.

BLOWING UP OF AVA BRIDGE—30 APRIL—2359 HOURS

In view of the danger to the Ava bridge and the unsatisfactory Chinese arrangements for the defence of the Myitnge position the 63rd Indian Infantry Brigade fell back to cover the bridge. This it did after

---
[13] General Alexander's *Despatch*, para 54.

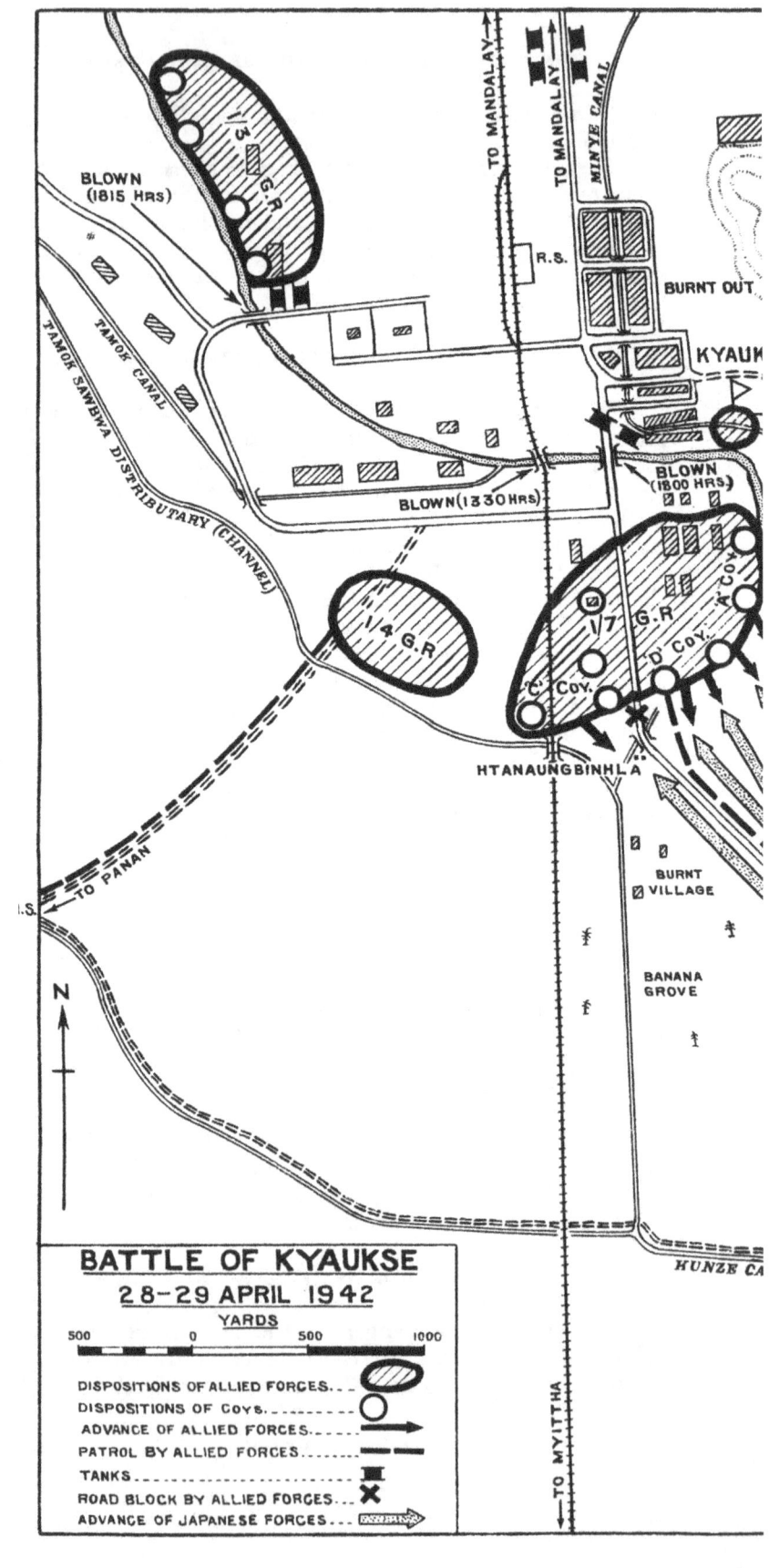

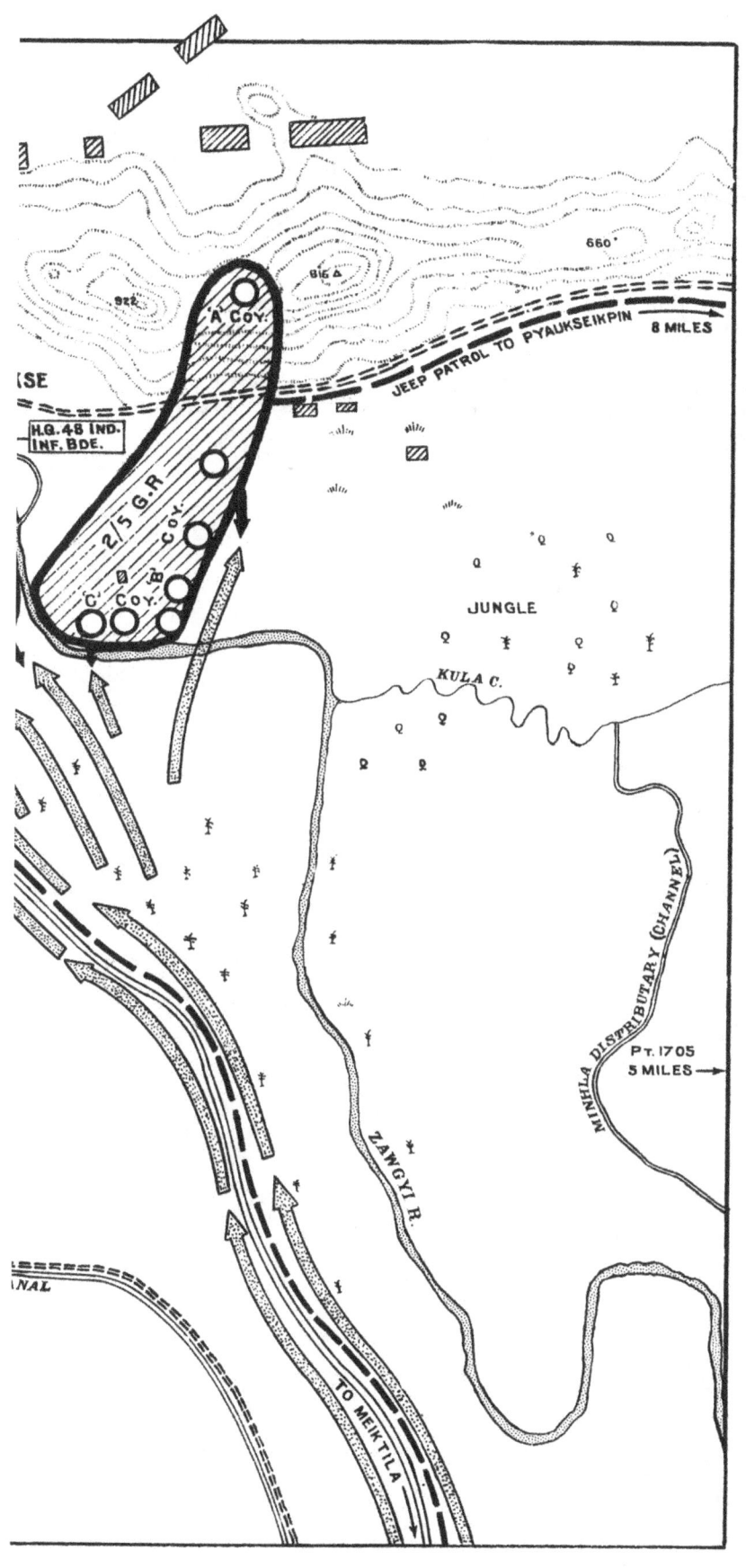

the 48th Indian Infantry Brigade had passed through it north of the Myitnge river. It then took up positions east of the bridge, a platoon being left on the Myitnge line.

During 30 April, the 63rd Indian Infantry Brigade remained on the east bank of the Irrawaddy, but it was evident that the destruction of the Ava bridge could not long be delayed. Japanese tanks were reported to be advancing on Mandalay from Lashio, other hostile forces were closing in from the south, and the Chinese 22nd Division was in no condition to fight.

After darkness that night the last elements of the Indo-British forces crossed the great bridge, and at 2359 hours it was blown. Two of its huge spans collapsed into the Irrawaddy.

CHAPTER XXII

Pursuit—Action at Monywa

JAPANESE PLANS

During the last stages of the First Burma Campaign, Japanese strategy was to cut off the routes of retreat of the Indo-British and Chinese forces and bottle them up in Upper Burma. As early as March the Japanese *Fifteenth Army* had made the following plan for a triple drive. The *18th* and *55th Divisions* were to advance as rapidly as possible and push the Allied forces up against the Irrawaddy bend south of Mandalay and capture Mandalay. The *56th Division* was to penetrate into the Shan Hills from Toungoo over the east side of the mountains and to advance quickly into the Lashio area. These moves would cut the retreat road of the Chinese Armies. The *33rd Division* was to advance up the Irrawaddy, capture Yenangyaung, cross over to the west bank of the Irrawaddy and "nail the Allied forces" in the area of Monywa or Shwebo.[1]

By the last week of April, it was clear to the Japanese that the Allied forces were going to abandon the Mandalay area. The *33rd Division* was therefore ordered to mop up the remnants of the forces moving westwards from Mandalay. The following orders were issued for 'the pursuit' which was to begin on 26 April. The main force of the division was to advance along the left bank of the Irrawaddy towards Myingyaung. The *Harada Detached Force* consisting of *215 Infantry Regiment*, one *Mountain Artillery Battalion*, one *Heavy Field Artillery* unit, one *Light Tank Company* and one *Transport Company* was to cross the Irrawaddy at Yenangyaung and to advance towards Pakokku and Monywa. A unit consisting mainly of one battalion of the *214th Infantry Regiment* was to proceed to Monywa by a large landing craft.[2]

IMPORTANCE OF MONYWA

The denial of Monywa meant the denial of retreat to India. It would cut off all the Indo-British forces west of the river Mu from direct approach to Ye-U through Monywa and also prevent the move of any force up or across the Chindwin. There was no regular formation of the Indo-British forces in position to oppose a direct Japanese advance on Ye-U.

FIRST ATTACK ON MONYWA—30 APRIL

On the evening of 30 April Monywa was garrisoned by a detachment

---

[1] *The Japanese account of their operations in Burma* (Dec. 41 to Aug. 45) edited by H. Q. 12th Army. 601/8255/H, p. 18.
[2] S.E.A.T.I.C. Bulletin No. 245—*History of the Japanese 15th Army.* 601/7785/H, p. 25.

of the 1st Battalion the Gloucestershire Regiment about one hundred and fifty strong, and the river patrol of the Royal Marines. In the town were a number of refugees waiting for steamers to carry them up the Chindwin. At Alon, six miles north of Monywa, was a party of eighty surplus officers, and over two thousand four hundred clerks and servants with their women and children sent off from the Army Headquarters at Shwebo the previous evening. This party also awaited transport up the river.

The civil authorities still functioned at Monywa. That day Burcorps Headquarters with a protective detachment and a Frontier Force column had opened at Songon, sixteen miles to the north, whilst Headquarters 1st Burma Division was at Ma-U four miles south-east of the town.

At 1910 hours machine-gun, mortar, and shell fire was directed on Monywa from the opposite bank of the river. No warning whatsoever had been received of the approach of the Japanese who had entered the village of Ywashe in motor vehicles accompanied by seven tanks. They were opposed by two men of the Royal Marines forming part of a guard of a launch moored on the west bank of the river. These two were last seen firing a Bren gun at the Japanese transport. It is stated that fire was opened across the river by the Japanese to prevent the escape of a steamer moored on the west bank. The serang in charge of this vessel cast off furtively in an attempt to cross to Monywa where his wife was. This move drew heavy fire from the Japanese and increased the threat to Monywa. Spasmodic fire was maintained on the town throughout the night; and the Japanese effected a crossing of the river to the south, setting up a road-block between the town and Headquarters of the 1st Burma Division.[2]

At 2045 hours as soon as it was informed of the situation Burcorps issued orders to the 1st Burma Division that it was to advance on Monywa as quickly as possible. It was then believed that Monywa had already been captured. The 1st Burma Division was ordered to concentrate at Chaung-U, and the 48th Indian Infantry Brigade, then at Myinmu, and the 63rd Brigade were placed under its command. The 63rd Brigade was expected to arrive at Chaung-U by train the following morning. The 16th Brigade was to proceed to Ye-U immediately by the quickest route. The brigade was then in the process of moving south from Ondaw to Muwa near Myinmu and, in fact, did not begin its movement towards Ye-U from Muwa until the following night, at 2200 hours. Meanwhile, on receiving information of the attack on Monywa, Army Headquarters ordered one squadron of the 7th Armoured Brigade to move on the town via Ye-U, and a second squadron to support the 1st Burma Division about Chaung-U. These orders were issued at 2359 hours on 30 April.

[2] About the action at Monywa *The Japanese History of the Fifteenth Army* (601/7785/H), S.E.A.T.I.C. Bulletin No. 245, p. 25, says "Harada detached force entered Monywa at dawn on 1 May and entered Monywa with little opposition. It was then surrounded by enemy forces which had retreated from Mandalay. The Division (33) main force immediately changed its line of advance, crossed the river at Sale and moved towards Monywa. The unit which had come up by landing craft landed at a point south of Monywa. The enemy force then abandoned its attempt to pass through Monywa and retreated towards Budalin".

1 May

At about 0500 hours on 1 May a mixed party of Japanese troops and Burmans (local guides) attacked the 1st Burma Division Headquarters at Ma-U, and captured a set. This somewhat disorganised the chain of command. The protective platoon, composed of raw Burmese troops, bolted; but a stout fight was put up by the officers, clerks and batmen. These withdrew fighting and went north of the railway line. Taking secret documents and ciphers with them they then made their way across country to Chaung-U.

At Monywa in the early morning a dozen hostile aircraft made a thorough reconnaissance of the town from a height of one hundred feet. the shelling increased, most of it being concentrated on the area of the landing stage. Three large launches were then observed to be coming up the river. They pulled up on the west bank and troops at once rapidly embarked in them, probably a couple of hundred men in each. The launches began to cross the river.

Monywa was then defended by the small detachment of the 1st Battalion the Gloucestershire Regiment, about twenty Royal Marines, and F.F. 1 which had been sent by Burcorps to the town during the night. On the south-eastern outskirts were some Sappers and Miners of the 1st Burma Division. This handful of troops opened small arms and light automatic fire on the approaching launches, and as soon as they did so, came in turn under heavy shell and mortar fire from the opposite bank of the river. The Bren guns in action could not prevent a Japanese landing. And once the Japanese were ashore they were soon in possession of the town.

In thus securing Monywa the Japanese made good use of the period when the direct line of approach from Pakokku lay unprotected. They had entered that town after the withdrawal of the 2nd Burma Brigade, on the night of 28 April. Obviously well supplied with information they struck suddenly at Monywa when they knew that it lay open to them. The organised nature of the attack on the town and on the Headquarters of the 1st Burma Division indicated a pre-arranged plan and not a haphazard dash. At the same time, by firing on Monywa for about twelve hours before carrying out their attack, they largely discouned the element of surprise and gave the Burcorps valuable time within which to group the forces against this unexpected threat. Even so, on 1 May, the road to the Ye-U lay unguarded save by the small force that had fallen back from Monywa. During the day this force was joined by a squadron of the 2nd Battalion Royal Tank Regiment which had moved on the receipt of orders from the Army-Headquarters.

The operations about Monywa were conducted by the 1st Burma Division, which was far short of its proper strength. Neither of its two available brigades was within striking distance of Monywa towards which they were marching. They were south of the Monywa-Myiumo road, and the shortage of motor transport precluded the possibility of ferrying. The most conveniently situated formation was the 63rd Indian Infantry Brigade since it could be taken forward by rail.

MORE TROOPS MOVED TO MONYWA—1 MAY

The 63rd Indian Infantry Brigade was at the moment being hurried towards Monywa from the area of the Ava Bridge. During the night of 30 April/1 May it proceeded by train from Sagaing to Chaung-U. On the morning of 1 May the 1st Battalion 10th Gurkha Rifles and the 2nd Battalion 13th Frontier Force Rifles detrained at Kyehmon, eight miles south-east of Monywa.[4] The Brigade Commander was then asked to advance on Monywa, with all speed by the Commander of the 1st Burma Division. The advance was made astride the road with the 1st Battalion 10th Gurkha Rifles to the right and the 2nd Battalion 13th Frontier Force Rifles to the left. A squadron of the 7th Queen's Own Hussars was to help them by moving ahead along the road and on the right flank. Instructions were left for the 1st Battalion 11th Sikh Regiment to follow on down the road. No sooner were the outskirts of Ma-U reached than strong opposition was encountered by the 2nd Battalion 13th Frontier Force Rifles. The advance was held up for some time. Eventually with the help of mortars which had by this time come up, the opposition was overcome and the advance resumed. After a march of another mile west of Ma-U the leading companies of the 2nd Battalion 13th Frontier Force Rifles came under heavy and accurate mortar fire. Two tanks of the 7th Queen's Own Hussars were lost, the Frontier Force Rifles Battalion sustained heavy casualties and the advance was brought to a standstill. It was also late in the afternoon and all ranks were exhausted. Order was therefore issued to halt on the line gained and to continue the advance the following day.[5]

The 1st Battalion 11th Sikh Regiment arrived at Chaung-U at 0830 hours and soon was on the march to Monywa. On approaching the village of Ma-U it was sniped from the surrounding jungle. One company was detailed for the task of combing the village and the jungle beyond it to the west. At 1500 hours the battalion went forward through the Frontier Force Rifles Battalion and took up an outpost position astride the road just west of Ma-U.

Meanwhile the 13th Indian Infantry Brigade had arrived at Ma-U[6] and received orders for a dawn attack next morning. The 1st Burma Brigade was then at Chaung-U. It was to continue its march to Monywa at 0500 hours and was to join in the attack. At night the Japanese shelled the area of the 1st Battalion 18th Garhwal Rifles.

The Japanese were active that night round the perimeter at Ma-U. Flares and tracer ammunition were fired by patrols and the usual noises indulged in. But the battalions of the 13th Indian Infantry Brigade kept calm and did not disclose their positions by firing. Two attacks were made on the Frontier Force Rifles, but these were successfully repulsed.

Events at Monywa were discussed at a meeting on the evening of 1 May between Gens. Sir H. Alexander and J. Stilwell at Ye-U. At this town were then assembled the Army Headquarters, and the Headquarters

---

[4] *War Diary*, 63 Brigade, Monywa.
[5] 7th Armoured Brigade HQ moved during the night of 1 May to an area four miles west of Ye-U followed by 2nd Royal Tank Regiment and the 7th Queen's Own Hussars.
[6] 13th Indian Infantry Brigade has a very short account of the action at Monywa.

of Burcorps and the 17th Indian Division.⁷ Gen. J. Stilwell agreed that a withdrawal from the Mandalay-Irrawaddy line could no longer be delayed. The situation created by the Japanese occupation of Monywa was serious since it cut off all the Indo-British forces west of the Mu river from the direct approach to Ye-U through Monywa. It also denied the use to them of the Chindwin, prevented the move of any of the forces across the river, and opened to the Japanese the means of cutting the line of withdrawal through Kalewa. It was further agreed that the situation required the withdrawal of the 7th Armoured Brigade from its position in support of the Chinese 38th Division east of the river Mu. Orders were therefore issued for the 7th Armoured Brigade to move forthwith on the axis Ye-U Monywa. The withdrawal from Mandalay-Irrawaddy line was ordered to begin at once. Gen. J. Stilwell informed Gen. Sir H. Alexander that he intended to withdraw the Chinese Fifth Army to the Katha area, but he was uncertain of his further plans. Preparations were, however, in hand for a possible withdrawal to India. This was the last occasion when Gen. Sir H. Alexander met Gen. J. Stilwell before the close of the campaign. Owing to the failure of Gen. J. Stilwell's wireless it was not possible to communicate again with him. He made his way to India by a route further north than that taken by the Indo-British forces.⁸

Attack by the 13th Brigade from the north-east 2 May

On 2 May the operations about Monywa were resumed. It was intended to attack the town on a two brigade front, the 63rd Indian Infantry Brigade advancing north-west astride the road and railway, and the 13th Brigade moving south-west on the town from Zalok down the road from Kyaukse. Its first objective was to be the railway line, and it was then to continue through the town to the river bank. The 1st Burma Brigade could not be available until the early afternoon when it was to support the attack by the 63rd Indian Infantry Brigade. To each brigade front a Mountain Battery was allotted and also a Field Battery (less a troop) of the 1st Indian Field Regiment, Indian Army. The squadron of tanks of the 7th Queen's Own Hussars was to co-operate with the 63rd Indian Infantry Brigade.

The town of Monywa lent itself to defence. Surrounded by flat, open country, much of it paddy land, it gave its defenders excellent fields of fire and good command of all approaches. The sparse vegetation of the dry zone afforded scanty cover for the attacking force. The Japanese had not been slow to seize upon these advantages, and were in strong positions in buildings and other points of vantage on the outskirts of the town.

At a conference held at 2100 hours on 1 May it was decided that the 13th Indian Infantry Brigade should carry out a night march from Ma-U to Zalok and make a dawn attack. Verbal orders were issued to this effect. Starting at 0400 hours the Brigade marched five miles north across country. The leading troops struck the Monywa-Kyaukka road

⁷ Gen. Sir H. Alexander's *Despatch*, para 65. For a brief account of action at Monywa see the *Despatch*, paras 61-69.
⁸ *Ibid.*

at 0545 hours. Their first objective was Shaukka, the intermediate one was the railway station and the final was the river bank. The advance from Zalok began at 0645 hours. The 5th Batalion 1st Punjab Regiment advanced on the right of the road.[9] Its 'B' company went left forward, 'D' company right forward and 'C' company in reserve. The 1st Battalion 18th Royal Garhwal Rifles advanced on the left of the road with the 1st Battalion Royal Inniskilling Fusiliers in reserve. Each forward battalion was to be supported by one Section 23rd Mountain Battery. The first objective, the village of Shaukka, one mile north-east of the railway station, was easily taken at 0740 hours. There were no Japanese there. Local Burmans proceeding east from Monywa estimated Japanese strength in the town at figures varying from nil to four hundred.[10] When they were six hundred yards north-east of the railway line the 1st Battalion 18th Royal Garhwal Rifles met heavy opposition. The forward companies took the village and pushed forward within fifty yards of the railway line. Meanwhile at 0800 hours the leading companies and the Advance Battalion Headquarters of the 5th Battalion 1st Punjab Regiment had advanced to within two hundred yards of the railway station. Soon they also came under heavy automatic and rifle fire from the Japanese positions which appeared to be on the railway line. The leading companies retraced their steps by a hundred yards. Thereupon one detachment of their mortar platoon opened fire on the railway station and secured several hits on the buildings there. The Japanese also replied with mortar fire. At about 0830 hours 'B' company worked its way forward and eventually succeeded, without any loss to itself, in dislodging the Japanese from the railway station. Meanwhile 'D' company had gone well out to the right and was attempting to gain the railway line there and attack the Japanese from the flank. However, on hearing that the artillery was about to engage the targets in that area it withdrew. 'B' Company was not only unable to advance beyond the railway line (the river bank was its final objective) but was also forced out of the station at 1030 hours.

Fifty yards away from the station 1st Battalion 18th Royal Garhwal Rifles was stopped by heavy Japanese automatic and mortar fire from a grove of palm trees to the left of the road and just east of the railway line. The leading company on the right, 'A' company, suffered heavy losses. 'C' Company was then ordered to attack astride the road with the object of turning the opposition's flank. It found the Japanese strongly entrenched behind the railway line with automatics and mortars. A mortar and infantry gun were observed, and the 23rd Mountain Battery was asked to shell these. After several rounds it forced the Japanese mortars to withdraw. At 1015 hours the reserve company, 'D' company, was ordered to work round the Japanese right flank through the palm grove. 800 yards away from the road, while advancing into the grove, the company came under mortar fire. The situation at 1030 hours was that neither battalion could make any progress towards the railway line. The Japanese were strongly entrenched just west of the railway line with

---

[9] There is a detailed account in the *War Diaries* of 5th Battalion 1st Punjab and 1st Battalion 18th Garhwal Rifles.
[10] This was an underestimate.

machine guns and mortars with strong points around the pagoda and a white house. They had organised excellent observation and had the range worked out along the whole front. Any forward movement of the 13th Brigade troops brought down heavy and accurate mortar fire.

There was a lull in the fighting for an hour. At 1050 hours a message from the Brigade Headquarters stated that 'tanks were coming to support left flank'. At 1130 hours the 5th Battalion 1st Punjab Regiment resumed the attack. 'B' company again worked forward and within half an hour occupied the railway station again. 'D' company reached the road running from Monywa north-east to Ettaw. On its way it forced small parties of the Japanese to retreat. At 1400 hours 'B' company was again forced off the railway station by superior numbers and returned to its old positions. For reasons unknown, 'D' company also returned.

On the 1st Battalion 18th Royal Garhwal Rifles front, at 1150 hours 'B' and 'D' companies on the left flank were ordered to infiltrate towards the railway line and report the situation. At 1300 hours 'B' company was holding the palm grove and 'D' company was trying to work round the Japanese right 1000 yards left of 'B' comapny. 'C' company was ordered to be prepared to push forward under cover of M.M.Gs at the bend of the road 400 yards east of the level crossing. But before it had fired two bursts, Japanese mortar fire forced it to withdraw.

ADVANCE OF THE 63RD INDIAN INFANTRY BRIGADE

The 63rd Brigade began its advance from Ma-U at 0840 hours. The 1st Battalion 11th Sikh Regiment moved on either side of the road with the 1st Battalion 10th Gurkha Rifles to its right and the 2nd Battalion 13th Frontier Force Rifles in reserve. During the advance the left forward company of the Sikhs observed hostile movement on the west bank of the Chindwin and some craft on the river itself. These were engaged by the battalion mortars and machine guns and by the artillery. Some vessels were sunk. At 1110 hours the forward companies (B and C) went through the village of Ywathit and reported that it was clear of the Japanese. But as the advance of 'B' and 'C' companies was about to recommence from the west end of the village, and as the Battalion Headquarters and 'A' and 'D' companies were entering the village, heavy fire came upon both the forward companies and the Battalion Headquarters from the village and trees surrounding it. Just ahead of the forward companies a tree previously prepared for felling was finally brought down by the Japanese and made into an effective road-block. The carriers ahead of the forward companies quickly turned round and got back without a shot being fired at them. All companies then moved to the village and drove the Japanese out of it.

At 1140 hours 'B' and 'C' companies pressed on towards their objective, the road-block. As it was covered by numerous machine-guns and mortars they suffered heavy casualties and were pinned to the ground about 100 yards from the hostile position. 'B' company lost its commander. All its platoon officers were wounded and eighty percent of its men were either killed or wounded. All this was the result of intense mortar fire. The two remaining companies tried to work forward,

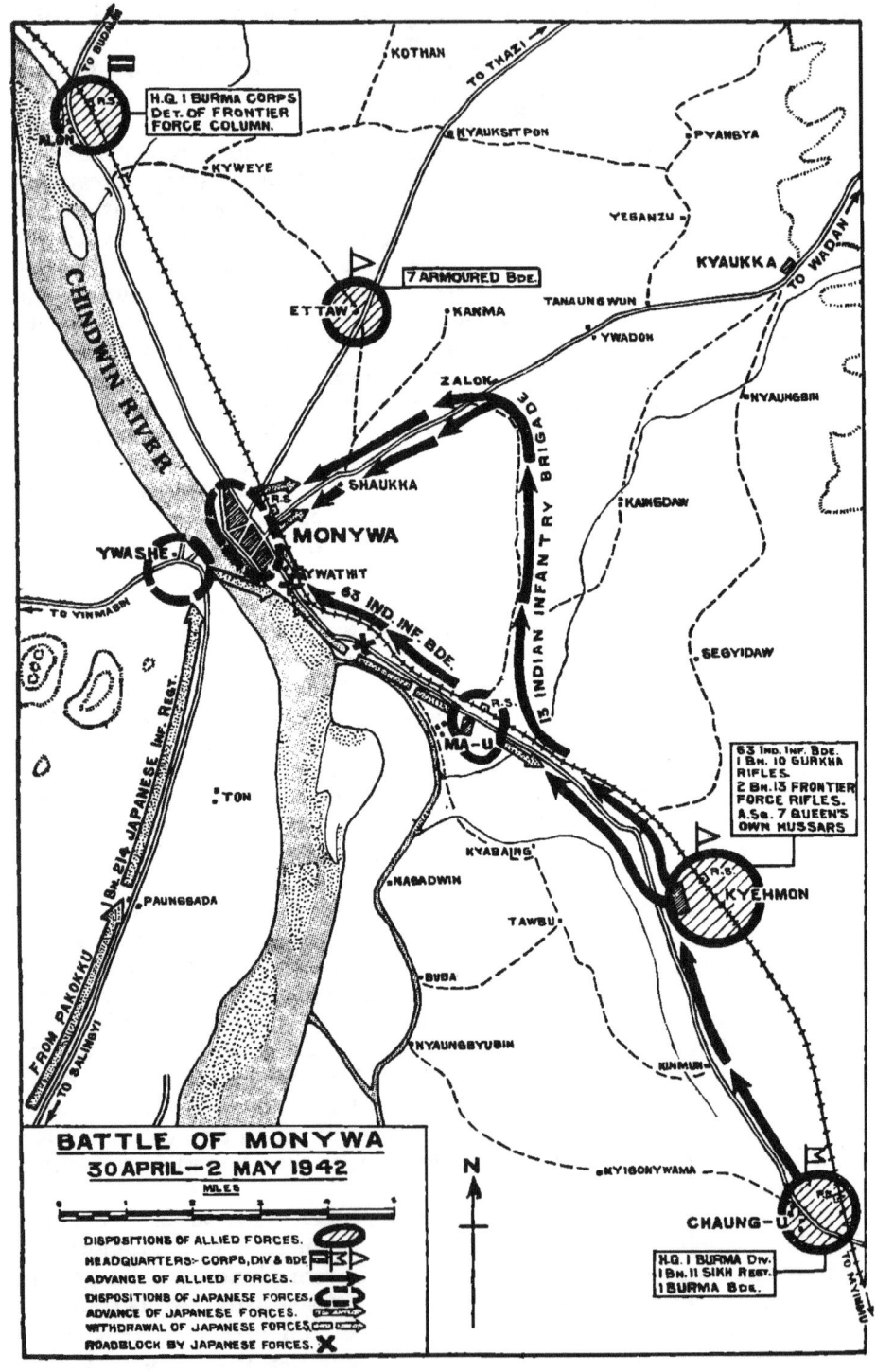

'D' company to the right of 'C' company and 'A' company to the left of 'B' company, but Japanese fire held them up. At 1400 hours two companies of the 2nd Battalion 13th Frontier Force Rifles arrived to be in reserve for the Sikh Battalion.

Hostile bombers guided from the Japanese Headquarters on the west bank of the river circled over the troops continuously but did not drop any bombs as the positions of the opposing forces were too close to be distinguished from each other.

At 1200 hours the 63rd Indian Infantry Brigade had ordered the 1st Battalion 10th Gurkha Rifles to attack from the north. But they had also been held up by heavy fire two miles south of Monywa. In the afternoon two companies of the Gurkha Battalion attacked in support of the 1st Battalion 11th Sikh Regiment but the attack was repulsed with a certain number of casualties. They soon lost touch with the rest of the brigade and moved clear of the eastern side of the town and joined the 13th Indian Infantry Brigade. The battalion carriers saw the Japanese moving in country boats. They opened fire with M.M.Gs. setting one or two of them on fire. Tanks of a squadron of the 7th Queen's Own Hussars were employed against the block. But they were unable to force it.

ATTACK BY THE 1ST BURMA DIVISION—2 MAY

The General Officer Commanding the 1st Burma Division thereupon decided to put in the 1st Burma Brigade to the attack through the 63rd Indian Infantry Brigade. It reached Chaung-U at 1700 hours on 1 May and moved out of it at 0500 hours the next day. This brigade consisted of the 1st Battalion the Cameronians, the 2nd Battalion the King's Own Yorkshire Light Infantry, and the 2nd Battalion 7th Rajput Regiment. The 1st Battalion 4th P.W.O. Gurkha Rifles also joined it that morning from the 48th Indian Infantry Brigade. The 1st and 5th Battalions Burma Rifles had been withdrawn from the brigade into divisional reserve after the Yenangyaung operations. These two battalions had each a strength of less than two hundred.

The 1st Burma Brigade attacked at 1545 hours on a two battalion front. It passed through the 63rd Brigade, but the left flank of its attack avoided the road-block. The 1st Battalion 4th P.W.O. Gurkha Rifles advanced between the main road and the railway, whilst on the right of it the 2nd Battalion 7th Rajput Regiment advanced northwards along the east of the railway which formed the dividing line between the two battalions. The two British battalions were in reserve. There was no artillery support as there was fear of shooting up the 13th Indian Infantry Brigade.

While orders were being issued several small launches and native craft were seen crossing the river. The 3.7" Howitzers scored a direct hit on one and M.M.Gs. of the 1st Battalion 4th P.W.O. Gurkha Rifles sank two fully laden boats.

The 1st Battalion 4th P.W.O. Gurkha Rifles passed through the 1st Battalion 11th Sikh Regiment and the 2nd Battalion 13th Frontier Force Rifles, but soon its leading companies came under heavy L.M.G. fire from the railway station area where a hollow pagoda was occupied as a machine gun nest. The 1st Battalion 4th P.W.O. Gurkha Rifles and the 1st Battalion 11th Sikh Regiment mortars opened heavy fire on the hollow pagoda area. Reconnaissance revealed a gap through which the Gurkha Rifles Battalion could safely and easily advance. The decision to put the reserve companies through this gap so that they might fan out in the rear of the Japanese lines while the rest of the battalion feigned an attack on the railway station was negatived by the brigade order to stand fast.

Similarly, the Rajputs also passed through the 63rd Brigade and cleared the outskirts of Ywathit of the Japanese. In the skirmish the battalion went wide to the north-east away from the railway line. Soon direction was restored and they were ordered to clear the railway station area. While so doing at about 1630 hours the Rajputs opened heavy fire on the 1st Battalion 18th Royal Garhwal Rifles and in spite of the signals from the latter the fire persisted. The Rajputs had not been informed of the 13th Indian Infantry Brigade's presence in that area.

WITHDRAWAL

Meanwhile at about 1500 hours on 2 May, the 13th Brigade had received an order to withdraw to Alon via Shaukka (where the Royal Inniskilling Fusiliers were holding reserve position) and Ettaw (held by Armoured Brigade). This order came through an officer of the 7th Armoured Brigade who stated that he had received it from the Army Commander. The order was passed by the 13th Brigade to the Divisional Headquarters. The withdrawal began at 1715 hours. There was no opposition and the Brigade reached Alon railway station at about 0200 hours (3 May).

At 1700 hours the Commander of the 1st Burma Brigade had also been ordered to stop his attack and to hold on to the gains already made. On his representing that the attacks should be allowed to continue, an extension of time until 1900 hours was given by the Divisional Headquarters. Both forward battalions of the 1st Burma Brigade were preparing to advance on the railway station and the area west of it. However, owing to the earlier order to cease the advance the impetus of the attack could not be revived, and the prior withdrawal of the 13th Brigade would have increased the difficulty of the task of the 1st Burma Brigade in any further advance. Also the casualties were heavy.

At 2000 hours the 1st Burma Infantry Brigade less Rajputs withdrew via main road and track skirting Monywa to the east via Takon to Alon and from there marched to milestone 9 on the road Monywa-Ye-U. There they took up a defensive position astride the road. The 2nd Battalion 7th Rajput Regiment received orders through one of its sections from the Division Headquarters to withdraw to Zalok. It arrived at Zalok at 2230 hours and later joined its brigade. The withdrawal was not followed up. The 63rd Indian Infantry Brigade also withdrew eastwards along the road for about one mile and then moved across country to Alon via Ettaw.

The divisional transport escorted by the battalions of the Burma Rifles during the day had by-passed Monywa, moving round it by cross-country tracks. The column was frequently dive-bombed by hostile aircraft. Towards evening the 1st Battalion the Cameronians was also detailed to cover the movement of the column.

The 48th Indian Infantry Brigade, which had been held in readiness at Myinmu to take part in the operations if required, was ordered to proceed to Ye-U via Shwebo. This it did.

A certain mystery surrounds the order to break off the attack on Monywa passed to the 13th Brigade. That this order came through an officer of the 7th Armoured Brigade is certain, but the Army Headquarters and Burcorps disclaim any knowledge of it. At the time when the attack was halted the Japanese were streaming out of Monywa and crossing to the west bank of the Chindwin. From evidence found by the troops on the outskirts of the town it was plain that the Japanese had sustained severe casualties. However, as the transport of the 1st Burma Division had been safely got away there was no particular advantage in continuing a costly operation.

The brigades of the 1st Burma Division carried out an arduous night march along rough bullock cart tracks through Zalok and Ettaw, and early on 3 May concentrated in an area north of Alon on the Monywa-Ye-U road. This area on the previous day had been held by the 7th Armoured Brigade with the 1st Battalion West Yorkshire Regiment. There was also the small detachment of the Gloucestershire Regiment and F.F.1 from Monywa. In the evening there had arrived a small force of the 1st Battalion the Gloucestershire Regiment, with F.F.7 under command, one troop of 15th Mountain Battery, and a battery of 77 mm. guns. This force took up a layback position south of Budalin astride the road and railway. Tank patrols were maintained about Alon on 2 May.

It was evident that the Japanese were losing no time in exploiting their success and that the line of withdrawal which necessarily cut the river near Kalewa was seriously threatened.

However, the 1st Burma Division began its withdrawal on Ye-U, the point from which the track to the Chindwin began. On 3 May, the 7th Armoured Brigade covered its movement and assisted in ferrying troops into Ye-U. The road was patrolled by the 7th Queen's Own Hussars which had a brush with some Burmese. The 2nd Battalion Royal Tank Regiment operating from the Alon area watched the northern and north-eastern exits from Monywa, whilst the 1st Battalion West Yorkshire Regiment observed the river and employed its mortars on hostile craft moving upstream.

Towards evening when all marching infantry was clear of the Alon area the 2nd Battalion Royal Tank Regiment began to fall back on Budalin. This encouraged the Japanese to follow up the withdrawal, and at 1830 hours one of our squadrons was in action east of the road against hostile tanks and anti-tank guns. The engagement was broken off, but two of the tanks were forced to make a wide *detour* to the east. One of these was subsequently lost by falling into a nullah in the dark.

At 0400 hours on 4 May tanks were heard approaching the lay-back south of Budalin, and were first assumed to be the two tanks mentioned in the preceding paragraph. When about one hundred yards distant these tanks opened fire. This was returned by the British tanks. The

Japanese fighting vehicles turned round and withdrew but not before setting alight a tank of the 2nd Battalion Royal Tank Regiment.[11]

Following on this incident the Japanese shelled this position with artillery and mortars. The mortars of the 1st Battalion the West Yorkshire Regiment replied with success. No attack developed, and after the last elements of the 1st Burma Division were clear, the 1st Battalion Gloucestershire Regiment withdrew. After this engagement at Budalin the Japanese did not again attempt to harass the withdrawal to Ye-U, which was completed on the same day. The two brigades of the 17th Indian Division not engaged at Monywa had already arrived at Ye-U, the 16th Indian Infantry Brigade arriving on 2 May and the 48th Indian Infantry Brigade less 1/4 G.R. the following day.

In addition to any craft they themselves had, the Japanese had also secured shallow draught vessels in Monywa. As it was evident that they were moving up the Chindwin it was essential for the Allies to secure Shwegyin, Kalewa, and Kalemyo at once. Consequently the 16th Indian Infantry Brigade was hurried forward in motor transport along the Ye-U-Shwegyin track to cover the Kalewa area. Brigade Headquarters and the 4th Battalion 12th Frontier Force Regiment left for Kalemyo on the night of 2/3 May. The remaining battalions left next day. The 1st Royal Battalion 9th Jat Regiment was to hold Shwegyin; the 2nd Battalion the Duke of Wellington's Regiment and the 7th Battalion 10th Baluch Regiment were to undertake the defence of Kalewa.

On the night of 3/4 May there was some sniping of the perimeter camp near Ye-U. At one time the firing was heavy. It came from a north-easterly direction. Whether Japanese or Burmese were responsible for this was not established.

THE 2ND BURMA BRIGADE MOVING ON THE WEST BANK OF THE IRRAWADDY

Whilst the operations recounted earlier were proceeding, the 2nd Burma Brigade was marching towards the Myittha valley. It then consisted of the 2nd and 8th Battalions Burma Rifles and F.F. 8. It moved with bullock cart and mule transport.

Arriving at Pauk on 1 May the brigade was in the centre of a disaffected area. Thakin elements were active. Pauk itself had been looted and burnt, bridges along the road for some distance west of Pauk had been systematically destroyed, and dacoits were numerous in the district. A party of about one hundred and fifty armed Burmans in improvised uniforms was encountered by the Brigade Intelligence Officer when he was alone some miles east of Pauk. This party was presumed to be marching for Pakokku. F.F. 8 on May 1 was engaged with a hostile force near Pauk. As a result of this engagement F.F. 8 largely disintegrated, and it is uncertain whether the opposition it encountered was Japanese or Burman.

After a difficult march the 2nd Burma Brigade on 12 May made contact with the Chin Hills Battalion of the Burma Frontier Force near

---

[11] *War Diary*, 7th Armoured Brigade.

Natchaung, south of Kalemyo. It was then picked up by motor transport and ferried onwards along the road to Tamu. Bullock carts were destroyed and all 'transport animals were handed over to the Chin Hills Battalion.

The 2nd Burma Brigade had marched from Pakokku to Natchaung, a distance of two hundred and sixteen miles, in fourteen days. It was the hottest period of the year, the brigade was already exhausted and it had only animal transport, while the track was not good. The marches had to be made by night. Considering these factors the performance was creditable.

If the Japanese had intended to carry out a dash for Kalemyo by this route they had now been forestalled by the 2nd Burma Brigade. After leaving Pauk the brigade made no contact with hostile elements, and there is no evidence that a Japanese advance along this route was initiated.

CHAPTER XXIII

End—Race for Kalewa

Following upon the despatch of the 16th Indian Infantry Brigade along the Ye-U-Shwegyin track the other troops began their general withdrawal along this route. Around Ye-U, the single point of entry, there was necessarily considerable congestion, which offered good targets for air bombing, but fortunately the Japanese did not take advantage of it. They had been active over Shwebo and in a series of raids had destroyed it when it was occupied by the Army Headquarters. Throngs of refugees at Kyaukmyaung on the Irrawaddy had been heavily bombed. So, too, were most of the towns on the railway between Sagaing and Katha. But at Ye-U aerial attacks were largely confined to the bridge that had been constructed across the Mu river just outside the town. Moreover, the Ye-U-Shwegyin track, beyond its first few miles, passed through a dense jungle which afforded protection to the heavy traffic that began to pass along it from the first day of May.

General Alexander's plan was to withdraw to Kalewa, and he fully realised that the operations henceforth would develop into a race with the Japanese for the possession of that vital point. He sent a warning to General Wakely at Kalewa to establish local protection and to block the river approaches. To prevent the Japanese forces reaching there, a boom was constructed across the Chindwin and the Royal Marines were despatched there with Breda guns to cover the obstruction. Further to prevent hostile landings at some points short of Kalewa in order to cut the Ye-U-Kalewa road, a force consisting of a detachment of the Bush Warfare School, some British infantry and two companies of the Gurkhas, was stationed at Maukkadaw. The General Headquarters India was asked to order air attacks on the Japanese craft moving up the Chindwin. Moreover, General Alexander also requested that the arrival of the 1st Indian Infantry Brigade to Kalewa from Palel be hastened to anticipate the apprehended Japanese advance on Kalemyo via the Myittha Valley. But he was disappointed when he learnt on 5 May that the brigade would not move to Kalewa owing to possible maintenance difficulties.[1]

On 3 May, India stated that a force could not be maintained in the Kalewa area, and Gen. Sir H. Alexander was ordered to take his troops back by motor transport to road-head one march north of Tamu as rapidly as the tactical situation permitted. The message to the Burma Army added that maintenance further south than Tamu could not be carried out, and that echelons of about three thousand daily could be dealt with at the road-head.

On the same day Gen. Sir H. Alexander received a visit at his Headquarters at Kaduma from Maj.-Gen. Li Jen Sun, commanding the Chinese 38th Division. This division as rear-guard to the Chinese Fifth Army

---

[1] General Alexander's *Despatch*, para 67.

had been carrying out a difficult task in its withdrawal north, and Maj.-Gen. Sun was anxious that his movements should be co-ordinated with those of Burcorps. Orders to this effect had already been issued, but Lieut.-General Slim was now again told that he must not withdraw from the Ye-U area until the Chinese rear-guard had passed north of Shwebo.²

Evacuation of the sick and wounded by rail and river to Myitkyina had been going forward. From Myitkyina casualties were being flown to India, but the rapid advance of the Japanese through the Shan States and the threat to Myitkyina closed this route. Casualties still with the main body of the troops and at the hospitals in Shwebo had to be taken out by the only route then available. No less than two thousand three hundred sick and wounded were sent out by motor transport along the Ye-U-Shwegyin track. They endured great suffering, but the fact that they were safely evacuated is evidence of the efficiency and tireless devotion of the Medical Services.

The 1st Burma Division with the 7th Armoured Brigade, less the 7th Queen's Own Hussars, held the rearguard position on the line of the canal about Ye-U whilst lay-backs were to be provided by the 17th Indian Division at Kaduma, Pyingaing, Shwegyin, and Kalewa. On 5 May at 1700 hours the rear-guard withdrew to Kaduma, the tanks of the 2nd Battalion Royal Tank Regiment covering this movement and the blowing of demolitions along the track. Next day the tanks patrolled from Kaduma back to the canal near Ye-U, but no contact with the Japanese was made.

The 1st Burma Division then continued its withdrawal towards Shwegyin, but the 1st Burma Brigade broke off from the division and carried out a flank march up the east bank of the Chindwin through difficult and waterless country. Leaving Pyingaing on 8 May it moved by Indaw to Pantha and there crossed the Chindwin. It then continued its march by Yuwa and the Yu river to Tamu, arriving at the latter place on 16 May.

The 13th Indian Infantry Brigade crossed the Chindwin on 9 May and that day began its march on Tamu.

From Kaduma the 48th Indian Infantry Brigade formed the rear-guard and was supported by the 7th Queen's Own Hussars. Motor transport by this time was very short but enough was available to move the 63rd Indian Infantry Brigade to Shwegyin. Simultaneously, the 48th Indian Infantry Brigade with Burma Military Police and Frontier Force units which were close-piquetting the route, marched forty miles from Kaduma to Pyingaing in thirty hours.

The dry sandy bed of the Maukkadaw Chaung which flows through Pyingaing gave an excellent approach from the Chindwin, and the country was ideal for the establishing of a road-block. To prevent any attempt by the Japanese to set up such a block a strong force was posted at the confluence of the Chaung with the Chindwin. This force consisted of Commando personnel and one company from the 2nd Battalion 5th Royal Gurkha Rifles and another from the combined Battalion 7th Gurkha Rifles.

² *Ibid*, para 68.

This force withdrew independently up the east bank of the river on the morning of 9 May after the rear-guard was clear of Pyingyaing. That village was abandoned on the afternoon of 8 May, the 7th Queen's Own Hussars leaving at 1500 hours.

The passage of the Indo-British forces through the vast and well-nigh uninhabited forests of the Chindwin was a remarkable achievement. Gen. Sir H. Alexander writes in his Despatch:

"This road (between Ye-U and Kalewa) was nothing more than a sandy track running from Ye-U via Kaduma, Pyingyaing and Thatkegyin to Shwegyin, eight miles south of Kalewa.... it was the lack of this last twelve miles of road, over which there was nothing more than a footpath, which caused the abandonment of the major portion of the M.T. and all tanks. The track from Ye-U passed through innumerable chaungs or nullahs, some of which were dry and sandy and some of which were wet. Between Pyingyaing and Thatkegyin there was a difficult hill section with many rickety bridges constructed only of brushwood or bamboo. Any one seeing this track for the first time would find it difficult to imagine how a fully mechanised force could possibly move over it"[3]

There is no doubt that only the urgent necessity of the occasion impelled the employment of the route. It crossed and recrossed and sometimes followed for considerable distances the sandy beds of innumerable chaungs. Often the deep sand brought vehicles to a standstill; some of them could not be extricated. There, until the engineers set to work to straighten out sharp hair-pin bends, traffic became inextricably blocked. The engineers also improved the going along the stream beds by laying corduroy tracks, and opened up a water point in the sand of the dry Maukkadaw Chaung near Pyingyaing.

Traffic control posts were established and sections of the track were organised for two-way and one-way traffic. Only the most persistent vigilance and insistence upon road discipline kept the track open. Every mile of the dense forests it traversed was littered with the wrecks of vehicles that had broken down under the strain.

The race for Shwegyin was all the more urgent because of the imminence of the monsoon which would have rendered the otherwise dry chaungs impassable and the track into a quagmire. It was essential, therefore, to gain the Chindwin as quickly as possible.

There was no shortage of rations along the route, and there was also sufficient petrol to carry all vehicles to Shwegyin. There was food, too, for refugees, some of them being army families. Gen. Sir H. Alexander was not prepared to abandon these unfortunate people either to the Japanese or to the tender mercies of the local population. They were carried to Shwegyin in military vehicles whilst many of the troops carried out forced marches.

From Shwegyin all troops, motor vehicles, and guns had to be transported to Kalewa by steamer. There were six of these streamers, each with a carrying capacity of some six or seven hundred men, but only on an average two lorries and two jeeps. This meant that few vehicles could

---

[3] General Alexander's *Despatch*, para 69.

be ferried across the Chindwin with the result that the transport problem from Kalewa onwards became acute. There was then barely sufficient transport to carry essential equipment and ammunition and to evacuate the wounded; but the establishment of staging camps stocked with supplies sent from India by motor transport eliminated the necessity for units to carry rations. The General Purposes Transport Company from India proved invaluable.

The embarkation point at Shwegyin was a small sandy bay where the Shwegyin Chaung entered the river. It was overlooked by steep jungle-clad hills. In this bay the engineers had built a jetty. A rise in the river submerged that, and there was much difficulty in loading on to the steamers the few vehicles and guns that could be taken. On 9 May the engineers constructed a more serviceable jetty.

The track approached the bay through a cup-like depression in the hills to the north-east. This depression, known as the 'Basin', was about half a mile long and some four hundred yards broad at its widest point. Like the bay it was commanded by escarped forest-covered hills. Its southern end opened on to the bay at the point where the Shwegyin Chaung joined the river. The flat land within the Basin afforded the only parking space for vehicles and as the withdrawal proceeded there collected a vast agglomeration of transport and equipment.

Hostile aircraft had located the activity at Shwegyin.[4] On 5 May they bombed and burst a protective boom that was placed across the Chindwin some two miles downstream, and on 7 May they bombed Shwegyin.[5] These attacks much restricted the work of ferrying by day, and many of the Burman crew were only prepared to operate at night.

On the night of 9 May, the 63rd Indian Infantry Brigade and the 7th Armoured Brigade, less the 7th Queen's Hussars, crossed the river to Kalewa. Before embarking, the 2nd Battalion Royal Tank Regiment destroyed its tanks which had rendered such splendid service during the campaign. One squadron of the battalion which had been unable to cross that night remained in Shwegyin with its vehicles undestroyed. To relieve the congestion in the Basin many units, guns, vehicles, and animals were retained in a harbour about two miles down the track near Mataik, northeast of Shwegyin. There were also located Advanced Headquarters of the 17th Indian Division, and the rearguard made up of the 7th Queen's Own Hussars, the 1st Battalion the West Yorkshire Regiment, and the 48th Indian Infantry Brigade.

Despite the endeavours of Royal Marines, officers of the Irrawaddy Flotilla Company, staff officers and others organising the embarkation, the lack of facilities made the work of loading vehicles on to the steamers painfully slow. On 9 May it was estimated that several days would still

---

[4] As regards plan of operations at Shwegyin and Kalewa the Japanese History of *33 Division* says the following:—

"To outflank the British and Chinese Forces retreating from Katha, Homalin, and Tamanthi the following operational orders were issued:

The main force of the Division was to move towards Budalin, and Ye-U; *Araki detached Force (Div. HQ, HQ 213 Inf. Regt. and one Mtn. Arty. Bn.)* was to advance to Kalewa Homalin and Tamanthi along the line of the Chindwin river; *the 2nd Bn. 213 Inf. Regt.* together with one *Mtn. Bty. Arty.* were to move by large landing craft to Kalewa." *History of Japanese 33 Div.* p. 25.

[5] Alexander's *Despatch*, para 74.

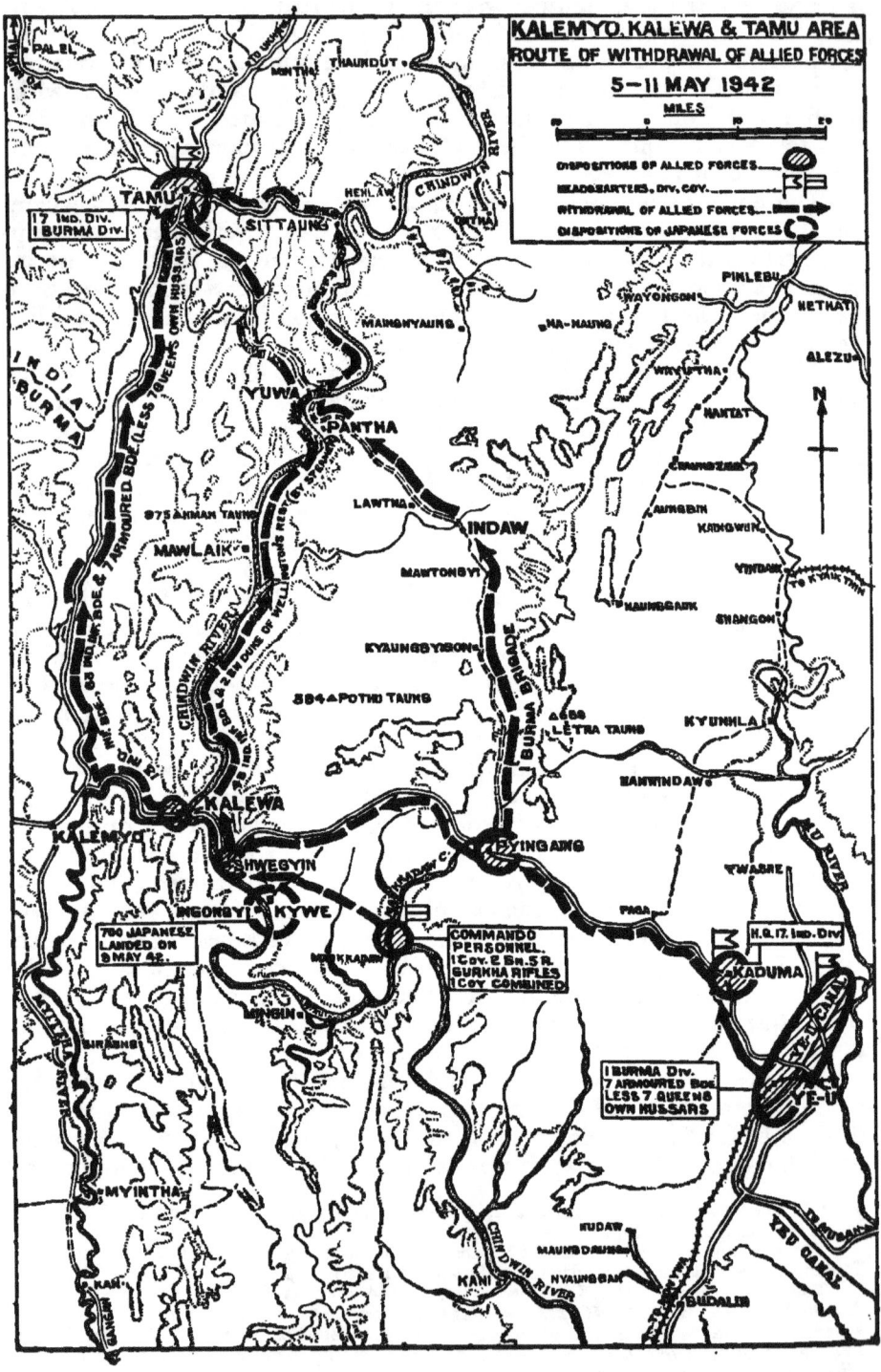

be required for the clearance of all the sick and wounded, troops, guns, animals, and vehicles and equipment not earmarked for destruction. The animal transport of both divisions still awaited ferrying across the river.

The 1st Royal Battalion 9th Regiment carried out the duties of covering troops at Shwegyin. It consisted of three weak companies, one of them on the west bank of the Chindwin. A large party was also continously employed in cutting firewood for the steamers.

Defensive positions were manned at the north end of the Basin where the track entered it through a long defile. The heights overlooking the east and southern sides of the Basin were protected, and there were posts astride the defile of the Shwegyin Chaung and on the hills immediately to the south of the confluence of the Chaung with the Chindwin. Downstream, covering the boom near Gaundi, were the 5th Battalion 17th Dogra Regiment and a handful of Royal marines. Both banks of the river were held and patrols went forward for some miles along the west bank.

The defence of the Basin was numerically weak, and on 9 May, Maj.-General Cowan decided to strengthen the garrison there. Accordingly, the Battalion of the 7th Gurkha Rifles was detailed to reinforce the Jats. It arrived in the Basin after dark on 9 May and was to take over the defensive positions the following morning.

THE FIGHT FOR SHWEGYIN

Meanwhile, unknown to this force the Japanese[6] had landed near Kywe, a village on the east bank of the river just south of Shwegyin. That was on the afternoon of 9 May. Men, ponies, equipment, and one or more infantry guns had been put ashore from fast moving landing craft, one of which flew the Thakin flag. No sooner was the disembarkation completed than the landing craft turned downstream, presumably for the purpose of bringing up more troops already on the Chindwin on slower moving vessels. After dark another and larger hostile force landed at Ingongyi on the west bank of the river almost opposite Kywe.

The first hostile force that landed at Kywe was estimated to number about seven hundred. It probably marched due north to the village of Thanbaya thus avoiding the covering troops astride the river at Gaundi. North-west of Thanbaya a path along a dry tributary stream-bed gave easy access to the lower reaches of the Shwegyin Chaung. An advance from the direction of Thanbaya was not expected by the defenders, and thus it gave an element of surprise.

---

[6] Japanese account is as follows:

Harada Unit after defeating an enemy force near Budalin advanced to occupy Ye-U. It continued its advance towards Wantho and Naba by way of Kinu, during which contact was made with the Chinese forces but little resistance was encountered. Araki Unit left Monywa for Kalewa, on about 4 May in its pursuit of enemy forces along the left bank of the Chindwin river.

The unit proceeding by craft landed at Shwegyin about 7 May; prior to the arrival of the main force of the Detached Force, it cut the Ye-U-Kalewa road. A three-day counter-attack by enemy forces retreating by Ye-U road was resisted successfully.

About 10 May the main force of Araki Detached Force arrived with one Bn of the Sakuma Force as reinforcement. "The British (now) fled towards Kalewa and Kalameyo leaving behind a considerable quantity of equipment including 126 tanks, 2300 motor vehicles and scores of field guns." *History of the 15th Army* (Japanese). 601/7785/H, p. 25.

The landing of this large hostile party was observed by the Commando force. It was then growing dark and owing to the exhaustion of his men the Officer Commanding decided not to attack, but to march due north to the track and rejoin the 48th Indian Infantry Brigade at Shwegyin. Not having a wireless set near him he could not convey the information of the proximity of the hostile force to the troops at Shwegyin. This force was however, split up in the dark and only a small party rejoined at Shwegyin.

Meanwhile, at 0545 hours on 10 May the 1st Royal Battalion 9th Jat Regiment encountered light machine-gun fire down the Shwegyin Chaung. The Japanese then attempted to advance towards the landing stage and into the Basin but were checked by machine-gun and mortar fire. As the light grew, hostile fire intensified. Crossing to the north of the Shwegyin Chaung the Japanese made some progress down the defile of the Chaung towards the Chindwin, suffering heavy casualties in so doing. Mortar shells fell in the Basin. There was heavy sniping from the south.'

Checked in their attempt to gain the jetty the Japanese began to work along the ridge dominating the eastern side of the basin, whilst still maintaining pressure in the area of the Chaung. The Jats were hard pressed, and the 7th Gurkha Rifles went forward to reinforce all their positions. Fighting was very confused on the hill tops to the south and east of the jetty and the Basin. Approaches were often precipitous, and in places the dense undergrowth reduced fields of fire to a few yards. Many small counter-attacks were put in by the Jats and the Gurkhas as the Japanese from time to time secured dominating positions on the hills. On one occasion men of the 7th Gurkha Rifles trapped about twenty Japanese in a nullah and destroyed them with bombs.

The Bofors guns of the 3rd Indian Light Anti-Aircraft Battery, were in position in the Basin. These guns for a considerable time were the only artillery support for the Infantry there. When a company of the 7th Gurkha Rifles went forward to the ridge east of the Basin their covering fire was of great assistance as the troops scaled the cliff-like hill. But the Japanese had established themselves on a prominent knoll there and could not be dislodged. However, Bofors and mortar fire kept them subdued, although one hostile party actually entered the Basin and for a time threatened the headquarters of the 1st Royal Battalion 9th Jat Regiment. They were driven out by the Jats and the 7th Gurkha Rifles.

Meanwhile Maj.-Gen. D. T. Cowan had gone forward from Mutaik to the Basin to ascertain the situation. He and his party came under automatic fire. Maj.-Gen. D. T. Cowan then ordered the 48th Indian Infantry Brigade to move on the Basin from Mutaik. It was also to cover

---

' As regards mopping up in the North Burma area the Japanese account gives the following details: 'After entering Naba, *Harada Detached Force* attacked Manshi with its main force, and at the same time despatched one Inf. Bn. to Homalin, and another (u/c Fuke Detached Force) to Tamanthi. Homalin was occupied round about 15 May.

With the completion of the operations around Kalewa, *Araki Detached Force*, immediately moved north, mopping up remnants of Chinese forces *en route* and contacted a part of *Harada Regiment* in Homalin about 18 May.

Div. HQ which was stationed in Shwebo organised *Fuke Detached Force* and despatched it to Mogaung and Myitkyina area., *History of the Japanese 15th Army* 601/7785/H, p. 26.

the track between these two places and the approach to the path up the east bank of the river by Kongyi to Kaing, the village opposite Kalewa.

The route between Mutaik and the Basin was close piquetted by the 1st Battalion 3rd Q.A.O. Gurkha Rifles (now only a single company in strength) and the 1st Battalion 4th P.W.O. Gurkha Rifles. The latter battalion was only just in time to prevent the Japanese from cutting the track just north of the Basin. It then held off repeated attacks by the Japanese and was well supported by the battalion 3" mortars and a section of the 12th Mountain Battery. Picquet positions were held throughout the day and were supported by tanks of the 7th Queen's Own Hussars.

The 2nd Battalion 5th Royal Gurkha Rifles marched down the track to the Basin and was held in reserve at its northern entrance. A squadron of the 7th Queen's Own Hussars also entered the Basin.

Firing from near Mutaik, 1 Battery of the 1st Indian Field Regiment supported the infantry. Despite the fact that only an inaccurate 1/4" map was available some most effective shooting was carried out.

The general situation in the early afternoon was that north of the Basin the Burcorps covered the track, and the path towards Kaing through Kongyi. Round the Basin and on the hills above the jetty the Jats and the 7th Gurkha Rifles were holding on grimly. Only on the knoll on the eastern edge of the Basin towards its southern end did the Japanese command its positions. On this knoll the Japanese had brought up an infantry gun, and from there were directing mortar fire, shelling the jetty and the Basin. However, before the infantry gun could open fire it was knocked out by a series of direct hits from a Bofors gun. After this incident hostile mortar fire was also much reduced, and at least one mortar was put out of action by Bofors guns of the 3rd Indian Light Anti-Aircraft Battery.

If further evacuation of troops and material was to be carried out, it was essential that the Japanese be cleared from the knoll, and at about 1400 hours a further attack was made on this position by the 7th Gurkha Rifles. Despite desperate attempts to dislodge the Japanese the attack failed. Meanwhile Japanese pressure on the positions about the Chaung covering the jetty had increased, and the Jats were hard put to it to hold their ground. Accordingly, a two-company attack by the 2nd Battalion 5th Royal Gurkha Rifles was planned, both to sweep this area and to recover the knoll. The attack was to be made at 1650 hours.

During the day it had not been possible to use the jetty, and the crew of some of the steamers could not be induced to work. Nevertheless, three steamers continued to operate the ferry by drawing in beneath an almost sheer cliff, some two hundred yards upstream. The troops continued to embark there. All the sick and wounded were evacuated although it was with great difficulty that some of those men could be sent down the cliff face.

Hostile reconnaissance aircraft were also active, but the anti-aircraft guns kept them at a distance. No bombing attacks were attempted. Once again the difficulty of the country and the close nature of the fighting probably deterred Japanese aircraft from attempting to support their troops.

The attack planned for 1650 hours was cancelled. Satisfied that the ferry could not be operated from the jetty that night and that the numbers

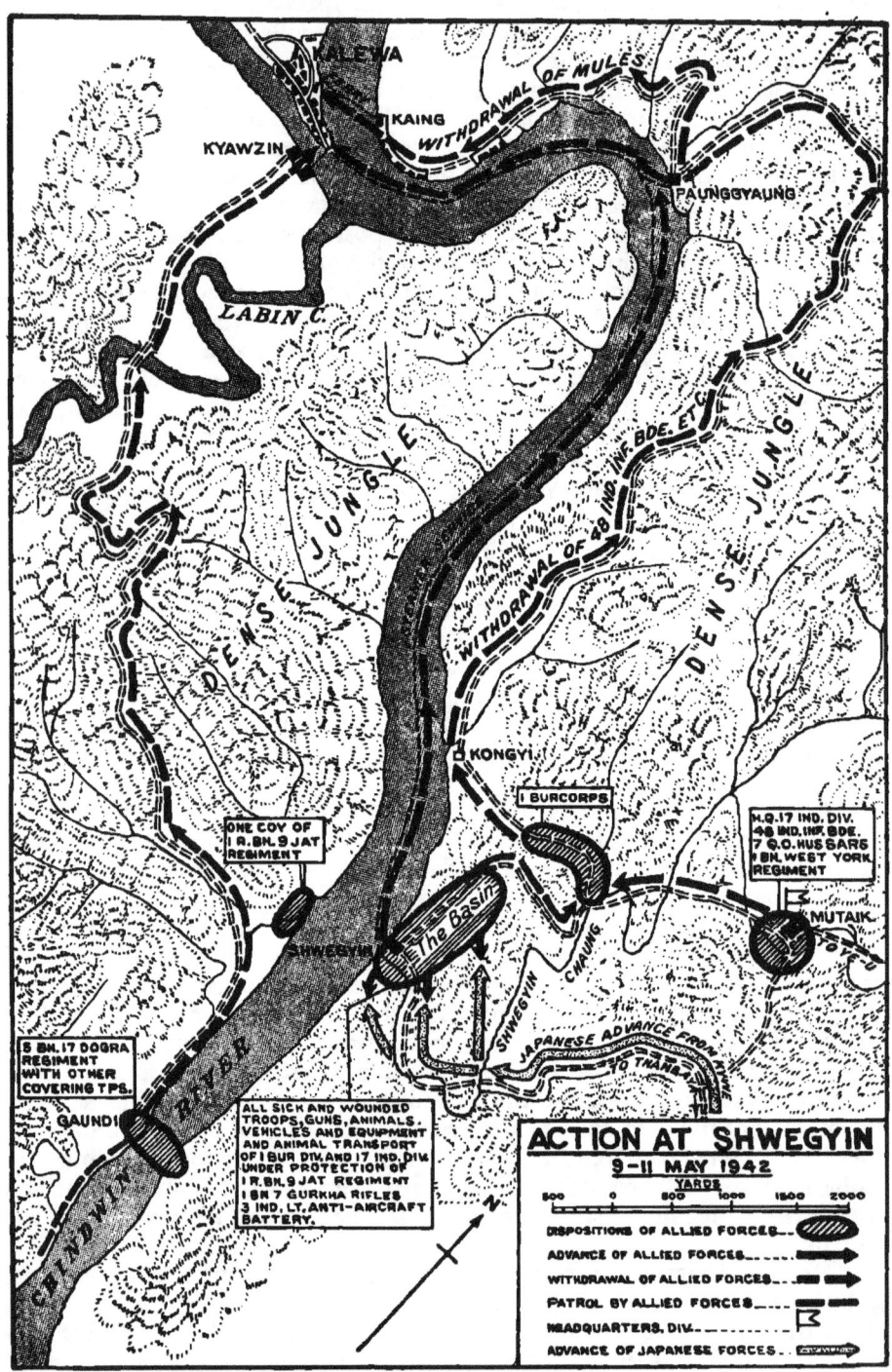

of the Japanese force had increased, Maj.-Gen. D. T. Cowan decided to fall back towards Kalewa along the Kongyi path.

The evacuation of the lines of communication and other unwanted troops remaining in the area began at once. The path was over precipitous hills known to be exceedingly difficult. Consequently, only the minimum of equipment could be carried. In the Basin and on the track towards Mutaik was the greater part of what remained of the motor transport, much of it still loaded with kit and equipment, rations, and ammunition. Apart from the artillery already mentioned, there were also present the 1st Heavy Anti-Aircraft Regiment R.A., B.A.F., the 8th Indian Anti-Tank Battery, the 8th Heavy Anti-Aircraft Battery R.A., one troop of the 5th Indian Anti-Tank Battery and the 15th Mountain Battery. Some of these units had not been actively engaged that day. Their guns could not be taken along the path and had to be destroyed.

At 1700 hours guns and mortars began wasting down their ammunition. Heavy fire was directed on all the Japanese positions. This had a quietening effect on the Japanese and the withdrawal of non-essential elements proceeded without interruption. At 1930 hours the path to Kongyi was reported clear, and zero hour for the withdrawal of covering troops was fixed at 1955 hours.

Two lay-backs were established by the 2nd Battalion 5th Royal Gurkha Rifles to protect the withdrawal of the forward troops through the northern exit of the Basin. The picquets along the track were to close in behind and follow the rear Battalion.

At 1955 hours every gun in the area increased its rate of fire. Ten minutes later they put down a devastating barrage on the positions evacuated by the Jats and the 7th Gurkha Rifles and on the hills surrounding the Basin.

Of this phase of the operations and of the barrage a War Diary mentions: "The chief contribution came from the Bofors whose tracer shells lit up the descending darkness. It was a cheering sound the like of which we had not heard during our time in Burma. At 2015 hours the guns ceased fire, and five minutes later we received the order to go. As we left the Basin enormous fires were getting a good hold on the dumps of stores and ammunition, tanks and lorries. It was an eerie sight in the gathering gloom and distressing to think that so much material had to be left behind. From the Japanese there wasn't a sound. They had apparently had enough".

It was as well that the Japanese had drawn off, for it soon became apparent that the path to Kongyi was hopelessly blocked. It was packed with troops and animals and the rear battalions could make no movement up to it. They were halted along the track north of the Basin.

The same unit War Diary continues:—"We were surrounded by cliffs three hundred feet high on two sides, difficult enough to climb by day, impossible to take against opposition at night. The 3rd Gurkha Rifles held the third side behind us, and on the fourth, to the east, ran the track back to Burma. On this track were several ammunition lorries burning furiously, lighting us up as we sat there. Small arms and mortar ammunition were exploding continuously for some three hours afterwards. Our only exit was up the narrow path on which, at the moment, movement was negligible . . . So there we were a sitting target".

Mules found it almost impossible to follow the steep and narrow path in the darkness. Many fell over the edge of it, others were pushed off to clear the way for troops. Progress was at the rate of about one mile an hour and it was dawn before the rear of the column was at Kongyi. There was no sign of the Japanese.

During the day the troops were ferried across from Paunggyaung to Kalewa, whilst mules were ferried over the river from Kaing.

A noteworthy feature of the arduous night march was the bringing out of a section of its guns by 12 Mountain Battery. Many mortars and much lighter equipment had been abandoned, and the carriage of these guns along the path to Paunggyaung was an outstanding performance.

On the other side of the river the 5th Battalion 17th Dogra Regiment with other covering troops there had carried out an equally difficult night march from Gaundi to Kalewa.

The total casualties in the Shwegyin action were difficult to estimate. In the area of the Basin there were about one hundred and fifty, and were therefore probably less than two hundred in all. On the other hand, records of the 17th Indian Division state of the Japanese casualties:—

"In the jungle no one could tell his casualties from shell fire but, from the infantry assaults, one hundred and seventy bodies were counted". Having regard to these figures and to the nature and extent of the fighting the first Japanese force that landed at Kywe must have been considerably augmented. There was no further contact with the Japanese. The last action of the campaign had been fought.

The 48th Indian Infantry Brigade together with the 2nd Battalion the Duke of Wellington's Regiment left Kalewa on the night of 11 May, proceeding by steamer to Sittaung and arriving there on 14 May. The Chindwin fleet was then sunk and the troops marched to Tamu.

The main body of the Indo-British forces withdrew to Tamu along the track from Kalewa, through the Kabaw valley. The 63rd Indian Infantry Brigade as rear-guard left Kalewa on 12 May and marched through Tamu on 19 May.

In the Chin Hills to the south-west and forward of the main force the tracks into India were covered by the Chin Hills Battalion, Burma Frontier Force. This battalion continued, unsupported, to protect the approaches to India along the western side of the Kalewa and Kabaw valleys. The other nearest troops to the battalion were then over a hundred miles away.

The first heavy rains of the monsoon fell on 12 May. By a narrow margin, therefore, had Gen. Sir H. Alexander extricated his troops. Had the campaign continued east of the Chindwin for any length of time after 12 May it is certain that only a very small proportion of the force could have survived a withdrawal to India.

The Army had brought out of Burma very little in the way of equipment or transport. It reported to General Headquarters India that it had ten twenty-five pounder guns, four anti-tank guns, fourteen 3.7" mountain guns, all with little or no ammunition ; no tanks, about fifty lorries, and thirty jeeps. All vehicles were badly in need of maintenance.

On 20 May IV Corps assumed operational command of all troops of the Burma Army. Gen. Sir H. Alexander's command then ceased to exist.

At Imphal the Kachins, Chins, and Karens remaining with the Burma Rifles were given the option of returning to their own homes. The majority of them elected to do so. Each man received three months' pay, his rifle, and fifty rounds of ammunition.

CHAPTER XXIV

The Chinese Front—2nd Phase

OPERATIONS CARRIED OUT BY THE CHINESE EXPEDITIONARY FORCE IN APRIL AND MAY, 1942

The operations conducted by the Sixth Army and other troops of the Chinese Epeditionary Force in the Shan States and Karenni were largely independent of those carried out by the Fifth Army on the front, south of Mandalay, where in April 1942 the Fifth Army was employed in opposing the Japanese advance from Toungoo. Behind it, in Mandalay, was concentrating the Sixty-sixth Army. The leading troops of this Army, the 38th Division commanded by General Sun Li Jen, entered Burma in the first week of April. From Mandalay the Division was sent to the British sector about Yenangyaung in support of Burcorps. Its operations are recorded in the description of events on the Indo-British sector. Its place in Mandalay was taken by the 28th Division. Headquarters Sixty-sixth Army and the 29th Division of that Army did not enter Burma until the end of April.

JAPANESE THRUST THROUGH KARENNI AND SHAN STATES

Before describing the Chinese operations south of Mandalay in April it is desirable to detail the course of events in Karenni and the Shan States. These had a decisive bearing upon the whole of the Burma Campaign and had their share in the withdrawal of the Allied forces from Burma. There was little co-operation between the Fifth and Sixth Armies, and in spite of the fact that the 55th Division was weak and the Japanese[1] were known to be advancing on Mawchi, the 3rd Regiment of the 55th Division was retained by the Fifth Army at Thazi for some time. It did not rejoin its division at Loikaw until 14 April. The 1st Regiment of the division was in Karenni disposed in depth along the road Mawchi-Bawlake-Loikaw. A battalion of the 2nd Regiment had also been moved up to Loikaw when the 3rd Regiment went to Thazi. There were accordingly four battalions, possibly one thousand rifles in all, in Karenni to meet the Japanese thrust along the Mawchi road.

---

[1] *56 Division* was operating in this region. It was raised in Kyushu in December 1941 with depots in Kurumed, Fukuoka and Omura. In February 1942 the Division less *3rd Battalion 146th Infantry Regiment* sailed to Nei and from here sailed to Siam and later Rangoon, and moved up to Toungoo in the wake of the 55th Division.

Here the *Fifteenth Army* ordered *56th Division* to penetrate into the Shan Hills over the east side of the mountains and to advance immediately into the Lashio area, take important positions on the Chungking-Burma Road, deliver decisive blows whenever possible and cut off the retreat road of the Chinese Armies—601/8255/H, p. 18. *The Japanese Account of their operations in Burma* (Dec. '41—to Aug. 45) Edited by H.Q. 12th Army.

Its first objective was Loikaw so that with other Divisions it might establish a line Loikaw-Yamethin-Yenangyaung.

The Karen Levies west of Mawchi could not delay the Japanese advance for long and the town was occupied by them on 4 April.² The company of Chinese troops there fell back on Kemapyu. Demolitions along the road were blown but not covered by the retiring force. The 1st Regiment then concentrated in the Bawlake-Kemapyu area which was one of considerable natural strength.

General Liang had reported the situation to the Sixth Army Headquarters on 6 April. He asked for immediate reinforcements. General Kan was at Lashio on a conference, and it was not until 9 April that the remaining two battalions of the 55th Division which were in Army reserve about Loilem were ordered to move into Karenni.

Immediately previous to this it had been decided to concentrate the 93rd Division (less one strong regiment to hold the Mongpayak area) and one regiment of the 49th Division at Loikaw. Owing to the long distances involved and lack of motor transport such a concentration would necessarily take a long time. The regiment of the 49th Division was to march across country, whilst the 93rd Division was intended to be moved by motor transport. The shortage of transport, the bottleneck of the Takaw ferry, and the poor condition of the road and vehicles made the transfer a slow one.

From Kemapyu the 1st Regiment was forced back to Pasawng, and shortly afterwards to positions covering the suspension bridge across the Htu Chaung just above its confluence with the Nam Pawn river. There it was relieved by the 2nd Regiment and went back to Bawlake and Namphe, where Field Headquarters of the 55th Division had been established.

Throughout these operations the Chinese appear to have failed to protect their right flank although there was always the possibility of a Japanese encircling movement from that direction. This actually occurred on 16 April after several direct attacks on the Htu Chaung positions had failed. In these engagements both sides incurred considerable casualties. The Japanese in their outflanking movement crossed the Htu Chaung north of the Chinese positions and thus compelled the 2nd Regiment to withdraw to a line just south of Bawlake. Next day, 17 April, the Japanese continued their cross-country advance on the west of the road and cut it between Namphe and Bawlake. In this latter place there was then only the 2nd Regiment. The remainder of the 55th Division, including the 3rd Regiment, was at Namphe. Casualties had been fairly heavy and at that stage the effective strength of the division was probably not more than four thousand.

At 0300 hours on 18 April, the 3rd Regiment was ordered to counter-attack the Japanese east of Namphe. Heavy fighting took place during the day. The Sixth Army Headquarters had been established at Loikaw, and there, on the evening of 18 April, arrived one battalion of the 93rd Division. It was immediately sent forward to Namphe in motor lorries. Information was also received that the 145th Regiment of the

---

² Of these engagements the Japanese account, *A short history of 56 Japanese Division* (including Div. Intelligence & Signal Organisation) says: "56th Division then switched across the Sittang in pursuit of three Chinese Divisions". The first engagement was at Alemyaung, the second was at Mawchi, (601/7249/H), p, 1.

49th Division had arrived at the To Sai Hka bridge on the road north of Loikaw.

That night telephone and wireless communication between the Sixth Army Headquarters and the 55th Division suddenly ceased. The Chinese force in the Namphe-Bawlake area had been cut off. Early next morning Japanese armoured vehicles were encountered at Ngwedaung, nine miles south of Loikaw. It was evident that the 55th Division had been overrun. In Loikaw were only a few guards and a company of sappers. These were disposed to cover the two bridges over the Balu Chaung and to carry out demolitions. Army Headquarters then left for the To Sai Hka bridge across the Nam Tamhpak. The bridge was prepared for demolition.

Karen Levies were in contact with a Japanese force at Yado, and there was a possibility that the latter would carry out an outflanking movement along the Mongpai-Pekon road and thus reach the Thazi-Loilem-Kengtung road behind the Chinese. A strong patrol was sent to Mongpai to prevent this. But it was too late, and the Japanese were already in possession of the road.

COLLAPSE OF THE SIXTH ARMY

The Japanese approached towards Sai Hka, and on the afternoon of 20 April crossed the bridge which had not been demolished. The Chinese retired on Hopong and took up a strong position some twelve miles to the east, astride the road at Htamsang. The available force was small, consisting of the remnants of the 145th Regiment, some Army troops, and a battalion of the 93rd Division. There were a few anti-tank guns.

The Japanese were in contact with the Chinese at Hopong on the evening of 21 April. Next morning they attacked the Htamsang position. Hostile aircraft took an active part in the operations on this front. The Chinese positions and approaches to them were almost continuously bombed during daylight hours. Loilem was also subjected to heavy dive-bombing attacks and a large part of the town was destroyed by fire.

That night the Chinese withdrew to a position at Kawng Nio, about eight miles west of Loilem. This was a position of great natural strength, but the Japanese outflanked it by moving along tracks to the south of the road. The Chinese were not in sufficient strength to stop this movement, and, although their forward troops continued to hold out, the Japanese were in possession of Loilem on the evening of 23 April. General Kan and the remaining elements of his force, amounting to about three hundred men, took up a defensive line on the Lashio road near Panglong.

At that time units of the 93rd Division approaching from Kengtung were only some twenty miles distant from Loilem. Hearing of the fall of that town they withdrew to Takaw. There they were met by General Kan who had marched across the hills with a bodyguard. From Takaw the remnants of the Sixth Army moved to Kengtung where were concentrated what remained of the 49th and 93rd Divisions. These forces were joined by General Chen and about a thousand men of the 55th Division who had made their way across country from the Bawlake area.

The Sixth Army then retired into China, and Kengtung was occupied by the Thais.

THE LAST STAGE OF THE FIGHTING IN THE SHAN STATES

Meanwhile, the fight in the Shan States had been maintained for a short period by other Chinese troops. Whilst advancing on Loilem the Japanese had also occupied Taunggyi with a mixed force reported to consist of Japanese and Burmans. This force opposed an advance by the 20th Division and one regiment of the 22nd Division of the Chinese Fifth Army moving east from Thazi. On the afternoon of 23 April the hostile positions west of Taunggyi were attacked under the personal direction of Gen. J. Stilwell, and on 24 April the town was retaken. Next day the 200th Division captured Hopong, and the Japanese were estimated to have suffered five hundred casualties. Loilem was then reoccupied by the Chinese.

The situation soon became very confused. Further north the 28th Division had been ordered back from Mandalay to the Hsipaw-Lashio area. It was accompanied by some tanks and anti-tank guns of the Fifth Army. With the exception of one regiment these troops succeeded in reaching the area by 26 April. The remaining regiment of the 28th Division, moving by road, was informed that the Japanese were in Hsipaw. Turning north just east of Maymyo it made for Mogok.

Headquarters Sixty-sixth Army and part of the 29th Division had arrived in Lashio and the Army Commander, General Chang, assumed command of all Chinese troops in the area. On 27 April, the 28th Division was moved south of Hsipaw to Namon, fifteen miles distant on the Loilem road. At 2300 hours that night it was in contact with a small lorry-borne force of the Japanese which was compelled to retire. However, fearing that his own small force would be outflanked, the commander withdrew on Lashio.

During this period motor transport and armoured vehicles of the Fifth Army from the front south of Mandalay were pouring through Lashio on their way to China. Nothing of this force was diverted for use against the oncoming Japanese, although General Chang was desperately short of troops and elements of his Army had still to arrive from China.

The Chinese destroyed their very considerable remaining stores left in Lashio. On 29 April after heavy fighting they fell back to Hsenwi, and later took up positions astride the road covering Kutkai.

---

[a] About the operations leading to the occupation of Lashio the Japanese account of *56th Division* says: After Alemyaung 'battles took place at Mawchi, Kemapyu and Namphe during which one Chinese Division was annihilated. Japanese casualties were slight. The advance continued north through Loikaw to Hopong, where the 2nd Battalion 146th Inf. Reg. was sent to deal with Taunggyi. The task completed it returned to the Division (56) and the advance continued. From Hopong *56 Division* pursued the Chinese through Mong Pawn, Loilem, Lai-Kha Mong Kung, to Kon Hai Nin (at the junction) of the Hsipaw and Lashio roads. At this point reached on 10 April 1942 the Division split up the main group taking the road through Tonglau and Namlan to the junction east of Hsipaw while 148 Inf. Regt. and 56 Recce Regt. (less the company on the way from Java with the 3 Bn. 146 Inf. Regt.) moved up the same road junction via

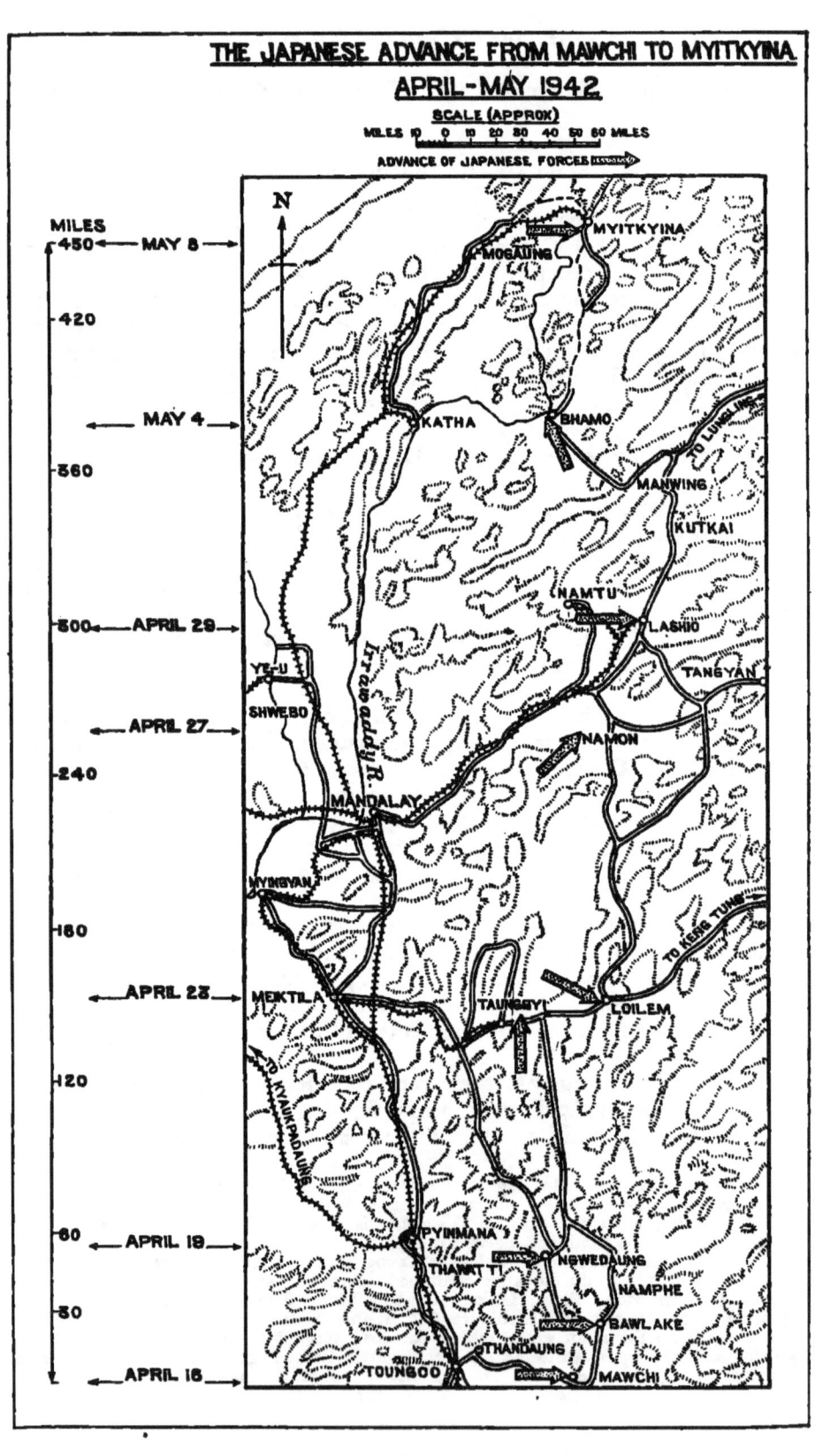

The Japanese occupied Lashio the same day.³ Their force was estimated at thirty light tanks, about a dozen 75mm guns, and two battalions of infantry.

The total force then available to General Chang could not have exceeded three thousand men and little resistance was made to the continued hostile advance. The Chinese withdrew into China through Kutkai and Wanting, having fought at both these places whilst the Japanese pressed on towards Bhamo in spite of the Shweli river which was a major obstacle.⁴

The Shweli river was bridged at Manwing, the bridge being held by the Northern Shan States Battalion, Burma Frontier Force. This battalion had been stationed in Lashio until the evacuation of that place. The necessary preparations for demolitions were made, but no officer trained in demolitions remained at the bridge. On 3 May the Japanese advanced in a column of lorries with machine guns mounted on the vehicles. The covering troops were rushed, the fuses of the demolition charges were damp and would not ignite and the bridge was lost. Further demolitions along the road had not been carried out and the Japanese went on to Bhamo. They occupied that town on 4 May. On 8 May they were in Myitkyina, no opposition being offered to them.

To complete the story of the Shan States operations it is necessary to refer briefly to the further movements of the Chinese 200th Division with its attached regiment of the 22nd Division. From Loilem this force moved on to Hsipaw. Finding the Japanese holding Lashio too strongly to be attacked it turned south-west and re-occupied Maymyo. From that place it went north to Mogok with the object of cutting its way out to China. At Mogok was the remaining regiment of the 28th Division.

Myitkyina is roughly four hundred and twenty miles due north of Bawlake, and the Japanese advanced over this distance in three weeks. In the earlier stages of this operation the Japanese *56th Division* was

---

Ke-hsi-Mansam, Mong-Yai and Hsawng Ke. When the Division had again concentrated it moved up to attack Lashio which was defended by four Chinese Disivisions. A fierce battle raged during which *56 Division* was supported by *14 Tank Regt.* from the *Fifteenth Army*. Lashio fell on 29 Apr. 42. *56 Division* casualties were very slight but the Chinese were almost wiped out'. *A short history of 36 Japanese Division*. 601/7249/H, p. 1. *14 Tank Regiment* which supported the forces attacking Lashio had been organised at Canton on 10 November 1939 with a total strength of 500 men and an allotment of 10 tankettes (type 94) for each of the three companies. The Commander of the Regiment was Colonel Kita. In July 1941 the unit was engaged in intensive training in co-operation with infantry. It was then thought that the Regiment would eventually be used in operations on the Manchurian front.

However it was transferred to Saigon and in August 1941 the Tankettes were replaced by 40 light tanks (type 95) and there followed a further period of training for the operations in Malaya. The Regiment moved by rail via Bankok to Malacca at the end of January 1942 where it detrained and joined the advance on Singapore. It landed at Singapore on 12 February. It sailed for Rangoon on 10 March and arrived there on 27 March. At this time its composition was as follows:—

(i) Regiment Headquarters 3 Light tanks and 6 trucks.
(ii) Each of the three companies consisted of 11 tanks and 8 trucks. There was an ammunition train of 13 trucks.

⁴ To give the further activities of *56th Division* "From Lashio it advanced to Hsenwi, where *56 Recce Regt.* slaughtered another Chinese Division. The advance continued through Kuktai, Namhpakka to Namkham. From the latter place the *3rd Battalion 146 Inf. Regt., 56 Recce Regt.* and the *1st Bn. 56 Field Arty.* were sent to capture Bhamo which fell on 10 May 1942. There Indian troops (F.F.) mainly cavalry were encountered for the first time." *A short history of Japanese 56 Division*. 601/7249/H, p. 1.

23

employed. Later the Japanese *13th Division*[5] also probably operated in the Shan States area. These divisions had entered Burma through Rangoon when considerable reinforcements were brought into the country early in April.

CHINESE FIFTH ARMY

It is now necessary to consider the operations undertaken in April by the Chinese Fifth Army on the front south of Mandalay. Upon the withdrawal of the 200th Division from Toungoo, the line was established by the 22nd Division on the Swa, south of Yedashe. The Japanese had been severely handled in the Toungoo fighting. Early in April their troops in that area were reported to have obtained reinforcements including artillery.[6] Air action continued to be heavy, and on 3 April both Pyinmana and Yamethin were severely bombed by them. After a brief interval the Japanese continued their forward movement and on 5 April were attacking the 22nd Division in Yedashe, where a battalion of the 66th Regiment was surrounded. There was hard fighting. In spite of strong hostile pressure the Chinese gave ground only slowly. The Japanese were held on the Swa river at Thagaya and again at Yeni. The Chinese then withdrew towards Pyinmana where General Tu was anxious to stage a "Changsha" battle. The plan for this involved the employment of all three divisions. One was to act as a forward screen, another was to hold Pyinmana as a strong point, whilst the third was to be held in reserve to deliver a counter-attack after the Japanese had carried out their inevitable pincer movement round the leading division. The weakness of the plan was that the Japanese with their almost complete air superiority were aware of the Chinese dispositions and refused to fall into the trap.

Early in April an important meeting took place in Maymyo between the Generalissimo and Gen. Sir H. Alexander. The former insisted that there must be no further retirements and undertook to stand at Pyinmana if the British would hold a line through Taungdwingyi and south of Magwe. Gen. Sir H. Alexander pointed out that Burcorps could not hold such a wide front, whereupon the Generalissimo promised to send one division across the Yomas to Taungdwingyi. But this promise could not be implemented probably due to General Tu's anxiety to carry out his

---

[5] There had been an 18th Division in the Japanese Army from the time of the Russo-Japanese War. It was demobilised in 1915 and remobilised 22 years later. Its recruits who were the best were drawn from the coal mining ship building and heavy industrial areas of the north and north-western prefectures of Kyushu with an admixture of farm workers. The code name chosen was *Kiku* or chrysantheum, the badge of the Imperial House.

The Division was organised on a square basis with 2 Brigades (23 and 35) and four Regiments *55, 56, 114* and *124 Inf Regiments. 12 Cavalry Regiment* and *18 Mtn Arty Regt., 12 Engineer Regt., 12 Tpt Regt.,* and *1, 2, 3 & 4 Field Hospitals* were attached to it. From 1937 to 1941 it saw service in China and for its services recieved thrice the diploma of merit.

After receiving intensive training in Canton, the Division took part in the Malaya Campaign. Here it became 'triangular'. It left Singapore on 1 April 1942 and landed at Rangoon on 10 April. It completed its concentration before Toungoo on 17 April and began its advance towards Mandalay two days later." *A short history of 18 Division* (Jap.). COL/7256/H, pp. 1, 2.

[6] 56 and later 18th Divisions.

"Changsha" plan. He did not send more than a single battalion to Taungdwingyi. The result was that Burcorps was too thin on the ground, and the Japanese passed through its line to cut off the 1st Burma Division at Yenangyaung. Gen. J. Stilwell was, however, determined to help the British and accordingly moved the 38th Division from Mandalay to the support of Burcorps. Elements of this division were able to render considerable assistance in the fighting round Yenangyaung.

Meanwhile, the Japanese had refused to enter General Tu's trap. Finding that they were unlikely to launch a direct attack on Pyinmana, Gen. J. Stilwell agreed to send the 200th Division to help Burcorps in a counter-attack in the Kyaukpadaung area. He was afraid that hostile pressure up the Irrawaddy valley might result in the outflanking of the Fifth Army from the west.

Great difficulty was experienced in transferring the 200th Division to its new area. Both British and Chinese Headquarters insisted that they were helpless and unable to provide the necessary transport. By the time that the division had reached Meiktilla, the threat against the Sixth Army had become so serious that General Stilwell was compelled to divert the division to the Shan States. Leading it in person he launched the attack on Taunggyi on 23 April.

It has already been stated that the Japanese in Burma had been heavily reinforced, and with the arrival of fresh troops they continued their pressure on the Fifth Army. The Japanese 18th Division was identified on this front.

On 20 April the Chinese were forced out of Pyinmana, and on that day the 96th Division was fighting twelve miles to the north of the town. The division had sustained heavy casualties and the Japanese had worked round behind it. Next day the division was fighting in Kyidaunggan, and behind it the 22nd Division was holding Pyawbwe. Moving by road to the west of Pyawbwe, a hostile force of tanks and armoured cars began to encircle that town on the afternoon of 25 April. The same evening British tanks surprised a column of Japanese lorry-borne troops several miles north of the town. The 22nd Division then withdrew.

The remnants of the two Chinese divisions passed through the 7th Armoured Brigade which covered their retirement. As a fighting force these Chinese divisions had almost ceased to exist and were reduced to less than half their effective strength. Opposed to a considerably superior force of the Japanese they had been in constant action since early in April. They had fought well.

The 48th Indian Infantry Brigade was in position at Kyaukse, and the 22nd Division was to occupy the line of the Myitnge river to defend Mandalay. The campaign had then entered upon its final phase. In the Shan States the Sixth Army had disintegrated, and the Indo-British forces with the Chinese 38th Division were withdrawing across the Irrawaddy. It was arranged that the 93rd Division with Army troops and some motorised units should also cross the Irrawaddy and move north through Shwebo. The 22nd Division was to follow by the east bank of the river through Mandalay to Singu, where it would cross the Irrawaddy to Kyaukmyaung, there rejoining the 93rd Division. The 38th Division was to act as rear-guard to the Fifth Army.

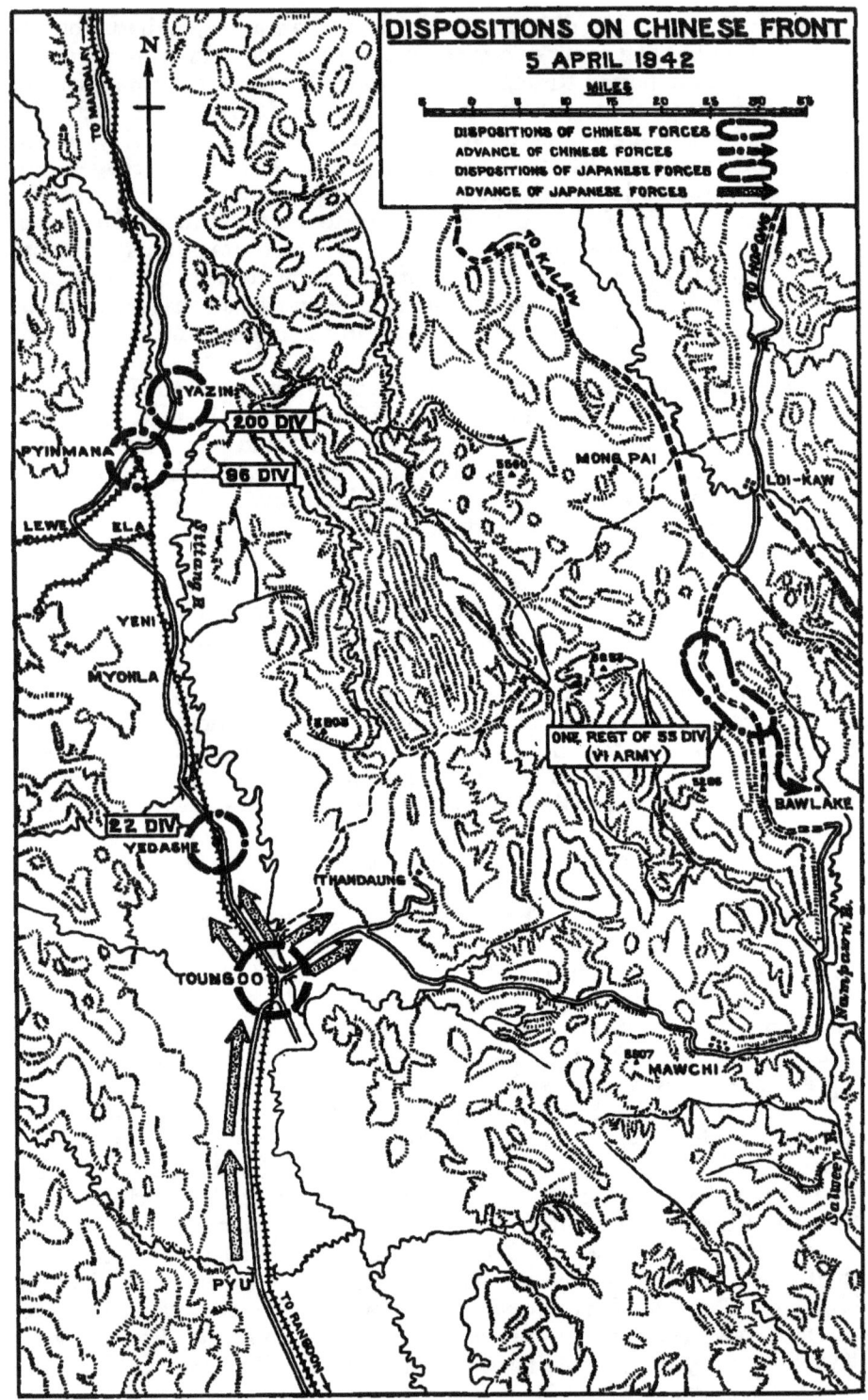

WITHDRAWAL

The original intention was to withdraw the whole force on Katha and Myitkyina. When it became apparent that Bhamo and Myitkyina were imperilled by the Japanese advance through the Shan States this plan was modified to the extent that the Fifth Army would make for India if it could not go north.

On 29 and 30 April the last elements of the Allied forces crossed to the west bank of the Irrawaddy, with the 22nd Division covering the east bank and Mandalay. At 2359 hours on 30 April the Ava Bridge was blown. The 22nd Division was then withdrawing through Mandalay. The road and rail bridges over the Myitnge river had previously been demolished.

The Chinese were in contact with the Japanese in the foot-hills to the east of Mandalay, but the withdrawal to Singu was not followed up and the river was crossed without opposition. Kyaukmyaung and points along the railway on the west bank of the river were repeatedly attacked by hostile aircraft which enjoyed unchallenged supremacy. These bombing attacks did much to complete the disorganisation of the railway and to interfere with the withdrawal northwards.

Realising that the Japanese had already reached Myitkyina, General Tu with his Headquarters and what remained of 22nd and 96th Divisions left the railway line about Naba and struck north-west through the Hukawng valley, eventually reaching India. The 38th Division, in much better fighting condition than the two divisions of the Fifth Army, turned south from Naba and regained contact with the Japanese at Wuntho where an engagement was fought. Then, with the 113th Regiment as rear-guard, the 38th Division crossed the hills to the Chindwin river. There at Paungbyin, on 11 May, it encountered a Japanese force moving up the Chindwin. Crossing the river, the division, less the 113th Regiment arrived in Imphal area on 24 May. The 113th Regiment was cut off east of the Chindwin, and all efforts to cross the river were checked by the Japanese.

Gen. J. Stilwell with members of his Headquarters and a bodyguard made his way independently across the Chindwin to India.

The assistance rendered by the Chinese Expeditionary Force led to a prolongation of the brief campaign in Burma which made possible the withdrawal of the forces to India. Without this aid the Indo-British forces alone could have been speedily enveloped after the fall of Rangoon.

CHAPTER XXV

Capture of Akyab

An account of the retreat from Burma would be incomplete without some reference to events in Arakan, and more particularly in the area of the port of Akyab. Some details of the work carried out by the Karen Levies and the Commandos, and of events in the Bhamo-Myitkyina area at the close of the Campaign are also necessary.

Akyab as a point of entry into Burma was of negligible importance. It was of value, however, as an air base, whilst its proximity to India and its position on the Bay of Bengal made it a prize of considerable importance to the Japanese. It was necessary, therefore, to deny it to them as long as possible. Akyab, for the defence of which General Headquarters, India, had assumed direct responsibility, was also the centre of a rice producing area. It had several large mills, and its main export was the grain crop of Arakan.

Prior to the fall of Rangoon the Japanese invasion of Burma had no vital effect on Akyab. At the end of January 1942 its defences had been augmented by the arrival of the 14th Battalion 7th Rajput Regiment which relieved 23 Garrison Company. Indian refugees from Rangoon and Lower Burma, crossing to the Arakan coast through the Taungup Pass from Prome, were crowding into the port. In the latter part of February the R.A.F., forced to evacuate the Rangoon airfields, strengthened its force in Akyab.

After the capture of Rangoon by the Japanese, Akyab was organised as a naval base under Commodore Graham, R. N. commanding Burma Coast. There were also stationed the R.I.N. sloops 'Sutlej' and 'Indus' and four L.N.D. vessels. From the base there operated five armed motor launches manned by the personnel of the B.R.N.V.R. to prevent hostile infiltration. But this force was not adequate for the task, which was made more difficult by the strain of evacuating a mass of refugees streaming out of Burma. Between the end of March and the beginning of May, thirty-five thousand persons were sent to India by sea from Akyab and the small island port of Kyaukpyu.

In view of the importance of Akyab as an air base it was decided early in March to strengthen further the forces there. Accordingly, Headquarters 109th Brigade with the 6th Battalion 9th Jat Regiment and the 9th Battalion 7th Rajput Regiment together with anti-aircraft guns were despatched to Akyab, arriving there on 18 March.

On 23 March the Japanese occupied the Andamans from which a small garrison had already been evacuated on 12 March under the orders of the ABDA Command. Although the islands were not occupied by the Japanese until 23 March the fact that they could not be defended constituted a serious threat to the security of shipping entering Rangoon river and was one of the factors bearing on the question of the evacuation of Rangoon. On 23 March, too, Akyab was subjected to a heavy air raid, this being repeated the following day. Just previous to it, the Magwe airfield had also been attacked. The result of the raids was the virtual extinction of the British air force in Burma, and the decision was made to employ Akyab only as an advanced landing ground. Headquarters 109th Brigade and the two newly arrived battalions were at once withdrawn. The remaining military garrison then consisted of the 14th Battalion 7th Rajput Regiment, one section 67th Heavy Anti-Aircraft Regiment, and two troops 1st Indian Light Anti-Aircraft Regiment.

From that date Akyab, its airfields and harbour, and the naval craft based on it were subjected to frequent air attacks. The first raids immediately resulted in a drop both in the military and civilian morale. There were numerous desertions amongst the troops and the civil police. Despite the protests of the naval and military authorities the Commissioner, Arakan Division, evacuated with nearly all his civilian officers on 30 March. The Deputy Commissoner of Akyab and some telegraph officers elected to remain at their posts; but civil administration throughout Arakan was then wholly at an end. Arson was not infrequent in the port. Rice mills were fired, and a large conflagration threatened the important oil installations of the Burmah Oil Company Limited. Civil unrest in Akyab and throughout Arakan increased. On 13 April the town and island of Akyab were placed under martial law.

Deserters from the Burma Frontier Force and the Burma Military Police joined the forces of unrest and, together with a gang of Arakanese, took part in the massacre of Indians, mostly women and children, at Gopethaung on 19 April. The general state of disorder was particularly marked south of Kyauktaw, and east of the Kaladan river. From about mid-April the prevailing unrest had assumed a definitely rebellious aspect, and patrols of the Rajputs were engaged in several skirmishes against parties of Thakins and others. On 21 April the Deputy Commissioner telegraphed a message to the following effect to the Burma Government:—
"This is report on situation in Akyab district. State of open rebellion exists which should be quelled only by military as owing to breakdown of civil (Administration) what is left of civil police is grossly unreliable. In Kyauktaw and Akyab sub-divisions gangs of rebels supported by deserters from Frontier Force with large quantities of arms and ammunitions and the extreme section of Arakan National Congress have done incalculable damage to life and property. Arson and looting are rampant and the ground is being prepared for enemy infiltration."

The existing garrison of Akyab and the naval patrols were of course quite inadequate to deal effectively with the situation or to prevent the advance of the Japanese. On 11 April a naval patrol from Kyaukpyu, learnt that two hundred and fifty armed Burmese with Japanese officers had arrived at Taungup on the previous day. They had launches and boats. This party proceeded to work its way up the coast via An to Minbya, a centre of rebel activity.

Towards the end of April Japanese aerial activity further increased, and there was no doubt left that a hostile force was concentrating in the Minbya area for an advance on Akyab. On 1 May two motor launches of the B.R.N.V.R. were separately engaged by this force near Minbya.

Four field guns were reported to have been employed by them and casualties were suffered on board the launches.

Next day the hostile force was in Kyauktaw and Ponnagyun. A Rajput patrol was sent out that evening in launches to locate the force. On the morning of 3 May these vessels were fired on by machine-guns on a reach of the Kaladan river below Ponnagyun. Several men were hit. The fire was returned and one of the launches brought its two pounder gun into action.

That day Akyab was subjected to a series of air raids, one of them by twenty-seven heavy bombing aircraft. This particular raid did appreciable damage to buildings, military stores, and equipment. Rations, mortars, and four armoured carriers were destroyed, and the reserve ammunition of the garrison was blown up. About twenty casualties were also sustained.

The role of the Akyab garrison was to defend the airfields as long as possible. If a serious attack was made on the port, demolitions were to be carried out and the garrison to be withdrawn overland towards Chittagong. The officer commanding the garrison considered that the retention of the port was no longer within the capacity of his force. The troops were in a low state of training; in addition, they were debilitated by malaria and shaken by the air raids. There were indications of the presence of regular Japanese troops who would probably attack Akyab before the morning of 4 May. The coast road was flooded and the inland route was already threatened, if not cut, since the Japanese were at Ponnagyun. Having regard to this state of affairs he determined to carry out an evacuation by sea that night. Demolitions were ordered to be effected.

Guns and heavy equipment were loaded on to the ships "Heinrich Jessen" and "Hydari", and after dark troops were embarked. Naval demolitions were carried out in the port and surplus vessels sunk. In the early hours of 4 May the forces had abandoned Akyab.[1]

KAREN LEVIES

The loyalty of the Karens towards the British has always been a marked characteristic. They had no love for the Burman who, in pre-British times, regarded them as a subject race. Speaking generally, the Karens were strong supporters of the British during the campaign, although one section of the community was reported to have pro-Japanese leanings. The religion of these people is Christianity. Their politics are often coloured by their religion, but by no means all the missionaries working amongst them had British sympathies.

Karenni lies astride the Salween north of Papun, but the Karens were to be found in all the hill districts of the Salween south of the Shan States, in the Pegu Yomas, and in the Irrawaddy delta. Their knowledge of

---

[1] The Japanese account, *History of the Japanese 15th Army*, p. 24 refers to the Capture of Akyab thus: "Despite its strategic importance Akyab was not strongly held. On orders from Army the Division (33) despatched one infantry company and one half of the M. G. Company to Akyab, by road and water transport and the town was occupied with little opposition." (601/7785/H).

the thinly populated areas, mainly inhabited by them, and their jungle craft was great. The organisation of these hill people for intelligence work and as irregulars would have been invaluable, yet nothing substantial was done until it was much too late. This was an instance of the absence of pre-arranged planning against the possibility of a Japanese invasion.

It was not until the Japanese entered Burma that any effective steps were taken to enlist the general aid of the hill tribes. Even in the case of the Chins and Kachins the time proved too short to meet the existing emergency, although these hillmen were to establish their value in a later stage of the war. With the Karens the results achieved within a brief period showed how dismally the Burma Army Command had failed to employ the excellent material available to it. However, at the end of 1940 and in 1941 a small force of Karen Levies was raised for intelligence work on the frontier and in Thailand. This body of men obtained very useful information in the Karenni area and in the adjoining part of Thailand.

In February 1942 Forest officers and others with an intimate knowledge of the Karens made contact with influential leaders for the purpose of raising Levies. The general direction of the work was under the Oriental Mission, an organisation formed for the conduct of operations through irregulars and behind Japanese lines. But by that time the Japanese were across the Salween and it was not possible to utilise them to the full. All that could be done was to distribute a scanty supply of rifles and guns with a little ammunition. However, in spite of the difficulties, a substantial number of Levies was raised.

It was on the road between Toungoo and Mawchi that Karens of the 1st Battalion Burma Rifles and Karen Levies were seriously engaged with the Japanese. The Karens of the Burma Rifles had been detached from their battalion at Toungoo where they took part in holding the Japanese surprise attack on the Kyungon landing ground. These men were armed with rifles and fifty rounds of ammunition apiece. They also had four Thompson sub-machine carbines. On 2 April this force, 135 men in all, of Burma Rifles, was covering the demolished road bridge at Paletwa on the road to Mawchi. Here it encountered a motorised Japanese force with armoured cars and estimated at some eight hundred men in strength. Allowing Japanese scouts to pass through their position, fire was opened on the main body at twenty yards range. Many casualties were inflicted on the Japanese. Then, when the left flank was overrun, the force withdrew. The road was blown in places and numerous booby traps laid. Wooden bridges were destroyed.

Next day the Burma Rifles and Karen Levies were in position just west of Kyichaung astride the road, the latter patrolling to the north and south. At 0230 hours on 4 April the Japanese attacked, employing mortars. An advance against the left flank followed. This was stopped by rifle fire. The Burma Rifles then put in a counter-attack, but weight of numbers compelled a withdrawal after more than forty casualties had been sustained. Only fifty-eight men of the Burma Rifles remained, while Japanese strength was about twelve hundred.

The Chinese Sixth Army then took over the defence of the Mawchi area, but the Karens continued to carry out patrols. On 5 April they

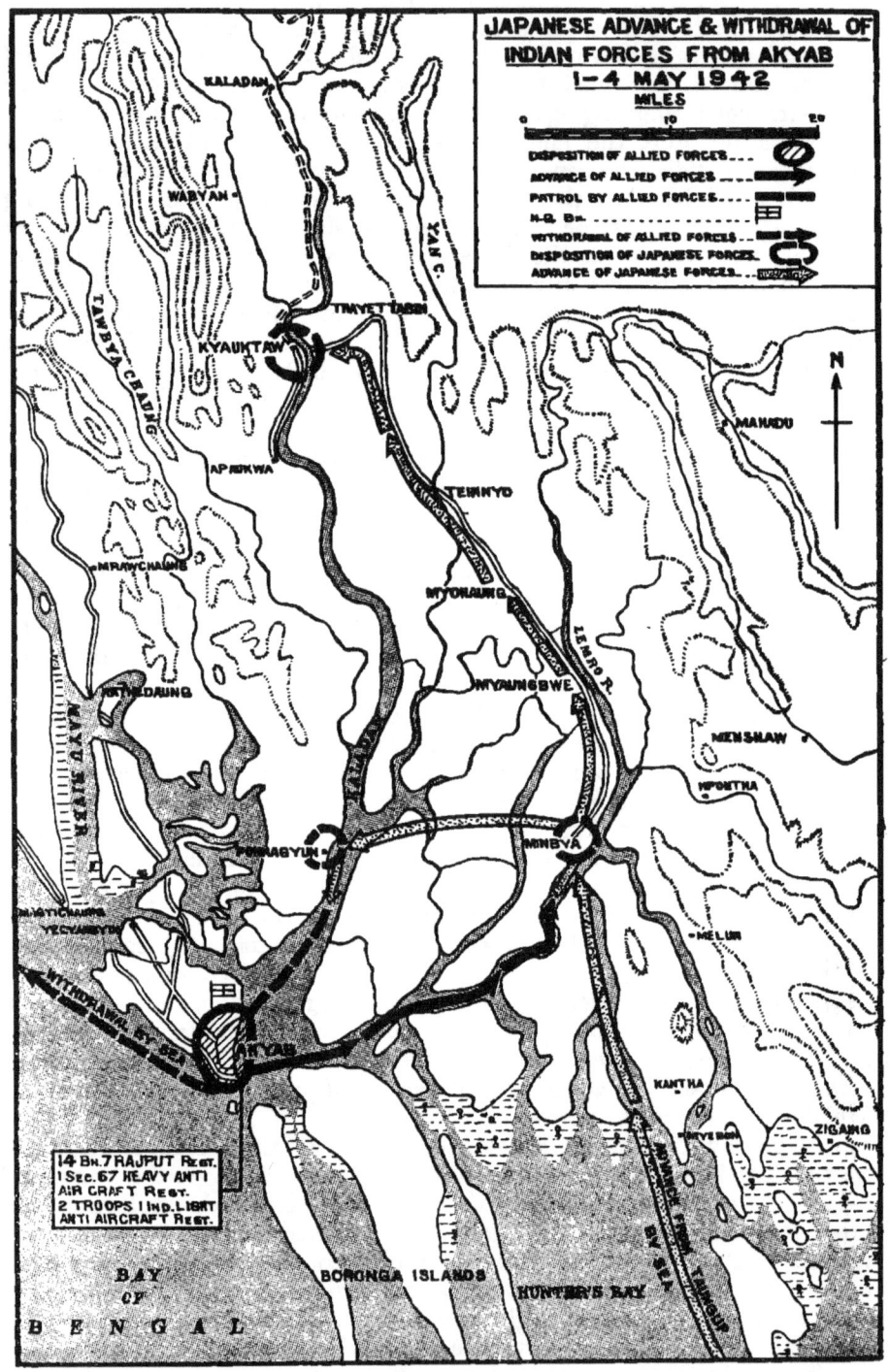

gave warning of an attempt by the Japanese to by-pass Mawchi to the north. Later, when the Japanese had gained Mawchi and were moving north along the road from Kemapyu, Levies and the remaining Karens of the Burma Rifles were patrolling and covering the tracks west of the main road. They were in contact with the Japanese at Yado and warned the Chinese of the threat to their right flank.

This brief account indicates that the Karens played by no means a negligible part in the campaign in their area. But owing to their inadequate equipment and insufficient organisation, they could not be effective in harassing the Japanese, which was intended to be their main role.

COMMANDOS

Three Special Service Detachments (Commandos) were also formed from the personnel of the Bush Warfare School. These units comprised specially trained and selected British officers and men, expert in guerilla warfare and demolition work. Towards the end of March these units were placed under the command of Colonel Wingate who, in view of his experience in Abyssinia, had been asked for by Lieutenant General Hutton to organise what were afterwards called Long Range Penetration Groups. Unfortunately conditions were such that it was not possible in the available time to organise anything very effective. However, Colonel Wingate put this experience to good use at a later date.

Two of these Commandos were employed in the Southern Shan States where they carried out one or two minor operations. Later, on the arrival of the Chinese Sixth Army, they remained to co-operate with these forces. In the final phase of the campaign they did much useful demolition work. The operations of the Commandos on the Irrawaddy valley front have already been described.

The success of deep penetration units depends to a large extent on their operating in a friendly country, but this condition did not exist in Burma at that time. Furthermore, as the Army was cut off from India, the only source of supply for suitable personnel was the depleted British battalions. In consequence, it was not possible to utilise these valuable Commando units to the full.

When the Japanese break-through occurred in the Shan States small parties of men from the Bush Warfare School, the only troops available, were sent to the Gokteik gorge to prevent a hostile advance on Maymyo. Later these small parties were reinforced by convalescents and other men from the British Infantry Depot. In early May some of these men were again employed to cover the mouth of the Maukkadaw Chaung on the south flank of the Ye-U-Shwegyin track.

EVENT IN BHAMO-SHWEBO IN THE LAST DAYS

When the Japanese air attacks towards the end of April rendered impossible the further regular employment of Shwebo airfield, the sick and wounded were sent by rail and river to Myitkyina for evacuation to India by air. Early in May there were also in Myitkyina numerous civilian refugees awaiting air transport to India. On 6 May Japanese aircraft twice bombed Myitkyina aerodrome. Two R.A.F. aircraft taking in wounded and evacuees were caught on the ground and destroyed. Most of the passengers and crew were killed or wounded. These raids put an end to evacuation by air and about two thousand refugees, including many Anglo-Indians, were stranded.

The only organised unit in this area was the Bhamo battalion of the Burma Frontier Force. This was really a depot battalion consisting of recruits and details and could not be regarded as fit for serious operations. Wholesale desertions from this battalion meant that no regular body of troops was available for the defence of the Bhamo-Myitkyina road. No attempt was made to hold it, nor were demolitions carried out. At many points this road lent itself to defence, and demolitions would have imposed substantial delay on the hostile motorised force.

Along the railway between Shwebo and Myitkyina were, at that time, thousands of refugees, military personnel, and casualties.

On 7 May Myitkyina was evacuated. Next day a force of about three hundred Japanese entered the town.

North of Myitkyina demolitions had been prepared along the road to Sumprabum. These were effected by a small band of officers, mainly of the Oriental Mission. No other opposition could be made to a further hostile advance.

It now remained for the refugees and military personnel along the railway north of Shwebo and from Myitkyina itself to make their way overland to India. The great majority of them followed the route through the Hukawng valley to Assam, others employed tracks further to the south, a handful crossed by the difficult Chaukan pass.

CHAPTER XXVI

Campaign in the Air

AIR FORCES IN BURMA—DECEMBER 1941

It has already been indicated that the employment of aircraft was always visualised as playing a large part in the defence of Burma. Here, again, the requirements of Burma were subordinated to other demands considered to be of a more pressing nature. The result was that in December 1941 the air garrison of the country was inadequate and wholly incapable of withstanding any heavy or long sustained attacks upon it. The RAF in Burma consisted of No. 67 Squadron with a strength of about sixteen Buffalo aircraft based at Mingaladon, and No. 4 Indian Flight equipped with a few obsolete machines. The only other flying unit in the country was the Communications Flight. This had two Moth type aircraft belonging to the Burma Volunteer Air Unit. No. 4 Indian Flight was stationed at Moulmein, the others at Mingaladon near Rangoon. There was also present in Burma the personnel of No. 60 Squadron, without its aircraft which were in Malaya when war broke out and which were not made available immediately.

In addition to the above, there was in Burma the 3rd Squadron of the American Volunteer Group which, with twenty-one P 40 (Tomahawk) aircraft, was based on Mingaladon for the defence of Rangoon. The primary role of the American Volunteer Group (A.V.G.) under Col. (later Brig-Gen.) C. L. Chennault was the defence of the Burma Road, its operational base being Kunming. Impressed with the importance of defending the port of Rangoon adequately, as supplies for China had to pass through it, Generalissimo Chiang-Kai-Shek specially detached the 3rd Squadron for the protection of that port. Besides these, there were no other aircraft in the country. "Reinforcing aircraft for the Far East were, however, flying through Burma to Malaya and the Dutch East Indies".[1] On 1 January 1942 the command of the enlarged Allied Air Force (Norgroup) in Burma was assumed by Air Vice-Marshal D. F. Stevenson.

AIRFIELDS

Geography determined the maintenance of air force in Burma. The port of Rangoon provided the only means of maintaining an air force in Burma and there were two valleys in which airfields could be made. The main line of airfields was therefore, Victoria Point, Mergui, Tavoy, Moulmein, Rangoon, Mingaladon; and up the valley of the Sittang were Toungoo, Heho, Namsang, Lashio and Loiwing. The last one was an American built airfield on the Chinese side of the frontier north of Lashio.

---

[1] Stevenson's *Despatch*; para 6.
The narrative in this chapter is largely based on this Despatch. Also see volume on the *History of the Indian Air Force* for details of the activities of the Indian Air Force.

Airfields under construction

There were other airfields at Akyab, Magwe, Meiktila, Shwebo and Myitkyina. Some of these were still under construction, but all, with the possible exception of Meiktila, were brought into use before the end of the campaign and rendered most valuable service. In general, the airfield development and construction undertaken by the Government of Burma showed an extremely good state of affairs. All airfields had one or two all-weather runways fit for modern aircraft of the heaviest type, and all-weather satellites were provided for most airfields. During the period of the campaign, too, the flat paddy lands of Burma were dry. Provided labour was available a runway suitable for fighter and bomber aircraft could be quickly prepared on these. Thus airfield accommodation for a considerable force was available in Burma. Consequently from the point of view of airfields, there was nothing to prevent the reception of considerable reinforcements as long as Rangoon was held. The weakness of the lay-out, however, was in the lack of adequate warning for the main line of airfields.[2]

WARNING SYSTEM

This line of airfields faced the Japanese in Thailand across the intervening jungle-clad and mountainous belt along the frontier. Hence, except in the case of Rangoon, adequate warning of the approach of hostile aircraft by RDF or telephone was impossible. Had Toungoo, Heho and Namsang been situated with the attendant satellites in the Irrawaddy valley, warning would have been satisfactory and possible as long as communications in the Sittang valley and along the Rangoon-Mandalay railway remained intact.

Observer Corps

The Burma Observer Corps could have provided an efficient warning system. But it was necessarily tied to the existing telegraph and telephone lines. Hence it could function only as long as the main centres of communication and telephone lines were not threatened by land attack. Aerodrome defence also was adequate. "Outlying station airfields such as Tavoy and Mergui had garrisons, while detachments of troops for land defence and anti-sabotage precautions had been provided at occupied airfields".[3]

ANTI-AIRCRAFT DEFENCE

At the outset of the camapign anti-aircraft defence was very weak. It consisted of one battery of the Burma Auxiliary Force whose equipment had only arrived at the end of December 1941. The arrival of the British and Indian light and heavy batteries later made it possible to organise a weak scale of defence at important vital points, but the defence was never in sufficient strength to provide adequate protection for all the

[2] *Ibid,* para 11.
[3] *Ibid,* para 16.

airfields. Except for a weak airfield detachment, the anti-aircraft artillery was deployed in the defence of vital points in Rangoon and of the troops in forward areas, to provide cover against hostile bombing. Light automatic defence against lowflying aircraft was provided at some aerodromes by hurriedly trained detachments of the Burma Auxiliary Force armed with a few Browning Arm machine-guns on anti-aircraft mountings. These were stationed at Mingaladon and Zayatkwin and later at Magwe. They were manned entirely by Burmese personnel of the 12th Battalion Burma Rifles. The training of these men was hurried and their number much under strength. The position as regards headquarters and station staffs was not good. Only a nucleus headquarters staff existed and Mingaladon was the only airfield having a station headquarters. All other airfields had only care and maintenance parties. There was no repair organisation.

AIR VICE-MARSHAL D. F. STEVENSON'S APPRECIATION—JANUARY 1942

On 14 January Air Vice-Marshal D. F. Stevenson completed his appreciation. He considered that Japanese air force would make a determined air attack on Burma, attempt a "knock out" blow against Rangoon in the event of the fall of Singapore, and that the scale of attack might reach as much as 600 aircraft a day at the maximum intensity. The air defence of Burma against an attack of this magnitude therefore required that the fighter force should be 14 squadrons—9 more than those already on the programme. But only the mixed equivalents of two Fighter Squadrons, one Bomber Squadron, two Army Co-operation Squadrons, and one-third of a General Reconnaissance Squadron joined action with the Japanese in the course of the campaign. Of seven Radio Direction Finder Stations proposed only one existed.[4]

RESOURCES AT THAT TIME

In addition to No. 67 Squadron the RAF fighter force later consisted of Nos. 17, 135 and 137 Squadrons, the last three being equipped with Hurricanes. There were never enough Hurricanes available in Burma to equip No. 67 Squadron and many of the machines received were obsolescent, worn-out Hurricane I aircraft. Consequently the maximum number of this aircraft ever in action was about thirty, i.e., the equivalent of two squadrons. The strength fell away rapidly due to lack of reinforcing aircraft, proper operational facilities, and absence of spares. On 15 February 1942 there were only fifteen serviceable Hurricanes, and on 5 March only six. For similar reasons the available effort of the A.V.G. fell away until, in March 1942, it was between seven and ten.

For the Bomber offensive, No. 113 Squadron personnel with Blenheim aircraft arrived in Rangoon in January and early in February 1942. But No. 60 Squadron could never be equipped owing to lack of Blenheims. The result was that only one Bomber Squadron was available for operations while the appreciation had placed the requirements at seven. The average daily bomber effort was six.

[4] *Ibid*, paras 21-22.

In respect of General Reconnaissance aircraft, No. 4 Indian Flight equipped with Wapiti and Audax aircraft arrived in Burma at the end of December 1941. This was later replaced by No. 3 Indian Flight which was armed with an initial equipment of 4 Blenheim I's. After the fall of Singapore, 139 Squadron, *en route* for Java, was held up in Burma. It was equipped with Hudsons; but there was no personnel or squadron equipment and the Hudsons were maintained by No. 3 and No. 4 Indian Flights.

Army Co-operation was carried out by No. 1 Indian Army Co-operation Squadron, and No. 28 Army Co-operation Squadron, both being equipped with out-of-date Lysander aircraft. Constant requests were made for the re-equipment of these squadrons with modern aircraft, but the Mohawks were not available.

The units of the Indian Air Force mentioned above were on active service for the first time in their history. They proved their efficiency and gallantry on several occasions. No. 1 Indian Squadron carried out forty-one bomber sorties against Japanese held aerodromes and direct support targets, but no Lysander was shot down by the hostile fighters. Accurate bombing was achieved. The General Reconnaissance Aircraft and in particular the Blenheim I's of No. 3 Flight carried out a considerable number of reconnaissances in the Preparis Channel and the Gulf of Martaban.[5]

JAPANESE AIR STRENGTH

In the opening stages of the campaign, and whilst the offensive in Malaya was in full progress, the Japanese strength within close range was estimated at a minimum of one hundred and fifty bombers and fighters as against thirty-five of the Allies. Japanese aircraft were disposed as follows:

Parachuab Khirikhan	10
Mesoht } Tak }	40
Bangkok	70
Lampang } Chiengmai }	30

Singapore fell on 15 February, but even before that date the hostile air strength had risen. After that they continued to bring up reinforcements and by 21 March it was estimated that they had a minimum strength of four hundred aircraft based largely on the Burma airfields south of the line Tharrawaddy-Toungoo and also in Thailand. Intelligence reports from China and other sources indicated the presence of some *fourteen Regiments* of the Japanese Army Air Force. This gave them an effort of at least two hundred and sixty, as compared to forty-two of the Allies on 21 March.

Types of Japanese aircraft

The Japanese employed three types of fighter aircraft; the Army 97

---

[5] *Ibid*, paras 29-37.

with a fixed under-carriage; the Army O.I. (an Army 97 with slightly improved performance and a retractable under-carriage) and the Naval 'O' Fighter. The former two were manoeuvreable with a top speed of two hundred and seventy miles an hour at fifteen thousand feet and had a climb of two thousand five hundred feet per minute. Armament consisted of two machine-guns.

The Naval 'O' had two 20mm guns in addition to two machine-guns, and was much superior in performance to the Army 97. It had a top speed of three hundred and fifteen miles an hour at ten thousand feet, a good climb, and good manoeuvreability. It was slightly inferior to the P.40 and Hurricane II at medium heights, and above twenty thousand feet the Hurricane II was definitely superior. None of the three types had self-sealing tanks or armour. All had a radius of action of over two hundred and fifty miles instead of the one hundred and thirty-five miles of the Hurricane II, and were also fitted with jettisonable petrol tanks which increased their radius to over five hundred miles.

The Japanese Army 97 heavy bomber was mostly employed. It had a radius of seven hundred and fifty miles and with a full load of petrol its lift was one and a half tons of bombs. It had no self-sealing tanks or armour.

COMPARISON OF THE ALLIED AND JAPANESE AIRCRAFT

Some Japanese fighter aircraft were able to reach out over great distances and to destroy first line aircraft on the ground. Consequently unless airfields had a good warning system these fighters could achieve an element of surprise and cause great damage to first line aircraft by low-flying attacks. This form of attack could be met by a good ground defence, but in Burma the Allies were extremely weak in this respect.

Japanese bombers with their range and bomb lift had a wide choice in their selection of objectives. Operating in formations of not less than twenty-seven, with a pattern of some twenty-seven tons of small, light anti-personnel and high explosive bombs, they caused great damage to first line aircraft and petrol, oil and lubricant supply even though dispersal and anti-blast protection had been provided.

The inferiority of the Allies was in the numbers of their aircraft, in the vital factor of the restricted range of the fighters, and in the range, bomb lift, and speed of the bombers. On the other hand, the Japanese were under the disadvantage of not having armour and self-sealing tanks. In addition, the Hurricane II and P. 40 in the air battle were decisive against the ill-defended Army 97 bomber, were much superior to the Army 97 fighter, and slightly superior to the Naval 'O'. The Blenheim bomber with its power-operated turret gave a good account of itself against hostile fighters. To sum up, fighter for fighter the Allies were much superior. But the Japanese could score against them when they were heavily outnumbered and had received no warning, and were without proper airfield protection.[6]

⁶ *Ibid.* Part II, paras 50-62.

FIRST AIR ATTACKS—DECEMBER 1941

Japanese aircraft raided Tavoy on 11 December but their bombs did little damage. On 13 December three air attacks were made on Mergui. On the same day a heavy raid was carried out against Victoria Point. Thereafter there was little or no hostile air activity until 23 December when between seventy and eighty bombers with an escort of some thirty fighters attacked the Mingaladon airfield and Rangoon. Another attack in about the same strength was made forty-eight hours later on 25 December.

In these attacks the Japanese did not escape without severe casualties. The P. 40s of the AVG and the Buffaloes of 67 Squadron RAF had taken a toll of no less than thirty-six first line bombers and fighters. On each occasion Japanese bombs had caused no substantial damage although on 23 December the Rangoon wharves and shipping area were attacked. There were, however, very heavy civilian casualties in Rangoon on 23 December, some two thousand four hundred persons being killed. This resulted, as has been previously mentioned, in the general exodus of labour and the almost complete stoppage of work in the port. In the first raid there were a few RAF casualties on the ground, and three P. 40s were shot down. On the second occasion four RAF fighters were lost. On 3 and 4 January 1942 two further significant air actions were fought. On 3 January nine Japanese aircraft attacked Moulmein, and as the raiders returned to their aerodromes they were overtaken by three AVG fighters. Three of the raiders were destroyed in the air and so, too, were four that had landed. The next day over thirty Japanese fighters attempted to break through to Rangoon. They were intercepted by the AVG and driven off with loss. The Japanese thereupon abandoned daylight attempts on Rangoon and for the next three weeks or so resorted to night bombing only, the effort varying from one or two bombers up to sixteen.

THE PLAN OF DEFENCE

After the bombing of Rangoon it had become apparent to Air Vice Marshal Stevenson that the main duty of the "small but growing fighter force (was to) defend the base facilities at Rangoon, the docks, the convoys arriving and departing and the air bases at Mingaladon and Zayatkwin. If these could be preserved from a damaging scale of day bombing attack, we should be enabled to secure our interests hereabouts and to get in our land and air reinforcements and maintenance."[7] There was also the additional task of aiding the army in its operations. So the Air Vice-Marshal's general plan was to keep his "fighter force concentrated in the Rangoon area, to accept such enemy bombing attacks as might be made on any other objectives in Northern Burma, to fight the enemy in the defence of the base, and lean forward to hit the enemy wherever and whenever I could with my small but total force".[8] To reduce the scale of attack it was decided to lean forward with a portion of the fighters, and

[7] *Ibid*, para 63.
[8] *Ibid*, paras 64-5.

by using advanced air bases like Moulmein, Tavoy and Mergui to attack hostile aircraft wherever found. Further to weaken the Japanese bombing action it was necessary to spread the Allied bombing in daylight to widely dispersed but important objectives such as Chiengmai, Mehohngsohn and Chiengrai in the north, and in the south to the aerodrome and railway communication system running down the eastern coast of the Malay Peninsula from Bangkok to Singora. Instructions were given accordingly on 2 January, 1942.[9]

This policy of attack was maintained throughout the earlier period of the Burma Campaign. It reduced the scale of attack against Rangoon and, later, against the Allied troops. At least fifty-eight hostile bombers and fighters were destroyed on the ground by the Allied fighters, and considerable damage must have been inflicted by the bombers in their attacks on grounded Japanese first line aircraft. This form of action was ultimately reduced in effort when the strength of the Buffalo squadron fell to only two or three serviceable aircraft and the P. 40s were suffering from a shortage of equipment. The effective range of the Hurricanes allowed them only to engage the closest hostile objectives.[10]

AIR BATTLE OVER RANGOON—23 DECEMBER, 25 FEBRUARY

The air battle over Rangoon lasted from 23 December 1941 until 25 February 1942. During this period thirty-one day and night attacks were made. Between 23 and 29 January a second attempt was made to overwhelm the small Allied fighter force, the Japanese using at least two hundred and eighteen aircraft, mostly fighters. During those six days some fifty of the hostile bombers and fighters were destroyed. This resulted in the Japanese taking to night operations, but a last attempt to attain air superiority over Rangoon was made on 24 and 25 February. The scale of attack then was one hundred and sixty-six bombers and fighters; and the Allied forces claimed to have destroyed thirty-seven of the hostile aircraft with another seven probably destroyed. On the second day (25 February), the AVG claimed to have shot down not less than twenty-four aircraft. Such wastage had been inflicted on the Japanese that thereafter they did not attempt to enter the warning zone round Rangoon until the city had been evacuated and the Mingaladon airfield was in their hands. Thus the safety of the convoys bringing in final reinforcements was assured, and the demolitions in Rangoon and Syriam and the final evacuation were carried out without any interference from hostile aircraft.

In the defence of Rangoon one squadron of P. 40s of the AVG, half a squadron of Buffaloes, and the equivalent of two squadrons of Hurricanes, which did not all arrive until midway through February, inflicted a loss on the Japanese of one hundred and thirty bombers and fighters with another sixty-one claimed as probably destroyed. The greater portion fell to the guns of the AVG which fought with a ready devotion and resolute gallantry.[11]

[9] *Ibid*, para 66.
[10] *Ibid*, paras 68-70.
[11] *Ibid*, paras 71-77.

AIR TACTICS EMPLOYED

As regards tactics, fighters in the correct proportion could be deployed against the hostile scale of attack. The AVG and the Hurricanes fought together and well. The Wing leader system was introduced. The general principles of fighting the air battle were those generally followed in the western theatre with but one difference. "On account of the manoeuvrability of the Japanese fighters the best method of attack was a dive and breaking away in a half roll or ailer-on turn before resuming position to carry out the attack again." Japanese escorted bomber raids were met on first interception; the bombers were attacked with a suitable proportion of the Allied forces, while the fighters were attacked and drawn off by the remainder. As regards night bombing there were no facilities for night interception. On the arrival of Hurricanes trained in night fighting later, some success was however achieved. No doubt "on moonlight nights—and the Japanese bombed on no other—considerable success would have been obtained from the fighter night system" had Rangoon held out.[12]

Air operations in support of the Army in Tenasserim

As regards air operations in support of the army, up to the fall of Rangoon, each evening at a general staff and air staff conference held at the Army Headquarters, Lt-Gen. T. J. Hutton and Air Vice Marshal Stevenson met to agree on joint action and review the changing situation. Subsequently the programme was adjusted according to requests made by the 17th Indian Division to which an Air Liaison Officer had been attached. Communication was by W/T and telephone. In general the system worked satisfactorily.

Much of the fighting by the 17th Indian Division in Tenasserim took place in close jungle country and it was often impossible for supporting aircraft to distinguish the troops. Navigators could not pin-point their targets with accuracy since there were no suitable land-marks. The situation was made more difficult by the impression in the mind of the crew that the Allied positions were frequently outflanked by the Japanese and there was a chance of the two forces being intermingled. In addition, recognition of Japanese troops was difficult owing to their use of captured uniforms and native dress, and their employment of the British transport which they had captured—bullock carts, launches, and private motor cars. However, promiscuous bombing of the jungle was known to have a good effect and this was frequently carried out, in spite of the risks involved.[13]

The fundamental requirement for the support of the Army in Tenasserim was the maintenance of air superiority over Rangoon and the bases and supply depots in its vicinity. This might have secured the line of communication from serious attack. On 20 January the attack on the Kawkareik position began. Air action in support of the troops holding the position was difficult owing to the density of the jungle. Accordingly the Japanese landing ground and base depot at Mae Saut were

[12] *Ibid*, paras, 78-85.
[13] *Ibid*, para 90.

attacked by bombers and fighters. Reconnaissance was also made towards Tavoy with the object of locating the two hostile forces in that area.

The withdrawal from Kawkareik took place on 22 January and on 21 and 22 January "Blenheims attacked Rahaeng aerodrome and village and Mesarieng. Fighter escort was provided with the object of clearing the air for short periods over the Army front and providing support for the bomber operations".[14] A strong escorted formation of hostile bombers attacked Moulmein and was intercepted by the escort of the Allied bomber raid on its outward journey. As a result seven Japanese bombers and nine fighters were destroyed.

From 23 to 30 January frequent low visual reconnaissance flights were made by the fighter aircraft over the battle area, the Japanese lines of communication, and the Tenasserim coast. But information was difficult to obtain over the jungle-clad areas, and in more open counry the Japanese only moved by night. The bomber force, a daily average of about six, acted in support of the army.

On the nights of 24, 27 and 28 January the bombers attacked the main base at Bangkok dropping a total of 42,000 lbs. of bombs. 113 Squadron had previously bombed Bangkok in the early morning of 8 January within a few hours of its arrival in Burma. Limited escort to the Allied ships coming into Rangoon, anti-submarine patrols and general reconnaissance in the Gulf of Martaban were also carried out from day to day. The fighter support which was provided over the forward army positions each day on a limited scale had accouned for at least 7 hostile aircraft shot and 13 damaged up to the end of January.

During January the main objective of the Japanese air force, outside Rangoon, had been Moulmein. The main target was the aerodrome, and seven attacks were delivered between 3 and 22 January, the first one by fighters and the rest by bombers. After the withdrawal of the land forces from Moulmein all available bombers and such fighters as could be spared were used for direct army support. Attacks were made on river craft on the Salween; and batteries, hostile concentration, troops, landing stages, railway stations, barracks and stores were strafed. Fighters, operating at a great distance from their base, attempted to intercept Japanese raids on the forward troops. Raids were carried out on Kado, Martaban, Pa-an, Moulmein, Minzi, Heinze, and the roads from Thaton to Martaban and Duyinzeik. The fighter effort was diverted from the Rangoon defence in support of the Army, and bombing operations continued to be from 6 to 12 per day.

The Japanese Air Force supported its land forces and from 8 to 12 February their bombers attacked the Allied troops, between Pa-an and Thaton, but generally with little effect. Four raids by bombers were also made on the Toungoo aerodrome on 3 and 4 February.

Air operations in support of the army continued at the maximum intensity possible during the withdrawal to the Bilin and Sittang positions, and the 17th Division was much heartened by the excellent air support it received during the operations on the Bilin river. With the loss of Moulmein, the forward air base in this area had been lost, and all

---

[14] *Ibid*, para 98.

operations had to be carried out from Rangoon. Also the warning system in Tenasserim was being rapidly rolled up, and the interception of aircraft supporting Japanese troops was impossible unless the attacks took place when the fighters happened to be over the line at the time.

Japanese air attacks in the Sittang area

The urgent need for air reinforcement was stressed by Air Vice Marshal Stevenson to General Wavell when the latter visited Burma at the end of January and again early in February. The main requirements were two reinforcing Hurricane Squadrons, two reinforcing Blenheim Squadrons, sixteen Blenheims for equipping No. 60 Squadron, allocations of twenty-four Hurricanes and twelve Blenheims a month from the Command flow of maintenance aircraft. But at that time the needs of Malaya and the Dutch East Indies were also of vital importance. Thus, Burma could not get the required reinforcements.

Further, with the fall of Singapore, the threat to Rangoon developed considerably which was aggravated, as related earlier, when the forces fell back to the Sittang line, because, save for the limited R.D.F. and Observer Corps posts, warning facilities had all gone.

Decision to base the air force in northern Burma

On 20 February when instructions were given for the withdrawal of the 17th Indian Division across the Sittang river, and for the evacuation of non-essential civil personnel from Rangoon, Lt.-Gen. T. J. Hutton had indicated to the Air Officer Commanding, the necessity of withdrawing the army northwards into central Burma. Arrangements were accordingly made to base a mixed wing on Magwe and another mixed wing on Akyab. These were to be supplied from a base organisation in India. The size of the Magwe wing was fixed on the maintenance already available in Burma, as on the fall of Rangoon there would be no sea or over land communication between Magwe and India. Akyab could, however, be maintained by sea. This decision to base the air force in northern Burma on Magwe was taken because Magwe was covered by two lines of Observer Corps telephone down the valleys of the Irrawaddy and the Sittang respectively. It was also the only aerodrome from which the withdrawal of the army from Rangoon up the Irrawaddy valley could be suitably protected. South of Magwe on this line were no bases of any kind for the operation of modern fighters and bombers with high wing loading. But Magwe itself had no accommodation, no pens, and no dispersal. Therefore, work on its improvement was at once put in hand.

The possibility of having to cover the withdrawal of the army had been foreseen, and a number of kutcha strips were cut into the hard paddy lands along the Rangoon-Prome line. The location of these strips was kept as secret as possible. They fulfilled a double purpose. At night all first line aircraft were flown from the parent airfields at Mingaladon and Zayatkwin to these strips. They were flown off the strips before dawn. This dispersal made the location of the fighting force difficult and consequently the damage by the Japanese night bombing of Mingaladon was avoided.

Importance of maintaining air superiority over Rangoon up to the last stage of its evacuation

It was very essential to maintain air superiority over Rangoon until the final phase of the important demolitions of oil and other plant in the area had been completed and the troops withdrawn. Thereafter it was equally necessary to cover the movement of the army away from Rangoon up the Prome road. To control the requisite fighter and bomber offensive action during these operations a special 'X' Wing Headquarters was formed. In spite of serious hostile effort, air superiority over Rangoon was maintained in the last few days of February. But owing to lack of maintenance and spares and the casualties sustained in the air, both the fighter and bomber efforts were fast dwindling.

In the first days of March when the Japanese followed the Indo-British troops across the Sittang, and fighting took place around Pegu, with the hostile forces infiltrating through the lower Pegu Yoma towards the Prome road, Hurricanes on reconnaissance observed that movement, and considerable activity was maintained over the battle area. Hostile air attacks were directed against Maymyo, Toungoo and Bassein.

On 2 March the RDF set was moved to Magwe, and the only warning then available in the Rangoon area was by observation from military posts and airfields. A 'Jim Crow' Hurricane was kept over Rangoon by day. The fighter force, as a protection against being surprised on the ground, was moved to the newly prepared strip known as 'Highland Queen' near Hmawbi. The bombers operated from Magwe, using 'Highland Queen' and 'John Haig' strips as advanced bases. To give the impression that the force was still at Mingaladon wrecked fuselage and dummies were parked there on the runways.

On 6 March a Japanese formation of at least twenty aircraft, protecting their troops moving through the Pegu Yoma towards the Prome road, overshot its mark and by accident discovered the 'Highland Queen' strip. Some Allied fighters, bombers, and general reconnaissance aircraft which were then on the ground, were attacked, but luckily the shooting was bad. Some Hurricanes were able to take off and to beat off the attack. Two of the Allied aircraft were destroyed on the ground, but the raid might well have made a decisive end to the small air force.

In the last days of the defence of Rangoon the bomber effort was directed against the Japanese wherever they could be found. Fighters accompanied the bombers to shoot up hostile objectives. 96,800 lbs of bombs were released, and troop concentrations, trains, transport columns, and boats on the Sittang were attacked with satisfactory results.

Withdrawal to Prome

On 6 March Headquarters of 'X' Wing was moved from Rangoon to Zigon, the first strip from which operations could be carried out in support of the withdrawal of the army along the Prome road. A demolition party then destroyed all facilities at Norgroup Headquarters in Rangoon and at the Mingaladon aerodrome.

The Army column withdrawing up the Prome road on 8 March was reported by air crews to be some forty miles long, mostly motor transport vehicles and tanks, and offered an admirable target for hostile bomb action in a country where there was little or no cover. There was also no possibility of getting off the long straight tarmac road. Hence, from Zigon the air force maintained fighter patrols over the line to Rangoon, whilst escort was provided for the sea convoy that left the port with the final demolition parties.

The rough surface of Zigon was unsatisfactory for Hurricanes, and on the night of 8 March 'X' Wing moved to Park Lane, a strip north of Prome, which could not be located by the Japanese who were carrying out reconnaissance over the eastern airfields, obviously searching for the Allied air force.

Meanwhile attacks on Japanese objectives in support of the army were being carried out, Rangoon and the Sittang valley were kept under observation, and the old air bases were watched for signs of the arrival of the Japanese air force.

MIXED WINGS AT MAGWE AND AKYAB

On 9 March Air Vice-Marshal Stevenson received orders from the Air Officer Commanding-in-Chief, Air Forces in India, to maintain the two mixed Wings at Magwe and Akyab, and also to organise the air defences of Calcutta, Asansol, and Tatanagar, and the Digboi oil installations in Assam, and to continue from India offensive bombing operations in support of the army in Burma. Reconnaissance over, and the attack of Japanese surface vessels in, the Bay of Bengal was also to be carried out.

The mixed Wing (Burwing) at Magwe comprising No. 17 Hurricane and No. 45 Bomber Squadrons, the elements of an Army Co-operation Flight, the numerically weak Second Pursuit Squadron of the AVG which had relieved the Third Squadron, and the RDF station were placed under the operational control of General Sir H. Alexander on 18 March.

The mixed Wing (Akwing) at Akyab then consisted of No. 135 Squadron armed with obsolete Hurricane I's and one Hurricane II, a General Reconnaissance Flight, and a small Air Communications detachment.

On 17 March Air Vice-Marshal Stevenson flew to Calcutta where his Headquarters reopened.[16]

ALLIED ATTACK ON MINGALADON—21 MARCH

On 20 March, when a reconnaissance disclosed more than fifty Japanese aircraft on the Mingaladon airfield, and their scale of air effort in Burma was estimated at a minimum of four hundred, an attack on Mingaladon was planned for the following morning to reduce the strength of their attack. Ten Hurricanes and nine Blenheims of Akwing took off. The Blenheims were intercepted by Naval 'O' fighters forty miles north of Rangoon, but they fought their way into Mingaladon, dropped their bomb lift of 9,000 lbs on the runways and then fought their way back to Tharrawaddy. Eighteen Japanese fighters were encountered, two of them

---

[16] Stevenson's *Despatch*, paras 179-181.

were shot down, two more were claimed as probably destroyed, and two damaged. Most of the Allied aircraft were hit but none was shot down, and the only casualty was one pilot wounded.

Meanwhile the Hurricanes carried out a low flying attack. Nine Japanese fighters were destroyed in air combat, whilst sixteen bombers and fighters were destroyed on the ground. Some of the Hurricanes were badly shot up and one of them crashed through lack of petrol.[16]

JAPANESE ATTACK ON MAGWE—21 MARCH

This was a magnificient air action and Officer Commanding Burwing was prepared to repeat the attack that afternoon. While final preparations were in progress Japanese aircraft themselves launched a heavy attack on Magwe.

Over a period of some twenty-five hours Magwe was attacked in force six times. In all, the scale of attack reached about two hundred and thirty fighters and bombers which included one hundred and sixty-six Army 96 and 97 medium and heavy bombers. Some two hundred tons of bombs were accurately released in patterns during these attacks.

There were twenty-one fighters in Magwe on 21 March when it was first attacked, but as a result of the action fought at Mingaladon that morning the number of serviceable aircraft ready to take the air was only twelve. When at 1330 hours twenty-one bombers escorted by ten fighters bombed and machine-gunned the airfield, the Allied fighters intercepted and destroyed four aircraft with one probable and one damaged, but the weight of the attack got home. This was followed by further raids at 1410 hours and 1430 hours. The scale of attack for the day was fifty-nine bombers and twenty-four fighters.

Next morning another attack developed at 0845 hours. Twenty-seven bombers with an escort of ten fighters attacked the airfield, and a quarter of an hour later similar formations repeated the raid. No warning of these raids had been received, but the Japanese formations were engaged by two Hurricanes that had been sent off to intercept a high flying reconnaissance aircraft heard earlier over Magwe.

Again considerable damage was done. The runways were rendered unserviceable, communications were broken down, and a number of bombers and fighters were destroyed on the ground. At this stage of the action only three P. 40s and three Hurricanes remained flyable, the Hurricanes alone being operationally serviceable. The Commander of the AVG Second Pursuit Squadron then reported to the Group Captain in charge of Burwing that, in view of the absence of warning and the scale of attack, he was compelled by the terms of his instructions from General Chennault to withdraw his remaining flyable aircraft to refit. That afternoon the AVG flew the P. 40s to Loiwing, the airfield on the Chinese frontier north of Lashio.

At 1330 hours two of the three remaining Hurricanes were sent up but failed to intercept hostile reconnaissance aircraft. Whilst they were returning to land at 1430 hours the Japanese again attacked with two

[16] *Ibid*, para 183.

waves of twenty-seven and twenty-six bombers respectively, each accompanied by fighter escort.

In all these attacks nine Blenheims and at least three P. 40s were destroyed on the ground, five Blenheims were rendered unserviceable, and three Hurricanes had been destroyed in the combat. The remaining aircraft were flyable but unserviceable owing to normal unserviceability or damage from hostile action. These, except the P. 40s, were flown out to Akyab.

This grave reverse was due to the weakness in fighters, the serious defects in the warning system, and the complete absence of aircraft pens and bad dispersal arrangements at the Magwe airfield. There were no Observer Corps posts to the west and north-east of Magwe, an outflanking avenue used by the Japanese in these attacks. It is understood, however, that for some of these attacks some warning was actually received but owing to the failure of land lines it did not get through to the aerodrome in time.[17]

ABANDONMENT OF MAGWE AIRFIELD

Early on 23 March Burwing left Magwe for Lashio and Loiwing for refitting. Loiwing was the only remaining aerodrome where a reasonable warning system still existed, but it was at a great distance from the area where the army was operating.

The hurried abandonment of the Magwe airfield and the resulting cessation of all air support for Burcorps and the Chinese Armies led to a definite drop in morale in the Allied forces. This was probably accentuated by the knowledge that earlier in the campaign signal successes had been scored over the Japanese in the Rangoon area. Troops now found it hard to understand why air protection was no longer afforded them, and the unopposed attacks by Japanese aircraft were a source of depression.

It was proposed to remedy the faults of the Magwe warning system and to put the airfield in a proper state of defence to enable Burwing to return to it for operations. But the rapid Japanese advance prevented this scheme from being carried through.

JAPANESE ATTACK ON AKYAB

Owing to the difficult nature of the country only the outlines of communication existed at Akyab where Observer Corps warning was poor. On 23, 24 and 27 March, the Japanese repeated the tactics employed at Magwe and overwhelmed the small RAF force at Akyab. The RAF fighters intercepted them on two occasions, inflicting a loss of four hostile aircraft destroyed and three probably destroyed at a cost of six Hurricanes. On 27 March, although warning had been received, low-flying fighters caught the RAF force on the ground. Two Hurricanes got into the air and engaged them but one was shot down. Seven Hurricanes and one Valencia were destroyed on the ground. After this Akyab was only

[17] Stevenson's *Despatch*, paras 186-198.

employed as an advanced landing ground for refuelling, and for enabling the Hudson reconnaissance aircraft to reach the Andaman Islands.[18]

The actions at Magwe and Akyab had in effect terminated the RAF activities based on Burma. The supply of aircraft to Burma now became the critical factor, as it was essential to build up the air defence of north eastern India and Ceylon. The lack of warning and increasing weight of the Japanese attack would only have resulted in the piecemeal destruction of any small force that could be maintained in Burma.

However, Burwing continued as an organisation and bombers were flown in to Loiwing and Lashio to operate for a few days. They then returned to Calcutta. Eight Hurricanes flown in on 6 April to Loiwing only lasted for a few days.

On the rapid advance of the Japanese on Lashio towards the end of April, Burwing was withdrawn to China to provide refuelling parties at the main Chinese air bases. The personnel of No. 17 Squadron withdrew to India via Myitkyina.[19]

JAPANESE REINFORCEMENTS IN APRIL

The Japanese in Burma had been reinforced on 6 April when a convoy of ships reached Rangoon. It was this reinforcement that enabled them to throw fresh troops into the attack and to speed up their advance. The passage of this convoy had been covered by vigorous air attacks on Ceylon and the Allied shipping in the Bay of Bengal. The RAF was unable to prevent its passage. Fortress aircraft of the USAAC, however, attacked a hostile force in the Andamans with five and a half tons of bombs and straddled a cruiser and a destroyer. Night flying attacks were also made on the convoy in Rangoon, and fires and explosions were caused in the dock areas.[20]

INCREASED JAPANESE ACTIVITY OVER THE AIR

After the Magwe air action the Japanese air force widely extended its patrols and attacked targets not only near the battle zone but also far behind it. Taunggyi, Prome, Mandalay, Lashio, Loiwing, Meiktila, Maymyo and several other places were accorded the main weight of their bomber attack. Great damage mainly to civilian property resulted, with much demoralising effect on local population. But no heavy and long-sustained attacks were made on the Allied ground forces, although considerable support was given by Japanese aircraft to their troops. The extent of the Magwe and Akyab successes does not appear to have been fully appreciated. The bases at Toungoo, Heho, Namsang, Lashio and Loiwing were constantly searched and attacked, but except for the last named they were unoccupied. As between 28 March and 5 April their flying boats based on the Andamans began attacks on Allied shipping in the Bay of Bengal.

[18] Stevenson's *Despatch*, paras 203-4.
[19] *Ibid*, paras 205-208.
[20] Stevenson's *Despatch*, para 211.

ALLIED EFFORTS IN APRIL AND MAY

Later in April and May the RAF bombers and fighters continued in action over Burma, but fighter action was limited to sorties that could be made within the range of the Mohawk Squadron based at Dinjan. Bomber action was exerted from the same aerodrome and from Tezpur and the Calcutta air bases. Chittagong was used as a forward landing ground. Long range bombers of the USAAC also took part, and fifty-eight raids were made in support of the withdrawing army. Most of the bombing took place on the right flank of Gen. Sir H. Alexander's forces; but three protective raids were made on the Chinese front, and places such as Mongpan, Laika, and Kongohaiping were attacked. The Chinese front was of course covered by the AVG operating from bases in China. They had bombed airfields in Thailand, notably Chiengmai on 24 March, and their constant attacks on advancing Japanese mechanised columns enabled the Chinese forces to consolidate their positions on the Salween front in May.

The airfields at Mingaladon, and later Akyab and Myitkyina when occupied by the Japanese, were also subjected to a harassing scale of attack. Operations against Akyab and Myitkyina were particularly successful, the airfields being made untenable by destruction of the Japanese first line aircraft on the ground. These later operations, however, had no material effect on the campaign. The Allied forces had already withdrawn from Burma.

In the final stages of the withdrawal of the army the Japanese attempted an outflanking movement along the Chindwin river. Steamers, launches, and barges were concentrated at Monywa for this purpose. These craft and the Monywa landing stages were bombed on 4 and 5 May. This supporting action by the Allied aircraft must have imposed delay and difficulty on the abortive Japanese encircling movement.

Air Transport Squadron No. 31

The work of No. 31 Air Transport Squadron must be mentioned. This was equipped with D.C. 2 and later some D.C. 3 aircraft. The daily effort was about three, and heavy transport requirements had to be met. The wounded were evacuated from Magwe, Shwebo and Myitkyina in turn as the battle moved north. A very large number of civilians was evacuated when there were no wounded to move. In all, two thousand six hundred wounded and an additional six thousand other persons were flown to India. Many thousands of refugees were streaming out of Burma along the difficult routes across the mountains into Assam. Food and medical stores were urgently required on all these routes both for refugees and troops. With the help of the American Air Force nearly one hundred and ten thousand pounds of supplies were dropped.[21]

---

[21] Stevenson's *Despatch*, paras 209-226.

CHAPTER XXVII

Civil and Military Administration

CIVIL ADMINISTRATION IN SO FAR AS IT AFFECTED MILITARY ADMINISTRATION

In considering matters of civil and military administration it is necessary to refer once again, very briefly, to the general situation in Burma immediately prior to the outbreak of hostilities with Japan. Incidentally, it is not proposed to discuss the civil administration save in so far as it affected the campaign.

Before December 1941 the possibility of war with Japan was realised, but it was by no means regarded as a probability. In Chapter IV the military appreciation of the situation has been discussed. As explained there, it was then believed that in the event of a war with Japan, the invasion of Burma was a somewhat remote possibility and that the main danger was from aerial attack. How far these views were justified is another question, but they certainly were the views of His Majesty's Government in the United Kingdom and of the command concerned. It was upon this reading of the situation that the Government of Burma made its preparations for a possible emergency.

In spite of the complete absence of assistance from His Majesty's Government some work was done both by the Army authorities and civil administration to prepare for war. The resources of both were, however, so thin that many of these preparations were incomplete, or the resultant organisation was so weak that it just melted away under the stress of war. There were too many notable omissions. Some of these might have been remedied if the work had been taken in hand earlier.

For all who cared to read, the writing on the wall was clear as soon as Japan entered Indo-China in September 1940. Thereafter readiness for war against Japan was a plain duty, but the Burma Government or the General Officer Commanding Army in Burma were not warned to expect and prepare to meet a full scale invasion. As far as is known, no directive was issued either by the Commander-in-Chief, Singapore or by His Majesty's Government setting out what preparations were to be made in Burma to meet the impending invasion. His Majesty's Government did increase its financial aid to Burma for defence purposes, but from a military point of view no material help was given to the Burma Government. Having regard to these facts and to the limited resources of the Burma Government and the inadequate staff, it would be unfair to criticise the authorities for their acts of omission. Admittedly more could have been done had the necessary knowledge and staff been available.

It may be mentioned that the defenceless state of Burma and the need for the provision of adequate staff and services to organise its defence had been the subject of repeated representations by the General Headquarters India, to the War Office. It is clear now that the demand made by the Chief of General Staff, India (Lt.-Gen. T. J. Hutton) when he visited the War Office in 1940, and again by Gen. Sir A. Wavell in the summer of 1941, that Burma should be placed under India, was the only correct solution. But this was done only after the outbreak of war with Japan when it was too late to undertake many of the necessary measures.

These factors led to a colossal unpreparedness which discounted the advantages which our troops had of fighting in their own country. Prior to the outbreak of war with Japan there was not that closest co-ordination which should have been established between civil and military departments. No arrangements existed for the militarisation of transport and other essential services, or for the organisation of the country as a whole against attack. The provision of an overland link with India was not regarded as an urgent matter calling for prompt and effective action. The great local knowledge of innumerable government servants and other reliable persons could be invaluable; but no plans existed for bringing it into immediate use. Little was done to raise irregular fighting forces amongst hillmen, such as the Karens. The immediate provision of an adequate number of guides and interpreters for troops operating in a strange country and ignorant of its language had not been made Even the supply of maps was grossly inadequate. Many were out of date, and units sometimes found themselves without any maps at all. When a few were available they were frequently on the scale of a quarter inch to a mile. In short, there had been a complete failure to comprehend the full implications of an invasion. Burma was never visualised as one vast battle-ground, and the possible hostilities with Japan were seen merely as an affair of frontier operations.

This lack of pre-war constructive forethought and preparation was to hamper the forces through the whole course of operations. In place of communications and local resources, Intelligence Services and all the specialised knowledge of the country, ready-organised against the invader, they had to fall back upon a series of hasty improvisations. Some of these withstood the strain tolerably well, others failed.

FAILURE TO PLACE CIVIL AND MILITARY ADMINISTRATION ON A WAR-TIME BASIS BEFORE THE START OF HOSTILITIES

A major lesson of the campaign, therefore, is the necessity for the placing of both civil and military administration on a war footing before the opening of hostilities. Peace time systems cannot adapt themselves at once to war conditions, and the speed of modern warfare does not permit of a leisurely change.

Speaking generally, civil officers European, Burman and Indian, stood by their posts when the emergency arose. They were, however, handicapped by the defection of many subordinates who fled at the first bombing of back areas by hostile aircraft. The result was a breakdown of police and essential services. It was not to be expected that many of the lowest rank of public servants would remain steadfast. They were bound by no particular ties of patriotism and loyalty to the foreign government, and to them the coming of the Japanese meant nothing more than a change of masters. Possibly it is a matter for surprise that so many did carry on with their duties.

EVACUATION PROBLEM

Men were often concerned not only for their own safety but for that of their families. Here the civil government was faced with a difficult problem which was considered but found to be insoluble. Pre-arranged plans for the removal of the families of essential public servants to areas of safety were not there. Hence the mass evacuations that took place were beyond the most strenuous efforts of the civil authorities to keep under complete control. At times they seriously impeded troop movements, brought about a breakdown in some essential services when they were most required, led to outbreaks of cholera which infected the troops (although energetic medico-military measures checked the spread of the disease), and facilitated the infiltration of hostile agents through the lines. It was not the civil administration alone that was confronted with the evacuation problem. It was equally the concern of the military authorities. But little seems to have been done by them either to make plans for it before the outbreak of war.

ASSAM-BURMA ROAD

The work on the road intended to link Burma with the Assam road and rail system was begun in a small way in December 1941 with the improvement of the existing tracks between Kalewa and Tamu. This work was undertaken in the first instance by the Deputy Commissioner with such assistance of the Public Works Department as could be provided locally and with local resources. The original proposal put to the Government of Burma was for a road from Tamu to Sittaung and thence to the railway near Wuntho. It was not until January, 1942 that this project was abandoned as impracticable, and the easier, though longer, alignment to Kalewa and thence to Ye-U was adopted.

Tools, plant, material, labour and rations for the labour employed, were always a difficulty. Even when they could be collected down-country, limited transport delayed arrival on the site. In accordance with the orders from India the exit of refugees by this route was sought to be limited to five hundred persons a day. But those who passed through had a disturbing effect on labour which tended to join in the exodus. Cholera broke out. In addition work on the Indian side of the frontier did not progress as fast as was expected, and consequently the help promised from India was not forthcoming in time.

The failure to have this road link with India was a major factor in the lack of maintenance and supplies, the movement of refugees and the withdrawal of forces. The completion of the road in time might have radically affected the situation.

MILITARY ADMINISTRATION AND OTHER MATTERS

Throughout the earlier part of the campaign the Government of Burma was opposed to the institution of Martial Law which in the minds of the people was associated with the existence of a state of rebellion. Its effects, therefore, might have been unfortunate. It had also recently been decided by His Majesty's Government and the Government of India to adopt a new attitude towards Martial Law, and in desiring to delay its application the Burma Government was only following the policy laid down. Later, however, certain Special Security Regulations were introduced with the effect but not the name of Martial Law. Much of the area to which they were applied was already in Japanese hands. Nevertheless, this attitude on the part of Government made little difference. Order was enforced by the military authorities from the early days of the campaign. Before the evacuation of Rangoon a Military Commandant was appointed, and looters were shot or otherwise punished. Similar action was taken in Mandalay; whilst in the forward areas occupied by the Allied forces, spies, fifth columnists, fire raisers, and similar agents were summarily executed. As the line receded and civil authority progressively ceased to function, military authority necessarily took its place.

In a previous chapter reference has been made to the change of command just after the opening of active operations. The new commander never had an opportunity to organise the defence and secure the administration on a sound footing. Even without considerable reinforcements or administrative units he could probably have done much if placed in command earlier and provided with an adequate staff. As matters stood neither the commander nor his staff had enough time to fully appreciate the defence problem or take stock of the available resources before becoming engaged in active operations.

That there was not a breakdown in military administration was due to the efforts of the administrative staff which kept its overworked machine functioning throughout the campaign in face of almost insuperable difficulties. Matters were in fact so serious that Lieut.-General Hutton, had to devote much of his time to a solution of these problems. Maj.-Gen. E. N. Goddard, was in charge of administration, and his successful efforts to keep the machine at work won the admiration of all concerned.

At no time were there sufficient administrative units. Transport, Supply, Medical, Movement and Transportation, Provost, Rest Camps, Mess, Ordnance and Labour units were all less than the number required for the force. Improvisation with all its attendant troubles was the only remedy. The problem would have been less complicated if the administrative plan had been drawn up before active operations began.

Some administrative and other matters together with the problems to which they gave rise are discussed below.

BASE

One of the main difficulties confronting all the Ordnance and Supply Services was the absence of a secure base. Before the outbreak of hostilities Rangoon was the sole Base and no similar installation had been sited in upper Burma. The course of operations at once proved Rangoon to be too far forward, whilst the advance of the Japanese entailed early organisation of another Base. The dislocation of labour and railways following on the bombing of Rangoon in December 1941, together with a shortage of other transport, made the establishment of a new Base far from easy. Such a Base should have been created in upper Burma before active operations began.

TRANSPORT AND SUPPLY

The army was mainly equipped with motor transport with little of animal transport, while, in the main, the terrain demanded a very comprehensive employment of pack animals. The absence of these in adequate numbers tied the force to the main supply routes, and had a marked influence on the course of the campaign. It was unable to disregard roads and could not move across country with the same freedom that the Japanese had. This fact gave the latter an advantage in their offensive movements and largely conditioned the nature of the defence.

Nevertheless, the force had no adequate motor transport either. Units often landed without their transport which sometimes did not even sail in the same convoy. In some cases troops had to be sent into battle as soon as they landed. Consequently, transport was necessarily improvised. This lowered the fighting efficiency, and therefore morale, and not infrequently resulted in the loss of much equipment and kit.

Vehicles for Supply Services were lamentably short. Prior to the outbreak of hostilities transport arrangements had been carried out with hired and requisitioned vehicles. When operations began, hired transport became unreliable. Vehicles were then bought, requisitioned, or in some cases acquired from Lease/Lend material. Only a proportion of mechanised transport units could be equipped as the heavy losses in Tenasserim and at the Sittang had to be made good. The loss of transport continued to be great as a result of fighting at road-blocks and through bombing. After the evacuation of Rangoon such losses were irreplaceable. As the Chinese Armies were virtually without transport and had to be supplied with rations also the added strain on the limited number of motor vehicles was severe. It must be remembered, too, that the distances to be travelled, particularly in the Shan States, were very long.

Much transport might have been saved from loss by the creation of a service of 'Road Officers', who would have functioned on all roads. Their duties would have covered the enforcing of road discipline, the direction of drivers who had lost their units, the carrying out of minor repairs, and the salvage of abandoned vehicles. Such a service could not be introduced owing to lack of both personnel and vehicles.

Due to the general shortage of transport and to the almost continual withdrawals, stocks of supplies were generally far forward, the main problem being to back-load surpluses and to get supplies into safe Bases. The rule, rather than the exception, was lay-backs based on an administrative time-scale fixing the number of days supplies to be held in forward localities. Only during the first short periods of stabilization could maintenance forward be carried out.

North of Rangoon the absence of lateral communications and the difficulty of persuading the crews of river craft to proceed down-stream added to the supply problem. Road convoys were sent out from Mandalay. The enormous task of supplying rice and other commodities for the Chinese Armies has already been frequently referred to. After the evacuation of Rangoon and the loss of its important mills this task increased. Up-country resources were limited and unorganised.

Very large quantities of supplies had been collected at Prome together with thousands of tons of rice both there and on the main railway line to Mandalay. Local resources were exploited to the full and an army purchasing agency, based on the peace-time organisation of Messrs Steel Brothers and Company Limited, was functioning. The administrative plan required the holding of a considerable amount of supplies in Prome. Much of these were lost when the town was evacuated.

Prior to this, at the end of March, a review of the stock situation had been prepared. It was then estimated that, by revising the scale of rations, stocks of imported and locally acquired supplies, with possible future purchases of indigenous supplies, would be sufficient to feed the army for six months from 1 April. This estimate was subject to the proviso that sources of supply could be held and that no loss of stocks took place. In fact the loss of the areas south of Mandalay, the destruction of stocks by air bombing in that city, and the earlier losses in Prome much reduced available supplies.

For the last phase of the campaign, with commendable foresight, supplies had been dispersed in depth on the Lashio-Mandalay Railway, on the railway from Shwebo northwards, and at Monywa and Kalewa on the Chindwin. The decision to fall back on India resulting in the withdrawal of Hospital and Administrative units from the Maymyo area, together with the movement of large numbers of evacuees, Chinese troops and supplies, threw additional heavy burden on railway services which were already fully stretched. As late as 22 April supplies and bombs were being despatched by rail in the opposite direction to stations on the Lashio branch. Much of the supplies east of the Irrawaddy, therefore, could not be transferred across the river and were handed over to the Chinese or destroyed. The sudden attack on Monywa cut off the stocks held at that town, but sufficient remained in the Shwebo area for the maintenance of the Indo-British forces on the Ye-U-Shwegyin track. After the forces had crossed the Chindwin supplies were received from India.

The supply of petrol, oil, and lubricants was a source of unending anxiety. Not only the requirements of the Indo-British forces, but also those of the Chinese Armies and the civil administration had to be met. On the fall of Rangoon the only source of supply was the oilfields which were not on the railway. Very few tank lorries were available and there was a shortage of containers. The prompt return of the latter became a vital necessity. Apart from direct distribution by road, oil barges and steamers went from the oilfields to Mandalay where all possible filling was done ex-bulk.

ORDNANCE

Rangoon Arsenal was itself unsuitable as a Base. It was intended for the maintenance in Burma of a small force of two brigades, and until the outbreak of hostilities the Ordnance staff was not warned to provide for more than an additional division. Consequently, stores and equipment were entirely inadequate for the forces that arrived later. Units arriving incompletely equipped could not have their deficiencies made up. Had the Chinese Government not released a supply of automatic weapons and three-ton lorries the situation would have been even far worse than it was.

The Ordnance staff at the Army Headquarters on the opening of the campaign consisted of an Administrative Officer (D.S.O.) and two officers on the engineering side. The Arsenal itself was working with an entirely civilian staff of clerks and labourers. As a result, after the bombing of Rangoon on 23 December 1941, the majority of the civilians disappeared, never to return. There was always a shortage of military personnel.

The Arsenal itself had no facilities for handling large quantities of stores, and being very near to the Mingaladon airfields, was subject to constant air attacks. For these reasons various subsidiary depots were opened in Rangoon and its environs. With the small staff available it was difficult to operate them fully.

Ammunition was dumped in a rubber estate near milestone 18 on the Prome road. On the evacuation of Rangoon lack of transport made it necessary to destroy much of this ammunition. Similarly, a large portion of other stores, mainly tentage and hospital reserves, had to be destroyed. Stores held in sheds near the Pazundaung creek were lost through arson before Rangoon was abandoned.

The only Base workshop facilities available consisted of the repair plant of a civilian motor agency in Rangoon. In the course of the campaign the Lashio workshops of Messrs Waston and Son Limited were taken over. There was a shortage of trained personnel but many suitable men were obtained from the Burma Auxiliary Force and British battalions to the detriment of the fighting efficiency of these units.

A fully rail served Base Ordnance Depot under construction at Meiktila was completed and opened up before the evacuation of Rangoon; at the same time work was pressed forward on an ammunition dump under construction by the Engineering Department of the railways, five miles north of Pyinmana. Later, a Central Ammunition Dump was established at Tonbo in the Shan foot-hills near Mandalay. But continued withdrawals necessitated a further removal to Katha, where the Ordnance Depot was eventually made over to the Chinese.

TRANSPORTATION AND MOVEMENT CONTROL

Prior to the outbreak of hostilities no plan existed for the militarisation of the transportation services. The Burma Railways Battalion, B.A.F. was only intended to meet security requirements during periods of internal disturbances. Soon after his arrival in Burma early in 1941, His Excellency Sir R. Dorman Smith asked His Majesty's Government for the services of a transport expert. Such an expert could not be made available as Burma was not considered to be on a very high level of priority. Work on the co-ordination of transport was then done by the Burma Government. After the outbreak of war it was proposed that Sir Johan Rowland, lately Chief Railway Commissioner, and at that time Director of Construction, the Burma-China Railway, should be placed in charge of transportation. For various reasons nothing came of this proposal, partly because it was thought preferable to appoint an officer with military transportation experience.

In December 1941, in response to an appeal from the Army Headquarters, a decision was made in India to form a Transportation Directorate for Burma and to send such personnel as could be made available. Eventually Col. F. J. Biddulph, Deputy Director of Transportation, Iraq, was appointed Director. He arrived in Burma on 27 January 1942. Colonel J. N. Soden, also from Iraq, had been appointed Director of Movements and he landed in Rangoon on 3 January. The absence of previous planning made the task of these officers difficult.

For the proper functioning of the Transportation and Movements Directorate, personnel trained in military duties was essential. To a very large extent it was not available, hence it was necessary to utilise the services of such officers as were then in Burma. Yet, many of these, taken direct from their ordinary civil occupations, carried out their duties most creditably.

The Burma Railways and the Irrawaddy Flotilla Company were highly organised and well equipped for peace-time requirements. They had large staffs of experienced and qualified officers. The same remarks apply to the Commissioners for the Port of Rangoon, the public body responsible for the maintenance and operation of the Port. In each case the subordinate staff consisted almost entirely of Indians.

Very early in the campaign the unreliability of civilian labour had been clearly demonstrated. Air raids and a reluctance to work in the forward areas soon led to desertions. Reference to this state of affairs has been made frequently earlier. In January 1942 Army Headquarters asked India to supply Railway, Docks, and Inland Water Transport units to remedy this situation. At that time the development of transportation in Iraq was considered vital, and India was also faced with her own defence problems. As with fighting troops, only a very limited number of units were available; and of these only three arrived in Burma viz. Headquarters No. 2 Docks Operating Group, No. 213 Docks Operating Company, and Headquarters No. 3 Railway Construction and Maintenance Group. In addition, a number of Inland Water Transport crew and locomotive drivers and firemen were flown in towards the end of the campaign. As no other units were available in India it was suggested that staff should be obtained from officers in Burma and that units be raised locally. It was far too late to do very much, but Headquarters No. 2 Docks Operating Group was available for recruiting and a company was formed from casual labour in Rangoon. Employed at once on dock work it received military training in spare time. The issue of three hundred Italian rifles greatly increased the morale of the unit. In his report the Director of Transportation writes, "Even this modicum of military training, the possession of uniform and arms, and the cohesion afforded by working as a unit with their own officers amply demonstrated the value of a military organisation in war. The Company worked through air raid alerts whilst their civilian comrades were under cover. Later on, during the last two weeks in Rangoon, only a proportion of the Company absented themselves at a time when there was a wholesale desertion of civilian labour".

An attempt at militarisation at so late a date did not commend itself to those in control of the transport organisations concerned. Difficulties were many and the effectiveness of the step at this stage was questioned. Consequently there was no general militarisation of the Transportation Services.

That a change in the control of the railways was necessary was indicated on 24 February when the Chief Railway Commissioner is reported to have declared in Rangoon that "the railways are finished and not another train can be run". He feared that increased desertions would occur in the lower grades of staff. The situation could not be accepted. The Governor sanctioned immediate militarisation of the railways south of Toungoo, and afterwards extended this to the whole railway system. Officials of the Burma Railways were commissioned, the Deputy Traffic Manager (Transportation) being appointed Director of Railways. These officers together with the remaining loyal staff maintained the essential railway services till the end of the campaign. In justice, however, it must be said that militarisation under the circumstances was in name rather than in fact for the army authorities found it impossible to feed, pay, clothe, or arm the staff. There can be no doubt, however, of the advantage of militarisation even in such circumstances. The morale of the personnel undoubtedly improved.

In the evacuation of Rangoon and throughout the remainder of the campaign there was always sufficient transportation for all personnel and goods brought to the loading points. This was so despite the defection of railway and river steamer subordinate staff. The limiting factors were lack of motor transport. Quantities of stores had to be abandoned in Rangoon and elsewhere, yet a sufficient quantity of what was available was got away to enable the army to live and fight. Had the campaign been further prolonged the loss of these stores would doubtless have been felt.

During the later stages of the campaign Transportation Services were maintained under increasingly difficult circumstances. Important railway stations on the main line, Toungoo to Mandalay, were frequently bombed, sustaining considerable damage. An engineering train in charge of an officer and with supervisory staff and labour, rations, equipment and stores, undertook essential repairs, moving up and down the line as required. An air attack on 3 April resulted in the wrecking of the Mandalay railway yard, though the station buildings received only minor damage. Telephonic and telegraphic communication was destroyed and was at the time irreparable. Working at night the railway staff repaired and brought into use six tracks, thus allowing the removal of a number of locomotives and loaded wagons which were despatched up-country. Thereafter, limited facilities at the small junction of Myohaung, three miles to the south, had to be used for the reception, marshalling, and despatch of trains. This was partly responsible for the halting of all through movements for twenty-four hours on two separate occasions during the most critical period of the withdrawal at the end of April.

As each town was bombed, the main lines of communication would fill with a fresh spate of refugees. Mandalay was a great clearing centre for these unfortunates. Forty thousand of them were sent north by river to Kyaukmyaung and Myitkyina; others travelled to the north by railway; yet another great stream went west towards India by way of the Chindwin river route. These mass movements further impeded the normal work of military transportation. Yet, that the railway services continued to function under chaotic conditions is a tribute to those officers and subordinates who stood by their posts. In the last days of April, when the desertions of operating personnel became very serious, administrative control was assumed by Sir John Rowland; and the activities of the railways were maintained as long as was humanly possible.

On the Irrawaddy and Chindwin rivers it became increasingly difficult to obtain steamer crews to go downstream, or even up the river to Bhamo. More and more were the minds of would-be deserters turning to the Chindwin river as a route of escape to India.

From Prome northwards the staging system of clearance was adopted on the river. No loaded craft were left for the Japanese. The Irrawaddy Flotilla Company had been requisitioned by the Government on 1 March 1942, the General Manager of the Company acting as the Director of Inland Water Transport. By his personality he retained the services of sufficient crews who, with the assistance of military personnel, complied with all civil and military demands. There were, however, periods of considerable anxiety, as when the Japanese unexpectedly seized Monywa and cut off part of the Chindwin Fleet. However, the majority of the steamers escaped and there were enough craft to operate the Shwegyin-Kalewa ferry.

Until January 1942 the Movements Staff in Burma was very small. On the erroneous assumption that the initial Japanese advance would be through Kengtung and Shan States the greater part of such staff as existed was in that area where most of its few officers had been detailed for other duties. One of the great difficulties that the Movement Control Directorate had to overcome was the complete ignorance of many commanders and staffs of their duties and functions. Movements were carried out with a total disregard for the Directorate. The usual overseas expedition is accompanied by some Movement Control Staff, but in Burma the staff assumed its duties after the campaign had begun. Peace-time methods were still in force, and it was some time before a proper control of movements could be introduced.

The disembarkation of troops in Rangoon, the transfer to upper Burma of the Base organisation and of the great accumulation of stores in Rangoon, and the movements of the Chinese Armies were heavy tasks for an attenuated Movements staff. In addition, arrangements had to be made for the move to upper Burma of essential stocks of supplies for civil needs.

One of the best administrative achievements of the campaign was the disembarkation of troops in Rangoon, particularly after 21 February. Lack of civil dock labour, frequent changes of orders, and transportation difficulties tested the staff to the full. Yet disembarkation was quickly and successfully carried out.

After the loss of Rangoon, movement control problems increased. Railway stations being the main targets for hostile aircraft, Transportation and Movement Control officers existed dangerously. As the railway line was usually destroyed and officers had no independent transport, upon a withdrawal they often got away only by good fortune or resource. The destruction of telephone and telegraph lines made communication difficult and, as in other branches of the army, contact had to be maintained by personal visits or a courier service. This did not make for efficiency.

Examples emphasising the importance of strict compliance with Movement Control orders were furnished during the campaign. Inspite of continuous orders to the loading services that railway wagons must be labelled, scarcely one wagon despatched from Rangoon bore a label. There were no staff officers available at the depots in Rangoon to check this. The resulting congestion on the railway at Mandalay and south of it was overwhelming. The Mandalay yards were full to capacity, and seventeen freight trains were stabled at adjoining stations. Sorting teams had to open and label every wagon before unloading or sorting could be carried out.

The heavy damage sustained in the Mandalay railway yard on 3 April was very largely attributable to non-labelling of wagons containing RAF bombs. Shortly after the air raid, wagons which had caught fire touched off a wogan-load of these bombs, the subsequent explosion causing more damage than did the raid itself.

The experience of both the Transportation and Movements Directorates pointed clearly to the necessity for the early planned militarisation of transportation services and to the provision of an adequate and efficient Movements staff from the outset of the campaign. The necessary organisation for the movement of fighting troops with equipment and stores is as essential as the presence of the troops themselves. The campaign proved the danger of relying on civil transportation services staffed by men without military training and not bound by ties of military discipline, yet exposed to dangers comparable to those encountered by troops fighting in the forward areas. Japanese dominance of the air established not only this fact, but also the further fact that, under the circumstances prevailing in Burma, a high standard of 'toughness' was most desirable amongst those whose duties required them to remain constantly in the neighbourhood of the main targets for hostile aircraft.

DENIAL OF RAILWAY AND RIVER SERVICES

As the Indo-British forces withdrew towards upper Burma, demolitions of river craft and the railways were carried out. The main portion of the Irrawaddy Flotilla Company's fleet was scuttled at Mandalay, and between that place and Katha. Over one hundred power-craft were sunk at or near Mandalay. Further sinkings were made at Kyaukmyaung, and on 3 May forty-four power-craft were scuttled at Katha. The fate of a few vessels left at Bhamo and Myitkyina is unknown. The greater part of the Chindwin fleet was sunk at Sittaung on 14 May.

On the railways, demolition was more thorough in the earlier stages of the campaign. Comparatively little damage was done to the main line bridges in relation to their importance. The speed of the Japanese advance combined with lack of engineer units and labour difficulties accounted for this, and many bridges scheduled for destruction were not, in fact, destroyed. Rolling stock in general was abandoned undamaged. Some wagons were burnt by the Commando units. Locomotives were usually immobilised by the removal of connecting rods and the destruction of injectors and other boiler fittings. Fire boxes were sometimes damaged by lighting up under empty boilers. Systematic destruction of the boilers and cylinders does not appear to have been carried out except by Commando units. It was estimated that well over a third of the locomotives owned by the Burma Railways were immediately or soon available to the Japanese, whilst those immobilised were probably repaired and put into use at an early date. Many of the undamaged locomotives were either handed over to the Chinese when they took over sectors of the railways, or were abandoned in the final stages of the campaign. At that time neither the Chinese nor the Indo-British forces carried out all the demolitions that could or should have been carried out.

The Japanese were in a position to operate important sectors of the railway very soon after occupying the areas they served. This was entirely due to the Allied failure to put into effect a comprehensive policy of demolition. It was not only upon the railways and waterways that general denial was not carried out. Enormous quantities of rice, both milled and unmilled, were left in godowns, mills, and villages. Valuable timber was abandoned in stacks or rafts; rubber plantations with their factories and smoke houses were often left untouched; the destruction of rice and timber mills was only spasmodic; livestock including elephants, a favourite means of transport with the Japanese, were left behind.

The systematic and controlled burning of towns and villages would have saved many casualties from snipers, hampered the work of spies and fifth columnists, and prevented heavy losses of stores in fires caused by air bombing.

Since a wholesale denial scheme was not enforced the supply problem of the Japanese, not only in Burma but elsewhere, was made easy. There is no doubt that more demolition work could have been done if a detailed plan had been prepared in advance and the task entrusted to a special organisation. Denial was carried out as far as possible, but divisional engineers were too occupied with other requirements to give this matter their detailed attention. There was neither the time and material, nor personnel to carry out a comprehensive scorched earth policy. The task would have been enormous and it is improbable that it would have made much difference to the length of the campaign. There was also the effect on the civil population to be considered. The policy of the Burma Government, with which the General Officer Commanding concurred, was not to interfere with the food supplies of the people. A general scorched earth policy would have spread panic and disaffection, and resulted in a large scale evacuation of the bulk of the population. Added to the existing stupendous refugee problem this would have had most serious effects on the conduct of operations.

SIGNALS

Signal communication in the field was never easy to maintain although the Signals Services acquitted themselves well. Again, the shortage of equipment aggravated the difficulties. Early losses led to a rapid worsening of the situation and in the final stages of the campaign the shortage was very acute.

Save for the slow system of runners, widely dispersed detachments and companies were frequently out of touch with their Headquarters. Patrols were unable to send back information at once, and were sometimes lost owing to sudden withdrawal orders which could not be passed to them in time. Higher formations were regularly compelled to maintain contact by couriers or liaison officers. It is obvious that where, as in Burma, operations essentially involve continuous movement, the rapid communication of information or orders is vital. Hence the inability to ensure rapid signal communication was a very heavy handicap.

The Burma Government Posts and Telegraph Department rendered great assistance to the army. The normal peace-time signal system in Burma fell short of military requirements, and on the outbreak of hostilities the department was hard put to it to expand the existing telephone connections. In the course of the campaign the staff of the Department was militarised. The conferring of military status did much to maintain morale. Members of the Posts and Telegraph Department were conspicious in carrying on with their tasks when other essential services were failing.

MATTERS AFFECTING DISCIPLINE AND MORALE

The lack of Provost, Rest Camp, and Mess Units tended to break down administration and, therefore, to impair discipline. No canteen organisation existed before the war, and the absence of amenities was a potent contributory factor in lowering the morale of both officers and men. During the campaign a Chief Amenities Officer was appointed, who was able to provide something in the way of comforts for the troops.

Constant withdrawals necessarily caused much straggling, and the need for a fully organised Provost service was acute, and was strongly represented to India on several occasions. The complete absence of any Provost personnel rendered it very difficult to maintain road discipline or to cope with stragglers. Eventually Provost Units were improvised locally.

The general unpreparedness of the army in Burma and the lack of essential equipment of all kinds meant decreased efficiency from the outset of the campaign. Several other factors too, affected morale and discipline. Many of the troops, both local and Indian, were young recruits only partially trained; British officers were often inexperienced and with insufficient knowledge of the languages spoken by the men. Frequent changes in the composition of brigades, brought about by an acute shortage of troops, were destructive of *esprit de corps*. It is significant that this spirit always remained high in the 7th Armoured Brigade and the 48th Indian Infantry Brigade formations which were well-trained, though not for jungle warfare, and were maintained virtually intact. Elsewhere, however, the utterly strange conditions of jungle warfare and lack of training for it engendered a state of depression which was heightened by the superiority of the hostile forces. Continued withdrawals, the knowledge that with the fall of Rangoon the army would in effect be cut off, and the air superiority enjoyed by the Japanese in the later phases of the operations, were other factors responsible for demoralisation. Most troops were employed without periods of rest as there were no reserves to render relief. It is not surprising, therefore, that there were few units which remained unaffected. Yet, there can be no doubt of the courage and intrepidity of a large part of the force. The last actions proved the ability of exhausted men to fight with courage and determination. This was demonstrated at Monywa and Shwegyin, whilst the holding of Kyaukse by the 48th Indian Infantry Brigade and its supporting troops must rank high as a model of a delaying action.

The conduct of certain battalions of the Burma Rifles and of other Burma units was not above reproof. There were however, extenuating circumstances. The majority of units included a very large number of raw recruits, whilst the Burma Frontier Force and Military Police were required to carry out tasks for which they had never been intended or trained. Undoubtedly desertions were heavy. They began in the opening phases of the campaign, and their example was catching. But the drastic measures taken to comb out unreliable elements from the Burma Rifles did have a wholesome effect.

Indian, Anglo-Indian, and Anglo-Burman personnel with families in the country suffered considerable anxiety. They feared not only the advent of the Japanese but definite acts of hostility on the part of the Burmese people. Owing to lack of transport there could be no general evacuation of their families out of Burma, and some of these men deserted the forces to accompany their relatives either to places of safety or to India. These considerations affected Indian personnel of the Burma Frontier Force and Military Police also, most of whom had families in Burma.

No definite figures are available, but many military families or members of them, particularly those of men in the Burma Frontier Force and Burma Military Police, were lost on the overland routes to India. Leaving Burma late, these families were exposed to the full rigours of the retreat, which caused a feeling of bitterness.

CASUALTIES

Officer casualties amounted to about four hundred. Sixty-three are reported to have been killed in action, seventy died of wounds or disease, one hundred and twenty-six were wounded, and one hundred and fifteen were originally stated to be missing.

Other casualties were as follows:—

	Killed	Wounded	Missing	Died of Wounds	Wounded and Missing	Prisoners of War	Presumed Dead etc.	Total
British Units	273	556	647	75	49	—	—	1600
Indian Army Units VCOs	60	60	80	—	—	3	3	206
Other Ranks	649	1678	5291	—	—	181	57	7856
Army in Burma Units	239	114	3052	10	12	—	—	3427
					GRAND TOTAL	...		13089

The large proportion of missing is no doubt partly accounted for by the fact that in jungle warfare, many of the wounded are necessarily shown under this head. No figures of the losses of the Chinese Expeditionary Force are to be had and no assistance is to be extracted from the brief Chinese official account of the Campaign. At Toungoo and elsewhere on the Sittang Valley front south of Mandalay the Fifth Army suffered severely; in Karenni and the Shan States the Sixth Army and the other formations engaged admittedly had heavy losses. The number of missing men must have been very high in Karenni and during the closing phases of the operations. Having regard to these factors the casualties of the Chinese may well have been not much less than those of the Indo-British Forces, although such an estimate must be little better than guess work.

APPENDICES

GROUP I

APPENDIX A

Location Statement

ARMY IN BURMA AS ON 1 DECEMBER 1941.

1. Headquarters Army in Burma   Rangoon.
   2nd Echelon (Burma)   Rangoon.
   Commando ...   Loilem.

2. Headquarters 1st Burma Division . . . . Toungoo.
   1 Burma General Hospital . . . . Toungoo.
          (Headquarters and one Section)
   Divisional Signals . . . . Toungoo.

   1 (A) UPPER BURMA AREA

   Maymyo
   Headquarters Upper Burma Area.
   Depot 2 Mountain Battery, I.A.
   Depot 2nd Battalion King's Own Yorkshire Light Infantry.
   Upper Burma Battalion, B.A.F.
   Headquarters and Two-Sections, Burma Sappers and Miners.
   Headquarters and Depot, Burma Signals.
   10th Battalion Burma Rifles.
   Militia Company.
   Burma Regimental Records and Recruiting Centre.
   Supply Depot.
   7 Supply Depot Section, B.A.S.C.
   5 Independent Sub-Section Field Bakery, B.A.S.C.
   5 Independent Sub-Section Field Butchery, B.A.S.C.
   2 Remount Detachment.
   British Military Hospital.
   Burma Military Hospital.
   Burma Army School of Education.
   Schools of Instruction.
   Bush Warfare School.

   Mandalay
   Station Staff Officer.
   One Company 1st Battalion the Gloucestershire Regiment.
   7th Battalion Burma Rifles.
   11th Battalion Burma Rifles.
   3 Garrison Company (less one Platoon).
   7, 11 Mechanical Transport Sections, B.A.S.C.
   Supply Depot, B.A.S.C.
   6 Supply Depot Section, B.A.S.C.

Burma Military Hospital with British Wing.
1 Ordnance Field Depot.
4 Supply Issue Section, B.A.S.C.
4 Independent Sub-Section Field Bakery, B.A.S.C.
4 Independent Sub-Section Field Butchery, B.A.S.C.

Meiktila
12 Reinforcement Camp.
9th Battalion Burma Rifles.
14 Mess Unit.
Burma Military Hospital.

1 (B) CENTRAL AREA

Akyab
Detachment Rangoon Battalion, B.A.F.
Burma Frontier Force Aerodrome Guard.

Bridge 392 Mandalay-Rangoon Railway.
Two Sections, 11th Battalion Burma Rifles.

Chauk
2 Garrison Company (less two Platoons).
Detachment 'D' Company, Upper Burma Battalion, B.A.F.

Kabyaung River Bridge
Two Sections, 12th Battalion Burma Rifles.

Kanhla
One Section, 1 Garrison Company.

Kutkai
F.F.1.

Lanywa.
Detachment 'A' Company, Upper Burma Battalion, B.A.F.

Lashio
Demolition Squad Upper Burma Battalion, B.A.F.
Burma Frontier Force, Aerodrome Guard.

Myitnge River Bridge
One Platoon 11th Battalion Burma Rifles.

Namsam Falls
Detachment 'C' Company Upper Burma Battalion, B.A.F.

Namtu
'C' Company Upper Burma Battalion, B.A.F. (less Detachments).

Pegu River Bridge
Two Sections, 12th Battalion Burma Rifles.

Pyu River Bridge
Two Sections, 12th Battalion Burma Rifles.

Samon River Bridge
Two Sections, 11th Battalion Burma Rifles.

Sinthechaung Bridge
Two Sections, 11th Battalion Burma Rifles.

Sittang River Bridge
Two Sections, 11th Battalion Burma Rifles.

Swachaung Bridge
Two Sections, 11th Battalion Burma Rifles.

Thayetmyo
6, 7 Garrison Companies.

Tharrawaddy
One Section, 1 Garrison Company.

Thegon
One Section, 1 Garrison Company.

Toungoo
Burma Frontier Force Aerodrome Guard.

Yenangyaung
Headquarters 1 Garrison Battalion.
1 Garrison Company (less one Platoon).
Two Platoons 2 Garrison Company.
One Platoon 3 Garrison Company.
'D' Company Upper Burma Battalion, B.A.F. (less Detachments).

Yonbinchaung Bridge
Two Sections, 11th Battalion Burma Rifles.

1 (C) RANGOON AREA

Mingaladon
Headquarters Rangoon Area.
1st Battalion the Gloucestershire Regiment (less two companies).
3rd Battalion Burma Rifles.
12th Battalion Burma Rifles.
Mechanical Transport Training Company and Depot, B.A.S.C.
3 Mechanical Transport Section, B.A.S.C.
Rangoon Arsenal.
'Z' Ordnance Detachment.
British Military Hospital (with Burma Wing).
Branch Veterinary Hospital.

Rangoon
Station Staff Officer.
One Company 1st Battalion the Gloucestershire Regiment.
Rangoon Field Brigade, R.A., B.A.F.

Headquarters and Detachments 1 Heavy Anti-Aircraft Regiment, R.A., B.A.F.
Rangoon Battalion, B.A.F.
Burma Railways Battalion, B.A.F.
Detachment Burma Army Signals.
Headquarters 2 Garrison Battalion.
5 Garrison Company.
Rangoon University Training Corps, Burma Territorial Force.
Supply Depot, B.A.S.C.
4 Supply Depot Section, B.A.S.C.
Supply Personnel Depot, B.A.S.C.
1, 2 P.O.L. Sections, B.A.S.C.
Detention Hospital.
Burma Hospital Company Headquarters and Depot.
13 Field Accounts Office.
Medical Stores Depot.
Reserve Base Engineering Park.
2nd Echelon (India).
Embarkation Staff Officer.

Syriam

One Battery 1 Heavy Anti-Aircraft Regiment, R.A., B.A.F.
4 Garrison Company.

1 (D) 16th INDIAN INFANTRY BRIGADE GROUP

Mandalay

Headquarters 16 Indian Infantry Brigade.
16 Indian Infantry Brigade Employment Platoon.
16 Indian Infantry Brigade Signal Section.
1st Royal Battalion 9th Jat Regiment.
4th Battalion 12th Frontier Force Regiment.
1st Battalion 7th Gurkha Rifles.
43 Mule Company.
34 Supply Issue Section.
160 Supply Personnel Section.
2 Rail Head Supply Depot.
112 Field Bakery Sub Section.
112 Field Butchery Sub Section.
3 Field Ambulance Troop.
37 Field Ambulance.
G. and Q. Sections Indian General Hospital.
'C' Field Hygiene Sub Section.
Mobile Veterinary Sub Section.
16 Indian Infantry Brigade Mobile Workshop Section.
139, 140 Mess Units.

Meiktila
Malerkotla Field Company.

Rangoon
135 Supply Personnel Section.
141 Mess Unit.

Taunggyi
27 Mountain Regiment.
50 Field Park Company.

Maymyo
5 Mountain Battery.

2 (A) 13TH INDIAN INFANTRY BRIRADE

East Taunggyi
Headquarters 13 Indian Infantry Brigade.
29 Mountain Battery, I.A.
13 Indian Infantry Brigade Employment Platoon.
13 Indian Infantry Brigade Signal Section.
1st Battalion 18th Royal Garhwal Rifles.
28 Animal Transport Company (Mule).
35 Supply Issue Section.
205 Indian Supply Section Field Bakery.
202 Indian Supply Section Field Butchery.
210 Supply Personnel Section.
Detachment 8 Motor Ambulance Section.
57 Field Ambulance.
1 Field Ambulance Mule Troop.
2 Mobile Veterinary Section.
15 Mess Unit.
38 Field Post Office.

Loilem
5th Battalion 1st Punjab Regiment.
2nd Battalion 7th Rajput Regiment.
17 Rail Head Supply Detachment.
Detachment, Burma Field Hygiene Section.
Detachment, 28 Animal Transport Company (Mule) 4 Casualty Clearing Station.

Mandalay
Indian General Hospital.

2 (B) SOUTHERN SHAN AREA

Taungyi
Headquarters Southern Shan Area and Headquarters 1 Burma Brigade.
Headquarters Lines of Communication Area.
2 Mountain Battery, I.A. ⎫
5 Field Battery, R.A., B.A.F. ⎬ Leaving for Laikha.
2nd Battalion The King's Own Yorkshire Light Infantry. ⎭
56 Field Company (less 3 Sections).
Brigade Signal Section (less 3 Detachments).
Southern Shan States Battalion, Burma Frontier Force.
13th Battalion Burma Rifles (less two companies, less two Platoons).
14th Battalion Burma Rifles.
Detachment 1 Animal Transport Company.

Detachment 2 Animal Transport Company.
1 Mobile Veterinary Detachment.
4, 5, 12, Mechanical Transport Sections.
1 Light Aid Detachment.
1 Company Field Ambulance (Leaving for Laikha).
Burma Military Hospital (with British Wing).
2 Field Hygiene Section.
Field Supply Depot.
2 Supply Issue Section.
2, 3, 6, Independent Sub Sections Field Bakery and Butchery.
4 P.O.L. Section.
2 Ordnance Field Depot.
Base Engineer Park.
Garrison Engineer.
Artizan Company, R.E.
2 Field Post Office (Leaving for Laikha).
Three Civilian Labour Gangs.

Aungban

Burma Frontier Force Satellite Aerodrome Guard.

Heho

Burma Frontier Force Aerodrome Guard.

Kunhing

One Company 13th Battalion Burma Rifles (less 3 Platoons).

Kengtung

One Company less two Platoons 13th Battalion Burma Rifles.
5 Ordnance Field Depot.
R.E. Dump.
5 Mechanical Transport Section.
Field Supply Depot.
2 Light Aid Detachment.

Loilem

F.F. 4 (less one column).
Commando.
Outposts Southern Shan States Battalion, Burma Frontier Force.

Loimwe

1st Battalion Burma Rifles.
Detachment Brigade Signals.
Outposts Southern Shan States Battalion, Burma Frontier Force.
F.F. 3.
One Section 56 Field Company.
One Company 2 Field Ambulance.

Laikha Area

209 Supply Personnel Section.

Mong Pan Area

One Column F.F. 4.

Mawchi
F.F. 5.

Monghpayak
One Column F.F. 3.

Mongping.
Detachment 13th Battalion Burma Rifles.

Namsang
Burma Frontier Force Aerodrome and Satellite Aerodrome Guards and Columns.
Burma Frontier Force Mounted Infantry two troops.

Nammawngun
One Section 56 Field Company.
Two Platoons 13th Battalion Burma Rifles.
One Company 5th Battalion Burma Rifles.
Field Supply Depot.
3 P.O.L. Section.
2 Supply Issue Section.
3 Light Aid Detachment.
4 Ordnance Field Depot.
R.E. Dump.
2 Casualty Clearing Station, (less one section).
One Civilian Labour Gang.

Pangkhem
5th Battalion Burma Rifles (less one company).
Detachment Brigade Signals.
2 Field Ambulance (less two companies).

Thamakan
Burma Frontier Force Column and Mounted Infantry Troop.

Takaw
One Section 56 Field Company.
One Platoon 13th Battalion Burma Rifles.
Detachment, enrolled ferrymen.

Tongta
Detachment 13th Battalion Burma Rifles.

2 (C) TENNASSERIM AREA

Moulmein
Headquarters Tenasserim Area and 2 Burma Brigade.
Brigade Signal Section.
Tenasserim Battalion, B.A.F. (less one company).
12 Mountain Battery, I.A.
One Section, 1 Field Company Burma Sappers and Miners.
One Section Artizan Works Company.
8th Battalion Burma Rifles.
Detachment Kokine Battalion Burma Frontier Force.
1 Animal Transport Company (less Detachment).

1, 2, 4, 6, 8, Mechanical Transport Section.
4 Light Aid Detachment.
1 Field Supply Depot.
1 Rail Head Supply Depot.
1 Supply Issue Section.
1 Independent Sub Section Field Bakery.
1 Independent Sub Section Field Butchery.
1 Field Ambulance.
1 Casualty Clearing Station.
1 Field Hygiene Section.
3 Ordnance Field Depot.
1 Field Post Office.
Station Staff Officer.

Mergui

2nd Battalion Burma Rifles.
F.F. 2
Detachment Kokine Battalion Burma Frontier Force.
Detachment Supply Depot.
Burma Military Hospital.
Station Staff Officer.

Tavoy

One Company Tenasserim Battalion, B.A.F.
6th Battalion Burma Rifles.
Detachment Kokine Battalion Burma Frontier Force.
Detachment 1 Annual Transport Company.
Detachment Supply Depot.
Burma Military Hospital.

Victoria Point.

Detachment Kokine Battalion Burma Frontier Force.

Thabawleik

F.F. 2.

Kawkareik

4th Battalion Burma Rifles.

APPENDIX B

Burma

ORDER OF BATTLE AT THE COMMENCEMENT OF HOSTILITIES
December, 1941.

1. 1st Burma Division—consisting of

    Maymyo Brigade
    - 2nd K.O.Y.L.I.
    - 1st Burma Rifles.
    - 6th Burma Rifles.
    - 7th Burma Rifles.
    - 12th Mountain Battery.
    - 56th Field Company (S and M).

    Tenasserim Brigade
    - 2nd Burma Rifles.
    - 4th Burma Rifles.
    - 5th Burma Rifles.
    - 8th Burma Rifles.
    - 2nd Mountain Battery.
    - Sec. Field Company.

    13th Indian Infantry Brigade
    - 5th/1st Punjab.
    - 2nd/7th Rajputs.
    - 1st/18th R. Garh. Rifles.
    - 23rd Mountain Battery.
    - 5th Field Battery, R.A., B.A.F.

2. Rangoon Brigade
    - 1st Gloucesters.
    - 3rd Burma Rifles.
    - Coast Defence Battery.

3. 16th Indian Infantry Brigade ...
    - 1st/9th Jat.
    - 4th/12th F.F. Regiment.
    - 1st/7th Gurkha Regiment.
    - 5th Mountain Battery.
    - Headquarters, 27th Mountain Regiment.
    - 50th Field Company (S and M).

4. Burma Frontier Force
    - Bhama Battalion.
    - Chin Hills Battalion.
    - Myitkyina Battalion.
    - Northern Shan States Battalion.
    - Southern Shan States Battalion.
    - Kokine Battalion.
    - Reserve Battalion.

5. Garrison Companies ...
    - 1st Garrison Company.
    - 2nd Garrison Company.
    - 3rd Garrison Company.
    - 4th Garrison Company.
    - 5th Garrison Company.

6. Burma Rifles (Territorials)　　11th Burma Rifles.
　　　　　　　　　　　　　　　　12th Burma Rifles.
　　　　　　　　　　　　　　　　13th Southern Shan States Battalion Burma Rifles.
　　　　　　　　　　　　　　　　14th Burma Rifles (forming).

7. Burma Auxiliary Force　　　　Rangoon Battalion.
　　　　　　　　　　　　　　　　Upper Burma Battalion.
　　　　　　　　　　　　　　　　Burma Railways Battalion.
　　　　　　　　　　　　　　　　Tenasserim Battalion.
　　　　　　　　　　　　　　　　1 A.A. Regiment (forming).

8. Burma Rifles　　　　　　　　　9th and 10th Battalions (forming).
　　　　　　　　　　　　　　　　Six Anti-Tank Troops.
　　　　　　　　　　　　　　　　One Field Battery.

9. Field Company　　　　　　　　Forming.

10. Armed Police　　　　　　　　Three Battalions.

SUMMARY OF STRENGTH OF ARMY IN BURMA, 7 December, 1941.

Infantry—

British	2 Battalions.
Indian	6 Battalions.
Burma Rifles (Regulars)	8 Battalions (4 of these just formed).
Burma Rifles (Territorials)	4 Battalions.
Garrison Company ...	5 Battalions.
Burma Auxiliary Force	4 Battalions.
Burma Frontier Force	6 Battalions.
	1 Reserve Battalion.

Artillery—

Indian Mountain Batteries.　　　3
Burma Auxiliary Force　　...　 1 Field Battery, 18-pounders.
Five Mobile Detachments Burma Frontier Force.

APPENDIX C
STATE OF INFANTRY 17TH DIVISION ON EVENING OF 24TH FEBRUARY 1942

Brigade	Battalion	British Officers	Viceroy's or Governor's Commissioned Officers	Other Ranks	Rifles	Bren Guns	Thompson Sub-machine Carbines
16	2nd Battalion Kings Own Yorkshire Light Infantry	6	—	200	50	2	2
	1st Royal Battalion 9th Jat Regiment	8	10	550	50	—	2
	1st Battalion 7th Gurkha Rifles	6	4	290	50	2	—
	8th Battalion Burma Rifles	3	3	90	60	2	—
	Total 16th Brigade	23	17	1130	210	6	4
46	7th Battalion 10th Baluch Regiment	5	3	200	90	—	2
	5th Battalion 17th Dogra Regiment	1	3	100	70	—	—
	3rd Battalion 7th Gurkha Rifles	5	5	160	30	—	—
	2nd Battalion, The Duke of Wellington's Regiment	16	—	300	150	4	6
	Total 46th Brigade	27	11	760	340	4	8
48	1st Battalion 3rd Q.A.O's Gurkha Rifles	3	4	100	40	5	8
	1st Battalion 4th P.W.O. Gurkha Rifles	12	18	650	600	30	30
	2nd Battalion 5th Royal Gurkha Rifles F.F.	6	6	215	30	2	2
	4th Battalion 12th Frontier Force Regiment	9	13	480	200	9	16
	Total 48th Brigade	30	41	1445	870	46	56
	Total for the Division	80	69	3335	1420*	56	68
	Approximate deficiency	100	65	4500	5800	300	300
	Immediate deficiency of weapons	—	—	—	1700	120	100

*Note the small number of rifles available.

APPENDIX D

CHINESE EXPEDITIONARY FORCE, BURMA 1942

Order of Battle—31 March 1942

Commander-in-Chief—General Lo Cho Ying

EXPEDITIONARY ARMY TROOPS

36th Division — Commander—Major General Li Chi P'Eng
  One Bn.; 20th Gendarme Regt. Inf.
  24th Eng. Battalion

V ARMY   *Locations*

22nd Division — Commander—General Tu Yu Ming   V Army Headquarters—Pyawbwe

22nd Division — Commander—Major General Liao Yao Hsiang
  64 Regiment
  65 Regiment   Yedashe/Kyungen
  66 Regiment
  Div. Troops

96th Division — Commander—Major General Yu Shao
  286 Regiment
  287 Regiment   Pyinmana
  288 Regiment
  Div. Troops

200th Division — Commander—Major General Tai An Leng
  598 Regiment
  599 Regiment   Yezin
  600 Regiment
  Div. Troops

Training Depot
  1 Reserve Regiment
  2 Reserve Regiment

Part III

Army Troops
  Cavalry Regiment
  Artillery Regiment
  Engineer Regiment
  Armoured Regiment
  Motor Regiment
  T.R. (1 Bn.)
  Signal Battalion
  A.A. Battalion
  Anti-Tank Gun Bn.
  Inf. Gun Bn.
  Sp. Ser. Bn.
  1 Coy.; of Fire B
  1 Coy.; of drivers
  Field Hospital
  1st Bn., of 10th Arty. Regt. (attached)
  1st Bn., of 18th Arty. Regt. (attached)

VI Army — Commander—Lieut.-General Kan Li   VI Army Headquarters—Loilem

49th Division — Commander—Major General Peng Pi Sheng — Mongpan Area / Karenni
  145 Regiment
  146 Regiment
  147 Regiment
  T.M. Battalion
  Eng. Battalion
  Tran. Battalion

55th Division — Commander—Lieut.-General Chen Mien Wu — Loilem / Thazi
  1 Regiment
  2 Regiment
  3 Regiment
  T.M. Battalion
  Eng. Battalion
  Tran. Battalion

93rd Division Commander—Lieut.-General Lu Kuo Ch'uan ⎫
  278 Regiment ⎬ Kengtung Area
  279 Regiment ⎭
  T.M. Battalion
  Eng. Battalion
  Tran. Battalion
Army Troops
  Liu Kuan-lung Detachment (277 Regt. from 93rd Division but strengthened)
  Sp. Ser. Battalion
  Engineer Battalion
  Transport Battalion
  Signal Battalion
  1st Bn. of 13th Arty. Regt. (attached)
  5th & 6th Coys. of 52nd Arty. Regt. (attached)

PART IV

The following Chinese Army entered Burma during April 1942.

LXVI ARMY Commander—General Chang Chen
28th Division Commander—Major General Liu Po Lung
  82 Regiment
  83 Regiment
  84 Regiment
29th Division Commander—Major General Ma Wei Chi
  85 Regiment
  86 Regiment
  87 Regiment
38th Division Commander—Lieut.-General Sun Li Jen
  112 Regiment
  113 Regiment
  114 Regiment
Army Troops
  1st Battalion 18th Arty. Regt.
  2 Coys; 1st Battalion, Firing Corps

APPENDIX 'E'

Order of Battle

(As issued by Headquarters Army in Burma)

ARMY IN BURMA

1st April 1942

1 BURMA CORPS (Burcorps)

Corps Troops

7 Armoured Brigade Group

7 Hussars.
2 R. Tanks.
414 Battery R.H.A.
"A" Battery, 95 Anti-Tank Regiment R.A.
1 West Yorks.
13 Light Field Ambulance.
65 Company R.A.S.C.
114 Butchery Independent Sub-section R.I.A.S.C.
7 Armoured Brigade Light Repair Section.
7 Armoured Brigade Recovery Section.
2 R.T.R. Light Aid Detachment.
7 Hussars Light Aid Detachment.
8 Field Post Office.

Artillery	8 Anti-Aircraft Battery R.A. 3 Indian Light Anti-Aircraft Battery (less one troops).
Engineers	1 Field Company, Burma Sappers and Miners. 17 Artizan Works Company I.E. 18 Artizan Works Company I.E. (less one Sect.) 6 Pioneer Battalion I.E.
Signals	1 Burma Corps Signals. 212 Line Construction Section, 'M' L of C Signals.
Infantry	Special Service Detachment No. 1 (Commando).
Supply and Transport	59 G.P. Transport Company R.I.A.S.C. 17 Divisional Troops Transport Company (less Detachment 47 Mule Company R.I.A.S.C. 4 Field Ambulance Troop R.I.A.S.C. 1 Local Transport Company (formed from 20 M.A.S. an impressed vehicles). 22 Motor Ambulance Section R.I.A.S.C. 115 Supply Personnel Section R.I.A.S.C. 1 and 18 Supply Personnel Sections B.A.S.C. Lower Burma Supply Section B.A.S.C. 112, 114 and 115 Bakery Independent Sub-section R.I.A.S.C.

	1 Bakery Independent Sub-section B.A.S.C. Lower Burma Bakery Section B.A.S.C. Lower Burma Butchery Section B.A.S.C. 1 Butchery Independent Sub-section B.A.S.C. 1 Rail Head Supply Detachment B.A.S.C. 2 P.O.L. Section B.A.S.C.
Medical	1 Burma Field Ambulance. 1 Burma Field Hygiene Section. 7 Anti-Malarial Unit (Indian). 2 Burma Depot Medical Stores.
Labour Misc.	Two Coys 18 Aux. Pnr. Bn. 2 and 7 Burma. Labour Coys. 85 Field Post Office. Mess Units. Advanced Base Stationery Depot (Burma).

1 Burma Division

1 Burma Brigade

2/7 Rajput.
1 Burma Rifles.
2 Burma Rifles.
5 Burma Rifles.

2 Burma Brigade

5/1 Punjab.
7 Burma Rifles.

13 Indian Infantry Brigade

1/18 R. Garhwal Rifles.

Divisional Troops

Artillery	H.Q. 27 Mountain Regiment. 2 Mountain Battery. 23 Mountain Battery. 8 Anti-Tank Battery.
Engineers	50 Field Park Company. 56 Field Company Sappers and Miners (less two Sections). Malerkotla Field Company.
Signals	1 Burma Divisional Signals.
Infantry	Special Service Detachment No. 2 (Commando).
Supply and Transport	1 Burma Division Headquarters Transport Section B.A.S.C. 3, 5, 9, 11 and 12 Mechanical Transport Sections B.A.S.C. 8 Motor Ambulance Sections R.I.A.S.C. 2 Animal Transport Company B.A.S.C. 28 Mule Company R.I.A.S.C. 1 Field Ambulance Troop R.I.A.S.C. 35 Supply Issue Section R.I.A.S.C. 1, 2 and 3 Supply Issue Sections B.A.S.C. 202 Butchery Independent Sub-section R.I.A.S.C. 2 Cattle Supply Section B.A.S.C.

Ordnance	7 Mobile Workshop Company I.A.O.C. 28 Infantry Brigade Workshop Section I.A.O.C.
Medical	2 Burma Field Ambulance. 27 Field Ambulance (Indian). 2 Burma Field Hygiene Section.
Veterinary	1 (Burma) Mobile Veterinary Detachment. 2 (Indian Mobile Veterinary Section.
Postal	1, 2 and 7 Field Post Offices (Burma). 38 Field Post Office (Indian).
Provost	1 Burma Division Provost Unit.

17 Indian Division

16 Indian Infantry Brigade

1. D.W.R.
1/9 R. Jats.
7/10 Baluch Regiment.
4/12 F.F.R.

48 Indian Infantry Brigade

1 Cameronians.
1/3 G.R.
2/5 R.G.R.
1/4 G.R.
1/7 G.R.
3/7 G.R.

63 Indian Infantry Brigade

1 Inisks.
1/11 Sikhs.
2/13 F.F. Rif.
1/10 G.R.

Divisional Troops

Artillery	1 Indian Field Regiment. H.Q. 28 Mountain Regiment. 5, 12, 15, 28 Mountain Batteries. 5 Anti-Tank Battery.
Engineers	24, 60, 70 Field Companies, Sappers and Miners.
Signals	17 Indian Divisional Signals.
Infantry	1 Glosters. 5/17 Dogra. 8 Burma Rifles 1, 2, 3, Frontier Force Detachments B.F.F. Royal Marine River Patrol. Rangoon Battalion, Burma Military Police. Special Service Detachment No. 3 (Commando).

Supply and Transport	46 Indian Infantry Brigade Transport Coy. R.I.A.S.C. 17 Divisional Headquarters Transport Section, R.I.A.S.C. Detachment, 17 Divisional Troops Transport Coy. R.I.A.S.C. 24 Mechanical Transport Section B.A.S.C. 45 Mule Company R.I.A.S.C. 5 Field Ambulance Troop R.I.A.S.C. 34, 36, 46 and 66 Supply Issue Sections R.I.A.S.C. 3 Butchery Independent Sub-section B.A.S.C. 1 Cattle Supply Section B.A.S.C.
Medical	23, 37, 50 Field Ambulance (Indian). 22 Field Hygiene Section (Indian).
Ordnance	59 Mobile Workshop Company I.A.O.C. 46 and 63 Indian Infantry Brigade Workshop Sections I.A.O.C.
Veterinary	4 (Indian) Mobile Veterinary Section.
Provost	17 Indian Division Provost Unit.
Labour	17 Auxiliary Pioneer Battalion (Less two Coys.)
Postal	40, 82, 97 and 100 Field Post Offices (Indian).

Army Troops

Artillery	1 Heavy Anti-Aircraft Regiment R.A., B.A.F. Detachment Rangoon Field Brigade R.A., B.A.F.
Engineers	1 Burma Artizan Works Company. Depot and Training Company Burma Sappers & Miners.
Signals	Depot and Training Centre, Burma Army Signals.
Infantry	Depot, British Infantry. 9 and 10 Bns. The Burma Rifles. Bhamo Bn. The Burma Frontier Force. Chin Hills Bn. The Burma Frontier Force (less Detachment). Myitkyina Bn. The Burma Frontier Force. Northern Shan States Bn. The Burma Frontier Force. Southern Shan States Bn. The Burma Frontier Force. Reserve Bn. The Burma Frontier Force. Kokine Bn. The Burma Frontier Force (less Detachments). Karen Levies.
Supply and Transport	56 Mechanical Transport Section R.I.A.S.C. A.H.Q. Mechanical Transport Section B.A.S.C. Mechanical Transport Training Centre B.A.S.C. Animal Transport Depot B.A.S.C. Base Supply Depot. H.Q. 15 Supply Personnel Company R.I.A.S.C. 135, 138, 153, 164 and 169 Supply Personnel Sections R.I.A.S.C. 4, 9, 12, 14, 15, and 16, Supply Personnel Sections B.A.S.C. 2 Rail Head Supply Detachment R.I.A.S.C. 3, 7, and 8 P.O.L. Sections B.A.S.C. 78 P.O.L. Section R.I.A.S.C. Supply Personnel Depot. 5 Supply Issue Section B.A.S.C. 22 and 23 Supply Personnel Sections B.A.S.C. 5 and 6 P.O.L. Sections B.A.S.C. 3 and 4 Cattle Supply Sections B.A.S.C.

Medical	1 Burma Casualty Clearing Station. 4 Burma General Hospital. ⎫ on loan to 3 Field Laboratory. ⎬ Chinese 2 Burma Staging Section. ⎪ Expedi- One Section, 41 Indian General Hospital. ⎭ tionary Force. Depot Indian Hospital Corps. Depot Burma Hospital Corps. H.Q. Detachment R.A.M.C.
Ordnance	Vehicle Distribution Group (Burma).
Survey	6 Indian Field Survey Company.
Misc.	Officer Cadet Training Unit. Burma Army Schools of Instruction. Burma Army School of Education. Bush Warfare School. Burma General Service Corps Depot. 1, 2 and 3 (Railway) Field Service Security Sections.

Line of Communication Defence Troops and Units

Artillery	2 Indian Anti-Tank Regiment (less two Batteries: no guns). 8 (Indian) Heavy Anti-Aircraft Battery. One Troop 3 (Indian) Light Anti-Aircraft Bty., Rangoon Field Brigade R.A., B.A.G. (no guns).
Engineers	1 Field Company, Burma Sappers and Miners. 56 Field Company Sappers and Miners. 6 Pioneer Battalion I.E. 18 Artizan Works Company. 107 and 108 C.R.E. Works (Indian). 310 Workshop and Park Company. 1 and 3 Engineer Stores Base Depots. Engineer Stores Depot.
Signals	213 Section "M" L of C Signals. Detachment Burma Frontier Force Signals. Burma Posts and Telegraphs L of C Signals.
Infantry	2 K.O.Y.L.I. 3, 4 and 6 Bns. The Burma Rifles. 11, 12, 13 and 14 Bns. The Burma Rifles B.T.F. Tenasserim Bn., Burma Aux. Force. Rangoon Bn., Burma Aux. Force. Burma Railways Bn., Burma Aux. Force. Upper Burma Bn., Burma Aux. Force. Mandalay Bn., The Burma Frontier Force. Detachments Kokine Bn., The Burma Frontier Force. Detachment Chin Hills Bn., The Burma Frontier Force. 1, 3, 4 and 5 F.F. Detachments, The Burma Frontier Force. M.I. Detachment, The Burma Frontier Force Headquarters 1 and 2 Garrison Battalions. 1, 2, 3, 4, 5, 6, 7, 8, and 9 Garrison Companies.

GROUP I—APPENDIX E

Supply and Transport

1, 2 and 3 Aux. Mechanical Transport Coys. B.A.S.C.
7, 13, 14, 15, 25 and 26 Mechanical Transport Sections B.A.S.C.
H.Q. 'A' and 'B' Sections, 3 Mechanical Transport Company B.A.S.C.
'C' and 'D' Sections, 3 Mechanical Transport Company B.A.S.C. (personnel only).
16, 17, 18, 19 and 20 Mechanical Transport Sections B.A.S.C. (personnel only).
21 Motor Ambulance Section R.I.A.S.C.
3 Field Ambulance Troop R.I.A.S.C. (personnel only).
43 Mule Company R.I.A.S.C. (personnel only).
1 Animal Transport Company B.A.S.C. (personnel only).
H.Q. 1, 3, 4 and 5 Supply Personnel Companies B.A.S.C.
2, 3, 5, 6, 7, 8, 10, 11, 13, 17, 19, 20, 21, 24, 25, 26 Supply Personnel Sections B.A.S.C.
114, 115, 116, 167, 209 and 210 Supply Personnel Sections R.I.A.S.C.
4 Supply Issue Section B.A.S.C.
3, 4 and 5 Rail Head Supply Detachments B.A.S.C.
17 Rail Head Supply Detachment, R.I.A.S.C.
1, 4, 9, 10, 11, 12, 13, 14, P.O.L. Sections B.A.S.C.
68 P.O.L. Section R.I.A.S.C.
2, 3, 4, 5, 6, 7, 8, 9, Bakery Independent Sub-sections B.A.S.C.
112, and 205 Bakery Independent Sub-sections R.I.A.S.C.
2, 4, 5, 6, 7, 8, 9, Butchery Independent Sub-sections B.A.S.C.
5, 6, and 7, Cattle Supply Sections B.A.S.C.

Medical

1, 2, 3, 5, 6, 7, and 8 Burma General Hospitals.
41, 59 and 60 Indian General Hospitals (less one section 41 I.G.H.)
1, 2 and 3 Field Laboratories (Burma).
2 Burma Casualty Clearing Station.
4 Indian Casualty Clearing Station.
1 and 2 Ambulance Trains.

Hospital Ships "Mysore" (staffed by 8 C.C.S.)
"Kalaw" (staffed by 8 C.C.S.)
"Fano" (staffed by 31 Indian Staging Section).
"Ebro" (staff of 3 Amb Train).
"Lady Innes"

39 Field Ambulance (Indian).
3 Field Hygiene Section (Indian).
1 Burma Staging Section.
2 British Staging Section.
16 Indian Staging Section.
British Convalescent Depot.
10 Mobile X-Ray Unit (Indian).
2 Ear, Nose and Throat Surgical Unit (Indian).
2 Opthalmological Unit (Indian).
Base Depot Medical Stores (Burma).
13 Depot Medical Stores (Indian).
District Laboratory (Burma).
Dental Centre (Burma).

Ordnance	Base Ordnance Depot (Burma). Base M.T. Repair Depot (Burma). 1, 2, 3, 4, 5 and 7 Ordnance Field Depots (Burma). 16 Indian Infantry Brigade Workshop Section I.A.O.C. 1, 2, 3, 4, 5, 6 Station Workshops (Burma). 1, 3, and 5 Light Aid Detachments (Burma).
Movement Control	2 Movement Control Area.
Veterinary	Burma Military Veterinary Hospital.
Remounts	2 Remount Detachment (Indian).
Provost	Provost Company (Burma).
Labour	18 Aux. Pnr. Bn. (less two companies). 1 Burmese Labour Company. Lahu, Wa, Shan and Gurkha Labour Companies.
Postal	Base Post Office (Burma). 3, 5, 6, and 9 Field Post Offices (Burma).
Misc.	Stationery Depot (Burma). Independent Rest Camp Sections. 9, 10, 12 and 18 Reinforcement Camps. Mess Units.

GROUP II

APPENDIX 'A'

Extracts from the Covering Memorandum to Far East Appreciation by the Chiefs of Staff Committee August 1941

DEFENCE OF BURMA

48. The possibility of a Japanese occupation of Thailand raises the question of the defence of Burma, since key points such as the Rangoon oil refineries and aerodromes on the Burmese section of the Singapore air route would be immediately threatened by air attack from bases in Thailand. The invasion of Burmese territory is a more distant threat, except in the extreme South where it would be possible for Japan to capture aerodromes. such as Victoria Point and Mergui.

49. To deal with these threats it may be desirable that air forces should be permanently established at bases such as Lashio, Rangoon and Tavoy and that additional troops (above those already earmarked) and air defences should be provided. The defence of Malaya must, however, have precedence over Burma and the provision of such forces can only be a very long term project.

50. On a shorter view the problem is to limit the Japanese threat with the resources likely to be available. It is necessary in the first place to ensure that the air route between Singapore and Rangoon is kept open. The aerodromes in Burma as far south as Tavoy and in Malaya as far north as Alor Star must, therefore, be held. If the aerodromes at Lashio, Rangoon and Tavoy are developed, stocked, and defended, it may then be possible, if the situation permits, to move air forces from Malaya or India to assist Burma in dealing with a sudden threat from the north. It will be important to deny the Japanese the use of the aerodromes at Victoria Point and Mergui, and we recommend that they should be prepared for demolition now.

51. We suggest that both the long and short term problems of the defence of Burma to meet a Japanese threat from Thailand should be reviewed on these lines by the Governments of India and Burma in consultation with the Air Officer Commanding in the Far East.

LAND FORCES

Burma

75. As regards the defence of Burma, we recommend (paragraph 51) that the Government of India and Burma should review the situation. Extra troops and anti-aircraft equipment will almost certainly be required, for the protection of air bases in particular.

China

76. We do not recommend that our garrisons in North China and at Hong Kong should be reinforced in any circumstances. In the event of a general settlement with Japan leading to the withdrawal of these garrisons, they would become available for employment elsewhere, *e.g.*, Malaya or North Borneo.

APPENDIX 'B'

Singapore Defence Conference 1940

EXTRACTS FROM REPORT, PART II

REVIEW OF DEFENCE REQUIREMENTS OF INDIA AND BURMA IN THE LIGHT OF POSSIBLE JAPANESE THREAT FROM THAILAND

I. THE THREAT TO BURMA AND INDIA

1. BURMA is of Imperial importance because of her oil and mineral resources, and because of sea and air communications with SINGAPORE. She is also the channel for supplies to the CHUNGKING Government.

2. The occupation of THAILAND by the Japanese will make BURMA liable to invasion by land as well as by sea and air, and will bring her within close range of aerodromes from which heavy sustained bombing could be carried out.

3. If Japanese troops advance into YUNNAN, BURMA will also be open to attack from the North-East by land and air.

4. For purposes of general defence, BURMA is an outpost of INDIA. Any threat to BURMA, or the occupation of BURMA by an enemy, is a direct menace to Eastern India and the installations of Imperial importance which are situated there.

II. PROBABLE ENEMY ACTION

5. Having occupied THAILAND, JAPAN will establish land bases from which, while MALAYA would be her primary objective, she could attack BURMA and Eastern India from the East. We consider that the immediate threat to BURMA and Eastern India will be

(a) Air attack on the oil refineries and docks at RANGOON, and possibly on the vulnerable point in Eastern INDIA (DIGBOI, CALCUTTA and TATANAGAR).

(b) Land, seaborne and air attack, including airborne troops, on TENASSERIM, to capture and/or destroy aerodromes on the SINGAPORE air route.

6. Attacks on the remainder of BURMA'S Eastern frontier would probably in the first place be limited to raids into BURMA territory, in which the Japanese might be assisted by the Thais. An attack from CHIENGRAI into the SOUTHERN SHAN STATES is a feasible proposition for a large force, against which defence measures must be taken.

7. As a long term project, the Japanese can attack BURMA from YUNNAN by land and air. To do this, they would either have to capture YUNNAN or come to terms with YUNNAN Provincial Government, who are believed to be inclined to favour the Japanese at the present time.

III. THE PROBLEM

8. The immediate problem is to limit the Japanese threat with the resources likely to be available in the near future. We must at any rate be prepared to

(a) deal with enemy air attack on BURMA and Eastern INDIA.

(b) hold and delay any land attack on BURMA until reinforcements arrive.
  (c) keep open the air route as far south as incl. Tavoy or MERGUI until TAVOY is ready for use.
  (d) receive air and land reinforcements to deal with a sudden threat.

9. The long term problem is to deal with a Japanese invasion of BURMA, which will entail the provision in BURMA of sufficient forces to repel an attack in force from THAILAND or YUNNAN.

IV. LAND DEFENCE

10. An examination of the coast line of BURMA reveals that the only likely objectives in coastal areas are
  (a) AKYAB aerodrome.
  (b) The RANGOON area.
  (c) TENASSERIM.

11. (a) AKYAB should be protected against raids, and for this the present Frontier Force and Military Police garrison will suffice.
  (b) The defence of the RANGOON area requires a Bde supported by a Fd. Bty., and a Fd. Coy.
  (c) In TENASSERIM, neither MERGUI nor VICTORIA POINT can be adequately defended or reinforced (except by air) owing to their geographical position and the absence of communications. MERGUI should be held if possible until TAVOY is ready for the operation of air forces. VICTORIA POINT is so cut off and so easy of access to big forces from THAILAND coming from JUBHORN via TAPLI that the defence of this place against serious attack is hardly a practical proposition. The aerodromes at MERGUI and VICTORIA POINT have been prepared for demolition in case of necessity. The defence of the rest of TENASSERIM (AMHERST and TAVOY Districts) requires four Bns., a Fd. Bty., a Mtn. Bty. & a Fd. Coy. An additional Bn. should be allotted for the defence of MERGUI until TAVOY is ready for the operation of air forces.

12. With regard to land frontier defence, troops required for the defence of the Eastern Frontier of TENASSERIM are included in the estimates given above. There remains the frontier from incl. SALWEEN District to MYITKYINA District. The defence of the SHAN STATES from attack, including the attack from CHIENGRAI mentioned in para 6 above, will require two Bdes with two Fd. Btys., a Mtn. Bty., an A/Tk Bty., a Lt. A. A. Bty., a Lt. Tank Coy. and two Fd. Coys.

13. The attack from YUNNAN mentioned as a long term project in para 7 would require two Bdes, a Fd. Regt., a Lt. A. A. Bty., two Med. Btys., a Lt. Tank Coy., an A/Tk Bty. and the necessary R. E. Unit.

V. ATTACK BY AIRBORNE TROOPS AND PARACHUTISTS

14. The existing aerodromes on the SINGAPORE air route and at LASHIO are all protected against landings by airborne troops. Garrisons are found by the BURMA Frontier Force, and are not included in the estimates above. In addition there are certain emergency landing grounds along the SINGAPORE air route. These will be rendered unfit for landing when war becomes imminent. Additional provision must be made for the extra aerodromes required under para 31.

VI. Internal Security

15. It is considered that unless there is a large scale rebellion a Bde. of Infantry acting in close co-operation with the police should be able to keep order in BURMA provided that strong action is taken at the first sign of trouble.

VII. A. A. Defence

16. We draw attention to the fact that the military targets in BURMA and Eastern INDIA are now within range of aerodromes in INDO-CHINA already occupied by the Japanese, from which sustained long range bombing by heavy bombers can be carried out, and that BURMA has at present no protection whatever, while that in INDIA is negligible.

17. We consider that it would be useless, in view of the resources likely to be available, to consider the problem in terms of other than deterrent effect. On this basis, and after expert examination of the problem of the A. A. Defence of SYRIAM Refinery and the dock area of RANGOON, so far as can be done from the map, and working on a minimum density of 12 Heavy Guns over SYRIAM and 8 Heavy Guns over the docks, we require

One Hy. A. A. Regt. of 24 Guns.

As regards Light Guns, 8 guns at SYRIUM and 8 guns distributed along the dock area should be sufficient as a deterrent, *i.e.*,

One Bty. of Light A. A. Guns.

18. If these guns cannot be provided, we consider that at least

Twelve Heavy Guns (3.7")
Eight Light Guns (40-mm.)

should be sent to this area as part of the immediate problem in order to raise the morale of the civil population, and to give some protection to the oil refineries.

19. We are advised that the proper scale of Searchlights is 72, with an absolute minimum of 48 lights, and that nothing less is worth having. In these circumstances, we consider that for the present RANGOON and SYRIAM should rely on protection from black-out until protection on the minimum scale can be provided.

20. We are advised that for climatic and other reasons, balloon barrages would not be practicable.

21. For mobile defence of troops operating against an invading force, at least one Lt. Bty. would be necessary, and for the defence of important bridges on the L. of C. two more Lt. Tps.

22. The protection of aerodromes mentioned in para 31, requires four Lt. A. A. Guns for each aerodrome. Until these are available, light automatic defence should be provided, on the scale of 16 L. as for MINGALADON aerodrome and 8 for each of the others.

VIII. Burma in Relation to Defence of Malaya

23. Apart from the operation of air forces against Japanese communications through THAILAND and the maintenance of the Imperial air route between BURMA and MALAYA, we cannot see that any contribution can be made by the forces located in BURMA to the defence of MALAYA against attack from THAILAND except raids against the L. of C.

IX. Summary of Army Requirements

24. The Army Reinforcements required are summarized in statement 'A'.[1]

X. Air Defence

25. In the Tactical Appreciation on the Defence of MALAYA a requirement for 566 aircraft was established, exclusive of those required "for

---

[1] See p. 403.

the protection of BURMA against Japanese attack by land, air or sea." This was based upon the necessity to meet Japanese air forces totalling some 617 to 713, as shown in the telegraphed summary of the Chiefs of Staffs' Appreciation, to meet Japanese seaborne attack in strength. Japanese forces of 617/713 are made up of carrier-borne 281 and landbased between 336 and 432.

26. It is unlikely that Japanese carrier-borne aircraft will operate against BURMA; should they do so we have sufficient G. R. strength to deal with them. This section of our report is, therefore, based upon the necessity to meet up to 432 Japanese landbased aircraft.

27. The C. of S. estimate of 336/432 landbased Japanese aircraft can be accepted as the maximum number the Japanese could find, so attack upon BURMA as well as MALAYA would entail splitting the Japanese effort; the stronger the attack upon MALAYA, the weaker the attack upon BURMA and vice versa.

28. Our Malayan forces were calculated upon meeting the full Japanese effort of 336 to 432, and if the Japanese divert a proportion of their aircraft against BURMA, we can similarly divert a proportion of ours to counter the attack on BURMA, provided that adequate operational facilities and stocks of fuel and bombs are already there. Such operational facilities will, in any case, be necessary to enable us to utilize BURMA aerodromes where, as in the South, these are more conveniently placed for our air offensive against a Japanese attack through THAILAND on MALAYA.

29. While it is possible for the Japanese to concentrate their full landbased aircraft strength in THAILAND and in INDO-CHINA for operation against BURMA, we think it unlikely that they will do so. It appears more probable that the Japanese will concentrate their main attack against the vastly more attractive and important objective of MALAYA. In these circumstances, and as we are aiming at maximum operational mobility, we think that the Air Forces to be located normally in BURMA can be provided on a limited scale as follows :—

One G. R. Squadron	RANGOON.
One Bomber Squadron	LASHIO.
One Fighter Squadron	for the RANGOON area.
One Bomber Squadron ...	MERGUI or TAVOY.
Detachment A. C. Squadron	as necessary.

Of these only the Fighter Squadron is in addition to the 566 already recommended.

30. The lines of approach to vital targets in BURMA are so widespread that it is impracticable to arrange for adequate forward fighter defence zones and we are, therefore, forced to fall back on some form of local air defence of the vital targets in conjunction with an efficient observer or warning system, which will have to be linked with INDIA'S system. This being so, we have only recommended the provision of one Fighter Squadron for the defence of targets in the RANGOON area. This Squadron should be supplemented by A. A. defences.

31. In the Tactical Appreciation on Defence of MALAYA stress was laid on the necessity for the maximum operational mobility throughout the Far Eastern area. We recommend immediate preparation and provision in BURMA of eight operational landing grounds fully equipped with fuel, explosives, communications and temporary accommodation, of which four will be occupied by the Units suggested in para 29. The exact location of the remainder must be decided after further investigation; they should be located in the vicinity of the Eastern Frontier of BURMA.

32. In the foregoing paragraphs, we have been mainly concerned with the defence against air attack, but the suggested provision of Air Forces will also, we consider, be adequate in conjunction with the land forces recommended to meet the scale of land attack likely to be encountered.

33. In the Tactical Appreciation on the Defence of MALAYA we have proposed to meet the Army Co-operation requirements of the Army in BURMA from the provision made for Army Co-operation requirements in MALAYA.

34. Provision for Trade protection and convoy work in the INDIAN OCEAN is referred to in para 39.

35. The air defences of BURMA may be considered as providing the first line of the defence of Eastern INDIA. As regards the A.A. and/or Fighter defence of certain areas in INDIA considered to be vital, *e.g.*, at DIGBOI in ASSAM and in the CALCUTTA-TATANAGAR-ASANSOL Area, we consider it is for the Government of INDIA to frame their own proposals.

36. The above requirements provide for the long term policy to be carried out as aircraft become available. For the immediate problem, we recommend that the aerodromes mentioned in para 31 should be at once developed and stocked in preparation for the forces which may be sent to BURMA FROM MALAYA, or elsewhere. At present, there are no air forces in BURMA, nor are adequate operational facilities available. BURMA is entirely unprotected from air attack, nor can reinforcements be spared from INDIA.

XI. NAVAL DEFENCE

37. (*a*) At this stage, it is difficult to assess the scale of Japanese Naval action against BURMA and in the BAY OF BENGAL, but it appears likely that so long as SINGAPORE remains in our hands, the main form of attack by sea would be an attempt to mine the approaches to RANGOON. This could be done by surface raiders or submarines. Mine laying submarines could approach RANGOON with little difficulty, provided their fuel supply was assured, as BURMA possesses no A/S vessels at present.

(*b*) Mines once laid would probably close the ports of RANGOON for some time as the only M/S vessels available are fitted with a modified form of sweep for "warning" purposes only. No magnetic sweeps are available.

(*c*) There are difficulties in the way of obtaining assistance from INDIA but in a case of grave emergency it is possible that a limited number of A/S and M/S vessels could be made available as a temporary measure for RANGOON, provided that the Japanese were not operating against INDIA'S ports at the time.

38. (*a*) Japanese fishing vessels already in these waters present a considerable menace. Motor vessels of some 70-80 tons, speed 10 knots, and capable of towing 4 to 5 large sampans, could transport up to at least 1,000 troops with stores and light guns from a point such as RENONG (N. W. THAI coast) to VICTORIA POINT, MERGUI and TAVOY. These craft have for years used the waters off BURMA and have operated in the ANDAMANS and NICOBARS and as far north as AKYAB. The motor vessels burn Diesel fuel which is easily transported in barrels and easily concealed in bases such as we must presume exist in the MERGUI ARCHIPELAGO and the ANDAMANS and NICOBARS. By using a route through the latter area, enemy troops could without great difficulty be transported as far to the Northward as AKYAB.

(*b*) The passage of such expeditions as those described above could not be opposed by surface vessels, as the Japanese would make use of little known and extremely shallow passages in which they would not be observed, unless a constant patrol by large numbers of small light-draught craft armed with say 3-pdrs, was maintained. Such craft are not available in anything like the required numbers.

(c) We regard it as essential that arrangements are made by the C.-in-C. concerned to round up all Japanese fishermen in these waters as soon as war is declared. As a first action, tighter control in peace of the granting of licences and increased supervision is necessary.

39. From what has been said in paras 37 and 38 above, it is clearly of the first importance that the necessary reconnaissance aircraft should be available in the ANDAMANS, NICOBARS and MERGUI ARCHIPELAGO areas. An additional and highly important duty to be carried out by these aircraft will be co-operation in the protection of supply convoys from INDIA, when these approach the meridian of 90°E. We recommend that wherever possible advanced bases and wireless stations, with small guards should be provided.

40. The immediate Naval requirements are for A/S patrols and M/S services in the approaches to RANGOON and every endeavour should be made to hasten the building programme already in hand.

XII. Preparations for the Reception of Reinforcements

41. We consider that Army Headquarters in BURMA should be strengthened to deal with the situation which will arise in the event of war with JAPAN, in order to provide for the control operations in addition to the day-to-day administration of the Army.

42. We consider that it is necessary to establish now a R.A.F. group Headquarters organization in BURMA for the command of Units to be located there and the maintenance of the additional operational facilities which we have recommended.

XIII. Command

43. The representative from INDIA raised the general question of command and control of the forces in BURMA.[1] While taking note of this statement, we consider that in view of the definite instructions contained in Telegram, dated 21/9/40, from Secretary of State for Colonies to Governor, STRAITS SETTLEMENTS, and Admiralty Telegram, dated 19/10/40, this question has already been settled in principle by the Chiefs of Staffs.

XIV. Financial Issues In Connection with Defence Preparations

44. If BURMA is to be dependent on some external authority for defence plans and for additional defence forces and preparations, it will be necessary to co-ordinate questions of financial incidence of cost and to provide adequate machinery to ensure that financial sanction for defence purposes is readily and rapidly forthcoming. It is not, we consider, for us to suggest the nature of the machinery required, but the urgent necessity for its provision is stressed, since on financial issues the Governments of BURMA, INDIA and MALAYA will be concerned as well as His Majesty's Government.

XV. Road and Rail Communications

45. Communications in BURMA are generally and strategically inadequate. It is essential that at least adequate roads be provided to the air operational bases selected, to permit of the maintenance of the air forces operating there, as well as of the troops for their protection.

---

[1] See the following Appendix 'C', p. 425.

Statement 'A' referred to in para (24) above.

ARMY REINFORCEMENTS REQUIRED IN BURMA

TOTAL IMMEDIATE REQUIREMENTS	ALREADY AVAILABLE IN BURMA (d)	IMMEDIATE REINFORCEMENTS REQUIRED	ADDITIONAL REINFORCEMENTS REQUIRED FOR LONG TERM PROBLEM
Five Inf. Bdes. with two additional Bns.	Two British Bns.	Two Inf. Bdes. with one additional Bn.	One Division. (c) less Div. Cav. Regt.
One Fd. Regt. and one Bty.	Four Burma Rifle Bns.	One Fd. Regt.	Two Fd. Regts.
Two Mtn. Btys.	One Mtn. Bty.	One Mtn. Bty.	One Fd. Coy.
One A/Tk Bty.	One Fd. Coy.	One A/Tk Bty.	One Inf. Bde.
One Heavy A. A. Regt. (a)	Four Burma Rifle Bns. (b)	One Heavy A. A. Regt. (a)	and with only one A/Tk.
One Lt. A. A. Regt. (non-mobile) of fourteen Tps. (a)	One Fd. Bty. (b) (Of four guns only).	One Lt. A. A. Regt. (non-mobile) of fourteen Tps. (a)	Bty. but with the addition of one Coy. Lt. Tanks.
One Lt. A. A. Bty. (mobile).		One Lt. A. A. Bty. (mobile).	
One Coy. Lt. Tanks.		One Coy. Lt. Tanks.	
Four Fd. Coys.		Three Fd. Coys.	

NOTES

(a) A minimum of 12 Heavy and 8 Light Guns should be provided for the RANGOON-SYRIAM area if the full requirements are not immediately available.
(b) Being raised—available at various dates during 1941.
(c) A Division organised in accordance with W.O. telegram dated 16/10/40 is assumed.
(d) Excluding Territorial and Auxiliary Forces allotted to internal security duties.
(e) The necessary Signal, Transport and Administrative Units will also be required.

XVI. Conclusion

46. The military garrison of BURMA is at present, based on Internal Security requirements alone. Hitherto, the defence of the country from external aggression has rested on the defences of MALAYA and INDO-CHINA.

47. With the forces at present available, the most that can be done is to hold the Northern part of TENASSERIM and RANGOON. The vital installations in the RANGOON Area, the oilfields and the vital installations in Eastern INDIA are entirely unprotected from air attack.

48. We stress the need for the provision of additional forces, particularly Air Forces, anti-aircraft defences, adequate local Naval defence and artillery to support the land forces.

APPENDIX 'C'

Singapore Defence Conference 1940

NOTE ON INDIA'S POSITION IN REGARD TO THE JAPANESE THREAT IN GENERAL AND AGAINST BURMA IN PARTICULAR

(By Major-General G. N. MOLESWORTH, Indian Delegation)

1. This note takes into consideration the following documents which are closely related:
    (a) The C.O.S. appreciation (telegraphed summary) dated 14/8/40.
    (b) The "Tactical Appreciation", dated SINGAPORE, October, 1940.
    (c) The appreciation prepared by the G.O.C., BURMA.
2. As regards (a) and (b) above, INDIA is interested in general and:
    (i) will require to know what requests may be made to her to supply troops, material or supplies for MALAYA or elsewhere.
    (ii) is closely concerned with any arrangements which may affect the security of her Eastern regions, her coasts, ports and territorial waters, which may be affected.
    (iii) is responsible for seeing that her troops sent overseas are adequately maintained and their general welfare safeguarded.

In other words, on general grounds, she is clearly interested in the security of INDIA itself, as it may be affected by the Eastern threat, in her capacity to contribute such aid as may be asked for without undue risk to her own essential commitments and in the adequate administration and maintenance of such forces as she may be able to supply.

As regards (c), INDIA is particularly interested since the defence of BURMA must be closely bound up with the defence of Eastern INDIA.

3. Although certain courses open to the Japanese are, perhaps, on balance, more likely than others and although, on balance, it would appear that an attack on MALAYA and SINGAPORE, is more likely than an attack on BURMA, it would be unwise to assume that what is likely will, in fact, take place, and therefore disregard other possibilities. If JAPAN establishes a foothold in THAILAND, and goes to war with us, an attack on vital targets in BURMA and Eastern INDIA is just as possible as on targets in MALAYA. On the other hand, land and sea attack against BURMA obviously offer much greater difficulties, though the former cannot be entirely discounted. Air attack is, therefore, the danger in which INDIA is closely interested and against which, she considers, adequate preparations should, primarily be made.

4. The targets against which an attack could be made from aerodromes in THAILAND and/or YUNNAN, in which INDIA is closely interested are:
   (a) SYRIAM (RANGOON). This is the site of the B.O.C. refineries. Damage or destruction would greatly affect INDIA'S requirements in P.O.L. of all kinds, including aviation spirit.
   (b) DIGBOI and TINSUKIA (North-East ASSAM). This is a smaller alternative oil supply to RANGOON. If DIGBOI and RANGOON refineries are destroyed, the bulk of INDIA'S P.O.L. and all aviation spirit would have to come from the U.S.A., entailing a delay of two to four months in delivery, even if tanker tonnage is available.
   (c) The industrial area of CALCUTTA and the LOWER GANGETIC PLAIN. This area contains a large proportion of INDIA'S industrial plant, and damage or dislocation of labour would have far-reaching effects on INDIA'S war effort.
   (d) TATANAGAR. This contains INDIA's largest single steel and industrial plant and is classed No. 1 of INDIA'S vital targets. Destruction or serious damage would dislocate INDIA'S production capacity for 12-18 months. The above targets are of Imperial as well as mere local importance.

5. The protection of these vital targets depends largely on the establishment in BURMA of
   (i) Bomber and fighter aircraft.
   (ii) A warning and observer system.

INDIA will, of course, provide her own more local defences, both air and ground, for the protection of targets (b), (c) and (d). But it is quite obvious that any defence in INDIA itself must be closely linked with defences in BURMA, and in any case, the bomber defence must be located in BURMA. Thus INDIA is closely interested in the plans made and the steps taken to implement them.

6. As regards land defence of BURMA, should air attack be supplemented by land attack from THAILAND or YUNNAN, such an attack presents obvious difficulties but might well be made with the object of creating a diversion to a main attack on MALAYA. In this event, it seems unlikely that BURMA could defend herself without land reinforcement. It seems, almost certain that such reinforcement would have to come from INDIA and that INDIA would be called upon to maintain BURMA. If this is correct, INDIA will require to know the extent and nature of the demands which may be made upon her, particularly, as they might be made at very short notice.

7. Finally, there is the question of operational control, operational planning and training. In this connection, the appointment of a C.-in-C. FAR EAST and his responsibilities are noted. It is, however, exceedingly questionable, whether BURMA should form part of the area for which he will be responsible. The main argument for such inclusion appears to be the position of BURMA—from the point of view of air action—on the North-western flank of Japanese forces which may operate from THAILAND and the obvious desirability of co-ordinating air action from BURMA with air action from MALAYA. From all other points of view, the advantages of placing BURMA under the control of INDIA preponderate. The main points in favour of the latter course are:
   (a) Strategically, the defence of INDIA and BURMA cannot be separated. The bulk of land and air forces for the defence of INDIA from the East must be located in BURMA and, therefore, INDIA should have a major voice in the preparations to be made.

(b) BURMA has only recently—some three years ago—been separated from INDIA, for political as distinct from strategical reasons. Her whole organization is entirely Indian in structure.
(c) It is almost certain that reinforcements for BURMA will have to come from INDIA and be maintained by INDIA.
(d) BURMA's resources are small and unless large sums are to be expended—perhaps unnecessarily—full use will have to be made of INDIA'S supply, storage, repair, production and training organizations.

From the point of view of land organization, INDIA would prefer to exercise operational control—with all that implies—in BURMA; the C.-in-C. INDIA working in this respect direct through the WAR Office and not through the INDIA Office, with adequate arrangements for the adjustment of financial questions between the Governments of INDIA, BURMA and the Treasury. As regards the air aspect of the problem, since the air defence of BURMA and INDIA will be closely linked, as also air protection of coasts and ports and convoys in the BAY OF BENGAL, there might be much to be gained, both operationally and administratively, if the air defence of INDIA and BURMA was under the A.O. C.-in-C. INDIA. In connection with preparations for defence and co-ordination of air action with air forces in MALAYA, there should be no difficulty in maintaining the closest liaison between the A.O. C.-in-C. INDIA and the C.-in-C. FAR EAST.

8. The above refers only to control in BURMA. It is a moot point—but one which requires careful consideration—as to whether responsibility for the ANDAMANS and NICOBARS, which are part of INDIA, should not also be an Indian responsibility. The desirability for this may be increased if MADRAS and PENANG are developed for maintenance and reinforcement from INDIA. This again raises a question of the final area of responsibility of the C.-in-C. EAST INDIA Squadron *vis-a-vis* the C.-in-C. CHINA.

APPENDIX 'D'

Headquarters, Army in BURMA,
RANGOON, 25th February, 1941.

To
GENERAL HEADQUARTERS,
FAR EAST,
SINGAPORE.

1. Reference your signal, dated 15th Feb., 41.
2. *Aerodromes.*

The following action has been taken regarding the protection of aerodromes.

(a) *Mingaladon.*
One concrete pill box has been constructed and a number of posts dug. The remaining pill boxes cannot be constructed until the work on the aerodrome is more advanced.
An officers' guard is on duty daily.
Permanent lookouts have been established and a mobile reserve has been organised in MINGALADON Cantonment.

(b) At each of the other operational landing grounds—
AKYAB   LASHIO
MOULMEIN   TAVOY
MERGUI   VICTORIA POINT

there are stationed two pls. of B.F.F. for the close defence of the landing area and installations. Each landing area is covered by two concrete pill boxes holding one V.M.G. each. Two A.A.L.M.Gs. are also sited.

The guards live in the immediate vicinity of their posts, which can consequently be manned in a very short time. As soon as an emergency is declared the pill boxes and A.A.L.M.Gs. will be manned permanently.

(c) MERGUI and VICTORIA POINT are the weak links in the chain of aerodrome defences. MERGUI has an excellent aerodrome and F.B. anchorage and is, therefore, suitable for R.A.F. operations. On the other hand, it is a most difficult place to maintain troops as communications are very bad.

VICTORIA POINT is worse still and would have to be abandoned if seriously attacked.

3. In addition to the guards for the close defence of the landing grounds the towns in which the operational landing grounds are situated are now garrisoned, the role of the garrison being the defence of the area against land, sea and attacks from the air.

4. *Denial Schemes.*
   (a) The foll. aerodromes are kept obstructed with bullock carts and other obstructions when not actually in use:
   SANDOWAY, BASSEIN, MOULMEIN, TAVOY, MERGUI, VICTORIA POINT and LASHIO.
   (b) At AKYAB obstruction material is kept available for immediate use.
   (c) Arrangements have been made with the Civil Authorities for the emergency landing grounds in TENASSERIM to be trenched as soon as the orders are issued from these H.Q.
   (d) MERGUI and VICTORIA POINT aerodromes have been prepared for demolition.

5. *Reinforcements for Frontier Posts.*
   (a) The troops in TENASSERIM are so located that they can reach the frontier on the possible invasion routes well within seven days.
   (b) One Bn. of the Burma Rifles with a Mtn. Bty. and certain administrative units now carrying out Bde. Training in the TAUNGGYI HOPONG area will remain there on the completion of training. Arrangements have been made for moving this Bn. forward to the frontier via KENGTUNG within seven days, should the need arise.
   (c) In the Northern Shan States, F.F. 1 is located at KUTKAI and can reach the frontier within two days or in a few hours by M.T.

6. *Offensive Raids*

Even if it was desirable to use them for the purpose, the Special Coy. is not likely to be ready in time to carry out the tasks envisaged.

The officer who is about to take over command of the Tenasserim Area is being instructed to take immediate steps to organise the raids in question making use of the troops already in the area.

(Sgd). D. K. McLeod,
Major-General,
General Officer Commanding BURMA.
Headquarters, Army in Burma.

APPENDIX 'E'

To
GENERAL HEADQUARTERS,
FAR EAST,
SINGAPORE.

Sir,

Please refer to C.-in-C., CHINA's Admiralty telegram.

1. General MORDAUNT's opinion expressed in para 2 of this telegram coincides with the opinion expressed by General SHANG.

2. The air and land forces required to resist an attack on BURMA are given in the Report of the SINGAPORE Conference, 1940, Part II.

3. Reports on the effect of air bombing in LYBIA and the SUDAN, especially dive bombing, make it clear that our troops will find themselves woefully deficient of A.A. fire which is necessary not only to keep off the enemy but to sustain the morale of the troops.

The long lines of communication on the probable areas of attack are also very vulnerable to air attack. The bombing of the SALWEEN and MEKONG bridges on the CHINA Road gives us a good lesson of the result of having no anti-aircraft guns.

We are very short of Artillery to support our Infantry and to provide mobile beach defence in TENASSERIM.

The enemy use of tanks will be confined to the KENGTUNG line and to seaborne landings on the TENASSERIM coast. Our anti-tank rifles have not yet arrived. We certainly require anti-tank guns to deal with the above.

The provision of more Infantry depends chiefly on the state of the country and how many troops can be spared for frontier defence. Apart from the defence of the RANGOON area, there should be a Brigade available for Internal Security. At present this Brigade is not in the country. It should be embarked in INDIA in order that the 13th Indian Infantry Brigade can be moved forward to the Frontier when required.

Finally, a company of light tanks should be available in order to deal with (a) tanks on the KENGTUNG line, (b) tanks landed on the TENASSERIM coast, or to (c) support a British offensive into THAILAND.

4. Taking these factors into consideration, the order of urgency of the reinforcements required is.—

    1 Heavy A.A. Regiment.
    1 Light A.A. Regiment of 14 guns.
    1 Light A.A. Battery (mobile) on each line of advance.
    3 Field Companies.
    1 Field Regiment R.A.
    1 Anti-tank Battery.
    1 Infantry Brigade.
    1 Company Light Tanks.

It is realised that these forces will not be available at once, but it is considered that plans should be formulated to get these troops from somewhere if an attack on Burma becomes imminent.

5. A land advance into BURMA during the rains is not a practical proposition for a force of any size, so that if the attack does not materialise before May, we should have until November to complete our preparations on land—this will require the Field Companies. Air attack will be possible in the rains, so that the A.A. units should be sent as soon as available.

I have the honour to be
Sir,
Your obedient Servant,
(Sgd.) D. K. McLeod,
Major-General.
General Officer Commanding
BURMA.

APPENDIX 'F'

Subject: JOINT PLANNING.
From : C/S.
To : G.H.Q. F.E.
Dated : 17th April, 1941.

With reference to your's of 7th April, F.E.C.B.'s appreciation is attached.

Japanese action against Aerodromes and Land and Sea Communication in Tenasserim Peninsula

General

1. It is assumed that the primary objects in undertaking operations in the Tenasserim Peninsula will be:—
   (a) To deny the use of aerodromes in the Peninsula to British forces.
   (b) To cause maximum disruption of land and sea communications and port facilities.

Own Information

2. *Moulmein.* (16° 29′ N, 97° 37′ E) in the district of AMHERST is 24 miles from the river entrance, which is navigable for ships with a maximum draught of 23 feet, dependent on tides and depth at the bars.

There are jetties with depths alongside of 4/21 feet at M.L.W.S. and one has a crane of 3-ton capacity. Others are fitted with small hand cranes.

3. 200 Lighters are available, capacities varying from 20-150 tons. There is a small slipway 110′ × 22′ and minor repairs can be undertaken.

4. The railway from Rangoon connects to Martaban, thence by ferry to Moulmein and from Moulmein to Ye in the South. There is a road to MYAWADI on the Thai border.

5. *Tavoy.* (14° 04′ N, 98° 11′ E). Tavoy town is about 32 miles from the sea and ships with a maximum draught of 7 feet can reach the town, dependent on the bar (3′ at M.L.W.S.) and tides. There are jetties available for lighters with one crane of 20 tons, and another of 5-ton capacity. Roads connect to Ye, Palau and Mergui.

6. *Mergui.* (12° 26′ N, 98° 36′ E). The anchorage is near the main wharf jetty, which can be used by small craft only. There is a 5-ton crane available.

A road connects to Tavoy.

Strategical importance of Tenasserim Peninsula

Aerodromes

7. Our own aircraft, with the possible exception of fighters, can fly direct from Rangoon to aerodromes in the Alor Star vicinity without using intermediary aerodromes for refuelling.

8. Shipping. Shipping using ports between Rangoon and Victoria Point consists of small coasters and fishing craft and is of no vital importance.

Facilities available to Japanese, Air

9. The following aerodromes in Thailand would be available:

PITSANULOKE	NAKON SAWAN
KOKE KATHIEM	NAKON PATHOM
DON MAUNG	CHUMPON
PRACHUAB KIRIKHAND	MESAUT
PETZHBURI	

10. Aerodromes available in the extreme south of Thailand are not included, as it is considered that these will be used for attacks on aerodromes in the Alor Star area.

Military

11. It is assumed that the Japanese have large forces in Thailand.

Naval

12. It is assumed that the Japanese will have no defended bases nearer than Thailand or French Indo-China.

Air

13. It is considered that the force necessary for the operation against the aerodromes in Tenasserim Peninsula would be:—
    4 fighter squadrons, 48 aircraft (for escort duties and aerodrome protection).
    4 light bomber squadrons, 48 aircraft.
    3 heavy bomber squadrons, 36 aircraft.

14. Owing to the short distances from base to target it is considered that, at a conservative estimate, aircraft could carry the following bomb loads on each sortie:—

Heavy bomber	1 ton.
Light bomber	½ ton.

Allowing three sorties per aircraft per week for sustained operations a total of 180 tons of bombs per week could be dropped. In the initial stages a slightly heavier scale of attack may be expected.

15. *Distribution of Attack.* It is impossible to forecast the scale of attack that may be expected on any particular target. Owing to the mobility of air forces the operation must be considered as a whole and the weight of

attack may be concentrated on any one target, or distributed over all. It is thought, however, that in the initial stages, attacks will be concentrated on bomb and fuel dumps at the various aerodromes, the road and rail communications to MOULMEIN, the docks at RANGOON and ships close in-shore or unloading on the Tenasserim coast. In view of the small amount of shipping that may be expected in and south of the BAY OF MARTABAN it is thought unlikely that air patrols will be established for attacks on shipping. The provision of 4 fighter squadrons should provide ample fighters for attacks on aircraft either in the air or on the ground.

Military

16. *Moulmein.* Moulmein in the district of Amherst is liable to either seaborne or land attack. The land attack would probably take place along the road from MYAWADI. This road could support one Brigade which could be provisioned by utilizing the air service to MESOD. The road between MYAWADI and KAWKAREIK is over mountainous country and could probably be held by two bns. and one mountain bty.

17. *Tavoy.* The coast from Amherst to Tavoy is suitable for sea landings though the approach to Tavoy by river is fairly difficult. The land approaches from Thailand are not good but it would be feasible for small forces, up to the strength of one bn. to attack from this direction during the dry season.

18. *Mergui.* Owing to its isolated position in regard to communications Mergui would be a difficult place to attack from Thailand. A raiding force possibly of the strength of two companies might make an attempt to destroy the aerodrome there, but it is not considered likely that any larger force would be employed.

19. *Victoria Point.* The proximity of Victoria Point to Thailand renders it very liable to attack. A first class road runs from Moeang Jumbhorn to the Burma border and it is considered that a mixed Bde. could advance along this route. It is considered that one Bde. of inf. and one bty. of field arty. would be required to defend Victoria Point.

Naval

20. As sufficient aerodromes and aircraft would be available in Thailand, it is very unlikely that any Carrier-borne aircraft would be employed even from carriers operating in the Gulf of Siam.

21. It is not considered that the strategical or commercial value of the Tenasserim Peninsula would justify a Japanese naval operation or landing on this coast as a preliminary move.

22. Submarine activity against coastal shipping is a possibility. As this is not important, it is more likely that submarines reaching these waters would attend to shipping on the ocean routes from India and Northern Burma.

F.E.C.B. Singapore.
17th April, 1941.

APPENDIX 'G'

DISCUSSION OF JOINT SINO-BRITISH ACTION TO BE TAKEN IN THE EVENT OF WAR BETWEEN THE BRITISH EMPIRE & JAPAN (JULY–AUGUST, 1941)

During the months of July and August 1941 certain conversations were held at Chung-King between delegates of the British and Chinese Governments in order to arrive at some measure of agreement regarding joint Sino-British action to be taken in the event of a war between the British Empire and Japan. The British delegation was led by Major-General L. E. Denys, Military Attache, and the Chinese delegation was composed of General Shan Chen, General Lin Wei and General Chowchi Jo. The first conversation was held on 24 July, the second on 30 July, the third on 6 August and the fourth on 12 August 1941. After prolonged discussions, one of which (2nd conversation of 30 July) was held during an eight-hour air alarm during which Chung-King was bombed four times, agreement was reached on certain points. The following is a summary (by Major-General L. E. Denys) of the points agreed upon and the recommendations made:—

Subject:	Serial No.	Agreements and Recommendations	Remarks
Strategical	1	China's future as well as Britain's depends on a British victory over Germany. British policy of not provoking war with Japan at present is the natural outcome of using all possible resources for the defeat of Germany.	
	2	Britain's difficulty of giving China assistance in men, and materials while she is at war with Germany is noted.	
	3	(a) If war breaks out between the British Empire and Japan, Britain's first task is to hold Singapore. (b) China's main contribution to the common cause will be to bring increased pressure to bear on the Japanese everywhere in China. (c) Britain will assist her to do so by providing British Officers and contingents of British troops, to augment and extend Guerilla warfare. (d) The British are stocking 4 aerodromes in YUNNAN area and 4 within operational distance of HONG KONG for use for limited periods by British bombers up to a maximum of three squadrons. The decision whether any squadrons can be employed in China and, if so, the number of squadrons and their objectives will rest with the C.-in-C. Far East, Singapore.	

Subject:	Serial No.	Agreements and Recommendations	Remarks
Defence of YUNNAN	4	Agreed that the defence of YUNNAN and of Northern BURMA is a single military problem, *i.e.*, the defence of land communications between RANGOON and CHUNGKING.	
	5	In response to a British request the Chinese delegates gave the British delegates details of their plan for the defence of YUNNAN. These plans include guerilla action against communications in INDO-CHINA and the Chinese would welcome some British Officer advisers for action with these Guerillas. Agreed that the best support Britain could give would be by bomber aircraft. The Chinese formal request was noted that British bombers should operate against Japanese bases in INDO-CHINA if the Japanese attacked the Burma road anywhere, *i.e.*, that they should operate for the defence of the road.	Note the proviso in Serial No. 3 (*d*)
Defence of BURMA	6	The British are pressing on with the defences of BURMA to ensure the safety of Chinese goods in transit and will do everything possible to ensure regular and swift transit of goods through BURMA.	
	7	(*a*) The Chinese agree to station a force of 10,000 men in the PUERHCHELI area for action East of the SALWEEN river against the flank and rear of any Japanese force advancing on or through KENGTUNG. This force will comprise a complete Central Government division and will begin to arrive about mid-November.	Under reference to G.O.C. Army in Burma.
		(*b*) The British will supply rice on payment for this force, from BURMA, including one month's reserve rations in advance. The Chinese request these rations may be delivered as far forward as CHELI.	Recommended to Burma Army.
		(*c*) Recommended that communication in war between this force and the British force in the KENGTUNG area should be by exchange of liaison officers supplemented, if possible, by a land line from PUERH-KENGTUNG.	

GROUP II—APPENDIX G 435

Subject:	Serial No.	Agreements and Recommendations	Remarks
		(d) The Chinese to provide details of their normal ground-to-air signals for recognition of troops. British to provide silhouettes for recognition of British Aircraft.	
	8	The Chinese agree to stocking aerodromes in Burma for use by International Air Force squadrons if Burma is attacked. The Generalissimo will decide whether any squadrons will be sent, and if so how many, and may withdraw them to China when he considers necessary.	Details of aerodromes to be stocked and amount of stocks remain to be settled.
Defence of HONG KONG	9	If HONG KONG is besieged the Chinese will undertake a strong offensive from the north-east to join up with the British garrison about KOWLOON, get supplies into HONG KONG and evacuate civilians. This plan pre-supposes that the Japanese in the CANTON-HONG KONG area have not been strongly reinforced. The British will give such Naval and Air support to the Chinese attack as is possible in the circumstances existing at the time.	Note proviso to serial No. 3(d).
Training facilities for the International Air Force	10	In response to Chinese requests the International Air Force have been allotted a second aerodrome at MAGWE, in addition to the aerodrome at TOUNGOO. They have been granted full facilities for assembling aircraft and training of pilots including mounting of guns and operational training.	
Transportation	11	The Chinese have accepted a tentative offer of assistance by Supply Base, Burma in seeing that International Air Force supplies are despatched expeditiously from Burma and in the right order of priority.	Details of exactly what assistance is required and the order of priority will be furnished by the Chinese.
	12	The Chinese have accepted in principle that they should transport British Air Force supplies from KUNMING to railhead near ISHAN provided the British will transport an equal amount of International Air Force supplies from LASHIO to KUNMING.	Details of the amount of supplies which are required to be transported will be furnished by the British.

Subject:	Serial No.	Agreements and Recommendations	Remarks
Communications	13	(a) Both Chinese and British realise the immense importance of increasing the intake of goods to China by the BURMA ROAD. The Chinese Government are taking urgent steps to reorganise the traffic on this road and improve the road surface. (b) The Chinese Government propose to complete the road BHAMO-TENGYUEN-PAOSHAN and request that the Government of Burma be asked to complete the portion of this road in Burma. (c) The Chinese have asked for assistance in making the India-Thibet-China Road.	

Miscellaneous	14	The following requests made by the Chinese during the conversations have been referred to H.M. Government:
		(a) A strong request that Britain should provide fighter pilots for the 144 Vultees released for China from British orders in America.
		(b) A request that 20 Radio D.F. sets be released for China from British orders in America.
		(c) A request that 20 T.R.9D. sets for ground use and 500 T.R.9D. sets for use in the air be loaned by Britain to China.
		(d) A request to increase the number of junior Chinese Naval Officers and ratings to serve with the Royal Navy anywhere in the world and so form the foundation of the Chinese Navy of the future.
		(e) A request for three experts as advisers in
		  1. Tactical training of guerillas.
		  2. Rapid demolitions in the field.
		  3. Mine making and mine laying in rivers.
		to be taken on contract with the Chinese Government with terms similar to those of Lt.-Colonel Dawson, adviser to the Tank Training School.
		(f) A request that Battalion and Company advisers now under training in Burma should come to China, if time permits, on contract to train Chinese Guerilla Coys.
			The S. of S. for Foreign Affairs has informed the Chinese Ambassador in London that pilots cannot be provided.
			
			The number previously under reference to H.M. Government was 6-8 Officers.
			
			The War Office have stated that this cannot be sanctioned at present.

APPENDIX 'H'

Telegram
From—Governor of Burma.
To—Viceroy.
Dated—12th December, 1941.

Appreciation from G.O.C., Burma

1. Enemy's object in attacking Burma would be (*a*) to cut air reinforcement route, (*b*) to cut Burma road, (*c*) to prevent reinforcements going to Singapore, and (*d*) to cause internal disturbances in Burma.

2. (*a*) Enemy forces available; ample, but limited by terrain—probably one or two divisions directed on southern Shan States and one division on TENASSERIM strongly supported by air. (*b*) Air attacks on aerodrome, Rangoon docks and oil refineries. (*c*) Raiders to stop supplies and reinforcements including lease lend for China.

3. Our plans hitherto have been on certain assumption (*a*) that Japan could not send convoys through Gulf of Siam because they would be too vulnerable to air and sea attack. Therefore, number of troops employed would be limited by land communications. This no longer applies. Japan is landing troops at Bangkok and at all ports on KRA and our forces are not able to stop them, (*b*) line of approach to Burma very vulnerable to British air attack; therefore, number of ground troops required could be cut down but this does not now apply as we have no bombers.

Comment. Enemy scale of attack can be increased over original estimate. Our scale of resistance considerably reduced by Absence of any air support.

4. *Conclusion.* Following additions are required to cope with present situation:

(*a*) Land forces for Tenasserim.
    1 Infantry Brigade.
    1 Field Battery.

(*b*) Land forces for southern Shan States.
    1 Infantry Brigade.
    1 Field Regiment.

(*c*) To support army after invasion by enemy we should have at our disposal
    3 Bomber Squadrons.
    2 Fighter Squadrons.

APPENDIX 'I'

Appreciation of the Situation in Burma by General Staff, India, on 15th December, 1941.

1. OBJECT

To resist a Japanese advance towards Burma and India and to cut Japanese communications down the Malaya Peninsula.

FACTORS AFFECTING THE ATTAINMENT OF THE OBJECT

2. COMMUNICATIONS

The main Japanese communications in Northern Thailand follow the Bangkok-Chiengmai railway. This is a metre gauge railway the capacity of which is calculated at 1,500 tons a day both ways. There is ample rolling stock. There is no road following the railway alignment.

Other communications leading northwards from Bangkok are confined to the River Chao Bhraya as far north as Paknam Po. On this stretch of the river I.W.T. could be used. Northwards of Paknam Po the strength of the current and the teak logs being floated down the river make it useless for navigational purposes.

There is no road north of Lop Buri until Lampang (on the railway) is reached. From Lampang a good motor road exists to Chiengmai in a north-westerly direction. Northwards from Lampang there is a first class two-way motor road to Chiengrai, and northwards from this place to the Burma frontier. From the Burma frontier the road continues to Kengtung and thence westwards to Taunggyi on the Burma railway. The portion of this road in Burma is only of a dry-weather standard for heavy motor traffic and there are no bridges over big rivers. The Salween crossing is carried out by ferry (one vehicle at a time). The current is between 10 to 15 m.p.h. and the breadth of the river is about 300 yards.

The estimated capacity of the road in Burma is one division maximum to the frontier, and then only in dry weather, two divisions from the frontier to Lampang.

From Chiengmai there is an all-weather route leading north-west to Taunggyi. Parts of this road are little better than a track. Japanese maintenance capacity one brigade maximum.

3. Communications leading westwards from Thailand into Burma are as follows:

   (a) A dry-weather road and track from Chiengmai to Mawchi across the Burma frontier. Maintenance capacity one Coy.
   (b) A dry-weather road and track from Chiengmai through Mesarieng to Papun in Burma which is connected by an M.T. route running south to Bilin on the Martaban Pegu railway. One brigade maximum could be maintained by this road in dry weather.
   (c) From the branch line at Sawarngalok a motor road to Reheng and thence by track to Mesoht and across the Burma frontier at Myawadi where an all-weather motor road leads to Moulmein or alternatively to Kyondo for communication with Moulmein by river. Estimated capacity one division if moved by brigade groups and also if maintenance is supplemented by air.

There are other routes leading into Burma from Central Thailand but these are not considered fit for wheeled traffic even in the dry season.

4. In the South Thai Peninsula, the Thailand State Railway follows the east coast to Singora where one branch continues to the Malaya border at Kota Bharu and another branch crosses to the west coast and joins with the Malayan railway system at Padang Besar.

The railway junction at Head Yai is, therefore, an important target. This is a modern metre gauge railway with frequent passing places and Diesel locomotives. Estimated capacity 1,500 tons a day both ways.

The following roads into Burma from Thailand exist:
- (a) From Prachuab Kirikhan there is a motor road to the Burma frontier. From there over the Mandaung Pass a very difficult track leads over the hills and from thence to Tenasserim and Mergui. There is an alternative river communication between Tenasserim and Mergui. This road is estimated to be able to maintain one battalion.
- (b) From Jumbhorn a motor road leads westwards to Taplee and from thence southwards to Victoria Point. From Taplee to Victoria Point is an alternative river route.

There is no through road communication from Bangkok southwards. There is a road from Hu Hin through Prachuab Kirikhan, Jumbhorn and Nagorn Sridharmrat which continues to Singora and thence via Yala towards the Malayan frontier at Tumpat.

5. From the above it is clear that the junctions of communications in Northern Thailand are at Chiengmai, Lampang and Bandara from which the branch line to Sawarngalok takes off. In the Southern Thai Peninsula the most important junctions are Prachuab Kirikhan, Jumbhorn and Head Yai.

Taking maintenance facilities into account, the most important junctions are Chiengmai, Lampang and Bandara.

The most vulnerable portion of enemy communications in Northern Thailand appears to lie between Lampang and Lop Buri where he has no road with which to supplement his railway communications. The country north of Lop Buri to Lampang consists of rice fields and dense jungle intersected by many rivers and is only approachable by the Moulmein-Raheng-Sawarngalok road.

6. CLIMATE

The rainy season in Thailand and Burma starts about May and clears up about October. Rains are exceptionally heavy and seriously impede movement. Dry weather is from November to April. It appears, therefore, that any large-scale operations must be undertaken during the latter period.

7. STRENGTH OF OPPOSING FORCES

Thai Forces
- 45 Infantry Battalions.
- 15 Artillery Regiments.
- 5 Cavalry Regiments.
- 1 A.A. Group (3 bns.)
- 2 Tank Regiments.

Note: (i) An Infantry Bn. consists of 450 men.
Note: (ii) An Artillery Regt. has four 75-mm guns and there is one Regt. with four 105-mm guns and eight 150-mm howitzers.

Air Forces
- 108 Fighters
- 52 Bombers
- 36 Army Co-operation
- 18 Floatplanes

Japanese Forces

It is estimated that there are now some 4 Japanese divisions in Thailand, 2 of which are operating against the North Malayan frontier.

Some 200 Japanese aircraft are already in Thailand at the moment and it is estimated that this number will be increased by at least a further 100.

Any operations undertaken by us into Thailand are likely to be opposed by the Thais.

8. BRITISH FORCES IN BURMA

Apart from units engaged on internal security duties, these consist of:
One Burma Division, H.Q. Toungu with Brigade Groups at Moulmein (less one bn.) and Kengtung, guarding the eastern frontier, with one Ind. Inf. Bde. in reserve at Taunggyi. In addition there is one bn. at Tavoy and another at Mergui in the Tenasserim area. 16 Ind. Inf. Bde. is arriving in the country as Burma Army reserve to be stationed initially in the area Mandalay-Thazi-Meiktila.

It is considered that the above troops on their present scale of transport and armament, particularly their paucity of artillery, would be unable successfully to undertake any offensive operations into Thailand.

9. THE IMPORTANCE OF RANGOON

Rangoon forms the only effective means of entry into Burma. Its protection is, therefore, of the utmost importance. The road now under construction between Assam and Burma can only be a supplement and can never be a substitute for the port.

10. COURSES OPEN TO THE JAPANESE

They already have four divisions in Thailand and possible elements of a fifth division. Two divisions are operating against Malaya and two have landed in the Bangkok area. The leading elements of these are reported to be at Lampang.

11. COURSE I

To continue the attack on Malaya and to reinforce this, if necessary, by rail from Bangkok. At the same time to sever communications between Burma and Malaya by cutting the air route down the west coast by capturing Tavoy, Mergui and Victoria Point. This course makes full use of Thailand communications to maintain forces operating against Malaya and avoids the dangers of sea communications to some extent. It leaves the forces remaining in Thailand free to push northwards to establish aerodromes from which Burma and the Burma Road can be attacked by air, thereby diverting forces which might possibly be sent to Malaya. It does not, however, allow Japanese forces to develop their full strength against Burma even by the limited approaches available. This is not a serious consideration so long as the momentum of the attack against Malaya can be maintained and the attacking forces in that area can be kept free from hostile air attacks from the north. The latter consideration is of paramount importance both as regards sea and land communications. As a short term policy this course has much to recommend it as the attack on Malaya must have first priority and forces in Thailand are in a position to support this. Forces not employed for this purpose are free to develop and stock aerodromes in Thailand from which far-reaching air attacks can be carried out against Burma and China.

12. Course II

To rely on the forces attacking Malaya being maintained and reinforced by sea. To employ the forces in the Bangkok area for the subsidiary purpose of capturing Tavoy, Mergui and Victoria Point and the main operation of establishing aerodromes in North Thailand with a view to giving the maximum support to an advance by land on Kengtung and Taunggyi at an early date before the rainy season. An advance on Moulmein via Raheng could be combined with the advance northwards to Kengtung.

This course would permit the Japanese to develop the maximum possible strength permitted by land communications against Burma and, if successful, should cut the Burma Road thereby eliminating China from the war and freeing considerable forces for operations elsewhere. India's main industrial areas would be under the threat of air attack and whatever stage had been reached in the operations against Singapore, reinforcements from India could not be spared for that place even if they could be sent, owing to the uncertainty of the internal situation in India itself.

13. As far as can be foreseen from the present situation the Japanese seem likely to adopt Course I followed by Course II. They may, however, consider that maintenance and reinforcement of their forces operating in North Malaya can continue to be carried out by sea. In this case Course II can proceed simultaneously with Course I.

14. Courses Open to Ourselves

The tasks before us are:
 (a) To defend Burma.
 (b) To cut Japanese communications down the Malaya, Peninsula.

Action with regard to (a) can be taken immediately but in respect of (b) actions must be comparatively long-term, especially in view of the organisation, equipment, and numbers of troops now in Burma.

15. Course I

To start preparing defences on the frontier at all places where useful routes lead from Thailand into Burma. These defences should be used as pivots of manoeuvre from which small mobile guerilla columns can operate into Thailand. This form of operation would be specially useful from the Tenasserim area against aerodromes and against railway communications south of Bangkok. It must be realised, however, that the cutting of the railway between Bangkok and Jumbhorn will not necessarily have any effect on the maintenance of Japanese forces operating towards Malaya.

The formation and training of these mobile columns should be put in hand at once. This course is the only one which admits of our taking some immediate action to comply with the first task set to us and, at the same time, admits of a minimum of offensive operations. If the static defences are skilfully planned they should be of great value as pivots of manoeuvre for future operations. As large a number of air forces as can be made available should be located in Burma at an early date so as to increase our offensive efforts and, at the same time, protect Burma from hostile air action.

16. Course II

Simultaneously with Course I above to build up a field force in Burma of not less than two divisions and, having completed this concentration to take action against Japanese forces in Northern Thailand. This operation would have to be staged before April 1942, and might take the form of moving one division on Lampang via the Kengtaung-Chiengrai route. At the same time the maximum force (probably only two brigades) to be moved from the Moulmein area via Raheng on Sawarngalok. This operation would result in cutting off all Japanese forces in the Chiengmai area. The disadvantages of this course are that the northern column would have to traverse a distance of some 200 miles from Kengtung, and would be forced to move on a narrow front for the greater part of the distance. It should thus be fairly easy for the Japanese to delay an advance from this direction. An advance from the Moulmein area suffers from the same disadvantage of being confined to a narrow front and in consequence, being fairly easy to delay.

For these reasons this course is not recommended.

17. Course III

To hold the northern frontier defences of Thailand and to carry out heavy bombing attacks against Japanese aerodromes and army concentrations in northern Thailand and, at the same time, to push forward small mobile detachments from the frontier defences with a view to giving the impression of a converging forward movement by all available routes leading into northern Thailand. Having drawn the maximum Japanese forces into northern Thailand, the main advance should be carried out by the route Moulmein-Raheng-Sawarngalok, if necessary as a methodical operation, improving the road as the advance takes place to a standard sufficient to maintain at least one division.

A successful advance by this route should enable us to cut the main railway line in northern Thailand, and to leave Japanese forces in the northern areas without maintenance except by air.

This operation would have to be accompanied by heavy air action against Bangkok and against communications running north from there to Sawarngalok. Continuous fighter cover would be necessary for the land forces operating on the Moulmein-Raheng-Sawarngalok route.

18. Course IV

To carry out the operation outlined above from Moulmein to Sawarngalok and to clear the Tenasserim area with infantry forces. The latter operation would be difficult from the point of view of maintenance as there is no railway south of Ye. Even if the Tenasserim area were cleared, it would not accomplish any important military object and would probably entail holding troops in this area in order to keep it clear. For this reason this course is not recommended.

19. Of the above courses, Course III appears to offer the best results.

20. The above review of courses open to us is of a local and limited character. The adoption of Courses I to III will enable us to defend Burma, but none of these courses will enable us to cut communications between Thailand and Malaya effectively.

21. It is, therefore, necessary to consider the wider strategic aspects of Chinese co-operation.

The Chinese armies in South China appear to be suitably situated to move southwards against Thailand and into China. A small Chinese force is already in Eastern Burma near Kengtung. From information available it appears that the main Chinese effort is being made towards trying to assist Hong Kong. While this is all to the good, it appears to be a dispersion of effort against what seems to be a somewhat doubtful task, unless the Chinese have sufficient forces to spare for the purpose without detriment to other operations. One of the main Chinese objects must be to keep the Burma Road open. The country south of this road appears generally to favour operations in a southerly direction and to be unfavourable to operations from west to east owing to the general lie of the land. It appears, therefore, that an initial move on the part of the Chinese from Yunnan into North Thailand might meet with considerable success, if carried out before the Japanese could consolidate themselves in that area. They will have to protect their left flank against Japanese attacks from Indo-China, but a successful operation into North Thailand might place them in a position from which they could extend their pressure against North Indo-China. The whole matter should be discussed as early as possible with the Chinese authorities with a view to formulating a strategic plan of operations in which we can co-operate to the maximum of our ability. Such a plan is urgently required and could not be drawn up without direct intercourse with the Chinese.

22. CONCLUSIONS

(*i*) Land operations from Burma into Thailand are limited by communications. Maintenance capacity of these communications indicates that a force of two divisions is about the maximum that can be employed against Thailand from Burma. (Paras 2 and 3).

(*ii*) Operations on land will probably not be possible after April 1942. (Para 7).

(*iii*) Our forces at present in Burma are insufficient to undertake any offensive operations in Thailand. (Para 9).

(*iv*) The importance of Rangoon as a means for entering into Burma cannot be over-stressed. (Para 10).

(*v*) The Japanese are likely to consolidate their position in North Thailand as soon as possible and to attempt to cut the Burma Road. An invasion of Burma may take place at a later date as soon as they have sufficient air support. Such an invasion is likely to be directed at Rangoon using the routes from Chiengmai and Sawarngalok. (Paras 12 & 13).

(*vi*) Our action at the moment must be defensive and should be designed to hold the main approaches into Burma from Thailand. Meanwhile, we should build up forces in Burma as rapidly as possible to a strength of at least two divisions with the object of taking offensive action at a later date in conjunction with the Chinese. (Paras 16, 17, 18).

(*vii*) Early conversations with the Chinese with a view to framing a strategic plan for the future are essential. (Para 22).

23. RECOMMENDATIONS

(*i*) The maximum air forces should be put into Burma as early as possible.

(*ii*) Burma should be ordered to construct defences at all approaches crossing the frontier from Thailand.

(*iii*) Mobile guerilla forces should be organised forthwith in Burma.

(*iv*) A force of two divisions should be transported from India to Burma at the earliest possible date.

(*v*) Staff conversations with the Chinese should be held at an early date with a view to formulating a strategic plan for the future and examining the possibilities of immediate Chinese action against the Japanese forces now in North Thailand.

APPENDIX 'J'

APPRECIATION BY GENERAL HUTTON, G.O.C., BURMA ARMY, MADE AT RANGOON ON 10 JAN. 1942.

OBJECT:

(1) To stabilise the position in Burma against enemy attack and to consider the steps required to enable an offensive from Burma to be undertaken.

CONSIDERATIONS AFFECTING ACHIEVEMENT OF THE OBJECT:

(2) Approaches to Burma—

The layout of the road and rail communications in THAILAND indicate certain places as concentration areas and Adv. bases for any attack in Burma.

These are:
CHIENGRAI and CHIENGMAI in NORTH THAILAND
RAHENG in WEST THAILAND.

An advance beyond CHIENGRAI would be carried out by the existing M.T. road from the border at TACHILEK via KENGTUNG on to TAKAW.

From CHIENGMAI no M.T. routes extend into Burma, but there are a large number of pack tracks and some cart tracks which would enable small columns on a pack basis to move across the SHAN and KARENNI hills on a wide front between KENGTUNG and TOUNGOO.

The approaches from RAHENG could probably be improved up to the border to take M.T. without much difficulty. At present it is a cart track only. A cart track, probably suitable already for light tanks, enters AMHERST Province some 100 miles SOUTH of the RAHENG road by the THREE PAGODA PASS and joins the RAHENG-MOULMEIN road WEST of KAWKAREIK.

There are subsidiary approaches from the BANGKOK-KRA ISTHMUS railway leading towards TAVOY and MERGUI. These are pack tracks only but distances are comparatively small and a threat against TAVOY might intervene at short notice.

The sea approach from the KRA ISTHMUS up the WEST COAST of TENASSERIM is important. Small craft can infiltrate up the inshore creeks, where they are immune from seaward attack and difficult to be seen from the air, as far as MERGUI. The Japanese have studied this and are known to be collecting small craft SOUTH of VICTORIA POINT.

Generally speaking, attacks against BURMA may be anticipated as under:

Based on CHIENGRAI aimed at KENGTUNG and TAKAW, possibly in some force on an M.T. basis.

Based on CHIENGMAI: Light Mobile colns.; on a pack basis moving on several tracks penetrating between incl. TAKAW and TOUNGOO.

Based on RAHENG: aimed at MOULMEIN and supported by subsidiary advances by the THREE PAGODA PASS and against TAVOY. This advance may further be supported by small craft infiltrating up the coast with MERGUI as their objective.

(3) CHARACTERISTICS OF THE OPERATIONAL AREAS

The whole of the country EAST of the SALWEEN river is for the most part heavily forested and extremely mountainous. Progress off tracks extremely arduous and difficult. The SALWEEN river is a major obstacle and there are no bridges across it. Local ferries with poor facilities only exist.

TENASSERIM is guarded by the DAWNA range also precipitous in places and heavily afforested. This range, however, has not the depth possessed by the mountains of the SOUTHERN SHAN STATES. All valleys are extremely malarious.

(4) WEATHER CONDITIONS

The best period for operations is Autumn and Winter. The rains start in May and after they have set in properly, waterlogged paddy is liable to seriously impede movement. TENASSERIM in particular is practically under water from June till September.

Rains do not affect operations in the SHAN STATES to the same extent but will considerably complicate maintenance.

(5) DEDUCTIONS
  (a) Approaches to BURMA from THAILAND in TENASSERIM offer the most direct and shortest approach with less depth in the natural obstacles to an enemy advance.
  (b) An advance into TENASSERIM can be assisted by sea-borne operations on the WEST COAST.
  (c) From the point of view of the defence the mountainous country in the SOUTHERN SHAN STATES offers great scope for delaying action and the further the enemy advances into BURMA the greater the difficulty he will have in maintaining his communications.
  (d) Active operations, particularly in TENASSERIM, are likely to stop after May owing to adverse weather.

(6) JAPANESE FORCES AND TACTICS

Present estimate puts Japanese forces in THAILAND at about three Divs. To this must be added the THAI Army which must be regarded as definitely hostile and probably anxious to co-operate with the Japanese with a view to regaining TENASSERIM for themselves.

There is no reason to suppose that the Japanese cannot bring considerably greater strength than 3 Divs. to bear against BURMA and the only limiting factor is really the difficulties of maintenance on the approaches to BURMA. There is evidence that the latter are being rapidly improved.

(7) The Japanese tactics have always been to envelop and to move on a wide front. Wherever possible they make full use of landing operations in rear or in the flank of their main advance. In attack they are enterprising and prone to take risks and their wide enveloping movements are often carried out without regard to possibility of support in face of counter-attack. They move very lightly equipped, require little maintenance and are prepared to live on the country with little regard to proper maintenance facilities and with no regard to bodily comfort.

Japanese, like the Germans, are fully aware of the importance of air superiority and their tactics to date have been designed to secure aerodrome areas from where they can deploy their air effort to the fullest extent. They have made use of parachute troops but not apparently with any outstanding ability.

(8) DEDUCTIONS
  (a) It is reasonable to assume that the enemy will deploy the greatest possible strength on as wide a front and on as many approaches as possible. It is unwise to assume that because we might have difficulty in maintaining a Bde. by any particular approach the Japanese will have similar difficulty. They will not, and may in effect maintain more than a Bde. on such an approach.

(b) Wherever possible a land advance will be supported by landings from the sea and we may expect this technique in TANASSERIM.

(c) We may anticipate that any major offensive will be prepared by attempts to secure aerodromes or landing grounds which will enable the enemy to push forward his air effort to render the greatest possible support to his troops and from where he can attack our vital centres. We may expect him to use parachute troops in support of his advance.

(9) INTERNAL SITUATION

The possibility of organised rebellion in BURMA at this particular time does not appear to be great. At the same time there are many disaffected elements and probably a number of Japanese sympathisers. There is a considerable Chinese population, particularly in RANGOON, and it is possible that a proportion of these may not be adherents of the Chiang Kai Shek regime.

The effect of air bombing and its consequent hardships is likely to have a considerable effect on the Burmese. Privation, compulsory or voluntary evacuation of bombed centres, and consequent lack of livelihood may result in considerable disaffection existing and possibly anti-British demonstrations.

(10) DEDUCTIONS

We must anticipate fifth column activity, sabotage and having to control large numbers of homeless and disaffected people. This will call for adequate protection of vital points, the maintenance of strong mobile columns and, above all, the availability of British troops in an Internal Security role.

(11) We must be prepared to take over with military resources transportation services, P and T road and ferry maintenance and all labour at important ports such as RANGOON.

BURMA COMMUNICATIONS

(12) LAND AND RIVER COMMUNICATIONS

Our present vital communications may be summarised as under:
Railway system between RANGOON and THAZI, between RANGOON and MARTABAN, between THAZI and MANDALAY.
River system between RANGOON and MANDALAY.

At present no communication by land exists with INDIA. Further, no road exists yet between MOULMEIN and YE, and an indifferent road fit for 30 cwt vehicles only exists between TAKAW FERRY on the SALWEEN and LOIMWE. There are a number of vital bridges or ferries on the above communications the destruction of which would probably prejudice the road or rail communications for a considerable time. The most important of these are:

Between Rangoon and Moulmein
　　　BILIN river bridge
　　　SITTANG river bridge
　　　PEGU river bridge
On Shan States Area L of C
　　　KUNHING BRIDGE
　　　TAKAW FERRY
　　　MARTABAN FERRY

(13) SEA COMMUNICATIONS

There is only one port at present in existence capable of dealing with the inflow of stores, equipment, reinforcements, etc., necessary for the security of

Burma. This is RANGOON. On the maintenance of facilities at this port further depends our ability to continue to pass Lease and Lend materials to CHINA and without this assistance it is not improbable that CHINA'S resistance might crumble.

Various factors affecting the ability of RANGOON to continue functioning as the main distributing centre for BURMA and CHINA are:
- (a) Our ability to secure it from destruction by air attack.
- (b) Our ability to prevent decisive threats to sea communications entering RANGOON Port.
- (c) Our ability to prevent minelaying attack from rendering RANGOON RIVER unusable.
- (d) Our ability to defend RANGOON against a sea-borne attack either by ship bombardment or landings.

The only alternative ports available are BASSEIN and MOULMEIN. The latter is unlikely to be of much value as it is difficult to give air protection to it and at present it is subjected to fighter escorted bomber attack.

(14) AIR COMMUNICATIONS

There are alternative air reinforcement routes:
- (a) CALCUTTA-AKYAB-RANGOON.
- (b) CHITTAGONG-MYTKYINA-RANGOON.

At present no landing ground exists in the ANDAMANS and consequently air communication with this island is limited to sea planes.

Air route exists to CHUNGKING in CHINA.

(15) CONSIDERATION OF COMMUNICATIONS AS A WHOLE

The importance of RANGOON is obvious from the above. The enemy will appreciate this fact and we may anticipate a heavy scale attack to be made on this port. There are also many opportunities for breaking communications outside RANGOON particularly at vital bridges. These must, therefore, be adequately protected.

(16) DEDUCTIONS

- (a) It is obviously a matter of primary importance to find if possible not only an alternative port to RANGOON but also an alternative overland route to INDIA. The most promising port is BASSEIN.
- (b) The need for keeping RANGOON going as a base port involves a heavy scale of fighter and AA defence, adequate coastal recce against submarine attack, ensuring the security of the ANDAMAN and NICOBAR islands, now under operational control of BURMA, against establishment of enemy air and submarine bases, a Mine Watching organisation in the RANGOON RIVER and finally preparations to defeat an enemy landing attempt against RANGOON.
- (c) Protection of vital points including bridges, on our vital road and rail system of communications involves provision of strong mobile columns and standing guards.
- (d) To minimise the results of successful attacks against these road and rail communications we must exploit to the utmost the possibilities of river transport.
- (e) Adequate supplies of all materials and reserves of ammunition equipment, etc., must be brought into BURMA as early as possible. These measures must include food supplies, etc., for the civil populations of RANGOON.
- (f) No congestion must be permitted at RANGOON. It must be treated as far as possible as a transit area.

(17) MILITARY SITUATION IN BURMA ON THE OUTBREAK OF WAR WITH JAPAN

Burma was under the Far East Command and relied for reinforcement, administrative assistance, etc., on the War Office. As a result of the occupation of Central THAILAND by the enemy, Burma was placed under operational and administrative control of India very early in the War.

The proximity of her frontiers to a strong enemy made a matter of pressing importance the strengthening of Burma's Defence Forces and the complete reorganisation of her military system. Plans were made with India for the immediate expansion of Army H. Qs. of subordinate H. Qs. for the provision of reinforcements of men, resources and equipment.

All forms of adm. installations, signal comms. transportation base depots and repair resources were found to be inadequate for field operations with an expanded force. Intelligence was practically non-existent. Plans for the immediate despatch of urgent requirements were made on an *ad hoc* basis, and before a proper appreciation either G or Q had been made. In the interim Burma was incorporated in the new Pacific Command and again divorced from India.

In addition Burma was given the additional responsibility of protection of the ANDAMANS and NICOBARS.

The fact remains that at present India is the only source of these urgent reinforcements and supplies for Burma which will enable her to defend her frontiers, and failing the arrival of these resources already allotted plus such other requirements which will become evident as a result of the plan framed from this appreciation, a serious state of affairs will ensue.

(18) DEDUCTIONS

Any plan must be based on the assumption that India will continue to provide the resources already promised. The exact position regarding Burma's future source of supply of reinforcements and equipment must be cleared up with the Supreme Command and India. The plan must include a statement of minimum forces considered necessary for the stabilisation of the Burma front.

(19) CO-OPERATION WITH CHINA
OFFER OF TROOPS

The Central Govt. offered early the co-operation of certain Chinese Troops. This was subject to the proviso that these troops should be given their own area of operations away from British or Burmese forces, and that the responsibility for maintenance should be taken on by Burma. The troops offered comprise the 5th Army 93rd Div. and 49th Div., and the 6th Army comprising three Divs.

Of these troops the 6th Army is well equipped and considered to be the best fighting formation in the Chinese Army. The 5th Army is poorly equipped. A mechanised force including tanks forms part of the 6th Army.

It is obviously advantageous to employ these troops in the North rather than in TENASSERIM. The difficulties of road and rail commun: anywhere EAST of the NAMPO River render their employment in force difficult unless they are given the TAKAW-LOIMWE road for maintenance. Nevertheless, the presence of the troops in number in the North of Burma constitutes a threat to any enemy advance westwards in the S.S.S.

(20) DEDUCTIONS

At present the only way of employing effectively the whole available strength of the 5th and 6th Chinese Armies would be to give them the TAUNGGYI-TAKAW-LOIMWE L of C. If this is not possible we can maintain in the operational area and keep the remainder back as a potential threat to the flank of an enemy advance.

The latter distribution is probably the best if we are considering offensive action later on, as it retains the well equipped 6th Army as a potential striking force.

(21) LEASE AND LEND MATERIAL

A great quantity of this material (some 100,000 tons) is at present congesting RANGOON dock area. There are reported to be a considerable number of ships en route from AMERICA bringing more. There is another large dump at LASHIO. The amount that can be taken up into CHINA, under existing conditions and including both rail and road facilities, is limited, and it is estimated that to clear RANGOON of its present accumulation, assuming no more shipments arrived, would take several months. Included in this lease-lend material there is a great deal of equipment greatly needed for the defence of BURMA. Such equipment includes sig. equipment of all natures, L. As, Light Carriers, explosive, M.T., etc. At present the policy is that BURMA may not touch this except by express consent of the Chinese Central Government, which is very difficult to obtain.

DEDUCTIONS

To keep RANGOON from being congested, lease-lend material must be removed urgently from the dock area to suitable storage accommodation, further shipments should be stopped until existing congestion is cleared, and a priority policy is necessary from WASHINGTON as to the best distribution of existing stocks to meet the present situation.

(22) OWN RESOURCES

The availability of fighting formations is summarised in the following table:

	Operational	L of C, I.S. and Static protection of V.P.s and aerodromes.
Available now.	2 Divs. each of two Inf. Bdes. 5 Bns. F.F.	About nine Inf. Bns. or their equivalent of which one is British.
Reinforcements By 20 Jan. By 10 Feb. By Mid March	One Inf. Bde. One Inf. Bde. Two African Inf. Bdes.	

We are short of Arty. all natures, tanks, R.E., M.T. and also of Inf. for I.S. and Static roles.

So far as Burma's resources are concerned, it is unlikely that any additional regular Burma Bn. could be formed owing to the existing paucity of reinforcements and inadequacy of recruitment.

The Territorial force units are of very questionable reliability and must be regarded only on the same level as Garrison Coys. There is only one B.I. Bn. available for I.S. duties. This is kept concentrated at RANGOON for use in emergency of Rangoon Fortress Area. The seaward C. D. Defences of Rangoon Fortress itself are limited to a Bty. of two six-inch guns. This is an examination battery only and has no counter bombardment role.

There is at present a lack of co-ordination in the Sea, Land, Air Defence of Rangoon, and resources available or even foreseeable, do not appear to be adequate against anything except a very light scale of attack.

The working of Rangoon Port including provision of labour, etc., is the responsibility of the Civil Authorities. Air raids, etc., have proved to have a disastrous effect on labour, which is apt to fade away in the night.

Railways, roads and Posts and Telegraphs, on which the Army must depend entirely for movement and to a large extent for inter-communication, are under the respective Civil Authorities. Powers do exist for militarising these organisations in emergency, but taking over would naturally place a great strain on Military Staff and resources. In each case air raids may cause almost complete immobilisation of the Army at short notice owing to the flight of civil sub-staffs and labour.

(23) DEDUCTIONS

(a) Even with the foreseeable reinforcements, that is up to the period mid-end March, our operational resources are so limited as to preclude anything except a defensive attitude possibly combined with very local offensives.

Further, until the security of our L of C the proper organisation of our Base port, transportation and inter-communication system is placed on a sounder footing, probably by the taking over, or at least, reinforcement of the civil organisations by the military, it would be inadvisable to attempt anything in the shape of an offensive with distant objectives.

(b) The requirements of troops, assuming a properly organised and protected L of C for an offensive against THAILAND requires a separate appreciation.

(c) More British Infantry are required for both operational and I.S. roles.

(d) The proper co-ordination of the Defence of Rangoon Fortress by sea, land and air, demands a separate investigation by a joint Staff Committee.

(24) COMMAND ORGANISATION AND PLANNING

There are three separate service commands in BURMA. The Resident Naval Officer who is under the command of the F.O. Eastern Fleet; the G.O.C., Army in Burma and the A.O.C. who are under the command of the Pacific Command. Both the G.O.C. and A.O.C. are under India for administration in its wider sense.

(25) DEDUCTIONS

It is necessary to devise a workable machinery for proper co-ordination and consultation as between the three service commands and their staffs.

(26) COURSES OPEN TO THE ENEMY

The scale of attack, and to some extent the direction of attack, by the Japanese, must depend a great deal on whether Singapore holds out. If Singapore continues to hold out any attack on objectives in the Bay of Bengal must necessarily be on a comparatively small scale. Further, it is reasonable to assume that Singapore will contain comparatively large forces of Japanese land and air resources which might otherwise be diverted against Burma.

The difficulties of the country will impose certain limitations on the forces employed against Burma, but there are adequate L. Gs. in THAILAND and INDO-CHINA, and we must expect any land offensive to be supported by a heavy scale of air attack.

Speed is probably the essence of any Japanese plan. This is forced on her by—
    (a) the fact that BURMA must be attacked before the monsoon breaks in May, if at all, this year; and
    (b) the advent of considerable reinforcements would make Japan's task very much more difficult.

(27) This need for a rapid decision in BURMA may, therefore, influence Japan to commence operations before the Singapore operations are concluded to her advantage. If this is so, her offensive will be limited from the point of view of sea-borne attack, and is likely to take the form of land attack against selected objectives in Burma backed by Air support. Other things being equal it is natural that with a rapid decision in view the Japanese will select the more direct routes into Burma. The shortest routes are RAHEN-MOULMEIN and CHIENGMAI-TOUNGOO. The seizure of MOULMEIN would give the enemy all the TENASSERIM aerodromes (*e.g.*, MOULMEIN, TAVOY, MERGUI, VICTORIA POINT) from which she could bring a practically continuous scale of air attack against RANGOON and make the use of this port for the reception of reinforcements practically impossible.

The seizure of TOUNGOO would split our forces in half and would deny us the only main road and rail commun: between NORTH and SOUTH BURMA.

Japan's available forces would probably enable her to use her traditional methods of wide front movements and whatever primary objectives were selected, it is probable that every approach across our frontiers would be utilised so as to extend the defence and ensure penetration.

(28) The possible scale of Air attack which would be available to the enemy to support his offensive will, no doubt, be examined in the R.A.F. appreciation now being made. It will, however, be heavy, and will possibly be directed against communs: so as to render difficult the movement of our reinforcements and resources. It is considered that probable targets might be MARTABAN railhead, the BILIN, SITTANG and PEGU Bridges, the railway junction at THAZI, and RANGOON itself.

It is probable that submarine and possible raider action would intensify on the CALCUTTA-RANGOON sea route, and this might be intensified by air action against convoys carried out by heavy bombers acting from VICTORIA POINT and THAI aerodromes.

(29) It is unlikely that Japan would commence this offensive with less than three and possibly four Divs. which she could easily concentrate from her available forces in INDO-CHINA and THAILAND.

The limiting factor of communications would probably prevent Japan from using more than one Div. for the principal thrust against MOULMEIN in the first place though this would almost certainly be combined with advances via the THREE PAGODA PASS and also against TAVOY.

As regards the Centre and North, a Bde. group is according to all previous appreciations, the maximum that could be developed by each of the pack tracks leading into TOUNGOO, and MONG PAN. Bn. colns. could, however, be used by various other tracks, particularly those running N.W. from MONG HSAT.

Again, by previous appreciation, a Div. could be used on the CHIENGRAI-KENGTUNG-SALWEEN route.

This would ensure the extension of all our defences and Japan would still have plenty of reserves to reinforce success.

(30) To summarise: Owing to need for rapid decision Japan may launch her offensive against BURMA before SINGAPORE is liquidated. Probable maximum scale of attack would be:

One Div. against MOULMEIN with subsidiary attacks by THREE PAGODA PASS and against TAVOY and MERGUI. The latter would be accompanied by seaward infiltration in small craft from VICTORIA POINT.

Bde. Gps. against TOUNGOO, MONG PAN, with Bns. moving by MONG HSAT and possibly other intermediate tracks.

One Div. against KENGTUNG.

Heavy scale air attack against bridges and railway junctions between RANGOON and MARTABAN, and RANGOON and THAZI. Parachute tps. might be expected to attempt sabotage in the area MARTABAN-SITTANG Bridges. Attacks on convoys ex INDIA by sea and air. In the event of SINGAPORE falling, a further appreciation will at once be necessary.

(31) COURSES OPEN TO OURSELVES

With existing resources we cannot do more than endeavour to stabilise the front and possibly carry out small scale offensive measures to delay enemy preparations for his offensive. We might concentrate sufficient tps. in TENASSERIM for a limited offensive to defeat enemy concentrations on the RAHENG route if we were prepared to use the Chinese 5th and 6th Armies on the line THAZI-KENGTUNG.

Failing this we can employ at most two Regts. of the Chinese 5th Army on our North flank about LOIMWE-KENGTUNG, keeping the rest of the Chinese in reserve in the NORTHERN SHAN STATES.

(32) By holding right forward to LOIMWE we expose our L of C LOIMWE-TAUNGGYI to infiltration by Bde. and/or Bn. colns. moving N.W. from CHIENGRAI and CHIENGMAI.

Similarly, in the South by holding the whole of the TENASSERIM peninsula south to MERGUI we use up tps. in small packets out of supporting distance of one another.

With our present weakness in tps. we must endeavour to concentrate as great a strength as possible at the really vital areas.

These would appear to be as follows:

MARTABAN-BILIN, YWATHIT-BAWLAKE, MONGPON, TAKAW.

All these areas, except MOULMEIN, are behind the formidable obstacle of the SALWEEN RIVER and are the main road and track junctions. By denying these four areas we virtually deny every practicable route into BURMA from THAILAND.

(33) The vulnerability of our communs. by road and rail between RANGOON and THAZI is a matter for some concern. The destruction of any one of the main bridges would render movement of reserves very difficult.

Apart from adequate measures to protect the vital bridges, etc., it may be necessary to split the reserves between the NORTH and SOUTH Defence systems and place them in positions from where they can ensure support to the forward defended areas. In the SOUTH the reserve for MARTABAN-BILIN should preferably be EAST of the SITTANG RIVER. In the NORTH either THAZI or TOUNGOO appears good locations.

The advantage of TOUNGOO is that it is within easy support of the BAWLAKE area which is the most direct route for an enemy attack, but which is not likely to sustain such a heavy scale of attack as the TAKAW area.

There are alternative routes from TOUNGOO towards TAUNGGYI. Either by the main road via THAZI, or by the MAWCHI MINES-BAWLAKE-LOIKAW road. Both routes are MT. roads.

The reserve at TOUNGOO could also, if necessary, be moved comparatively quickly to the SOUTH if the situation in TENASSERIM deteriorated, and provided the bridges remained intact.

THAZI is a main railway junction and movement either EAST towards TAKAW, or SOUTH towards BAWLAKE, is simple and not prejudiced by dangerous defiles. Also there are alternative routes. It is, however, a probable target for heavy scale air raids, and, therefore, not altogether suitable for a troop concentration.

On balance TOUNGOO area is probably a better location for the Northern reserve than THAZI.

(34) To Summarise:

Our Defence system must aim at concentration in the vital areas.

These areas are MARTABAN-BILIN, BAWLAKE, MONGPAN TAKAW.

We must delay forward of these areas but fight in these areas.

Adequate protection for our communs. between incl. THAZI, RANGOON and MARTABAN is essential.

Army reserves should be situated EAST of SITTANG RIVER and TOUNGOO.

Plan

1. Prepare defence areas at important strategic points to deny the line of the river Salween to enemy penetration. Vital areas on this line are as follows:

    Area MARTABAN-BILIN.
       „   YWATHIT-BAWLAKE.
       „   MONGPAN.
       „   TAKAW.

These areas to be prepared as all round fortress areas, stocked and provisioned for protracted resistance.

2. Occupy forward delaying positions on main approaches leading into these areas.

3. Establish Army reserves on the SITTANG River and at TOUNGOO.

4. Survey existing resources available for protection of L. of Cs. and internal security with a view to adequate defences of road and rail system between RANGOON and MANDALAY, RANGOON and MARTABAN, and THAZI and LOIMWE, and river system between RANGOON and MANDALAY.

5. Work out and demand from India minimum requirements in military transportation units, L. of C. communications and labour, to cope with the possibility of complete disintegration of civil labour.

6. Obtain, if possible, an additional two British Infantry Bns. for internal security in Burma.

7. Distribution of troops likely to be available for defence of Burma up to beginning of monsoon will be as under:

    South: TENASSERIM area: One Div. plus at least two additional Bns. for Divisional reserve.
    North: SOUTHERN SHAN STATES   One Div.

Army reserve two Bdes. and Chinese reinforcements.

8. Form a Joint Commanders' Committee with machinery to implement their decisions.

Undertake urgently detailed investigation of the defence of RANGOON fortress by air, land and sea, with the object of co-ordinating existing resources available and ascertaining additional requirements.

9. Consult Supreme Commander urgently on need for stopping at source, further supplies of lease and lend material destined for BURMA, and obtaining a priority policy as to best distribution of existing stocks.

10. Take immediate measures to clear Port of RANGOON of a proportion of its military equipment and reserves, including lease and lend equipment as soon as possible.

11. Plan for alternative base area in dry zone in the North. Push on with road KALEWA/TAMU to provide alternative overland communication with INDIA.

12. Advise Civil Government to arrange for adequate food supplies in Northern BURMA and in RANGOON.

13. Improve the port of BASSEIN with a view to using this Port as an alternative to RANGOON.

14. Consider with Irrawaddy Flotila Coy. the possibility of increasing capacity of river for movement of troops and stores between RANGOON and MANDALAY.

15. Clear up with Supreme Commander the exact position regarding BURMA'S future source of supply of reinforcements and equipment.

16. Prepare a separate appreciation regarding accommodation of troops likely to be in BURMA during the monsoon.

17. Prepare a separate appreciation regarding the possibility of undertaking offensive action against THAILAND in co-operation with Chinese troops allotted to BURMA at the end of the monsoon period.

18. Obtain early information regarding position in ANDAMAN and NICOBAR ISLANDS, including a reconnaissance of PORT BLAIR, with a view to determining resources necessary for protection of the Islands and prevention of their use by the enemy as submarine or raider bases.

APPENDIX 'K'

Tel.
Dated 22/12/41.
From: Rangoon Burma.
To : Secretary of State Burma.

Personal for Chief of Imperial General Staff from General WAVELL.
Following is appreciation of situation in Burma:

1. Burma is essential base for operations against Japan, it is only route for supplies to China, it is integral part of defence of Eastern India, where large proportion of munitions FACTORIES are sited. Its security is, therefore, absolutely vital to effective prosecution of War against Japan.

2. At present time Burma is very far from secure. From lack of aircraft and breakdown of intelligence system based on Singapore, information of Japanese moves and intentions is completely lacking. At present moment G.O.C. Burma is working blindfold.

3. Little has been done to make defensive works on main line approach. Fighting qualities of great proportion of forces available are quite unknown quantity. Defensive plan seems to have been based largely on hope that our Air Forces would make enemy approach difficult or impossible by bombing. This is contrary to all experience of this War and anyway, we have now no BOMBERS.

4. Great weakness in Burma from defensive point of view is local single port of entry in most exposed position. Defence of Rangoon against attack by air, sea and land is primarily considered.

5. Burma Command has many administrative deficiencies. Staff is inadequate in quantity and quality and over twenty officers Staff and Services have already been sent from India to supplement since India assumed

responsibility. Repair organization to transport is almost entirely lacking and there are serious deficiencies in medical services.

6. Present intention is to render Burma secure base from which offensive organization can later be built up. *Immediate* requirements are:
   (a) At least two bomber squadrons of BLENHEIM IV or equivalent, these should arrive within next week or two.
   (b) Two modern fighter squadrons for defence of Rangoon. Pending arrival will endeavour to secure return of one or two of CHENNAULTS squadrons of International Air Force.
   (c) Two Brigade Groups and divisional headquarters. Will wait for these from remainder seventeen division provided no further demands to Malaya are made.
   (d) Apparatus for making efficient warning system, telegram has already been sent about this.
   (e) Anti-aircraft guns for defence of aerodromes, Rangoon port etc. I am sending Burma seven BOFORS which are only mobile A.A. guns available in India, A.A. artillery from convoy W 12 Z on which I was counting have been diverted to Singapore. When can expect replacement?
   (f) I will endeavour to supply from India Burma's main deficiencies in staff and administrative services as far as possible, replacements from England must be sent early.

7. I trust that importance of defences in Burma and its many deficiencies will be realised and that every endeavour will be made to meet them especially in Aircraft which are really urgent.

APPENDIX 'L'

From: War Office to C.-in-C. India.
Cable. Dated 26/12/41.

Following is summary of J.I.C. Paper on the Threat to BURMA:
1. Japanese objects in attacking BURMA would be:
   (A) To cut the BURMA ROAD.
   (B) To establish naval and air bases in the Indian Ocean.
   (C) To cut our air routes to SINGAPORE.
   (D) To disturb our position in INDIA.
   (E) To deny us and gain for themselves important raw materials.
2. ECONOMIC IMPLICATIONS
   (A) Cutting of BURMA ROAD would deprive CHINA of all outside supplies and deprive us and U.S.A. of part of Burmese and all Chinese supplies of Tungsten. Capture of Tavoy and Mergui would deprive us of remainder of Burmese tungsten productions.
   (B) INDIA gets one-third of her oil from BURMA. Burmese oil now of increased importance to us due to loss of Borneo supplies. This oil would also be useful to Japan for supply possible bases in Bay of Bengal.
   (C) INDIA would be cut off from substantial supplies of lead and zinc.
3. LINES OF APPROACH AND OBJECTIVES

Thai-Burma frontier country is thickly forested, mountainous and traversed by few routes capable of supporting military operations. There are also other tracks passable only Dec. to March, but these latter unsuitable for military forces of any size. Following are probable lines of approach:
   (A) From Northern Thailand through Kengtung to Meiktila—to cut Burma Road and rail communications Rangoon to Northern Burma and oilfields.

(B) From central Thailand to Moulmein—to threaten Rangoon and Southern terminuses of the BURMA ROAD route and of the pipe line.
(C) Short but indifferent routes leading to
  (i) Tungsten mines at TAVOY and MERGUI.
  (ii) Anchorages suitable for submarine and raider bases in Bay of Bengal.

SCALES OF ATTACK

(A) LAND
  (i) Route (A) can support two Divs. Route (B) can at present support up to 1 Div. in dry weather. Route (C) can support one Div. in dry weather by tracks. These forces are already in THAILAND and available at short notice irrespective of operations elsewhere.
  (ii) A.F.V.'s would be confined to roads. Otherwise movement off roads presents no greater difficulty than Japanese have surmounted in MALAYA. River SALWEEN is a formidable obstacle.

(B) AIR
  (i) If operations continue on present scale against MALAYA, PHILIPPINES, HONG KONG and BORNEO, scale of attack would probably not exceed 100-150 aircraft.
  (ii) If Japan obtained dominant air position in areas above but had to retain containing air forces there scale is likely to be some 250 to 300 aircraft.
  (iii) If Japan had eliminated air opposition in above areas and strong air opposition from other islands of N.E.I. could not be offered scale might reach 400 to 450 aircraft.
  (iv) Japanese might reinforce above forces by carrier-borne aircraft and carrier-borne sea-planes up to a total of some 100 to 150 aircraft which could operate from Gulf of Saigon against lower Burma.

(C) SEA. Submarines will probably be used against our forces in Bay of Bengal. M+T.B.'s small craft and midget submarines may be transported across the KRA ISTHMUS for local operations.

(D) LIKELIHOOD OF ATTACK. Attack on Burma would be sound strategy and likely to be part of Japanese plan. Likely to be attempted as soon as attack on MALAYA has reached a stage which would enable necessary air forces to be diverted. Independent small forces will probably attempt to move towards TAVOY and MERGUI even before major operations against Burma.

APPENDIX 'M'

EXTRACT FROM CABLE FROM WAR OFFICE TO G.H.Q., FAR EAST, 8-1-42.

For General Wavell from Chiefs of Staff in Washington:

"Ref. para 6 (A). We do NOT altogether agree with line you propose taking on BURMA. It is of highest importance CHIANG KAI SHEK should be given every possible support and encouragement. We must in conjunction with him ensure that the BURMA Road is kept open and that a flow of warlike stores reaches him. Continuation of Chinese resistance is indispensable and will pay good dividend. Americans feel very strongly on this."

APPENDIX 'N'

Tel.
Dated 18/2/42.
From: Burmarmy,
To : ABDACOM.

Appreciation

PART I. Present situation is that 17 Div. is holding line of Bilin R and has inflicted severe check on enemy which may hold him up for some time unless he has fresh troops available which appears probable. 17 Div. are mostly tired and have suffered a good many casualties. In event of fresh enemy offensive in the near future I cannot be certain of holding present positions though every effort will be made to do so. If this battle should go badly enemy might penetrate line of R Sittang without much difficulty and evacuation of Rangoon would become imminent possibility. We have now three British Bns. for defence of Rangoon from R. Sittang to delta with a Garrison coy. at Bassein and two weak Bns. of little fighting value forming an observation line on R. Sittang N. of Sittang village. I Bur. Div. is reduced to four Bns. plus Frontier Force detachments and therefore no reserves. Date of arrival of Chinese fifth army in lower Burma uncertain. One British Bn. and armoured Bde. arrives 21st, S. African Bde. 28th and 63rd Bde. 2nd March.

PART 2. Probably the best that can be hoped for is that we shall be able to hold line of R. Sittang possibly with bridgeheads on E. bank. Effect of above will, however, be to interrupt or seriously interfere with use of railway to Mandalay through Pegu which is main route of supply to China. Alternative route beyond Prome depends on use of road and river and will be most seriously congested if evacuation of troops, RAF stores and H.Q. from Rangoon are carried out by this route. Alternatively to start moves now and possibly prematurely with obviously bad effect on morale of civilians and troops. Movement of stores and non-essential offices is already proceeding.

PART 3. To hold R. Sittang line permanently or to undertake offensive both 17th and 14th Divs. will be necessary but it should be noted that latter does not arrive till early April. In meantime, Chinese fifth army may fill the gap. For defence against seaborne attack on scale now becoming possible at least one division is required and one more is necessary to provide army reserve and I.S. troops. Third target should, therefore, be five divisions.

PART 4. The major problem is whether the prospects of holding Rangoon and denying oilfields justify efforts to despatch the above scale of reinforcements at the expense of the defence of India. In my opinion they do provided we can get impending reinforcements and in addition some more British Bns. more quickly than is at present visualised. Failing this the risk of losing Rangoon within the next few weeks is, I think, considerable, especially in the event of seaborne attack.

APPENDIX 'O'

Tel.
Dated 20/1/42.
From: Burmarmy.
To : ABDACOM and INDIA.

FIRST. Ref. appreciations by AOC and myself and your directive must stress importance of Burma and China as Air and Military base for eventual reduction of Japan as well as our defence of India. It is, therefore, essential to provide *now* sufficient Air Forces and troops to hold Burma in all circumstances.

SECOND. Experience in Malaya seems to show that paucity of communications will not prevent employment of very large numbers of Japanese and these comns. are being rapidly improved. Previous estimates of scale of attack are thus invalid. There is no reason why Japan should not launch at any time an attack greater than we can withstand with troops and air forces now available. There are signs that this may have already started and I cannot guarantee safety of Burma with forces now available.

I have, therefore, asked India to accelerate despatches. If Malaya and Philippines fall greatly increased resources will become available to Japan. Owing to lack of intelligence and difficulty of air recce over Jungle surprise attack is always possible. Scale of attack on shipping by air, sea or submarine may become serious at any time and it is most desirable to get reinforcements in while conditions are good.

THIRD. Consider a total of four Divisions should be completed earliest possible and that priority should be given to provision of necessary shipping. Total includes Bns. Burma Rifles which are very immature and weak and with practically no trained reinforcements and thus unfit for serious fighting.

Request that in view of urgency HMG and India be asked to give absolute priority to Burma's needs over those of Mid. East and Iraq. Also that one additional Div. should be got ready by India for despatch to Burma if necessary.

FOURTH. If investigation shows it to be practicable request authority to bring in 49th Chinese Div. of 6th Army in addition to 93rd and for these to become responsible for the whole N.W. Frontier of Thailand.

FIFTH. Above dispositions and reinforcements should provide reasonable degree of security and may enable some offensive action to be taken before monsoon. Am considering possibilities.

SIXTH. Provision of Air forces to meet A.O.C.s needs is equally urgent and there is so far little sign that adequate provision is being made. Burma's situation is particularly favourable for effective air attack even after loss of Tavoy.

SEVENTH. Consider Navy should be able to take some action to control coastal waters. SNOs resources are almost negligible but he can state what is needed.

APPENDIX 'P'

Tel.
Dated 20/1/42.
From: Burmarmy.
To : ABDACOM BATAVIA.

Continuation my telegram of 19 Jan., following is brief appreciation:
Approaches to TENASSERIM offer most direct route with less depth natural obstacles and likely be assisted by sea-borne operations off West coast. Southern Shan States country offers great scope for delaying action by defence. Monsoon beginning May will stop active operations. Japanese believed have three divs. THAILAND of which two in South plus Tank Regt. His tactics normally include penetration wide front and we must anticipate he will use all possible approaches with greatest weight against TENASSERIM. His object probably to secure aerodromes. He may use air-borne troops.

Chinese 5 and 6 Armies offered to co-operate with BURMA forces. Must use Chinese armies on Northern line but should aim at using them to release as many own tps. as possible for operations in South. Internal situation fifth coln. activity and sabotage is possible also movement large numbers refugees. Labour has already disintegrated and anticipate we shall have to take over all u/m services civil sig. communications, road and ferry maintenance with mily resources. RANGOON port and river vulnerable and obvious air target. Of primary importance develop alternative port and overland route to INDIA. Heavy scale of fighter and A.A. defence required for RANGOON also coastal recce against submarines and maintenance security ANDAMAN and NICOBAR Islands. Protection of vital road and rail bridges between MOULMEIN RANGOON and MANDALAY requires strong L of C. protective element. Early accumulation in BURMA food reserves both military and civil necessary.

RANGOON must be used as transit area and no congestion allowed. BURMA'S only immediate source of supply INDIA. Essential flow of reinforcements, etc., should continue without interference with agreed programme. Great quantities Chinese lease and lend material now at RANGOON. This must be cleared and if possible further shipments stopped till congestion docks removed. Priority policy necessary for best distribution as between Chinese and ourselves in present situation.

Following is availability fighting formation. Now two Divs., one of two Bdes. only, plus five Bns. BURMA F.F. Following additional reinforcements expected:

  Early Feb. 48 Ind. Bde.
  End Feb. One African Bde.
  Early March one African Bde.

Have asked INDIA for one additional Inf. Bde. earliest possible. Consider whole of 14 Ind. Div. will probably be required. No expansion BURMA Bdes. possible and fighting to date has shewn they are below standard. Evident no offensive action can be expected from BURMA before end rains.

Lack of British Bns. of which only two in country great handicap especially if I.S. situation deteriorates or extensive withdrawal becomes necessary. Two have been asked for but INDIA state unable to provide, we are short of Arty. of all natures, but anticipate reinforcements to complete us eventually to two Mtn. Regts., three Field Btys. and one A-Tk. Regt.

Enemy courses. Owing need for rapid decision anticipate enemy attack before SINGAPORE is liquidated. Probable maximum scale of attack. One Div. against MOULMEIN with subsidiary attacks against TAVOY and MERGUI. This has already started. One Div. against KENGTUNG with possibly Bde. Gps. operating against TOUNGOO and MONGPAN. Heavy scale air attack against commns. and port and attacks on convoys by sea and air.

In event of fall of SINGAPORE evident that possible scale of attack especially by sea much heavier and ANDAMANS-NICOBARS probably first objective. In this event reinforcement will become difficult and must, threfore, be provided for in advance.

Our courses. We must endeavour stabilise front till monsoon. Defence system must aim at concentration of forces in vital areas, these are MOULMEIN, MARTABAN, BAWLAKE, MONGPAN and TAKAW. We must delay and inflict casualties forward of these areas but fight in the area.

Summary of plan. Distribution of tps. by end March as under:

  TENASSERIM One Div. plus one Bde.
  SHAN STATES One Div.

Balance internal security and Army reserve. Chinese forces
    93 Div. under comd. North and S.E. of KENGTUNG.
    49 Div. in reserve WANTING to move South to concentration area N.W. of TAKAW if necessary.
    6th Chinese Army in reserve on BURMA Road about Chinese border.
Concentration L of C protective tps. on road rail communs. between MOULMEIN-RANGOON-MANDALAY. Obtain minimum requirements military Transportation units L of C commn. and Mily. labour to cope with anticipated breakdown of civil labour. Details of these have been sent to ARMINDIA, they include urgent request for two British Bns.

Obtain early policy regarding lease and lend material including stopping at source till present congestion clear and allocation between Chinese and ourselves.

Push ahead with development BASSEIN port and KALEWA TAMU road estimated latter through by end March. BASSEIN now available as reinforcement port requires development to take stores of M.T.

Plan for alternative base area in dry zone about MEIKTILA. Arrange with civil Govt. for collection food reserves in North BURMA and RANGOON.

Early recce of ANDAMAN NICOBARS with view to concerting necessary defensive measures.

Prepare separate appreciation for possible offensive action after monsoon and additional forces necessary for such an offensive.

APPENDIX 'Q'

Tel.
Dated 26/1/42.
From General Wavell in Batavia to C.O.S. and
To Washington for combined C.O.S.

Returned this morning from Rangoon. Do not consider situation immediately serious provided certain steps outlined below are taken as early as possible. Japanese advance in Tenasserim probably made by comparatively small force. Our main force south has been withdrawn across Salween and Japanese occupation of Moulmein is probable but have instructed Hutton to take offensive action as soon as he has organised sufficient force.

2. Following steps for defence of Burma essential:

NAVAL. Anti-submarine flotilla based on Rangoon to keep approaches clear. Should eventually consist of two small destroyers, four sloops or corvettes and six trawlers or similar craft, at least half of above are required at once. None available from present Abdacom resources.

LAND. Reinforcements in sight from India and Africa with Chinese assistance should suffice if convoys continue to arrive safely.

AIR. Reinforcements promised should suffice for present provided they arrive speedily especially Hurricanes from Middle East. It is essential that A.V.G. Squadron which Chennault is endeavouring to withdraw should remain at Rangoon at least until further Fighter Squadrons are available. This Squadron has been doing invaluable work. Can I please be informed under whose orders it is to be regarded? Some Hudson aircraft for coastal reconnaissance required immediately.

3. Internal situation reasonably satisfactory. Rangoon docks have been cleared and sufficient labour available for immediate purposes but liable to disappear under bombing attacks. Railways working well.

4. Squadron long range bombers operating from Burma would have excellent targets and propose to send one as soon as possible.

APPENDIX 'R'

Tel.
Dated 21/2/42.
From: ABDACOM.
To : Burmarmy.

Personal for Hutton from Wavell

One. You should draw up at once plans for counter-offensive with Armoured Brigade and all available troops. If at all possible SITTANG River must be crossed and counter-offensive be made East of River. In any event plans must be made to hit enemy and hit him hard if he ever succeeds in crossing. He will go back quick in face of determined attack.

Two. Do not understand why you are turning back convoys, surely you want all possible resources to attack enemy with.

Three. Have you organised Armoured train for railway?

Four. All possible support is being sent you and we must and are going to hold RANGOON.

APPENDIX 'S'

Tel.
Dated 21/2/42.
From: War Office.
To : ABDACOM.

One. Our object is to maintain a front in BURMA with particular object of keeping open a supply route to CHINA preferably through RANGOON but failing that through ASSAM.

Two. It is at best doubtful whether we shall be able for long to continue to get convoys to RANGOON in face of the air threat and of the naval threat which the JAPANESE can develop through the MALACCA STRAITS.

Three. Nevertheless, the holding of RANGOON is very important to us so long as our supplies can get through to BURMA and CHINA. Even afterwards its denial to the JAPANESE as a port will be vital to the achievement of the object in para 1 in so far as the defence of the northern route is concerned.

Four. It, therefore, seems to us that port should be held as long as its retention can contribute to the achievement of our main object but that rather than continue to hold it after this stage has passed you should consider the possibility of blocking the port preparatory to establishing all forces on a front to the north. In short we do not consider that the delay which would be imposed on the enemy by our attempting to hold RANGOON after it had been isolated would justify the loss of the forces in RANGOON from the fighting strength in BURMA.

Five. You are aware that if we lose the port of RANGOON the capacity of the overland supply route will limit the size of the forces which can operate in BURMA.

Six. Assuming the AUSTRALIAN GOVERNMENT agree to the postponement of the return of the 7th Australian Div. to AUSTRALIA do you in view of the considerations set out above wish this Div. to be directed to RANGOON? It could reach there by 27th February. Telegraph clear the line YES or NO.

Seven. Please also telegraph your comments on our above appreciation and send us your plan for the defence of Northern BURMA in event of withdrawal from RANGOON.

APPENDIX 'T'

Tel.
Dated 22/2/42.
From: Wavell.
To : War Office, G.H.Q. India and Burma.

I have no longer responsibility for BURMA but following are my views:
- (a) Neither RANGOON nor BURMA will be held by defensive methods and maintaining a front. Only prospect of success is vigorous counter-offensive at early date for which 7th Australian Div. is required as well as 7th Armoured Bde.
- (b) I see no reason why air action should close RANGOON Port. TRIPOLI and BENGHAZI still function and I consider Japanese Air Force less effective than R. A. F.
- (c) Nor do I see why Naval action should close it. Surely our Eastern Fleet can prevent Japanese singeing our beard at RANGOON.
- (d) BURMA is far better provided with air bases than THAILAND, if we and Americans put on all we know in the air as soon as possible we should be able to turn Japanese air fields in this theatre into grave yards for their Air Force.
- (e) If RANGOON is lost we can maintain few troops in BURMA and do little to help CHINA.
- (f) We have got to fight these Japs some time somewhere. BURMA not ideal geographically but represents almost our last chance to show the Japs and the world that we do mean to fight.

APPENDIX 'U'

Dated 23/2/42.
From: ABDACOM BATAVIA.
To : Armindia.

For Hartley from Wavell

Have no large-scale maps of BURMA here and little knowledge of nature of country but send you following ideas for consideration:
- (a) Now that we have fallen back to SITTANG, battle for RANGOON must be fought somewhere in area between river and railway PEGU-NYAUNGLEBIN. It must be offensive battle on our part to drive enemy back into river with heavy loss if he succeeds in crossing it.
- (b) Battle must be planned and prepared now, *i.e.*, country must be carefully reconnoitred, use of various water lines studied, material for crossings prepared etc.
- (c) Supply problem must be studied, *e.g.*, PEGU made into Advanced Base, depots of supplies placed along railway line etc.
- (d) Suggest best methods in this wide area not to operate by divisions but by widely separated Mobile Brigade Groups or even smaller columns operating from railway as base and converging rapidly on any body of enemy between railway and river. By such methods wide area can be covered offensively and enemy infiltration tactics defeated by immediate attack often from several directions. Use can be made of natural obstacles to protect flanks and to drive enemy against. We have advantages of Railway Base and better communications.

(e) For protection of area East of RANGOON-PEGU against landings from GULF of MARTABAN small Mobile Force should suffice based on PEGU-THONGWA railway. Understand coast here very unfavourable for landing.
(f) Improvised armoured trains might be useful.
(g) Close co-operation with Air Force essential and there must be arrangements to distinguish our troops from enemy from air. Coloured umbrellas of local type might be useful. I believe by such tactics with reinforcements now arriving enemy can be heavily defeated. But immediate preparations required.

APPENDIX 'V'

Tel.
Dated 7/3/42.

For C.O.S. from General Wavell

Following is my general appreciation of course of war in East on which I should be glad to have your views.

ONE. Immediate Japanese objectives after occupation Java likely to be
(a) Rangoon, Andamans, Northern Sumatra for naval (mainly submarine) and air bases facing Bay of Bengal; and
(b) Upper Burma to cut communications between India and China and establish air bases against India.

I believe these objectives more probable than attack on Ceylon or Australia.

Two. I have always considered Burma as most vital area in war against Japan
(a) to maintain connection with China;
(b) to protect North Eastern India with its war industries; and
(c) as essential air base from which Japanese air bases can be attacked and aircraft passed through to China to attack Japan itself.

For above reasons I have continually endeavoured to place defence of Burma on secure footing but I fear without success. When India became responsible for Burma after outbreak of war with Japan reinforcements of land and air troops earmarked by India for Burma were diverted to Malaya. Later efforts to put 7th Australian division into Burma and to induce Americans to put bomber aircraft there failed. As result fear Rangoon will have to be abandoned and it is doubtful whether hold on Upper Burma can be maintained since reinforcement and supply will become matter of extreme difficulty. Troops and aircraft required for Burma and N.E. India are now being diverted to Ceylon.

With Rangoon in their possession Japanese can abandon long and difficult line of communications through Thailand and Tenasserim and supply and reinforce by sea. They can increase their forces up to 7 or 8 divisions if necessary while we shall be hard put to it to supply the comparatively small forces we have in Burma.

THREE. I anticipate, therefore, early attack on Upper Burma which may be difficult to hold up indefinitely. How far the enemy will push his advance will depend on resistance we and Chinese can offer but I consider he will aim at Mandalay and possibly Lashio so as definitely to cut connection between India and China. He is also likely to raid Akyab and possibly Chittagong.

Four. If enemy succeeds in Burma he will probably attempt attack on N.E. India by land, by sea-borne forces and by air attack. Whether or not he can make landings on large-scale in Bay of Bengal will depend on situation at sea and I have at present little knowledge of composition or plans of our Eastern fleet.

Five. I will do everything possible to maintain hold on Burma and to organise defence of N.E. India but we are very thin on ground and in air and if troops and aircraft continue to be diverted elsewhere my difficulties are increased.

APPENDIX 'W'

Tel.
Dated 13/3/42.

From: War Office to G.H.Q. India.

One. We agree with your conception of forming bastion in North East India but the problem is to decide what portion of our slender resources it is right to allot to this area *vis-a-vis* Ceylon of the importance of which you are fully aware.

Two. In our view the security of our Indian Empire depends in the last resort on our ability to control sea communications in Indian Ocean. For this we must have secure naval bases and the only ones in sight for some time to come are in Ceylon. Both COLOMBO and TRINCOMALEE are necessary owing to limited capacity of each and it will be necessary to operate air striking and reconnaissance forces from the island. ADDU ATOLL not yet adequately developed.

Three. For these reasons we consider that defence requirements of Ceylon must be given priority although we agree that North East India is very important and also appreciate potential internal security problems with which you may be faced in Bengal and Eastern India. Estimated scale of attack on Ceylon under review in light of recent developments.

APPENDIX 'X_1'

Tel.
Dated 15/3/42.
From: ARMINDIA.
To : CHIEFS OF STAFF.

First. Agreed that present resources are utterly inadequate for defence of India, therefore, more reason that we should consider their distribution with greatest care and on best policy which should be as offensive as resources allow. Present policy seems to be to crowd unduly large proportion of slender resources, land and air, into Ceylon where their purpose is purely defensive to protect fleet which will certainly be unable to venture far into Bay of Bengal if we lose command of air in Burma and N.E. India.

Second. Agreed that naval bases in Ceylon are of vital importance and must be protected but we cannot afford to over insure. My reasoning is that if we lose command of sea and air round Ceylon to such extent that Japanese can bring sea-borne expedition to island no number of troops are likely to save bases. Without even landing Japanese can destroy bases by air attack as American base at Manilla was destroyed.

Third. Whole history of Japanese advance so far is that they do no move their warships and transports outside protection of land-based air forces nor until they have destroyed or greatly reduced enemy air forces covering their objective. To attack Ceylon they must depend on carrier-borne aircraft against land-borne aircraft and must risk fleet action within range of hostile land-based air forces. This seems most unlikely.

FOURTH. If their objective is India they will surely attack where they will have cover of land-based aircraft both for their land forces and ships. This they can do by working up Burmese mainland and West coast and establishing successive air bases at Rangoon, Akyab, Upper Burma and perhaps Chittagong. With these in Japanese possession our fleet will be unable to venture near N.E. India and will be powerless to prevent sea-borne invasion of Bengal. This as I see it is India's chief danger.

FIFTH. Though I am responsible for defence of India I have so far been given no indication of naval appreciation or naval intentions. I am unaware of proposed strength of Eastern fleet date of its assembly or its strategy when assembled. Nor have I any idea of how far its action will be combined with that of American Pacific Fleet. It appears to me, however, that if the two fleets work on some combined plan, it should be made difficult and dangerous for Japanese to detach sufficiently strong fleet to risk fleet action in Bay of Bengal or Indian Ocean and that without such action invasion of Ceylon is unlikely.

SIXTH. Conclusion is that Japanese attack on India will be made via Burma. Burmese coast and waters close to Burma under cover always of shore-based air superiority which will make it dangerous for our warships to interfere. Ceylon will be threatened or raided but not attacked.

SEVENTH. From above reasoning following are conclusions:
(a) Ceylon should have sufficient defence to prevent raid of Pearl Harbour or Port Darwin type from aircraft carriers and to protect ports and aerodromes against possible smash-and-run landing parties.
(b) Our main air forces must be concentrated on securing air superiority in Upper Burma and N.E. India.
(c) As large land forces as possible should be made available for defence of N.E. India where our main war industries are concentrated. If sufficient troops are provided, there is good prospect of defeating Japanese forces even if they succeed in landing or in penetrating through Burma. Forces at present available are unlikely to be sufficient. Appreciation of forces required will be sent shortly.

EIGHTH. Establishment of air superiority in N.E. India will have following results:
(a) It may enable us to maintain hold on Upper Burma and connection with Chinese.
(b) It will protect Calcutta and our war industries.
(c) It will prevent large sea-borne landings in Bengal and Orissa.
(d) It will enable Navy to operate in Bay of Bengal.
(e) It will allow us to strike blow against Japanese air force which is their weakest point. Nowhere else can we do this effectively.

NINTH. Immediate steps necessary are in my opinion as follows:
(a) Release Brigade 70 Division from Ceylon for India. I consider Ceylon with two Indian Brigades, two Australian Brigades, one British Brigade, one African Brigade and local troops will be over insured compared with remainder of India. On arrival second African Brigade should like also to consider withdrawal one Indian Brigade from Ceylon.

(b) Provide Ceylon with Beaufort Squadron asked for by C.-in-C. This is far more effective defence than infantry brigades.
(c) Ask Americans to place at India's disposal all fighter and bomber forces as they become operationally ready. In particular bomber forces in Bangalore area would contribute to defence of Ceylon.
(d) Concentrate with utmost urgency largest possible air force in N.E. India. This is vital for security of India and is only form of offensive action we can take at present.
(e) Provide me with naval appreciation especially as regards defence of India. Destroyers and other small craft are urgently required for N.E. India.

APPENDIX 'X.'

Tel.
Dated 25/3/1942.

For C.O.S. from General Wavell

1. Must warn you that position regarding defence of Burma and N.E. India has seriously deteriorated during last few days as result enemy action against our air forces and arrival enemy convoy with cruiser escort in Andamans. There are indications from secret sources that AKYAB may be Japanese objective in near future.

2. Situation of which I gave warning in my telegram of 14th has in fact occurred in Burma. We raided enemy aerodromes at Mingaladon on March 21 with 8 bombers and 10 fighters our maximum available effort. Enemy retaliation was 60 bombers and over 40 fighters and four raids of approximately this strength, two on Magwe two on Akyab, have been made in last few days causing us heavy loss in aircraft. Every indication that enemy air force has been strongly reinforced and that raids on this scale will continue.

3. I had hoped to build up air forces at Magwe and Akyab to contest control of air with enemy and to make use of Rangoon port hazardous for him. Now air force at Magwe has been almost destroyed and Akyab has been made temporarily unusable as air base. My bomber force immediately available in Burma area to meet new Japanese threat is six Blenheims and my fighter force about equivalent one squadron Hurricanes. Am sending separate telegram on air situation. Reinforcements at present in sight and proposal in telegram from S. of S. India will not suffice to restore situation or give hope of building up effective resistance to Japanese air strength.

4. Immediate problem is Akyab. I have placed there brigade to hold air base and two sloops and other available small craft to check Japanese infiltration up coast in small boats. If, however, enemy send landing force escorted by cruisers and covered by large air force which is quite possible, it is unlikely that Akyab can be held for long. As occupation by enemy would constitute serious menace both to Burma and India I must try to hold it though I regard both troops and ships there as hostages to fortune. Eastern fleet, according to appreciation received, is unable to afford any resistance.

5. Unless something can be done very soon to provide adequate air force, defence of Bengal and N.E. India will be seriously compromised as well as Burma.

APPENDIX 'X₃'

Tel.
Dated 4/4/1942.
From: G.H.Q. India.
To : C.O.S. from General Wavell.

Following is summary of appreciation by Alexander:

ONE. Japanese object will be first to occupy oilfields to deny petrol to Chinese and ourselves. Second to cut road communications between China and India. Latter involves initial advance to Mandalay to cut Kalewa road and ultimate advance to Myitkyina to cut the northerly road. Japanese possibly intend to go as far as Lashio in order to secure aerodrome but seems doubtful whether they will attempt to go as far north as Myitkyina in view of the great distance and fact that northerly road cannot be completed for many months. If Japanese advance to Lashio occupation of Shwebo area by them will be necessary to cover flank of advance.

Two. Japanese will probably attempt to advance simultaneously by both Prome and Toungoo routes with subsidiary advance by Kengtung or Mongpan or both.

THREE. Owing to Japanese possibility of reinforcement via Rangoon weak strength of Allied forces and lack of air support gradual withdrawal northwards seems inevitable.

FOUR. Mandalay will be covered as long as possible but if force has to withdraw further plan under consideration as follows. Corps H.Q. Armoured Brigade and one Infantry Brigade of 4 battalions to withdraw on Lashio acting as rear-guard to Chinese armies. Remainder of force to area Chindwin Valley-Shwebo to cover the Kalewa approach to India and to operate on flank of Japanese advance to Lashio. Former force might withdraw into China which will involve supply by air in view of famine conditions in Yunnan or to Bhamo area where they would constitute threat to Japanese advance into China. Portion of latter force might also withdraw to Bhamo area or whole force might withdraw via Kalewa into India. From Bhamo connection with India would be by route now under construction from Ledo.

FIVE. I have accepted above appreciation in principle and instructed Alexander to make his administrative preparations accordingly. Eventual decision must depend largely on situation at time.

SIX. Reinforcements. Maximum use is being made of air transport but only small numbers can be carried. Situation will improve with arrival of D.C. aircraft from Middle East.

APPENDIX 'Y'

Tel.
Dated 14/4/42. From General Wavell to General Alexander. Appreciate great struggle you and your troops are making against difficulties and am confident you will succeed in defeating enemy attack. Your determined resistance is of vital importance to the defence of India.

APPENDIX 'Z'

From
General Sir H. R. L. G. Alexander,
K.C.B., C.S.I., D.S.O., M.C.

Headquarters, Army in Burma,
SHWEBO, 29th April, 1942.

I have given very careful thought to future operations and I can see no other alternative which will allow me to carry out my objectives:

The defence of INDIA, maintain touch with the Chinese and keep one or more jumping off places in BURMA.

The present situation on the battle front is as follows:

The Imperial Forces, or rather what is left of them, are acting as rear guard on a front from the Mandalay-Rangoon road about KYAUKSE to well WEST of the IRRAWADDY at PAUK, a distance of 175 miles. For the defence of the MANDALAY position, we shall have 17 Div. Bur. Div. (less detachments sent to cover the approaches to KALEWA), 38th Chinese Div. and broken-up remnants of the 96th and 22nd Chinese Divs. These latter have no guns and have already had a severe handling. My orders are that the maximum delay must be imposed on the enemy by our present rear guards and that the MANDALAY-IRRAWADDY Front will be held until I order otherwise. I require every day to backload, prepare and stock the road from YE-U to KALEWA, which is but a bad track and has no water on its 105-mile stretch.

The Administrative situation at KALEWA is a very serious problem. I am sending by boat what I can collect in the time available from MONYWA, but the main supply must come from INDIA by road and via the YU river and, if things go badly, provisions will have to be dropped by air.

The Chinese forces will withdraw up the valley towards KATHA. I wanted to keep the 38th Div. (the one which fought with BURCORPS at YENANGYAUNG) and send it back to INDIA to be properly equipped. It is a very good Division and both our chaps and theirs got on very well together, but owing to shortage of tps. in the centre of BURMA, they will have to move back up the valley on SHWEBO and then KATHA. With the Chinese I shall send a detachment so that British forces and Chinese can still maintain a front together.

I am planning to go myself with a small staff and a small detachment to MYITKYINA, because I feel sure that the political situation demands that I stay in BURMA as long as I am nominally in command of the allied armies.

Now a word or two about this Force. As I originally said, it is full of good fighting material if properly trained but, owing to exhaustion due to the results of last four months—loss of equipment, shortage of supplies of all types, lack of all air support, battle casualties and general war weariness, they are not up to much more. In fact, it is not an exaggeration to say that as a fighting Force it has reached the end of its tether. When it can be done they must be relieved on the KALEWA front and rested, reorganized and equipped. And more important still—they must be *trained*. They *DO NOT* know their job as well as the Jap, and there's the end of it. Individual units and individuals have fought extremely well—especially the 7th Armoured Bde. whose morale is still very high. The Inf. now rely almost entirely on the tanks and will do nothing without them, which is quite wrong. Incidentally, I don't think we shall save any of our remaining 70 Tanks but they are mechanically worn out and have an average life of 500 more miles left in them. In any case, there are no roads NORTH of SHWEBO.

And now we must quickly and with all energy regroup and consolidate our positions round KALEWA, KATHA, BHAMO and MYITKYINA—and during the rains prepare plans for the future.

Sd./- X X

To
General Sir P. Archibald Wavell, G.C.B., C.M.G., M.C.,
   Commander-in-Chief, INDIA.
   P.S. I have discussed plans with Gen. Stilwell and General Lo, C.-in-C., Chinese Forces, and they are in complete agreement with me on every point.

GROUP III

APPENDIX "A"

17 DIV. OPERATION INSTRUCTION NO. 5

1 Feb. 1942

INFORMATION

1. The enemy is in considerable strength in the MOULMEIN area. He is in possession of a number of rafts, launches and other river crafts, and may possibly try and make landings between MARTABAN and the SITTANG river estuary.

2. Our tps. have been withdrawn from MOULMEIN.
Two extra Bns. have already arrived and 48 Bde. is expected shortly.

INTENTION

3. The Div. will stop any further enemy advance from MOULMEIN. Any attempts to cross SALWEEN R. or to land tps. from the Gulf of MARTABAN will be dealt with by immediate counter-attacks. MARTABAN, THATON, PA-AN, BILIN, KYAIKTO and PAPUN will be strongly held and the main rd. and railway from incl. MARTABAN to incl. SITTANG BR. will be patrolled under bde. arrangements.

4. Areas of 16 and 46 Bde. as given in sketch map att. to 17 Div. Op. Instruction No. 4 of 29 Jan. 42, remain unaltered. (NOTE: Op. Instruction No. 4 has been cancelled but sketch map holds good in respect of 16 and 46 Bdes.).

5. Patrolling responsibilities of 2 and 48 Bdes. as under
   - *2 Bde.* From incl. KYAIKTO to incl. SITTANG BR.
   - *48 Bde.* From excl. KYAIKTO to incl. THEBYUCHAUNG BR. about mile 72 rd. KYAIKTO-BILIN.

METHOD

6. Bdes. will be eventually organised as in Appx. A. In the meanwhile, however, organisation and Tasks will be as follows:

16 Bde.   Bde. HQ. THATON.
Area of responsibility—KAMAMAUNG-PA-AN-MARTABAN-THATON-DUYINZEIK.

Tps.
- 2 KOYLI
- 1/7 G. R.
- 1 R. Jat.
- 4 Burif.
- 8 Burif.
- 5 Mtn. Bty.

Until 8 Burif. are ready to come into the bde. 3/7 G. R. less two coys. will remain under comd. 16 Bde.

TASK OF 16 BDE.

MARTABAN will be strongly held.
The ferries at SHWEGUN and KAMAMAUNG will be watched and guarded.
Some armd. cars will shortly be available for use on the rd. THATON-MARTABAN.

46 Bde.   Bde. HQ. HNINPALE.
Tps.
- 5 Dogra
- 7 Baluch (after relief by KOYLI)

2 Coys. 3/7 G. R.
7 Burif.

TASKS OF 46 BDE.
(a) Will hold PAPUN strongly and ferries over SALWEEN. R. at DAGWIN and KYAUKHNYAT. They will use 7 Burif. for this purpose which will be placed temporarily under comd.
(b) Will patrol the rd. BILIN-THATON and watch approaches from the sea in that area.

2 Inf. Bde.
Tps.
4 FFR.
3 Burif will guard SITTANG BR. Relief to be carried out as soon as possible.
2 Burif (Div. Tps.) will
    (i) take over local protection round KYAIKTO from 3/7 GR. with two coys.;
    (ii) have one coy. watching the SITTANG. R. estuary for possible sea landings; and
    (iii) keep a reserve of one coy.

ADM.
7. *Tpt.*
All inf. bns. will shortly be brought on to the following scale of tpt.
Staff Car—1
15-cwt trucks—25
Lorries—13
Mules—40
Further adm. instruction will be issued later.

          Sd./- Lt.-Col.
          G.S. 17 Ind. Div.

APPENDIX A TO ABOVE

Div. TPS. F F 2.
46 Ind. Bde.
    7 Baluch
    3/7 G.R.
    5 Dogra (on arrival from INDIA).
16 Ind. Bde.
    2 KOYLI
    1/7 G.R.
    1 Jat
    8 Bur. Rif.
48 Ind. Bde.
    1/3 G.R. ⎫
    1/4 G.R. ⎬ (on arrival from INDIA).
    2/5 R.G.R ⎭
    2 Bur. Rif.—under orders to move to KYAIKTO.
2 Inf. Bde.
    Cameronians (on arrival from INDIA)
    4 F.F.R.
    7 Bur. Rif.
    3 Burif.
F.F. 2 after complete reorganisation will be sent from PYAWBWE to join 17 Div. as Div. & Recce tps.

APPENDIX "B"

DIVISIONAL COMMANDER'S INSTRUCTION
H.Q. 17 Ind Div, 6 Feb. 1942.

TACTICS AND MOBILITY

1. *General Wavell's Visit*

    The Chief points made by General Wavell were as follows:
    - (a) We must allow the enemy no further advance.
    - (b) Offence is the best means of defence.
    - (c) The Jap must not be made out to be a superman.
    - (d) We must eventually get back that part of TENASSERIM we have lost.

2. *Tactics and Mobility*

    The above points conform to the principle of 17 Div. Operation Instruction No. 8. Now to get down to further details as to method.

    Defensive
    - (a) There are certain key points which must be held strongly and counter-attacked for if lost.
      These are SITTANG BR, KYAIKTO, BILIN, THATON, MARTABAN, PA-AN, PAPUN.
    - (b) The line of the R. SALWEEN must be watched.
    - (c) The main MARTABAN-THATON-KYAIKTO-SITTANG road must be patrolled. Strong road-blocks must be established protecting the key points in para (a) above.
      Instances occurred in MALAYA of Japanese tanks going straight down the road without let or hindrance.
      The C. R. E. will also prepare certain demolitions in consultation with Brigade Commanders.

    Offensive
    - (d) We must push out our patrols to gain contact with the Jap.
    - (e) We must obtain information of Jap numbers and concentrations by means of local agents.
    - (f) 46 and 16 Bdes. will start as early as possible mobile columns consisting of one coy. from each bn.
      These columns will move very light with radius of action of about 3 days, of which one day should be, when possible, living on the country.

    Object
    - (i) To gain control over the no man's land between ourselves and the Japs.
    - (ii) To train our troops in jungle warfare.
      Bdes. will give each column an area to work in.
    - (g) In order to carry out the above tasks Bde. Comds. must keep in close touch with their local D.C.s and D.S.P.s and demand from them all the help and advice they can give.
      It must always be remembered that good information has to be sought for—it does NOT just "come in".
    - (h) *Interpreters and Guides*
      Bde. Comds. will obtain from their affiliated Burma Rif. Bns. 1 NCO and men for each Indian Bn. to act as interpreters and guides. For this purpose Burma Rif. Bns. are affiliated as follows:

3 Burifs	2 Bde.
4 Burifs	16 Bde.
2 Burifs	16 Bde.
7 Burifs	48 Bde.

3. *Mobility*

We are still very M.T. minded. Most of the units of this Div. had been training for warfare in the big open spaces and feel rather lost without their M.T.

We must of course make full use of M.T. whenever we can but we must always be prepared to leave it well back and operate on foot by jungle tracks.

4. *Observation*

Bdes. will think out and recce suitable O.P.s in their areas from which the sea coast and the area towards the SALWEEN can be continuously observed.

Div. Sigs. will then consult and co-ordinate.

5. *48 Bde.*

Will train and act in the spirit of the above paras. Bde. and Bn. recce parties will visit fwd. Bdes. and become familiar with the country and the tactics.

6. *2 Bde.*

Have for the moment certain defensive and training tasks to carry out.

They will, however, be thinking continually on the lines of the above instruction.

Sd./- Maj.-Gen.,
Comd., 17 Ind. Div.

APPENDIX "C"

17 DIV. OPERATION INSTRUCTION NO. 12

14 Feb. 42.

INFORMATION

1. It appears probable that the enemy is preparing to launch a strong attack on 46 Bde. at DUYINZEIK and THATON.

INTENTION

2. 17 Div. will concentrate behind the BILIN River.

METHOD

3. (a) 46 Bde. will start withdrawing tonight to KYAIKTO area.

   (b) Comd. 46 Bde. will conduct the withdrawal until his tps. have passed through 16 Bde. on the line of the BILIN river. As many wooden bridges as possible will be fired and destroyed.

   (c) One bd. 48 Bde. will proceed by train to THATON arriving there about 21.00 hrs. this evening.

      This bn. will be used by Comd. 46 Bde. as a lay back and will be withdrawn under his orders.

      The train will be used to send back excess ammunition and any personnel or material Comd. 46 Bde. does not require for his withdrawal.

   (d) On arrival at BILIN the following units of 46 Bde. will come under Comd. 16 Bde.
      5 Mtn. Bty.
      Sec. 18 Pdr. Bty.
      Sec. Armd. Cars.
      KOYLI
      1/7 G. R.

   (e) On arrival KYAIKTO Comd. 46 Bde. will take over comd. of the KYAIKTO defences from Lt.-Col. EDWARDS 4/12 F.F.R. Troops now forming part of the KYAIKTO defences will come under Comd. Brig. EKIN. He will be responsible for road protection from excl. SITTANG Bridge to incl. landing Ground at about mile 75.

4. *16 Bde.*
   (a) Will hold a strong defensive position behind the BILIN river from approx. LEIKKON to PAYASEIK.
   (b) MENEGONHTA must be watched. (G8103 North of *P* in IB (PWD).
   (c) Particular attention will be paid to demolitions and A/Tk. defences.
   (d) Patrols will work well fwd. to watch all approaches.

5. *48 Bde.*
   Will act as Div. reserve and will also recce, and be prepared to hold, a defensive posn. from TAUNGZUN—behind the river THEBYU.
   They will patrol the road from excl. landing ground to excl. BILIN during the hours of daylight.

6. *F.F. 2*
   No. 1 column will continue to operate on the coast as far as the BILIN river.
   No. 2 column will be based on MELAN G 7705 and will watch all approaches towards the left flank of our area.

7. *2 Burif and detachments on R. SALWEEN*
   2 Burif will remain at PAPUN and will be controlled direct by Div. HQ.
   They must be prepared to withdraw if necessary either on to SHWEGYIN or TOUNGOO.

8. The coy. 8 Burif now at KAMAMAUNG will remain at that place but will come under the orders of 2 Burif and will be withdrawn if necessary by them.
   The coy. 4 Burif at SHWEGUN will remain in its present posn. If forced to withdraw it will join the above coy. 8 Burif.

SALVAGE

9. All civil comn. eqpt. will be collected from ry. stas. and Post Offices en route.

DEMOLITIONS

10. Permanent route will be demolished at frequent intervals and in particular at stations and post offices.

11. Posn. of HQ. 16 Bde. will be notified later.

Sd./- Lt.-Col.,
G.S. 17 Ind. Div.

APPENDIX "D"

17 DIV. OPERATION ORDER NO. 3

10 March, 42

INFORMATION

1. *Enemy*
   (a) 55 and 33 JAPANESE Inf. Divs. have been operating against 17 Div.
   (b) 33 Div. is now in occupation of RANGOON with the task of using it as a base for operations against PROME.
   (c) 55 Div. is based on MOKPALIN, with, it is understood, the task of operating against TOUNGOO.
   (d) Corps Tps.—incl. tanks and a FORMOSA Mortar Unit are in the PEGU-MOKPALIN area according to the most recent and reliable information.

(e) We must expect infiltration on our flank from the PEGU YOMAS and possibly rd. blocks by parties 2-500.[1] These will be destroyed at once by the mobile and armd. forces.

2. *Own Tps.*
   (a) The following units are placed or remain under comd. forthwith:—
      1 W Yorks   Under Comd. 7 Armd. Bde.
      1 D W R   "   "   16 Inf. Bde.
      Cameronians   "   "   48 Inf. Bde.
      Inniskilling Fus.   "   "   63 Inf. Bde. (on arrival).
   (b) Under Div. Recce Regt.   1 Glosters.
   (c) Other units in Bdes. as at present except that as or when units become over strength through arrival of reinforcements and re-equipping, amalgamated bns. may be split off and pulled into Div. Res.
   (d) Under Comd. Div. Recce Unit from 12.00 hrs. 11 Mar.—One Col. F. F. Gp.
      Also Maj. DONALD of the BURMA Police will report as Adviser to HQ. 1 Glosters.

INTENTION

3. 17 Ind. Div. will deny the line HENZARD-SANYWE-THONZE R. until further orders and reorganise during this period.

METHOD

4. The organisation of the Defensive Zone will be in the form of Bde. Gp. Areas acting as bases from which mobile Gps.—especially 7 Armd. Bde. Gp.—can operate—the whole being covered by a screen of irregular forces and patrols.

5. *Strong Base*
   (A) *Fwd. Zone. Right.*   62 Inf. Bde. with under comd. one tp. A Tk. Bty. (2 prs.); in support 1 Ind. Fd. Regt. less one bty. in conjunction with 16 Inf. Bde.
      Area.   ANYASU-YELE NYAUNGWATNG.
      Tasks.   (i) Close patrolling for local protection.
               (ii) Rest and reorganisation.
               (iii) Creating of striking force of the Bn. as soon as possible on a marching basis. If full motorization is necessary 17 Div. will provide M.T.
      Centre.   1 *Glosters* with under comd. one coln. F.F. Gp.
      Area.   THONZE.
      Tasks.   (i) Form rd. block at main rd. and river crossing.
               (ii) Patrol deep on 24 hrs. basis towards OKHAN.
      Left. 16 Inf. Bde. Tps. under comd. and in support for as 63 Bde.
      Area.   North of THONZE CHAUNG from approx. PANZWE—1½ miles East.
      Tasks.   As for 63 Bde.
              Comd. will recce direct MT route North of CHAUNG to THARRAWADDY.

---

[1] 200 to 500 strong.

(B) *Rear Zone.* 48 Inf. Bde. with in support one bty. 1 Ind. Fd. Regt.
    Area.   LETPADAN.
    Tasks. (a) Protect Rd. and Rail Juncs. at LETPADAN.
            (b) Close patrolling East, West and North East.
            (c) Act as reporting and rallying centre for BMP Gps. operating N.E. and East.
            (d) Rest and reorganise.

(C) *Tharrawaddy Area*
    1 Cameronians will be allotted by 48 Inf. Bde. for special task of protection of and maintenance of law and order in THARRAWADDY.

General Note All Areas. Slit trenches will be dug—but the posns. will NOT be wired or prepared for static defence.

6. *Outer Screen*
    (a) This will be provided by F. F. Gp.
                           B. M. P. Bn.
                            Forest watchers.
    (b) *Areas and Distribution*
        HENZADA   One Coy. B. M. P. one tp. M.I.
                           One coln. F. F. Gp.
                           Dividing line of reponsibility.
                           Ry. HENZADA-BASSEIN incl. to B. M. P.
        PEGU YOMAS from 3 Coy. B. M. P.
        excl. OKHAN-excl. Forest Watchers.
        PROME.

7. *Div. Res.*

7 Armd. Bde. Gp.	THAINDAWYO R. F.
12 Mtn. Bty. less one sec.	THARRAWADDY.
One Bty. A. Tk. (77 mm.)	THARRAWADDY.
All R. E.	THARRAWADDY.
One Coln. F. F. Gp.	Div. HQ. Area.
One tp. M. I. F. F. Gp.	Div. HQ. Area.
One Coy. B. M. P.	THARRAWADDY.

8. *R. A.*
    (a) As allocated above.
    (b) A. A. protection.
        By Bofors over THONZE Br. Area.
                        "   THARRAWADDY.
                        "   THAINDAWYO R. F.
        By 3   "   "   THARRAWADDY Area.
    All A.A. Bty. will be under comd. A.A.D.C.

9. *R. E.*
    (a) Separate instructions have been issued re. Rd. blocks and demolitions West of R. IRRAWADDY.
    (b) Water recces will be carried out at MINHLA-LETPADAN.

10. *IRRAWADDI River Patrol*
        Comd.   Maj. JOHNSON R.M.
        Tps.   R. Marines River patrol.
    will come under comd. 17 Div. on arrival HENZADA Area.
    Reports to 17 Div. by W/T.
    Patrol will liaise with B.M.P. Comd. at HENZADA R.S.

11. *Armed. Train*

Manned by 1 W. Yorks, this train will patrol line between excl. THONZE and excl. PROME.

It will also be used on demand to HQ. 17 Div. by B.M.P. or F.F. Gp. on the line LETPADAN-THARAWA.

Adm. Arrangements

Sd./- Lt. Col.,
G. S. 17 IND. DIV.

APPENDIX "E"

17 DIV. OPERATION INSTRUCTION NO. 19

14 March 42

Information

1. *Enemy*

No further information is yet available.

Own Tps.

The following additional units now form part of 17 Div. Tps.

    5 Dogra.
    8 Burif.
    Karen Commando.
    Musgrave's Contingent.

Intention

2. 17 Div. will occupy a defensive posn. in the OKPO-GYOBINGAUK area from which it can detach strong mobile and armd. forces to act against any enemy located in this area.

Method

3. *Locations*
    (a) The areas occupied by formations is shown in the att. tracing, Appx. A.
    (b) 7 Armd. Bde. is concentrated in the area East and North of GYOBINGAUK.
    (c) The garrison of OKPO R.S. will be 5 Dogra.
    (d) The garrison of ZIGON where certain wkshop installations have been formed will consist of 8 Burif.

8 Burif will be reformed in this area. Arrangements are being made for the despatch of reinforcements as soon as possible.

4. *System of Defence*
    (a) As attack may be expected from any side, the defensive posn. must be based on a series of Bdes. areas in which Bns. and Coys. are sited for all round defence.
    (b) Slit trenches with alternative trenches will be dug and as soon as available tactical wire will be put up.
    (c) Primary consideration will be concealment. This applies especially to sentry posts.
    (d) During the day trenches need not be occupied but, provided adequate sentry and defensive precautions exist, men may rest in scrub areas.

- (e) Scrub obstructing field of fire will be burnt down.
- (f) There will be no firing at night inwards within Bde. defensive perimeters, but all unit posns. will be so sited that if one bastion is overrun, fire from the others can cover this.
- (g) To avoid any incidents of our units shooting each other the most careful liaison to establish posns. of posts on right and left will be carried out.

5. *Patrolling*

Deep patrolling day and night will be carried out by all Bdes. in additions to the Div. Recce Regt.

48 Bde.	West and N.E.
16 Bde.	East and N.E., S.E.
63 Bde.	East and South.
5 Dogra	West and S.W.

6. Every effort will be made to ambush and destroy small parties of the enemy, especially recce parties who will try and discover the extent of our posn.

Units are reminded that it is a favourite trick of the enemy's to use Red Tracer from automatics at night fired at random to draw the fire of our posns. thus disclosing our flanks.

7. Details of the outer irregular screen of "scouts" and informers will be issued tomorrow.

Lt.-Col.
G.S. 17 Ind. Div.

APPENDIX "F"

DIRECTIVE

Based on BURMA ARMY Appreciation Dated 26.3.42.

1. In order to cover the possibility of a further withdrawal, it is necessary to issue instructions for the proper co-ordination of the action of the British and Chinese Armies in this event.

This directive deals only with movement North of the road KYAUKPADAUNG-MEIKTILA.

The general direction of movement, during which the utmost possible resistance will be afforded to the enemy's advance, will be as under:—

2. *1 Bur. Corps*
   - (a) A small column consisting of CHIN tps. (Burma Rifles) to move North from PAKOKKU via PAUK on KALEMYO. Role to cover the right flank of 1 Corps, to hold up the enemy's advance on the ASSAM road by this route with the assistance of CHIN irregulars and to threaten the flank of any Japanese Troops or traitor forces that endeavour to work up the West bank of River CHINDWIN.
   - (b) One column to move from PAKOKKU on the West bank of the River IRRAWADDY and River CHINDWIN to cover the movement of shipping on the latter and our installations at MONYWA. It will be most important to keep open the L. of C. from MONYWA to KALEWA as long as possible.

Columns (a) and (b) above should hold Pakokku as long as possible.
   - (c) One column to move via MYINGYAN-MYOTHA TADA-U and NGAZUN to cover MANDALAY to the West of the PANLAUNG River, crossing the River IRRAWADDY if necessary by the ferry

at NGAZUN or the AVA bridge at MANDALAY. This force will then operate West of River MU in the angle between the River IRRAWADDY and River CHINDWIN to cover the withdrawal of non-essential units and personnel via River CHINDWIN on KALEWA. Subsequently this force will either move by the KALEWA route or on YE-U. It is suggested that (*a*), (*b*) and (*c*) should be carried out by 1 Bur. Div. In view of the difficulties of this route and river crossings M.T. should be kept to a minimum. Reconnaissance should be carried out at an early date and an administrative plan made.

(*d*) One column to move via MEIKTILA-KYAUKSE to assist the Chinese in the defence of MANDALAY. It will subsequently split and one portion will co-operate with the Chinese in opposing the enemy's advance up the LASHIO Road. This latter portion should consist of 7th Armd. Bde. and one Inf. Bde. of 17 Div. The remainder, i.e., the balance of 17 Div. shall cross the AVA Bridge and after holding SAGAING as long as possible will cover the SHWEBO-YE-U Road. The subsequent movement of the above columns will be:—
  (*i*) Via LASHIO-BHAMO, 7 Armd. Bde. and 1 Inf. Bde.
  (*ii*) From SHWEBO via track, rail or river towards INDAW-KATHA, 17 Div. less one Bde.

(*e*) *Command.* Chindwin Force (Paras (*a*), (*b*) and (*c*) above)—Comd. HQ. 1 Bur. Div.
  Defence of MANDALAY (Para (*d*) above)—Comd. HQ. 1 Bur. Corps.
  Defence of LASHIO Road (Para (*d*) (*i*) above—Comd. HQ. 1 Bur. Corps.
  Defence of SHWEBO Road (Para (*d*) (*ii*) above)—Comd. HQ. 17 Div.
  A.H.Q. will command each of the above direct.

(*f*) *Administration.* The necessary reconnaissances and formation of dumps North of MANDALAY and River IRRAWADDY will be carried out by A.H.Q.

3. *V Chinese Army*
This will move by the main BURMA-CHINA road and will be responsible for the defence of MANDALAY East as far West as River PANLAUNG.

4. *VI Chinese Army*
For troops West of the R. SALWEEN routes:—
From LOIKAW and MONGMAI to LOILEM and thence North to HSIPAW and LASHIO.
93rd Chinese Div. should withdraw on PUERH.

5. Reserves of supplies for the Chinese Armies will as far as possible be accumulated at LASHIO and KENGTUNG.

6. *Communications*
The following work is urgently required in addition to the completion of the TAMU-KALEWA-YE-U road. Recce and information of tracks and roads as under:—
  (1) From YE-U Northwards.
  (2) PANTHA-INDAW-KAWLIN.
  (3) SITTAUNG-PINLEBU.
  (4) MONYWA-YE-U.
  (5) THABEIKKYIN-MOGOK-HSIPAW.

(6) THABEIKKYIN-KINU.
(7) BHAMO-MYITKYINA.

Of the above (1) and (4) should be made into fair weather M.T., (2) and (3) into cart tracks in the first instance, (5), (6) and (7) should be made into all-weather M.T. roads as soon as possible.

Sd/- xxx
Lt.-Col.
for C.G.S., Army in Burma.

APPENDIX "G"

1 BURCORPS DIRECTIVE NO. 2

27 April, 42

INTENTION

1. To hold a bridge-head covering the KALEWA route to INDIA so that reinforcements may arrive, first to relieve units of Burcorps, and in due course to resume the offensive.

METHOD

2. Formations are directed into areas as under:

3. *1 Burdiv* will move by the SAMEIKKON ferry to MONYWA and will pass a strong Bde. Gp. (13 Bde.) to the WEST bank of the CHINDWIN. 1 Burdiv, less 13 Bde. and 2 Bur. Bde., will concentrate at MONYWA where it will be joined by one Bde. Gp. (probably 63 Bde.) from 17 Div. This Bde. will come under comd. 1 Burdiv.

Task of 1 Burdiv will be to delay the enemy astride the CHINDWIN as far SOUTH as possible, in any case holding line astride the river at KANI about 35 miles NW of MONYWA.

4. *2 Bur. Bde*, in supercession of previous orders will move via PAKKOKU and PAUK to TILIN where it will prevent any enemy movement up the MYITHA valley.

5. *17 Div.* less one Bde. (*vide* 3 above) will move through 38 Chinese Div., in SAGAING area, by the main SHWEBO rd. to YE-U where one Bde. will establish itself in a defensive posn. covering the MU crossing, the remainder of the Div. remaining in mobile reserve.

6. *38 Div.*, after 17 Div. has passed through will move back on SHWEBO covered by 7 Armd. Bde., subsequently passing behind 17 Div.

7. *Corps HQ.* moving by the SHWEBO axis will proceed to YE-U.

8. Grouping of Burcorps subsequent to above movements will be as follows:

2 Bur Bde.	... TILIN
1 Bur. Div. (less 2 Bur. Bde. and with 63 Bde. under comd.	Astride CHINDWIN MONYWA area.
17 Div. (less one Bde.)	YE-U.
38 Div. and Armd. Bde.	... SHWEBO en route to YE-U.
Corps HQ.	... YE-U area.

9. Subsequent moves depend on arrival reinforcements from INDIA.

10. *ADM.*

2 Bur. Bde. will be maintained from KALEWA on arrival TILIN.

1 Burdiv. will stock up as far as possible from stocks at MONYWA and will subsequently be maintained by river from KALEWA.

Both the above formations must obtain all available local supplies and be prepared to live in the country as far as possible.

Remaining formations will be supplied from YE-U or SHWEBO.

Sd./- BRIG.,
GS. HQ. BURCORPS.

1 BURCORPS DIRECTIVE NO. 3

28 April, 42.

(NOTE:—THIS DIRECTIVE CANCELS DIRECTIVE NO. 2 OF 27 APR.)

1. INTENTION

To delay enemy on the line of IRRAWADDY River, to permit reorganisation in rear and the regrouping of the Forces.

METHOD

2. Formations are directed into areas as under.
3. (a) *1 Burdiv.* (less 2 Bur. Bde.) will move by the SAMEIKKON Ferry to Monywa. On arrival MONYWA 13 Inf. Bde. will pass across the CHINDWIN and will operate SOUTH and SOUTH-WEST from SILINGYI down to the general line of the NGA KONYAMA Chaung.
    (b) *1 Bur. Bde.* (as reorganized with KOYLI and Rajput) will move by ship direct from MONYWA to KALEWA where it will come under comd. L of C Area for the defence of KALEWA bridge-head.
    (c) *One Bde. Gp.* from 17 Div. will be moved by rail under Corps arrangements to CHAUNG-U where it will come under comd. 1 Bur. Div. and will operate SOUTH from CHAUNG-U towards MYAUNG and MOGYIBOK with the object of preventing enemy penetration and protecting rd. and ry. SAGAING-MONYWA. Div. will report entraining strength and maundage of Bde. to Corps HQ. immediately.
    (d) *2 Bur. Bde.*, which will remain under comd. 1 Bur. Div., will move via PAKKOKU and PAUK to TILIN where it will prevent any enemy movement up the MYITHA valley.
4. (a) *17 Div.* (less one Bde.) will move to area MYINMU ALLAGAPPA and will prevent enemy infiltration between incl. the MU river and incl. ALLAGAPPA.
    (b) *F.F. 9* now in posn. at NYAUNGBINWUN and on the KYAUK-TALON and NGAZUN ferries will come under comd. 17 Div.
    (c) 17 Div. will recce routes leading NORTH through AYADAW to YE-U with a view to making use of them in event of withdrawal NORTH.
5. 38 Chinese Div. will hold the area ONDAW-SAGAING-YWATHGYI and prevent enemy penetration across the river from AMARAPURA or TADA-U.
6. (a) *7 Armd. Bde.* less one Sqn., will be in support to 38 Chinese Div. and will operate from ONDAW area.
    (b) One Sqn. 7 Armd. Bde. will come under comd. 1 Burdiv. for operations in the CHAUNG-U area.
7. Corps HQ. will move to MONYWA about 30 April.

GROUP III—APPENDIX G

8. Grouping of Burcorps subsequent to above moves will be as follows:—

2 *Bur. Bde.*	... TILIN.
1 Burdiv. (less 2 Bur. Bde. and with one Bde. Gp. from 17 Div. and one Sqn. Armd. Bde. under Comd.)	MONYWA-CHAUNGU-SALINGYI area.
17 Div. (less one Bde.) with F. F. 9 under Comd.	MYINMU-ALLAGAPPA area.
38 Chinese Div.	ONDAW-SAGAING-YWATHGYI area.
7 *Armd. Bde.* less one Sqn. (in support 38 Div.)	ONDAW.
CORPS HQ.	MONYWA.

9. ADM. (*a*) Divs. will report to Corps immediately ration strengths of their respective Divs. after the above regrouping.
  Showing Nos.:—BT. IT. Bur. T. and Animals.
  (*b*) Army are arranging move by ship of 1 Bur. Bde. to KALEWA from MONYWA.
  (*c*) Army are arranging for maintenance of 2 Bur. Bde. at TILIN from KALEWA.

10. 1 Burdiv. (less 2 Bur. Bde.) and 17 Div. will be supplied from MONYWA.

11. 38 Div. and 7 Armd. Bde. (less one Sqn.) will be supplied from SHWEBO.

12. All formations will make fullest possible use of local resources, requisitioning wherever possible.

It is essential to lay in stocks in the KALEWA-YE-U area from future maintenance of the force: and all concerned must be informed that saving of resources in the immediate future is a matter of *vital* importance to every individual member of the Force.

The strictest economy will be exercised in the running of M.T. and the consumption of M.T. spirit.

Sd./- BRIG.,
GS. HQ. BURCORPS.

GROUP IV

APPENDIX "A"

A Brief Account of the Defence of Martaban and Subsequent Withdrawal

The 3 Bn. 7th Gurkha Rifles and an attached company the K.O.Y.L.I. were surrounded at Martaban and after a two coy. attack, we eventually made our way out. Subsequent accounts have not been very accurate, so the writer who commanded the MARTABAN Garrison offers this account which is written entirely from memory. When MOULMEIN was evacuated on the night 30/31 January and following day I was temporarily commanding the 46th Bde. but on return of the Commander the next day I went down to Martaban to rejoin my battalion.

On the way down, at THATON special orders were given to me by 16 Bde. Comdr. to take over command of the Martaban defences. We had the 3/7 G.R. (less two Coys. away on Div. HQ. protection) the 1st battalion 9th Jats under Lt.-Col. Hay and later Major Gerty, a Mountain Bty. RA and a contingent of the Burma Auxiliary Force, I made my HQ. with the Jat Bn. who were holding the forward positions. We had a very big front, eight miles along the north bank of the Salween—the wharves and warehouses at the mouth of the river all held by the Jats, to about eight miles up the coast from the estuary patrolled by the Gurkhas who were then in reserve about 3 miles North on the main road.

We also had to watch the jungle behind us, west of which ran the main road and railway back to Bde. HQ. at THATON, thirty-eight miles away by road. The Bty. O.P. was near a pagoda on the high ridge overlooking the whole position with a grand view of MOULMEIN. The Bty. was at M.S. 3 near the reserve.

Our water-front was not wired though the field of fire in some places on the East side was only 50 yards and the river being tidal, at low tide, and flats and shallow water between some small islands and the main-land made wading possible and gave us still more area to watch. After a day or two, more troops were sent down, the 7/10th Baluch Bn. under Lt.-Col. Dyer and my remaining two companies arrived, which eased things considerably and allowed us to patrol the close country along the SALWEEN RIVER towards NATHMAW.

From the first day of the defence our troops, including 3/7 G.R. sustained casualties from air action, after several days we were shelled by enemy artillery and mortars. The troops in trenches near the warehouses and M.G. posts were under continuous enemy observation by day. Parties of the enemy in large sampans, taking advantage of the dark hours or early morning river fog, came close to our shore before they were observed and engaged by defensive fire. During the next week many officers and soldiers survivors of the MOULMEIN Garrison, some in Burmese dress, came trickling through us—one B.O. crossed by swimming from island to island. They had been left behind when MOULMEIN was evacuated.

We were very thin on the ground but in spite of alarms and occasional Jap boat patrols and inadequate air support, we held the position for 9 days. Our wireless was always giving trouble so that usually we had to use the existing civil telephone line which was an unreliable and too convenient a means of communication.

By about the 6th Feb. all the other troops and eventually the gunners also, were removed for duty elsewhere. That left our Bn. and a Coy. of British Infantry to carry on the defence of MARTABAN.

Patrolling on the West side which faces BILUGYUN was extremely difficult owing to many creeks; even at low tide wide detours inland were necessary. As far as I know 17 Div. had no boat patrols along the coast but had watchers at OKPO, about 10 or more miles N.W. from Martaban. Until the last day our O.Ps. were established in the hills. On the 6th Feb. one Pl. 3/7 G.R. was detached and established in the pass (c) (see diagram) across the range of hills 10 miles North of Martaban to give warning of undetected infiltration around the flanks of the MARTABAN Garrison. M.T. patrols up to 7 miles along the road leading north on the East side of the range, and daily establishment of an Intelligence Group was arranged, and this was responsible for the first definite information of Jap forces having crossed the River SALWEEN and infiltration around our East flank, on the 8th February. On that day before noon the telephone line was cut and a party including British and Gurkha Signaller under Capt. STOURTON went out to investigate; they bumped a strong Japanese road-block about 8 miles up the main road. Only one man returned at about 3-30 p.m. My observation posts were meanwhile busily reporting barges and boats from BILUGYUN a small steamer

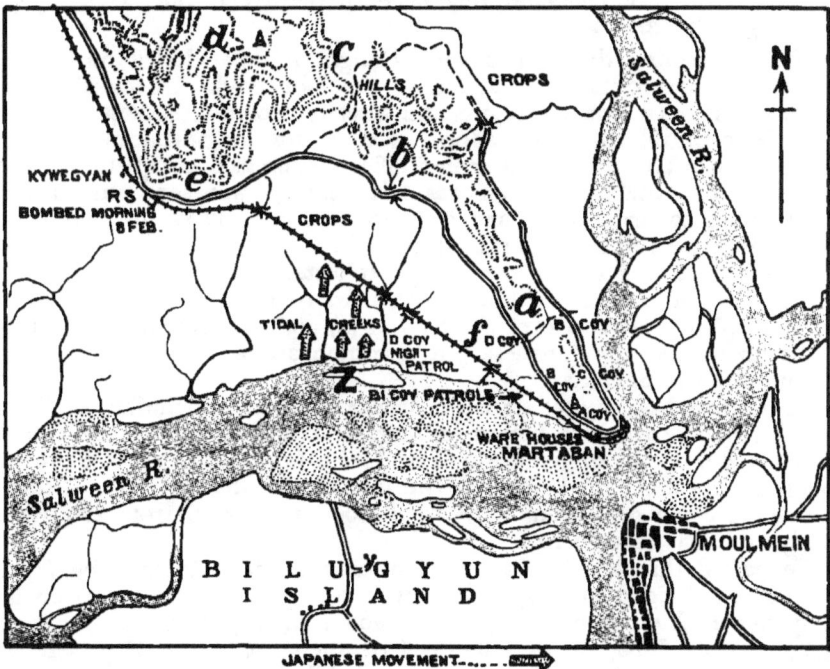

SKETCH OF MARTABAN

or motor boat landing men on the seaside. On the river side, at about 13.00 hours news came that a Jap Officer had been contacted on the east road which runs up North some eight miles and then comes to an end. Two British Officer 2/Lts. CARVER & BLAIR and their Orderlies, who went out in a truck to reconnoitre, had a narrow escape; BLAIR was wounded but they brought back news of Japs on the road about four miles from our left Coy.

Shortly after 2 p.m. I gave orders for two Companies under CARVER to attack these fellows and moved the company of Br. Inf. to a position about 3 miles up the main road on the other side, to face North on the West side of the hills. It should be remembered that the defence of the long water-front was our main task.

At about 5 p.m. a report from Carver said he had chased the Japs off his road into the jungle towards hills East of (b) & (c) and had a truck-load of trophies including a small gun. This was the first gun captured and the first bayonet charge in the Burma Campaign, I believe. At about 6 p.m. Major Haughton K.O.Y.L.I. and I climbed to (a) and observed considerable dust and movement from Z. We estimated that about one to two thousand Japs were moving across the plain.

Of the situation reports and messages handed into the Div. Sigs. Mobile W/T Unit during the developments that day, only one was reported to have been accepted at about 16.45 hours on 8 Feb. by Div. HQ. at KYAIKTO. Subsequent enquiry produced a denial which shows that it was probably NOT received and certainly not passed to 46 Bde. (just relieved 16 Bde. HQ.). MARTABAN Signallers stated at 16.00 hours that throughout 8 Feb. their offer of messages to Bde. HQ. was repeatedly refused, though the possibility of Japanese W/T Sigs. masquerading as our own Bde. HQ. was not unlikely.

The Japs observed advancing from the West were moving not towards us but towards their road-block (b) and the hills (d). It appeared that they were moving to a position from which they could attack Martaban the next day. There was practically nothing between them and Bde. HQ. to whom we could give no message.

After confirming these facts with Haughton (later killed on the Bilin river) and a short conference including my 2-in-comd. I decided to break through on the east side where we had already scored a success and where the jungle to the North would afford us cover for the withdrawal after the break-through. The other two senior officers expressed complete agreement with this plan. One Coy. which was left near (f) was sent out to oppose any Jap move towards (a). They were to have gone N.W. to gain contact, but went West and did not gain contact.

At 8-15 p.m. I had all the troops collected on the East road facing North and we advanced. Although two pairs of runners were sent to order the Coy. at (f) to withdraw over the pass at (a) and to follow up, the company did not do so and the Japanese put a cordon across the hills at (c) which they bumped the next day.

We destroyed our motor transport trucks and lorries including Lt. Carver's truck of Japanese trophies before leaving, as I had considered that because of being a Bn. on the higher scale of M.T. the Jap would expect us to break through on the main road side and we intended to mislead him. I doubted also that we could get through the road block, reinforced from the West so strongly as it was sure to be.

We passed through the East road block without incident; the Japanese had evidently decided to stay in the jungle covered hills. One post on a hill put up a flare but we were very quiet and evidently mistaken for a large fighting patrol. Most of us got through then; only the Coy. left at (f) appeared not to have caught up with us. We then crossed wide streams, muddy rice fields and skirting the edge of the jungle through marshes, made as much distance North as we could. I have no maps now, but believe our main party covered about twenty-five or more miles before we made a proper halt.

At about 06.30 hours the next day we took up a position in square formation on a ridge and had about 6 hours rest. We found that many men had dropped behind and "A" Coy. and some sub-units had avoided crossing a march and had become detached.

Shortly after mid-day we set out again and as we came across no water, that part of our march through dry jungle up and down hill was exhausting. At about 6 p.m. hearing there was a well near our track we had an hour's halt. The Second-in-Command who had been urging on the tail of our column reported many more stragglers and recommended a halt to collect them, for which the order was then given. The Adjutant and I made a short reconnaissance and posted some sentries and then rested till men brought us water in 'chaguls' (canvas bags). We were terribly thirsty.

We started off again round about 16.30 hours and about 18.00 hours observed troops coming towards us from the East. We got into open formation, after some difficulty owing to extreme fatigue, and my Orderly 10156 L/Nk. Bhimraj Limbu went towards these troops, using my binoculars, to identify them. They turned out to be Burma Rifles who on questioning said they were patrolling West from a point (NATHMAW) on the river some 16 miles from MARTABAN. Their officer, said to be a Jamadar, though sent for, appeared to avoid us, but we heard from a Havildar that the Japs had not been seen near their out-post on the river. I remember on first sighting these troops, I though I could see two Officers with them who appeared to be looking at us through binoculars.

In the village some of them took up a position as if to fire at us but Capt. MacCabe and I having recognised them shouted to them.

They did not join us but continued due West. As the Japs contacted and charged on the 8th must have come across the river between KADO and MARTABAN, I still have the impression that some information of the Japs had been received by these particular troops. Two doubtful guides were obtained from a village who seemed keen to lead us East so they were dismissed and continuing North we reached the road leading to THATON that night. We slept soundly in spite of much shivering with cold. The next morning, 10th February, a truck passed along the road and we send word to THATON to say where we were. Most of us were later conveyed in motor transport into the town.

We learnt that the preceding day, 9th February, my liaison officer had been killed North of the main road-block when trying to bring me orders in an armoured car and that an attack organised by Bde. to get through to MARTABAN had been unsuccessful. Apparently, there was no landing at MARTABAN Wharves on the 9th February, because some odd men who had not received the order to withdraw subsequently came in and told us they had remained in MARTABAN till some time on the 9th February. One thing which is mystifying was the move of enemy troops from (z) towards (c) and (d) and, perhaps to the Railway Station* (SHWEGYIN) at (c) which was reported by the Intelligence Group and personally observed by Major HAUGHTON and me, and yet the small relieving force including the platoon left at (c) say they did not contact the Jap till they attacked the West road-block at (b) on the 9th February.

Shortly after our arrival at THATON the Japanese attacked and overwhelmed a battalion at PA-AN some twenty-six miles to the East and this is considered to have been his main thrust. Another unconfirmed report states that be made his main thrust through KADO and confirms the landing North of MARTABAN on the West side from BILUGYUN Island. On the 7th February Jap forces in MOULMEIN were reported to be about 20,000 but this had not been confirmed.

CONCLUSION

Here are a few points for comment on the MARTABAN position:

(*i*) Wide frontage; dispersion of defending forces; active patrolling; ultimate fatigue of troops; distance between Bde. HQ. with support and the forward Bn. was 38 miles which was difficult even for W/T communication; breakdown of communications, undetected infiltration S.W. of NATHMAW, between PAAN and MARTABAN, also by boats and launch from BILUGYUN on the sea-slide.

(*ii*) The force had orders to hold on as long as possible, and unknown to the Commander, the liaison Officer from THATON was alleged to be bringing definite orders from the incoming Bde. HQ. to stay in Martaban. The withdrawal as effected was easy though when formed up for the break-through at 20-15 hrs. on 8th Febry., we were expecting heavy opposition. In any case, the withdrawal was not done without casualties.

(*iii*) If we had waited for the Jap to attack us, he would probably have done the opposite and made straight for Bde. HQ., advancing up the main road.

(*iv*) He may have attacked us on the 9th after preparation. Had we stayed in the position we could not have avoided infiltration and out-flanking by considerable Japanese forces.

(*v*) As it happened, no direct attack on MARTABAN was made from MOULMEIN on the 8th or 9th, so we would not have been called upon to prevent a landing at the Wharves while being out-manoeuvred, thereby remaining at MARTABAN the battalion and British Coy. would ultimately have been overwhelmed to little or no purpose.

(*vi*) Actually the Japs apparently decided to bye-pass MARTABAN and to make their main thrusts above MARTABAN and at PAAN.

(*vii*) In my opinion the decision to evacuate MARTABAN and fight our way through was the correct tactical solution and once made, the plan was successful owing to its prompt execution. We had held MARTABAN for 9 days. Where else in Burma was a stand made for this length of time?

(*viii*) The actual march back through crops, marshes and jungles was a telling performance, more than 50 miles in two days on little or no food. The carriage of Anti-tank rifles, MGs and mortars could not be attempted but fortunately all mortars had been sent back to dump as their range was inadequate to harass Japs in MOULMEIN and on the islands in the river. Two MGs were there also, waiting to be delivered to the Battalion, so that except for the losses of D Coy. not many weapons were lost.

This has been written from memory without reference to maps, except the Road Map of India, so there may be small inaccuracies. On the other hand no other individual had received continuous reports and knew the position so well, except the outgoing Bde. Comdr. at THATON who had visited us almost daily.

"A" company. Kings Own Yorkshire L.I. rejoined the Unit at THATON and Col. KEEGAN later said that the men were proud to be their first Coy. in action and glad to have made a firm friendship with Johnny Gurkha.

All ranks were footsore because of the hard going. Most of D Coy. 3/7 GR got back during the next few days, also several BOs and GOs. There were a number of cases of hostility from Burmans but just as many acts of kindness. A Coy. were given plenty food by villagers who declined payment. Some of the troops were captured by the Japs and a few of these had been beaten and released but all forgot hardships and were happy to rejoin the Battalion. Actual numbers are difficult to obtain but the 3/7 GR casualties for this action were believed to be about 80 of whom 2 BOs Capt. Stourton and Lt. Joliffe were killed and one Lt. Blair was wounded.

H. R. Stevenson,
Lieut-Colonel,
Comdg. 3/7th Gurkha Rifles.

18 Feb. 1942.

APPENDIX "B"

SOME NOTES ON THE WITHDRAWAL FROM PROME—

April 1942

1. As a result of a General Staff Appreciation, made during the withdrawal of the Army of BURMA from RANGOON, it was decided to concentrate the 1 Bur. Div. and the 17 Ind. Div., with the 7 Armd. Bde., in the PROME Valley, to form a Corps HQ. to be known as 1 BURCORPS, to control the operations of the above formations, and to make the CHINESE Vth and VIth Armies, then in the TOUNGOO Valley and the SHAN STATES respectively, responsible for the protection of Eastern BURMA. The PEGU YOMAS formed the dividing line between the BRITISH and the CHINESE Armies.

2. It was further decided that a system of Area defence was to be built up. The I BURCORPS were to prepare and deny a defence system which was to be based on the defended Areas, of PROME and ALLANMAYO, with the 17 Ind. Div. in the PROME area and the 1 Bur. Div. in depth at ALLANMAYO, 7 Armd. Bde. was in hand as a Corps reserve. The CHINESE Armies were to base their defence system on a defended Area at TOUNGOO with other defended Areas protecting the EAST flank at MAWCHI and in the SHAN States.

3. Very considerable delay was caused in getting the 1 Bur. Div. over from the TOUNGOO Valley. This Div. got mixed up in the fighting then proceeding between the JAPANESE and the CHINESE Vth Army about TOUNGOO, and time was lost in extricating it, with the result that only two weak Bdes. and no artillery of the 1 Bur. Div. were available at the time of the PROME battle.

4. During MARCH the JAPANESE did not follow up the withdrawal of the 17 Ind. Div. from RANGOON towards PROME. This Div. established itself about LETPADAN south of PROME where it carried out some much needed re-organization, and from where a very complete Intelligence system watching the PEGU YOMAS and the IRRAWADDY River, was constituted.

5. During the latter part of MARCH, however, the JAPANESE began to move NORTHWARDS towards LETPADAN from RANGOON and early in APRIL (query) it was decided to withdraw into the PROME-ALLANMAYO Area. PROME had been adequately stocked by the time this withdrawal took place, and some of the 1 Bur. Div. had arrived in the ALLANMAYO-THAYETMYO area but the 13 Bde. and all Arty. were still with the CHINESE in the TOUNGOO area. Early in April the Chinese Vth Army planned to carry out an offensive against the Japanese South of TOUNGOO. To assist in this offensive 1 Burcorps was ordered to carry out limited offensive operations from PROME against the Japanese then in the vicinity of LETPADAN.

6. In pursuance of these instructions 17 Ind. Div., with 7 Armd. Bde. under comd., organized a completely motorised force comprising (I think) four British Bns. and the 7 Armd. Bde. less one Regt., with the task of securing LETPADAN and destroying the enemy in that Area.

7. This force was to operate from the secure base of the PROME-ALLANMAYO defended Area system. The motorised force advanced down the main PROME-LETPADAN road, and found that the enemy were themselves advancing by the railway line and EAST of the town. Simultaneously a considerable force of Japanese and hostile Burmans crossed the IRRAWADDY at Swadaung, about 10 miles South of PROME, and cut in

behind the motorised force on the PROME road. Here this force was attacked and stopped by the 63 Bde. holding PROME, but they continued to occupy the road and thereby interposed themselves between the 63 Bde. and the motorised force. The question as to whether the motor force, finding itself in the rear of the main Japanese advance up the railway, should not have attacked the rear of this force instead of spending its effort in breaking through the JAP-BURMAN force on the PROME road, is one which you have probably already dealt with in detail.

8. The results of the subsequent operations, however, were that the motor force did break through the regained PROME (with considerable loss of M.T.) and the main Japanese force disappeared somewhere in the hill forests South of PROME from which fastness it did not appear again until it attacked PROME in concert with a simultaneous advance up the Irrawaddi River on the left banks a few days later.

9. 63 Bde. was holding PROME at the time of this attack. I do not think any attempt had been made to establish a system of Bn. defended areas in depth. Anyway, the attack came in at dusk against the SOUTHERN edge of PROME. I believe the 3/17 Dogras were holding this sector, and they gave way during the night. Confused fighting took place all night and at dawn the situation, as reported to Corps HQ. was that the enemy had secured the South and waterfront areas of Prome and *that a very large Japanese column was moving due North along the left bank of the river.*

10. Comd. 17 Ind. Div. was, I believe, laying on a counter-attack to regain PROME when this information arrived. The information about the Japanese force advancing up to river bank, I believe came from a B.M.P. Officer, one Major CHAPPELL, who reported he had personally seen this JAP column moving North through PROME. The road PROME-ALLANMAYO led through dense reserved jungle for some 15 miles NORTH of PROME, ideal country for JAPANESE road block tactics.

11. The decision that had to be made therefore, and made instantly, was whether the counter-attack on PROME should proceed or whether the whole 17 Ind. Div. and 7 Armd. Bde. should withdraw immediately behind the thick jungle belt North of PROME onto the 1 Bur. Div. then in position at, and South of, ALLANMAYO.

12. The following factors were pertinent in making this decision. The counter-attack against PROME would take some time to stage. The 48 Bde were, I think, the most immediately available tps. and they could have been supported by part of the 7 Armd. Bde, though the country round PROME itself was most unsuitable for armoured operations. Anyway, the 48 Bde. were at least 10 miles from PROME, so it is unlikely that the counter-attack could have taken place before the evening.

13. It was not known in what shape 63 Bde. were in. They had been fighting all night and were thoroughly disorganized. I do not know if they still had anything left in hand. A strong Japanese column (estimated at a Regt.) on the road behind 17 Div. in that thick jungle country would have been a very serious thing. In fact it would have meant that a really decisive battle would have taken place in the course of which we should either have destroyed the Japanese 33 Div., or the 1 Burcorps would have ceased to exist as a fighting formation.

14. In the latter event the JAPS would have been made present of the YENNANYAUNG Oilfields, which were not ready for destruction.

15. I Bur. Div. comprised only two weak Bdes., with no artillery. They were capable of holding a lay back position and of delaying the Japanese advance but they were not an offensive formation and could not be expected to bring much pressure to bear if it came to an all in fight in the jungle.

16. With these factors in mind the Corps Comd. agreed with Comd. 17 Div. that it would be unwise to risk everything on a major battle with the Japanese in between the 17 and 1 Bur. Divs., and that an immediate withdrawal by 17 Ind. Div. was to take place. This withdrawal was carried out with great skill by 17 Div. who passed through I Bur. Div. concentrated about ALLANMAYO.

17. Now some personal comments—

I do not consider that the defence layout of PROME as made by the 63 Bde., was at all effective. The country was dense, it is true, but there were certain areas which if held in strength by concentrated Bns. would have been easy to defend and from which vigorous offensive action could have been taken against enemy bye-passing them. The whole WEST flank of the PROME position was secured by the IRRAWADDI River.

18. I have personally always doubted the accuracy of the report by the B.M.P. Officer concerning the advance of a JAP Regt. up, the river bank. This force never appeared subsequently and it certainly never made any attempt to secure the road behind 17 Div.

19. As the whole series of decisions taken depended on this report, it is obviously most important to know whether it was, or was not true.

20. IF *NOT* true then PROME was evacuated prematurely and without reason, and a strong position from which we had an excellent chance of dealing the JAP a bad rebuff, possibly of stopping him altogether, was abandoned on a false report.

21. It is not possible to say what effect on the campaign a successful action at PROME would have had, but I feel that it might have exercised a decisive effect, and if this is so you will appreciate what an important effect was exercised by that report by the B.M.P. Officer.

Sd/- Davies,
Maj.-Gen.

Bibliography

In the short time that has elapsed since the close of the Second World War, numerous publications have appeared, purporting to tell the story of the Allied retreat from Burma in 1941-42 and the subsequent offensive by the Allies (1944-45) resulting in the recapture of Rangoon. Though useful for obtaining a general picture of the campaign, these books do not form a primary source of information for a detailed narrative of the different Burma campaigns. The best source for this type of information is, of course, the war diaries of the various units which took part in the actual operations. Though the nearness to actual events described prevents the writers of these diaries from having a proper perspective, yet there is no better source for the day to day account of events as they occurred and the tactical military situation as it developed. The Historical Section possesses an almost complete set of these diaries, especially of the Indian units and a full use has been made of these for the writing of this narrative.

Next in importance to the Diaries are a large number of appreciations, mostly unpublished, which were written from time to time by military officers and men at the top in this theatre of war. Forming, as they do, the basis for higher policy, these are invaluable for a proper appreciation of the strategic situation.

In addition, there are various Despatches written by the commanders soon after the completion of operations. Some of these have been published but some are still in manuscript form. As many of these as were available were consulted for this narrative and a list of the more important of these is given below.

Translations of Interrogations of Japanese prisoners, and captured documents, some of the latter containing Japanese accounts meant for their own Government, are another very useful source of information. These also provide material for checking up certain facts and clearing up some obscure points, which would not otherwise be clear, during the operations on account of the defective intelligence system of the Allies. The reports by Japanese Generals and the answers to interrogations are generally very brief, but they are probably the only evidence of Japanese overall conduct of the war in Burma and their processes of reasoning and methods of working. Their intrinsic value is thus very great.

When the Historical Section was formed letters were written to many military officers who had taken part in the operations to give their personal accounts of certain important events of which they were eyewitnesses. Many of these officers were good enough to send their accounts which were found of considerable use. Though some of these accounts have been written from memory, there are very few or no inaccuracies and the accounts are invariably interesting. A list of these is given below and two of these have been reproduced in the appendices.

Since ample documentary sources of a primary nature were available, much use has not been made of the secondary published sources or accounts, except perhaps for describing Allied strategy and diplomacy at the highest level. However, a list of these secondary sources which have been consulted is also given below.

War Diaries

War Diaries of all the units that took part in the campaign, and particularly of the following:—Burcorps; Burma Army; 14th and 17th Indian Divisions; 1st and 2nd Burma Infantry Brigades; 7th Armoured Brigade Group; 13th, 16th, 46th, 48th and 63rd Indian Infantry Brigades; and their subordinate units. Also diaries of administrative units such as Medical, Ordnance, RIASC, Engineers, Signals Corps etc. etc. These are too numerous to be listed in detail.

Appreciations, Reports and Plans

Appreciations and Plan of the Operations for *the Defence of North East Frontier of India*, 1927.

Burma Policy—Sub-committee reports on:
   (a) *Rail connections between Indian & Burma.* May 1936.
   (b) *Road and Rail connections between India and Burma.* June-Sept. 1936.
   (c) *Strategic implications of proposed Yunan-Burma Railway.* Nov. 1936.
   (d) *The future position of the Garrison in Burma after separation.* Feb.-March 1937.

Question of the Separation of Burma from India. Government of India Defence Department—G.S. Branch, 1932-1936.

The internal security scheme for Burma. Annexure, 1-B, Maymyo. Military Keep Scheme 1939.

Army in Burma, Mobilisation Scheme, (Provisional). 1940.

Report of the Anglo-French Conference held at Singapore. June 1939. G.S. Branch.

Report of the Singapore Defence Conference. October 1940.

Report of the Anglo-Dutch-Australian Conference held at Singapore. Feb. 1941.

Defence of the Eastern Frontier, 1941. G.S. Branch M.O.

American, Dutch & British Conversations, Singapore. April 1941.

Report on the Administrative layout of the Army in Burma, with particular reference to 'Q' Services and units. November 1941.

Minutes of General Staff Branch Daily Conference. 6 to 29 April 1942.

Report on the Evacuation of the Northern and Eastern Districts of Burma, by Routes leading to Northern Assam. (Appendix II). Administrator, Refugees Areas (North Assam). Govt. of India Press Simla, 1942.

Japan—Threat to the British Empire. Secret Telegrams (from 24-10-41 to 1-12-41).

Most Secret Telegrams (Cipher) between General Wavell & General Hutton regarding *South Burma Operations* from December 1941 to March 1942.

Most Secret Telegrams regarding *Burma Operational Control.*

Report on the lessons of the Burma Campaign, administrative and tactical, which are based on the experiences of 17th Indian Division, by a Committee convened by order of Major General D. Tennant Cowan, M.C., General Officer Commanding, 17th Indian Division.

Report on the Burma Campaign. Brigadier Eabs, D.D.S.&T. (Burma Army).

Report on the Civil Defence Organisation of Burma. January 1943.

Situation reports from Burma Army, Rangoon, to Troopers. 12-12-41 to 30-4-42.

Report on the Burma Campaign, 1941-42. His Excellency, The Right Honourable, Sir Reginald Dorman Smith, G.B.E., Governor of Burma.

Appreciations of the situation in Burma by General Staff India on 15th December 1941: *To resist a Japanese Advance towards Burma and India and to cut Japanese communications down the Malay Peninsula.*

Air Command, South East Asia, Bombing Operations 1941-42. R.A.F. & U.S.A.A.F. Units based in India and Burma.

Brief Note on *The Part the Public Works Department of the Government of Burma played during the War, 1939-42.*

Progress Reports, Headquarters Army in Burma. June 1939 to April 1942.

Topographical Report re: Routes Across the Burma—Siam Frontier. Burma Command Intelligence Summary No. 2.

Report on the effect of Denial and Demolition Schemes in Burma. H. G. Wilkie, ICS, 1942.

Report on the Burma Frontier Force, 1939-42. Brigadier J. F. Bowerman.

Report on the Naval Operations in Burma Coast Area, from 7 to 25 March 1942. Commodore Graham, 3 June 1942.

Report on the Burma Railways with Special Reference to the hostilities in Burma, 1-11-42. G.H.Q., New Delhi.

Appreciation by Lt.-Gen. T. J. Hutton, C.G.S., Army in Burma, dated 26-3-1942, *To consider future policy as regards the defence of upper Burma.*

Appreciation G.O.C. (General Hutton) Burma Army, made in Rangoon on 10th Jan. 1942, *To stabilise the position in Burma against enemy attack and to consider the steps required to enable an offensive from Burma to be undertaken.*

Protection of Syrian Oil Refinery, correspondence file, G. S. Branch, 1941.

Report of a conference between the Commanders of the British Forces in Burma and the Commanders of the Japanese Forces in Burma, held at the Headquarters Burma Command on 12 Feb. 1946.

Despatches

Despatch by Sir Robert Brooke Popham *on Operations in the Far East, from 17 Oct. 1940 to 27 Dec. 1941.*

Despatch by General Sir Archibald Wavell, GCB, CMG, MC, ADC, *on Operations in Burma, from Dec. 1941 to May 1942.*

Despatch by Lt.-Gen. T. J. Hutton, *on Operations in Burma, from 27 Dec. 1941 to 5 March 1942.*

Despatch by H. R. L. G. Alexander, KCB, CSI, DSO, MC, *on the Operations in Burma, from 5 March 1942 to 20 May 1942.*

Army in Burma, Mobilisation Scheme, (Provisional). 1940.

Despatch by Air Vice-Marshal D. F. Stevenson, CBE, DSO, MC, *on Air Operations in Burma and the Bay of Bengal, from 1 Jan. to 22 May, 1942.*

Japanese Accounts, Documents and Answers to Interrogations

Japanese Methods (Interrogation Reports Nos. 6 & 7 of 12th Army Intelligence Summary Nos. 9 & 13).

Interrogation Reports of Japanese Officers.

Japanese Operations of 18th Div. in Hukawng and Mogaung Area 1941-45. F.E.C., A.T.I.S.

Japanese Divisional Intelligence (18 Div.).

The Japanese Account of their operations in Burma, Dec. 41 to Aug. 45. Edited and issued by HQs 12th Army from documents submitted by HQ Japanese Burma Area Army.

History of the Japanese 15th Army.

A short History of Japanese 18 Division.
History of 33 Japanese Division.
Short History of Japanese 55 Division.
Short History of Japanese 56 Division.
A short History of Jap 14-Tank Regiment.

PERSONAL NARRATIVES

Prome Road-Block on 7-8 March 1942. Lt-Col. G. T. Wheeler.
Tavoy, from 13th Jan. to 18th Jan. 1942. Capt. W. R. Andrews, 6 Burif.
Mergui and the Japanese Invasion, Dec. 1941 to Jan. 1942. F. Yarnold, I.C.S.
Operations, Prachuab—Kirikhan. Capt. E. J. Stephenson, 5 Bur. Regiment.
Kawkareik. M. A. Maybury Esqr, B.C.S.(I)—Sub Div. Officer, 20-22 Jan. 1942.
Kawkareik and Comments on above. Brig. J. K. Jones, DSO.
Sittang, Feb. 1942. Lt-Col. F. C. Simpson.
Operations in Tavoy and on Moulmein Aerodrome. Capt. N. R. Watts, MC (6 Burif), Jan. 1942.
Narrative Account. Lieut Brown, B.R.N.V.R.
Narrative of Actions at Martaban and Pa-an and withdrawal from Thaton to Bilin River, 9-17 Feb. 1942. R. G. Ekins.
The Defence of Martaban, and the withdrawal when surrounded. Lt-Col. H. A. Stevenson—Officer Commanding 3/7 Gurkha Rifles, Feb. 1942.
Experiences of Lieut-Colonel H. Chappel, 2nd Battalion, the Burma Regiment *during the withdrawal from Burma to India in 1942.*
Account of the operations of 1st Bn. the Sikh Regiment in the 1st Burma Campaign.
Chinese operations in Burma, March 29 to June 1942. Compiled from extracts from the "Statesman".
Account of the Operations of Force "Viper" in Burma Campaign. Major D. Johnston, RM, O.C. Force "Viper". 1942.
Account of the Defence and Evacuation of Moulmein. Brig. R. G. Ekins —2-1-1943.
17 Indian Division Account of Operations in Burma, 1942. War Information Circular No. 28-A (G.S., India), 1942.
Diary of Lieut-Colonel W. E. V. Abraham, Liaison Officer from Mid East regarding *South Burma Operations, Dec. 41 to March 1942.*

UNIT HISTORIES

History of 17th Indian Division, July 41 to Dec. 45.
Official History of 3rd Battalion The Rajputana Rifles, Nov. 41 to Oct. 44.

SECONDARY SOURCES

The Burman—His Life and Notions. Shway Yeo, 1896.
The Story of the Kachins, including a Kachin Military venture. A note on Burmese Military employment. Enriquez, 1911.
Contemporary politics in the Far East. Stanley K. Hornbeck, B.A. (Oxon): Ph.D., 1916.
The Karen People of Burma, A study in Anthropology and Ethnology. Rev. Harry Ignatius Marshall, M.A., 1922.
Burma—A handbook of Practical Commercial and Political information. Sir J. G. Scott, KCIE, 1921.
The Military side of Japanese Life. Capt. M. D. Kennedy, 1924.

Some aspects of Japan and Her Defence Forces. Captain M. D. Kennedy, 1928.
The Karen People of Burma—Study in Anthropology and Ethnology. H. I. Marshall, M.A., 1920.
A Burmese Loneliness—A Tale of Travel in Burma, The Southern States and Keng-Tung. Capt. C. M. Enriquez, F.R.G.S. ("Theophilus"), 1918.
A Burmese Wonderland—A Tale of Travel in Lower and Upper Burma. Major C. M. Enriquez, F.R.G.S. (Divisional Recruiting Officer, Burma), 1922.
The Province of Burma. Aleyne Ireland.
British Burma. Forbes.
The Chin Hills. B. S. Carey.
The Silken East. O'Connor.
Burmese Arcady. C. M. Enriquez.
Burma and the Karens. San C. Po.
Japan must Fight Britain. Ishimaru, 1936.
Races of Burma, Handbooks for the Indian Army, Compiled under the orders of the Government of India by Major C. M. Enriquez, 1933.
Far East in Ferment. Guenther Stein, 1936.
Burma Hand Book. Govt. of India Press, Simla, 1944.
Howard Journal of Asiatic Studies, 1938.
War Moves East. Strategicus.
U.S.I. Journal, July, 1943—"*The Start of the War in Burma*". Maj.-Gen. T. G. Smyth.
British Rule in Burma, 1824-1942. G. E. Harvey, Late Indian Civil Service.
Japan's Emergence as a Modern State. E. Herbert Norman, 1940.
Japan and the Modern World. Sir John Pratt, 1942.
The War with Japan Part I—Dec. 41-Aug. 42. Department of Military Art and Engineering, U. S. Military Academy, West Points, New York, 1945.
Trek Brack from Burma. W. G. Burchett.
This War Against Japan. Ian Morrison, 1943.
A Million Died, A Story of War in the Far East. Alfred Wagg, 1943.
The War with Japan. Department of Military Art and Engineering, United States Military Academy, 1945.
Keesing's *Contemporary Archives.*
The old Burma Road. Dr. Neville Bradley, 1945.
Burma. John L. Christian, 1945.
Behind the Japanese Mask. The Right Hon. Sir Robert Craigie, GCMG, CB, His Majesty's Ambassador to Japan (1937-42), 1945.
Burma Pamphlets, 1943.
Through Japanese Barbed Wire. G. Priestwood, 1944.
Burma. Ma Mya Sein, 1944.
"Speaking Generally" Broadcasts, orders and addresses in time of war. General Sir Archibald Wavell, C-in-C, India (1941-43), 1946.
The Lost War—A Japanese Reporter's Inside Story. Masuo Kato, 1946.
The Stilwell Papers. Joseph W. Stilwell, 1948.
Japanese Offensive in Burma. Chapter XVII.
The Census of Burma, 1931.

INDEX

Abdacom, 354. Burma placed under, 78. Closed down, 184.
Act of 1919, 15.
Act of 1935, 16. First elections (1937), 17.
Airfields in Burma, 365.
Air Forces in Burma (Campaign in the air),
    No. 67 Squadron, 367.
    No. 4 Indian Flight, 368.
    3rd Squadron of American Volunteer Group, 53, 204, 222.
    Fighter Squadrons, 222, 367.
    Bomber Squadron, 222, 367.
    Army Co-operation Squadrons, 222, 367-8.
    General Reconnaissance Squadron, 367-8.
    Hurricanes, 163, 204, 238, 240, 367.
    Blenheims aircraft, 163, 238, 240, 367.
    Wapiti and Audax aircraft, 368.
    Plan of Defence, 370.
Air Transport Squadron No. 31, 380.
Akyab Landing Ground, 11, 55, 204, 376.
    Capture of, 358-61, 363-4. Under Martial Law, 359.
    Air raids on, 360, 378.
Alebo Village, 280-1.
Alexander, Lt. General, Sir H., 241-2, 258, 277, 297, 303, 311, 376.
    Appointment as a Commander, 184.
    Meeting with Lt. Gen. Hutton, 192.
    Plans to infiltrate across Pegu Yoma, 192.
    Meeting with Gen. Wavell, 209.
    Decision for evacuation of Rangoon by, 210.
    Orders 17th Ind. Div. to carry out operations at Waw, 210.
    Remarks of, about the retention of Rangoon, 210.
    Orders the road-block to be opened at Rangoon by tanks, 216.
    Concentrates the Indo-British Forces in Irrawaddy Valley, 229, 231.
    Task of retaining Upper Burma, 233.
    Plan and views of, on the defence of Irrawaddy, 237.
    Conference with Gen. Wavell at Allanmyo (1.4.42), 260.
    Requests Gen. Tu to send one Regiment to hold Taungdwingyi (4.4.42), 274.
    Remarks about the operations, 286.
    Plans in the event of loss of Mandalay, 303-4.
    Meeting with the Generalissimo at Maymyo (21-4-42), 305.
    Views on problem of Ava Bridge, 306.
    Plan of a withdrawal north of Mandalay (25/26-4-42), 308.
    Visits Burcorps HQ (28-4-42), 311.
    Meeting with General Stilwell, 321.
    Meeting with General Stilwell (1-5-42), 326-7.
    Plan to withdraw to Kalewa, 336.
    Meeting with Major General Li-Jen Sun (3-5-42), 336.
    Remarks about the passage of Indo-British Forces through Chindwin, 338.
    Extricating his troops from Chindwin (12-5-42), 346.
    Command ceased, 347.
    Meeting with Generalissimo Chiang Kai-shek, 354.
Allanmyo Village—Evacuation of, 370.
Anglo-Burmese Wars, 2, 12.
Animal Transport Company, 107.
Anstice, Brigadier A., 245, 247-9, 313.
Anti-aircraft Battery, 33, 55, 289-91, 299, 342-3, 345, 359.
Anti-aircraft Defence in Burma, 366.
Anti-tank regiment, 57, 316.
Appreciations and Plans of Defence, 31, 33-4.
    Burma Command—Appreciations by, 35.
    Appreciation by General Staff, India, 36.
    Plans for defence of Burma, 37.
    Troop dispositions in Burma, 39.
    General plan of defence, 39.
    Appreciation and plan of Lt. Gen. T. J. Hutton, 81-3, 85.
    Appreciation of Brig. R. G. Ekin in Moulmein, 114.
    Appreciation of Lt. Gen. T. J. Hutton about Salween Line, 118.
    Appreciation of Lt. General T.J. Hutton about Bilin Line, 149-152.
    Appreciation of GOC Burma Army regarding Pegu Area, 187.
    Plan of General Sir H. Alexander to check enemy infiltration across Pegu river, 192.
    Plan of Air Vice-Marshal D.F. Stevenson, 203-4.
    Views of General Hutton on evacuation of Rangoon, 206.
    Appreciation of General Wavell for Allied capacity to hold Burma indefinitely, 220-2.
    Appreciation of Lt. General T.J. Hutton giving position of Army in Burma, 241.
    Appreciations of Lt. Gen. T.J. Hutton, 303-4.
    Plan of Gen. Sir H. Alexander for withdrawal north of Mandalay, 308. Plan altered, 311.
    Appreciation of Air Vice-Marshal D. F. Stevenson, 367.
Arakan National Congress, 359.
Archibald Campbell, Comdr. Indo-British Forces, (1825), 13.
Armoured Brigade, 7th, 57, 152, 157-8, 176, 184-9, 192, 194, 196-7, 214, 220, 224, 234, 237, 243, 263, 267, 270, 274,

282, 285-6, 289-90, 303-11, 313-4, 324, 327, 332-3, 337, 339, 355.
Auchinleck, General Sir C., 41.
Australian Division 7th—Non-arrival of, 187.
Ava Brigade, 306, 310-1, 314, 320-1, 326.
  Proposals for blowing up of, 321.
  Blowing up of, 357.

Baluch Regiment, 120-1, 124-27, 130-1, 133-4, 142, 158, 162, 166-7, 181, 185, 237, 243, 262, 334.
Ba Maw, Dr., As Chief Administrator of Burma, 19.
Bangkok, 63, 127.
Bassein—Port of, 3.
Battery, 414 R.H.A., 57, 186, 194, 196-7, 243, 245, 247-50, 285, 290-1, 296, 300, 313-4, 316.
Bhamo Town, 10.
Biddulph, Colonel F. J., Director, Transportation Directorate for Burma, 388.
Bilin Line, 118, 126, 134, 136-7.
  Defence of, 139.
  Forces at, 140, 142.
  Japanese advances on 142-52.
  Withdrawal from, 152-6.
  Air Operations on, 373.
Bokpyin Village, Japan's raid on, 70-2. See also, 64, 67, 80.
Bombay Burma Trading Corporation, Fine of £230,000 on, 13.
Bourke, Brigadier A.J.H., Commander 2nd Burma Brigade Group, 50-1, 225.
Bruce Scott, Major General J., Commander 1st Burma Division, 51, 290, 296, 298-9.
Buddha Hill, 169, 171, 175.
Burma Brigade, 39, 72, 89, 92, 106, 109, 120, 122, 190, 226, 228-9, 253, 261, 274, 280-3, 285, 296, 310-1, 326.
Burcorps, 229, 234, 237, 242, 246, 250, 260, 269, 272, 274, 276-7, 283, 291, 301, 305, 307-9, 324, 343, 354.
Burma, Topography, 1. Geographical Divisions, 2. Rainfall and weather conditions, 4. Population, 4. Agriculture, production of rice, teak, 6. Petroleum and tin, 6-7. Communications, 7. Roads, 9-10. Water-ways, importance of, 11. Early History of, 12. British Associations with, 12. After the first Burmese War, 12. Anglo-Burmese Wars, 12-4. British Rule, 14. Danger of invasion of, 31. Armed Forces in, 42. Before separation, 42-3. After separation, 43-4. Controversy over India's help to Burma, 44. Creation of forces in, 44-5. War Time Expansion in, 45-53. Burma Royal Naval Volunteer Reserve, 53. India's contribution for defence of, 54-57.
Defence—Its transfer to India Command, 70. Preparedness for War, 79. Under ABDACOM, 78. Under C-in-C, India, 184. Campaign in the air, 365-80.
Civil & Military Administration, 381.
Transport & Supply, 385-6. Ordnance 386-7. Discipline and Morale, 393-4,
Casualties, 394-5.
Burma Army Service Corps, 49-50.
Burma Auxiliary Force, 39, 44-5, 85, 106, 124, 140, 175, 207, 223.
Burma Division, 1st, 51, 186, 192-3, 210, 223-229, 231-3, 236, 255, 257, 261, 269-70, 290-1, 305, 315, 324, 331, 333, 337.
Burma Frontier Force, 17, 33, 39, 46, 48, 88, 107, 109, 186, 207, 210, 364, 394.
Burma Independent Army, 209, 247, 250.
Burma Military Police, 42, 46-7, 150, 186, 207-8, 234, 242-3, 249-50, 261, 265, 337, 394.
Burma Rifles, 3, 39 42, 44-5, 47, 71, 85-6, 90, 92-3, 98, 100, 103-6, 109-13, 115-6, 118, 120-2, 127-8, 134, 137, 140, 142, 145, 154, 158, 162-3, 166-7, 170-1, 173-8, 176, 178, 186, 181, 185, 207-8, 223-9, 231-2. 394
Burma Sappers & Miners Detachment, 42, 44, 177, 207, 211, 223, 243, 290, 298, 325.
Burma Territorial Force, 45.
Burma Volunteer Air Unit, 53.
Burmese Buddhism, 1.
Bush Warfare School for Training at Maymyo, 52, 334, 363.

Cameron, Brigadier R. T., Commander, 48th Indian Infantry Brigade, 262, 314.
Cameronians Force, 56, 122, 185-7, 190-2, 194-5, 198, 200, 234, 237, 254, 258, 260, 282-3, 293-4, 331, 333.
Cavalry Regiment, 58.
Central Ammunition Dump at Tonbo, 387.
Chang, General, 351.
Changsha Battle—General Tu's Plan for, 354-5.
Chauk Village, 6.
Chaung-Yu, Village, 324, 326, 331.
Chen, General, 351.
Chennault, Brigadier Gen. C.L., 365, 377.
Chiang Kai-shek, Generalissimo, 78, 162. Meeting with, 189, 241-2, 252, 365. General H. Alexander, 354. Detaching 3rd Squadron for protection of Rangoon, 364.
Chiengmai, Town, 34, 64, 81, 223.
Chiengrai, Town, 10, 32, 81, 223.
China, China's complaint against Japan to League of Nations (Lytton Commission), 24. Proclamation of National Government in (Aug. '40), 25.
Chindwin River, 3, 336.
Chinese Fifth Army, 82, 135, 229, 233, 241, 252-5, 257, 276, 303, 305, 316, 321, 327, 348, 351, 353, 357, 395.
Chinese Sixth Army, 82, 186, 223-4, 252-7, 303, 348, 350, 361, 363, 395.
Chinese Expeditionary Force, 58. Entry into Burma of, 252-9. 93rd Division, 72, 77, 223, 252-9. 55th Division, 252-9, 305. 49th Division, 252-9. Withdrawal of, 357.
Chinese 38th Division, 291, 296, 305-6. 309-11, 321, 327, 355.
Chinese 227 Regiment, Taking over defence of Mekong river, 223.
Chungking,—General Sir H. Alexander's visit to, 241.

INDEX

Commando Force, 53, 236, 250-1, 342, 358, 363, 392.
Committee of Imperial Defence, 43, 46.
Conferences, Anglo-French Conference, 31. Singapore Defence Conference, 32. Indo-Burma Conference (1941), 35. Inter-Service Conference in Rangoon, 46. Between C-in-C India & GOC Burma Army, regarding Victoria Point, 66. Between General Wavell, Lt-General Hutton and Air Vice-Marshal D. F. Stevenson at Magwe reg: prematurity of Rangoon's evacuation, (1-3-42), 188. Between C-in-C India & General Sir H. Alexander at Allanmyo, 258. Between Generalissimo Chiang Kai-shek and General H. Alexander in Maymyo, 354.
Cowan, Brigadier D. T., Commander, 17th Ind. Division, 137, 177, 189, 192, 210, 268, 341-2, 345.

Denial and Demolition Schemes.
  In Rangoon, 130-2, 205, 210.
  In Yenangyaung Area, 287-8.
  In Upper Burma, 391.
Divisional Employment Platoon, 290.
Divisional Infantry Group, 58.
Divisional Reconnaissance Regiment, 234.
Divisional Signals, 58.
Docks Operating Company No. 3, 388.
Docks Operating Group No. 2, 388.
Dogra Regiment 17th, 56, 120-2, 130-4, 136-7, 140, 142-3, 145, 149, 158, 171-4, 181, 185, 261-4, 341, 346.
Dorman Smith, Sir R., 387.
Duff Cooper, Mr., 33.
Duke of Wellington's Regiment, 56, 160-2, 164, 166-7, 170-4, 176, 234, 243, 245-8, 250, 262, 301, 334, 346.
Duyinzeik—Attack on, 134-6.

East African Brigades, 56.
Edwards, Capt. J.O.V., Commander of Burmese Column No. 1, 69.
Ekin, Brigadier R.G., 56, 116, 135, 137, 173, 180. Control of Operations in Moulmein of, 111-3. Appreciation of the situation in Moulmein by, 114.
Engineer Regiment, 58.

Far East, Japanese aggression in, 21-30.
Far East Command, Instructions on Japanese attack, 35. Its creation at Singapore, 40.
Far East Conferences, 31-3.
Farwell, Brigadier G.A.L., M.C., Commander, 1st Burma Brigade Group, 51.
Field Ambulance (39), 167.
Field Battery, 2nd, 175, 214, 216, 264, 278.
Field Company, 62, 115-6, 122.
Field Company, 70th Indian Engineers, 264.
Field Company Sappers and Miners, 107, 109, 122, 243, 316.
Field Regiment, 33, 220.
Forster, Mr. W.L., for Demolition Scheme, 211, 287.
Frontier Force Regiment, 17, 39, 51, 89, 93, 104, 109-10, 112-3, 115-6, 120, 122, 149-51, 154, 158, 161-2, 164-7, 170-1, 176-7, 185-6, 192, 212, 216, 223-4, 228, 232, 234, 236-7, 243, 247, 249-50, 257, 261-3, 265, 280-2, 289, 324-5, 333-4, 337, 346, 353.
Frontier Force Rifles, 56, 215, 247, 249-50, 261, 264, 274, 277, 326, 328-9, 331, 334.

Garhwal Rifles, 18th Royal, 51, 72, 77, 224, 281, 293-5, 297, 311, 326, 328.
Garrison Battalion, 207.
Garrison Company, 55, 207.
Gloucestershire Regiment, 39, 47, 186, 207, 215, 218, 234, 236-7, 242-3, 245-8, 250, 262, 281, 289-90, 324-5, 333-4.
Goddard, General, 309, 384.
Graham, C.M., Commander Burma Coast, 53.
Graham, R. N., Commodore, 358.
Gurkha Rifles, 51, 56, 77, 93, 96-8, 100-1, 103-5, 107, 110, 118, 120-2, 124-5, 134, 136-7, 140, 142-50, 152-5, 158, 163-4, 168-81, 185, 192-3, 196, 198-200, 214, 237, 243, 249, 261-3, 265-7, 277-80, 301, 315-20, 326, 329, 331-2, 337, 341-3, 345.

Hallet, Capt. J.I., Naval Officer I/C, Rangoon, 53.
Hasegawa, Lt-Col., Commander Syriam Force of Japanese, 189.
Heavy Field Artillery Regiments, 58.
Hlaing River, 7, 12.
Hlegu Village, 188-9, 192-3, 197, 200-2, 210, 213, 215, 218, 256.
Hong Kong—Japanese invasion of, 61.
Htu Chaung, Stream, 349.
Hume, Major J.G.L., R.A., Commanding, 12th Mountain Battery, 115.
Hutton, Lt-General, T. J., Commander of Burma Army.
  Assumes Command of Burma Army (27-12-41), 77.
  Makes appreciation of military situation in Burma, 81-84.
  Decision to strengthen defences of Moulmein, Kawkareik and Tenasserim, 93.
  Comments on attack on Tavoy and Kawkareik, 105.
  Views on holding of Moulmein, 108.
  Appreciation regarding Salween Line, 118.
  Views on withdrawal from Bilin Line, 152.
  Views about the retention of Rangoon, 159.
  Appointment as Chief of General Staff, 184.
  Comments about Burmese Forces active part in operations, 187.
  Visits HQ., 17th Ind. Div. holding Pegu, 191-2.
  Meeting with General H. Alexander, 192.
  Favours evacuation of Rangoon, 206.
  Policy to concentrate Indo-British Forces in South of Burma, 223.
  Sets out position of Army in Burma, 241.
  Visits Keng Tung, (15-1-42), 253.

Seeks permission to move 5th Army to Lashio, 253.
Flies to Lashio to meet Generalissimo, 254.
Visits Taunggyi, 255.
Appreciation regarding Mandalay, 303.
Meeting with Air Vice-Marshal Stevenson, 372.
Indicates necessity of withdrawing Army into Central Burma, 374.
See also 54, 117, 157, 160, 162, 363, 384.
Ilda Shojiro, C-in-C, Japanese 55th Division, 63.
Imperial Ordinance of 1889, 21.
Indian Anti-tank Regiment, 56.
Indian Division, 14th, 56.
Indian Division, 17th, 55-6, 70, 108, 120-1, 124, 128, 135, 137, 142-3, 149, 155, 157, 162, 164, 175, 177, 180-1, 184-90, 192, 210, 214-5, 218, 223, 225-6, 233-4, 236-7, 242, 247, 251, 260, 263, 268, 270, 282, 285, 301, 303-5, 309, 314, 334, 337, 339, 346, 372.
Indian Field Regiment, 57, 214-5, 234, 243, 247, 249, 262, 264, 278, 316, 320, 343.
Indian Infantry Brigade 6th, 192.
Indian Infantry Brigade, 13th, 39, 51, 193, 224-5, 229, 274, 280, 292, 295-6, 298-9, 311, 326, 331, 337.
Indian Infantry Brigade, 16th, 51, 77, 93, 99-100, 103, 118, 121-2, 135-7, 140, 145-9, 152-5, 161, 165, 169, 171-6, 181-2, 185, 188, 192, 234, 237, 262-3, 267-8, 270, 314, 324, 334.
Indian Infantry Brigades 44th & 45th, 107.
Indian Infantry Brigade, 46th, 56, 107, 120-2, 135-7, 140, 142-3, 153, 160, 160-1, 165, 169, 171-2, 176, 181-2.
Indian Infantry Brigade, 48th, 56, 120, 122, 135-6, 144-6, 148-9, 152-5, 158, 160-1, 163, 166, 168, 185, 192-3, 196-201, 234, 237, 262, 266, 278, 282, 290, 313-4, 320, 324, 333, 337, 339, 346, 355, 394.
Indian Infantry Brigade, 63rd, 56, 188, 192, 195, 215, 220, 234, 261, 264, 268-9, 310, 313-6, 320-1, 324-5, 327, 329, 331, 337, 339, 346.
Indian National Army, 309.
Indian Territorial Force, 42.
India's contribution for defence of Burma, 54-7.
Indo-China—Japan's attacks on, 26-7.
Irrawaddy Flotilla Company, 14, 212, 241, 280, 282-3.
Irrawaddy River—Usefulness of for irrigation, transport 3, Line of Communication, 11. Defence of, 237. See also, 2, 222, 233, 334.

Japan—Japanese influence, 18. Aggression in the Far East, 21. Imperialism, 21. Armed Forces, 21-2. Aggression on Korea (1895), 22. Russo-Japanese War 1904-5, 22. Consolidation, 22. Gains in World War I, 23. Washington Agreement, 22. Control over Manchuria 23-4, Anti-Comintern Pact with Germany (1936) and Italy (1937), 25.

Japan—War with China (1937), 25. Doctrine of Co-Prosperity in East Asia, 25-6. Neutrality Pact with Russia (April, 1941), 30. Japanese Forces in Burma, 57-8. Air Forces in Burma, 59-60. First attack on Burma, 61. Invasion of Thailand, 62. Invasion of Tenasserim, 64. Raid on Bokpyin, 70-2.
Japanese Air Strength—Fighter aircraft, Army, 100, 368. Fighter aircraft Army O.I., 369. Fighter aircraft Naval 'O', 369. Japanese campaign in the air, 368-80.
Japanese Forces—
  33rd Division 76, 92, 95, 126, 136, 143, 160, 182, 189, 193, 210, 213, 218, 220, 250, 286, 292, 315, 323.
  Fifteenth Army, 57, 63, 189, 323.
  55th Division, 57, 63, 95, 117, 127, 142-3, 182, 189, 213.
  213th Infantry Regt., 127, 276.
  Sakuma Detached Force, 276, 300.
  Imperial Guards Division, 63-4.
  114th Infantry Regiment, 63.
  3rd Coy. 55th Cavalry Regiment, 63.
  1st Coy. Engineer Regiment, 63.
  55th Division Medical Section, 63.
  143 Infantry Regt., 63, 65.
  112th Infantry Regiment, 76, 84, 95.
  Oki Branch Unit, 76, 84.
  215th Infantry Regiment, 131.
  14th Tank Regiment, 63.
Jat Regiment, 9th, 51, 93-4, 100-4, 118, 121-2, 124-6, 134, 140, 145-6, 152-4, 158, 171, 174-5, 178-9, 185, 207, 262, 334, 342.
John Rowland, Sir, 387, 390.
Jones, Brigadier J. K., Commander, 16th Indian Infantry Brigade, 93, 99, 140, 153, 173-5, 177-9.
Jones, Brigadier N. Hugh, 48th Ind. Infantry Brigade, 56, 146, 152-4, 167-8, 171, 176.
Jwala Singh, L/Nk—Appreciation of situation at Moulmein by, 111.

Kalewa Village, 10, 221, 327, 334. Race for, 336-9, 341-3, 345-7.
Kan, General, 349-50.
Karenni sector, 186, 255. Operations in, 223-9, 231-2.
Karens—Population in Burma of, 4. See also 225.
Kawkareik Sector, 9, 372.
  Troop dispositions at, 92, 95.
  Japanese movements, advance and attack on, 95-9.
  Withdrawal of troops to Kyondo, 99-105.
  Effects of withdrawal of, 105.
Kings Own Yorkshire Light Infantry, 47, 50, 109, 114, 118, 120-2, 124-6, 134-5, 137, 140, 142-9, 154-5, 174, 181, 185, 214, 223, 298, 331.
Kokine Battalion, Burma Frontier Force, 66, 109, 112, 207.
Koyli Force, 122, 126, 132, 155, 171, 175, 181, 282-3.
Kyadoe, Major, (a Karen) Commander, Company of 7th Bn., 229.

Kyaikto Town, 9, 109, 114, 118, 137, 149, 153-6, 160, 224.
  Defences in, 142. Japanese attack on, 162.
Kyaikto-Kinmun-Sakan Line, 162-4.
Kyaukpadaung village, 8.
Kyaukse Village, 327, 355. Action at, 314. Disposition of forces at, 315. Japanese attack on, 317. Withdrawal from, 320.
Kyondo (Village)—Attack on, 96, 99-103.

Lashio Airfield, 8, 11, 58, 189, 239, 241, 253, 257, 303, 307, 321, 353.
Leslie, Brigadier R. B., Commander of Rangoon Fortress, 207.
Lewis, Major General H. V., CB., CIE., DSO., Commander, 17th Indian Division, 107.
Liang, General, Vice-Commander, 55th Division, 349.
Light Anti-aircraft Battery, 34, 243.
Lin Wei, General—Generalissimo's Principal Liaison Officer, 305.
Loilem Village, 10, 350-1.
Loiwing Aerodrome, 238.
Lou, General, Commander of Chinese force on Pyawbwe front, 306-7.
Love, Major, S.W.A., Attack on Bokpyin by, 71.

Madauk Village—Operations in, 228-9.
Magforce, 290, 292.
Magwe Aerodrome, 53, 56, 222, 238, 240, 258, 292, 301, 359, 374, 376.
  Japanese air attack on, 377-8.
Maha Bandula—Burmese General in 1824, 13.
Malaya—Invasion of, 61-2.
Myamyo Village—Bombing of, 242. See also 42, 49, 208, 211, 353, 357.
Mandalay—Railway and Communication Centre, 7-8. Bombing of, 242. Retreat North of, 303-11, 313-22. Plans for resistance south of, 307. Order for withdrawal north of, 308. Other references to: 7, 14, 77, 208, 212, 355.
Manekshaw, Capt. S.H.F.J., Commanding Officer 'A' Company—Award of Military Cross to, 167.
Martaban Range, 8, 77, 80, 96, 112, 116, 118, 121-2.
  Forces at, 124-6. Bombing by Japanese and counter attacks, 128-9. Evacuation of, 129-30.
Martin, Brigadier, 307.
Mawchi Village, 10, 193, 224, 226, 258-9, 348-9, 361, 363.
Ma-Yu Village, 326, 329.
McLeod, Lt.-General, D.K., CB., DSO., 51, 54, 62, 77.
Mehar Das, 2/Lt., Anti-aircraft Battery, 115.
Meiktila, 305, 310, 313-4, 355.
  Road Junction, 10. Bombing of, 242.
Mekong River, 223, 253.
Mergui Aerodrome, 7, 13, 32, 40, 62, 203, 370.
  Japan's air raid on, 67.
  Evacuation of, 89-91.

Mesoht Town, 9, 80, 92, 95, 99.
Migyaungyi—Occupation of, 281.
Minhla-Taungdwingyi Line, Disposition of forces at, 274. General situation, 276. Japan's thrust to the oilfields of, 276-83, 285-6. Withdrawal from, 285-6.
Mingaladon Airport, 11, 53, 74, 184, 203, 205, 211, 213, 238, 240, 367, 376.
Mongpan, 34, 255.
Mokpalin Village, 95, 161, 164, 166-7, 170, 172-5.
  Battle of Sittang at, 162-79.
Monywa, 8. Action at, 323. Japanese Plan for advance to, 323. Importance of, 323. First attack on, 323. Monywa-Myinmo Road, 325. Monywa-Kyaukka Road, 327. Withdrawal from, 322.
Moulmein Aerodrome, 7, 31, 37-8, 70, 76, 80-1, 92, 95-6, 125, 128, 142, 149, 203, 224, 373. Defence of, 106. Forces at, 106. Plan of defence at, 106. Japanese attack on and defence of, 109-14. Evacuation of, 114-7.
Mountain Battery, 33, 42, 44, 56, 72, 106, 109, 112-3, 115, 118, 121-2, 124-5, 130, 140, 144, 147, 153, 169, 175, 215-6, 224, 227, 231-2, 243, 257, 261-2, 264, 281, 283, 294-5, 299, 328, 333, 343, 345.
Mountain Regiment, 57-8, 227.
Myawadi Village, 96-7.
Myitkyina Town, 8, 203.
Myitnge River, 8.

Namtu—Silver lead mine of Burma Corporation at, 7.
Netherland East Indies—Japanese attack on, 28.

Pa-an Village, 105, 118, 124.
  Forces at, 126-8. Japanese attack on Pa-an and counter-attack, 130-4. Attacks on Thaton and Duyinzeik, 134-6. Withdrawal from Duyinzeik, 136-9.
Pedigon Village, Action at, 243, 245-7.
Pagoda Hill, 169-71, 175.
Pakokku Village, 311, 323, 325, 334.
Punjab Regiment, 1st, 51, 224, 228-9, 231, 283, 285, 293-5, 328-9.
Paungde Village—Action at, 243, 245-7.
Payagyi Area—First clash at, 190-1. Attacks near, 197.
Pearl Harbour, 61.
Pegu River, 165, 210, 213, 220, 234, 375.
  Location of, 7. Operations in, 183. Changes in Command at, 184. Reorganisation of 17th Division at, 184-5. Forces and their dispositions at, 186. Plans to evacuate, 188. Japanese moves and attacks on, 194. Withdrawal from, 198-201.
Philippines—Japanese invasion of, 61.
Pin-Chaung, 9, 289-92, 296-9.
Prendergast, Major General H.N.D., V.C., 14.
Prome—9, 13, 185, 204, 206, 210, 229, 247, 249, 251, 258. Bombing of, 241. Withdrawal from, 260. Dispositions of troops in, 261. Japanese moves, 263.
Puerh, Burmese Border, 77, 252-3, 303.

Pyinbon Village, 190.
Pyu Village, 193, 232, 256.

Queen's Own Hussars Regiment, 57, 186, 191, 197-8, 218, 243, 245-7, 249-50, 285, 301, 309, 313-4, 316, 320, 326-7, 331, 333, 337-8, 343.

Railway Construction & Maintenance Group, 388.
Rajput Regiment, 7th, 51, 55, 227, 229, 280-1, 283, 297-8, 331, 359.
Ranbir Bakshi, Capt., 320.
Rangoon, 46, 149, 159, 182, 187.
 Capital, Commercial and industrial centre, 7.
 Japanese Air raids on, 73-5. Inadequacy of Civil Defence Organisation in, 75.
 Demolitions in, 188.
 Fall of, 202-18. Importance of, 202.
 Air raids on, 220-2. Plan for evacuation of, 205-6. Voluntary evacuation of, 206.
 Garrison at, 207. Under Military, 208.
 Japanese movements towards, 213-8, 220.
 Effect of loss of, 220-2.
 Air battle over, 371.
 Importance of maintaining air superiority over, 375.
Rangoon Field Brigade, 47.
Reconnaissance Unit, 33.
Reginald Dorman Smith, Sir, 54.
Robert Brooke-Popham, C.-in-C., Far Eastern Command, 40.
Roughton, Commander, Central Area, 290.
Royal Battalion, 1st, 262.
Royal Engineers, 207.
Royal Inniskilling Fusiliers, 56, 234, 243, 250, 262, 281, 293, 295, 297-8, 328, 332.
Royal Marines River Patrol, 207, 234, 236-7, 242, 250-1, 290, 324-5, 336, 339, 341.
Royal Tank Regiment, 57, 186, 189, 191, 194-5, 214-5, 218, 249, 265-6, 270, 278-9, 281, 285, 289-91, 294, 296, 298, 300, 313-4, 325, 333-4, 337, 339.
Sakurai Shoso, Lt.-General, Commander, Japanese 33rd Division, 127.
Salween Line—Martaban and Pa-an, 3, 137, 303.
 Troop dispositions at, 118, 120-1. Reorganisation of forces in, 121-2, 124. Difficulties of defence, 124.
Shan States & Karenni, 3-4.
 Operations in, 72, 223-9, 231-2, 255. Chinese Front, 348. Japanese thrust through, 348. Last stage of fighting in, 351.
Shans, Population in Burma of, 4.
Shwebo Village, 8, 304-5, 324, 336, 363.
Shwedaung Village, 247, 249-50.
Shwegyin Village, 336-9. Attacks on, 226-8, Fight for, 341.
Sikgyi, oilfields at, 6.
Simon Commission (1930), 15.
Separation of Burma from India, 15.
 Reaction of parties and General Council of Buddhist Association to Separation, 17.
Sikh Regiment, 11th, 56, 193, 216, 218, 261-2, 264, 326, 329, 331-2.
Siri Kanth Korla, Capt., Commanding 'C' Company, 132-3.
Sittang River, 120, 148, 186, 210, 213, 225.
 Characteristics of, 3. Importance of, 157. Battle of, 162-77. Blowing up of the bridge, 177. Withdrawal from, 178-82. Air operations, 373. Japanese air attacks, 374.
Slim, Lt.-General W. J., MC., Commander Burcorps, 234, 268, 276, 285-6, 296, 307, 337.
Smith, Sir R. D., Governor, 75.
Smyth, Major J. G., V.C., 55, 114, 135, 139.
Sodan, Colonel J. N., Director of Movements, 388.
St. John's Ambulance Brigade in Burma, 75.
Stevenson, D.F., Air Vice-Marshal, 203, 365, 367, 370, 372, 374, 376.
Stevenson, H. R. (Lt. Colonel), Commander of Martaban Defence, 124-5.
Stilwell, General J.
 Orders regarding Chinese 200th Div. and 22nd Division, 305.
 Meeting with General Alexander at Shwebo, 321.
 Meeting with General Alexander at Ye-U, 326-7.
 Attack on position West of Taunggyi, 351.
 Moves 38th Division from Mandalay to support Burcorps, 355.
 Crosses Chindwin, 357.
Sun, Major General Lie Jen, Commanding Chinese 38th Division, 291, 336-7.
Syriam, Burma Oil Company's plant at, 6, 186, 188-9, 207, 210-1.

Tai, General, Commander 200th Division Chinese Army, 257.
Tenasserim, 3-4, 6, 14, 62-3, 76-7, 81, 90-1, 209, 223, 253-4, 372.
Taungdwingyi Village, 8.
Tavoy, 7, 13, 40, 62, 64, 70, 81, 203, 370, 373.
 Japanese attack on, 84-6, 88. Evacuation of, 88-9.
Thadon Village—Japanese attack on, 279.
Thai Force.
 Infantry Battalions Artillery Regts., Cavalry Regiments, Tanks Regts., Anti-aircraft Group, Aircraft, 36.
Thailand, 223-4. Japan's aggression on, 28-30. Japan's invasion of, 62.
Thakauchi Hiroshi, Lt. General, Commander Japanese 55th Division, 63.
Thakin Party, 191, 238, 311, 334, 359.
 Anti-British attitude of, 19-20.
Tharrawaddy Village, 214, 216, 220, 236.
 Detachments sent to, 187.
Thaton Town, 118, 129-36, 143. Forces at, 122. Air raid on, 128.

Thazi Junction, 8, 34.
Thazi-Keng-Tung-Tachilek Road, 35.
Thilwa, Oilfield at, 6.
Toungoo Airfield, 10, 51, 53, 135, 186-9, 223, 225-6, 229, 253-6, 361, 373. Loss of, 257-9.
Transport Regiment, 58.
Treaties :
    Archibald Campbell's treaty with Bagyi-daw, re: Burmese surrender to East India Company, 13.
    Thailand's treaty of alliance with Japan, 64.
    Trade Treaty between Japan and America, 27.
Tu Tu Ming, Commander Chinese Fifth Army, 255, 270, 354-5, 357.

U Pu, Premier, 17.
U Saw, Premier, 18. Detention by British, 19.

Victoria Point, 9, 32, 64, 77, 82, 370.
    Japanese invasion of, 65-67.

Wakely, Major General, Commander, Line of Communications Area, 309, 336.
Walton, Major, Gloucestershire Regiment, 208.
Wanting Village, 10, 252, 255, 353.
Washington Naval Treaty, 24.
Wavell, General Sir A.
    Recommends transfer of defence of Burma to India, 41.
    View about Burma's preparedness for defence, 77.
    Appointment as Supreme Commander of Abdacom, 78-9.
    Recommends defence of Burma to remain responsibility of India, 78.
    Comments after withdrawal from Kawkareik, 105.
    Comments re: necessity for holding Moulmein, 107.
    Views regarding situation and instructions to General Hutton (Jan. '42), 108.
    Approval for the evacuation of Moulmein, 117.
    Proposal for taking the offensive, 122.
    Suggests counter-offensive at Sittang river, 160.
    Remarks about the withdrawal from Bilin river, 161-2.
    Remarks after the visit to the Salween, 185.
    Conference with Lt. General T. J. Hutton & Air Vice-Marshal D. F. Stevenson at Magwe (1st March 1942), re: holding of Rangoon, 188.
    Countermands Divisional Commander's plans to evacuate Pegu, 188.
    Visit to Hlegu, 189.
    Proceeds to Lashio. Interview with Marshal Chiang Kai-shek, 189.
    Orders retention of 48th Bde. at Pegu, 189.
    Countermands evacuation of Rangoon, 208.
    Issues directive re: importance of Rangoon's retention, 209.
    Gives a resume of positions in Burma to General Sir H. Alexander, 209.
    Intervention for postponing evacuation of Rangoon, 220.
    Views for the defence of Calcutta & Ceylon, 240-1.
    Visit to Chungking to discuss Military situation with Generalissimo Chiang-Kai-Shek, 241.
    Flies to Chungking to meet Chiang Kai-shek (23-12-41), 252.
    Conference with General Sir H. Alexander at Allanmyo on 1/4/42, 260.
    See also, 33, 54, 57, 77, 223, 240, 252, 254, 259-60, 305, 382.
Waw (Village), 9, 184, 186, 190-3, 210.
    Fighting about, 187, occupation of, 189.
West Yorkshire Regiment, 56, 186-8, 191-2, 194, 196, 198, 200, 234, 243, 245, 248-50, 263, 281, 285, 290-1, 296, 298, 310, 313, 316, 333-8, 339.
White, Lt. Colonel B.J., Commanding Officer 1/7 G.R., 199.
Wickham, Brigadier J., Commander, 63rd Ind. Infantry Brigade, 56, 193, 195.
Wingate, Colonel, 363.
Winterton, Major General, Chief of Staff of Burma Army, 304.
Wundwin Village, 313-4.

Yacht, Scheme for defence of Burma, 68-70.
Yenangyaung Village, 6, 305, 355.
    Orders for the destruction of, 277. Fighting in, 287-302. Japanese air attacks on, 288. Forces at, 289.
Ye-U Village, 8.
Yin-Chaung Stream, 283.
Yomas Intelligence Service, 237.
Yoshizawa, Mr., Japanese Ambassador to Indo-China (Nov. 1941), 27.

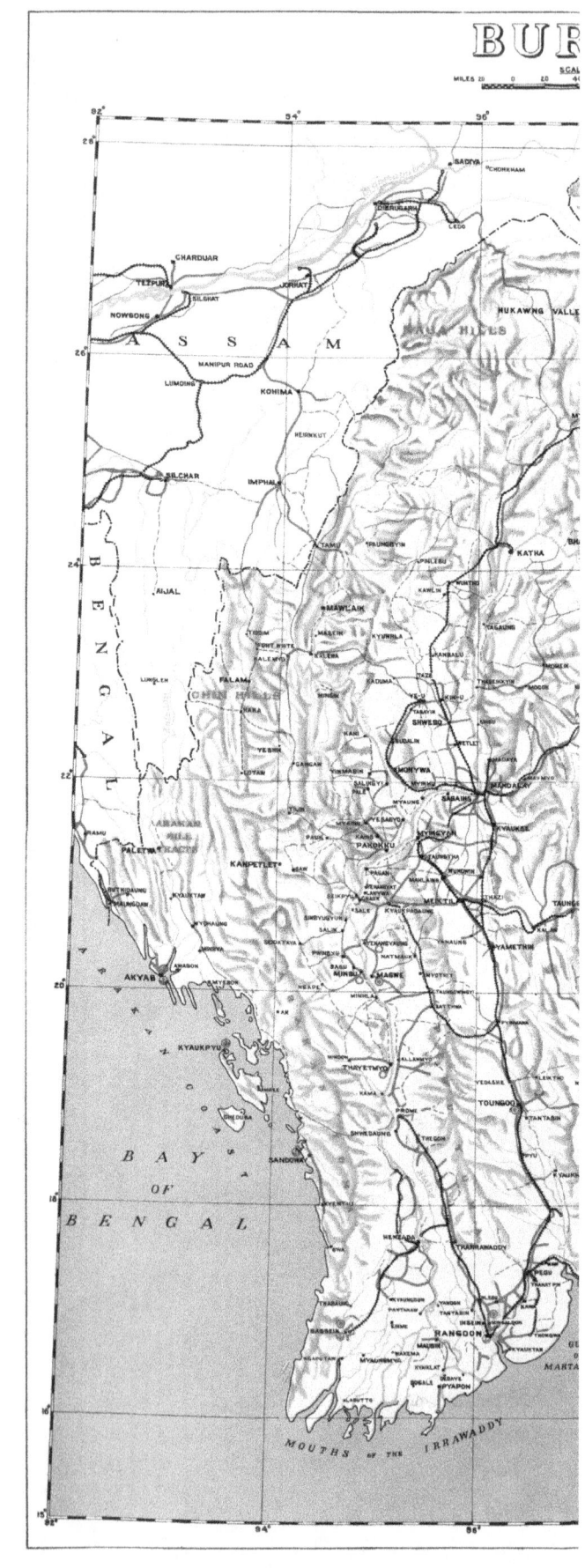

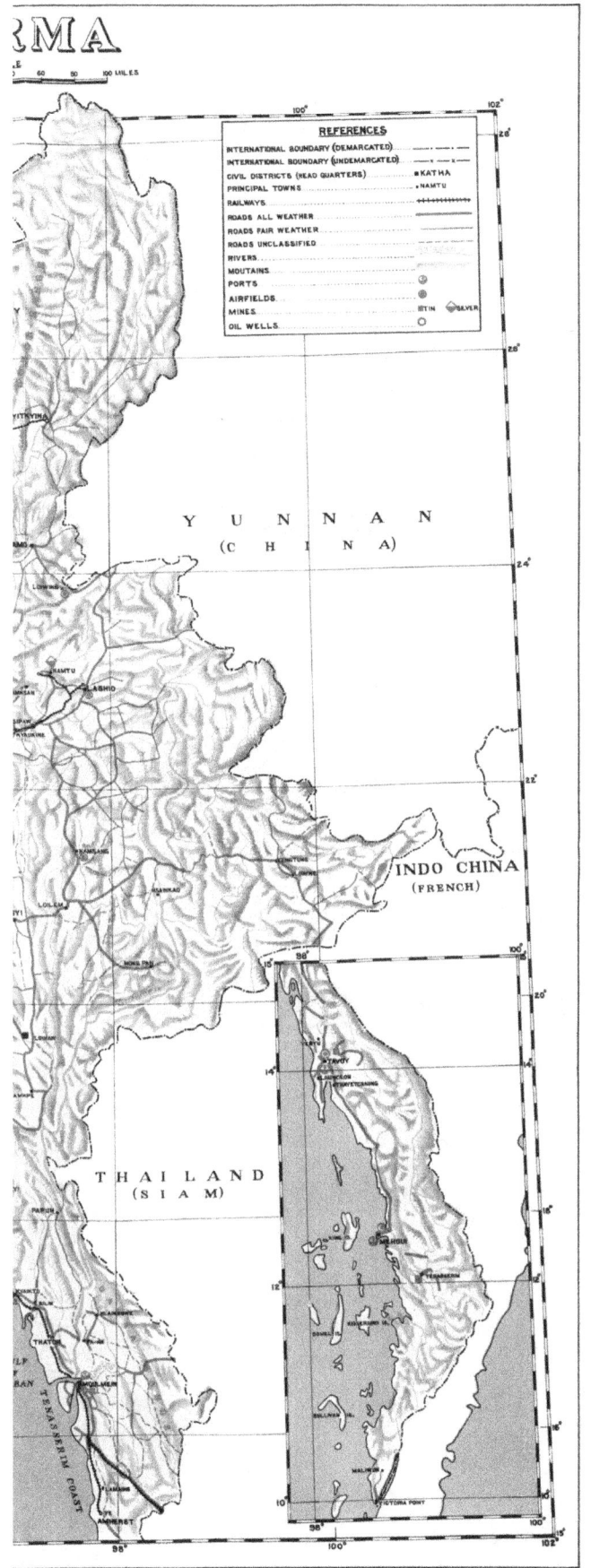

INDIAN DIVISIONS WON A FINE REPUTATION IN WORLD WAR TWO

Field Marshal Auchinleck, Commander-in-Chief of the British Indian Army from 1942, asserted that the British *"couldn't have come through both wars (World War I and II) if they hadn't had the British Indian Army"*.
British Prime Minister Winston Churchill also paid tribute to *"the unsurpassed bravery of Indian soldiers and officers"*.

Between 1945 and 1947, the Director of Public Relations, War Department, Government of India, published a series of short publications covering the individual histories of the WWII Indian Divisions. They followed a consistent format, having between 44 and 48 pages within illustrated soft card covers. They have an average of 50 monochrome photographic illustrations, and each has a full colour centrespread depicting a scene from the Division's wartime operations (drawn by official war artists). They were printed at various presses in Bombay and New Delhi, and each contains at least one map.

As condensed histories they are useful – particularly those which relate to Divisions for which no other record was ever produced.

The British Indian Army during World War II began the war, in 1939, numbering just under 200,000 men. By the end of the war, it had become the largest volunteer army in history, rising to over 2.5 million men in August 1945. Serving in divisions of infantry, armour and a fledgling airborne force, they fought on three continents: in Africa, Europe and Asia.

This Army fought in Ethiopia against the Italian Army, in Egypt, Libya, Tunisia and Algeria against both the Italian and German Army and, after the Italian surrender, against the German Army in Italy. However, the bulk of the British Indian Army was committed to fighting the Japanese Army, first during the British defeats in Malaya and the retreat from Burma to the Indian border; later, after resting and refitting for the victorious advance back into Burma, as part of the largest British Empire army ever formed. These campaigns cost the lives of over 87,000 Indian service- men, while another 34,354 were wounded, and 67,340 became prisoners of war. Their valour was recognised with the award of some 4,000 decorations, and 18 members of the British Indian Army were awarded the Victoria Cross or the George Cross.

RED EAGLES
The Story of the 4th Indian Division
9781474537520

During the Second World War, the 4th Indian Division was in the vanguard of nine campaigns in the Mediterranean theatre, Egypt, Eritrea, Syria, Tunisia, Italy and Greece. The 4th Division captured 150,000 prisoners and suffered 25,000 casualties, more than the strength of a whole division. It won over 1,000 honours and awards, which included four Victoria Crosses and three George Crosses. Field Marshal Lord Wavell wrote: "The fame of this Division will surely go down as one of the greatest fighting formations in military history."

THE FIGHTING FIFTH
History of the 5th Indian Division
9781474537513

As described in much greater detail in Anthony Brett James's book 'The Ball of Fire', the division saw active service in East Africa, North Africa and Burma.

GOLDEN ARROW
The Story of the 7th Indian Division
9781474537506

The role of this division is also duplicated by a much larger work: the book by Brig. M. R. Roberts. However, this booklet gives a good account of Kohima and Imphal and the crossing of the Irrawaddy. In 1945, the division was flown into Siam, so becoming the first Allied formation to re-enter South East Asia.

BLACK CAT DIVISION
17th Indian Division
9781474537483

This formation was committed to Burma from the early days when the British were in full flight from the invading Japanese. It remained in Burma right through to the end, when the starving remnants of the Japanese Army were making their own desperate retreat.

ONE MORE RIVER
The Story of the 8th Indian Division
Biferno, Trigno, Sangro, Moro, Rapido, Arno, Senio, Santerno, Po, Adige

9781474537490

The 8th Indian Division started its overseas service in the Middle East in the garrisoning of Iraq and then the invasion of Persia to secure the oil fields of the area for the Allies, before moving to Italy in 1943. Landing at Taranto, it pushed up the length of the peninsula in a series of major battles: breaking the Sangro Line, forcing the Rapido and turning the defences at Cassino, breaking the stubborn German resistance at Monte Grande and, finally, forcing the Po River. It won four VCs, 26 DSOs and 149 MCs along the way. During the war the 8th Indian Division sustained casualties totalling 2,012 dead, 8,189 wounded and 749 missing.

TIGER HEAD
The Story of the 26th Indian Division
Arakan, Ragoon

9781474537452

This is a history of the division said later by the Japanese to have been the opponent which they most feared. The 26th held the Allied monsoon line in the Arakan during two such seasons, repulsing every attack launched against it. Later it made a series of leap-frog landings down the coast to clinch the issue in the Arakan. It was the first division to enter Ragoon, invading the city from the sea.

THE TWENTY THIRD INDIAN DIVISION
"The Fighting Cock Division"
Burma, Malaya, Java

9781474537469

The Fighting Cock Division is well recorded in the book by Doulton. This book gives coverage of the heavy fighting at the Kohima Battle, the capture of Tamu, the reoccupation of Malaya in August 1945, and then its strange role on the island of Java – concurrently disarming the Japanese garrison, fighting the insurgent Indonesian nationalists, and caring for 65,000 former internees pending the arrival of a new Dutch administration.

A HAPPY FAMILY
The Story of the Twentieth Indian Division,
9781474537476

One of the few Indian divisions in the 14th Army trained specifically for the war in Burma. Raised in Bangalore in 1942, it commenced active operations in late 1943 and served from Imphal through to the end. It established the 14th Army's first brigade-head across the Chindwin and its second such brigade-head across the Irrawaddy. Its final task was to round up the Japanese in French Indochina.

TEHERAN TO TRIESTE
The Story of the Tenth Indian Division
9781783317028

This History deals with the 10th Indian Div's exploits in Iraq (under Maj Gen "Bill" Slim) its role in the Libyan battles leading up to El Alamein, the following two years of garrison duties in Cyprus and Syria, and finally, its fighting services in the Italian campaign (from Ortona onwards).

THE STORY OF THE 25th INDIAN DIVSION
The Arakan Campaign
9781783317585

Formed in Southern India in August 1942 for defence of that area in case of Japanese invasion, the "Ace of Spades" Division had its baptism of fire in Arakan in February 1944. It served throughout the remainder of that campaign the climax being the battle of Tamandu. Its victorious fight for the Kangaw roadblock was considered by many to have been the fiercest battle of the entire Burma war, while its liberation of Akyab was the first convincing proof to the rest of the world that the tide had turned against the Japanese.

DAGGER DIVISION
The Story of the 19th Indian Division
9781783317035

Raised in the late 1941, the 19th was the first "standard" Indian Division. Its troops were the first to breach the Japanese defence line in Burma and to raise the flag at Fort Dufferin. It crossed the Chindwin in November 1944, driving on to Mandalay and Ragoon during seven months of continuous fighting. The 19th's exploits are graphically described also in John Masters' personal memoir, *The Road Past Mandalay*.

www.ingramcontent.com/pod-product-compliance
Lightning Source LLC
Chambersburg PA
CBHW060415300426
44111CB00018B/2860